Gender, Genre, and Power
in South Asian Expressive Traditions

SOUTH ASIA SEMINAR SERIES

Recent volumes in this series include:

Identity and Division in Cults and Sects in South Asia. 1984
Science and Technology in South Asia. 1985
Making Things in South Asia: The Role of Artist and Craftsman. 1988

Publications of the American Folklore Society
New Series

General Editor, Patrick Mullen

Gender, Genre, and Power in South Asian Expressive Traditions

Edited by Arjun Appadurai, Frank J. Korom, and Margaret A. Mills

upp

University of Pennsylvania Press
Philadelphia

Printed in the United States of America

Library of Congress Cataloging-in-Publication Data

Gender, genre, and power in South Asian expressive traditions / edited by Arjun Appadurai, Frank J. Korom, and Margaret A. Mills.
p. cm. — (South Asia seminar series)
Includes bibliographical references and index.
ISBN 0-8122-3082-5 (cloth). — ISBN 0-8122-1337-8 (pbk.)
1. Folklore—Asia, South—History and criticism. 2. Folk literature—Asia, South—History and criticism. 3. Women—Asia, South—Folklore. 4. Sex role in literature—Asia, South—History and criticism. 5. Sex—Asia, South—Folklore. 6. Power (Social sciences) I. Appadurai, Arjun, 1949– . II. Korom, Frank J. III. Mills, Margaret Ann. IV. Series.
GR302.G46 1991
398′.095—dc20 91-2711
CIP

Contents

Part II: Genres: Identification and Identity

Part III: Tradition: Persistence and Divergence

Preface

The South Asia Seminar at the University of Pennsylvania has a long and venerable history. Over the past four decades, the Seminar has involved intense, yearlong discussions of major topics of interest to those who study South Asian history, society, and culture. Its approach has generally been interdisciplinary and its results have been disseminated in a variety of formats. The Seminar has unfailingly been a central contributor to the vitality of South Asian studies in the United States.

During 1987–88, the title of the Seminar was "Knowledge, Performance and Transmission in South Asian Folk Traditions," and about twenty-five scholars presented papers on a variety of aspects of the subject. We were particularly pleased not only by the diversity of approaches but also by the inclusion of papers about Pakistan, Bangla Desh and Afghanistan, which offset the frequent Hindu bias of such colloquia. This volume is based on the 1987–88 Seminar but papers by William O. Beeman, Dan Ben-Amos, Carol Breckenridge, Constance Fairbanks, Henry Glassie, Kathryn Hansen, Edward O. Henry, Kathryn March, and Regula Qureshi could not, for a variety of reasons, be included. We thank all of them, however, for having shared their ideas with us in the course of the year. The remaining papers have been considerably revised and recontextualized.

The editors owe thanks to many individuals for helping in the organization and success of the Seminar and for making this volume possible. Alan Heston, Chairman of the South Asia Regional Studies Department, has been a source of good things, both moral and material, throughout. Patricia Smith, of the University of Pennsylvania Press, has been a patient, tactful, and collegial editor, who has in many ways helped to strengthen this volume. Victoria Farmer was of invaluable assistance in handling the logistical details of the Seminar, as were the staff of the South Asia Center, notably Richard Cohen, its Associate Director. Sagaree Sengupta Korom provided valuable technical help throughout the process of transforming the papers into publishable form. Two anonymous readers for the Press gave us thoughtful criticisms and suggestions which provoked us to refine the logic that underlies the volume. We are grateful, above all, to the faculty, students, and visitors who attended the Seminar regularly, asked searching questions, and set both authors and editors to rethinking their views. This last contribution, though collective, is probably the most important ingredient of the vitality of this volume.

Arjun Appadurai
Frank J. Korom
Margaret A. Mills

Note on Transliteration

A number of diverse languages are represented in this book. We have attempted to follow the Library of Congress system of transliteration, as spelled out in the series of *LC Cataloging Service Bulletins,* as much as possible. However, some of our contributors have chosen to represent local speech forms in some cases, and others chose to modify the LC system to suit their own specific needs. The same word may therefore appear in different forms in this volume, depending on the linguistic environment in which it is being used by each individual contributor. We hope, however, that consistency in each essay shall prove less ambiguous than standardization across the volume.

Introduction

Arjun Appadurai, Frank J. Korom, and Margaret A. Mills

Introduction

This introduction is being written in the midst of the worldwide furor over the publication and sale of Salman Rushdie's *The Satanic Verses* (1988). Battles are being fought over censorship and freedom of speech, politics and fantasy, blasphemy and terrorism, individual authorial rights and collective readings, as well as riots in remote corners of the world. The volume we present appears at first glance to be far from the blood and passion of the Rushdie issue. But this book explores powers and processes of expression in the very part of the world where riots first broke out over the sale of *The Satanic Verses,* where Salman Rushdie spent the crucial years of his childhood, and where a major nation-state (India) first banned *The Satanic Verses.* If there is one lesson we learn from all this, it is the following: we had all better understand the ways complex civilizational traditions, like those of South Asia, have engaged the problems of fiction and of fantasy, of the authority of writers and audiences, of the connection between affect and expression, of the aesthetic prerogatives of men and women, and of the problems of irony and satire within a complex set of performance traditions.

In short, this volume is ultimately about the pragmatics of folk sensibility in a rapidly changing world. Its authors engage many topics, but through all of the chapters there runs a series of crucial intra-civilizational debates: about the past and its uses, about the multiplicity of canons which performers may invoke (or subvert), about the varieties of "magic realism" in South Asia, and about the politics involved in the resilience of oral forms in a society where literacy is highly valued. The authors engage these topics in rich and context-sensitive case studies, and draw the reader into the dense and heteroglossic world of South Asian aesthetic expressions. Readers will be directed to textual, historical, and interpretive minutiae that do not make for light reading, but for those who genuinely wish to engage the "otherness" of other worlds of folk knowledge, expression, and performativity, the essays offer an uncompromisingly unsentimental overture. If we wish to be intelligent citizens and critics in the world after *The Satanic Verses,* we need to take the folksiness out of our perception of folk traditions. This entails engagement with dense historical materials, complex aesthetic issues, and subtle problems of textuality and history. The essays in this collection are an invitation to such an engagement.

The Context

This book stands at the confluence of two important streams of scholarship, and though not all the authors are equally self-conscious about the background against which they are working, there are two major bodies of literature that this volume presupposes.

The first is the scholarship, produced largely in the last two decades, during which folklore has become transformed from a rather conservationist exercise in collecting traditions to a radical enterprise which explores the dynamics of folk reproduction in the study of a variety of expressive forms. In this revitalized form of folkloristics, key terms such as the folk, genre, text, performance, and tradition itself, have become problematized. Perhaps as a consequence, folklore has become more than ever a field in which contestation between disciplines can and does occur: in the topos of folklore, the questions of authenticity and invention in regard to tradition have become problematized (Abrahams 1986; Handler 1988; Handler and Linnekin 1984; Herzfeld 1982; Kirshenblatt-Gimblett 1988; Korom 1989a; Whisnant 1983); the question of text and textuality has become, once again, a topic of contestation (Bauman and Abrahams 1981), as sociolinguists, folklorists, ethnopoeticists, anthropologists, and historians of religions seek to negotiate over what "texts" are, how much they can and must be read as parts of lived experience, and so forth (Ricoeur 1971a, b; Hanks 1989). Finally, performance as a term has come to be richly multivalent, and a new dialogue is emerging between earlier meanings of performance (which simply stressed the activity of producting folk expressions rather than the static products of such activity) and newer meanings, which stress sensitivity not only to situated language use but also to the problems of dialogue, voice, heteroglossia, and the like, which emerge once a text is itself seen as a constructed experience and social experience is reconceived dialogically (Bauman 1986; Briggs 1988; Schieffelin 1985). Clearly, the study of performances, however we construe them and whatever approaches we utilize, must be envisioned as a multidisciplinary hermeneutic process (Malbon 1983; Sullivan 1986). The point is not that everything is up for grabs in the current situation of folklore, but rather that folklore has become the locus and critical nexus of important interdisciplinary debates and contests pertaining to the expressive dimension of social life. The authors in this volume could not have produced their essays, whatever their topics, without the benefit of these ongoing debates, some of which are explicitly programmatic, others of which are more embedded in interpretive specifics. But suffice it to say that, taken as a whole, these essays are produced in an era when terms such as "genre," "performance," "tradition," and "text" are no longer markers of terminological common sense but point, rather, to large areas of intense debate. The field of folklore is host to these debates and, moreover, has participated in opening them up to even larger debates in the fields of critical theory, media studies, and cultural studies.

There is yet a second stream of work that has nourished the chapters in this volume, and it has come out of South Asia. In the last decade, South Asia has seen an unprecedented flowering of work in folklore, construed broadly. There have been two major collections produced in the United States (Blackburn and Ramanujan 1986; Blackburn et al. 1989) and two significant edited volumes in India (Claus et al. 1987; Das 1986); they reveal a generation of scholars who have brought together folkloristics, anthropology, history of religions, and Indology in dramatic new ways. This has been a quiet revolution, but its results are dramatic: women have moved to the center stage of this work, Dravidian India has moved out of the shadow of the ever-hungry classicizing North, nonverbal genres have begun to edge into the privileged territory of verbal material, and oral materials have begun to compete for attention with written ones. These inversions of our conventional thinking, and of others', did not, of course, descend on the scholarly world ex nihilo. They built on earlier debates about "great" and "little" traditions, about Sanskritization and its variants, about the role of classical models and meanings in a polyglot, vernacular world, about *bhakti* as a counter-system to orthodox Hinduism, and about the hidden alternative discourses of Untouchables, poet-saints, and women in the subcontinent. Still, though it is tempting to see history as necessity, there would have been no way to predict, say in 1980, that this past decade would have seen an immense flowering of scholarship in South Asia folkloristics. Here it must be acknowledged that the sociology of this development involves, at least in part, a kind of internal disciplinary restlessness, which led many of the finest minds in anthropology, linguistics, comparative religion, and Indology to become renegades in their own disciplines and look to folkloric materials for new energies to bring to their areal concerns.

Here the two streams come together, for this move to the margins within several disciplinary fields in the South Asian area converged with a rich period in the ongoing dialogue of folkloristics, discussed above, creating a juncture between a series of classic problems in an areal field and a series of new debates and discoveries in a disciplinary field. Many of the contributors to this volume have been part of this happy circumstance, and their work builds on problems and issues from both streams of scholarship. But like all original scholarship, the essays in this volume are not simply mechanical products of the encounter between folkloristics and South Asian studies in the late 1970s and 1980s. These essays also extend our understanding of key issues and problems, both for South Asianists and for folklore "at large." Of course, it might be noted at this point that disciplinary concepts, especially in the human sciences, never represent the "view from nowhere," and always represent the crystallization of empirical work in particular places, which by a mixture of quality, serendipity, and academic politics, become seen as "theory-at-large," for a while (Appadurai 1986). Then, theory-at-large moves on, because work done in new areas creates new configurations of theory and method to which scholars working in yet other areas will have to respond.

We believe that this volume and the recent ones that precede it represent such a moment in the spatial politics of disciplinary development. It is not that these essays turn the study of folklore, or any part of it, on its head. Rather, they are invitations to those who work on "general" theory to take note of the twists that attend their concerns in this locality. Not all work can issue such a challenge. But work that is carefully contextualized, and is aware of developments elsewhere, invites the folklorist "at large" to rethink the politics of citation. Building on the major volumes in South Asian folklore that have preceded them, these essays should help in a radical reconfiguration of the master terms of folklore scholarship, terms that otherwise tend to become quickly normalized, as if they had become part of everyone's common sense, and contained the strange epistemological privilege of the "view from nowhere." On matters of gender, of genre, and of the dynamics of long-term cultural reproduction, South Asian work in folklore studies needs to be seen not as more data to be digested, but as potentially interrogating existing disciplinary understandings framed around data from other major cultural areas.

Thus, these essays stand at an interesting conjuncture of place and theory in folkloristics, a conjuncture which can be savored only in its specifics. In this introduction, we point to a few major themes that run through the essays and provide a brief guide to the contents of the volume. Far be it from us to claim that the way we have organized the essays is the only possible way. Yet, some essays do speak more forcefully to one another than others. So we have divided the contributions into three sections, each consisting of five chapters: one on gender, one on genre, and one on tradition. These sections are followed by an afterword. What follows is a brief discussion of each of the sections.

Gender

The essays on gender (by Ramanujan, Mills, Grima, Gold, and Claus) are about men and women, and also about gender, taken as a problem of relating, of contrast, and of relationships between ethnobiological categories. Each of the essays spins gender out in a different direction, yet they resonate with one another in interesting ways, while filling a geographical gap in the growing literature on gender studies.

The last decade and a half have seen the U.S. publication of one major bibliography and several collections of feminist folklore scholarship, endeavoring to integrate the subject of gender with folkloristics (de Caro 1983; Farrer 1975; Jordan and Kalčik 1985; special issues of *Journal of American Folklore* [100], *Journal of Folklore Research* [25]), but almost none of this work cast its gaze east of Suez. De Caro's bibliography, listing 1,664 items, identifies only 19 which deal directly with either India or Nepal, one of which is a general bibliography on Indian women, and three others being general works on women dedicated to some geographic region. Certainly there is a great deal more published work pertinent to women and folklore in South Asia, but it has remained relatively obscure to American folklorists who are not South Asianists. No doubt much older material concerned with the portrayal of women and/or women as folk artists and performers exists in collections that are not indexed in such a way as to make that content obvious to a nonspecialist. Even Marta Weigle's far-reaching comparative studies on women and mythology (1982, 1989) make only passing mention of Indic mythology, despite such recent provocative comparatist work as that of O'Flaherty (1980).

South Asian folklorists and textually oriented anthropologists have nonetheless produced a number of recent studies of fundamental interest to Western folklorists concerned with gender. In *Another Harmony* (Blackburn and Ramanujan 1986) alone, seven out of nine contributions substantively and innovatively address gender issues. Of particular interest in juxtaposition to Western theoretical developments (e.g., Stoeltje 1988) is the consideration that patriarchal structure in South Asia is not the product of colonial presence, yet colonial and postcolonial experience is crucial to current developments in gender roles and the expressive systems which both reflect and partly constitute the gendered nature of social life. The female aspect of deity is abundantly represented in South Asian traditions and for this reason, among others, the current study of gender issues in South Asian folklore has no trouble, *pace* French feminism, turning up examples of women as gazing and enunciating subjects, not just as gazed-upon objects (cf. Ramanujan, Wadley, Claus, and Egnor in *Another Harmony;* Ramanujan, Trawick, Grima, Mills, Claus, Flueckiger, this volume). It is to be hoped both that South Asianists can turn their attention more systematically to an assessment of Eurocentric feminist theory apropos of folk (and now public) culture and that the present volume, together with work already in print, will make South Asian expressive traditions and scholarly activities more accessible for the enlargement of American and European folklorists' perspectives on gender issues.

The division of social roles along gender lines is, of course, nothing new to the social sciences. But the role that gender plays in performance is still a fertile area of exploration. Limon and Young (1986) predicted, accurately, with regard to the essays anthologized here, that gender should and would become a central focus for future folklore studies. Gender ideology is such a basic resource in the making of all kinds of cultural meanings that virtually no chapter in this collection can proceed without reference to it. Besides the chapters gathered in Part I of this volume, explicitly entitled "Gender: Voices and Lives," several others in the anthology take gender as a central issue, including those of Hiltebeitel, Salomon, and Flueckiger.

The role of gender in cultural expression is so basic and pervasive as to defy generalization beyond an observation of its pervasiveness, but a rough topical division might be made between scholarly considerations of gender in the act of performance (including not only performers, but also audience composition and differential response) and representations of gender roles in the "texts" as performed. Clearly, neither of these areas of interest can be addressed without addressing the other; in particular, attention to gender in the organization of performances may help to reveal, as it does in several of these essays, alternative voices and points of view in verbal art productions (the "texts") and in their indigenous interpretations. Alternative voices are a topic never far from the center of attention throughout this volume; gender is one of the basic parameters of alterity.

As Ramanujan reminds us in his essay on south Indian folktales in Part I, the predominance of a theme in the expressive culture of one subgroup does not preclude its popularity in other groups, but interpretations of narrative themes and images may vary widely between subgroups. Ramanujan defines "women's tales" as tales told by and centered around women, which does not preclude male exposure to and interest in them. A general theme such as fate, worked out in a fictional woman's life in his first example, has relevance for both women and men. In the example he presents, the theme of separation and suffering, dramatically rendered, ascribes the heroine's suffering not to character or *karma,* but to "Mother Fate." The untangling of a fated life is often accomplished by the heroine recounting her misfortunes within the tale, a recounting which makes her a person, according to Ramanujan's interpretation. In this regard, whether Tamil (Trawick), Kannada (Ramanujan), or Paxto (Grima), women's personal narratives may be seen to share the general function of recapitulation in fictional narratives: the construction of a self. Referring to a story about an old widow whose mental and bodily functions deteriorate precisely because she is not able to tell anyone her story, Ramanujan points out that "the whole tale is the tale of her acquiring her story, *making a person of her, making a silent person a speaking woman*" (p. 42, our emphasis). Benedicte Grima, whose essay is included in this section, suggests the same about the function of *tapos* narratives. Fictional tales and narratives grounded in concrete personal experiences overlap in these examples, suggesting that fantasy and reality often address similar concerns. Thus, normative biological categories such as gender and culturally constructed ones such as genre, are not as taxonomically distinct as one might presume, for as Ramanujan reminds us in his contribution, "genders are genres." Finding a personal voice in male-dominated galaxies of possibilities seems to be at the center of female-related gender issues in the general study of folklore (cf. also Mills, this volume), as well as in the description and analysis of the emergent production of genres.

Margaret Trawick (whose chapter in Part II is discussed at greater length in the following section), also bridges the gap between emotionally laden accounts of individual experience and genre production. She detects a tangible transformation between life and song: song clarifies and strengthens certain life events, in this case fragmentation and suffering in human relationships. The song of an Untouchable Tamil woman (analyzed by Trawick), and the *gham* performances of Paxtun women discussed by Grima, reconfigure the relations between social margins and centers, superiors and subordinates. The thematic congruences among these essays challenge us to seek a fine-grained comparativism that can take simultaneous account of gender with caste, class, or ethnicity as conjoined determinants of women's lived experience and self-representations. Along parallel thematic lines, Heston (discussed in the next section) notes the pervasively tragic themes of separation peculiar to Paxto chapbook romances, composed and performed by men, in contrast to the happy endings popular in Persian, for instance.

Three of the chapters in Part I cohere around this point, the construction of an experiential or moral self, or both, through autobiographical narrative; the particularities of the selves so constructed remain grounded in local cultural preoccupations which, as Ramanujan points out in distinguishing the causal role of fate (in stories) from the invocation of *karma* (in other types of daily verbal exchanges), may actually encompass rather divergent world views (cf. Abu-Lughod 1986). These counter-systems may operate in different spheres of one person's expressive life, or differentially among different subgroups, including male and female. Ramanujan's observation that marriage is often the concluding point of male-centered adventure tales, and the starting point of female-centered ones, can be extended to other traditions (cf. Mills, this volume, 1983, 1985 for similar patterns in a corpus of oral tales from western Afghanistan).

Mills addresses issues raised by Ramanujan concerning the gendered distribution of folktale themes, but also points out that the gendered division of access to expressive media (in this case, reading and writing, cassette tape recorders) must be taken into account to assess differences in men's and women's oral performances, the stylistics, genesis, and distribution of oral genres and subgenres. Technological transformations can be expected to change women's exposure to different types of performative speech, even within the functioning institution of *pardah*. The effect of this new exposure on the gendered differentiation of speech styles, however, cannot be expected to be a mechanical one, since gendered differentiation of speech styles is part of a larger system of gendered cultural distinctions, and is not simply driven by technology.

Themes of gender roles and the ambivalence of power, rather differently handled, are also evident in the Rajasthani Gopi Chand narrative explored by Ann Grodzins Gold. It is not clear to King Gopi Chand, as hero, whether remaining a householder or becoming a renunciant is the appropriate path (cf. also Blackburn, this volume, on the discussion of transcendence and balance in a Tamil folk *Rāmāyaṇa*). Gopi Chand is compelled by the terms of his birth to become a yogi, but, unlike his guru, he has experienced both the attached and the detached life, and for him the choice remains real. Attachment is evoked by "women, especially beloved women" (wife and sister) who "cause him, weeping, to cling to the world he must leave—a world of mortality in which love is illusion but no less potent for being so" (Gold, p. 102).

These attachments, and the episode of a contest between the yogis and a group of malevolent female magicians, provide a dual vision of *māyā*, illusion which is also creative power in ways that are distinctly female. Gold presents these facets of illusion or *māyā* as an inherent property of women (viewed from a male perspective) and put into motion by them. The creations of female *māyā* are tangibly real, with enduring consequences, countered only by superior male creative forces.

Peter Claus's chapter extends the discussion of indigenous interpretation by exploring the relevance of certain genres of traditional fictional narratives from Tulu-speaking south Karnataka to local conceptualizations of kinship and gender relations. But these are not the timeless, architectonic conceptualizations of kinship which predominated in the older analytic ethnographies. In Claus's observation of the relationship between story and history, oral narrative often draws on the conflicts experienced by people in their day-to-day lives. The Tulu *pāḍdana* describes and comments upon the explosively real tension that exists between *podderü* groups, consisting of brother-sister siblings sets, which remind us that gender is not just a matter of conjugal relations, though a conjugal power struggle figures largely in the *pāḍdana* examples that Claus examines. Authorial voice is also at issue here, as in several of the chapters in this volume. Although the performer is a woman, the story, according to the female audience's evaluation of the female main character's actions, warns against female defiance of male dominance in Tulu society. Women's performances cannot be mechanically assumed to stand in counterposition to male-dominated ideologies. As Ramanujan suggests, system and counter-system may be expressed in different domains of speech performance.

Claus invites us to pay close attention to the context of *pāḍdana* performance in order to interpret its multiple meanings. The *pāḍdana* is a cross-gender genre that has the intertextual sense and force of a ballad in some situations, an epic in others, or a tale in still others. The generic designation, *pāḍdana,* encompasses a number of distinct song forms, which allows the story structure and content to vary as the situation demands. Claus's identification of genre, subgenre, and sub-subgenre relies upon a detailed exploration of the diversity of performance contexts.

Genre

As Claus's chapter in Part I demonstrated, genre is a taxonomic problem, but not merely classification is at stake (Abrahams 1976; Gossen 1971; Voigt 1980). As a problem of ethnopoetics (Hymes 1971, 1981; Tedlock 1986), genre analysis is also a metafolkloristic problem (Dundes 1966), because central to the study of narrative expressions is the understanding of what system of expressions they fit into locally (Ben-Amos 1976). Without such an understanding, we misclassify. And when we misclassify, we misunderstand and distort.

With a few major exceptions (e.g., Boas 1914; Malinowski 1926), genre analysis, however critical it may be to a holistic understanding of expressive culture, was not a pressing issue in the anthropological and folkloristic study of verbal art until fairly recently, owing to ongoing spurious assumptions concerning the unified nature of tradition (cf. Honko 1968, Ben-Amos 1976). Such misunderstandings led to homogeneous, static, and cross-cultural models of genres based on Eurocentric literary notions of aesthetic form and sociologically construed ideal types. But the essays in Part II, by Flueckiger, Wadley, Trawick, Salomon, and Heston, address the problematics of genre in context in a variety of ways and contribute important South Asian generic information to the further comparative refinement of this elusive problem that has preoccupied folkloristics "at-large" for the past few decades.

Joyce Flueckiger's discussion of genre and community in Chhattisgarh points out ways in which the claiming of different forms of folk verbal art is a part of self-perceived regional identity, and the ways in which genres so claimed then form systems. The "we" in common statements, such as "We dance the *suā nāc*" or "we sing songs at our weddings," becomes problematical. Proprietary claims to traditional verbal arts cannot be taken as transparent identifications of actual practitioners: they are actually much more than that, operating, with actual performance, across boundaries of gender and caste to articulate regional and other forms of community identity. Flueckiger's perspective yields not only a refreshingly flexible approach to genre but also an equally supple model for community identification. For instance, she captures differences in male and female tendencies to claim genres which they do not in fact perform, and reflects on the possible grounds for those differences in concepts of community inflected by gender, including caste membership.

The performance forms themselves are changing as the settings for performance and the region's economic and demographic picture change. Genre designations are also problematical: genres are seen to be clustered not by similarities of form but by social categories of practitioners (unmarried girls, married women, men) in indigenous thought. As these groups' expectations for themselves transform under changing social and economic conditions, their claims to particular genres also shift. Nontraditional performances and performance settings are emerging, sometimes more evidently in action than in folk reflection. Increasing school-based literacy, with its concomitant expectations for appropriate status behavior, and the emergence of mass media (video halls, All-India Radio performances of *suā nāc*) compete with older traditions of public performance. Performance forms related to ritual, such as *suā nāc,* are being simultaneously privatized (as newly literate *ādīvāsī* girls decline to perform outside their own neighborhoods) and commodified (through decontextualized radio performance). The Candainī epic, claimed as a distinctively Chhattisgarhi form, is also undergoing changes in caste of performers, preferred forms of performances (from dual-voice sung recitation to *nācā* dance dramas), language of performance, musical style, and perhaps story line (though the latter is hard to trace in a tradition with no literate modality). Audience composition is becoming more inclusive, as the epic is claimed as a regional property.

Flueckiger's concept of regional isogenres helps organize a systematic discussion of variation within complex multigenre systems. It might be scaled up, and its limits tested, in application to discussions of transregional phenomena such as *qawwālī* or classically derived epic performance (*Mahābhārata* and *Rāmāyaṇa;* cf. Brenneis, Blackburn, Hiltebeitel, this volume). The flexibility of her model responds to the fluidity of tradition in Chhattisgarh, a fluidity which no portrayal of South Asian expressive culture can afford to ignore.

Susan Wadley's chapter, while not primarily concerned with historical change, opens up the question of the simultaneous presence of multiple genres within an established (in this case, epic) performance form, and poses basic questions about the differential impact on listeners of distinct modalities of performance. Whereas Peter Claus demonstrated (Part I) the interrelationships between genre and social ideology determining the message of the text, Wadley observes how the dialectic among the prose narrative and the melody, sung text and instrumentation, operates in the audience's multichanneled reception of a coherent communicative event. In this light, she explores the dynamics of genre shifts during *ḍholā* epic performance. The *ḍholā* (a chanted couplet) is skillfully manipulated by the singer to focus attention on critical points in the story. The singer has a number of alternative paths that he might take in constructing his performance, which he creatively utilizes to convey certain essential truths about the content of the narrative. Drawing on the work of Bloch (1974) and Wheelock (1982) on ritual language, Wadley seeks to tease out the logic of genre shifts, especially movements between song and prose. Wadley sees prose as more explanatory or information-oriented, song as more situating and contextual, but she is cautious not to overemphasize the distinction, recognizing that formal language can *in*form and well as *per*form (Gill 1987). She concurs with Wheelock that the intention of the speaker ultimately determines a crucial distinction in the making of meaning.

Wadley's attention to musical texture as well as prosody in sung *ḍholā* invites us to reflect on possible extensions of this investigation to, for example, the examination of Tulu *pāḍdana*s (see Claus, this volume) with regard to musical texture, along with the relationship of verbal content and social structural ideology. Wadley's vision of epic as characterized by the constant shifting and manipulation of genres might help us understand why the overarching category of *pāḍdana* can be understood in so many ways. Her complex view of meaning-making in epic offers a general perspective on the openness of traditional texts, an important element to be taken into consideration in case studies of social change and concomitant changes in emotionally laden expressive systems.

The rise of mass media and popular culture challenges our understandings of the role of the individual in cultural production and reproduction, at the same time that postcolonial energies are being invested in the empowerment of previously unheard voices. At the ethnographic level, life history (especially in its traditional forms) stands revealed as a powerful genre for communicating personal experience and points of view, as well as for delineating generic cultural configurations. Given the history of biography in the modern era in the West, Western readers might normally expect an individual's life story to reflect feelings and attitudes of an individual (as defined in our culture) relating the events. Margaret Trawick's paper points out some limitations in our received notions of autobiography. As she tells us, her informant Cevi's life history speaks more about other people than about herself. Nevertheless, Trawick argues that we can learn much about Cevi's own life as an Untouchable Tamil Paraiyar through her relationships to other actors in the narrative. Trawick observes that artistic performance might be understood as an intensified expression of the performer's experienced life (pp. 224, 242). In Trawick's case, reality and fiction converge in interesting ways, not unlike the concerns expressed by Ramanujan and Grima in Part I. Items of a performer's repertoire may also reflect personal experience through the choice of specific items to sing.

By focusing on the artistic composition and sociolinguistic texture of the life history text, Trawick discovers an interesting set of parallels between Cevi's delivery style and her life. The core around which the narrative revolves is the problem of hopelessness related to Untouchable status. Trawick suggests that in Cevi's life story, "to be in the house" means to be stable and secure (p. 237), a theme that both Grima and Gold also uncover in their discussions of departures and separations as undesirable experiences in women's self-portrayals. While Van Gennep (1960 [1909]) and Turner (1969, 1974a, 1974b) have treated transitory ritual status of separation as conditions defying definition with (at least putatively) uncertain consequences, Cevi's uncertainty is chronic, her future not just periodically liminal or even liminoid (in Turner's terminology; cf. Bynum 1984), but incontrovertibly marginal and insecure as she moves about from place to place, trying to secure a place of her own.

Uncertainty takes the form of ambivalence and illusion in the Bengali Baul songs of Lalan Fakir that Carol Salomon examines in her essay. Like *qawwālī* (cf. Qureshi 1986), the aims of Baul songs are, variously, religious instruction and the inducement of mystical experience (the mix of the two depending on the degree of initiation of the hearer; cf. Wadley's discussion of representational and relational meanings, this volume). But many of the present hearers of Baul songs, now claimed as a national poetry, appreciate them aesthetically, as clusters of poetic images, without grasping their propositional content to any degree, or subscribing to the particular devotional path which they enigmatically map (Capwell 1986). The pithy song lyrics themselves quite often mock religious authority and learning as illusory. At most, *bāul saṅgīt* ambivalently presents a path to follow toward enlightenment through the use of paradox. The musical poetry of the Bauls acts as a vehicle for paradoxical and elliptical statements that refer not only to cosmological doctrines but also to practices meant to embody those doctrines, some of which are highly repugnant to the noninitiated appreciators of Baul songs. As in Cevi's songs of complaint, points of view unacceptable to some powerful sectors of the audience are presented in veiled or enigmatic form (cf. Radner and Lanser 1987).

Baul songs, transmission, and singing practices also aid in maintaining the canonical status of the texts themselves. As Salomon points out, performers of Lalan's songs strive to adhere as closely as possible to the original texts in order to present Lalan's message accurately (and paradoxically?) as the tradition allows. The intentional ambiguity of Lalan's songs stems ultimately from the difficulty of achieving mystical awareness, the Baul path appearing ineffable to its adherents (but all too physical to its detractors). Lalan depicts this ineffability by employing a symbolic medium of word play, presenting paradoxical riddles which nonetheless, in Salomon's analysis, yield to specific (though often multiple) symbolic interpretation. For the genres, or subgenres (to follow Claus's lead), of *dhā̃dhā* and *hẽyāli*, conveniently translated in English as "riddle," are more like Zen *koāns* (Zug 1967), rhetorical questions that do not necessarily require an answer. One of the aims of Lalan's songs is didactic, it seems: the listener must struggle to work out his or her own answer to the enigmatic proposition without aid from the questioner. As Salomon demonstrates, such answers become possible only with intimate and specific knowledge of doctrines that are themselves paradoxical. Salomon relates the possible dual meanings of the often contrary words and concepts employed to the philosophical ideals which most likely motivated Lalan to use them. She keeps in mind the eclectic origins of these concepts in Hindu, Sufi, and Buddhist thought, a key to their ambiguity and paradox. Lalan's choice of homely metaphors—images of fishing, farming, and sailing—brings the project of synthesis into the daily, concrete world of his audience without diminishing its complexity. The resulting literature brings together and reinterprets different levels of tradition so that its appeal is broad and sustained, among people of different religious beliefs, over a hundred years of dramatic social change.

Wilma Heston's chapter, "Footpath Poets of Peshawar," provides another case study regarding the transmission of verse. As she points out, studies of such literature to date have concentrated on thematic analysis rather than on creation, transmission, production, and distribution (and by inference, audience reception) of South Asian traditions (pp. 305–6). Heston focuses on the historically identified Bazaar of the Storytellers in Peshawar as the still-current center of Paxto language popular literature publishing. From it she traces patterns of marketing and secondary centers of production of cassette and chapbook romances. Heston found a continuous interaction between oral and written song and print in Peshawar (cf. also Mills, this volume). Additionally, some forms of Paxto poetry sold on the footpaths are not indebted to classical Persian models, whereas others, such as *cārbaytī,* differ substantially from Persian prototypes. The dynamics of Paxto poetic genres disseminated in print and sound recording cannot be understood as simply the peripheral derivatives of a classical tradition.

As Heston observes, music is as integral to the performance of *qiṣṣa* narratives as it is to *ḍholā, qawwālī,* and *ghazal,* but the specifics of that musical dimension remain to be explored. The data that Heston provides offer insights into the cottage industry of cassette production and the changing nature of the authorial claims of poets and the charisma of performers. Heston observes that, prior to the cassette boom, transmission was predominantly oral in an overwhelmingly nonliterate community. Now, as a result of the onslaught of cassettes, we are confronted with a blurred line between personal/direct and impersonal/mass media transmission. On the basis of interviews with poets recorded in recent years, we know that certain singers and poets learned their craft from records, cassettes, and films, or were at least motivated by these models. Such singer-poets themselves may later become researchers, valuing the felt historicity of their subject matter enough to seek out the location where a story is said to have taken place in order to get the facts straight from local (oral) authorities.

The advent of the cassette, as Heston and Manuel (in the next section) show, has had a powerful impact not only on the dissemination of sung material but also on the styles of individual performers. Cassette marketing and packaging can be seen as a continuation of the chapbook tradition in one sense, since packaging has a problematical relationship to contents. Apart from entertainment genres, Roy Mottahedeh (1985) has shown how cassettes can serve as a powerful force in mobilizing people during times of crisis in another Islamic context; David Edwards (1987a, b) traces similar uses of cassettes in the Afghan revolution. It seems likely that mass media, especially cassettes, will emerge elsewhere in South Asia as media for engaging individuals in political discourse; their cheapness of production and ease of amateur duplication provide for fluid communication from grassroots to mass-audience arenas and back.

Tradition

Tradition is a term which has now become fashionable to deconstruct. The Hobsbawm and Ranger volume *The Invention of Tradition* (1983) is perhaps the strongest push in this direction. But tradition has been generally studied and problematized elsewhere (Shils 1981; Ben-Amos 1984), while the excesses of the Hobsbawm and Ranger argument have recently been tempered by Abrahams (1986). The critique of tradition as a fixed and natural bedrock or backdrop against which change unfolds has rightly been criticized, along with such related concepts as authenticity (cf. Adorno 1964; Appadurai, this volume; Handler and Saxton 1988). Yet societies do manifest certain configurations because they have come to be shaped in certain ways, not just by values and beliefs but by styles and genre conventions. The chapters in Part III all concern the landscape against which the problem of tradition, especially in a complex civilization, must be understood. This landscape consists of widespread and more local forms, the *longue durée* and the brief performance, the certainties of histories and the illusions of narrative. The chapters by Manuel, Brenneis, Blackburn, Hiltebeitel, and Narayana Rao and Shulman all concern tradition, loosely imagined, but in very diferent ways.

Peter Manuel's research addresses quite specifically the relationship between changing social structure and changes in musical genres, in this case, the Urdu *gh̲azal*. Manuel argues that, along with the decline of Indian feudal society and its patronage system and the emergence of capitalism, the advent of industrial technology, especially mass media (radio and recordings), has affected virtually every aspect of the development of urban Indian music. He takes *gh̲azal* as a special case for historical examination, because it is as popular now as it was in the nineteenth century. The transition from concert to cassette, from salon to concert hall, demonstrates the plasticity of the *gh̲azal*, its ability to expand and adapt over time to meet the aesthetic demands of the growing urban audience. One reason for the genre's adaptability might be the fact that a canonical aesthetic code for its performance never developed; yet the audience has always had expectations which were utilized in the past, as in the present, to evaluate performances.

As audience aesthetics change, performers must meet new demands or fade from popularity. At the same time, new technologies (such as amplification) facilitate new styles of performance (reflective, crooning intimacy at 95 decibels). The *ghazal* succeeded in bridging the gap between the tastes of the educated urban elite and those of the mostly illiterate working class. The Urdu *ghazal*, like the Paxto and Urdu narrative romances called *qiṣṣa* (Heston, this volume; Pritchett 1985), may owe part of its cachet to its Perso-Arabic roots. Drawing on literary, religious, and oral sources, the genres were able to generate an appeal cutting across social divisions and historical periods.

Manuel shows how the *ghazal* diversified into a "continuum of styles" after the initial impact of commercial gramophone recordings, but then became more generic as producers began to grasp its broad-based appeal. Yet while the *ghazal* may have become more homogeneous as it became mass-produced in films and recordings, there was a concomitant development of levels of complexity. Especially as cassettes, cheap to produce and easier to duplicate and listen to in a variety of settings, began to take over the music market from gramophone recordings, greater diversification appeared in sales and production because cottage cassette industries could address diverse needs of subgroups of consumers. Compared with the *qiṣṣa* romance narrative, which also has a double life in cassette recordings and popular print (Heston, this volume), the *ghazal* is a compact form with an emphasis on oral performance and highly personal emotive impact; yet the *ghazal* itself enters the realm of the fantastic in its important role in Hindi film. The *filmī ghazal*, in its elaborately visual frame, invites temporary entrance into a world that is enchanted and posed as unique and alien to the everyday lives and commonsense experiences familiar to its mass audience. But film, expensively mass-produced, is a primary factor in the homogenization of modern *ghazal*.

Donald Brenneis's essay considers diachronicity and spatial movement in an analysis of cultural diversity and the stories a community tells itself. With regard to east Indians in Fiji, he asks, how does knowledge get transmitted in a community far removed from its self-perceived origins? Does tradition in such a community disintegrate or innovate? Brenneis's model emphasizes not cultural loss of tradition, as many of Fiji's indigenous east Indian population would express it, but an exploration of the discourse which leads to "conceptualizing culture." Brenneis examines innovation rather than simple continuity in order to highlight the active role people play in the social construction of tradition (cf. Handler and Linnekin 1984). Brenneis reiterates that in performance, it is not just the performers who are actively engaged as interpreters, critics, and respondents, but the audience as well. All parties contribute to the shaping of successful performance events.

Brenneis describes the total configuration of Fiji Indian aesthetics as a complex of factors in three dimensions: performance, emotion, and experience, linked by the indigenous concept of *bhāv,* which has an Indian philosophical precedent and is itself a conjunction of feeling and display (Gerow 1977). In exploring the concept of *bhāv* and the performance forms known as *kavvālī* and *gālī* in Fiji, Brenneis reveals that even though Fiji Indians place great emphasis on the canonical status of printed texts used in performance and the historically Indian origin of expressive modes, their understandings of such texts and performances and their interpretive goals and performance settings, differ markedly from the corresponding Indo-Pakistani understandings of the parent institutions and concepts, not to mention the expectations for emotional and intellectual engagement with them. Differences in performance context, in particular, are critical to understanding the nexus of text, performer, and audience.

Stuart Blackburn, drawing on one of the most variegated and pervasive of Hindu India's religious storytelling traditions, the *Rāmāyaṇa,* undertakes to understand how classical religious tenets are incorporated into the quite different world view of a local or folk tradition. His thesis is that the classical devotional theology of perfection gives way to a principle of balance, which results in the construction of powerful ironies over and around the philosophical structure of the classical source text, Kampaṉ's Tamil *Rāmāyaṇa.* The local interpretation of *rāmāvatār* (the Rāma incarnation) does not merge the classical ideal of perfection with the folk conception of balance, but accentuates their difference. This equilibrium, and its interruptions, are expressed both by subtle adjustments in the narrative plot and by the visual array of puppets on the performance stage. According to Blackburn, the classical concept of the *avatār* as presented by Kampan "violates the basic principles of the local world view." The reworking of the classical conception of the *avatār* into a balanced world view results in a creative tension between *bhakti* and folk streams of Indian culture. Such creative tension amounts to what Jonathan Z. Smith (1982) has termed "situational incongruity" in religion, a context in which a preexisting set of beliefs no longer makes sense. When this happens, the incongruity in question must be creatively altered to flourish and expand. Blackburn presents an elegantly expanded example of the alternation of folk and classical value systems, a topic previously invoked by Ramanujan (Section I). Blackburn's example, like Ramanujan's discussion here and elsewhere (1986), points out the central importance of shifts in the portrayal of gender relations and roles in the articulation of folk versus classical cosmological views.

Alf Hiltebeitel likewise draws on one of Hindu India's most pervasive themes, the veneration of Draupadī, to examine the folk-classical relationship in India with particular reference to her cult in Tamilnadu. Ultimately he raises the issue of the need for a pan-Indian perspective (an admittedly huge undertaking) for the fullest understanding of the genesis and integrity of local forms. While Hiltebeitel feels that certain themes, such as Draupadī's hair and sarees, link regional epics, he concludes that if there is a "folk *Mahābhārata*," it cannot be monolithic because it has no prototype. Hiltebeitel thus asks how the classical *Mahābhārata* is transmitted and performed, and how themes diffuse from the pan-Indian tradition into the vernaculars and vice versa (cf. Blackburn and Ramanujan 1986, "Introduction"; Ramanujan 1986).

Hiltebeitel concurs with Blackburn and Ramanujan in recognizing the potential in local folk traditions for autonomous and even opposing interpretations of the vision of a parallel classical text. The *akam/puṟam* distinction explored by Ramanujan (1986) serves Hiltebeitel in his analysis of local *Mahābhārata* performances as fittingly located at the *puṟam* (public spectacle) end of the private/public schema: if read in the home, the *Mahābhārata* is said to cause domestic conflict, whereas the *Rāmāyaṇa* conduces to family harmony. (Claus's argument might, however, place some limits on the applicability of Ramanujan's schema; see Claus, this volume.) Hiltebeitel, like Claus and Wadley, presents material that confounds any mechanical approach to folklore genres. As he shows, epics are intertextual, especially conducive to incorporating such other genres as riddles, tales, proverbs, and songs (cf. also Korom 1989b). The study of multiple lines of transmission must therefore be multigeneric, as Hiltebeitel suggests. Furthermore, multigeneric performance formally accommodates within itself a diversity, and perhaps contestation, among the voices used in what Ramanujan calls the "construction of consciousness." The exploration of the polysemy of epic performances will be served by systematic attention to their complexities (cf. Lutgendorf 1986; Wadley, this volume).

In their contribution, Velcheru Narayana Rao and David Shulman also address the folk-classical relationship, in the most literary-historical offering in the volume. They find a strong, albeit ambivalent, relationship between south Indian folk stories and the courtly literature of the Nāyaka period in late sixteenth- and seventeenth-century Tamilnadu. They suggest that a folk counter-system with its own autonomous logic comments upon the courtly literature and functions not simply as a derivative foil to the classic tradition, or in dismissive satirical fashion, but as parody, which simultaneously sustains and critiques courtly values. Historically, the authors see the parodic commentary as part of a cultural trend associated with a bundle of other social changes occurring during the Nāyaka period. Nāyaka-period folk literature, suggest Narayana Rao and Shulman, presents a well-known theme in Indian tales, namely, the unforetellable future of kingship through role reversal, and also a counter-vision of power informed by ambivalence and sustained by its own illusions, whereas the Nāyaka literature demonstrates a gradual disintegration of illusion, which only briefly becomes reality to make a point. Illusion in Nāyaka literature recreates itself as only temporarily real, articulated through male manipulations of caste differences in the illustrative texts given, within which gender relations are a basic but secondary resource. The Nāyaka farce takes illusion apart and puts it back together again.

* * *

In the end, these essays recommend that tradition is an ever-receding point of social reference. Tradition is about "pastness" (Halbwachs 1980 [1950]) and not just about the past. It is not a positive discourse but a reflective and reflexive one. In it, and through it, societies explore the limits of their histories, and replay the points of tension in these histories. It is a metadiscourse, which allows the past to cease to be a "scarce resource" (Appadurai 1981) and allows it to become, to borrow an adjective from ecologists, a renewable resource. Tradition is another zone of contestation, though not about selves (as with gender) or about forms (as with genre), but about temporal boundaries themselves.

The problem of pastness itself changes as the modes of cultural reproduction change. As traditions become mass-produced, as cultural artifacts become commodified, as intimate performances become available to large audiences, the pastness of the present becomes itself a plastic relationship, bendable by the forces of singularization (Kopytoff 1986) and "commodification." The deep, creative force that now drives the reproduction of cultural forms in South Asia, and elsewhere, is the friction between singularization and commodification, as the culture industries seek to commodify and domesticate local voices, and local voices seek to incorporate the very commodified forms they are forced to consume. This global cannibalization of sameness and difference constitutes a complex dynamic which cannot fully be explored here (but see Appadurai 1990). What is worth noting is that tradition, heritage, and authenticity are all now terms proper to a landscape of heteroglossia and one of intense contestation. Such controversy in this volume, is seen in discussions of the ontological construction of the self, of genre fluidity, and of the internal politics of pastness.

This volume marks several developments: a further step in the newfound vigor of South Asian folkloristics; an invitation to savor more of the multiplicities of South Asia's folk voices; and a recognition that these readerly pleasures must co-exist with the fact that such folkloric production is inevitably political. This politics is not the politics of blood and glory, but it is no less political for being about selves, about narrative strategies, and about the fictional realities and the realities engendered by fiction. For the study of South Asia, this is an important step, because earlier conventions of scholarship had striven to keep the heat of politics out of the cool world of Indic texts and the gentle warmth of folk expressions. This comforting compact between Indology, folklore, and anthropology has come unglued as fieldworkers begin to see the fissures and fractures that characterize the links of text to social life, past to present, gender to genre.

We began this introduction with a reference to the controversy over *The Satanic Verses* by Salman Rushdie. We then conducted the reader through some of the terrain covered by this volume. The voices and expressions of many South Asian traditions are evoked here, as are the voices and styles of analysts who represent a wide variety of disciplines and interpretive stances. No introduction ought to simplify such a heteroglossic collection and to draw from it any simple moral or model. Yet there is a lesson in such a volume, a lesson that is elementary and valuable in a world where literature has become an occasion for xenophobia and terror on a worldwide scale. The traditions that have developed outside the Euro-American aesthetic orbit are extraordinarily diverse and complex, and they do not succumb easily to preconceived ideas of genre, readership, or style. From the materials in this volume, we are reminded that resistance can be silent or subtextual; that sorrow can be the occasion for entertainment; that some stories cannot exist if their tellers have not lived certain kinds of lives; that some tales and songs can subvert the common sense of their audiences and their performers; that history and illusion can be linked in many ironic ways; that mechanical reproduction changes but does not erase the politics of voice and genre; that life stories need not be about the self. These may not all be startling observations, and this volume contains many others. But they are a reminder that long-standing traditions of singing and storytelling outside the West constitute another world of textuality, in which the complicities of text, performer, occasion, and audience can be as subtle as they are diverse, and can be deeply different from our own. In the afterword, Arjun Appadurai reflects on where such considerations might lead, in future studies of folk expression in South Asia.

Arjun Appadurai
Frank J. Korom
Margaret A. Mills

References

Abrahams, Roger D.

1976 [1969] The Complex Relations of Simple Forms. In *Folklore Genres,* Dan Ben-Amos, ed., pp. 193–214. Austin: University of Texas Press.

1986 Complicity and Imitation in Storytelling: A Pragmatic Folklorist's Perspective. *Cultural Anthropology* 1:223–237.

Abu-Lughod, Lila

1986 *Veiled Sentiments: Honor and Poetry in a Bedouin Society.* Berkeley: University of California Press.

Adorno, Theodor

1964 *Jargon der Eigentlichkeit: Zur deutschen Ideologie.* Frankfurt am Main: Suhrkamp Verlag.

Appadurai, Arjun

1981 The Past as a Scarce Resource. *Man* (n.s.) 16/2:201–219.

1986 Center and Periphery in Anthropological Theory. *Comparative Studies in Society and History* 28/2:356–361.

1990 Disjuncture and Difference in the Global Cultural Economy. *Public Culture Bulletin* 2/2:1–24.

Bauman, Richard

1986 *Story, Performance and Event: Contextual Studies of Oral Narrative.* Cambridge: Cambridge University Press.

Bauman, Richard, and Roger D. Abrahams, eds.

1981 *"And Other Neighborly Names": Social Process and Cultural Image in Texas Folklore.* Austin: University of Texas Press.

Ben-Amos, Dan
1976 Analytical Categories and Ethnic Genres. In *Folklore Genres,* Dan Ben-Amos, ed., pp. 215–242. Austin: University of Texas Press.
1984 The Seven Strands of Tradition: Varieties in Its Meaning in American Folklore Studies. *Journal of Folklore Research* 21/2–3: 97–131.
Blackburn, Stuart H.
1988 *Singing of Birth and Death: Texts in Performance.* Philadelphia: University of Pennsylvania Press.
Blackburn, Stuart H., and A. K. Ramanujan, eds.
1986 *Another Harmony: New Essays on the Folklore of India.* Berkeley: University of California Press.
Blackburn, Stuart H., Peter J. Claus, Joyce B. Flueckiger, and Susan S. Wadley
1989 *Oral Epics in India.* Berkeley: University of California Press.
Bloch, Maurice
1974 Symbols, Song, Dance and Features of Articulation: Is Religion an Extreme Form of Traditional Authority? *European Journal of Sociology* 15: 55–81.
Boas, Franz
1914 Mythology and Folktales of the North American Indians. *Journal of American Folklore* 27: 374–410.
Briggs, Charles L.
1988 *Competence in Performance: The Creativity of Tradition in Mexicano Verbal Art.* Philadelphia: University of Pennsylvania Press.
Bynum, Caroline Walker
1984 Women's Stories, Women's Symbols: A Critique of Victor Turner's Theory of Liminality. In *Anthropology and the Study of Religion,* Robert L. Moore and Frank E. Reynolds, eds., pp. 105–125. Chicago: Center for the Scientific Study of Religion.
Capwell, Charles
1986 *The Music of the Bauls.* Kent, Oh.: Kent State University Press.
Claus, Peter J. et al., eds.
1987 *Indian Folklore II.* Mysore, India: Central Institute of Indian Languages.
Das, Veena, ed.
1986 *The Word and the World: Fantasy, Symbol and Record.* New Delhi: Sage Publications.
de Caro, Francis A.
1983 *Women and Folklore: A Bibliographic Survey.* Westport, Conn.: Greenwood Press.
Dundes, Alan
1966 Metafolklore and Oral Literary Criticism. *The Monist* 50/4: 505–516.
Edwards, David
1987a Words in the Balance: Honor and Sacrifice in the Poetry of the Afghan Jihad. Delivered paper, American Anthropological Association Annual Meeting.
1987b Poetics of Order in the Afghan Resistance. Delivered paper, American Ethnological Society Annual Meeting.

Farrer, Claire
1975 *Women and Folklore*. Austin: University of Texas Press.
Gerow, Edwin
1977 *Indian Poetics*. Wiesbaden: Otto Harrassowitz.
Gill, Sam D.
1987 *Native American Religious Action: A Performance Approach to Religion*. Columbia: University of South Carolina Press.
Gossen, Gary
1971 Chamula Genres of Verbal Behavior. *Journal of American Folklore* 84: 145–167.
Halbwachs, Maurice
1980 [1950] *The Collective Memory*. Translated by Francis J. Ditter, Jr., and Vida Yazdi Ditter. New York: Harper & Row.
Handler, Richard
1988 *Nationalism and the Politics of Culture in Quebec*. Madison: University of Wisconsin Press.
Handler, Richard, and Joycelyn Linnekin
1984 Tradition, Genuine or Spurious. *Journal of American Folklore* 97/385: 273–290.
Handler, Richard, and William Saxton
1988 Dyssimulation: Reflexivity, Narrative, and the Quest for Authenticity in Living History. *Cultural Anthropology* 3/3: 242–260.
Hanks, William F.
1989 Text and Textuality. *Annual Review of Anthropology* 18: 95–127.
Herzfeld, Michael
1982 *Ours Once More: Folklore, Ideology, and the Making of Modern Greece*. Austin: University of Texas Press.
Hobsbawm, Eric, and Terence Ranger, eds.
1983 *The Invention of Tradition*. New York: Cambridge University Press.
Honko, Lauri
1968 Genre Analysis in Folkloristics and Comparative Religion. *Temenos* 3: 48–66.
Hymes, Dell
1971 The Contribution of Folklore to Sociolinguistic Research. *Journal of American Folklore* 84: 42–50.
1981 *"In Vain I Tried to Tell You": Essays in Native American Ethnopoetics*. Philadelphia: University of Pennsylvania Press.
Jackson, Bruce, ed.
1987 Folklore and Feminism. *Journal of American Folklore* 100/398 (special issue).
Jordan, Rosan A., and Susan J. Kalčik, eds.
1985 *Women's Folklore, Women's Culture*. Philadelphia: University of Pennsylvania Press.
Kirshenblatt-Gimblett, Barbara
1988 Mistaken Dichotomies. *Journal of American Folklore* 101: 140–155.
Kopytoff, Igor
1986 The Cultural Biography of Things: Commoditization as Process. In

The Social Life of Things: Commodities in Cultural Perspective, Arjun Appadurai, ed., pp. 64–91. New York: Cambridge University Press.

Korom, Frank J.

1989a Inventing Traditions: Folklore and Nationalism as Historical Process in Bengal. In *Folklore and Historical Process,* D. Rihtman-Augustin and M. Povrzanovic, eds., pp. 57–83. Zagreb: Institute of Folklore Research.

1989b Review of *Oral Epics in India. Karnataka Folklore Newsletter* 1/4 : 15–19.

Limon, Jose, and M. Jane Young

1986 Frontiers, Settlements, and Developments in Folklore Studies, 1972–1985. *Annual Review of Anthropology* 15 : 437–60.

Lutgendorf, Philip

1986 The Life of a Text: Tulsīdās' *Rāmcharitmānas* in Performance. Ph.D. dissertation, University of Chicago.

Malbon, Elizabeth S.

1983 Structuralism, Hermeneutics, and Contextual Meaning. *Journal of the American Academy of Religion* 51/2 : 207–30.

Malinowski, Bronislaw

1926 *Myth in Primitive Psychology.* New York: W. W. Norton Co., Inc.

Mills, Margaret A.

1983 The Lion and the Leopard: The Composition of a New Fable in Traditional Style Articulates a Family Dispute. *ARV: Scandinavian Yearbook of Folklore,* 1981, pp. 53–60.

1985 Sex Role Reversals, Sex Changes and Transvestite Disguise in the Oral Tradition of a Conservative Muslim Community. In *Women's Folklore, Women's Culture,* Rosan A. Jordan and Susan J. Kalčik, eds., pp. 137–213. Philadelphia: University of Pennsylvania Press.

Mottahedeh, Roy

1985 *The Mantle of the Prophet: Learning and Power in Modern Iran.* New York: Simon and Schuster.

O'Flaherty, Wendy

1980 *Women, Androgynes, and Other Mythical Beasts.* Chicago: University of Chicago Press.

Pritchett, Frances W.

1985 *Marvelous Encounters: Folk Romance in Urdu and Hindi.* Riverdale, Md.: Riverdale Company.

Qureshi, Regula B.

1986 *Sufi Music of India and Pakistan: Sound, Context and Meaning in Qawwali.* Cambridge: Cambridge University Press.

Radner, Joan N., and Susan S. Lanser

1987 The Feminist Voice: Strategies of Coding in Folklore and Literature. *Journal of American Folklore* 100 : 412–425.

Ramanujan, A. K.

1986 Two Realms of Kannada Folklore. In *Another Harmony: New Essays on the Folklore of India,* Stuart H. Blackburn and A. K. Ramanujan, eds., pp. 41–75. Berkeley: University of California Press.

Ricoeur, Paul
1971a The Model of the Text: Meaningful Action Considered as a Text. *Social Research* 38/3:529–562.
1971b What Is a Text? Explanation and Interpretation. In *Mythic-Symbolic Language and Philosophical Anthropology,* D. Rasmussen, ed., pp. 135–152. The Hague: Martinus Nijhoff.
Rushdie, Salman
1988 *The Satanic Verses.* New York: Viking.
Schieffelin, Edward L.
1985 Performance and the Cultural Construction of Reality. *American Ethnologist.* 12:707–724.
Shils, Edward
1981 *Tradition.* Chicago: University of Chicago Press.
Smith, Jonathan Z.
1982 A Pearl of Great Price and a Cargo of Yams: A Study in Situational Incongruity. In *Imagining Religion: From Babylon to Jonestown,* pp. 90–101. Chicago: University of Chicago Press.
Stoeltje, Beverly J.
1988 Introduction: Feminist Revisions. *Journal of Folklore Research* 25:141–53.
Stoeltje, Beverly J., ed.
1988 Feminist Revisions in Folklore Studies. *Journal of Folklore Research* 25/3 (special issue).
Sullivan, Lawrence E.
1986 Sound and Senses: Toward a Hermeneutics of Performance. *History of Religions* 26/1:1–33.
Tedlock, Dennis
1986 *The Spoken Word and the Work of Interpretation.* Philadelphia: University of Pennsylvania Press.
Turner, Victor
1969 *The Ritual Process.* Chicago: Aldine Press.
1974a *Dramas, Fields and Metaphors.* Ithaca, N.Y.: Cornell University Press.
1974b Liminal to Liminoid in Play, Flow, and Ritual: An Essay in Comparative Symbology. *Rice University Studies* 60:53–92.
Van Gennep, Arnold
1960 *The Rites of Passage.* Translated by Monika B. Vizedom and Gabrielle [1909] L. Caffee. Chicago: University of Chicago Press.
Voigt, Vilmos
1980 On the Communicative System of Folklore Genres. In *Genre, Structure and Reproduction in Oral Literature,* Lauri Honko and V. Voigt, eds., pp. 171–188. Budapest: Akademiai Kiado.
Weigle, Marta
1982 *Spiders & Spinsters: Women and Mythology.* Albuquerque: University of New Mexico Press.
1989 *Creation and Procreation: Feminist Reflections on Mythologies of Cosmogony and Parturition.* Philadelphia: University of Pennsylvania Press.

Wheelock, Wade T.

1982 The Problem of Ritual Language: From Information to Situation. *Journal of the American Academy of Religion* 50:49–71.

Whisnant, David E.

1983 *All That Is Native and Fine: The Politics of Culture in an American Region*. Chapel Hill: University of North Carolina Press.

Zug, Charles G., III

1967 The Nonrational Riddle: The Zen Koan. *Journal of American Folklore* 80:81–88.

Part I

Gender: Voices and Lives

A. K. Ramanujan

1. Toward a Counter-System: Women's Tales

Although educated in the Indian "classics" like the *Mahābhārata*, the *Rāmāyaṇa*, the *paurāṇik* mythologies, and so forth, Indians are also exposed to customs, tales, and beliefs that may be quite contrary to what they find in the classics. These alternative forms embody ways that together encompass the possibilities envisaged by the culture. They may present different selections, viewpoints, and solutions, expressing "finite provinces of reality" (in Alfred Schutz's phrase) which bracket off *temporarily* other such provinces and forms. In each of the following examples, I shall explicitly contrast a well-known classical or Sanskritic story or point of view with forms I found among women, peasants, illiterate workers, and others in Karnataka. This does not mean that these different kinds of materials are exclusively the property of one class or another. It is not useful to work with terms such as "classical" and "folk" as terms in simple opposition, but instead they should be seen as parts of a cline, a continuum of forms, the endpoints of which may look like two terms in opposition.

Many of these tales (from my field notes) are women's tales. By "women's tales," I mean two things: (1) tales told by women and (2) tales that are centered around women. Sometimes the tales that are told by women are also told by men, but a single inquiry makes it clear that, invariably, the men had heard them first from a woman in a domestic setting, usually in childhood. Young boys and girls are told such tales by older women who feed them in the evening, in the kitchen—which is exclusively the realm of women. Boys, as they grow older (often no older than six or seven), may drop out of these tale-telling sessions, while girls continue until adolescence. Thus, these nonprofessional tellers of tales tend to be predominantly women. There are tales I have heard exclusively from men in a public setting: often long, romantic ones or more intimately bawdy tales. Even among these there are some that are women-centered. The focus of this chapter is on the nature of such tales whose protagonists are women—tales about mothers and daughters, mothers-in-law and daughters-in-law, wives and concubines, fathers and daughters. To these should be added village myths about goddesses, the lives of women saints, oral epics with heroines, women's retellings of the epics.[1] I shall speak here only about a small number of domestic oral tales and explore three themes: *karma* and its alternatives, stories about stories, and chastity.

Karma and Its Alternatives

Much attention has recently been paid to the technical category of *karma* (O'Flaherty 1980b). The term is used and discussed widely in epic, didactic, and philosophic texts in Sanskrit as well as in Tamil and other regional languages. It is often chosen as a, if not *the,* representative pan-Hindu, even pan-Indian, concept. Let us see how it appears in the light of Kannada folktales. But first let us consider the components of this cluster called *karma.* I suggest that *karma* can be usefully analyzed into at least three independent variables:

(1) *Causality:* Any human (or other) action is nonrandom; it is motivated and explained by previous actions of the actors themselves.

(2) *Ethics:* Acts are divided into "good, virtuous" and "bad, sinful"; the former accrue *puṇya* ("merit"), the latter *pāpa* ("sin [?], demerit").

(3) *Rebirth or re-death (punarjanma* or *punarmṛtyu):* Souls transmigrate and have many lives in which to clear their ethical accounts. Past lives contain motives and explanations for the present, and the present initiates the future. The chain or wheel of lives is called *saṃsāra,* and release from it is *mokṣa* (salvation, liberation), *nirvāṇa* ("blowing out"), or *kaivalya* ("isolation"), in different systems.

Each of these three elements may, and often does, appear in India and elsewhere in different combinations. For instance, Freudian psychoanalysis depends on causality, a version of ethics (e.g., a punitive superego), and no rebirth. Utilitarian ethics depends on element 1 and a version of 2 in its "calculus of consequences." Biblical sayings such as, "Whatsoever a man soweth, that shall he also reap," depend on elements 1 and 2, without 3.

Certain theories of rebirth may or may not involve (1) and (2), as in ideas as varied as the phoenix rising from its own ashes, or Śaṅkara's conception that "the Lord is the only transmigrant" (Zaehner 1969).

It seems to me that the combination of *all* these three elements (considerations of causality, ethics, and rebirth) makes for the special force of the *karma* doctrines of India. The following is a report on my search for this explicit category, as defined above, in Kannada folktales. Here is a folktale with variants recorded for six different districts, told by different castes:

THE LAMPSTAND WOMAN [*dīpada malli*]

A king had an only daughter. He had brought her up lovingly. He had spread three great loads [*khaṇḍuga*] of flowers to lie on and covered her in three more, as they say. He was looking for a proper bridegroom for her.

In another city, another king had a son and a daughter. He was looking for a proper bride for the prince. The search was on. Both the kings' parties set out, pictures in hand. On the way, they came to a river, which was flowing rather full and fast, and it was evening already. "Let the river calm down a bit. We can go at sunrise," they said, and pitched tents on either side of the river for the night.

It was morning. When they came to the river to wash their faces, the two parties met. This one said, "We need a bridegroom." That one said, "We need a bride." They exchanged pictures, looked them over, and both parties liked them. The bride's party said, "We spread three great big measure of flowers for our girl to lie on and cover her in three more. That shows how tenderly we've brought up our girl. If anybody promises us that they'll look after her better than that, we'll give the girl to that house."

To that, the boy's party replied, "If you spread three great measures of flowers for her, we'll spread six." They made an agreement right there.

When they were getting the town ready for the wedding, the rain god gave them a sprinkle, the wind god dusted and swept the floors. They put up wedding canopies large as the sky, drew sacred designs on the wedding floor as wide as the earth, and they celebrated the wedding. It was rich, it was splendid. And soon after, the princess came to her husband's palace.

The couple were happy. They spent their time happily—between a spread of six great measures of flowers, and a cover of six more.

Just when everything was fine, Mother Fate appeared in the princess's dream and said, "You've all this wealth. No one has as much. But who's going to eat the three great measures of bran and husk?" So saying, she took away all the jasmine and spread green thorn instead. The girl who used to sleep on jasmine now had to sleep on thorns. Every day Mother Fate would come, change the flowers, make her bed a bed of thorns, and disappear. No one could see this except the princess. The princess suffered daily. She suffered and suffered, got thinner and thinner till she was as thin as a little finger. She didn't tell anyone about Mother Fate's comings and goings, or about the bed of thorns she spread every night. "My fate written on my brow is like this. Nobody can understand what's happening to me," she said to herself, and pined away.

The husband wondered why his wife was getting thinner by the day. Once he asked: "You eat very well. We look after you here better than they do at your mother's house. Yet you're pining away, you're getting thin as a reed. What's the matter? The father-in-law, the mother-in-law, and the servant maids all asked her the same question. When Mother Fate herself is giving her the kind of trouble that no one should ever suffer, what's the use of telling it to ordinary humans? "It's better to die," she thought, and asked for a crater of fire. She insisted on it.

She was stubborn. What could they do? They finally did what she asked. They robed her in a new sari. They put turmeric and vermillion on her face. They decked her hair in jasmine. They piled up sandalwood logs for the pyre, sat her down in the middle of it, and set fire to it. Then, a most astonishing thing happened. Out of nowhere, a great wind sprang up, picked her out of the burning log-fire, raised her unseen by others' eyes into the sky, and left her in a forest.

"O God, I wanted to die in the crater of fire, and even that wasn't possible," she said, in utter sorrow.

When the wind died down, she looked around. She was in a forest. There was a cave nearby. "Let a lion or tiger eat me, I can at least die that way," she thought, and entered the cave. But there was no lion or tiger in there. There were three great measures of bran and husk heaped up—and on the ground were a pestle and a pot. She wondered if this is what Mother Fate meant when she had asked in her dream: "Who's going to eat three measures of bran and husk?"

What could she do? She pounded the bran each day, made it into a kind of flour, and lived on it. Three or four years passed that way. All the stock of bran and husk disappeared.

One day she said to herself, "Look here, it's three or four years since I've seen a human face. Let's at least go and look." She came out of the cave, and climbed the hill. Down below, woodcutters were splitting wood. She thought, "If I followed these people, I can get to a town somewhere," and came down. The woodcutters bundled their firewood and started walking toward a nearby market-town, like Bangalore. As they walked on, she walked behind them, without being seen.

As the men walked, the sun set in the woods. They stayed the night under a tree. She hid herself behind a bush. Then she saw a tiger coming toward her. "At least this tiger will eat me up, let it," she thought, and lay still. The tiger came near. But he just sniffed at her and passed on. She felt miserable, and she moaned aloud, "Even tigers don't want to eat me." The woodcutters heard her words.

They got up and looked around. They saw a tiger walking away from where she was. They were stunned, terrified. When they could find words, they came close and talked to her. They said, "You must be a woman of great virtue. Because of you, the tiger spared us also. But you are crying! What's your trouble? Why do you cry?"

She begged of them: "I've no troubles. Just get me to somebody's house. I'll work there. It's enough if they give me a mouthful of food, and a twist of cloth. Please do that much, and earn merit for yourself."

They said, "All right," and took her with them.

Nearby was a town, like Bangalore. The woodcutters went to the big house where they regularly delivered firewood, and talked to the mistress there. "Please take in this poor woman as a servant here," they said. She said, "All right," and took her in. The woodcutters went their way. She started work in the big house, doing whatever they asked her to do.

One day the mistress's little son threw a tantrum. The mistress said to her, "Take this child out. Show him the palace. Quiet him down." So she carried him out and, as she was showing him this and that to distract him, a peacock pecked at the child's necklace, took it in its beak, and swallowed it. She came running to the mistress and told her what happened. The mistress didn't believe her.

She screamed at her, "You thief, you shaven widow, you're lying! You've hidden it somewhere. Go, bring it at once, or else I'll make you!"

The poor woman didn't know what to do. She cried piteously. "No, no, I swear by God. It's that bird, that peacock, it swallowed the necklace," she said.

They didn't listen to her. The mistress said, "This is a tough customer. She won't budge for small punishments. We'll have to give her the big one."

And she proceeded to punish her most cruelly. She had her beaten first, then had her head shaved clean and naked, asked them to place a patty of cowdung on it, put an oil lamp on it, and herself lighted the wick.

She was given household chores all day. At night, she had to carry the lamp on her head, and go wherever they asked her to go. Everyone called her Lampstand Woman, Lampstand Woman. Time passed this way.

One day, the mistress's elder brother came there. He was the Lampstand Woman's husband. But he didn't know anything. He came to his younger sister's house, dined there, and sat down to chew betel leaf and betel nut. The mistress sent the Lampstand Woman to light the place where he was sitting, enjoying his quid of betel leaf.

She knew at once that this man was her husband. She swallowed her sorrow and stood there, with the lamp on her head. Though he looked at the Lampstand Woman, he didn't recognize her. She had changed so much. He believed that his wife had perished in the fire. He thought this was some shaven-headed servant woman getting punished for some wrong she had done. Without even looking at her, he asked her, "Lampstand Woman, tell me a story."

"What story do I know, master? I don't know any story."

"You must tell me some story. Any kind will do."

"Master, shall I tell you one about what's to come yet or what's gone before?"

"Who can see what's to come? Tell us about what's gone before."

"It's a story of terrible hardships."

"Go ahead."

The Lampstand Woman told him about the palace where she was born, how she got married, slept between cartloads of flowers; how Mother Fate appeared every night in her dream and tormented her on a bed of thorns; how she thought she could escape it all by dying on a pyre of sandalwood; how the wind miraculously carried her to a forest, and how she lived there on a meal of bran and husk; how she came with the woodcutters to this place and entered service; how the peacock swallowed the necklace when she was consoling the child; how she was called a thief and made to look like a shaven widow; and how she was condemned now to walk about as a Lampstand Woman. All this she told the prince, in utter sorrow. As he heard the story, he listened to her voice and began to see who she was. He recognized that this was his long-lost wife. He took down the lamp from her head, lovingly hugged and caressed her. He scolded his younger sister and brother-in-law for punishing his wife so cruelly. They fell at his feet and asked forgiveness—but he put his wife on his horse and left at once for his own town.

Everyone was very happy to see that the princess hadn't really perished in the fire. (Liṅgayẏa 1971:16–20; tr. Ramanujan, forthcoming)

The story of the Lampstand Woman is told in the Kannada, Tamil, and Telugu areas. I have an example each from Tamil and Telugu and six variants from several Kannada districts. Of the several points that can be made about it, the relevant one here is the mainspring of the action. What happens to the heroine has nothing to do with her character. It is made clear she is blameless. There is no villainy, no fault. Mother Fate seems a bit jealous of the woman's good fortune. Her speech in the girl's dream makes that clear: "You've all this wealth. No one has as much. But who's going to eat the three great measures of bran and husk?" A psychologically oriented interpreter might see in the dream an expression of the heroine's guilt over the prosperity, a need to earn it by suffering and hardship. That is plausible, but the storytellers (when I ask them) tell me it's all because of "what's written on the forehead," or the will of Mother Fate (*Vidhiyamma*). Character is not destiny here, nor does the character have to "learn through suffering" as in Western (Greek or Shakespearean) drama.

Vidhi, or Fate, is usually imagined as a woman, *Vidhiyamma* in South

Kannada; *Śeṭivi tāyi* in North Kannada and Marathi (Karve 1950). She writes on a newborn child's forehead all that is going to happen to him or her. Sometimes the *Vidhi* function is performed by Brahma. Several expressions refer to this writing on the forehead: *talaividi* ("head-fate"), *talaiyeḻuttu* ("head-writing") in Tamil; *haṇeli barediddu* ("what's written on the forehead"), *haṇebareha* ("the writing on the forehead") in Kannada; *phālalikhita* ("what's written on the forehead"), *brahmalipi* ("Brahma's Script") in Sanskrit and the Sanskritized dialects of various Indian languages. Some of the former phrases are also used as interjections and exclamations when misfortune strikes, like "*vidhi!,*" "*talaividi!,*" "*talaiyeḻuttu!*"

In another Kannada story, "Shall I Come at Seventy or at Twenty?" (Type 938B, in the international Aarne-Thompson index of tale types; see also Thompson 1964), a young king, his queen, and two children are at the height of their prosperity. On her way to the river, the queen is accosted thrice by a bird which says, "Ask your husband when I should come—at seventy or at twenty?" The husband decides that whatever it is, it is better if it comes at twenty when their bodies are still firm and can endure anything. So he asks her to tell the bird he would prefer it to come at twenty. When the bird hears this, it follows the queen to the palace, flies in through the front door and goes out through the back. And their misfortunes begin. Suffering defeat, exile, poverty, the king becomes a poor woodcutter. The queen works as a menial maidservant, is molested, abducted, and imprisoned in a ship by a merchant. The king is disgraced and separated from his wife for many years. Finally one of his sons wins a kingdom, the sons meet up with the merchant's ship, rescue their mother from her abductor, and reunite with their father (Hegde 1976).

In this tale, fate is not mentioned; only a sinister mysterious bird of ill omen brings misfortune. But it gives the king a choice of time, and he wisely chooses to suffer hardships in youth rather than in old age. Here too, there is no sense of past causes or moral responsibility. Compare this with the *Mahābhārata,* where the characters act and suffer for reasons of past *karma;* celestial Urvaśī's curse makes Arjuna serve as an effeminate dancing master for one year in Virāṭa's court. The exile itself is caused by Yudhiṣṭira's wager at the dice-game, which in turn is caused by Śakuni's vengefulness and, in some versions, by the acts of his and others' past lives. The Kannada folktales depict action within the span of a single life, no more.

A god like Śani (Saturn) or a goddess like Lakṣmī, if offended, may also bring misfortune. Many of the *vrata* stories and stories about Śani's power are of this type, called the Offended Deity stories. The Śani story is intimately related to astrological beliefs regarding the planet Saturn and his seven-and-a-half-year sway over a person's life. As a variant, some tales begin with an astrologer's prophecy of misfortune. The story works out the prophecy, despite the protagonists' struggle to escape it. An Indian Oedipus tale (Ramanujan 1983) begins this way. A girl is born and an astrologer prophesies she will marry her own son and bear him children. The rest of the story tells of the fulfillment of the prediction. The prophecies are seen as indicators of future events and there is no question of causality.

Thus instead of past *karma* as an explanation of present action, exemplified in both epic story and philosophic debate, folktales seem to depend on another set of explanatory notions: (1) arbitrary *vidhi,* or fate, who writes on the newborn's forehead, often personified as a goddess or Brahma; (2) an offended deity who wants a defiant person to toe the line; (3) a prophecy that cannot be evaded. Even curses are quite rare in these folktales, for they too are often earned by the individual's own acts, as in the classic case of Śakuntalā.

The overwhelming impression here is of the mysterious power of a fixed fate, which can only be obeyed and allowed to run its course. *Karma* seems to belong to another tradition altogether—with its complex intertwining of individual responsibility, multiple lives, the inexorable chain of ethical judgment and causation. The characters of these folktales live in a different ethos.

Not that our storytellers did not know about *karma.* Whenever Mother was angry with one of us, she (and all her fellow-mothers) scolded us with phrases such as, "You are my *karma,* my *prārabdha* [accumulated bad deeds] come now to torment me in this life." Terms of abuse as well as the Sanskrit epics were full of *karma* and its consequences—so one had to be careful to do good deeds and accumulate *puṇya,* or merit, and avoid bad ones which would heap up *pāpa,* or sin (for want of a better word), with evil consequences in our divine accounts. We also believed when we were children that if anybody was thirsty and needed water, we should not refuse that person—if we did, we would surely be reborn as lizards. But in the stories Grandmother told us there was no mention of *karma* or rebirth at all. They confined themselves to a single life span and seemed to work on a theory of action rather different from the karmic theory.

Donald Davidson (1980) and other philosophers speak of the difference between "actions" and "events." I find the distinction useful here. Actions have actors; actions express actors. Actions have reasons. Actors are responsible for what they do. Here character is destiny. But events happen *to* people. They have no reasons, only causes. Narratives motivated by *karma* convert all events into actions; in them everything has a reason, as in the *Mahābhārata*. But there is much in human reality that is not controlled by individual human beings—accident, social and economic institutions, nature itself, especially nature in its most intimate human form, one's own and others' bodies. This latter kind of reality, the uncontrollable part of it, cannot be rationalized, especially in the moment of crisis. It can only be accepted, or watched, laughed at or sidestepped and bypassed by human ingenuity. In these tales, this reality is not reasoned away, but faced. Here actions, even human actions, are seen as events. They have causes, no reasons. By enduring them, and watching for a moment of change that is the apt moment for action, and then acting—usually by speaking out and telling one's own story—one comes through. That is why many of these tales end with the heroine telling her story to "the significant other" (often through a device, such as a talking doll or lamp), resolving the crisis, enduring her separation, reuniting her with her husband and her kin. The tale has now become her story. Till then she had no story to tell. The whole tale is the tale of her acquiring her story, making a person of her, making a silent woman a speaking person. This may be why it is crucial that stories should be told, and why there are stories about not telling stories and why *they* should be told.

Stories About Stories

Here is one such story about stories.

> A poor widow was living with her two sons and two daughters-in-law. All four of them scolded and ill-treated her all day. She had no one to whom she could turn and tell her woes. As she kept her tales of woe to herself, she grew fatter and fatter. Her sons and daughters-in-law mocked at her growing fatter by the day and asked her to eat less.
>
> One day, she wandered away from home in sheer misery and found herself in a deserted old house outside town. She couldn't bear to keep her miseries to herself any longer. She told all her tales of grievance against her first son to the wall in front of her. As she

finished, the wall collapsed under the weight of her woes and crashed to the ground in a heap. Her body grew lighter as well.

Then she turned to the next wall and told it all her grievances against her first son's wife. And down came that wall, and she grew lighter still. She brought down the next wall with her tales against her second son, and the remaining fourth wall too with her complaints against her second daughter-in-law.

Standing in the ruins, with bricks and rubble all around her, she felt lighter in mood and lighter in body. She looked at herself and found she had actually lost all the weight she had gained in her wretchedness.

Then she went home.

This Tamil tale begins with a woman beleaguered and enclosed, and ends with her in the open, all her four walls demolished. The old woman tells her stories, her family secrets, only to lighten herself, not to enlighten anyone. Nothing is said about her cruel family being converted, becoming kinder; only she has changed, unburdened of her sorrows.

In our classical literature, too, stories are told performatively—they are not merely utterances, they are part of the action, they change its course, but they affect the *addressee*. In this Tamil folktale, the tale of woe is told to express and affect the speaker's own mood, to change one's own state. It is cathartic for the teller in the tale. Such a notion of catharsis is not part of Indian classical aesthetics. Note also how emotions have weight, literally—not metaphorically—"burdened," "heavy-" or "light-hearted." Tales and dreams take metaphors literally. Such literalization is not merely a literary device. It implies the sense that emotions and thoughts are substances. Material and non-material things are part of a continuum of *sthūla* and *sūkṣma,* "gross" and "subtle" substance allowing transformations. One may become the other.

In another tale, a barber, while he is shaving the king, discovers that the king has a donkey's ears. The king orders him never to tell anyone about it on pain of death. So he keeps the secret, but the more he keeps it to himself the fatter he grows. His wife is alarmed and, after much trying, wheedles the secret out of him. At once she begins to grow round, looking more and more pregnant, till one day, unable to bear the burden any longer, she digs a hole in the ground and tells her secret to the hole and covers it up. Out of the buried secret springs a tree. One day the palace drummer breaks a branch of the tree and makes drumsticks for his drum. When he beats his drum in the palace assembly, the drum says, "*Dum dum dum,* the king *dum dum* has the ears *dum dum* of a donkey, *dum dum* the king has the ears *dum dum* of a donkey *dum dum!*" Nothing is lost, only transformed.

A STORY AND A SONG

A housewife knew a story. She also knew a song. But she kept them to herself, never told anyone the story nor sang the song.

Imprisoned within her, the story and the song wanted release, wanted to run away. One day, when she was sleeping with her mouth open, the story escaped, fell out of her, took the shape of a pair of shoes and sat outside the house. The song also escaped, took the shape of something like a man's coat and hung on a peg.

The woman's husband came home, looked at the coat and shoes, and asked her, "Who is visiting?"

"No one," she said.

"But whose coat and shoes are these?"

"I don't know," she replied. He wasn't satisfied with her answer. He was suspicious. Their conversation was unpleasant. The unpleasantness led to a quarrel. The husband flew into a rage, picked up his blanket, and went to the Monkey God's temple to sleep.

The woman didn't understand what was happening. She lay down alone that night. She asked the same question over and over: "Whose coat and shoes are these?" Baffled and unhappy, she put out the lamp and went to sleep.

All the flames of the town, once they were put out, used to come to the Monkey God's temple and spend the night there, gossiping. On this night, all the lamps of all the houses were represented there—all except one, which came late. The others asked the latecomer, "Why are you so late tonight?"

"At our house, the couple quarreled late into the night," said the flame.

"Why did they quarrel?"

"When the husband wasn't home, a pair of shoes came into the veranda, and a coat somehow got on to a peg. The husband asked her whose they were. The wife said she didn't know. So they quarreled."

"Where did the coat and shoes come from?"

"The lady of our house knows a story and a song. She never tells the story, and has never sung the song to anyone. The story and the song got suffocated inside; so they got out and have turned into a coat and pair of shoes. They took revenge. The woman doesn't even know."

The husband, lying under his blanket in the temple, heard the lamp's explanation. His suspicions were cleared. When he went home, it was dawn. He asked his wife about her story and her song. But she had forgotten both of them. "What story, what song?" She said. (Lingaṇṇa 1972)

That story tells us why stories should be told, according to domestic tellers. Stories must be told because they are crying out to be told. For without transmission they suffocate, they die. Untold stories transform themselves and take revenge. They fester, create an atmosphere of rancor and suspicion, as they did between the husband and wife of this story. Note also that stories are physical things: they can take the shape of objects. The immaterial and the material are part of a continuum, interchangeable. Furthermore, neither flames nor stories are ever put out. They change shapes or move to the Monkey God's temple—with interesting consequences. The Hindu law of the conservation of matter seems to read not "When a candle burns, nothing is lost" but "When a candle is put out, it goes to the temple—for a gossip session."

In classical literature, stories (or texts) must be recited because they produce results. One recites the *Rāmāyaṇa,* or certain sections of it, for the prosperity of one's family or other such worldly results, or to propitiate a god by remembering his story. Every such text comes with a *phalaśruti,* a recital of results, telling one what one might expect from a recitation. Texts are magical, instrumental. Their reading has a purpose outside themselves, because they are efficacious. Their recitation has an efficacy similar to a Vedic or domestic ritual. But in the woman's tale, a story is a form of existence, it cannot be neglected, killed, or wished away. It has a life of its own and insists on being told and kept alive. Otherwise it can change into something else and take revenge.

Such stories also tell you that tales have to be told because they have an existence of their own, a secondary objectivity, like other cultural artifacts. They are part of the Popperian Third World or World 3, neither subject nor object, but a third realm that depends on and enters into the construction of both subjects and objects. It is in this sense perhaps that "myths think themselves through humans," as Lévi-Strauss would say. (1969 : 12) They hate it when they are not passed on to others, for they can come into being again and again only in that act of "translation." If you know a tale, you owe it not only to others but also to the tale to tell it, or else it suffocates. Like chain letters, traditions have to be kept in good repair, transmitted, or beware, such tales seem to say, things will happen to you. You cannot hoard them.

In another story told all over south India, a son cannot understand why his poor mother gives away half the food she earns each day. She says that she is, after all, an ignorant old woman, only Śiva knows the answer to such questions. So he sets out to go and ask Śiva the question about giving away food. On the way, he meets a king who has built a tank, but it is dry; a snake who is stuck in a hole, unable to move in or out; a tree that is unable to produce any fruit; and a man whose legs are crippled by paralysis. As he meets each of them, each one asks him to ask Śiva the cause and cure for his special problem. When the boy gets there, Śiva (who is chewing betel nut with Pārvatī after a hearty meal) tells the boy that each of them has been keeping something to himself—the king has a grown daughter whom he has not given away in marriage, the snake has a jewel in its hood he must give away, the paralytic has all sorts of knowledge that he is hoarding, and the tree is hiding a treasure in its roots. As you can guess, they are eager to give the young man the jewel, the learning, the treasure, and the princess—all, of course, thanks to his mother's *puṇya,* the merit gathered by her daily gifts of food with which the tale begins.

Daughters, wealth, knowledge, and food must circulate, these are *dānas*, or gifts, that, in their nature, must be given. Communities and generations depend on such exchanges and transfers. Stories are no different.

Such notions are not confined to grandmothers, peasants, and such other unlettered types in the culture. In a largely nonliterate culture, persons of every kind and from every stratum have large nonliterate subcontinents within them. Thus folktales and other genres, such as proverbs, riddles, and songs, each in its own contextual slot, are "constitutive of consciousness"—not only for the illiterate but for everyone. Oral literature precedes other kinds in India, offers forms, "presumptions of meaning," that are filled out by later living. We need to study Indians' favorite folktales and their role in modeling and "scripting" their psychic and relational lives.

Chastity

The Sanskritic classics of India, the two epics and the *purāṇas*, are peopled with examples of chaste wives, *pativratās*, who are devoted to their husbands. Any transgression of chastity is punished swiftly and surely, as in the case of Ahalyā. Ahalyā is seduced by Indra, who comes to her in the shape of her husband, Gautama comes home, discovers the erring couple, and curses Indra to lose his testicles. In the Tamil *Rāmāyaṇa* by Kampaṉ, the curse covers his body with a thousand vaginas. Ahalyā, the erring wife, is cursed to wander bodiless or, as in Kampaṉ, to become a stone.

But see what happens in a folktale told in several south Indian languages.

THE SERPENT LOVER

There was a young woman named Kamakshi. Her husband was no good. He went after a concubine. She was patient—she thought that the man would mend his ways and return to her tomorrow, if not today. But he got more and more deeply infatuated with his harlot, and took to staying with her night and day. His wife thought, "This is God's will, it's His game," and held her tongue. Two or three years passed.

One day, an old woman who lived next door talked to her.

"What is this, my dear? How can you take it, when your husband lies in the pigsty of a harlot's house? We must do something about it. I'll give you some love medicine. Mix it with his food and serve it to him. Then your man will be your slave. He'll live at your feet, he'll do whatever you wish. Just watch."

The despairing young wife thought, "Why not?"

She brought home the old woman's potion and mixed it with sweet porridge. But, to her horror, the porridge turned blood red. She said to herself, "This stuff, whatever it is, instead of making him love me, may make my husband crazy. It may even kill him. Let him be happy with anyone he wants. If he is alive, by God's grace, he'll come back to me some day."

And she poured the blood-red porridge into a snake hole behind her house.

It so happened that there was a snake in that hole, and it drank up the sweet porridge. The love potion acted on it and the snake fell madly in love with her. That night, it took the shape of her husband and knocked on her door. Her husband, as usual, was out. She was startled by the knock. Who could it be? Should she let him in? When she peeped at him through the chink in the door, the man outside looked like her husband. When she talked to him, he talked exactly like her husband. She took him in without asking too many questions and he made her very happy that night. He came to her night after night, and in a few days, she was pregnant.

When the snake came to know of it, he wanted to tell her the truth. He said, "Kamakshi, who do you think I am? Your husband? No, I'm the king of snakes. I fell in love with you and came to you in the shape of your husband."

Then he shed her husband's form and became a five-headed serpent. She was terrified and shut her eyes. He changed back into her husband's form again.

"You know now I'm the king of snakes. I live in that snake hole behind your house. I drank your porridge, and I don't know what you put in it, I fell in love with you. I couldn't help coming to see you and making love to you. You're pregnant now, but there's no need to panic about it. I'll see to it that everything goes well. Your husband will come back to you and live happily with you. I'll also arrange for that harlot of his to come and be your servant," he said, and went back to his hole in the ground as a snake.

The place buzzed with the news of the woman's pregnancy, and the errant husband heard about it too. He flew into a rage. "How could she do this to me?" he screamed. He came straight to his father-in-law and protested, "Father-in-law, I haven't slept in the same bed with your daughter for three years now. She has taken a lover, the whore. How else did she get pregnant?"

The father-in-law summoned his daughter and asked her, "Your husband is saying these slanderous things. What do you say?"

She replied, "He has never been good to me. But I've done nothing wrong."

Her father wasn't convinced.

That night she talked to the king of snakes, who said, "Ha, that's very good. Don't you worry about it. Tomorrow the king's court will be in session. Go there bravely, and say, 'The child in my womb is my husband's, no one else's.' If they don't believe you, say then, 'I'll prove it to you by taking the test of truth. In the Śiva temple, there is a king cobra. I'll hold it in my hand and prove to you the truth of what I say. If I'm false, I'll die.'"

Next day the raja's court assembled. The raja said to the husband who was there with his complaint, "Tell us what your suspicions are. The elders can clear the doubts."

The husband got up and said, "Elders, I have not slept in the same bed with my wife for three years now. How did she get pregnant? You tell me what you think."

She rose and expressed utter surprise. "O elders, if my husband is not with me in this, where can I go for witnesses? He comes to me every night. That's how I got pregnant. If you don't believe me, I'll go handle the cobra in Śiva's temple. If I've done any wrong, may it bite me and kill me."

The elders agreed to the test.

The whole court adjourned to the Śiva temple. There was an awesome five-headed cobra coiled round the Śiva-*liṅga*. Kamakshi concentrated all her mind and senses, and prayed aloud so that everyone could hear, "O lord, the child in my womb is my husband's. All other men are like brothers to me. If what I say is false, may you sting me to death."

Then she put out her hand and took the cobra, who was no other than her lover, the king of snakes. He hung around her neck like a garland, opened all his five hoods, and swayed gently. The onlookers were awe-struck. They said, "*Che, che,* there has never been such a chaste wife. There never will be another better than her," and saluted Kamakshi. They were ready to worship her as a paragon of wives, a *pativratā*. The husband was bewildered and felt like a fool.

Several months passed. She gave birth to a divine-looking son. He glowed and was beautiful. The husband took to playing with the child every day for a long time after dinner. The concubine became anxious about his coming later and later each day, and so asked a maid to investigate the matter. The maid reported, "He has a lovely son. Your man plays with him a lot after dinner. That's why he comes late."

The concubine too wanted to see the child. She sent a message through a discreet maid to Kamakshi that she would love to see the child of the man they both loved. Would she kindly send him with her maid for a short time?

Kamakshi, coached by her serpent king, said she would send the child on one condition.

"I've put a lot of jewelry on my son. I'll weigh him when I send him to you, and I'll weigh him again when he is returned. If anything is missing, that concubine will have to become my servant and haul pitchers of water to my house."

The confident concubine agreed and said, "Who wants her jewelry? She can weigh him all she wants." Before she sent the child, Kamakshi took him to the king and weighed the child with all his ornaments in the king's presence. The concubine was very taken with the child, took him home, played with him for half an hour, and sent him back carefully without tampering with any of his ornaments.

On his return, Kamakshi and her maids weighed the child again in front of the king. The king of snakes had done his bit meanwhile. Several ornaments were missing and the weight came up short. The king at once summoned the astonished concubine and ordered her to haul water to Kamakshi's house.

Her husband gave up the concubine's company, favored his wife in all things, and was supremely happy with her. In the happiness of regaining her husband, Kamakshi forgot the king of snakes. She was wholly absorbed in her husband and son now.

One night, the king of snakes came to see how Kamakshi was doing. He saw her lying next to her husband and child, fast asleep, contentment written on her face. He couldn't bear this change: he twisted himself into Kamakshi's loose tresses, which hung down from the edge of the cot, and hanged himself by them. In the morning, on waking, she felt that her hair was heavy. Wondering what was wrong with it, she shook it, and the dead snake fell to the floor. She was grief-stricken.

Her husband was surprised by her reaction. He asked, "Why do you weep over the carcass of a snake? How did a snake get into our bedroom anyway?"

She replied, "This is no ordinary snake. I had made offerings to him so that I may get my husband back. It's because of him you're with me now. He's like a father to my son. A snake is like a brahmin, twice-born. Therefore we should have proper funeral rites done for this good snake and our son should do it."

The husband agreed, and the son performed all the proper funeral rites, as a son should for a father. Kamakshi felt she had repaid a debt and lived happily with her husband and son. (Ramanujan, forthcoming)

Note how the lover in the folktale is never discovered, helps the wife get a son when she could not do so by her husband, helps bring the husband and wife together, and gets rid of her rival, the concubine. He even dies in a fit of jealous rage over her happy union with her husband, that he himself so nobly arranged.

The wife gets everything—a husband, a passionate fantasy lover, a child. She does everything right, too—she even has her lover, the true father of her child, cremated by her own son, which is the proper thing to do.

The story also mocks the classic chastity test, the test of truth. In the *Rāmāyaṇa,* Sītā comes through the ordeal of fire because she is truly chaste and faithful. Here, the woman comes through the ordeal of handling a venomous snake only because she has a lover—it is her very infidelity that is used to prove she is a *pativratā,* a faithful wife.

It looks as if it takes a lover to unite a man and wife who are caught in an indifferent marriage. The audience is sympathetic to the woman in this story and enjoys her triumph over all the conventional wifely requirements.

The split in the male figure between the sullen husband by day and the passionate lover by night seems also to hint at a common phenomenon in a joint family. When a couple lives in an extended family, the man is usually forbidden to show open affection to his wife during the day, with his mother and other relatives watching; sometimes the mother may explicitly frown on or mock the wife for encouraging public demonstrations of amorousness. But at night, in the privacy of the bedroom, or at least in the dark, the husband may change into an amorous and passionate lover.

If one were psychoanalytic, one could say that the classical Ahalyā story is told from the point of view of a punishing superego, which punishes pleasure and rewards asceticism. The folktale is told from the point of view of the pleasure principle, even the id, which uses all of the sanctioning devices of the culture (like chastity tests) to get its way. The two kinds of stories represent two points of view, and they need to be taken together. The ego needs both the superego and the id. The same tellers know both kinds of stories and tell them in different contexts.

One more interesting motif deserves comment. In such woman-centered tales, the snake is a benign figure. He is often a transformed brother, a grateful helper, a father figure, and, as in the present tale, the best of lovers who gives the woman everything—child, husband, even a reputation for chastity. On the other hand, in many male-centered tales, the snakes are rivals whom the hero kills or who try to kill the hero. The motif of the lethal first night is a characteristic example: anyone who marries a certain princess is found dead after the wedding night. And the king, her father, has issued standing orders that anyone who survives the wedding night will be rewarded with half his kingdom. Then comes our hero, armed with a father's precept, something like "Never fall asleep in a strange bed." He offers to marry the lethal princess and does. On the wedding night, he remembers his father's precept and keeps awake. When the princess sleeps, snakes come out of her nose (obvious euphemism? upward displacement?) and are about to bite him. He cuts them up with his sword. Next morning, everyone is astonished to see this bridegroom alive and they give the couple a big gala wedding. Here, certainly, is the male fear of the first night, the terror of the *vagina dentata,* the danger of female sexuality. Such differences in the meanings of motifs ought to make us rethink the simple snake = phallus equation. It means different things in male-oriented and in women-centered tales.

In addition, the well-advertised South Asian split of the women's image between the erotic and the fertile, between mother and whore images, between Wendy O'Flaherty's sacred cow and profane mare (1980), just is not there in these tales. When I told a brahmin woman the above tale about a snake lover, she told me that this story is a ritual tale (*vratakathā*) regularly recited on Subbarāyana Śaṣṭhi, the sixth day of the moon dedicated to cobras and to vows ensuring fertility.

These are what I would call woman-centered tales. Such tales share special characteristics. While tales that feature princes who go off on a quest for the golden bird in the emerald tree invariably end in wedding bells, tales with women at the center of action never do so. The women meet their husbands and are married formally or informally in the first part of the tale, often at the very beginning, and then the real story, usually nothing but trouble, begins. In this matter, they are unlike European tales of the Cinderella or Snow White type, which always end in marriage. The characteristic pattern of woman-centered tales begins with a first union, often a marriage, followed by a separation, and ending in a reunion and a firmer bonding between the woman and her spouse. In several of them, the middle part features the death of the husband, separation of the most drastic kind, as in this one (and in the classical tale of *Sāvitri*), and in the latter part the wife restores him to life. In this story the separation reaches its worst phase, her suffering its lowest depth, when the acrobat woman usurps her place and becomes her husband's lover. An upper-class woman's fear of the rivalry of a supposedly more vigorous lower-class woman is also evident here.

For the prince on his quest, a kingdom and a bride are the prizes he wins after his adventures and hardships—that is his initiatory scenario. But in the woman-centered tales, as in their classical analogues of *Śakuntala* or *Sāvitri,* it does not seem enough for a woman to be married. She has to earn her husband, her married state, through a rite de passage, a period of unmerited suffering.

I have used the term "counter-system" in my title. The term probably makes too strong a claim, but I have used it for want of something better. It implies a concerted system, while I wish to assert only that these stories present an alternative way of looking at things. Genders are genres. The world of women is not the world of men.

Some of these tales are creations of women's fantasy that deny in imagination the restrictions of reality, the constraints of family and custom, even within themselves. In these tales they bypass their own superego, and try to gain wish fulfillment that is unavailable outside the world of the stories. The woman with the serpent lover manages to have both lover and husband; and the lover provides her with everything she lacks in the beginning of the tale—a male child, her husband's attentions, a reputation in the whole town as a *pativratā.* And her rival ends up as her servant, hauling water to her door. Even her conscience is clear because her lover is a double, a lookalike of her lawfully wedded husband, and conveniently kills himself in the end. The woman begins with nothing and ends with the best of all worlds.

By means of these stories, women may be partly reconciled to the reality of their lives. Freud[2] quotes Plato as saying, "Good men dream what wicked men do." These are the dreams of good women.

As in the stories about *karma,* here is an alternative set of values and attitudes, theories of action other than the official ones. In an indissolubly plural culture like that of India, one may look for context-sensitive systems. As in diglossia and multilingualism, different dialects or even different languages are used in different sites, occasions, and functions. In a south Indian wedding, a Vedic fire ritual is presided over by male priests and conducted in Sanskrit. But after the solemn ceremony is over, other ceremonies are conducted by women with the bridegroom the only man present. There he is teased, posed riddles, shown mirrors. The in-laws sing, often scatological, certainly insulting, songs in the mother-tongue dialects to each other; the singing is dominated by especially the bride's party, which has been all this time forced to be ultra-courteous and hospitable to the groom's party. They remind one of the double plots of Shakespearean or Sanskrit plays, with a diglossia articulating different worlds of the solemn and the comic, verse and prose, the cosmic and the familial. The second alternate world speaks of what the first cannot—incest, the secret wishes of good men and chaste women, the doubts and imperfections of idealized heroes.

Such a presence of reflexive worlds; such a dialogic response of one tradition to another; the copresence of several of them in one space, parodying, inverting, facing, and defacing each other, sharing and taking over characters, themes, motifs, and other signifiers but making them signify new and even opposite things—this is characteristic of Indian creativity. I shall end with Mikhail Bakhtin's words about Dostoevsky's heroes, which also capture some sense of India's many dialogic traditions: "Every thought senses itself to be from the very beginning a *rejoinder* in an unfinished dialogue. Such thought is not impelled towards a well-rounded, finalized, systematically monologic whole. It lives a tense life on the borders of someone else's consciousness" (Clark and Holquist 1984 : 242).

Notes

1. For some of these materials, see Ramanujan 1985, 1986, 1988, 1989a, b).

2. In *The Interpretation of Dreams,* James Strachey's translation; see, e.g., the 1976 edition (New York: Basic Books).

References

Blackburn, Stuart H., and A. K. Ramanujan, eds.
1986 *Another Harmony: New Essays on the Folklore of India.* Berkeley: University of California Press.

Clark, Katerina, and Michael Holquist
1984 *Mikhail Bakhtin.* Cambridge, Mass.: Harvard University Press.

Daniel, Sheryl
1983 The Tool Box Approach of the Tamil to the Issues of Karma, Moral Responsibility, and Human Destiny. In *Karma: An Anthropological Inquiry,* E. Valentine Daniel and Charles Keyes, eds., pp. 27–62. Berkeley: University of California Press.

Davidson, Donald
1980 *Essays on Actions and Events.* Oxford: Clarendon Press.

Hegde, L. R., ed.
1976 *Namma Janapada Kathegalu.* Mysore: Institute of Kannada Studies.

Karve, Irawati
1950 A Marathi Version of the Oedipus Story. *Man* 99 (June): 71–72.

Lévi-Strauss, Claude.
1970 *The Raw and the Cooked.* Translated by John and Doreen Weightman. New York and Evanston, Ill.: Harper Torchbooks.

Lingaṇṇa, Simpi, ed.
1972 *Uttara Karnāṭakada Janapada Kathegalu*. New Delhi: Sahitya Akademi.
Lingayya, D., ed.
1971 *Paḍineḷalu,* Siḍlaghaṭṭa: Kannaḍa Kalā Sangha.
O'Flaherty, Wendy Doniger
1980a *Women, Androgynes and Other Mythical Beasts*. Chicago: University of Chicago Press.
1980b (ed.) *Karma and Rebirth In Classical Indian Traditions*. Berkeley: University of California Press.
Popper, Karl
1980 *Unended Quest: An Intellectual Autobiography*. Glasgow: Fontana/Collins.
Ramanujan, A. K.
1983 The Indian Oedipus. In *Oedipus, A Folklore Casebook,* L. Edmunds and Alan Dundes, eds., pp. 234–61. New York & London: Garland Publishing Co.
1985 On Folk Puranas. Paper presented at the Festival of India Conference on Puranas. Madison, Wisconsin.
1987 The Relevance of South Asian Folklore. In *Indian Folklore II,* Peter J. Claus, J. Handoo, and D. P. Pattanayak, eds. Mysore: Central Institute of Indian Languages.
1989a Telling Tales. *Daedalus: Another India* 118/4 (fall): 239–261.
1989b Where Mirrors are Windows: Toward An Anthology of Reflections. *History of Religions* 28/3 (February).
forthcoming. A Flowering Tree and Other Kannada Folktales.
Thompson Stith
1964 *Types of the Folktale*. Helsinki: Suomalainen Tiedeakatemia.
Thompson, Stith, and Warren Roberts
1960 *Types of Indic Oral Tales*. Helsinki: Suomalainen Tiedeakatemia.
Zaehner, R. C., trans.
1969 *The Bhagavad-Gita*. Oxford: The Clarendon Press.

Margaret A. Mills

2. Gender and Verbal Performance Style in Afghanistan

This chapter takes a peripatetic route to its central subject of gender, because it is precisely in, around, and through other sorts of social observations that gender asserts itself as a necessarily primary consideration. Close examination of a body of verbal art will reveal subcategories of the genre or genres under study and different predilections among performers and audiences within the range of subjects and styles of performance presented. Persian-language verbal arts in particular have thrived in an environment in which the boundary between oral and written productions is highly permeable, but reading and writing skills, never widespread, are also very unequally distributed among men and women. An understanding of the forms and values of oral tradition in Persian, therefore, entails a close look at the history and present state of literary pedagogy and of patterns of primary and secondary access to literacy skills, in which gender is implicated. This essay argues for the necessity of further detailed, wide-ranging sociolinguistic study in order to understand Afghan Persian oral narrative performance in particular, and illustrates that need on the basis of work already done, which provides at best only a partial picture of the complex social mechanisms involved in the formation of genres, subgenres, and styles of performance.

Among fashionable topics, primary attention to gender surfaced in folklore, as in the other social sciences and humanities fields, about twenty years ago. The half-life of intellectual fashions in the humanities and social sciences being fifteen years, gender studies should be declining into obscurity by now. That has not happened, however, because gender distinctions are a basic element in the organization of communications within any human group. Gender is, therefore, not so much a current topic as a necessary, integrated component in any adequate consideration of expressive processes. Just to review a few basics: gender is to be understood not as a biological fact but as a cultural construction. Biological differences between male and female humans are everywhere apparent, but each culture (or subculture) has its own notions of what constitute the "natural" differences between males and females, and how those differences do or should affect behavior, expressive or otherwise. Other societies' sexual divisions of cultural labor may appear to us to be more radical or pervasive than our own, in part simply because they are different from our own, and thus in our view striking, marked categories, with our own procedures as the unmarked, taken-for-granted ground. One of the potential benefits of a mature feminist scholarship, grounded in comparatism that integrates gender with other social dimensions, will be to enable Western academics to reverse that all-too-natural figure-ground organization in our own comparative studies, and thus remind ourselves how gender operates in our own taken-for-granted mental and social procedures.

To narrate a bit about my entry into the topic of gender: I did not go to Afghanistan with any feminist scholarly agenda. My introduction to oral narrative composition and performance, from Albert Lord, was largely silent on the subject of gender, save to observe that women in Yugoslavia did not perform the sort of long verse narratives that lent themselves to Parry-Lord style "oral theory" analysis (Bynum 1976). My preliminary research design for Afghanistan was simply to find out what types of narrative were most prevalent among Persian-speakers in the area of Herat, in western Afghanistan, to study their forms, learning, and performance patterns. I chose Herat on cultural and linguistic grounds, as I wanted to work in Persian language in a locale with a well-entrenched literary tradition and relatively little penetration by mass media. Influenced by Lord's thinking of the 1960s (Lord 1960), I was struck on my arrival in Iran in 1968 by what was by all accounts a long-standing symbiotic relationship in Persian between oral and literary narrative traditions. Such a sustained, mutual cross-fertilization of oral and literary traditions was not supposed to persist over time, according to the then-current dichotomous Parry-Lord processual model, which regarded the development of literacy (individual or societal) as antithetical to certain processes of oral composition and transmission.

I speculated then, and subsequent research has tended to corroborate, that procedures in traditional Islamic pedagogy, especially the development and use of certain mnemonic techniques in conjunction with reading and writing, sustain this relationship, whereas the pedagogy developed in the West over the last 200 years tends not to do so (Eickelman 1978; Wagner and Lotfi 1980; Street 1984). Research in the ethnography of literacy in the last decade and a half has revealed the complexity and variety of intellectual procedures which had hitherto been viewed as monolithic (Goody 1968; Havelock 1982; cf., Street 1984, Pt. 1; Scribner and Cole 1981; Stock 1983). Research on different oral traditions has similarly complicated the picture on oral poetics, composition and mnemonics developed by Parry and Lord in their original work in Serbo-Croatian (Finnegan 1976; cf. Blackburn 1988 for a study of the traditional use of written texts in one South Asian oral epic performance form). To date, however, Street (1984) is the only detailed ethnographic work available on traditional Persian-language pedagogy in a village setting. Further systematic research is needed to round out the picture of how oral and visual skills combine in learning in and out of school in the region.

Herat, less affected than Iranian cities were by mass media in the mid-1970s when I undertook my field research, seemed a good place to look at the oral-literate symbiosis in its pre-electronic form. The focus of that first research effort, which resulted in my dissertation (Mills 1978), was oral narrative tradition, with some preliminary attention to its literary connections. The ongoing study anticipated as a follow-up to that work, covering traditional Islamic pedagogy in Afghanistan more generally, is still pending due to the political disasters of the last decade.

Several developments brought my original research design for Herati folk narrative beyond the simple "go see what's there" rubric. First of all, extended verse narrative was not performed in Herat in any quantity. Since the Parry-Lord model of composition in performance was only intended for application to extended verse narrative, and such poetry was scarce in Herat, I primarily examined oral-literary relations in prose narrative, rather a different matter from the adaptation or composition in performance of verse. (I have recently analyzed two short oral performances of literary poetry, one in highly context-sensitive, edited verse form, the other, similarly reshaped by performance context, paraphrased in prose; Mills forthcoming.)

Seeking the loci of traditional narrative performance, I was directed by Afghan helpers and friends to two contexts: pilgrimage sites (especially certain large shrines managed by Sufi orders) and homes. There was virtually no public tradition of entertainment narrative (e.g., in tea houses) in Herat at that time. As a matter of fact, there were even ethnic jokes about Heratis' lack of interest in public entertainment, or rather, their tightfistedness in refusing to sponsor it (this notwithstanding H. L. Sakata's [1983] finding of abundant professional music in Herat in those years). The master storytellers (male) I met corroborated my impression of the undeveloped state of professional storytelling by remarking with surprise that I was the first person who had ever offered them money to tell stories. Although storytelling was not normally a paid entertainment form, when I asked people to record for me over periods of several days or evenings, I compensated them for their time. This sometimes had the effect of lengthening performances, when certain performers realized that they were essentially being paid by the hour.

Initially, I gravitated toward domestic storytelling, not because the shrine tradition was less rich, but because of local customs bearing on gender. My female presence was highly disruptive to the normal social interaction of male shrine gatherings, though I nonetheless enjoyed several productive narrative recording sessions at shrines under the unusual conditions of my own presence. Women I contacted at one shrine, gathered with the female relatives of the shrine's *khalīfah,* or guardian,[1] expressed interest in my work, but declined to be recorded. I inferred, perhaps prematurely, that women did not normally share traditional narratives at shrines, as men did, or that perhaps the devotional nature of their visits, compounded by the definition of the shrine as a public space, made women more attentive to restraints on their behavior, which they regarded as religiously based, especially the general prohibition of women performing or speaking publicly. Mernissi (1977) reports forms of women's talk at Moroccan shrines, especially personal experience narratives. Doubleday (1988) reports on a shrine visit in Herat with women she knew, including trancing and other verbal exchanges. Attention to other genres of narrative would probably have given me a different picture. It may be that while shrines are sites for ongoing avocational study of religious texts for Sufistically inclined men, they are not so for women, and thus the narrative component of traditional pedagogy which can take place there for men does not have a corresponding activity pattern among women. This is the sort of differential pattern that needs to be explored in future research.

The only women who willingly appeared in traditional male gatherings of any kind were a few professional singer-dancers who performed at weddings, and they were generally considered to be prostitutes. My presence as a guest in people's homes (while still somewhat anomalous) could be better integrated into local patterns of social contact than could my attendance at public gatherings of males. Hospitality to strangers is a value that Afghans regard as enjoined upon them by Islam, and so my presence was graciously received in the context of private hospitality. Furthermore, the mixed-gender domestic settings to which I had access were not open to my male counterparts, either foreign or Afghan (with the exception of Afghan men socializing with their own female relatives), so it became no liability but an opportunity to be steered in this way toward domestic rather than shrine settings and traditions. Finally—and I came to realize this fully only while writing my dissertation—the observation of the processes I found most interesting, story learning and story invention among adept narrators and the shaping of personal repertoires within a tradition, required a degree of intimacy and spontaneity between myself and my principal informants which was easier for me to achieve with women than with men. I wanted to be allowed to watch people flounder through stories they did not know well, or question each other about stories, or otherwise display behind-the-scenes aspects of narrative learning and performance. Generally speaking, my relations with male storytellers and the performances they offered me were more formal and less mixed with other kinds of communicative activities, and so the creative processes that interested me were kept rather off the stage of our verbal interactions.[2] Some women, by contrast, became familiar enough with my project to let me be present for these behind-the-scenes activities among themselves and other storytellers or members of their family audience. Not least because neither men nor women were much disposed to talk in the abstract about these processes, direct observation was crucial for my understanding of them, and it was women, not men, who let me see the processes. Gender relations were thus deeply implicated in the view of oral narrative that I or any other researcher could gain in this community. Domestic settings were more accessible to me as a woman, and women were more ready to reveal to me the messier processual aspects of narrative organization. Thus the exploration of the topic of orality (or of literacy) itself becomes a function of gender, of the researcher as well as the informants.

The pattern of formality and informality that I experienced is explicable from several viewpoints: one is that women rarely performed narratives to adult nonfamily members in Afghanistan, so their total approach to performance might be assumed to be more exclusively informal, personal, and interactive than men's. This generalization parallels Sakata's (1983 : 19) observations of women's musical performance and the asymmetrical distribution of both professional performance and audience participation in the various types of musical performance in which women and men engaged. Both aspects of female informality are corollaries of the general fact that women rarely or never socialized with nonrelatives (the exception being relatives-to-be, at engagement or wedding parties, and, for some city women, attendance at the public women's parties at the women's park during the spring New Year festivities). Men, by contrast, had regular occasions for communication with nonrelatives in the mosque, the bazaar, and in travel for military service, business, or educational purposes. Any sustained communications among women were mostly predicated on kinship bonds or on the near prospect of having such bonds, or occasionally on patron-client relations.

Male storytellers also performed for me in domestic settings (we were usually both guests in some mutual male friend's guest room), often performing the same genres, even some of the same items, as women, but the men's turns on the conversational floor tended to be longer, with fewer interruptions from children or others present either to comment on the story or to demand a halt in storytelling for other purposes. Making tea, caring for young children, and other intermittent domestic chores interrupted individual women's performances, but not the men's. Having no model for communications with another adult woman besides domestic intimacy, women shared with me unpolished as well as polished performances. Men, lacking any model at all for conversation with female nonrelatives, fell back on more formal interactions. Were the social status of the observer's own activities not factored into the observational picture, one might infer either that Afghan men do not indulge in informal or experimental performances, or, more absurdly, that these men do not experiment or struggle with narrative material at all. If such inferences seem absurd on their face, I would only point out the many inaccurate allegations made in the past by male researchers about women's lack of involvement in performance in cultures that maintain degrees of separation between women's and men's cultural activities. Such allegations are generally founded on a similar lack of opportunity for observation (Bell [1984], for example, examines the pervasive inaccuracy of the literature on aboriginal Australian religious practice in this regard). While Herati women's tendency toward informality in narrative performance was probably part of their larger pattern of socializing, some degree, at least, of male formality in the performances I witnessed was a direct function of my presence.

Into this picture must also be factored the formalizing influence of the tape recorder, an influence more visible among men than among women. Generally speaking, cassette tape recorders were familiar objects in Herat by the time I got there, but they were generally owned and operated by young men. Young men would take their tape recorders—often the fruit of stints as guest workers in Iran—to parties or concerts, either to play and copy tapes or, if live entertainment was offered, to record that. The stages for evening concerts in the fasting month of Ramazan, very public, formal, commercial affairs, would sprout a veritable forest of portable recorders brought by audience members. These young men had developed ideas about what was worthy of recording: performances were rather strictly bounded. Recording was limited to the actual instrumental piece or song, or, on a few occasions when young men gathered with me to record stories and brought their own tape recorders, they would turn them on with a tale's opening lines and off with its closing formulas. Both my male research assistants, who accompanied me to male gatherings at different stages of my work, discouraged me from leaving the tape recorder on after the narrative or song had ended. In their view, tape and batteries ought not to be wasted on surrounding conversation, commentary, or preparatory activities associated with the performance. So my introduction of a tape recorder into domestic storytelling sessions, which were not normally taped, tended to associate storytelling with the more formal, bounded organization of public performances as exemplified by music, and accentuated, and perhaps created, boundaries between conversation and narrative performance, at least in the company of men who were part of the "radio cassette" subculture.

Women, young or old, were less likely to manipulate tape recorders for their own entertainment, and were generally reluctant to have their voices taped unless they were assured that no males in Afghanistan would hear the tapes (an expectation I honored). A few elderly women I recorded did not initially relate the sound they heard on the tape to their own voices: one asked whether it was a little man or a little woman speaking out of the machine, then, listening closely, remarked with amazement, "It remembers every word!" This degree of naïveté was somewhat extreme (her younger female relatives teased her), but generally, women were not used to thinking of their own voices as separable from themselves. Women's gatherings did not yet participate in the production end of the taping culture whereby privately made tapes became public documents, circulated and copied among circles of (male) friends, though they listened with pleasure to tapes of male performance when they were played at home. In conformity with women's avoidance of this new sort of public exposure, I promised not to circulate any tapes made of women performing. Thus my taping of women had less effect on the "stagedness," formality, or boundedness (or interactiveness) of women's domestic performances. Like other gender-based differences in communicative habits, access to tape recorders precipitated differences in the style of performances I was offered by men and women.

Within the traditional setting, effects of gender on performance in different genres vary, partly according to the degree to which a performance genre is displayed in public. Islamic Herat, both Shi'a and Sunni, rather strenuously upholds the segregation of unrelated men and women. Unlike women in some other communities in Afghanistan and Iran, rural women in the Herat area are excluded from work in the fields and confine their productive activities to the home compound and its immediate environs. Nor do women normally attend the weekly Friday prayer and sermons in the congregational mosque. Other public movements of women are similarly limited.

Gender, just as it conditions the social access that individuals have to one another, is likely also to condition their technological access to different communicative resources. The differential use of tape recorders is part of a larger, long-standing pattern of gender-based differences, which pertain even in the absence of such cultural anomalies as myself or new, foreign gadgets. According to Afghan educators I met in those years, and others I have interviewed recently in the Peshawar-area Afghan refugee community, one of the most frequently voiced traditional objections to teaching females to write is that the skill would enable them to write love letters and thus promote illicit contacts. The connections between social rules and access to technology require more systematic examination, both the ideologically self-conscious connections, as in the case of differential access to writing skills, and other patterns that may be less self-conscious but are implied by articulated ideological constraints. For some educational and technological reformists, the dismantling of traditional social patterns is a hidden (or not-so-hidden) agenda in development schemes, while others rather optimistically argue that technology can be transferred without ideological transfer. But even observational fieldwork, with no component of intentional social intervention for change, affects the patterns of communication within the group being studied. A correct assessment of traditional gender-based patterns can only be approached when full cognizance is taken of the degree to which the recording or other observational processes (and their agent or agents) introduce anomalies. Susan Slyomovics's recent (1987) work on Bani Hilal epic performance in Egypt provides another example of the importance of such considerations in the analysis of performance.

In Herat in the 1970s, instrumental music had a strong tradition of professionalism, clearly distinguished from amateur performance, with various occasions during which professionals performed publicly, sometimes joined by amateurs. These artists were overwhelmingly male. Professional musicians (and traditional play-actors) were either recruited from the pseudo-ethnic subgroup known as *jat* (roughly equivalent to Gypsies in European stereotype) or recruited *to* that group by virtue of their musical professionalism (Baghban 1977). There were a few troupes of female musicians, from the same families as the male bands, who mainly performed for the women's parties at the larger weddings, as well as some single female singers or dancers who performed with male musical troupes before male audiences (Sakata 1983; a moving and informative portrait of the premier professional woman musician in Herat, both as a performer and as a member of her extended family, can be found in Doubleday 1988). But for the most part, women guests at weddings and circumcisions supplied their own entertainment, taking turns playing the tambourinelike *dāyirah* hand drum (a women's instrument), singing traditional wedding songs and folk quatrains (*chārbaytī*), and dancing either singly or in groups. The women professionals, when present, generally played the drum and sang in order for female guests to dance and sing along together the traditional wedding songs. The male half of such celebrations more strictly divided guests from performers when professionals were present. Male musical troupes, with or without female dancer/singers, would perform and the male audience would watch. Guests who were known to be particularly gifted singers or dancers might be cajoled to perform individually with backup from the professionals, which they would do only with shows of reluctance. Male musicians also played a wider range of instruments than their female counterparts, including various stringed and percussion instruments. The simplest male ensemble, for less elaborate events, consisted of the *sāz* or *sūrnā* (oboe) and *dohol* (a hand-held drum beaten with a single stick). Women's music was thus less professionalized, less diversified, and more participatory than men's, even when professionals were present.

Narrative, unlike music, lacked a highly professionalized dimension at that time in Herat, though it had an equally rich and intricate tradition. The types of material I heard performed, prodominantly in domestic settings, included extremely numerous fictional folktales, generally called *awsānah* (lit. Persian *afsāneh*). This indigenous genre designation, as used by some informants, encompassed not only wonder tales similar to European *Märchen,* but also tall tales and humorous anecdotes (including those of the famous trickster-fool, Mulla Nasr ud-Din), sometimes also animal and other fables (designated *masal* in literary contexts), and chain tales, the latter told primarily for or by children. Besides those stories which Heratis readily identified as *awsānah* and considered fiction (also *dorūgh,* "lies"), there were legends of the Prophet and of local saints; legends of other historical figures, such as the famous King Mahmud of Ghazni or the Iranian Shah ʾAbbās; a few stories derived from the Persian national epic *Shāhnāmeh* or related epic material; and the long, multi-episodic prose adventure tales or romances called *dāstān* in Iran and on the subcontinent (but not so specifically designated, so far as I could tell, in Herat). Although these latter complex tales, told almost exclusively by men, functioned as a genre, Herati informants usually designated them only by individual titles, mainly the name(s) of one or more of the main characters, rather than by a single generic term.

Besides a range of narratives, women also performed bodies of traditional quatrains (*chārbaytī*) and other verses appropriate for the bride's family and groom's family, respectively, at weddings. Both men and women commanded repertoires of mainly romantic *chārbaytī* not tied to any ritual occasion. Some women performed mimetic songs in which sung verses accompanied the motions of harvesting or other activities. I did not encounter men who performed the latter sort of songs, though they may exist.

To return to narrative, *awsānah,* broadly defined, together with most of the other types of stories from the above list, are told by both men and women. Traditional folk drama was exclusively male in its public forms, but I was told of forms of comic skits, perhaps an extension of the mimetic songs, performed by and for women at home (cf. Baghban 1977, a comprehensive study of folk theater in Herat). Performances of *Shāhnāmeh* epic stories in either prose or verse were few, and I only heard them from men, though my sample of three male performers was too small to be definitive. *Dāstān* prose romances, on the other hand, were quite popular but, clearly, men predominated in their performance. The plot structures and subject matter of many of the *dāstān* popular in Herat at that time did not differ materially from that of many romantic stories designated *awsānah* and performed by women. (The basic plot is, boy falls in love with girl, sometimes in a dream or through other magical intercession; boy meets girl, boy loses girl and goes on quest; boy gets girl back, usually to the consternation of some false suitors and at least some of her relatives.) The difference between the many *awsānah* concerned with courtship quests and the *dāstān* commonly performed in the Herat area seemed to be mainly in length and intricacy of descriptive development and in the types of poetry likely to be included, rather than basic plot structure. This lack of complexity seems to distinguish the Persian *dāstān* then popular in Herat from the more elaborated ones Frances Pritchett (1985) has described in Urdu written form from the subcontinent. Multivolume literary *dāstān,* including the *Hamzanāmeh,* which reached even greater levels of elaboration in Urdu, did exist and were orally performed in Herat, but less frequently than the shorter examples. One feature which characterized many of the best-known *dāstān* was the inclusion of substantial amounts of sung poetry, in the form of lyric *chārbaytī* quatrains exchanged between the romantic couple, sung by the narrator without accompaniment.

I met a few women who knew all or part of a single *dāstān,* but no women who had multiple *dāstān* in their active repertoires, whereas a number of men knew multiple *dāstān* as well as other types of narratives. Since there was no prohibition on women singing lyric *chārbaytī* quietly at home, and women had repertoires of such poetry not associated with narratives, I am still puzzled as to why women, in a performance tradition that was predominantly domestic for both men and women, did not perform these more extended narratives. Nor does the women's relative exclusion of *dāstān* from their repertoires seem to relate to complexity of plot, since women do perform complex, multi-episodic folktales with great relish. While romantic *awsānah* averaged twenty to thirty minutes in length, the shortest *dāstān* performances were about an hour long, not necessarily because of greater density of plot incidents but because of more elaborated dialogue and descriptive detail and the verse inclusions, which lengthened the dialogue sequences. One young male informant, with whom I worked extensively transcribing tapes, was not a performer himself but an audience member in his own social circles; when asked why women did not perform this type of story, he laughed and said, "They just can't—it's too difficult for them."

Intricacy of plot seems to be less at stake in this distinction between male and female narrative fluency than are certain kinds of ornamentation of incident, ways of talking. I am still investigating these differences in repertoire in my collection of recorded performances, but one can begin to connect these gender differences to gender-based differences in access to literary narrative of various kinds, thus to literacy-influenced vocabulary and speech styles, and perhaps also to gender-based differences in the length of turns to talk, which may be unrelated to literacy or nonliteracy, except insofar as literacy is prestigious and those with prestige can more readily claim the conversational floor. Simple allegations of gender-based natural capacity or incapacity such as my young male informant offered may figure in local interpretations of the distribution of social, intellectual, and cognitive skills, as indeed they are prominent in the debates on gender within our own society. However arbitrary or nonexplanatory they may appear from an extracultural vantage point, as part of indigenous social-organizational maps these statements should be carefully noted, with attention to the age, gender, social status, ethnicity, occupation, and training of each informant who furnishes such observations. More systematic inquiry into the whys and hows of cultural divisions of labor at this level of detail (here, the gendered distribution of morphologically and topically similar subgenres of oral narrative) would both lead to and depend on a more comprehensive inquiry into traditional learning and pedagogy of all kinds, not just that directly concerned with the transmission and performance of oral entertainment narrative. More informative answers to a question such as "Why don't women perform *dāstān*?" should ultimately come in the form of comprehensive descriptions of the overlapping domains of male and female discourse. An answer such as "Because it's too difficult for them" verifies the existence of such domains and invites their study. The perspectives of individuals on the exact composition of the expressive map are likely to differ systematically in relation to their age, gender, and social position. Attention to individual perspectives on the reasons for the map's configuration (as they see it) will also produce a finer-grained sociolinguistic picture than has hitherto been available to outsiders.

Regarding the oral-literary connection, many of the *dāstān,* unlike *awsānah,* exist in written form in small, lithographed Persian-language chapbooks that are printed mostly in Iran and northwest Pakistan and sold in the bazaars of Afghan cities and towns (cf. Heston, this volume). Reading stories aloud is a recognized form of entertainment in households where there are readers (a small minority—fluent readers probably numbered between 5 and 10 percent of males and less than 1 percent of females in 1974–76). Besides their limited edge in access to education, men also have regular access to written words through reading and discussion of religious writings, often narratives, in connection with mosque sermons. Women do not normally attend mosque prayer, although they do visit shrines, mainly for votive purposes.

Regarding entertainment literature, nonliterate men reported to me that they had learned certain stories from the reading of other men, while literate and nonliterate storytellers alike often readily and accurately identified stories that existed in written versions ("had a book," in Persian) and could readily recall whether they had learned individual stories from reading or from hearing others' oral performances. No woman reported learning a story from hearing it read (except perhaps for a few folktales performed on Kabul radio), nor were any of my primary female informants literate. Although not all *dāstān* exist in written versions, many do, and in the repertoires of some adept male storytellers, use of "bookish" (*ketābī*) lexical forms in performance was more pronounced when they told *dāstān* than when they told *awsānah,* implying to me that some storytellers at least associated these long romances with literary language. There are numerous differences between classical Persian, as it is written even in popular literature, and spoken Persian in any of its current dialects. The most obvious differences between written Persian and spoken Herati are lexical, and morphological in such features as verb inflections and plural formations, but also evident are some syntactical differences, greater elaboration of syntactic parallelism and compound-complex sentence structure in written Persian. Framing devices are also more elaborated in written than in non-written narratives, oral constructions being more constrained by time limits, but the manipulation of frames and subplots is aesthetically valued in performance whether the source is oral or literary.

Male-performed romances were longer than *awsānah* in part because of a greater use of ornamental language whose models are to be found in literary style. Men's greater command of these forms conforms with their generally greater involvement with formal social interaction, as well as with their somewhat greater access to formal education, but it must be stressed that many of the men who used literary or pseudo-literary verbal styles were not themselves literate. Gender-appropriateness in speech behavior seemed to accommodate men's laying claim to "bookish" forms, whether or not they were formally educated, while women tended not to appropriate such speech patterns.

Now that women have greater exposure to formal speech in the home through radio broadcasts (news, narratives, sermons) and tapes of such things as sermons of famous preachers, which circulate privately and commercially, it remains to be seen whether women will appropriate more literary forms into their own narrative performances (cf. Webber 1985). Women's narrative performances certainly are conceived by both performers and audience members to have aesthetic worth, but it remains to be explored how far the use of literary-style speech is itself a gender-bound language pattern with aesthetic implications rooted in gender-appropriateness rules, independent of gender-bound patterns of exposure to such speech. Individual women's relative nonuse of literary forms cannot even be assumed to indicate lack of knowledge of the forms. Folklorists of various traditions have for some time noted the existence of "passive bearers," individuals who make up a critical audience for traditional performance because they know the material of performance well and interact with performers knowledgeably, but do not themselves perform. The case of the distribution of oral narrative genres in Persian invites a close investigation of women's (and men's) attitudes toward language and especially their notions of aesthetically pleasing and powerful speech. In Iranian Persian, speech appropriateness is highly nuanced according to the relative status of speaker and listener (Beeman 1986). Afghan Persian usage is no less complex, though the aesthetic and underlying social values are somewhat different and not yet the subject of systematic study. Beeman was primarily concerned with conversational exchanges, but social relations of speaker and audience are no less implicated in the language and subject matter of extended narrative performance, its indigenous evaluation and interpretation.

The spread of government-sponsored formal education has had some paradoxical effects on attitudes toward speech (cf. Ghani 1988 for a historical overview of this transition from the point of view of elite literature). Two young male schoolteachers of my acquaintance, trained in the French-modeled government school system, heard me recording a male master storyteller who used literary and pseudo-literary language forms extensively. He was a master of *dāstān* who knew at least fifteen different romances. The two schoolteachers criticized his speech style as pretentious, pseudoliterate, and verbose. One of them arranged for me to hear stories from his own very elderly, blind aunt (the woman who wanted to know whether it was a male or female voice in the tape recorder), because he found her simple, somewhat taciturn village Persian more aesthetically pleasing than the elaborate language of the male romancer, whose pseudoliteracies and tendencies to hypercorrection particularly annoyed him. I asked one of my research associates, an economics student at Kabul University who, like one of the two young schoolteachers, had known this romance storyteller well since childhood, what people in their circle of acquaintance thought about his storytelling language. He responded, "They like it—people like to hear unusual words."

Yet there was some tendency toward rejection of pseudoliterate language in oral performance even by traditional literates. One of the most highly literate storytellers I recorded, an elderly mullah with a traditional religious education who was widely read in religious and classical literary narrative texts, substantially eschewed the use of literary forms in his oral performances that I recorded, even when he was performing literary-derived material (Mills forthcoming; 1991).

Gender distinctions in speech are of course intimately linked to speech communities and subcommunities. Ravan Farhadi, a Sorbonne-trained Afghan linguist, observed to me in 1974 that in Afghanistan as in other traditional societies, dialectologists' interests were best served by studying the speech of women, since they tend to speak in purer regional styles, having less exposure to speech styles of people outside their own immediate kin groups.[3] Mass media can be expected to alter this picture somewhat, but it remains to be seen whether diglossia will become a more visible feature of women's speech under these influences. Such a development might imply a greater formalizing of women's performance forms, among other things, but formalization is a matter not simply of aesthetic preference but of the larger social dimensions of performance context, in which appropriateness rules (including aesthetic standards) operate. Exposure to speech forms does not automatically cause their adoption into active use. The adoption of speech styles by segments of a population that did not previously use them potentially changes not only the status of the group but also the status of the forms so adopted.

Besides lexical and morphological variations related to literary influence, intonation and vocalization patterns also vary between men and women and between narrative and non-narrative speech in both gender groups. In general, Herati Persian tends toward vowel placement that is higher, more frontal, and in some cases more nasalized than, for example, Kabul dialect. Herati also appears to have a wider total tonal contour than Kabuli (though probably not as wide as Tehran dialect). These tendencies appeared to me to be more pronounced in women's speech than in men's, though such things are hard to quantify, and if true, this differential may be part of the relatively greater regionalism of women's speech which Farhadi noted.

Extended narrative speech of both women and men has intonational patterns (pitch contours and cadences) that differ from conversational speech. At present, I am more cognizant of the individual differences in narrative pitch contours (which amount almost to signatures or fingerprints of individual storytellers) and am not yet confident of generalizations differentiating male from female storytellers on this basis. But in general, the pitch contours of narrative tend to cluster breath-segments (clauses, what we would call sentences, or long phrases), ending each with a pitch configuration that signals semi-closure ("there's more to come"), rather than a full closure which would permit or invite another speaker to take the floor. In narrative, full closure bounds a cluster of four, five, or more semi-closed phrases, but the speaker often follows it with a conjunction or interjection that discourages interruption (for example, "*Kho*—" or "*Khey*—," "Well, then—"), or a chaining clause ("X did Y [full stop]. After X had done Y . . ."). Semi-closures vary in shape from person to person, but tend to avoid what one can perceive as the speaker's "tonic" pitch, generally hovering above it somewhere within a major third. These pitch contours, like pause patterns (cadences), are relative within the narrative, influenced by factors such as rising excitement or suspense in the plot.

All this makes narrative intonation appear to be quite individually variable, but a comparative analysis of a number of speakers would, I think, reveal systematic male/female differences as well. I would hypothesize, as a preliminary impression only, that women on average use more full stops, while men tend to construct longer semi-stop clusters, and women use fewer linking interjections and chaining clauses after full stops. If accurate, this would be simply a configuration of mechanisms that is part of the general picture of men as the tellers of lengthier narratives and holders of longer turns to talk than women. This sort of impressionistic observation needs testing by detailed study of recordings of single-sex and mixed-sex groups of speakers (keeping in mind the potential effects of recording and of the presence of non-native listeners: formalization tends to reduce audience interruptions; perhaps speakers signal the inappropriateness of interruptions more strenuously when they are being recorded). It is my hypothesis that relative involvement with literacy or pseudoliteracy, which varies among men, may account for more of these differences in intonation and periodicity than gender alone would do. That is, taking into account the extent to which gender may determine or constrain access to literacy, I would expect that the narrative speech patterns of men not involved with "*ketābī*" ("bookish") speech styles would more closely resemble those of women. The genderedness of speech need not induce all men to "talk like books." Indeed, one of my most literate informants avoided obvious literate *forms* in his narrative, but his intonation may be another matter. All such observations are hypothetical at present, however, because intonation studies are new ground for me and for Persian in general. But it seems clear that literacy and the gendered distribution of formal education and speech training are deeply implicated in anything one might say about gender and oral narrative performance styles.

A second, more readily observable difference between men's and women's narration patterns manifests itself at the content level. Some years ago, I compared the incidence of narratives with male and female main characters, in the repertoires of the eighty or so storytellers of various ages whom I recorded, mainly in Herat and Kabul (Mills 1985). A sample of about 140 stories told by women were divided almost evenly between male-centered and female-centered tales. The 250 or so men's performances in the sample, by contrast, were male-centered by a ratio of about nine to one. Furthermore, among those few tales told by men which had female heroes, about half those female characters impersonated men, performing heroic deeds in a male environment, usually in male disguise. Women's interest in transsexual disguise, in either direction, was much more limited. Women's stories with female protagonists often centered on the domestic sphere and on the agonistic potential of kinship relations after marriage. Courtship tales are also prominently represented in women's storytelling, of course, but male narrators are overwhelmingly interested in the winning of wives and other picaresque adventures, and conspicuously less interested in the complex social adjustments that follow the acquisition of a spouse. Women readily identify dramatic potential in the women's world (however fancifully portrayed, and it is quite fanciful when one's in-laws are fairies and demons), and tend less than men do to cast women in male roles in order to make them active characters.

Brenda Beck (1986) has offered a provocative analysis of dyadic clusters of dramatis personae in folktales from the subcontinent, but she uses printed sources and thus has to operate without the discriminator of narrator's gender in the patterns she traces. Among her findings are differences in sibling rivalry (brothers tend not to be violent rivals, sisters tend to be quite violent, even murderous toward each other) and in child-parent solidarity (fathers tend to be friendly toward daughters, not toward sons), and the social roles of active women characters (predominantly negative in the corpus she examined). In my own collecting experience, underlying psychodynamic patterns of this kind (initiatives, solidarities, and rivalries distinguished by kin relations, gender, and age) sort out quite differently in the repertoires of male and female narrators. If bodies of folk narrative can be distinguished by gender of narrator, different perspectives on social organization and nuances in the predominant psychosocial themes emerge. Other recent work in India, such as that of Narayana Rao (1986) on folk epics in Telugu, and also Margaret Trawick Egnor's work on crying songs (1986), have analyzed differences in gender roles as functions of narrative genre or subgenre, and have cross-indexed the variables with differences in social status of performers and/or audiences. This status-distinction question seems a very productive line of research, if less overtly expressed, still potentially highly significant for those of us working in nominally egalitarian Muslim communities. According to Narayana Rao's findings, martial, male-centered values more prominent in upper social strata (agricultural castes) coincide with more passive roles for positive female characters, in comparison to the presence of positive, active roles for women in the epics performed by and for the trading castes, which are of lower status. Not surprisingly, these portrayals correlate with relatively permissive or restrictive customs regarding women in their respective caste groups.

To the extent that genres are gender-specific, one might also look for intracaste variation in portrayals of the dramatic roles of men and women, and male-female relations within the kin group. My own observations suggest that gender of traditional performers and/or audience, genre, and distribution of roles among male and female characters co-vary in complex ways within social groups as well as between them. Blackburn and Ramanujan (1986), in drawing together the considerable information on gender in performance and narrative structure from their recent collection, link variations in gender roles with general distinctions to be made between classical and folk, or better yet, elite and lower-caste narrative traditions (for there are folk traditions in high castes as well). In general, they see more elite productions as stressing control and decorum (and by extension, a more passive role for women), while lower-caste genres admit stronger statements of themes of defiance, social disorder, and emotional intensity: hence Sītā, for instance, is passive in high-caste formulations, active and even martial in lower-caste Telugu versions of the *Rāmāyaṇa*. In Ramanujan's (1986) terminology, the tooth goddess of the lower castes is replaced by the breast goddess in elite formulations.

On the surface, Hindu India appears to offer a more complex field for this type of distinction than does Muslim Afghanistan, in part because Muslim society is more univocal about the proper ritual role of women. Here I am sidestepping a potentially rich topic in religious practice, that of votive activities in Islam, where women have a major, informal, and, in some views, heterodox role in religious activities deemed beneficial to the whole community. Most of the published information on these activities, which often involve ritual performance of traditional folktale-type narratives, comes from Iran, so this issue is somewhat beyond the scope of the present discussion (cf. Jamzadeh and Mills 1986, and citations), but I would very much like to see further discussion of the role of gender in Muslim votive activities on the subcontinent, which would no doubt complicate and enrich the picture derived from the Persian side.

Despite the comparative stress in Islam on social equality and the condemnation of castelike distinctions among coreligionists, values which idealize uniformity of devotional practice among other social activities, I would point out that intracommunity differences are evident in Afghan expressive traditions (both religious and not) regarding male and female roles, and such intracommunity differences probably occur in single-caste Hindu communities as well. With regard to narrative, the inter-*gender* analysis which uncovers such patterns tends to be inter*generic* as well, but even where both women and men perform the same genres of narrative, gender-based, *intra*generic differences may also be found, as in the case of Afghan *awsānah*. These differences may be manifested in style, themes, or both, and call for caution when one undertakes comparative and historical analysis of materials recorded or transcribed in previous times, when gender-sensitive research methodology was not such a recognized priority as it is now.

In dealing with an Islamic community, I have focused more on intragroup and intragenre distinctions in communicative styles and subjects. Looking at the work being done in non-Muslim communities in South Asia, I am excited by the possibilities for intergroup and intergenre studies. I believe we have things to learn from one another, reciprocally, with regard to the diversity of cultural voices not only among but within groups. In this dimension, gender will continue to be of crucial interest.

* * *

The author gratefully acknowledges support from the Fulbright-Hays Dissertation Fellowship Program, Harvard University's Sheldon Fund, the AAUW Education Foundation, the NEH Translation Grants Program, the Research Fund of Pomona College, and the University of Pennsylvania's Literacy Research Center and Research Foundation, all of which have supported phases of the above research. I thank the South Asia Seminar attendees, my co-editors, and especially Richard Bauman for helpful advice on revisions of this chapter.

Notes

1. The *khalīfah,* or guardian, is sometimes a lineal descendant of the saint whose shrine it is, or if not a lineal descendant of the saint, then a leader of the Sufi mystical order which maintains the shrine, if the shrine is affiliated with a particular order.

2. My experience caused me to question the accuracy of earlier claims to "classificatory male" status made by some female ethnographers operating as outsiders in highly sex-segregated societies. In village Afghanistan, gender is never taken out of account, but individual women who, as outsiders with special training, seek access to male gatherings will be tolerated to varying degrees depending on their area of concern. Their presence is invariably disruptive to the normal social interactions of such groups, however.

3. Coates (1986: 41–46) summarizes the conflicting views of European dialectologists concerning the relative conservatism of male and female speakers and suggests the political dimension of such debate. Farhadi subscribed to one side of this debate among historical linguists, perhaps the most appropriate one for the Afghan case.

References

Baghban, Hafizullah

1977 The Context and Concept of Humor in Magadi Theater. Ph.D. dissertation, Indiana University. Ann Arbor, Mich.: University Microfilms (no. 77–10,977).

Beck, Brenda

1986 Social Dyads in Indic Folktales. In *Another Harmony: New Essays on the Folklore of India,* Stuart H. Blackburn and A. K. Ramanujan, eds., pp. 76–102. Berkeley: University of California Press.

Beeman, William

1986 *Language, Status and Power in Iran.* Bloomington: Indiana University Press.

Bell, Diane

1984 *Daughters of the Dreaming.* Melbourne: McPhee Gribble/George Allen & Unwin.

Blackburn, Stuart H.

1988 *Singing of Birth and Death: Texts in Performance.* Philadelphia: University of Pennsylvania Press.

Blackburn, Stuart H., and A. K. Ramanujan, eds.

1986 *Another Harmony: New Essays on the Folklore of India.* Berkeley: University of California Press.

Bynum, David

1976 The Generic Nature of Oral Poetry. In *Folklore Genres,* Dan Ben-Amos, ed., pp. 35–58. Austin: University of Texas Press.

Coates, Jennifer

1986 *Women, Men and Language.* London and New York: Longman.

Doubleday, Veronica
1988 *Three Women of Herat*. London: Jonathan Cape.
Egnor, Margaret Trawick
1986 Internal Iconicity in Paraiyar "Crying Songs." In *Another Harmony: New Essays on the Folklore of India,* Stuart H. Blackburn and A. K. Ramanujan, eds., pp. 294–344. Berkeley: University of California Press.
Eickelman, Dale F.
1978 The Art of Memory: Islamic Education and Its Social Reproduction. *Comparative Studies in Society and History* 20 : 485–515.
Finnegan, Ruth H.
1976 What Is Oral Literature Anyway? Comments in the Light of Some African and Other Comparative Material. In *Oral Literature and the Formula,* B. A. Stolz and R. S. Shannon, eds., pp. 127–66. Ann Arbor: Center for the Coordination of Ancient and Modern Studies, University of Michigan.
Ghani, Ashraf
1988 The Persian Literature of Afghanistan, 1911–78, in the Context of Its Political and Intellectual History. In *Persian Literature,* E. Yarshater, ed. New York: Bibliotheca Persica, New York University Press.
Goody, Jack
1968 Introduction. In *Literacy in Traditional Societies,* J. Goody, ed., pp. 1–26. Cambridge: Cambridge University Press.
Havelock, Eric A.
1982 *The Literate Revolution in Greece and Its Cultural Consequences*. Princeton, N.J.: Princeton University Press.
Jamzadeh, Laal, and Margaret Mills
1986 Iranian *Sofreh:* From Collective to Female Ritual. In *Gender and Religion: On the Complexity of Symbols,* C. W. Bynum, S. Harrell, and P. Richman, eds., pp. 23–65. Boston: Beacon Press.
Lord, Albert B.
1960 *The Singer of Tales*. Cambridge, Mass.: Harvard University Press.
Mernissi, Fatima
1977 Women, Saints and Sanctuaries. *Signs* 3/101–22.
Mills, Margaret A.
1978 Oral Tradition in Afghanistan: The Individual in Tradition. Ph.D. dissertation, Harvard University. Garland Press Harvard Folklore Dissertation Series, 1990.
1985 Sex Role Reversals, Sex Changes and Transvestite Disguise in the Oral Tradition of a Conservative Muslim Community. In *Women's Folklore, Women's Culture,* Rosan A. Jordan and Susan J. Kalčik, eds., pp. 187–213. Philadelphia: University of Pennsylvania Press.
forthcoming Folk Tradition in the *Mathnavī* and the *Mathnavī* in Folk Tradition. In *The Heritage of Rūmī,* A. Banani, ed. Cambridge: Cambridge University Press.

1991 Sit Down with People of Wisdom . . . . In *Rhetorics and Politics in Afghan Traditional Storytelling*. Philadelphia: University of Pennsylvania Press.

Narayana Rao, Velcheru

1986 Epics and Ideologies: Six Telugu Folk Epics. In *Another Harmony: New Essays on the Folklore of India,* Stuart H. Blackburn and A. K. Ramanujan, eds., pp. 131–164. Berkeley: University of California Press.

Pritchett, Frances W.

1985 *Marvelous Encounters: Folk Romance in Urdu and Hindi.* Delhi: Manohar.

Ramanujan, A. K.

1986 Two Realms of Kannada Folklore. In *Another Harmony: New Essays on the Folklore of India,* Stuart H. Blackburn and A. K. Ramanujan, eds., pp. 41–74. Berkeley: University of California Press.

Sakata, Hiromi Lorraine

1983 *Music in the Mind: The Concepts of Music and Musician in Afghanistan.* Kent, Oh.: Kent State University Press.

Scribner, Sylvia, and Michael Cole

1981 *The Psychology of Literacy.* Cambridge, Mass.: Harvard University Press.

Slyomovics, Susan

1987 *The Merchant of Art.* Berkeley: University of California Press.

Stock, Brian

1983 *The Implications of Literacy: Written Language and Models of Interpretation in the Eleventh and Twelfth Centuries.* Princeton, N.J.: Princeton University Press.

Street, Brian

1984 *Literacy in Theory and Practice.* Cambridge: Cambridge University Press.

Wagner, Daniel A., and Abdelhamid Lotfi

1980 Traditional Islamic Education in Morocco: Sociohistorical and Psychological Perspectives. *Comparative Education Review* 20, 2:238–251.

Webber, Sabra

1985 Women's Folk Narratives and Social Change. In *Women and the Family in the Middle East: New Voices of Change,* E. W. Fernea, ed., pp. 310–316. Austin: University of Texas Press.

Benedicte Grima

3. The Role of Suffering in Women's Performance of *Paxto*

Paxtuns were studied and described first by British colonialists stationed in what they called Northern India (present day Afghanistan and Northwest Pakistan) in the mid-nineteenth century. Later, they became of interest to anthropologists as a tribal society and were studied by Jon Anderson (1982), Fredrik Barth (1959, 1981), Akbar S. Ahmed (1980), Charles Lindholm (1982), the Tappers, and others. What most of these studies have in common is that they are conducted by men and focus on male culture and society. Paxtun areas, as viewed from the outside public realm, seem at first very hostile and harsh, and most unaccompanied women do not feel comfortable there. Indeed, the outsider among them is treated with utmost suspicion and aggression, particularly if she happens to be female. The language is difficult and little instruction exists. The result is that few women have chosen to do fieldwork in that area, and so the Paxtun world is presented largely as a men's world. Those women who have written about Paxtun women's culture have so far presented the institution of marriage (Lindholm and Lindholm 1979; Tapper 1987), the position of women in Paxtun tribal society (Ahmed and Ahmed 1981), and women's rebellion in folk poetry (Boesen 1980, 1983).

Anthropologists, travelers, and generalists writing about Paxtuns have never failed to mention the code of honor and modesty/shame, a code with rigid behavioral requirements sometimes referred to as *paxtunwali*. The word *paxto* itself designates not only the language but also the behavior defined by the code. Almost every Paxtun is familiar with the proverb: "You don't speak Paxto; you do *paxto*." Indeed, people daily refer to "having" or "doing" *paxto* in describing others or in socializing children. *Paxto,* in this sense, is equivalent to honor. *Paxto,* the code of honor, and not just Paxto, the language, defines the person.[1]

So what does it mean to have, do, or perform this *paxto?* I shall summarize what the existing literature tells us, and then talk of one aspect of it which pertains specifically to women and has therefore been overlooked in the general discussions to date. Those who have written about the code, such as Atayee (1979), Janata (1975), Kieffer (1972), Lindholm (1982), Spain (1962), and Steul (1981), have unanimously agreed on several points which constitute the male code of honor. One is *melmastia*, or hospitality, which calls for lavish entertainment often beyond the means of its provider. Having a guest reflects one's own status and influence, as it also creates a relation of dependence. Along with hospitality is usually mentioned *nənawātay*, or the right of refuge, which must be granted to anyone who asks for it. It is an institution on which the favored patron-client relationships among Paxtuns thrive. The third point always present in any discussion of the Paxtun code is *badal*, normally referred to as revenge. Revenge homicide is common and highly regarded as honorable, just as not performing it leads to a man's disgrace and loss of influence. *Badal* is a crucial notion behind most action and interaction in *paxto*, and I shall return to it in order to redefine it from a woman's perspective. *Paxto* and *gheirat* are the words used for honor, for what one does when one acts according to *paxto*. It is key to social acceptance within the community.

The doing of *paxto* for men, then, generally means showing oneself as strong, combatant, generous, and hospitable. It is the side of the code which has been elaborated by male ethnographers relying on data from male informants. I now turn to what *paxto* means for women.

Just as the gun and turban are typically used as images to exemplify Paxtun manhood, I suggest that tears and the endurance of hardship exemplify Paxtun womanhood. This is true both in the image of women as created by men in popular culture (films, romances, songs, poetry) and in women's images of themselves. I would like to illustrate this notion of honor in suffering by discussing two types of narrative in which women present themselves to each other.

First I focus on narratives of the self among Paxtun women. I shall begin by introducing the life story as it is perceived and performed. Then I shall discuss a particular genre of personal-experience tale relating illness and misfortune and occurring in a formal emotion ritual called *tapos*. This is a women's visit of sharing sadness over someone's misfortune. I shall explain the visit and the narrative genre within the context of *badal* or institutionalized exchange, and then do a quick exegesis of the appended narrative. I am using this data to suggest that the display, or performance, of emotion, in this case of loss and suffering, is related to identity: Paxtun,

Muslim, and feminine. It is these stories and events that inform us about people.

When I first did formal fieldwork in 1982, I began by looking for women's performances of the popular romances with which I had previously worked. Actually, I was looking for any kind of household narratives. The following is a passage taken from field notes at that time.

> Shama Babi is both criticized and widely acclaimed in her village for being a great narrator of *qessa* [stories]. Almost daily, she comes to visit the household where I am staying as a guest, and takes and holds the floor for hours with stories defaming other women, or with tragic personal narratives, most of which have been heard numerous times before by this community of women, but which they urge her to tell for me. The first time I expressed interest in Shama Babi's narrative and asked to tape it, she delightedly responded: "Oh, that's the kind of *qessa* you wanted. You should have said so. I thought you wanted *qessa* like *Adam Khan* or *Yusuf Khan* [popular folk romances], and I don't know any of those. This kind, I can tell you many of, and make you cry like no one else can."
>
> I sat with Shama Babi and recorded her for three days. She narrated, and groups of women would come and go in her courtyard as time allowed. Her tales were mostly sad and personal ones, recounting the painful events of her husband's death, her son's car accident when he was a child, and her daughter's wedding. It became clear as I listened and watched the audience that the more personal suffering she could express, aided by tears and outcries and occasional wailed verses, the better her tale was esteemed by the small audience of women.

It was Shama Babi and others like her who slowly led me to acknowledge this neglected genre as what was most told and valued by women. I began to see the personal-event narratives and life stories emerge as the major performance genre both in ritual contexts, which I later describe, and in informal contexts of intimacy. It was a private genre told by women to women, and the more I made my loyalties to the women's domain known by eliminating my interaction with men, the more I became privy to these personal tales. Not only did I become privy, I also gained a reputation as "the one who is interested in our sad tales," which is how I was often introduced to new women by those wanting to have me record all the best stories.

These narratives are a performed and framed genre with defined social contexts and rules. Each time they are told, it is with the implicit message of asserting and reasserting membership and reputation as a good Paxtun in the community. Each is saying: "Look what I've been through. I've suffered one hardship after another, and endured it. I'm still here." The quest for honor is a quest for reputation. In fact, the motivation behind most behavior among Paxtuns is a concern for one's reputation, a fear of being accused of not performing *paxto*. We can extend this interpretation to the way women present themselves in their personal narratives.

In her work on the Bedouin discourse of self and sentiment, Abu-Lughod (1985, 1986) proposed that there exist two ideologies, each with its own models of and for different types of experience.[2] She juxtaposes the poetic discourse of self and sentiment, on the one hand, and the ordinary, everyday discourse of honor and modesty, on the other. Her clear-cut distinction, however, leaves one curious about the array of possible narrative genres among the Bedouin that she does not mention. The life stories told by Paxtun women are also vehicles for sentiment and emotion that are inappropriate to tell out of specific contexts of intimacy and privacy, but at the same time, they are a discourse of honor that gains them reputation. This can perhaps best be illustrated in discussions evaluating the type of narrative being collected, such as the following dialogue I had with a major informant in Ahmadi Banda[3] who was deciding, along with her friends, whom to send me to for a good story. It is the metafolklore that supplies crucial data for research:

> Selma: You must go see X. She's really got the best story to tell.
> BG: What makes her story so good?
> S: She's undergone so much *gham* [sorrow, pain, hardship, suffering]. She's really endured a lot.
> BG: Can you or someone else tell her story?
> S: No, only the person herself, or someone who knew her very well. The best story is always told by the person herself.

As Selma demonstrates, a longing for truth and for knowledge of each other and of events outside their compound has created a requirement for accurate reporting among women. There is a thirst among Paxtun women for autobiography. There is also a correct way to "seek the person out" with questions. One day, when my daughter's nanny had observed me eliciting a life story from someone, she later tried to correct me on the grounds that I did not know how to interrogate properly. "You foreigners don't know how to search [*latawəl*] each other," she reproached me. "When we Pakistanis[4] ask a person's story, we don't let a single detail go by. We dig in all the corners, high and low. We seek the person out. That's how we do things. We are storytellers and story seekers. We know how to draw out a person's heart." Finally, there is a great appreciation for the skilled teller of her own life story. This skill lies mostly in her ability to move her listeners to tears.

I often asked about and sought out the women communally known to have the best stories and to be the best tellers. As it turned out, most of the women with this reputation had experienced difficult and sad lives. Their experience itself, its beauty judged by the appropriateness according to *paxto*, along with the fact that they had not run from the hardship, made for the best story in community evaluation.

Here is an example of how a life story often begins, and the way it advances:

—The story goes like this, *kana*, that my name is Naseema.
—My mother died when I was a child. Those orphan children remained in my care. My father remained in my care.
—My mother, she died. She died in childbirth. My brother remained, only a year old. I took care of him. Then he grew up, *kana?*

—Then I got married. Then my father gave me away. I got married. Those orphans stayed in the house with their father. I have no mother.
—My brother stayed with my father and I would climb over the roof so he could see me. Like, he was sad, *kana?* His mother was dead. He didn't know his mother. He was still crawling on all fours.
—A husband took me. A man married me. My father gave me to him. They all stayed behind.
—Now, they would wait, and I'd bring them bread by way of the rooftops. Bread, which I'd throw down to them. He'd come crawling on all fours, and then would eat it.

—Now, I came by the road. My father beat me. He said, "Why are you running a stranger's house and coming here looking after this boy? You've become a non-kin woman to us. Don't come to my house. You run your stranger's house."

—Now, I had another sister. I had another sister. Then my father gave her away, too. They [father and children] stayed alone.
—Then my father died. I brought them all over with me.

—Then my house fell apart. I had three children. I became a widow with three children. I was a young widow. Then I stayed.

—Then I got to it and took another husband, that fish man.
—My brothers got upset with me. They left. They said that, "You've left us, just like that."
—Now, they cut off relations with me for four years.

—Now, my father went and fell down in the road. His heart failed. He died.
—A whole lot of people came. My father died.
—I cried. My other brother came. I cried. I cried a lot. I cried that: "My father died upset with me. My father died vexed."
—Like, lots and lots of people cried.

—Then, in the meantime, time passed and passed. I left home and went to Kalam. My seven-year-old son died. Then he died in the meantime.
—Lots of people kept coming for us. They all came. The people cried. The boy was dead. Three days. People kept coming for many days. He was dead.

—Then, some time later, my husband performed the *hajj* and took my co-wife.
—My daughter cried. I cried. All my neighbors were upset for me, that he had taken her and not me.
—Then he came back. He had hidden the dates, and those garlands.
—Then again I cried and was filled with grief.

—Then my daughter got married very young. I cried after her. She used to help me with the children. She does that for me, like, the housework. My brother went with her.
—I came in that grief and again cried after my daughter because I'd given her away in tribal area. I'd sold my own daughter. I'd done her an injustice. I cried again.

—Then their father jumped up and he broke my arm. I cried again for a month.
—Then I got upset and I cried a whole lot.[5]

In contrast to the autobiographical life story, I have also collected a few biographical accounts of other local famous women, told by women. These were told with more distance, not so much as a series of woeful events. They were also told after expressing tremendous reluctance to do so. Responsibility for another's life is a burden not many want to be accountable for. Selma's comment above was often repeated to me, that the best story is by the protagonist herself, because only she, as narrator, can tell and elicit from her listener(s) the amount of sympathy needed to make a good story.

Discussions with contemporary Paxtun writers, critics, and audiences have yielded similar conclusions in regard to the story line in novels, romances, television or radio dramas, folk tales, and poetry. *Gham* (pain, suffering) is what determines the best story in any of these.

In an interview with a thirty-year-old unmarried rural school teacher, when I asked her about her own life story, I received the following answer: "I have no story to tell. I've been through no hardships." And when I asked her what gave a woman renown, she replied, "Her hardships. How else can she prove herself? If she takes any independent action to better or escape her situation, she'll be stigmatized and even ostracized, and certainly not held in praise. With age and hardship, a woman gains respect, her story becomes known, and she is respected by all in the community for having undergone so much suffering. Her suffering is perceived as action according to the code of honor and morality. If she goes through troubles, it's for the sake of honor. Otherwise, she could be free and take care of herself."

Both *paxto* and Islam, which supply the grid through which action and experience are determined and evaluated, dictate that women should bear with their hardship and not seek to escape or ameliorate it. This endurance is what earns a woman honor and reputation among other women, and makes her worthy of being called Paxtun by them.

Gham, then, along with shame and modesty, is a key cultural term in women's everyday performance of *paxto.* In a woman's life, *gham* and *taklif* (misfortune, hardship) begin with her marriage, when she is cast from the security of her mother's house into an environment of hostile relationships with a mother-in-law, sister(s)-in-law, and even a co-wife, living day after day in the same house with no release from them. It may also begin with her mother's death, but most often with marriage. Before that, she is not expected to know anything about life, or to share in *gham.* She neither considers herself, nor is she considered by the community, to have begun living or to have any kind of story to tell. She is frequently referred to, in this regard, as *kam-ʿaqla,* or ignorant.

Just as marriage marks the introduction of *gham* into a woman's life, so does it mark the opening in the story of her life. In fact, the phrase used most often by women to speak of their lives is *taklifuna che mā bānde ter shəwi di* (the misfortunes which have befallen me), as opposed to the more literary Urdu-Persian word for autobiography, *ḥāl-e zendegī.* Many informants, when I asked them for their story, began before I had even set up my taping equipment with a line such as: "My life has been nothing but misery," or "My life has been that of a dog," or "There's been no joy in my life."

The following are some responses I received when I asked women, toward the end of their tragic tales, if they could recall any joy in their lives at all:

> —"None. Since I learned good from bad, there's been no joy at all."
> —"No. Only unhappiness has come into my life. All unhappiness."
> —"I've never seen any joy. My birth itself is a sorrow, a sorrow. There is no joy at all."

Most of the answers to the question were of this nature. A woman's life is perceived almost entirely within a framework of hardship and suffering, beginning with her being severed from her mother. Many women agreed, upon my asking, that the time before marriage had been one of happiness. But hardly any women admitted remembering anything of this period.

The perception and organization of life as a chain of crises and stresses is particularly true of rural and older women. In urban centers, among the younger generations of upper and upper-middle class, educated and working women, there is resentment about perceiving their lives within this framework. I often tried to elicit life stories from these young women, but they claimed they had no story to tell, as the schoolteacher's reply above, "I have no story to tell. I've been through no hardships."

These women expressed the pressure they felt from relatives in the villages and from their elders in the family, to perform a discourse they no longer identify with. One elite Paxtun woman, divorced and working in a women's hospital in Peshawar, complained that she often felt pressured by her patients who wanted to hear her story in terms of the hardships she had encountered as a result of her divorce. She resented these pressures because she did not perceive the experience as being anything other than positive. "These women like to hear life stories," she told me, "but I have none for them." Another young upper-class urban mother originally from Peshawar and now living in Islamabad complained to me that she felt pressured by her mother-in-law to tell the story of her children's birth to relatives in terms of the pain and difficulties she had experienced. It angered her because she had, on the contrary, perceived the births as elating. She also added that she felt more consciously pressured to display a distressed persona among her relatives in Peshawar than among the younger, less traditional ones in Islamabad.

Although my work was conducted mainly among rural, poor women, the dozen or so urban women I spoke with had responses similar to the ones discussed above and told me they had no story. I could elicit no life narratives. However, they were quick and eager to refer me to an old servant woman or to other women from their family villages who were known to tell the "saddest and most beautiful stories." They appreciated the aesthetic of the *gham* but did not personally identify with the genre, as if the life story, defined in *paxto* as a story of *gham,* could only be told by those who still molded their existence into the traditional pattern. There is no new model for the Paxtun life story. Thus not having a life story to tell becomes a statement in itself. It may be saying, "I defy the traditional cultural model, but must remain silent until a new one is formulated."

Having suggested the link between honor and suffering for women, I would like to illustrate it with an example. I turn to a specific moment in life that is marked by a ritual of emotion, as I call it, and a woman's personal-experience narrative. I present it alongside the life story not only because it is in itself a little piece of the story, but because it is important both to see how people understand themselves and to see their actions and behavior as in some ways the creations of those understandings.

When I first arrived in Peshawar in 1982 and lodging was found for me with an older couple, the wife was preparing her son's wedding and was also suffering from migraines. Groups of women came daily to see her and ask about her, and she would lie on the bed, hands to her head, moaning about her aches, diet, and anxieties. The guests would drink tea, shake their heads and sigh at the story, and leave when their obligation was terminated. With the women gone, she would get up and resume her usual activities, as well as her usual voice. The performance, consisting of a near-verbatim repetition of the narrative, would be repeated as many as five to seven times a day for the guests. I meanwhile remained baffled and amused by what I perceived as her theatrical abilities and by her husband's seeming lack of concern. He would even laugh and wink to me, as he disappeared at each new arrival of women. This scene, though I was unaware of its importance to my later work, provided my first contact with a tradition of expressive behavior and ritual tied up with the aesthetic of suffering.

The type of visit described above is called *tapos*[6] in Paxto. Literally, the word's dictionary definition is "question" (*tapos kawəl* = to ask). Its social meaning, however, refers to a specific event, an obligatory visit of enquiry about someone ill, injured, dying, or suffering a loss.

Although Paxtuns recognize that *tapos* originates in Islam and is practiced in various forms throughout the Muslim world, they believe it has appropriated a role of major importance in *paxto,* perhaps exceeding its position in other Muslim societies. One reason for this is that Paxtuns perceive their system of *purda* (veiling, seclusion, and segregation of women) as stronger and more active than among other Muslims. This makes *tapos* one of the few licit occasions for women's mobility beyond the immediate family compound. (I might add that *tapos* is considered strictly women's work. Men can perform it casually over a handshake in the street.) Another reason women give for *tapos* being so meaningful to them is that, unlike in other Islamic contexts where it is just meritorious (*sawāb*), in *paxto* it is believed to operate by the strict rules of reciprocity and can be the source of hostility and even of feud if it is neglected. I suggest the importance of *tapos* is that it provides the key stage for women to display emotion, which reaffirms for the community their kinship tie with the ill person and hence their identity within the community of good Paxtuns.

Tapos is only one type in a wide variety of visiting patterns called *gham-xādi* (lit., sorrow-joy). Visits are governed not by individual choice but by the constraints of social relationships and of exchange. They belong to the actions of doing *paxto*.

To begin, the phrase *gham-xādi* means far more to its users than just the rites of passage (Barth 1959) or the reciprocal obligation to attend funerals and weddings (Lindholm 1982). It implies the event as well as the visit and the appropriate response. The words *gham* and *xādi* are two words that do not evoke for Paxtuns an image of internal emotional states, but instead an image of a particular public and cultural event that calls for a certain behavior. One goes to a *gham* or to a *xādi.* A *gham* event calls for crying, wailing, and exchanging stories of loss, while a *xādi* event calls for dancing and singing. Apart from this, the combined terms, particularly in women's language, refer to the wide array of visits possible for and demanded of them in daily life. To do *gham-xādi* with someone means to have good relations with them or, at least, not to have bad relations, and to have an ongoing record of reciprocal visits at major life events (births, circumcisions, departures and arrivals from far away, engagements and weddings, deaths, passed exams, illness, misfortunes, and so on). It does not necessarily imply closeness, but only that there is no hostility.

Of all the *gham-xādi,* there was no doubt in anyone's mind, men or women, that *gham* outweighs *xādi* in importance, significance, and social demand. This measuring of sorrow against joy is continually recalled in the culture. In Islam itself, which feeds a great part of Paxtun ideology, pain and suffering are meritorious and redemptive for the pious (Ayoub 1978).[7] The Qur'an often reiterates that the pious will be tried with hardship as a measure of their faith, as in S.II: 155–156, "Be sure we shall try you / with something of fear and hunger / and loss of wealth and life / and the fruits [of your labor]; / but give tidings of happiness to those who have patience. / Who say when assailed by adversity: / 'Surely we are for God, and to Him we shall return.'" (Ali 1984: 30). And it says that those who persevere will be rewarded by God, as in S.XXXIX: 10, "Only those who persevere / will get their reward measureless." (Ali 1984: 392)

A prominent Ahmadi scholar and poet, whom I have known personally since 1982, spoke to me about *gham* in the following way: "Man's greatness is judged from the point of view of his *gham.* Not his joy, but his reactions to tragedy, make him great." And he quoted a *tappa,* a popular form of two-line poetry, often with a proverbial intensifying intent:

gham de də tā na wafādār day
tə kəla kəla gham de tal rāsara wi na

(Your sorrow is more faithful than you;
you are only passing, but your sorrow is eternally with me)

Finally, numerous proverbs in Paxto indicate the priority of sadness over joy, for example, "*gham tal day; xādi kəla kəla wi*" (Sorrow is eternal; joy is a sometime thing), or "*gham də ṭolo, xādi də yaw co day*" (Sorrow belongs to everyone; joy only to the few). As we saw earlier, younger girls and women participate in *xādi* events only. Until marriage, or an older age for unmarried women, they are considered not to know about life, and are excluded from *gham* events. And certainly, the life story is dominated by *gham* events.

One cannot discuss *gham-xādi* in *paxto* and exclude the notions of exchange, or *badal.* I mentioned, in the beginning of this chapter, that the existing literature on the Paxtuns usually presents the code of *paxto* from a purely male perspective, so that we are led to believe that *badal* just means blood revenge. Lindholm (1982) has a full discussion of the types of exchange in Swat, in which he suggests that "all relationships contain elements of hostility or contempt, or both" (p. 159). He claims that it is this extreme hostility and jealousy of Paxtuns that counteracts itself in the seemingly contradictory behavior of generosity and hospitality. Because Lindholm understands *badal* purely as revenge, he assumes it plays no role in women's lives. In effect, most men's immediate definition of *badal,* when I asked them about the term, was one of revenge, with the example, "If you kill someone from my family, I'll kill you, or someone from your family." Data from women, however, yield a very different notion of a phenomenon whose narrower meaning has become standard and generally accepted in the anthropological literature on the Paxtun.

Not a single woman ever gave the interpretation of blood revenge when asked to explain *badal.* For many women, the first response was that it is an exchange of women in a marriage alliance, either to mend a hostility or to create and seal a bond between two families.[8] They maintained that *gham-xādi* was a form of *badal.* Most women would end the discussion claiming that everything in their lives was *badal.* For men, the notion of *badal* as reciprocity of gifts, visits, and emotional display belongs to the realm of women's domestic lives and is less significant to them. It is passive rather than active information for them. Men's honor is played out in avenging those who threaten their family reputation, while women's honor is played out in maintaining relations through the reciprocity of gifts and *gham-xādi* visits and in displaying appropriate behavior and narratives. Since *badal* is a major notion in the definition of *paxto,* as we saw earlier, and doing *paxto* constitutes different behavior for men from that for women, it is understandable that men and women would have different active information in their descriptions of such a crucial notion. It also explains why male ethnographers who have traditionally described *badal* on the basis of data collected from men have failed to mention how institutionalized exchange operates beyond revenge. Certainly among the Paxtun *badal* is a key cultural concept that lies at the heart of most communication and social exchange, including tears, tales, and emotions.

I now return to the *tapos,* the specific type of visit, which is the context for the illness and misfortune narratives, as well as the life stories, in which hardship and suffering are welded into ethic and aesthetic, "beautiful stories" telling of good, *paxto*-abiding women.

Tapos visits are required by relatives and neighbors and anyone doing *gham-xādi* with the affected party. There are rules dictating who can and cannot go, the accepted manners of dress and of gift-giving, and other details which I will not elaborate upon here. The necessary exchange is between the visitor and the visited, although many other women may be present. The visitor makes the inquiry and the visited gives the story. The visited is usually not the ill person, but his or her mother or next senior female relative. As the stories provide an important source of social validation for the narrator, they focus on her caretaker role.

The narrative appended to this paper is taken from fieldwork done in 1986. Nur-ol Amin is the youngest son of Shiriney, a woman whom I have known since 1978 in Swat, and whose family has always hosted me or provided me independent housing at a low cost. Nur was eighteen and still unmarried at the time of this event. He was involved in a car accident and suffered minor injuries. He spent the first night in the hospital and walked up to the house (a steep walk uphill from the village) the next morning.

In a previous article (1985) I described a *tapos* event from the perspective of the visitors. In this case, I observed it from the perspective of the injured boy's mother, Shiriney. I was then living in a separate annex of their house and was therefore immediately informed of the accident; I was also able to remain with her and witness her telling the same narrative twenty-two times in three days.

This telling of the story was recorded on the fifth visit, the morning after the accident. It was narrated by Shiriney to women visitors (Shiriney's sister, with her daughter-in-law, and two neighbor women) who had come for Nur's *tapos*. Nur was lying on the bed in our midst, silent. No one ever asked him how he was, nor did he volunteer any story. His three sisters-in-law and I sat on low stools, while the visitors and Shiriney were seated on the cot and chairs, and children ran in and out during the event.

The *tapos* exchange, as I said, consists of both the inquiry and the narrative. The inquiry, without which the visit may not count as a *tapos,* consists of three parts, in which the visitor announces:

—how I found out (i.e., who brought the news)
—how I responded upon finding out (expression of devastation)
—what I did (i.e., come as soon as I could for *tapos*).

The narrative told in response by the visited contains five essential parts:

—what happened (third-person report)
—how I found out (either found the person, or was told by someone else)
—how I responded upon finding out (expression of devastation)
—what I did
—resolution.

These five parts can be arranged into any order, although they most often follow the sequence just mentioned. In the appended narrative, however, Shiriney does quite a bit of jumping around.

She begins immediately with her first-person account (A), in which she sets the scene for when and how she found out about her son's accident. She did not usually start her narrative this way, but in this case, her sister, who had made the inquiry, had visited Nur in the hospital and knew the facts of the accident in detail. Still, just before getting to the announcement of the news, Shiriney breaks here into her third-person account of "what happened" (B), as if to satisfy the other listeners. She then returns to her first-person account of how she found out (C). It is her other son who enters the scene, pale and frenzied, looking for his older brother. Shiriney skillfully portrays the escalating sense of disarray before she finally quotes her son's announcement to them: "Now, a car has fallen and Nur-ol Amin is in it."

The response to finding out (D) is typical of the way most women portray their behavior. Cries, wails, and exclamations often occur at this point in the narrative. Women tell of fainting, dropping their food, or, as in this case, striking themselves.

The section marked "what I did" (E) is where the narrator is given a chance to show herself strong and capable of transgressing a number of social rules in a desperate attempt to be near the ailing person. In one narrative, a woman proudly tells how she rented a pick-up to go from her village to the main city hospital, how she then bribed the hospital guards and argued her way to her son's room (see Grima 1985). Shiriney tells us she tried to leave the house, but her sons and husband objected, so that all she could do was remain at home in a fretful worried state ("My heart burned and burned . . . I beat and beat myself. I was sitting outside, crying . . . I couldn't bear to eat the slightest thing"). Here she begins a resolution (F), at which point her sister's neighbor seizes the floor to tell a story of her own, at the end of which Shiriney abruptly switches to section G, back to "what I did," and section H, "what happened."

Finally, *tapos* narratives, where no death occurs, conclude with recognition and thanks to God, as Shiriney says, "Great God showed mercy," and "Great God was very virtuous."

Nur-ol Amin's accident offered his mother the opportunity to publicly (in the form of her narrative performed for many groups of women) demonstrate her *paxto* in the role of a mother devoted to her son and grief-stricken by his misfortune. A comparative analysis of many *tapos* narratives shows that they all share the same structural elements. This is not to disparage or doubt the sincerity of the grief, but to recognize that the form it takes is coded. It is learned gender-related behavior and responds to the aesthetic of suffering expected of women. We must be able to evaluate Shiriney's story in light of the way she has chosen to relate the experience and draw that portrait of herself in the public context of *tapos*. Neglecting this public display of distress could lead to suspicion about her relationship to the injured person, her son. Hence, the type of illness story we see occurring in *tapos* serves to reaffirm the strength of that tie and gives the woman status. It brings smiles and nods of approbation to her audience members, who refer to the most tragic accounts as *khkwle qesse* (beautiful stories). Ethic and aesthetic are here combined in the experience story.

As was mentioned earlier, suffering and enduring hardship are aesthetic criteria of honor for Paxtun women. Mothers must suffer over their sons to gain status and recognition as good mothers. Events such as illness, accidents, and loss provide visits that serve as a stage for narrative performance. And the personal-event narrative in turn acts as a vehicle through which the mother can publicly display her actions for the benefit of the community. Hence, performing the narrative within a ritualized situation, for a large audience in the *tapos* context, becomes crucial. Once we understand the ethic/aesthetic of pain and suffering, it is easy to see why the *tapos* visit becomes the ideal setting for this type of statement of Paxtun feminine identity.

Women thus have two channels for expressing their social and personal selves: the illness and misfortune narrative of the *tapos* ritual on the one hand, and the life story, told in a more informal, private, and intimate context, on the other. In both of these we have sentiments of suffering and hardship as elements that determine and shape their direction.

What is the significance or the relationship of the *tapos* narrative to the life story? Every life crisis is heightened by a ritual that requires the closest female relative to transform it into a personal crisis in which she demonstrates in narrative performance that she has suffered and endured with God's help. The precedence given to pain and suffering as opposed to joy, and the ritual and narrative around each *gham,* also shape the memory and perception of one's life. These were the important moments which gave recognition and status, and they are the ones told in the life story. The life story, like the *tapos* narrative, is told as an attestation of having and doing *paxto*. It is told as a chain of *ghams*. Recall the segment of a life story I read earlier: almost each event the narrator finds worthy of telling is one that was marked by crying and visits, during which (no doubt) she had to tell the story of "what happened."

* * *

To conclude, my research (and this essay) speaks to issues of feminist folklore and anthropology in that women's culture deserves separate attention and cannot be subsumed under the dominant male models (either endogenous or exogenous). It also adds to the claim recently made by some scholars pursuing the links between language, culture, and affect: one must look beyond the private interior of the self, and to the processes of social interaction and discourse, to see the why and the how of emotion as learned, culturally coded and performed behavior, rather than as a phenomenon opposed to cognition (see Beeman 1985; Good, Good, and Fischer 1988; Irvine 1982; Lutz 1986; Shweder and Levine 1984; White 1987). This is why I have tried to present the formulation of the self in the life story as well as in a genre of narrative publicly performed in a ritual context.

Shiriney, Nur-ol Amin's mother
Madyan, Swat 6/86

A. "How I found out."

—When he told me . . . Peda Mahmad came.
—We had cooked the food for the feast of the dead [food offered to the poor in memory of the recently deceased, during the three last

days of Ramadan]. I was cooking bread. I'd told her: "I'll cook that bread. Your daughter is crying, and I can't calm her. And it's that she's sick, too. And I can't always be calming that child." So I said I'd cook the bread.

—When I'd cooked the bread, I was so tired, and my knees ached. So I came and spread the felt rug. I sat on the felt rug.

—When I'd cooked the bread and come to sit down, I hadn't even stretched out my legs when I looked and saw Peda Mahmad, looking completely pale and breathless.

B. "What happened."

—Just then he had gone to Fatehpur, so I thought he could bring some rice and meat to Bakhtsardara [daughter].

(X:[9] Peda Mahmad had gone?)

—It was Khan Amin. It was Nur-ol Amin. I thought he could bring Nasrat [niece] back with him.

—When he brought her and she came, then in that very moment, he disappeared. He went for prayers, and that's when he climbed in that car, and went with that boy.

(X: His time had come.)

—His time had come.

—His father had given that boy the keys, [saying]: "Park the car in the garage. It will get ruined."

—Then he went. Then he came back. Then he took him. Then they went there.

—As they were coming from Satal, then they fell.

(X: They fell at Mian Sheikh Baba [tomb of a holy man]?)

—No, no, at the Friends Hotel.

(X: Huh! The one that used to be yours?)

—No, not the one that used to be ours. The Khan's.

(X: Yes, yes. Sardar's.)

—Now, they were on their way back from there. Now, they had gone as far as if going from here to Alim Allah's house.

(Z: That place is very high. Dangerous.)

—It's high, and they went where it's steep. But they said: "If we'd fallen over, we'd have died."

—But Great God guided them straight on those rocks. He guided

them straight, and they rose and fell onto those rocks. And when they went, they fell into the river.
—Now, two tires were in the river.
(Z: That's a very dangerous place.)

C. "How I found out," cont.

—But, when Peda Mahmad came, then he said: "Halai!" [an exclamation of alarm used in Swat]. He was completely pale, that boy. He arrived at full speed. I thought he'd gone pale from the climb.
—I said: "Eh, son, don't you say hello to Nasrat?"
—He said, "Yes. Hello, girl."
—Then he said, "Where is Spin Dādā?" [house name often given in Madyan to the oldest brother and used by all those younger than him, as it is improper to use the proper name of an elder].
—I said, "He's climbed up on the roof."
—Now, when he came back down, now his father said, "What's the matter?" We also said, "What the matter?" He said, "There's nothing the matter."
(BG: Like, everyone was at home, *kana?*)
—It was evening, *kana*. There were five minutes left before breaking the fast.
—Now, he said . . . he said: "Hurry up. Where's Spin Dādā? Now, a car has fallen and Nur-ol Amin is in it."

D. "How I responded upon finding out."

—Halai! I struck myself. I beat my head. And I got ready to go with them. I didn't even think of taking my veil or anything else.
—When I got set to go, the three of them left.
—Then he didn't let Moambar's [oldest son] father go. He didn't let me go, either. He told Moambar, "The boy is not talking. And neither your father should come with me, nor your mother.
—But like, we'll go, but the boy is unconscious. He's not talking."
—Meanwhile, I was looking, but he forcefully pushed me back. I was sitting on the edge of the path. I yelled and his father, he came from down below. He hadn't allowed him to go, either.
—I was still looking when Khan Amin [other son] came and said,

"I've come to break the fast. The boy is all right. Tell Mother not to come."

E. "What I did."

—Now I was about to go. Three times I went down the steps and then climbed up again.

(X: I figured you were coming but they wouldn't let you.)

—I thought up until that moment I'd lost my heart.

—I thought, "How do I know that he's alive, that he's still alive?"

—I thought maybe he was alive, but, God forbid, close to death, and that's why they didn't want to let me go. My heart burned and burned.

—Morning is coming, time to start the fast. We were up all night.

(Z: May God not break a single branch of the forest. Last night I was so like that. And then that happened, my heart was like that. And I thought, "May God keep him well." What more do we have? Just these children!)

—We have nothing more than our sons. We have no fields of any kind. But God, may God give them life.

(Z: What's a generous husband? But children . . .)

—I was, like . . . I beat and beat myself. I was sitting outside, crying.

—Meanwhile, that younger son, Sher Banu's husband, came.

(Z: What did he know? Did he know of the car falling over?)

—Yes.

F. "Resolution."

—Now, they went from so far away. But Great God showed mercy. And the saints must have been watching from somewhere. And God preserved them.

(Z: They had bought a jeep from Ranzre. Now, two people in it were wounded. And Kharo's sister's son was the third.)

[Z takes the floor and tells her own story of a car accident in which her nephew was killed some time back. Although Shiriney has officially given up the floor by concluding her story with the resolution, she struggles to get it back, interrupting Z several times to continue her own story. But the floor is not given to her. While Z keeps talking to her, she looks to me for an audience.

Seeing that I am looking at her, she continues her story, ignoring Z who is still talking to her.]

G. "What I did," cont.

—Now, last night we . . . [Z talks]
—And everyone told me he's talking. And I said, "He's not talking. You are just telling me that."

(Z: That baby is as dried up as an old stick.)

—Yes, he's very skinny. God has kept him that way. God keeps us. No one can do anything.

—Then our . . .
—I wasn't expecting him to come back alive.
—Now, I was beating myself. Now, my sons come individually and say, "He's okay."
—Peda Mahmad came hurriedly. "Mother, he's okay. I came to reassure Mother that the boy is okay. And he's eaten a little."
—I ate . . . I ate just this little bit. I ate just one mouthful. And the second they forced me to sit and eat. It got caught right here [points to esophagus]. It's been hurting me right up until now, from that mouthful getting caught.
—I drank tea after it. I drank water after it, but it didn't go down.
—And I was so hungry and then I couldn't bear to eat the slightest thing. And I drank a cup of tea.

(Z: That's due to great anxiety.)

—It was great anxiety. Only with great force did it go.
—When they came back, then we killed a chicken. They brought it to him. And the boys were with him until 11:00. They didn't break their fast until 11:00. They were that way, too.

(X: And it's a good thing that they underwent such a shock and weren't too wounded. But our hearts were jolted.)

H. "What happened," cont.

—Oh, God! And I tell you that when it took off. . . . That car took such a shock, *kana*. And it bashed into the mountain. Then it bounced back off the mountain and spun around in that sand. Then they say it headed straight for the mountain . . . for the river. He says he doesn't know what happened after that.
—He says, "I didn't have any idea what was happening to me. Then

they brought me. Then they bandaged me. I had no idea what was happening to me. . . ."

(Z: Almonds! You should get almonds for him. [Almonds are believed to be good for the mind and memory.])

—"I was gone in the air."

(Z: Get a lot of almonds for him.)

—Huh!

(Z: He underwent a shock. Moshtar's brother was not too hurt, but his speech was permanently impaired.)

(X: She tells her son.)

(Z: He suffered a shock, *kana*?)

—Huh! And Great God saved him like that. That one boy fell on the road. The driver, that boy fell on the road.

(Grandson: The door opened up, and he fell from it.)

I. "Resolution."

—Now, Great God . . . He [driver] wasn't hurt anywhere. And he [son] was hit here by the glass and was hurt. I thought that God can heal a hurt, as long as he doesn't die. I was terrified at the thought of his death. Great God showed mercy. I am ever grateful to Dear God. Great God was very virtuous.

[Another guest from next door enters who, after shaking hands with the visitors, right away takes over with her story of how she had found Shiriney when the news came, and had cried with her and then rushed to inform me so I could go over and sympathize.]

Notes

1. *Paxtun* is the adjective and proper noun. *Paxto* is the word used for the language and the code of honor/modesty. For the language, I have used upper case *P*, and for the code of honor lower case *p*. I have used the symbol *x* to represent the Paxto letter ښ, which is spoken as "*sh*" or "*kh*" depending on the speech group. I represent the letter *shīn* by "*sh*," and *khe* by "*kh*," both of which are invariable sounds in Paxto.

2. See Geertz (1973: 93–94) for a discussion of models of and for. He differentiates symbolic models or parallels of social or psychological systems (i.e., theories) that represent patterned processes and provide sources of information, from models *for* cultural patterns (i.e., rites, doctrines, melodies) that are required in the communication of pattern.

3. A Khattak village in the Karak district of NWFP, Pakistan, where I conducted most of my fieldwork in 1982–83 and 1986–87.

4. This woman was not originally Paxtun, but Bengali, and had married into a Paxtun family. Although the Paxtun milieu was that which she knew best and which fed her information on Pakistan, she alternated between presenting herself as Paxtun and as Pakistani. On this particular occasion, in private, she was accentuating the difference between me, a foreigner, and her, a Pakistani. When other women were present, she tended more to speak of herself as Paxtun.

5. The full version of this narrative appears in Grima, *"The Misfortunes Which Have Befallen Me": Paxtun Women's Life Stories.*

6. See Grima (1985) for a longer description of the visit and a sample narrative.

7. Although Ayoub examines redemptive suffering from a Shi'a perspective, he postulates in his introduction that "redemption plays a vital role in the actual life of the Muslim community and has been a dynamic force through the acceptance and understanding of suffering. Purposeful suffering is the holy struggle (*jihād*) of man in the way of God. This is so regarded both at the personal level and at the social level." He is referring here not only to Shi'a Islam, but to Sunni Islam and Sufism as well. Qazi Mujeeb ur-Rahman, of the Islamic Institute of Peshawar (Sunni), also presented me with the same argument.

8. See Anderson (1982), Lindholm and Lindholm (1979), and Tapper (1987) for further discussions of marriage within the larger system of exchange and control among Paxtuns.

9. X, Y, and Z refer to three other women in the audience who comment within the narrative.

References

Abu-Lughod, Lila

1985 Honor and the Sentiments of Loss in a Bedouin Society. *American Ethnologist* 12:245–261.

1986 *Veiled Sentiments: Honor and Poetry in a Bedouin Society*. Berkeley: University of California Press.

Ahmed, Akbar S.

1980 *Pukhtun Economy and Society: Traditional Structure and Economic Development in a Tribal Society*. Boston: Routledge and Kegan Paul.

Ahmed, Akbar S., and Z. Ahmed

1981 "Mor" and "Tor": Binary and Opposing Models of Pukhtun Womanhood. In *The Endless Day: Some Case Material on Asian Rural Women*, T. S. Epstein and R. A. Watts, eds., pp. 31–46. Oxford: Pergamon Press.

Ali, Ahmed

1984 *Al-Qur'an: A Contemporary Translation*. Princeton, N.J.: Princeton University Press.

Anderson, Jon W.

1982 Cousin Marriage in Context: Constructing Social Relations in Afghanistan. *Folk* 24:7–28.

Atayee, M. Ibrahim

1979 *A Dictionary of the Terminology of Pashtun's Tribal Customary Law and*

Usages. Translated by A. Mohammad Shinwary. Kabul, Afghanistan: International Center for Pashto Studies.

Ayoub, Mahmoud

1978 *Redemptive Suffering in Islam: A Study of the Devotional Aspects of Ashura in Twelver Shi'ism*. The Hague: Mouton.

Barth, Fredrik

1959 *Political Leadership Among Swat Pathans*. London: Athlone Press.

1981 *Features of Person and Society in Swat: Collected Essays*. London: Routledge and Kegan Paul.

Beeman, William O.

1985 Dimensions of Dysphoria: The View from Linguistic Anthropology. In *Culture and Depression: Studies in the Anthropology and Cross-Cultural Psychiatry of Affect and Disorder,* Arthur Kleinman and Byron Good, eds., pp. 216–43. Berkeley: University of California Press.

Boesen, Inger W.

1980 Women, Honour, and Love: Some Aspects of the Pashtun Woman's Life in Eastern Afghanistan. *Afghanistan Journal* 7, 2:50–60. Also in (1979–80) *Folk* 21/22:229–239.

1983 Conflicts of Solidarity in Pashtun Women's Lives. In *Women in Islamic Societies: Social Attitudes and Historical Perspectives,* Bo Utas, ed. London: Curzon Press; Atlantic Highlands, N.J.: Humanities Press.

Geertz, Clifford

1973 *The Interpretation of Cultures*. New York: Basic Books.

Good, Mary-Jo Del Vecchio, Byron Good, and Michael M. J. Fischer, eds.

1988 Emotion, Illness and Healing in Middle Eastern Societies. *Culture, Medicine and Psychiatry* (special issue).

Grima, Benedicte

1985 The Pukhtun Tapos: From Biography to Autobiography. *Asian Folklore* 44:241–267.

Forthcoming *"The Misfortunes Which Have Befallen Me": Paxtun Women's Life Stories*. Austin: University of Texas Press.

Irvine, Judith

1982 Language and Affect: Some Cross-Cultural Issues. In *Contemporary Perceptions of Language: Interdisciplinary Dimensions,* H. Bynes, ed., pp. 31–47. Washington, D.C.: Georgetown University Press.

Janata, A., and R. Hassas

1975 Ghairatman—Der gute Pashtune. Exkurs über die Grundlagen des Pashtunwali. *Afghanistan Journal* 2/3:83–97.

Kieffer, Charles M.

1972 *Über das volk der Pastunen und seinen Pastunwali*. Berlin: Mitteilungen Institut für Orientforschung 17, no. 4.

Lindholm, Charles

1982 *Generosity and Jealousy: The Swat Pukhtun of Northern Pakistan*. New York: Columbia University Press.

Lindholm, Charles, and Cherry Lindholm

1979 Marriage as Warfare. *Natural History* 88/8:11–21.

Lutz, Catherine
1986 Emotion, Thought, and Estrangement: Emotion as a Cultural Category. *Cultural Anthropology* 1:287–309.
Shweder, R., and R. LeVine, eds.
1984 *Culture Theory: Essays on Mind, Self, and Emotion*. Cambridge: Cambridge University Press.
Spain, James W.
1962 *The Way of the Pathans*. Karachi, London, New York: Oxford University Press.
Steul, Willi
1981 *Paschtunwali: Ein Ehrenkodex und seine rechtliche Relevanz*. Wiesbaden: Franz Steiner Verlag.
Tapper, Nancy
1987 Direct Exchange and Brideprice: Alternative Forms in a Complex Marriage System. *Man* 16:387–407.
White, Geoffrey M.
1987 Constructing and Deconstructing Emotion: The Discourse of Disentangling. Paper read at the American Anthropological Association conference as part of a session entitled "Emotion and Discourse."

Ann Grodzins Gold

4. Gender and Illusion in a Rajasthani Yogic Tradition

Introduction

A recurrent motif in the Rajasthani version of the pan-North Indian tale of King Gopi Chand[1] is the spreading (*phailnā*) of the "net of illusion" (*māyājāl*). This net entraps or snares (*phaṃsnā*) the human spirit, and obstructs its passage to liberation from cycles of birth and death (*saṃsāra*). King Gopi Chand's story is largely concerned with relations between its central figure and various female characters and types. Women, especially beloved women, evoke in Gopi Chand those passionate attachments that cause him, weeping, to cling to the world he must leave—a world of mortality in which love is illusion but no less potent for being so.

This regional recension of Gopi Chand's tale, which I recorded as it was sung and told by a bard of the Nath caste, contains an elaborately narrated conflict between male yogis and female magicians (*jādūgāriyāṃ*). Both sides in this conflict hurl effective spells of transformation—a manipulation of apparent reality, and thus a wielding of *māyā,* understood as magical art.[2] Therefore, the Rajasthani oral performance of Gopi Chand demonstrates and comments on two kinds of *māyā,* and links them with the ways different kinds of females interact with them. I shall explore some subtle and complex connections between the nature of illusion and relations between the sexes which emerge in the narrative of King Gopi Chand's trials as he strives, halfheartedly, to become a true world-renouncer.

Gopi Chand is the story of a king who must become a yogi, although he would rather not. The reason for his balkiness—as his guru frequently reminds him—is that he is still enmeshed in the snares of illusion. Yoga itself, a self-disciplined path to higher knowledge, may be construed as cutting through or dispersing illusion. But yoga is also a technique for accumulating personal power, and thus potentially of controlling illusion. The nature of illusion, or *māyā*, is appropriately elusive and distinctly feminine. Frequently embodied as a, or the, goddess (Coburn 1982; Goudriann 1978:46–47; Kinsley 1986), *māyā* is also a concept of multiplicities of name and form which exuberantly mask a monistic reality. It is closely allied with *prakṛti*, or nature as female, a principle associated with the differentiation entailed by an emergent universe. From the single, eternal, inactive *puruṣa* (cosmic man) arise diverse, populous, and proliferating created worlds: all *prakṛti*. As the flux of creative energy, *māyā* is also identified with *śakti*, that is, power as female, without which the universe and its gods would be lifeless.[3]

The Gopi Chand text makes numerous direct references to the snare of *māyā*'s net, describing it as "always very bad" (*ḫargaj bahut burā*). It also offers a panoramic view of women in relation to the king-turned-yogi, in contexts ranging from home to dangerous foreign lands. Even relations with familiar women at home are not "normal," for the tale is entirely premised on the severing of such connections. Nonetheless, the mode of separation is determined by the previous quality of the bond between those separating. *Māyā*'s spreading net is a recurrent image, used in connection with clinging, loving women. The statement "the noose of *māyā*'s net is always very bad" precedes the most painful partings: husband from wife, brother from sister. By contrast, *māyā* as the power to bewitch is wielded by ruthless, amoral females who have no previous connection with Gopi Chand, strangers who playfully trap him in snares of their own device. However, females who manipulate power wisely, and who themselves slip through ephemeral, worldly tangles, emerge as the tale's most stable and admirable figures.

Through an overview of King Gopi Chand's relations with women and a detailed account of some of the more vividly antagonistic intersexual confrontations depicted in the tale, I propose to examine the ways in which an oral performance may forge and transmit a coherent if complex understanding of gender—one where conflicting paradigms, or fluidly context-dependent ones, may alternate or meld. The yogic sources of Rajasthani Nath traditions contain characterizations of women as temptresses and worse; but they also valorize divine power as female, and teach its internal discovery. These elements of a distinctive yogic perspective, I shall suggest, blend with images of vigorous and noble women predominant in regional folk traditions performed by and for householders to generate some altered visions. By focusing on configurations of gender and illusion, and the manner in which the bard presents and his village audience understands them, I hope to illuminate some of the qualities that cluster around femaleness as construed in rural South Asia and the relation of these qualities to both householders' and renouncers' world views.[4]

Folk performances instill as well as articulate cultural values. In rural Rajasthan, the audience for a tale such as Gopi Chand's consists largely of farmers, herders, artisans, unlettered and spiritually humble folk. These listeners are eager to acquire some religious instruction (*śikṣā*), as well as enjoy an evening's entertainment (*manorañjan*), when a performance is offered by someone who, like the Nath singer of Gopi Chand, has privileged access to particular knowledge (*gyān*). My project here is predominantly an old-fashioned one: to search for meaning in a recorded and transcribed text. However, I attempt to do this without losing awareness of the dynamic performance context so central to modern folklore theory, even as I probe for other less tangible settings, such as world view or value systems.[5]

Let me briefly set the stage. The bard, Madhu Nath, from whom I recorded this Rajasthani version of Gopi Chand's tale, belongs to a caste of householding farmers with yogic affinities and antecedents.[6] Madhu wears the special glass earrings of an initiated ascetic but was married and the father of two sons (he is now a widower and one of his sons died in 1980).[7] For the edification of the village, and for a share in the grain harvest, Madhu regularly performs Gopi Chand.

Madhu's usual performance never takes place in a single location. Rather, he goes from place to place—a process called *pherī lagānā,* or making rounds. During several nights he sings and tells fragments of King Gopi Chand's story outside private homes and at public gathering spots in front of neighborhood temples. Madhu does not give the entire story in sequence to his village audiences. Some favorite parts are, by request, repeated more frequently than others. Nevertheless, most listeners are cognizant of the whole plot, essentially a very simple one.

Like so many folklorists before me, I created a semi-artificial or "induced" performance context in order to record all Madhu knew of Gopi Chand's tale.[8] Within the frame of my exotic patronage, the Naths organized a situation comfortable and satisfying to them. It was winter (January), and for each session a small group gathered around a fire in the entrance way of my research assistant Nathu Nath's house. Nathu was closely related to the bard, as were all the Naths of our village. The audience included various other members of the village's Nath community, neighbors belonging to other middle-level peasant castes, and me. Women (Nathu's wife and mother and other relatives of the men present) felt free to join the listeners. We did not form a large group; rarely were more than ten or twelve persons there at one time. The bard's son faithfully attended, offering a faint vocal accompaniment to the sung parts, but I heard comments to the effect that he would probably never learn and be able to perform the whole tale properly, as his father did.

The fire was frugally fueled with small sticks, dying down to embers as the evening wore on. I supplied the ingredients for a tea break, and also some raw sugar for the bard to suck when his throat got dry and *bīḍīs* (local cigarettes), which he smoked at intervals despite a bad cough. It took five nights of recording sessions, varying from three-and-one-half to five hours, for Madhu to complete the saga to his satisfaction. The first two portions he sang for me were actually the first and third parts of the tale—reflecting his desire to give me the best, lest we be unable to complete our work. He then had to leave for another village where land-holdings required his attention, but he returned within two weeks and sang the second and fourth parts on two consecutive nights.

The transcription of Madhu's Gopi Chand, in handwritten *devanāgarī* on legal-size paper, is 465 pages long, and the rough, double-spaced typescript of my English translation about 250. However, this bulk has much to do both with performance style and with the poetic style of the bard's language. Madhu's performance alternates between segments of sung, metrical lines, accompanied by *sāraṅgī* music which he plays himself, and a prose *arthāv,* or "explanation," in which he retells everything he has just sung using more colorful, prosaic, and often vulgar language. He also inserts questions to the listeners—a technique of all Rajasthani storytellers—to make sure they are alert. Occasionally he expands on particular points of interest, and engages those present by giving anonymous characters the names of audience members.[9] The *arthāv* is the more dynamic part of the performance, demanding greater artistry and flair from the bard. While singing, his tone is uniform even at the most dramatic moments, but during the *arthāv* emotions such as grief, rage, and wonder, as well as considerable humor, play in his voice. All the passages I cite here are from the *arthāv.*[10]

Unlike several epics of royalty and divinity indigenous to Rajasthan,[11]

Gopi Chand has a small cast and a straightforward plot. The four parts into which Madhu divides his performance are as follows:

(1) the circumstances of Gopi Chand's birth (27 pages);[12]
(2) Gopi Chand begs alms from his own palace and calls his wife "mother" (53 pages);
(3) Gopi Chand goes to Bengal to meet with, and part from, his sister (106 pages);
(4) Gopi Chand's body-soul becomes immortal (66 pages).

For general orientation I provide a bare skeleton of the plot now. In the later discussion of gender and illusion some lengthy passages will be translated, so that style and flavor, necessarily omitted in this summary, may emerge.

In segment 1, King Gopi Chand learns from his mother, Manavati, that he must abdicate his throne and abandon his wives and slave girls to become a wandering yogi, a disciple of the guru Jalindar Nath. She reveals to an incredulous Gopi Chand the reason for this cruel fate: because no son was written in her destiny, Manavati, after performing very difficult ascetic feats in order to win the boon, received Gopi Chand as a loan from Jalindar. The loan had a limit of twelve years of childhood and beyond that twelve years of rule. Time has run out; if Gopi Chand does not become a yogi, he will die. He accepts this edict only after testing the warning and experiencing death, from whose clutches he is barely rescued by the powerful gurus Jalindar and Gorakh Nath.

In segment 2, Gopi Chand, now an initiated disciple, is sent by his guru to beg alms from his own palace and call his wife "mother." This is a very painful experience for him and he almost lapses back into householderhood as he sits, himself weeping and surrounded by weeping queens and slave girls, with his little daughter sobbing and clinging to his neck.

In segment 3, Gopi Chand tells his guru that he intends to visit his sister, Queen Champa De, in Bengal. Jalindar chides him for this evidence of persisting entanglement in the net of *māyā* and warns him that he will never get there anyway because of the female magicians who deny all yogis passage through Bengal. Gopi Chand stubbornly insists on going, and of course, he no sooner reaches the border than he encounters the lady magicians and suffers greatly at their hands. At the close of this episode he does finally meet with his sister and then goes off to immortality.

Segment 4 is largely concerned not with the further adventures of Gopi Chand but with those of other Nath yogis—especially Gorakh Nath and his guru Macchindar Nath. Gorakh rescues Macchindar from a (seemingly different) Bengal ruled over by magician-queens who have so bewitched him with their *māyā* that he—who should be a celibate yogi—is a happy householder with four wives and two sons. By turning Macchindar's wives into various other beings and establishing his sons as temple icons, Gorakh is able to free himself of the shame of having a guru who is "an enjoyer of women."

In each of these segments, as should be evident even from this rudimentary summary, various kinds of women play various important roles. Indeed, except for the gurus Jalindar and Gorakh, all the movers and shakers in Gopi Chand's tale are women. And except for Manavati Mother, all these women—whether loving, devoted wives or dangerous sorceresses—are shown as impeding the success of Gopi Chand's world-renunciation (and in the Gorakh-Macchindar episode are correspondingly destructive of Macchindar Nath's yogic prowess).

Again and again, the temptation to "tangle" in illusion's net is seen to arise from bonds with women and is directly opposed to yogic detachment. *Māyā* as practical magic is controlled by both female magicians and male yogis who wield verbal spells as weapons, and are thus able to transform humans into animals.[13] Although the male yogis participate fully in this power "contest," it is definitely the women who start it. However, *māyā* is not only delusion, not only the "spoiling" of one form to replace it with another, equally false. *Māyā* is also creativity, in a positive sense,[14] and here its association with females may be positive. Women in Gopi Chand's tale often display wit and ingenuity far livelier than men's. Just as the bard's (and audience's) sympathies are clearly with attached humans over detached yogis, despite the tale's yogic orientation, so the construction of femaleness that is generated may be a vigorous and positive one, even though it emerges from an apparently misogynous text.

The Women in Gopi Chand's Life

The female characters who appear in the Rajasthani version of Gopi Chand's tale run the gamut from powerful and destructive, seductive and selfish, to wise, nurturing, and enlightened. A far cry from pliable *pativratās* (husband-worshipers, one version of an ideal Hindu female), women in this tale talk back to their spouses, abandon their domestic chores, threaten men with both physical and magical violence, and develop themselves as yogic adepts. No lasting social or cosmic disasters result from these manifestations of women's independence. Although the most radical ladies, the Bengali magicians, are the cause of some significant disruption to the well-being of their kingdom, affairs are set to rights on the initiative of another, equally outspoken but impeccably virtuous female: Gopi Chand's sister, Champa De Rani.

By contrast with this variety of interesting women, men in the tale are of considerably less distinction. Essentially, two kinds of males appear: ordinary ones, including Champa De's husband the Bengali king, who all talk and act like country bumpkins; and yogis. The best of the yogis display definitely superior powers, crude but effective: they can turn dirt into gold and bring the dead to life. But most of them are not much more impressive, in wit or courage, than the householders. Gopi Chand himself, a markedly unheroic hero, is neither fully householder nor yogi (A. Gold 1989). Despite the sexual capacity implied by his having eleven hundred wives and sixteen hundred slave-girls, Gopi Chand is strikingly "womanly" in his endless weeping, his utter dependence on the guru, his concern with personal appearance, his unquenchable love of hearth and home. He is also significantly lacking in a male support system. He has no brothers, no father, no male advisors or comrades of note.[15] Gopi Chand is either solitary (and usually quite miserable for being thus), complaining to his caretaker guru Jalindar Nath, or struggling in various ways with various women.

The yogic tradition in which Gopi Chand's tale has its roots rejects all of *māyā*'s spreading web, opposing it by withdrawal (established in the text by lowered eyelids) and inner concentration on god or *smaraṇ* (which the bard conveys by muttering "*ŚivŚivŚivŚivŚiv*"). This typical self-removal from the world by male yogis may be one cause of women's prominence in the society depicted in the tale. For example, Behri Yogin, guru of the Bengali magicians, has a husband, Asmal Yogi, who is described as "absorbed in meditation on the music of sixteen flutes" while she goes about her nefarious business, running (or ruining) the kingdom of Bengal. However, she too is a yogi who presumably has acquired her power through some kind of meditative practice.

In fact, no tidy oppositions are possible here, such as withdrawn men versus worldly women. In this regard, Manavati Mother and her complex part in the tale are particularly important. Gopi Chand's mother outdoes even Jalindar in keeping her eyelids lowered for a long time, yet her withdrawal has the worldly goal of obtaining a "protector of the kingdom"—a son and heir. When it becomes clear that she must lose him again, to yoga if not to death, she does not perish from grief (as does his sister), because, as she puts it: "For twelve years I served the guru and I served Śiva, the Simple Lord." Thus her ascetic practice, although life-oriented, gave her the experience of inner detachment and outer devotion to ascetic guru and god that allows her to be philosophical about the destruction of her hard-won happiness. A typically hated mother-in-law to her son's eleven hundred queens, she blames them for almost succeeding in luring Gopi Chand back to certain doom in the world of mortality.[16] Yet she consigns her son to yoga only in order to prevent his death. Despite her calm resolution to make Gopi Chand a yogi, she also suffers from this loss. The king himself, when reciting the woeful results of his fate, refers several times to "my old mother weeping in the palace."

Schematically, Gopi Chand's tale is composed of a series of nine conflicts between males and females, sometimes as individuals, sometimes as groups; sometimes emotional, sometimes magical, and sometimes physically violent. The major opposing parties (in order of appearance) are these:

Gopi Chand / Manavati Mother
Gopi Chand / his slave-girls
Gopi Chand / his queens
Gopi Chand / the *jādūgāriyāṃ*
Jalindar Nath's disciples (represented by Carpat Nath) / Behri Yogin and the *jādūgāriyāṃ*
Jalindar Nath (represented by Hada Nath) / Behri Yogin and the *jādūgāriyāṃ*
Gopi Chand / Champa De Rani's slave-girls
Gopi Chand / Champa De Rani
Gorakh Nath / Macchindar Nath's queens

In the first of these encounters, Gopi Chand stolidly defends his place in the world, while his mother, Manavati, advises him of that world's illusory nature: "Be a yogi, my son," she repeatedly insists, "and you'll become immortal. If not, time will eat you." In the second two sets of encounters, Gopi Chand confronts first his slave-girls and then his queens. These wailing women embody *māyā,* and Gopi Chand's frail grip on yoga is almost destroyed by their hypnotic power. Desiring only that Gopi Chand remain their husband, the eleven hundred queens are devastated (symbolically and effectively widowed) by his becoming a yogi. When the unknown beggar at their gate reveals himself as the former king, the queen's slave-girl reports to her mistress: "Lady, now you must break and throw away your ivory bangles. Lady, your husband has become a yogi and your fortune has burst."

Patam De, Gopi Chand's chief wife, goes weeping and fainting to meet her former husband, taking his renunciation as a personal rejection: "Hey king, so I seem sour [*khāṭī*] to you . . . but you met some yogi who seemed good." The other queens echo her lament: "Grain-giver, we seem sour to you, but that yogi who seems just fine has wrapped your ass in a loincloth, and pierced your ears and put in great big yogis' earrings. . . . Grain-giver, these palaces have become sour for you and the guru has made the jungle seem fine." The queens use Gopi Chand's daughter, Phulam De, as ammunition for their onslaught, and he is helplessly re-ensnared until Jalindar Nath's arrival. Deposited by Jalindar in the palace of his sympathetic mother, Gopi Chand has a brief respite from struggles, and a good meal.

Gopi Chand's next encounter with dangerous women is in Bengal, where seven lady magicians use black magic to enslave him and prevent him from getting to where he wants to go. The difference between the loving queens and these hostile enemies becomes blurred in the bard's language. Accusing the queens of wanting to kill her son, Manavati Mata has called them "sluts," the same term that is regularly used for the lady magicians.

Just as Jalindar had to rescue Gopi Chand from the queens, his virtuous and loving wives, so the guru, who is blissfully if ignorantly free from all ties with women, must also rescue him from his captivity with the magicians. The attempts to rescue Gopi Chand—first by fourteen hundred of Jalindar's disciples led by Charpat Nath, who fail; and then by fourteen hundred more led by Hada Nāth and backed up by the presence of their all-powerful guru, who succeed—involve an escalating war between the sexes in the kingdom of Bengal. This is a pitted battle of spells versus spells, with no holds barred: *māyā* against *māyā*, a brute test of power. In the next section I examine in detail Gopi Chand's own encounter with the *jādūgāriyāṃ* as well as the global battles of yogis versus Bengali women.

Gopi Chand's skirmish with his sister's slave women is structured very similarly to the previous one with Patam De's, but the conflict becomes more intense. Both begin with the chief slave approaching the king-as-yogi with sweet words and seductive dress. When her offering of jewels is rejected by Gopi Chand, who asks instead for stale bread, she heaps terrible threats and abuses upon him.[17] At his sister's, these abuses so enrage the former king that he strikes the slave-woman.

The bard's description of Gopi Chand's disastrous encounter with Moti De Dasi, chief maidservant of his sister Champa De Rani, shows the slave as explicitly seductive:

> Moti De Dasi put on a skirt with eighty pleats, and wrapped herself in a flowered Gujarati sari. She put on jingling silver ankle bracelets, and threaded pearls in her hair; she used all sixteen cosmetics. Finding a golden platter, she filled it with diamonds and rubies.
>
> If the wind blew this way then she dropped this way and if the wind blew that way then she dropped that way, and if it blew from all four directions she would break into pieces. And if a big opium eater saw her, he would take her for a single dose and consume her.

Although the fact that Gopi Chand ignores her delicate charms and refuses the jewels might indicate a proper yogic stance, the former king is, in fact, lost in a regretful reverie about his ruling times. Speaking as a king, he calls Moti De "*golī*," a stronger term than the usual *dāsī* for slave-woman, and one carrying the explicit implication of sexual access. She takes offense at being thus casually addressed by a begging yogi.

Here the potential for violence between the sexes explodes, first verbally and then physically.

> "O yogi, the mistress of the kingdom doesn't say '*golī*' to me, and the people of the city don't call me 'girl' either, princely yogi. Yogi, I will string you up, and I will rub your skin with bitter leaves and salt. Many such as you come. What do you mean by calling me '*golī*,' yogi?" . . .
>
> When Moti De said this, the yogi got mad, Gopi Chand was filled with rage, the yogi got furious. Gopi Chand struck her hard with his iron tongs and the slave-woman fell on her face in the entranceway. Stumbling she went, and her platter of diamonds and rubies were scattered about the entranceway. He had given the slave-woman just a single blow but two welts had risen, as if she had been branded like a sick animal. From the back of her neck two welts rose, running right down to her buttocks. Stumbling the slave-woman went, falling she went, and crying she went into the palace.

Violence is inappropriate behavior for a holy man (as is most of Gopi Chand's behavior). "What kind of a yogi is this in whose heart there is no pity?" muses the Queen Champa De. "If he has no pity, then how is he a yogi?" She then summons all her female servants and instructs them to take bamboo sticks and drive this undesirable out from their palace. Gopi Chand is surrounded and threatened by these hostile women:

> "Yogi, we'll rub salt in your flesh, O yogi, you'll remember well what your iron tongs did. We'll beat you with sticks, we'll make your skin fly." . . .
>
> Dying of fear, the yogi told them he was Gopi Chand. [They don't believe him.]
>
> "Yogi, we will hang you high from the bitter *nīm* tree, and rub salt in your flesh."
>
> The eleven-hundred slave-girls surrounded him, and some grabbed his locks, and some prodded him, and some punched him. Gopi Chand was crying hard, a rainstorm in his eyes. "Guru, hear my prayer and come, Baba Nath, these [women] nourished on my scraps are spoiling my honor."

Gopi Chand's abject fear is mingled with royal outrage. The slave-girls are part of a pool of women whose sexual favors Gopi Chand the king might have enjoyed. Although like all women they are forbidden to Gopi Chand the yogi, he nonetheless feels a self-righteous superiority over them. By referring to their being "nourished on his scraps," he claims the king's paternal role of protector-provider. When, after Jalindar Nath's intervention, the women realize his true identity, it is their turn to weep and abjectly beg forgiveness.

The former king's reunion with his sister, Queen Champa De, is singularly melodramatic: she dies of grief clinging to his neck, embodying the snare of *māyā* but also demonstrating the absolute "truth" of a sister's love. However, Jalindar is able to revitalize her with his elixir of life, and the readiness with which this is accomplished may be the ultimate put-down of illusion.[18] She then does all she can to prevent Gopi Chand from going off to be a yogi. He slips away from her by employing an old ruse: "Hey, your palace is on fire," he shouts. She turns her head out of concern for her precious home, giving Gopi Chand the chance to "become wind" and vanish. The bard comments disparagingly at this point: "Such is the female species!" However, as soon as she realizes what has happened, Champa De herself puts on ocher robes and goes wandering in the forest in search of her lost brother.

The coda tale of Gorakh Nath and Macchindar, which Madhu Nath counts as segment 4 of his Gopi Chand, seems designed to reinforce antihouseholding and concomitantly antifemale motifs in the strongest possible way. Taunted by Jalindar's disciples with the accusation that his guru is "over there in the land of Bengal, enjoying himself with sluts," Gorakh Nath feels compelled to alter this situation. He must sneak into a Bengal guarded by watchmen instructed to prevent all yogis from entering, and awaken his guru from the pleasures of *māyā* to the reality of yoga. This mission requires extreme resourcefulness and slyness on Gorakh's part, for Macchindar is less than delighted at being rescued.

After successfully concluding the adventure during which he effectively destroys, through various transformations, all four magician-queens and Macchindar's two sons as well, Gorakh Nath breathes a sigh of relief. He is once more easy in his mind, for now no one can say to him, "Look, your guru enjoyed sluts and had sons." In stressing the need to rid Macchindar of his sons as well as his wives, this episode denies one of the householder's chief religious aims. For householders, it is the son who gives salvation, indeed immortality, to his father; for yogis it is a different story.[19]

On the surface, Madhu Nath's Gopi Chand sounds some rather crude sexist notes: the low-born women, both magicians and slave-girls, are regularly referred to, in both the sung and spoken versions, as *rāṇḍ,* or "slut" as I translate it—a term of abuse deriving from "widow" with implications of "prostitute" or "loose woman." Episodes of violence, such as Gopi Chand's abuse of Moti De, are described with a kind of relish that might be seen as playing to sadistic sexual fantasies. However—and this may be what initially captivated me about the tale—the women in it not only have genuine power, they also have character. They speak their minds and act accordingly.

Within the social universe of the tale, such vigorous women appear at all levels of the social hierarchy. The magicians who oppose Gopi Chand are laundress, potter, oil-presser, and their ilk; those who captivate Macchindar are queens. Although all the lady magicians are ultimately defeated, and King Gopi Chand ultimately released from his attachments to women, the end of the story does not neatly force its powerful females to revert to roles of subservience or restricted domestic lives. Fated to be left without an heir to the kingdom, Manavati Mother remains a good, dharmic ruler; in the fourth segment we do not see her but learn that she has sent several cartloads of rich treats to feast visiting yogis, and she is praised for this action. In Bengal, if renegade women turn things upside down, an equally vigorous but virtuous female, Champa De, restores order by telling her husband the king exactly what to do. Only the queens who seduced Macchindar Nath are permanently removed from society as Gorakh Nath fanatically obliterates all reminders of his guru's straying from the ascetic path. The low-caste lady magicians are merely forced to vow to play no more contests with wandering yogis.

Trouble in Bengal[20]

Unlike Manavati Mother, whose rituals and ascetic feats are single-mindedly undertaken to achieve the boon of a son, the seven lady magicians of Bengal who impede Gopi Chand's arrival at his sister's palace seem to have no motivation other than pure sport, or "art for art's sake." While *māyā* is traditionally associated with divine creative power in a playful mode, and also with human practices of aim-oriented magic, the Bengali *jādūgāriyāṃ* are playful magicians.[21] But they are also casually portrayed as wives who at times labor diligently at their caste trades, while what little we learn of their husbands demonstrates those unfortunates' irresponsibility. The guru of all the lady magicians has a husband who does nothing much but meditate on flute music; the washerwoman's man is in debt to the wine-seller because of his fondness for drink.

Madhu Nath lingers over the lady magicians. Responding to as well as evoking his listeners' appreciation, the bard expands on the *jādūgāriyāṃ* with particular relish and comic flair. We first hear about these dangerous women from Gopi Chand's guru, Jalindar Nath, when he tries to talk Gopi Chand out of visiting his sister in Bengal:

> "Look, son, Gopi Chand, your sister Champa De lives in the land of Dak Bengal. Over there they won't let you meet your sister."
>
> "Who won't allow me to meet her, Baba?"
>
> "Over there is a land of magicians, seven lady magicians."
>
> "Who?"
>
> "Behri Yogin, Gangali Telin, Kapuri Dhobin, Setali Khamari, Luna Chamari, Bajori Kanjari, Chamani Kalali.[22] They are seven guru-sisters, and son, they will never allow you to meet with your sister."

Gopi Chand knows a flattering answer to this: "Hey Guru Maharaj, I have in you such an all-powerful guru, so should I be afraid of magic mantras?" At this the guru relents and gives Gopi Chand the standard advice to yogis, involving a desexualization of all females: "Don't stray from the road and call all women 'mother' or 'sister.'" For Gopi Chand, who has just finished the ordeal of calling his actual wife "mother," such advice seems superfluous. However, it may obliquely presage the vague sexual threat posed by the magicians.

When Gopi Chand arrives in Bengal, he sits down by the water to meditate. The seven magicians happen by, on their way to fill their double water pots.[23]

> The seven lady magicians were coming to the water-place to get water, and they were talking. In front of all the rest was Behri Yogin, for she was the guru of them all. Among them was Gangali Telin, who looked onto the water-place and spotted Gopi Chand. That yogi appeared to be doing *tapas* [ascetic practice].
>
> Now Gangali Telin spoke: "Sisters, listen! Burn up all other matters and listen to me."
>
> "What is it?"
>
> "Look, over on the water-place, there's a yogi doing *tapas*. Many days have gone by since we've played a contest, and today our fortune has opened. So burn up all other matters and let's hurry to the water-place, for today we'll have a contest with this yogi."
>
> As soon as she said this everyone got excited, and going to the water-place, they put down their double water pots. There was Gopi Chand, seated in meditation, his eyelids lowered, reciting. So they surrounded Gopi Chand, all seven of them.
>
> Then Behri Yogin said to Gopi Chand, "Yogi, where are you from? You look like someone well established. Raise your eyelids, Baba Nath, I have come to take your *darśan* [divine vision]."
>
> As soon as she said this, Gopi Chand thought, "Brother, some devotee has come to offer service to me." He was hungry too, and thought, "Someone must have brought food for me to cook, and then I will eat."
>
> Gopi Chand raised his eyelids and looked around, and everywhere he looked he saw women. Silently he counted them and there were a full seven.
>
> As soon as he had counted a full seven, Gopi Chand, who was hungry, stopped feeling hungry. "Uh-oh, Guru Maharaj said some-

thing about 'seven lady magicians' and they seem to have come right here to the water-place. They didn't even let me into the city. They look like lady magicians and I don't even know magic, I don't even know mantras. And now, who knows what they will do? Oh Brother!" So right away he lowered his eyelids again.

As soon as he had lowered his eyelids, Behri Yogin spoke: "Hey yogi, where are you from? Raise your eyelids, Baba Nath, I have come to take your *darsán*. Why do you shut your eyes now? Talk a little with your mouth. Who is your guru? What is your village and what is your name? Tell everything or else we will have a contest with you."

As soon as she had said this, Gopi Chand spoke: "O Sisters, I don't know contests nor do I know contesting, O Bengali women. And I am a yogi who was shaved only yesterday; I am a new-made yogi. So I know neither contests nor contesting. And I have come wandering aimlessly into Bengal."

Then Behri Yogin said, "Yogi, it seems you are a powerful magician, a death-spell wielder, since you have come into Bengal; otherwise you wouldn't even have glanced over here in Bengal. If you knew nothing, then how did you come into Bengal?"

"O Sisters, I came to wander."

"Does this look like some public meeting place?[24] Without asking you have come to Bengal, and this is hardly a public meeting place. This is Bengal! How did you arrive if you know no magic and mantras?"

"O Sisters, I know nothing. I came only to wander."

"Yogi, now watch out for your magic, watch out for your mantras! If you don't tell me all about yourself, then I will send you flying, I will send your campfire flying, I will make your iron cane into a crow, I will make your sack into a vulture, and that gourd of drinking water I will turn into a tortoise.[25] And I will send you flying in the sky. How did you come here into Bengal if you know nothing?"

Then Gopi Chand said, "Sister, I am a new-made yogi. Do as you please with me, sister. If you wish to fly me in the sky, that's fine; and if you wish to keep me on the earth, that's fine."

Behri Yogin said, "Brother, nobody is allowed to come here."

"So is this your father's kingdom? Do you give the orders here?"

"Yes, I give the orders."

"Fine, sister, I won't come again, sister, I've come and now I'll go."

> "Yogi, you seem to be a powerful magician, a death-spell wielder, and now watch out for your wisdom."
>
> So right away Behri Yogin recited magic, and she recited mantras, and she struck the magic blow. Gopi Chand, poor thing, he knew nothing, he was a new-made yogi. And no one had taught him magic mantras, and he had just come to meet with his sister. Behri Yogin struck the magic blow and made Gopi Chand into a parrot. Yes, she made him a parrot, and put him in her sack.
>
> Then on the water-place all seven lady magicians filled their double water pots, put them on their heads, and returned to the city.

Notice the closure here. After their sport with and victory over Gopi Chand, the magicians resume their interrupted work of bringing home water. As the conflict between women and yogis escalates, the women eventually abandon domestic routines. Before that happens, however, several of the lady magicians are able to use (and abuse) Gopi Chand for their own purposes, conscripting his labor for their low-caste work. First, Gangali Telin talks Behri Yogin into giving her the parrot, promising to treat it well. Instead, she transforms it into an ox, pierces its nose, and inserts a nose-rope. She then scolds her servants:

> "You sluts, how can you be so slack, when I am standing here with an ox who has never before worked. Take this ox and yoke him to the oil press and drive him day and night. Don't let this ox go, because he cost a lot of money. He was very expensive, and he is an unworked ox."
>
> After she said this several of her slave-girls came running and surrounded the ox. They grabbed him and bound his eyes,[26] and making soothing sounds they took him to the circular track and delicately put the yoke on him. They put on the yoke and the leather harness, and struck his back with the nine-tailed whip, and as soon as they struck him, Gopi Chand leaped forward so that twenty kilos of oilseeds were pressed in just a few minutes. He had been a ruler [and therefore was very strong].
>
> "Girls," said Gangali Telin, "don't set the ox free. Grind oilseeds in twenty-kilo batches, one after another. Make him go day and night, and if he goes slowly, then beat him with the nine-tailed whip and poke him with the iron prod. Push him forcefully from behind. Don't let him go, this is an ox who has never worked before."

Gopi Chand ground up one batch of seeds and a second one and a third. While he was grinding the fourth batch, Gopi Chand's spirit withered. And Gopi Chand began crying hard, a rainstorm struck his eyes, and they rained water. Plop, plop, his tears were falling and he went slowly and they beat him with the nine-tailed whip and shoved him from the rear with the toothed iron prod, so that the moon and the sun were printed on both his buttocks.[27] Gopi Chand was beginning to get hungry and he was tired; he had pressed four batches of seed, and the fifth was poured into the press. Now how far could he go? Gopi Chand was crying hard, and he beseeched his Guru Maharaj:

"Hey Guru Maharaj! Oh, Father of a Daughter! [a curse] How nicely I have met with my sister! Here I am yoked to the oil press and the sluts, they are poking all over my body. Wherever they please they are sliding the iron prod and striking me with the whip, and I am dying of hunger. Hey Guru Maharaj, now my life's breath will leave me. Guru Maharaj, I beseech you, come quickly, Baba Nath, for my breath is leaving me and now I am in no condition to turn the oil press."

Next to acquire the living prize is the laundress, Kapuri Dhobin. Becoming angry with Gangali Telin, the washerwoman-magician recites spells that change the ox into a donkey.

She made a donkey and grabbed its ear and took him to her house. She tied him to a stake and went running all through Bengal, and from some she took full skirts, and from some turbans, and she also took wraps from all the women of Bengal. The washerwoman took them in order to wash them. She brought them and loaded them on top of the donkey. She piled them on the donkey, and sat on top of the pile and went to the water tank. There she tied up the donkey and washed the clothes and then she piled the wet clothes back on him, and she, the washerwoman, sat on top.

Then, Gopi Chand was crying hard, a rainstorm struck his eyes and they rained tears. Gopi Chand wailed, "Oh ho ho, Guru Maharaj, you must come. Your eyelids are closed over there in Kajali Woods, but I am your disciple, and how my condition has been spoiled today! The clothes from all of Bengal, full skirts and wraps, are on top of me, on top of the king. It doesn't seem possible that someone would pile

> up full skirts and wraps on top of King Gopi Chand, but there it is, Guru Maharaj.[28] And what's more, the washerwoman has seated herself on top of me—a washerwoman is seated on top! So Grain-giver, if this were my ruling time, and a washerwoman sat down on top of me, then I would bury her deep and have horses trample her, or else I would make her fly from a cannon's mouth. But I am being controlled by others, and Guru Maharaj, I beseech you to hurry today, Baba Nath, O sorrow-giver, take care of me, Lord knows how much my condition has been spoiled by now."

Not Jalindar but Chamani Kalali, the wine-seller's wife, rescues the donkey. Transforming him into a rooster, she seats him on her roof and teaches him to crow in the morning.[29] There King Gopi Chand remains until Behri Yogin retrieves him, makes him a parrot once more, and shuts him up in a cage.

The lady magicians are depicted as ruthless and heartless. But they are not without their feminine graces, as the first view of them carrying double waterpots indicates. Although none is ever described in terms of her individual appearance, en masse they and their disciples make a pretty as well as an imposing sight. When they learn of the arrival in Bengal of Charpat Nath, leading fourteen hundred disciples to the rescue of Gopi Chand, the lady magicians muster their forces.

> Each person had seven hundred disciples, and they brought along those who were not disciples, too, to see the show. "Come along with us, we're going to have a contest with the Babajis."
>
> Some wrapped themselves in striped wraps, some put on ones with silver trim, some wore flowered skirts. Dressed like that they came, in brilliant multicolors [*raṅg raṅg raṅgilā*]. They gathered at the water-place, on the pretext of getting water. Then they went to the garden, and in front of them all came their guru-queen, Behri Yogin.
>
> In the garden, the fourteen hundred yogis had lowered their eyelids, and their campfires were crackling and they were reciting "*Śiv Śiv*." Then the garden filled with all the women of Bengal. As soon as she arrived, Behri Yogin went up to the yogis and said, "Hey Yogis, where are you from? You look like established Naths. Raise your eyelids, for I have come to take your *darśan*."
>
> Charpat Nath raised his eyelids and looked: "O ho, as in the

> month of Śrāvan clouds coming from the place of Indra mount in the sky, so these women all in red and yellow, like clouds gather and draw near. O Lord," thought Charpat, "if they are all magicians, then there won't be enough of us to go around! How will they share us out?"

Despite these qualms, Charpat easily defeats the masses of women, turning them into donkeys, but Behri Yogin remains standing before him. Thus, it comes down to a contest between Behri Yogin, the women's guru-queen, and Charpat Nath, the chief disciple among Jalindar's first batch of fourteen hundred. Behri Yogin challenges Charpat Nath:

> "As much wisdom as you've got, let it come over me. As much wisdom as there is, let that much come now. You have made all the city's women into donkeys. But now let your wisdom come on me."
>
> Charpat Nath once more recited magic, recited mantras, gave the magical puff, [recited] mantras into many pebbles and threw them, but not one struck Behri Yogin. After a bit she said, "Have you finished?"
>
> "Lakṣmī, my magic doesn't go over you."
>
> "So, Charpat Nath, now comes my skill, and you be careful." And Behri Yogin recited magic, she recited mantras, she struck a magic blow, and as soon as she struck a magic blow, she turned all the disciples into donkeys. Charpat Nath remained standing, and only Behri Yogin remained facing him. The others were made into donkeys.
>
> While she alone remained standing, if he had given her two or four blows with his iron cane, then from doing that much he would have been able to stop the lady-yogi. But he missed his chance. So right away, Charpat Nath again recited magic and recited mantras but nothing happened; he was defeated. "Enough, enough, now what can I send over you, Lakṣmī?"

Why at this juncture does he call her Lakṣmī—the name of that most gracious Hindu goddess who bestows luck and wealth on those who attain her favor through worship and service? It seems to be highly ironic. While it is popularly said that to call someone Lakṣmī is to identify her with good fortune having arrived in the form of a woman, I often heard men derisively address or speak of women who caused them trouble as "Lakṣmī."[30] In any case, trouble is coming for Charpat Nath. Behri Yogin turns all fourteen hundred disciples into donkeys and makes Charpat himself into a camel.

She restores the women who Charpat made into donkeys to human form, and then drives the whinnying camel and braying asses into the wilderness.

> Having left them in the jungle she came back, singing a song of victory. She was happy and she and the rest of the women returned to the town.
>
> To those who had not gone they said, "My sister-in-law, if only you had come with us! Fourteen hundred yogis were made into donkeys and driven into the jungle. We played a contest today and had a lot of fun."
>
> The women who had stayed home said, "O big sister-in-law, take me with you next time, take me with you. Next time, sister-in-law, don't leave me behind."

Jalindar's second batch of disciples, like the first, are afraid of the Bengali women. When their guru instructs them to go to Bengal and rescue Gopi Chand, they reply: "Hey Guru Maharaj, we will shit right here but we won't put one foot in Bengal, not one foot. We will shit water [from fear] but we will not go to Bengal." The macho guru becomes angry at his cowardly disciples' fear, and declares, "Well, sister-fuck! If you can't win with magic and mantras, then use iron tongs! Give those sluts your iron tongs, beat them!"

Jalindar determines to go along himself this time. When he arrives in the Bengali garden he discovers the abandoned, smoldering campfires of the vanquished yogis he had sent before and mutters: "The sluts have eaten all of them, they have devoured all fourteen hundred disciples, those lady magicians." Jalindar devises a way of sending his challenge to the magicians. He has his disciples pile green wet wood on the campfires and he has them cry "Alakh!"—the yogi's cry—in unison. The billowing smoke darkens Bengal and the sound of the yogis' voices shakes the land. Perceiving Jalindar's powerful presence, the magicians prepare to answer his challenge. The bard also describes the ordinary townswomen's response to this turn of events:

> They were dying from anticipation. If one slut was grinding flour, she left the flour in the mill; and if one was rolling bread, she left the flour in the dough-dish, she left the dough: "Later I will roll it." And if one was nursing a boy or girl, she tied him in the cradle: "We will be late for the show, and miss the fun, so let's go now and nurse later." The sluts, all the women of the city, acted this way.

The women's triumphant vacation is short-lived. Even Behri Yogin is defeated by the spells of Hada Nath, who is directly backed and guided by the all-powerful Jalindar. The female yogis—now merged effectively with all the women of Bengal—are sent as she-asses into the wilderness. But they are then missed at home, for the domestic scene is left in chaos:

> All the women of the city were made into donkeys. You couldn't have the vision of a Bengali woman anywhere; in the villages there was nothing you could even call a woman. Now only men were left, and the boys and girls in the cradles were crying.
>
> Some men said, "My sons' and daughters' mother hasn't come here." And some said, "Oh no! Mine left the dough in the kneading bowl." Others said, "O dear, at my house the bread is burning on the griddle." But others shouted: "Let the bread burn, but my boys and girls are crying in the cradle and whose breast will suckle them, where has she gone?"[31]

The men resolve to reclaim their women. "Let's all go now and aim our sticks at the yogis. We haven't any mantra-magic, but we men have straight stick magic, and from one blow with a stick five loincloth-wearers will fall." This is sheer bravado. Confronted by the angry men, the yogis play coy, but reveal their contempt: "O sons, why do we need your women, O sons. Because of women-trouble we became yogis. O Brothers, if there are women, search for them."

Jalindar easily defeats the men, turning them too into donkeys. A few remaining old folks petition the king to do something about the depopulation of Bengal. Rather than confront the yogis, the cowardly king reiterates the cowardly disciples' protest: "I'll shit right here, but I won't go [to see Jalindar Nath]." His wife, Gopi Chand's sister, after roundly denouncing his improper rule, tells him that he must approach Jalindar barefoot with his hands behind his back. She also instructs him to propose making a copperplate edict outlawing contests with yogis in the kingdom of Bengal.

The king of Bengal thus humbly approaches Jalindar: "Hey Great King, I will have an inscription engraved: 'No sluts will play any games with any robe-wearers. The punishment [for disobedience] is burial and to be trampled by horses. I will require a vow, Hindus on cows and Muslims on pigs, not to play any contests with any yogis at all.'" Jalindar agrees. Eventually the donkeys are herded back and restored to their original forms. The kingdom resettled, Gopi Chand—rescued from his parrot's cage, but thoroughly disheartened and weeping still—proceeds to meet with and part from his sister.

What does the bard Madhu Nath's excursion into the land of Bengal teach his audience about women? Masters of magic, the lady magicians of Bengal have gained unlimited power over that "ill-fated" kingdom—as Gopi Chand's sister Champa De refers to it again and again. A number of misogynous cultural stereotypes are confirmed here, the most evident and homeliest of which is that powerful women make bad wives. Also striking is the contagion factor: what begins as the sport of a few bad characters soon influences all the women of the land. Concomitant with these notions is the more wide-reaching implication that a precarious male dominance, endangered by the greater wit and strength of women, must be maintained lest all of society descend into the condition of animals.

These negative impressions are not, however, the whole story, or the whole story's impact. The solution to the donkey disaster is contract, rather than punishment, vows rather than violence, and significantly, this settlement is proposed by a woman. The men with their big sticks and abject fears are totally ineffectual. The yogis, except for Jalindar, have not much more poise. Gopi Chand himself, not just in Bengal but everywhere, is constantly manipulated by women. Some seek his well-being, while others are less beneficent; but all of them, until the moment he evades Champa De and achieves immortality, seem wiser, trickier, or more resolute than he is.

Conclusion

When Madhu Nath performs the tale of Gopi Chand, his audience—respecting him especially as a wearer of yogis' magical earrings (*darśanī, mudrā*)—take in his song and explanation as lore containing knowledge (*gyān*), conducive to acquiring merit (*puṇya*) and promoting morality (*dharma*). As part of a body of tradition that disparages family bonds as ephemeral, insisting that mortality ends all human love, the message of Gopi Chand is peculiarly double-edged.[32] For what is compelling about its central figure is not his achievement of immortality as a renouncer, but rather his all-too-human sufferings in the process of renouncing.

Gopi Chand's deepest sufferings—which arouse evident empathy in the audience—are the result of his attachments to the illusory world spun out by *māyā*. And, although the yogic tradition may firmly devalue such attachments, the peasant-householder listeners well understand their pull and worth. In the episode of the magicians, which so swells Madhu's version of the tale's third segment, the hero's sufferings at the hands of women are externalized. Bondage is no longer emotional but physical (ropes and cages); and the pain entailed by it becomes similarly corporeal. Rather than beloved household members, these women are enemy-strangers, so much easier to hate. And illusion itself is reduced from the nearly divine power of love to the particular and limited efficacy of spells. It seems as if the Rajasthani Naths' version of Gopi Chand needed the Bengali magicians in order to promote a detachment from *māyā* that did not violate bonds of husband to wife, brother to sister, son to mother so valued by its village-householder audience. The popularity of the Bengali magician portion of Gopi Chand as entertainment may then be in part a reflection of its complementarity to some of the tale's deeper messages.

Although there is no way of knowing the exact sources of Madhu Nath's particular version of Gopi Chand, I suggest that the configurations of gender and illusion emerging from the performed text have their sources both in yogic renouncers' traditions and in regional folk traditions, particularly women's lore. The knowledge absorbed by Madhu's audience, then, possesses the power of yogic certainties, enhanced by the familiarity of home truths. In both these currents come views of females and male-female relationships that hold considerable potential for flexible rather than rigid identities and attributes.

Originally, the Nath tradition was an esoteric one, and it may also be described, loosely, as an "antistructural" one. By "antistructural" I mean simply that it offered access to spiritual power in ways reacting against and controverting aspects of a more rigidly conceived socio-moral hierarchy crowned by male Brahman ritual experts.[33] In the structured social world defined by Brahmanical textual tradition, women were equated with Śudras—or low-born persons lacking spiritual capacity—and accordingly denied access to religious knowledge except through marital union. Within antistructural trends in Indian religion such as *bhakti* and *tantra*—streams which overlap and commingle at times with the Naths' yogi traditions—neither sex nor caste necessarily prohibited spiritual development, and a different set of attitudes toward women accrued.[34]

Certainly, antiworldly yogic traditions, including the Naths', may denounce the effects on men of paying attention to women in the world; but they also contain a high valuation of power as feminine, and their teachings often include cultivation of female power within—as *śakti* or *kuṇḍalinī*.

Such female energy is understood as complementary and vital to divinity, both on the macrocosmic scale and within each human body. To find empowered females ambivalently perceived in a popular tale having roots in such traditions should not be surprising.

In regional South Asian folklore, especially those stories and songs performed by and among women, positive valuations of femaleness as auspicious and life-affirming predominate. They are less related to abstract concepts of the Goddess or female power than to very earthy associations of women with reproduction and communal fertility. Women's public rituals bring well-being, prosperity, and, above all, renewed life to the village as a whole (A. Gold 1988a: 123–32), even as their domestic ones promote similar boons in the more limited arenas of husbands' (and brothers') families (Wadley 1980). Neither sexuality nor the bonds of affection are necessarily devalued in these traditions; rather both are intrinsically linked to the well-being brought about by women's worshipful arts and domestic graces.

The pool of witty and resourceful females appearing in women's tales, whose devotional habits (*niyam*) persuade the gods to effect all kinds of miracles, must surely have influenced the Rajasthani Gopi Chand as its distinctive regional traits developed over time. Performances would be affected by expectations held by audience and bard, deriving in part from such shared traditions.[35] Those clever brides, self-sacrificing sisters, and triumphant daughters-in-law who populate the world of women's tales have something in common with Gopi Chand's wise, spiritually adept mother and ingenious, loving sister. Echoes of plucky folk heroines also sound in Queen Patam De's vigorous remonstrances with her spouse, in the slave-girls' sudden, defensive anger when the unknown beggar ill-treats one of their number. Even the magicians' gaiety and esprit de corps has a certain resonance with the prevailing atmosphere during Rajasthani womens' gatherings on festival days.

A reasonable if unverifiable supposition is that the ways in which Madhu's version of Gopi Chand portrays female characters and shows them interacting with men derive from a confluence of yogic sources and regional folklore. That is, the devaluation of women as "snares" of illusion or emblems of a seductive world is modified by the high valuation of women as resourceful, blessed, and life-giving, which is such a strong current in local tales and songs. Tantric exaltation of female power would have an immediate affinity for such folkloric persuasions. Moreover, the goddess as *mahāmāyā*— a pan-Hindu theme well known in this region where the dominant Rajput caste is strongly associated with Devī-worship—provides a "role model" for both views of femaleness. Creative grace and delusive power are two sides of the same great *māyā*.

As a whole the Rajasthani Gopi Chand transmits a world view in which gender is construed flexibly, the attributes of the different sexes are at times interchangeable, and misogyny coexists with a view of women as definitively the better half. Both in love and in magic, women command the power of *māyā*, and no ordinary male can overcome this—although the very best of yogis can outdo women by rejecting the former and co-opting the latter. However, though his spells prevail, even Jalindar's superiority may be open to doubt. Frequently, when the guru chides Gopi Chand for tangling in illusion's net, the king retorts: "You were thrown from the sky and Earth Mother caught you, so you have no mother, you have no father, no sister or niece, to which would your spirit cling?" Most of Jalindar's ignorance seems to lie in the realm of attachment to women, and Gopi Chand, who is after all the hero, insists that the knowledge of this love means something. Such ignorance as Jalindar's may indeed be yogic bliss, but it flaws the guru's omniscience (although we might suspect that it also enhances his power). Manavati Mother, by contrast, knows what she is talking about when she tells Gopi Chand to become a yogi. Not only has she served the guru, but she has been a wife and mother too.

Thus a tale intended to elevate world-renunciation becomes a tale of nostalgia for the world; a tale dominated by yogi-magicians absorbs a tradition of free-thinking, nearly victorious female magicians; a tale in which women embody the snare of illusion's net becomes one in which some of them boldly manipulate that net; and some, like Manavati Mother, are able to see quite vividly the truth beyond it. I have tried here to untangle some of the ways in which illusion's net is associated with gender in a regional version of a popular tale, showing also how such associations may fluctuate within converging traditions.

* * *

Thanks to Daniel Gold, Ruth Grodzins, Kathryn Hansen, and the editors of this volume for many helpful comments and suggestions on this chapter's style and content. My greatest debt and thanks are owed first to the bard Madhu Nath for his generous cooperation, and to Nathu Lal Nath for patient transcription work and Bhoju Ram Gujar for his help in translation.

Notes

1. Temple presents a Punjabi version and English translation of this popular North Indian legend (1962, vol. 2:1–77). Grierson (1878) contains a text from Bengal with translation and commentary; Grierson (1885) contrasts two texts recorded in Bihar. Gopi Chand's story told in simple Hindi prose appears in Dikshit (n.d.: 131–218; 355–356); a dramatic version in Hindi verse is published in Yogishvar (n.d.). Bengali versions of Gopi Chand's tale are summarized in Briggs (1973), Dasgupta (1969), and Mahapatra (1971); Sircar (n.d.) provides an unpublished translation from one Bengali text. Rose briefly treats Gopi Chand in his entry on "Jogis" (1970:393–95). Hansen (1986) describes printed Hindi scripts for dramatized versions of Gopi Chand's story that belong to the repertoire of popular theater in Uttar Pradesh. While the basic plot remains the same, different episodes are weighted differently and the emotional tone may vary greatly from one text to another. See A. Gold (1990) for a complete annotated translation of Madhu Nath's Rajasthani version of Gopi Chand and a comparative consideration of selected variants across north India.

2. As far as I know, only the Rajasthani version incorporates the lady magicians of Bengal (but see Temple [1962, vol. 2:435–439] for a brief episode in the legend of Puran Bhagat in which women change yogis into bullocks and are changed into she-asses in return by Gorakh Nath).

3. For a useful discussion of *prakṛti* and *śakti* in relation to the construction of gender in the Hindu world view, see Wadley (1977). For the relation between *māyā, śakti,* and *prakṛti,* see Kinsley (1986). For the yogic view of *śakti,* see Woodroffe (1964).

4. See Burghart (1983) for a critique of interpretations of Indian world-renunciation that take into account only the householder's perspective, and an attempt to correct that deficiency. Since Gopi Chand's tale clearly partakes of both, and represents the severe tensions between them, it may also cast some light on these matters.

5. The vital inseparability of context, style, and meaning in performed oral traditions has received much attention in recent years. See, for example, Bauman (1977), Tedlock (1983), and (with an Indian setting) Ramanujan (1986) for particularly well-reasoned and powerful statements.

6. Alone among village farming castes, the Naths wore turbans dyed ocher, a color restricted to ascetics. They were, moreover, the only group in the village who buried, rather than cremated, their dead—burial being classically enjoined for world-renouncers. This caste and its oral traditions are more extensively treated in A. Gold (1988a:99–123) and D. Gold and A. G. Gold (1984).

7. Thus, the tale of a yogi born a king but fated to renounce his kingdom was performed by a bard who was born and lived as a householder, but had ritually acquired the split ears and magico-religious powers and burdens of an ascetic. This resonance between tale and tale-teller is discussed in D. Gold and A. G. Gold (1984).

8. See Goldstein (1967) for discussion of the usefulness of an "induced natural context" in folklore fieldwork. Talking with Madhu in the winter of 1988, I learned that sometimes a rich patron or a whole village might pay him to perform

nightly for a week or a month; on these rare occasions he would, as he did for me, give the complete tale. Madhu recalls one such month-long period from his youth, while traveling with an uncle in a kind of informal apprenticeship, as the time when he really learned to sing all of Gopi Chand.

9. For a rich analysis of how a storytelling modern guru uses this technique see Narayan (1989).

10. My decision to translate Madhu Nath's spoken explanation (*arthāv*) rather than his singing for the purposes of this chapter was based in part, I admit, on a desire to avoid dealing with versification. More important, however, it was a result of my perception of Madhu's spoken elaborations as surpassing his sung narrative in engaging qualities, charm, and humor. In my full translation of the Gopi Chand tale (Gold 1990) (a project funded by the National Endowment for the Humanities), I discuss and exemplify musical and poetic aspects of Madhu Nath's performance.

11. Whether it is more correct to call the Gopi Chand tale a legend or an epic is a terminological quandary that I shall refrain from attempting to solve here. The bard called it a *byāvalā,* meaning the "wedding song of a god" (Platts 1930). However, rather than lauding the marriage of a god, Gopi Chand is essentially about unmaking a human marriage. Another long narrative in Madhu Nath's repertoire is "The Wedding-Song of Lord Shiva" (*Śivjī kā byāvalā*)—and he probably refers to Gopi Chand as *byāvalā* because of this association. Villagers sometimes refer to Madhu Nath's performance of Gopi Chand as *vārtā,* a term used locally for recitations of episodes from epic tales of Rajasthani hero-gods (but see Pande [1963] for a much broader scope for *vārtā*). Dev Narayanji, Pabuji, and Ramdevji are probably the best known of these regional deities. Kothari (1982) briefly discusses their tales in relation to their worship at local shrines. Miller (1980) has worked on several aspects of the performance traditions surrounding both Pabuji and Dev Narayanji. Joshi (1976) provides a plot summary for the Dev Narayanji tale of which the extreme density testifies to its truly "epic" proportions. There are so many striking differences between Gopi Chand's tale and those of Dev Narayanji, Pabuji, and Ramdevji that I originally felt that, if the latter were epics, then the former was not one. However, according to recently proposed, sensible, informed, and flexible definitions for South Asian epics, the Gopi Chand tale falls beyond doubt in the epic genre (Blackburn and Flueckiger 1989:2–4; Wadley 1989:76).

12. Enumerated pages refer to the typescript of my translation draft.

13. See Pritchett (1985:72–74) for the motif of "transformation combat" in Urdu and Hindi folk romances.

14. See Gonda (1959:119–93) for a detailed investigation of the concept of *māyā* from Vedic through current usage. He argues persuasively that the term "be defined somewhat as follows: 'incomprehensible insight, wisdom, judgement and power enabling its possessor to create something or to do something, ascribed to mighty beings" (126). See also O'Flaherty (1984) for an appreciation of some positive attributes of illusion.

15. Male solidarities are often important factors in other South Asian epic tales. The bonds between brothers, the unity of a patrilineage, and the ties of male friendships may all be motivating causes for action, and such loyalties are an impor-

tant component of heroic character. See, for example, Beck (1982); Waterfield (1923); and, for the twenty-four Bhagaravat Brothers of Rajasthan, Joshi (1976) and Miller (1980).

16. While Madhu does not lay great stress on the competition and estrangement between Gopi Chand's mother and his wives, other versions of the tale elaborate it, having the angry queens attempt—and repeatedly fail—to do away with Manavati Mother (Sircar n.d.). Some Bengali Nath traditions represent Manavati (called Mayanāmatī) as an accomplished yogi-magician, initiated by Gorakh Nath and herself possessed of an immortal body (Dasgupta 1969: 226–27).

17. See A. Gold (1989) for a closer look at the semiotics of food and jewels, kinship and sexuality in this scene.

18. See Gray (1904) for the story of Gopi Chand's mother's brother, King Bhartṛhari, who tests his queen's "truth" by sending a false message of his death. When she spontaneously dies on hearing this news, proving herself a real *satī,* Bhartṛhari is mad with grief. Enter Gorakh Nath, who is able to bring the queen to life. However, Gorakh's demonstration of the meaninglessness of life and death as ordinary mortals understand them influences the king so strongly that he deserts his now despairing, if alive, queen, to follow the renouncer's path. Madhu Nath knows and performs a Rajasthani version of this tale.

19. For these "two immortalities" see O'Flaherty (1973: 76–77). The *Devī-Mahātmya*—chief Sanskrit text for worship of the goddess—is surrounded by a frame story in which a king and a merchant, both disenchanted with their families and with the world in general, turn to a seer for help with their problems. The seer tells them:

> "O best of men, human beings have a craving for offspring, / Out of greed expecting them to reciprocate; do you not see this? Just in this fashion do they fall into the pit of delusion, the maelstrom of egoism, / Giving (apparent) solidity to life in this world (*saṃsāra*) through the power of Mahāmāyā. / . . . . / This blessed Goddess Mahāmāyā, having forcibly seized the minds / Even of men of knowledge, leads them to delusion. / Through her is created this whole universe, that which both does and does not move. / Just she is the gracious giver of boons to men, for the sake of (their) release (*mukti*). / She is the supreme eternal knowledge (*vidyā*) that becomes the cause of release / From bondage to mundane life; she indeed is the queen (governing) all who have power" (Coburn 1984: 124).

Thus the goddess as *māyā* is identified with the ignorance of desiring sons, yet simultaneously praised as eternal knowledge and the cause of release.

20. That the place "Bengal"—from the perspective of western India—is a dangerous land inhabited by the mysterious and unpredictable "other" is an assumption shared by bard and audience. (See Korom 1989 for some cultural and historical aspects of Bengali otherness.) In the Rajasthani Gopi Chand tale, the strangeness of Bengal emerges through the presence there of women whose unbridled power has upset the socio-moral order. The worst evidence of this—the height of amorality from a yogi's point of view—is that these women prevent yogis

from wandering freely and taking alms. Bengal is perceived by rural Rajasthanis today as a land of mystery and loose women. When a "Bengali magician" came to a town near the village where I worked and put on a sleight-of-hand show, he was accompanied on stage by a skimpily clad dancing-girl. His skills at "mantra-tantra" and her shamelessness both provoked a great deal of comment. For Gopi Chand himself, however, Bengal is not only a dangerous foreign land but his sister's *sasurāl,* or marital home. Rajasthanis consider their sisters' homes as places where they must never accept hospitality, and may visit only when bearing costly gifts. Gopi Chand worries about this explicitly as he approaches Champa De's palace. There is thus a consonance for him between Bengal as a place where yogis are not welcome to beg and Bengal as his sister's marital home, where it is shameful for him to appear as a beggar.

21. Goudriaan, in his study of *māyā* as magic, notes that usually it has an aim, but he also acknowledges its playfulness and in doing so implies an alignment with the playfulness of the gods (divine *līlā*): "The magician acts as god. He enfolds creation as his own. He might indeed boast of changing a rope into a snake. He displays his powers, and as it were plays with objects and creatures; his is a 'playful' existence" (1978 : 248–49). The female Bengali magicians have some godlike powers, but their basically unprincipled behavior might put them in a class with lesser spirits, such as ghosts and witches, whose antics, when they enter and control human bodies, are referred to as their "play" (*khel*) (A. Gold 1988b).

22. The caste names of these women translate as Yogi, Oil-presser, Laundress, Potter, Leather-worker, Butcher, and Wine-seller. See Crooke (1926 : 134, 437–438) for references to a "noted witch," called Lona Chamārin, or "the salt one," who among other things strips naked in order to plant rice seedlings. I am indebted for this reference to David White, whose research on alchemical imagery in yogic teachings convinces him that "she is in some way a demonization of the corrosive powers of caustic substances" (personal communication). *Lūṇ* is the Rajasthani word for salt.

23. Bringing home water is a daily task for rural Rajasthani women, one which becomes in village rituals strongly associated with fertility (A. Gold 1988a : 247–260). To meet a woman with double waterpots on her head is good luck, and thus this initial view of the magicians is not an inauspicious one.

24. The term used is *paṭelāṃ kī poḷ*—the entranceway to a headman or *paṭel*'s house. Inevitably involved in factional politics and dispute-settlement, a *paṭel* must keep open house for enemies as well as friends.

25. These items comprise a Nath yogi's standard equipment, and it is significant that Behri Yogin address her threats to virtual emblems of yogic identity (A. Gold 1989).

26. Oxen attached to oil presses are normally blindfolded—the only way, I was told, to fool them into walking in endless circles.

27. In his ruling condition Gopi Chand is always described as having the moon on his forehead giving off such brightness that it is as if the sun were rising. Therefore, this branding of his rump has especial pathetic and ironic power. The conjunction of sun and moon carries sexual significance in Tantric yoga (Dasgupta 1969 : 238).

28. In Rajasthan the mention of soiled women's clothing cannot help but evoke the potential of menstrual pollution. I was told that even the skirt of a nonmenstruating woman was polluting because at some time it must have come into contact with menstrual blood.

29. All the abuses the lady magicians inflict on Gopi Chand seem to have some sexual associations: whipped and prodded buttocks, soiled skirts with a rider on top, and teaching a captive cock to crow. In the only printed reference to these lady magicians in Rajasthani folklore of which I am aware, sexual predation is confirmed. This is a tale about Kala Gora Bhairu (Black Bhairu and Fair Bhairu; all Bhairus are considered to be emanations of Śiva). Kala Bhairu is trapped by one Gangali Telin and compelled to turn her oil press by day and to serve her as a husband at night (Bhanavat 1968; thanks to B. R. Gujar for help in reading this Mewari source). On the theme of sexual bondage by Bengali women, the modern novel *Midnight's Children* contains an episode "In the Sundarban," or "beautiful forest"—explicitly Bengal—where apparitions of four beautiful women nightly treat four male characters to sexual bliss that completely entrances them but later leaves them "transparent" (Rushdie 1980: 438–439; it was Connie Fairbanks who called this to my attention).

30. My male research assistants occasionally addressed me thus when my demands seemed irrational or irritating to them (but then I was also a source of wealth).

31. Modern feminist rhetoric in India has much to say on the subject of housework, which traditional culture so strongly allocates to females that more equitable distribution of duties seems even more remote from reality there than here (Kishvar and Vanita 1984: 40, 118–119, 154). For a horrifying, many-faceted approach to woman as breast-giver in feminist fiction and theory see Spivak (1987: 222–268).

32. See A. Gold (1988a: 106–119) for a set of funeral hymns performed by the Nath community to which Madhu belongs. These consistently and scathingly deride family bonds, praising the guru within or the formless Lord as the only remedy for humankind.

33. Even today the village Naths are associated, in whispers, with two "cults" (*panth*) involving intercaste commensality and extramarital sexuality. A recently deceased Nath of my village, famous for his spells and mind-reading abilities, was reputed to have developed his talents by living in cremation grounds. All of these associations imply a seeking of unusual power through channels abhorred by structured society. For antistructure (and counterstructure) in one Indian religious movement see Ramanujan (1973). For sociological and religious aspects of Naths see Briggs (1973); Vaudeville (1974).

34. See Ramanujan (1982) for women saints in *bhakti* traditions having life histories distinctively different from the normative, prescribed Hindu patterns. Bhattacharyya (1977) writes that tantra is "free from all sorts of caste and patriarchal prejudices. All women are regarded as manifestations of Prakṛti or Śakti, and hence they are objects of respect and devotion. . . . A woman and even a Śūdra is entitled to function in the role of the preceptor" (1977: 224–226).

35. See Flueckiger (1987a, b) for helpful demonstrations of the concept of "a

folklore community" and the insufficiency of looking at any single piece of tradition in isolation.

References

Bauman, Richard

1977 *Verbal Art as Performance*. Prospect Heights, Ill.: Waveland Press.

Beck, Brenda E. F.

1982 *The Three Twins: The Telling of a South Indian Folk Epic*. Bloomington: Indiana University Press.

Bhanavat, Mahendra

1968 *Kālā Gorā ro Bhārat*. Udaipur: Bhāratīya Lok-Kalā Maṇḍal.

Bhattacharyya, N. N.

1977 *The Indian Mother Goddess*. New Delhi: Manohar.

Blackburn, Stuart H., and Joyce B. Flueckiger

1989 Introduction. In *Oral Epics in India*, Stuart H. Blackburn, Peter J. Claus, Joyce B. Flueckiger, and Susan S. Wadley, eds., pp. 1–11. Berkeley: University of California Press.

Briggs, George W.

1973 *Gorakhnāth and the Kānphaṭa Yogīs*. Delhi: Motilal Banarsidass.

Burghart, Richard

1983 Renunciation in the Religious Traditions of South Asia. *Man*, n.s. 18 : 635–653.

Coburn, Thomas B.

1982 Consort of None, Śakti of All: The Vision of the Devī-māhātmya. In *The Divine Consort: Rādhā and the Goddesses of India*, Jack Hawley and Donna M. Wulff, eds., pp. 153–165. Berkeley: Berkeley Religious Studies Series.

1984 *Devī-Māhātmya: The Crystallization of the Goddess Tradition*. Delhi: Motilal Banarsidass.

Crooke, William

1926 *Religion and Folklore of Northern India*. London: Oxford University Press.

Dasgupta, Shashibhusan

1969 *Obscure Religious Cults*. Calcutta: Firma K. L. Mukhopadhyay.

Dikshit, Rajesh

n.d. *Navanāth Caritra Sāgar*. Delhi: Hind Pustak Bhaṇḍār.

Flueckiger, Joyce B.

1987a Brave Daughters, Bound Kings: A Tradition of Disguise and Reversal in Central India. Paper presented at the Annual Meeting of the Association for Asian Studies, Boston.

1987b Land of Wealth, Land of Famine. The Suā Nāc (Parrot Dance) of Central India. *Journal of American Folklore* 100 : 39–57.

Gold, Ann Grodzins

1988a *Fruitful Journeys: The Ways of Rajasthani Pilgrims*. Berkeley: University of California Press.

1988b Spirit Possession Perceived and Performed in Rural Rajasthan. *Contributions to Indian Sociology,* n.s. 22/1:35–63.

1989 The Once and Future Yogi: Signs of Rule and Renunciation in the Rajasthani Tale of Gopi Chand. *Journal of Asian Studies* 48/4:770–786.

1990 *A Carnival of Parting: The Tales of Gopi Chand and King Bharthari as Sung and Told by Mathu Natisar Nath of Ghatiyali, Rajasthan, India.* Unpublished manuscript.

Gold, Daniel, and Ann Grodzins Gold

1984 The Fate of the Householder Nāth. *History of Religions* 24/2:113–132.

Goldstein, Kenneth S.

1967 The Induced Natural Context: An Ethnographic Folklore Field Technique. In *Essays on the Verbal and Visual Arts,* June Helm, ed., pp. 1–6. Seattle: University of Washington Press.

Gonda, Jan

1959 *Four Studies in the Language of the Veda.* The Hague: Mouton.

1965 *Change and Continuity in Indian Religion.* The Hague: Mouton.

Goudriaan, Teun

1978 *Māyā Divine and Human.* Delhi: Motilal Banarsidass.

Gray, Louis H.

1904 The Bhartṛharinirveda of Harihara. *Journal of the American Oriental Society* 25:197–230.

Grierson, George A.

1878 The Song of Manik Chandra. *Journal of the Royal Asiatic Society of Bengal* 47:135–238.

1885 Two Versions of the Song of Gopi Cand. *Journal of the Royal Asiatic Society of Bengal* 54:35–55.

Hansen, Kathryn

1986 Nautanki Chapbooks: Written Tradition of a Folk Form. *The India Magazine* (January): 65–72.

Joshi, Om Prakash

1976 *Painted Folklore and Folklore Painters of India.* Delhi: Concept Publishing Company.

Kinsley, David

1986 *Hindu Goddesses: Visions of the Divine Feminine in the Hindu Religious Tradition.* Berkeley: University of California Press.

Kishvar, Madhu, and Ruth Vanita, eds.

1984 *In Search of Answers.* London: Zed Books.

Korom, Frank J.

1989 Inventing Traditions: Folklore and Nationalism as Historical Process in Bengal. In *Folklore and Historical Process,* D. Rihtman-Augustin and M. Povrzanovic, eds., pp. 57–83. Zagreb: Institute of Folklore Research.

Kothari, Komal

1982 The Shrine: An Expression of Social Needs. In *Gods of the Byways,* pp. 5–31. Oxford: Museum of Modern Art.

Mahapatra, Piyush Kanti

1971 The Nāth Cult of Bengal. *Folklore* 12:376–96.

Miller, Joseph C.
1980 Current Investigations in the Genre of Rajasthani Paṛ Painting Recitations. In *Early Hindi Devotional Literature in Current Research*, Winand M. Callewaert, ed., pp. 116–125. New Delhi: Impex India.

Narayan, Kirin
1989 *Storytellers, Saints, and Scoundrels: Folk Narrative in Hindu Religious Teaching*. Philadelphia: University of Pennsylvania Press.

O'Flaherty, Wendy D.
1973 *Asceticism and Eroticism in the Mythology of Śiva*. London: Oxford University Press.
1980 *Women, Androgynes, and Other Mythical Beasts*. Chicago: University of Chicago Press.
1984 *Dreams, Illusion, and Other Realities*. Chicago: University of Chicago Press.

Pande, Trilochan
1963 The Concept of Folklore in India and Pakistan. *Schweizerisches Archiv für Volkskunde* 59:25–30.

Platts, John T.
1930 *A Dictionary of Urdū, Classical Hindī, and English*. London: Oxford University Press.

Pritchett, Frances W.
1985 *Marvelous Encounters: Folk Romance in Urdu and Hindi*. New Delhi: Manohar.

Ramanujan, A. K.
1973 *Speaking of Śiva*. Baltimore: Penguin Books.
1982 On Women Saints. In *The Divine Consort: Rādhā and the Goddesses of India*, Jack Hawley and Donna M. Wulff, eds., pp. 316–324. Berkeley, Calif.: Berkeley Religious Studies Series.
1986 Two Realms of Kannada Folklore. In *Another Harmony: New Essays on the Folklore of India*, Stuart H. Blackburn and A. K. Ramanujan, eds., pp. 41–75. Berkeley: University of California Press.

Rose, H. A.
1970 *A Glossary of the Tribes and Castes of the Punjab and North-West Frontier Province*. Punjab: Languages Department.

Rushdie, Salman
1980 *Midnight's Children*. New York: Avon Books.

Sircar, Kanika, trans.
n.d. Gopicander Pancali. University of Chicago, Department of South Asian Languages, mimeographed manuscript.

Spivak, Gayatri C.
1987 *In Other Worlds: Essays in Cultural Politics*. London: Methuen Inc.

Tedlock, Dennis
1983 *The Spoken Word and the Work of Interpretation*. Philadelphia: University of Pennsylvania Press.

Temple, R. C.
1962 *The Legends of the Punjab*, 3 vols. Patiala: Languages Department, Punjab.

Varenne, Jean
1976 *Yoga and the Hindu Tradition*. Chicago: University of Chicago Press.
Vaudeville, Charlotte
1974 *Kabir*. London: Oxford University Press.
Wadley, Susan S.
1977 Women and the Hindu Tradition. In *Women in India: Two Perspectives*, pp. 113–39. Columbia, Mo.: South Asia Books.
1980 Hindu Women's Family and Household Rites in a North Indian Village. In *Unspoken Worlds: Women's Religious Lives in Non-Western Cultures*, Nancy Falk and Rita Gross, eds., pp. 94–109. San Francisco: Harper and Row.
1989 Choosing a Path: Performance Strategies in a North Indian Epic. In *Oral Epics in India*, Stuart H. Blackburn, Peter J. Claus, Joyce B. Flueckiger, and Susan S. Wadley, eds., pp. 75–101. Berkeley: University of California Press.
Waterfield, William
1923 *The Lay of Alha: A Saga of Rajput Chivalry as Sung by Minstrels of Northern India*. London: Oxford University Press.
Woodroffe, John, trans.
1964 *The Serpent Power*. Madras: Ganesh and Company.
Yogishvar, Balakrām
n.d. *Bhakt Gopīcand Bharatharī*. Delhi: Agraval Book Depot.

Peter J. Claus

5. Kin Songs*

The Tulu-speaking people who inhabit coastal Karnataka have recorded the stories of their heroes and heroines, their local deities, their great families, and their tragedies in an oral tradition called *pāḍdana*. As the term (derived from the verbal root *pāḍ-*, "to sing") implies, the stories "must be sung." Tulu speakers never developed a writing system or a written literature in their own language. Still, although not written, the *pāḍdana*s are the closest thing the Tulu speakers have to a "national" literature. In recent times the genre has lent its stories and themes to other performance and literary traditions, even to the first Tulu films. For the Tuluva people, many of the stories are regarded as history as much as they are literature. Since many of the characters in the stories are today worshipped, and known and remembered through their stories, the tradition carries the weight of religious dogma as well.

The unique stories themselves number into the hundreds and are of widely varying lengths, taking from less than an hour to as much as several evenings to sing. Some of the forms of presentation qualify as epic, while others more resemble ballad, dirge, and even chant. Even a single story may be presented in different styles that embrace a wide variety of verse form and meter. Thematically, all are tragic. Longer ones tend, additionally, to be strongly heroic in character.

The *pāḍdana*s are essentially a performance tradition, with the performance context defining the selection of particular pieces and their form of presentation. A broad distinction can be made between the contexts in which women sing and those in which men sing.[1] Men sing primarily in the context of a village ritual called a *bhūta nēma*, or *bhūta kōla*. Their singing narrates the exploits of spirits of heroes and of gods—both called *bhūta*s—and evokes their presence. The singing leads to a state of posses-

*The transliteration of Tulu words in this chapter follows the Library of Congress standard for Indian languages, with the addition of ü (a vowel midway between back u and front i) and é (a vowel between e and a). Aspirates are not pronounced as such in normal speech, but are represented here for easier recognition.

sion during which the singer then portrays the spirit in a costumed dance, and the singing shifts to the first person as the spirit tells his or her own story. In this ritual context, the singing and dancing is performed only by professionals of certain castes.

Women sing as they work in teams transplanting paddy in the fields. Among women singers there is no professionalization and little caste distinction. Women of many castes (nearly all except Brahmans) work together in the fields, and all may participate in the singing. A woman of any caste may lead the singing, while the others repeat her verse in a chorus.[2] The lead singer is usually an older, more experienced woman. Singing the chorus provides younger women ample opportunity to learn the stories and the techniques used to elaborate them in verse. The *pāḍdanas* women sing in the field are also usually about *bhūtas*, but their songs are longer and more richly poetic than are those of the men.

In ritual,[3] song is often attenuated to make room for the other concerns of the ceremony. In the fields, elaboration of poetic verse and imagery alleviates the tedium of the work. Often one finds the same stories sung in both contexts, where the women's versions are elaborate while the men's versions make only brief reference to the longer episodes. Even in a ritual context, when the singing itself is important, it may be given over to women of the performer's family, while the performer applies his elaborate makeup and prepares to dance. In such cases the women would normally sing episodes of the same stories they sing in the fields, and in the same fashion they would in that milieu.

The *pāḍdanas* I discuss in this chapter are primarily heard as field songs that are sung by women.[4] I wish to demonstrate the following points: (1) that there is a constancy to the themes these *pāḍdanas* contain, (2) that these themes usually revolve around a certain kinship structure, and (3) that there is a strong relationship between the content of the songs and the context in which they are sung.

Genre and Content: Preliminary Remarks

I am not alone in grappling with the particular problems of identifying the themes and moods of Indian folk genres. Most of the researchers who have worked on the material have sensed that certain genres concentrate on certain themes, accentuate certain emotions, and revolve around certain types of social ties. Many of the papers written on Indian folklore in the modern era—what I have called the "new folklore" (Claus 1986a)—have dealt with this problem in one way or another.[5] There are at least two dimensions to most of the thinking that has gone into the matter: that there is something about the way themes in Indian folklore distinctively represent Indian society and thought; and that different genres (literary as well as oral) speak to different kinds of issues.[6] So the problem, put in other words, is that Indian folklore seems to address peculiarly Indian concerns in peculiarly Indian ways and in contexts (genres) peculiar to the lines of Indian society, and we should be able to describe in theoretical terms the regularities that occur in these relationships.

Brenda Beck, in "Social Dyads in Indian Folktales" (Beck 1986), presents a survey of some four thousand Indian folktales listed in the Thompson and Roberts index.[7] Her purpose is to identify some themes unique to the folktales of India as a whole and then to identify other themes with particular regional and subregional areas within India. In order to do this, she develops a new coding approach which, first of all, groups tales according to their core social relationship, a social dyad (e.g., mother-son, brother-sister, friends, lovers, and so forth). Then,

> By counting and sorting the different types of social dyads that receive attention in the folktales, one can develop a rough measure of their proportional importance in a given story collection. . . . I shall discuss the various interaction patterns and sentiments found between the characters in specific dyads. Such generalizations will provide us with a set of background norms. (Beck 1986 : 77)

I will not here try to discuss her findings or criticize her approach, except to note that the selection of a social dyad, which she herself sees as a "relatively culture-free concept," is a completely arbitrary criterion for classifying folklore. As it turns out, however, it is not a bad one for the folktale, resting as it does on Olrik's law of Two to a Scene.[8] Social dyads are not, however, "culture free": categories of kin or categories of friends or lovers (and the like) in India are patently not to be understood as being in any sense the same as those identified by the same English words used to describe Western relationships. What we are led to believe is that there is a measure of comparability here that does not exist in fact.

In a more recent paper, Beck again discusses core structural patterns, but this time in the epic genre.

> Students of the epic need to develop some hypothesis about the common structural underpinnings of this genre. What types of character patterns typify epics in general, and what subtypes among these are found especially well

> developed in India? . . . The search for general principles . . . can help us think about our epic materials, and aid with the knotty problem of what we mean by the concept of "distinctive" Indian cultural traditions. (Beck 1989 : 155)

For the epics she sees a core *triangle* of characters. She then shows how the "permutations of this core triangle help to describe the relations of major characters in Indian epics more generally" (Beck 1989). The core triangle involves a central hero(ine), one secondary male character, and one secondary female character. For example, in her *Aṇṇanmār Kathai* (see Beck 1982), the characters are Cankar (hero and younger brother), Ponnar (elder brother), and Tankal (younger sister), respectively.

Again, this is not the place to criticize her approach. I want only to point out that here, too, she uses broad categories to characterize the diversity and uniformity in a folk genre. This time, for the epic genre, she uses social triadic relationships, but one has the feeling it is not as arbitrary a choice for sorting out the different epics. I feel sure she would, as before, characterize the general relationships as being "relatively culture free." Indeed, this time her categories *do* seem relatively culture free, but I question whether her core triadic relationship of two male and one female characters really does hit at the "common structural underpinnings" of the genre. But my real objection to Beck's dyads and triangles is that they are not sufficiently sensitive to the themes and moods of the genres they are meant to characterize and categorize. At least they neither characterize nor differentiate the various epiclike Tulu *pāḍdanas*.

A. K. Ramanujan, in his contribution to *Another Harmony* (1986), entitled "Two Realms of Kannada Folklore," also addresses the relationship between content and (genre) context. In his view, the relationship in India is distinctively Indian, cognate with the distinction of *akam/puṟam,* "domestic and public," complementary distinctions in ancient Tamil Sangam literature. Domestic genres—folktales, for example—are perpetuated by women, in the home (*akam*), and are regarded as secular (not preceded by prayer); they do not use names for the characters, and are told in a style close to ordinary speech. Public genres, such as epics, are transmitted by males, usually professional bards, in public (*puṟam*), ritualized settings, using poetic verse in song and instrumental accompaniment. They use specific names for the characters. Although some of the distinctions might be common to European or Trobriand or any other culture's genre distinctions, Ramanujan argues that the specific list of characteristics is distinctively south Indian. And the content (themes, characters, language) found in the genres is correlated with the social person of the performer and the restrictions on the performance context in a way that can only be expected to be found in Indian society.

I find Ramanujan's approach, although limited by being so culturally determined, especially attractive since it speaks to the coherence between a number of aspects of text and context, especially social context. My only problem with it is, again, that the Tulu material does not seem to fit his divisions. The field song *pāḍdanas*, a women's genre, are curiously both public and domestic. The stories always are about named characters and always sung in poetic verse, in a style quite different from the way the story would be told in conversational narrative form.[9]

There must be something else going on here. But before I go into what I think it is, I must describe some features of the Tuluva social structure, especially its matrilineal kinship system, and introduce the *pāḍdanas* themselves. I will then try to demonstrate that the songs revolve around a certain kind of kinship structure common to all Dravidian social systems.

Tuluva Kinship and the *Pāḍdanas*[10]

Unlike most of India, but like its more famous neighbor, Kerala, to the south, Tulunad favored the development of matrilineal families. Inheritance and succession to the managership of the family property passes from a man to his sister's son in a system called *āḷiya santāna* (sister's son succession). Although at the time of marriage a woman traditionally leaves her matrilineal estate and lives at her husband's house, she maintains strong ties to her natal home, and there is a strong tendency for her and her children to gravitate back there as the children get older. In any case, she and her children return to live at her natal home at the time of her husband's death. Neither she nor her children have the right to stay at her husband's house, which is, after all, the property of his maternal relatives; his sisters and their children are by this time shifting back to what is their natal home. Thus the tie between a woman and her natal house remains strong throughout her life. She and her children always retain the right to live there. Her ties and her children's ties to her husband's house are temporary. The husband and his family are entrusted with the responsibility of caring for the woman and her children in return for her services. For a number of reasons, it is a delicate situation for both sides.

The tie between brother and sister also remains very strong throughout their lives. A brother has a strong moral obligation to see that his sister is well provided for and that her children are taken care of. He is willing to expend much of the family's wealth to see to it that she is able to obtain a husband at least as well-off as they are.

But despite these matrilineal emphases—which have mostly to do with how wealth and property are handled—Tulu kinship shares many of the characteristics of other south Indian (Dravidian) peoples. Tulu kinship terminology, for example, in common with other Dravidian languages, makes a distinction between cross-cousins (mother's brother's children, father's sister's children) and parallel cousins. Terms for the latter are the same as those terms used for one's own siblings. The former terms imply marriage. And notable, at least in the Indian context, is their practice of cross-cousin marriage. It is possible for the children of a brother and sister to marry. That is, a person may marry someone in the same category (addressed by the same kinship term) as his or her mother's brother's child or father's sister's child.[11] One way to interpret this practice is by saying that a brother and a sister share the same ritual status as their mother. If their children marry, that ritual status is preserved into the next generation. This is not to say that the people of south India *always* marry their cross-cousins, but if they do otherwise, they usually have compelling reasons, such as to marry a person of a higher ritual status or of greater wealth, and now, of course, for love.

It is not necessary that we pursue a discussion of Tulu kinship terminology any further. The *pāḍdanas* deal with *sets* of kin, not dyadic relations between *individual* kin, as described in Figure 1. Tulu identifies these sets of kin by distinctive vocabulary, the most important being literally translated as "older brother–younger sister" (*tagé-tangaḍi*), "a-woman's-older-brothers" (*tagéḍlu*), and "brothers-in-law" (*nanikéḍlu*). Two further sets of relationships that are important are: (1) between groups who are the descendants of sisters (*kavaru*) and (2) between groups who are the descendants of siblings who are brother and sister (*podderü;* singular *poddé*). The former may be thought of as branches of a larger matrilineage, or a *kuṭumba* (the descendants of one woman, their mother or ancestors of an earlier generation). The latter may be thought of as a relationship between in-laws, since preferential cross-cousin marriage links the children of a brother and sister in marriage.

In keeping with the Tuluva man's obligations toward his sister (whose ritual status he and all members of a *kavaru* share), he should see that she marry someone of equal status (i.e., a cross-cousin).[12] If he does not, then

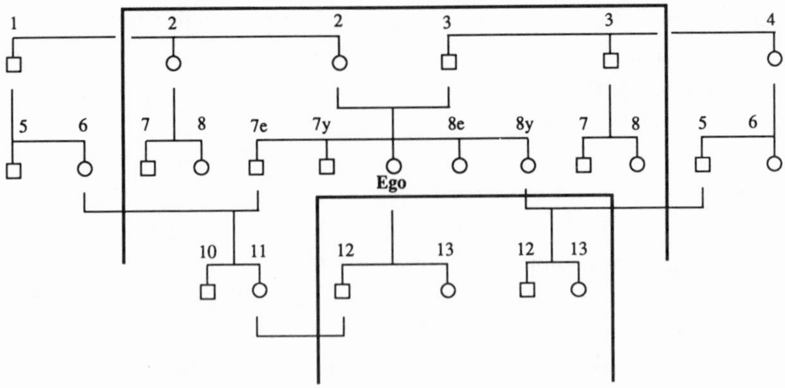

Key (In relation to female **Ego**):

1 - 4 Parental generation, divided into cross (1 & 4) and parallel (2 & 3) relatives.

5 - 6 "Cross cousins," potential or actual marriage partners.

7 - 8 "Siblings," elder (e) and younger (y).

10 - 13 "Children" and "children of siblings of the opposite sex," depending on Ego's own sex, falling in cross or parallel groups.

= Siblings. Bold lines separate Cross and Parallel Groups.

= Marriageable.

FIGURE 1. Dravidian kin terms and cross-cousin marriage.

he should try to have her married to someone of a higher status, and he and the whole *kavaru* are apt to spend a great deal of wealth to do so. In turn, for his own marriage, he may accept for a price, a dowry, a marriage to a woman of a lower ritual status whose family is similarly seeking to offer him its wealth in exchange for *his* more prestigious status. At this point there would be a difference in status between the children of the brother and the children of the sister—with the children of the sister being of higher ritual status and possibly the children of the brother having greater wealth—but they are nevertheless obliged to accept their (cross-cousin) intermarriage. Thus, for the Tuluvas, it is the sister's son (Kannada *āḷiya,* as in *āḷiya santāna;* Tulu *arawatté,* or, in the context of marriageability, *hakküda arawatté,* "rightful sister's-son") whose claim on his mother's brother's daughter replenishes the wealth of the *kavaru* and maintains the arrogation of status between the two sets of *podderü* (see Figure 2).

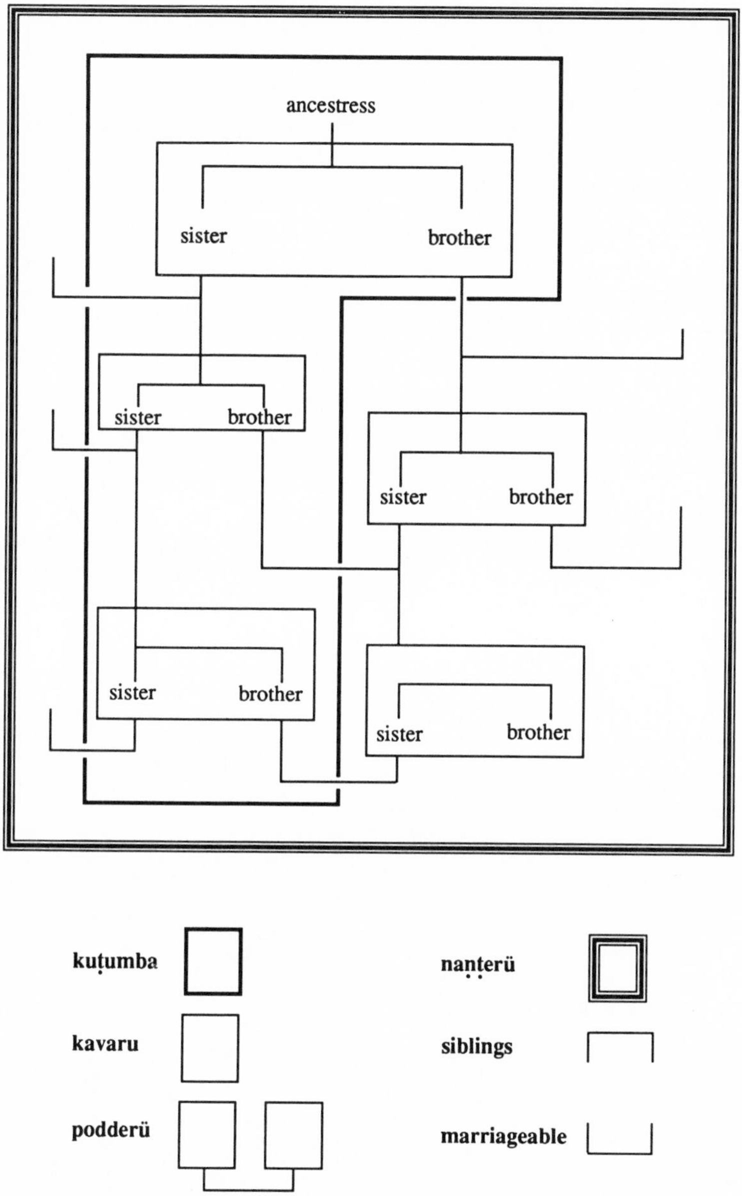

FIGURE 2. Tulu kin groups.

Thus, two groups of siblings—the children of brothers and sisters—are very important to one another. For each the other is called *podderü* in Tulu. If they marry according to the rules, one's *podderü* are not only those with which your group has had marriage ties, but with which one will likely seek marriage ties in the future (they are "cross-cousins"). People related as *podderü* exchange wealth and marriage partners generation after generation. Together they call themselves *naṇṭerü* ("kinsmen"; singular *naṇṭé*).

But each *podderü* group is also part of a matrilineal descent line that owns property and wealth. The children of brothers and sisters belong to different matrilineal families, called *kuṭumba,* and they constitute a "branch," or *kavaru,* of their respective families. The brother is the manager of his sister's *kavaru,* an office he will pass on by the rules of *āḷiya santāna* (matrilineal inheritance) to his sister's son—who will manage the property on behalf of *his* sister, and so on.

There is thus a considerable tension between *podderü* with regard to their separate claims on property. At this point in our discussion, it would be better to let the Tulu people speak for themselves on these matters. The *pāḍdanas* themselves revolve around *podderü* and their relationships as part of an ongoing generational relationship between families. Let us look first at the story of Paramale Ballal.[13] I will present it in prose form, but the reader should remember it is properly something which "must be sung."[14]

The Story of Paramale Ballal

Paramale Ballal suggested to his wife, Maniga, that they while away the time with a game of *cenne.** She objected that she couldn't possibly play on an ordinary board made of wood, with seeds for playing pieces, that in her house they had a board made of gold and playing pieces of silver.

Shamed, the Ballal rose early the next day, dressed, and went to the goldsmith and had a board made of gold, playing pieces of silver. When he returned, he again challenged her to a game. She again refused, saying that she didn't play on a common wooden board. This time, however, the Ballal was able to tell her he, too, had a board of gold and pieces made of silver.

She won the first round. He admonished her against foul play. She

*The game of *cenne* (known as *mancala* in international folklore scholarship) is, in Tulu culture, a complex symbol of sexual activity and competition used in a number of Tulu folktales and ballads. For a discussion of its meaning see Claus (1986b).

won the second and third game. He rose up in anger. "Ah, so you want a struggle, do you?" he said, and started beating and kicking her.

After he had had his fill, she just lay there, covering her face. She refused to get up. She refused to work. The hearth fires went out. The calves bawled for their milk. The buffalo called for their food. The cocks went unfed. Soon word of this state of affairs went around the village and everyone was talking about the "strike" at the Ballal's house.

The Ballal himself went to the hillsides where women were gathering leaves for the cattle sheds. "Tell me, women, is there even one among you who, like my wife, just because she got a beating, would refuse to do the work of her husband's house? Isn't she wrong? Don't you agree? Would you refuse to work if your husbands beat you? You are god-fearing women, tell me." He went to the fields and asked of the men who were plowing, "Are your women like my wife? Would they refuse to work if you hit them?"

The women of the neighborhood got together and called upon Maniga. "Sister, listen to us. We are women like you. Get up and get back to work. Stop acting like this." But Maniga didn't listen, she lay there, her face covered, refusing to work. The men of the village came and urged her to work, but she wouldn't listen.

Finally, some cowherd boys came and asked for water to quench their thirst. Even for this she refused to rise. So they went around the town, beating a drum, calling out the faults of Maniga. Maniga heard this and rose up. She lit the hearth fires, fed the animals, and went to work making dinner. The Ballal, having finished his work in the fields, came home and saw that dinner was prepared and waiting for him.

After dinner, Maniga asked to go and visit her (maternal) uncle at her natal house, Paddelü. The Ballal agreed. He sent her off in proper style, in a palanquin, wearing fine cloths and jewels and all. As she was leaving he asked her, "Will you return by evening, Maniga?" She assured him she would, and off she went. When she got to her natal home, she breaks off her bangle, removes her *tāli** and nose-ring and takes off her wedding ring. She puts these things in the palanquin and sends it back to the Ballal.

When the Ballal sees the palanquin coming, he thinks it is Maniga, true to her word, returning by evening. When he looks in the palanquin, he realizes his wife's intentions for going home. In anger he calls out to Sarala Jumadi, the *bhūta* of his household: "I sent her off in honesty, believing her. In truth does she return as she said, or does she make fun

* A *tāli* is a pendant worn as a mark of being a married woman.

of the way I sent her off? You are the guardian of truth in this manor, Jumadi, do you hear?"

On the fifth day after she had gone to her uncle's house, Maniga began to have pains throughout her body, her vision was blurred. She told her uncle that she must return to the Ballal's manor.

The Ballal sees her coming and meets her in front of the manor. "Maniga, if you left with an honest intention, you may enter with one." But as she enters, she trips on the door sill, falls, and dies. "So the guardian of truth, Jumadi, has shown truth to be with me. You see, people, she has eaten her own acts [*karma*], my truth has won."

* * *

I collected this short *pāḍdana* several years ago and have a number of very similar versions. For a long time I thought this was the complete *pāḍdana* as, I am sure, my singers and Tulu folklorists believe.[15] Although it is widely known, I suspect it may also be a "modernization," since I heard it primarily from younger women.[16] In many ways, as it stands, the story resembles a Tulu folktale. Like a tale, it focuses on a single kin relationship, husband and wife. But for the connoisseur, it leaves several questions unanswered which a *pāḍdana* would normally provide. Who is this Maniga and who is the Ballal? How did this marriage come about to begin with?

As it is, Maniga's character is clear from the very first line. She is an arrogant and outspoken woman with a strong sense of her individuality. But does she deserve the fate she receives? And the Ballal's character is established by the time he beats his wife. But his character is not that of "wife-beater" but as a reasonable, patient, and just man! In the singers' eyes, Maniga is the one who is bad from the start, and not just because she beats her husband at *cenne*. This is confirmed by the community, the men and women of the *pāḍdana*. It is also confirmed by the women who sing the *pāḍdana*. How they formed these opinions on the basis of the information in the text was a mystery to me. I presumed there was a tradition of folk exegesis to accompany the text.[17]

Indeed, there is, but I now know this is what might be called a "short version" of a much longer *pāḍdana*. The longer version of the *pāḍdana* makes these facts clear. At the time, I was right in feeling that this *pāḍdana* must be seen together with dozens of others, because there is something in this version which should have led me to suspect it was incomplete in itself. The portion left out of this short version is the beginning, in which Maniga's character is fully developed. The following portion clarifies what I mean:

> Paramele Ballal lives all alone at Malla Palace. "No one to serve him, no elder sister to lead the way, no younger sister to follow." He calls on his people to find him a wife. They suggest women of the four directions, but he rejects them all, claiming that because of their strange ways they would bring ruin on his house. But up in the Ghats in the Meggima Kingdom there is one who is his uncle's daughter, his *maitidi* [cross-cousin]. She is the niece of Bikrama of Paddelü Palace, a girl by the name of Jewu Maniga. So he sends his relatives off to speak for this girl.
>
> Arrangements are made and a date is set for the marriage, and when the time comes the Ballal goes to Paddelü Palace for the marriage. The wedding is a grand one and when it is over, the Ballal, Bikrama, and Maniga set off for the Ballal's palace. As is customary among the high matrilineal caste of Tulunad, the bride then immediately returns with her uncle to her natal home. The Ballal sends them back in a decorated palanquin. The Ballal tells them that on the way they will meet Bangera women who will offer them milk in a pot. Maniga is to give them a handful of flowers. Back at Paddelü Palace, Maniga declares she will not return to the Ballal's house. The reason she gives is that she will not sit in the palanquin her mother sat in, not wear her mother's gold or her mother's sari. So her uncle, Bikrama, goes in and gets some money and goes to town, where he buys new gold ornaments and the finest silk sari and brings them for Maniga. Again Maniga refuses to return to the Ballal's house, this time claiming it is because of the Bangera women.
>
> So Bikrama writes a letter to Maniga's brother, Baladanda, to come at once. When Baladanda arrives, he says to Maniga that he has never seen his brother-in-law's house, and that Maniga should come and show it to him. She cannot refuse her older brother's request. After they arrive at the Ballal's house, Baladanda asks Maniga to heat water for him to bathe in. Then they eat. As soon as they are finished eating, Maniga wants to go back, but Baladanda says no, that it is too hot and they should rest for a while. While Maniga is asleep, Bala-

danda gets up and tells the Ballal to go awaken her. Then, as he leaves, he tells the Ballal that if she gets sad and lonely he should play a game of *cenne* with her.

From there, the stories are much the same. Clearly what is left out of the shortened version is the web of kinship that surrounds the Ballal and Maniga.[18] The story now is one between two families. The link is called *podderü* in Tulu. Maniga is the Ballal's *maitidi* (cross-cousin). Bikrama is her maternal uncle (see Figure 3).

The jewelry and gold and the provision of a palanquin mentioned are presentations extended to Maniga's *podderü* group on the part of Paramale

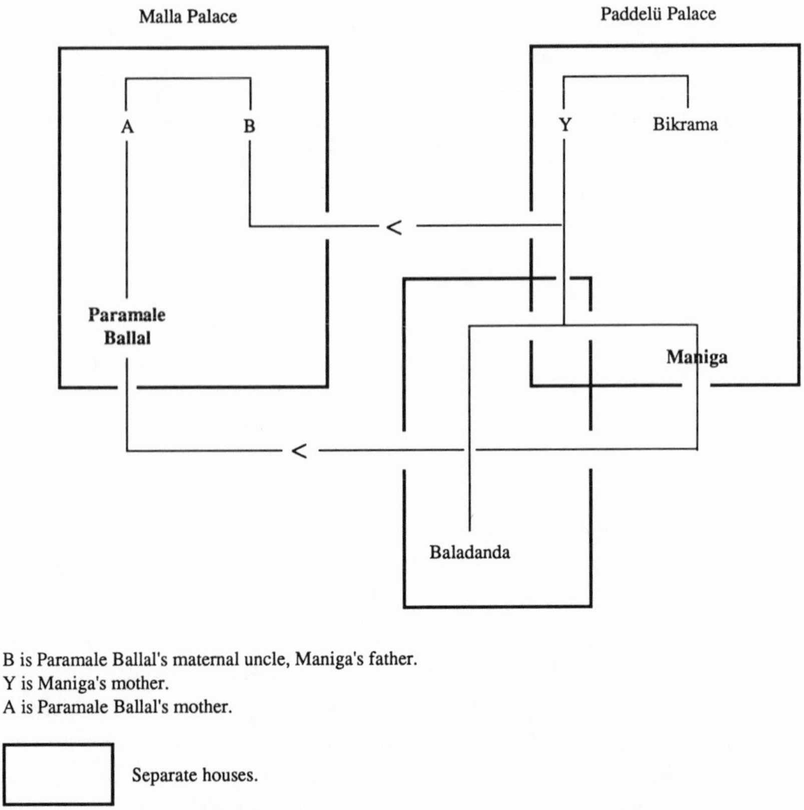
Malla Palace
Paddelü Palace
A
B
Y
Bikrama
Paramale Ballal
Maniga
Baladanda
B is Paramale Ballal's maternal uncle, Maniga's father.
Y is Maniga's mother.
A is Paramale Ballal's mother.
Separate houses.

FIGURE 3. Kin ties in Paramale Ballal.

Ballal's *podderü* group. The gifts are costly ones, requiring (as is indicated when Bikrama had to give them to Maniga himself) the conversion of wealth to a gift that creates alliance. They are given as bride-price (*sirdesi*) to Maniga's mother, to be inherited by Maniga in any case. In a sense, they represent the father's contribution to the children. And since the items are female items, they become the permanent property of her *podderü* group (and since they regard property, her *kavaru*). Now, Paramale Ballal is her paternal cross-cousin, and he has a right to her in marriage. He need not present her with a bride-price (one interpretation of the type of marriage called *dharma dāre*), and that is what she wants. She does not want "her mother's" gold necklace and silk sari. She already regards these as hers (it may be they were kept by the women of Malla at her mother's death). Her demand is an understatement of her greed for Malla property, which her father had managed and which she apparently felt he should have directed toward her via her mother. Her uncle's offer of a gold necklace and silk sari is hardly a substitute, since these were purchased with her matrilineal wealth, which is intended for her in any case. In short, she wanted something for herself, at the expense of the alliance between the two houses, and in defiance of Ballal's right to her in marriage.

There is, furthermore, a matter of hierarchical status involved. Among the high matrilineal castes, it is implied that wife receivers are higher in status than wife givers. To describe it from the perspective of any given matrilineage, the children of daughters are superior to the children of sons; or the mother's brother's children are of a less favored status than the mother's own children. Maniga refuses to accept this. She will not live in her husband's house, where the women of that house would make her feel inferior.[19]

Here is the source of her damaged pride. From her point of view, she and her *podderü* group are superior to the Ballal; from his point of view, his is. The matter is decided then, over demonstrable wealth and obligation, which is exactly the concern of the fight they later have: a *cenne* board and her obligations to cook for him.

The reference to the Bangera women is a historical one. Whether it is a reliable reference I cannot say; but it serves to show that particular marriages are sometimes seen to be enmeshed in larger political arenas—between, in this case, the kingdom of the Bangeras and its neighbors. Maniga's refusal to live with the Bangera women is also a political act her male kinsmen rush to avoid. She sees them as compromising her status and the status of her descendants—their descendants, as well.

Her kinsmen, however, apparently feel they are not ready to declare themselves independent of the Bangera. So we have another dimension to the emotional and attitudinal aspects of the kinship expressions in the *pāḍdanas*; that between the men and women of a descent group, in which we can see the ways a woman can take independent action of great consequence, even in political spheres. Their actions have consequences that men must try to control. They are not simply matters of ritual purity, but matters of social and political consequence. In the matters of status, women not only stand for absolute, uncompromising maintenance of status, whereas men are compromising (for their own personal political ends), but women have the upper hand in that it is their *person* which is the medium of the expression of status. Only a woman's brother, the person whom she trusts above all others and with whom she shares an equal status, can try to convince her to take a certain course of action. He is the only male whose interests are identical to her own. In this case, he is ordered to do what he does (trick his sister into compromise) by their maternal uncle for the sake of male concerns (political alliances). Ultimately, she must obey him. It is a case of male authority over women: a power play. And this is the source of the tragedy. It is not simply that Maniga is a headstrong, overly proud, and selfish woman, but that she is caught in a conflict of principles, and as she stands up for her rights as a woman, she is brought into conflict with men. Men, standing on their right to control women, to insist on the subservience of women to men, force her to compromise. In the end she refuses and loses her life. But in the end, the *podderü* and their alliance are also severed. All lose. In some versions, the Ballal regrets his action.

So there are dimensions to the relations between women and the actions of women toward one another that appear to be largely ritual in form, but have great social and political significance. Women are not the inconsequential passive beings in social, political, and economic spheres one sometimes supposes, and Maniga's actions have their equivalent in every living real-world family.

My next selection, the story of Parnderü, is longer and more mythical. I have collected eight versions of this piece from various regions of Tulunad.[20] Some of the versions are identified as the Karnaga *pāḍdana* and consist of what may be regarded as a short form, covering only the death of Parnderü's niece, Kannyagé, or, as she is called in these versions, Karnaga.[21]

The Story of Parnderü

Parnderü and his sister, Bare Parndédi, lived at Mallara Guttu.[22] Their father had died and their mother died giving birth to Parndédi. Parnderü, himself, raised his younger sister with great care and affection.

Mattara Mayinda Heggadé lived at Mattara Guttu. He was thinking, "My mother's brother's [*tammale*] children are at Mallara Guttu. I should make a marriage alliance (*poddu barpené yānü*) with that place." So he sets off from Mattara Guttu to speak to Parnderü.

"You are the children of my mother's brother. Uncle has died and Auntie has passed away. What will you do with that motherless child? I am having to cook myself and eat alone in my manor. Your sister is my rightful bride [*maitidi*]. By birth she is the daughter of my mother's brother: by right, one I might marry. You must give her to me in marriage [*dharma dāre*]. You have to have her sent to Mattara Guttu to do the cooking there."

Thus they were married and Heggadé brought her home to Mattara Guttu. One day, he told her he was going out to adjust the water in the fields. Meanwhile, Bare Parndédi prepares to cook. She cleans the house and bathes. The hearth fire had gone out, so she took a coconut shell and fiber and went to the neighbor's to get coals for starting the fire.

The neighbor women see her coming at a distance, and she calls to them. But Bare Parndédi was not the mother of a child, yet. She had not attained maturity, not yet begun her menstrual cycles. It was now a year and she hadn't given birth. The neighbor women insulted her. "Hide your children! Close the door!" they said.

Hearing this, Bare Parnedédi threw away the coconut shell and fiber which she was carrying and came back to Mattara Guttu. She entered the bedroom, put down a mat, and lay face down on it.

When Heggadé returns from his work he looked for her. When he finally finds her hiding in a dark room, he asks her what the trouble is. She tells him that the neighbor women insulted her by calling her a barren woman.

Mattara Mayinda Heggadé thought about this. "Fix your hair and put on a sari," he says. "Let us go to Mallara Guttu." There, Parnderü says they must go to their *mūlastāna** and make an offering. So the three of them

*"Place of origin," meaning a temple (or its tank or a sacred grove there) at the place where the family originated. This place and the deities there are felt to be the source of generation and continued regeneration.

go and make the required offering and return. Parndédi takes holy water of the family deity, Jumadi, from the tank at Mallara Guttu. As she climbs the stairs of the tank, when she reaches the 16th step, she attains maturity. Then she went to the courtyard of Mallara Guttu and wrapped her arms around the pillar of the pavilion [*dampada kamba*] and bowed her head.

When her brother, Parnderü, invites her in to eat she tells him that she is menstruating. So Parnderü's wife, Duwu, brings out food: rice left over three days, a water mango that a widow had touched, and a chili pepper in which two stones had been put [all very defiling and inauspicious—Duwu is attempting to bring ruin on Parndédi's descendants].

But Parndédi doesn't touch her food. Her brother comes and asks, "Why are you just sitting and staring? Eat!"

"I'm not hungry," she replies. "I have a terrible pain in my stomach. Take the food and put it in the trough for the buffalo. Husband, get up! Let us go to Mattara Guttu." Heggadé takes leave of his brother-in-law and they return home.

They are coming back to Mattara Guttu. On the 30th day of the month Parndédi has her period and goes to the river to bathe. That month she became pregnant. On the sixth month she tells her husband her stomach is heavy with child. On the eighth month Heggadé tells her he will perform the pregnancy ceremony [*bāyaké*] and that she must then return to Mallara Guttu.

Parndédi says: "I won't go to Mallara Guttu. Even if I died, I would stay at Mattara Guttu." Heggadé performs the *bāyaké* ceremony, buying Parndédi a silk sari and a gold chain. The neighboring women are called to serve Parndédi special foods and to bless her with offerings.

On the ninth day of the tenth month, on the ninth minute of the ninth hour, she calls out to her husband that she is in labor. The midwife comes. From her one stomach she bore two children. As the babies are born, Parndédi died.

Heggadé weeps and mourns her death. He sends a letter to inform Mallara Guttu. Duwu receives the letter. She tears it up and throws it away. When the messenger returns back to Mattara Guttu, Heggadé wonders why there is no reply to the letter he sent. He sends another letter, but again Duwu gets it and tears is up. At the time, Parnderü was out adjusting the water level in the paddy fields. When he returns, he sees a bit of the torn up letter. He is able to read a few words of it and learns of the news. He cried out in grief and races to Mattara Guttu. "Ayyo brother-in-law! What's news? What's the story? You have to cut the babies' umbilical cords and clean them up. You have to give them names. If they are to come and live at Mallara Guttu the first born has responsibility for watching after matters inside the house and should be called Kannyagé. The second born will have responsibility for matters outside and should be called Kapora."* Parnderü had a funeral pyre and Parndédi was cremated.

Heggadé then tells Parnderü, "I will not give the children, I will raise them and care for them." Parnderü then said that he would return when the children were grown.

The children matured quickly. When they were seven years old, Heggadé called his brother-in-law. "I have raised and cared for the children whose mother died. These are the descendants of your shrine [*adikodi*]. For the past seven years, I have raised them in Mattara Guttu. Take them to Mallara Guttu, brother-in-law. Go and be in peace." But Parnderü tells him, "You should bring the children to Mallara Guttu." When they reach Mallara Guttu, Parnderü calls out to Duwu, "I have returned and brought along our nieces." Duwu does not get up and look. Parnderü asks his brother-in-law to sit down. "Let us eat whatever there is ready." He gives him a glass of water. "I don't want it," replies Heggadé, "I will be going now." At this Parnderü takes offense and insists that he sit and stay. Heggadé stays for the meal. Duwu brings and serves the food she has prepared. Heggadé and Parnderü ate, and when they were finished they chewed betel. Heggadé again says he will be going, and tells Parnderü to watch after the children carefully. Before he leaves Heggadé embraces the girls. They cry, but he tells them to stay and he will return; that their uncle, his brother-in-law, is there to watch after them. After reassuring them, he leaves.

After some time, there was a gathering of the important people of the region and Heggadé had to attend. He called to his wife, Duwu, and told her, "Listen, a messenger has come with a letter for me. I have to go to a meeting. You have to prepare food for me immediately."

But Duwu replies, "Husband, I am old. I can't see. I can't walk. I can't move my arms. There are your nieces. The first born, Kannyagé, has responsibility for watching after matters inside the house, and the second born, Kapora, takes responsibility for matters outside. Tell them."

So Parnderü calls Kannyagé and tells her to prepare a meal before his journey. Kannyagé chooses the finest rice from the storeroom and goes to the garden to choose the best vegetables for the curries. When Kannyagé

*I have not encountered this custom of assigning responsibilities and corresponding names to children by the order of birth in other *pāḍdanas*. Nor do I understand the relationship between the names and the responsibilities. His concern is clearly for the children, his descendants, not for the loss of his sister.

went out, Duwu leapt up and got a handful of unhusked paddy and a handful of pebbles and put them in the plate of rice which Kannyagé had prepared and set aside. Kannyagé returns and cuts up the vegetables and rinses them and brings them to the hearth to cook. When everything is finished, she brings the food out and serves her uncle. Parnderü takes up a handful of rice, but all he gets is a handful of paddy. "Kannyagé! Come here. What kind of rice is this?" he asks. "There is unhusked paddy in the rice," she replies, "so that you may become famous as an arbitrator at the council."*

Parnderü takes up another handful of rice, and he gets hair. "What is this in the rice, Kannyagé!" he asks again. "There is hair [*tare*] in the rice so that you will get a reputation for being a leader with a good head [*tare*]," she replies.

He takes a third handful of rice and he gets pebbles [*kallü*]. Again he asks Kannyagé, "What is this in the rice?" This time she replies, "There are stones in the rice, Mamaji, so when you go to the meeting you will be changed to stone [i.e., adamant in decisions]."

Hearing this, Parnderü is furious. His anger fills the seven worlds. "Listen, child, may that which was made for me, be the rice for Jumadi, who sits in the shrine of our house."** He left the meal and leapt up, saying, "Give it to Jumadi!" He dressed and went to the council meeting.

Meanwhile, Kannyagé calls for her sister, Kapora, to come and bathe, and together they go off to the Mallara tank. Kannyagé and Kapora go down the steps. They let their hair down loose and lower their heads into the water. As the girls bend their heads, the goddess of the house, Jumadi, comes and pushes them into the tank. Then, in the form of a red hawk, Jumadi flies to the council meeting. There, in a vision, she tells Parnderü, "I have finished the work you were thinking of."

In a flash, Parnderü realizes what has happened. "But I didn't mean what I said in anger!" says Parnderü. "Because of a curse uttered in anger, your lamp, too, will go out." He races home.

There he calls out to Kannyagé and Kapora. They are not there. He calls to Duwu. He is afraid for Kannyagé and Kapora. Duwu says to him, "Husband, there is a saying, 'When a frog becomes too large it searches for a bigger pond. When a girl becomes proud, she won't stay in the house.'

* She apparently does not realize the truth of her uncle's claim, and responds to it as if it were a joke, or possibly jokes, to cover her embarrassment. The replies all contain puns.

** This statement is a curse (*wāk*). It is not that he wishes ill toward the household deity, but that he offers this feast prepared for him to the deity. If there is fault in it, let Jumadi take action. See Claus (1979b).

As soon as you went off to the council meeting they said, 'Let's go to the Mallara tank and bathe.'"

So Parnderü went to the tank. There he sees the pair of flower pods of the areca-nut palm, dancing and playing on the water of Mallara tank. "Rama! Rama!" he cries, "The children whose mother died when they were born, the children my brother-in-law raised for seven years and I took in for eight—you took them today, Jumadi? A bud so carefully cared for; can it be so quickly snatched away? Who is to keep your lamp lit from now on?" He takes the silk shawl from his shoulders, goes down to the tank, and holds it in front of him. "If you children are innocent, you must come ashore, you must come to my silk shawl." The two corpses, in the form of two areca-nut flower pods, dancing and playing on the water, come to the edge of the tank and into his shawl.

He sends a letter to Mattara Guttu. "The children whom you raised with such love and beauty fell into the tank at Mallara Guttu and died today." As Heggadé reads it he thinks, "Did you take the life from these innocent children, brother-in-law? The children whose mother died when they were born, the children whom I raised with such care?" He leaves Mattara Guttu and rushes to the Mallara tank. "It appears your Jumadi doesn't want a lamp lit. Your family line has ended, the bud removed. What is the use of just standing here looking?"

The two corpses of Kannyagé and Kapora are taken and placed on the pyre and are cremated.

Heggadé then says: "I will go to Samderü and ask to have my daughters back." Going to the place of Samderü, he asks, "Hear me, Samderü. Your nieces, two Siris, you must give to me." Samderü replies that there are two Siris, the highest in Medima Loka, his nieces and that he will give them for a price. "For each step you must give a fine of one sovereign." Heggadé agrees to give the amount. Thus Samderü created from two Siris of Medima Loka two girls of the lower Siri Loka [the earth], saying to them, "Go to the lower Siri Loka, to the Budu of Mayinda Heggadé. They will give a fine for each step and a sovereign for each *ajje* [footprint]."*

*This is clearly reference to a ritual of some kind. Neither the singer nor I could recall anything exactly like it in existence today. However, the scene bears some resemblance to what transpires at a Siri *jātre,* where women who are afflicted with various illnesses and unwanted spirit possession become possessed by Siri spirits and are able to air their problems so that others may hear. Furthermore, in some of the myths associated with that cult, there is reference to Siris being granted to devotees as children (descendants) and, after they die a tragic death, returning to Medima Loka to take their original forms. The presiding deity in these myths is, however, called Bermerü. See Claus (1978a).

So Heggadé returns to the cremation grounds along with the two Siris. The Siris gathered the ashes of the pyre into a heap. Then they created water in a vessel. They created a stick of *nāgara darba* [a reference to a Sanskritic ritual item]. Then they put the water on the ashes. The two girls, Kannyagé and Kapora rose up and sat. "May you return to life," said the Siris. Then they touched the *nāgara darba* to the top of their heads and Kannyagé and Kapora stood up. "Ayyo," cried the girls, "where did you come from? Our aunt removed us. She put paddy and stones and coconut in the rice we made. Then our uncle got angry, sisters. 'This is not food made for me, but for Jumạdi,' our uncle said. Then our Jumadi took us."

Heggadé heard these words. He gave the Siris the price he had agreed: a fine for each step and a sovereign for each *ajje*. Then he brought the girls back to Mallara Guttu, where they tell Parnderü the story. Parnderü calls Duwu to come out. He takes her by the neck and pushes her. She falls onto the courtyard floor. "You can go wandering the villages begging. Never enter my house again," Parnderü tells her.

* * *

The kinship relationship between the two houses is described in Figure 4. The matrilateral marriage alliance between the two houses is per-

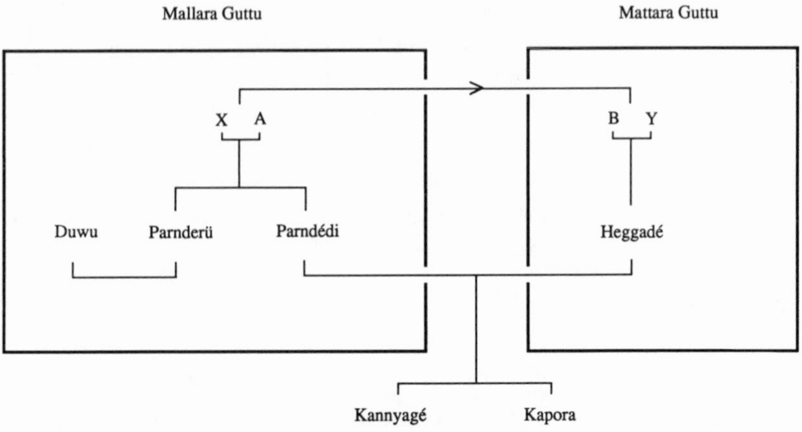

A, Parnderü and Parndédi's father, is Heggadé's mother's (i.e. B's) brother.
X is Parnderü's mother.
Y is Heggadé's father.

FIGURE 4. Kin ties in the Parnderu *Pāḍdana*.

petuated with Heggadé's claim on his uncle's daughter. He expresses this claim with the understatement that he needs someone to cook for him. He loves his wife, though, and meets all of his responsibilities toward her *kavaru* (property group). He does what is necessary to insure his wife bears children and that they are raised properly and sent home at the appropriate time. He loves his children. If this were all there were to the story, it would be a happy one, but not a good *pāḍdana*.

Duwu, Parnderü's wife, is the obvious villain in this story. Her actions cause the death of her husband's sister and then his nieces. It appears she is childless, a barren woman. In Tulu story traditions a childless woman is not only despised (as at first Parndédi is) but is also portrayed as an evildoer, similar to a witch or a wicked stepmother in European traditions. Here we are given a picture of the strong jealousy she feels toward the women of Mallara. Her jealousy would make sense if she had children and desired that Parnderü lavish as much care and attention on them as he does his nieces. And it would make sense if she resented that her marriage to Mallara implied that she and her people were inferior to the women of that house (as it seems Maniga felt). But as a barren woman there is an additional, mystical intensity to her jealousy. In many a Tuluva household such women and jealousies of this sort are not uncommon (see Claus, 1986b).[23] But, again, if this were all there were to the story, then, though it might have made a good folktale, it would not have been a good *pāḍdana*. In a folktale the narrative would have concentrated on the relationship between these two women and the men would have been alluded to only indirectly.

In fact, the real tragedy comes about in Parnderü's character and actions. First of all, he is too easily duped by Duwu. One gets the feeling—as indeed, I think Parndédi and Heggadé come to realize—that he *is* favoring his wife over his sister. At his sister's death (possibly caused in a magical sense by his wife having given her spoiled food at the moment of her first menstrual period—a moment at which Parnderü should have held an important life-cycle ceremony and given her auspicious food), his concern is for his descendants, over whom he might exercise a claim. He acts selfishly in two regards: favoring his wife, with whom he has a strong personal (either sexual or magically induced) attraction, and favoring his nieces, over whom he has authority. A man's concern for his sister is the closest thing to a purely altruistic concern, since it has no immediate benefit to himself, only for his descendants, his matrilineal line. That he acts selfishly, rather than in the interest of his descent group, is a source of tragedy. We have a male equivalent to Maniga of the previous *pāḍdana*.[24] But, of course, the central tragedy occurs when he brings about the death of his nieces, who are the source of his own social perpetuity and authority. We know that Duwu instigated this and Parnderü's nieces innocently played into it, but it is directly a product of his own incredible stupidity and headstrong emotions (an element of the individual's character) that brings it about.

And what about the family deity? These spirits act mechanically, carrying out the consequences of human requests no matter what the result (see Claus 1973, 1979b). We know this from other *pāḍdanas* (e.g., Paramale Ballal, above), and Tulu-speakers would know that the line "Give it to Jumadi!" is the line around which the tragedy revolves. They gasp at this utterance. Nothing could be more devastating, and at the same time nothing could be more self-defeating. As Heggadé observed, "It appears your Jumadi doesn't want a lamp lit. Your family line has ended, the bud [*kavaru* means 'branch'] severed." But it is not Jumadi who is stupid, despite the fact that she will suffer in the exact way as Parnderü will.[25] Parnderü is stupid because, in a fit of anger, thinking an insult has been caused to himself, he transfers it to the emblem and source of his own real power and authority, his family deity. At the meeting—to which he has been invited because of his family's authority and power—he realizes his stupidity.

And what about Heggadé? I have already indicated that he has acted appropriately as a *poddé* throughout. It is he who, through his love and affection toward his daughters, has the power to go to the giver-of-children to have the daughters brought back to life and have the source of the family difficulties brought to justice. Two final notes: Duwu is, despite her bad character, something of a scapegoat in the end. And it is noteworthy that Samderü and the Siris have the capacity to override Jumadi's act. Jumadi offers no objection or comment. Family dynamics contain the problems, rather than the family deity (*bhūta*, a much-maligned category in the literature: see Claus 1973, 1979a). This is also the case in the Siri cult activities, with which this *pāḍdana* has strong association. (See Claus 1975, 1979a, 1986b for my ongoing interpretation of this important religious cult.)

My final selection is the story of Kelinji Bale. The translation is highly abridged and leaves out much of the specific imagery.

The Story of Kelinji Bale

Kelinji Bale desired to see her cousin (her father's sister's son), Kelinji Rayerü. Her mother and her brothers warned her not to go, that she was too inexperienced to cope with his seven sisters, who would be jealous of her.

Still she insists on going: "If you send me in a palanquin it will honor your name, but I am satisfied with walking." So, they send her off dressed as a bride, in a beautifully decorated palanquin.

When the seven sisters see her coming, they are indeed jealous that their brother will never pay any attention to them if he sees her. They plot to kill her before he comes. They make *dōsa** and heat up milk and lace them with snake poison. When Kelinji Bale arrives, they offer her this to quench her thirst and hunger after the long ride in the heat of the day.

She refuses the food. Stymied, they go to their mother and ask her to offer it to Bale. "How can I do this?" she asks, "I have only one niece to marry my only son." But she relents at their insistence.

She offers the poisoned food. Bale declines. Her aunt forces the situation: "If you won't take from me, then who will you take food from?" Bale takes some of the *dōsa* and gives it to a cat. The cat dies. She gives it to a rooster and it too dies. She gives it to a dog and it dies. "Why, Auntie, have these animals died?" "They have died of disease," replies the aunt. She takes a few drops of the milk and puts it on her anklet and it bursts. "Shall I drink this, Auntie?" she asks three times. Hearing no reply from the aunt, she drinks it and dies.

The aunt and her daughters put the body on the golden mat in Rayerü's room and cover it with a cloth. They pretend nothing has happened.

Rayerü returns from the fields and asks who came in the palanquin. When then tell him it was Kelinji Bale, he is anxious to see her. They tell him, no, she had her first menstrual period once she arrived, and is in a room and he can't go in. Happy at that news, he sends word to her brothers that they should come and celebrate the event.

They come and want to see her. The aunt again says no. But they point out to her that since she is their sister, they cannot be polluted by her condition. So they go and gather around her cloth-covered body. They soon notice she is not breathing, that she is dead. They call to Kelinji Rayerü to come. When he hears the facts, he is overcome with grief. He asks how this happened, but his mother evades his questions, saying she is sick, she doesn't know how this happened. But Rayerü is furious.

The dead girl's seven brothers tell him to calm down, keep his wits about him. The body must be cremated, there is work to do. The body is washed, she is prepared for cremation in the dress of a bride. Kelinji Rayerü is asked to perform the rituals as if he were her husband. The funeral over, the brothers return home and Rayerü goes to his room in grief.

* *Dōsa* is a pancakelike food made from a fermented batter of rice and black gram flour.

From the ashes of the fire Kelinji Bale goes to the heaven of Narayana in the form of a beetle. There she pleads with God to allow her to return to Siri Loka. Narayana relents and gives her the boon to return in the form of a 16-year-old woman.* So, still in the form of a beetle, she returns, buzzes around Rayerü's head three times, and takes her form beside him on the bed.

He is overjoyed to see her again, but wants to know the whole story. She tells him of the poisoning. He gets up, sends word to her brothers to come, that their sister has returned and he must marry her. He then goes and gets his sword, kills his mother and sisters, and buries them.

The brothers arrive and the marriage is performed and everybody lives happily ever after.

* * *

Kelinji Bale's character and the relationship between her and her husband, Rayerü, is the exact opposite to that of Maniga and her relation to her husband, Paramale Ballal (see Figure 5). The two *pāḍdanas* look at the same family relationships from opposite perspectives. Kelinji Bale and her husband are deeply devoted to one another. Cross-cousins, they regard one another as husband and wife even before marriage: she is cremated as a bride.

Although Kelinji Bale, unlike Maniga, shows no animosity toward her "sisters-in-law" (her cross-cousins), they are jealous of her from the start. Why? A brother—their brother—is the manager of matrilineal wealth. There is always the suspicion that he might siphon this off and give it to his wife and children. We have seen in the *pāḍdana* of Parnderü something of the obligations of a man to his wife and her kin in the relationship between Heggadé and Parndédi and Parnderü. We have also seen that a man can be deceived by his wife, as Duwu deceived Parnderü. A wife may be very possessive of her husband's property and his relationship to his sister and sister's children. She can be jealous of her status in her husband's household, not wanting to relinquish any rights to the rightful heirs. In this case, the fears are unjustified. The seven sisters are bad, but their badness is not uncommon. If that were all that this narrative was about, it would have been a good folktale, but not a good *pāḍdana*.

The key figure in the *pāḍdana* is the mother. What motivates her?

*The singer has inadvertently created a confusion of images here: Kelinji Bale went as a 7 1/2-year-old girl, but reincarnated as a 16-year-old woman; Rayerü clearly recognizes her as his wife and accepts her present form as that which she had before.

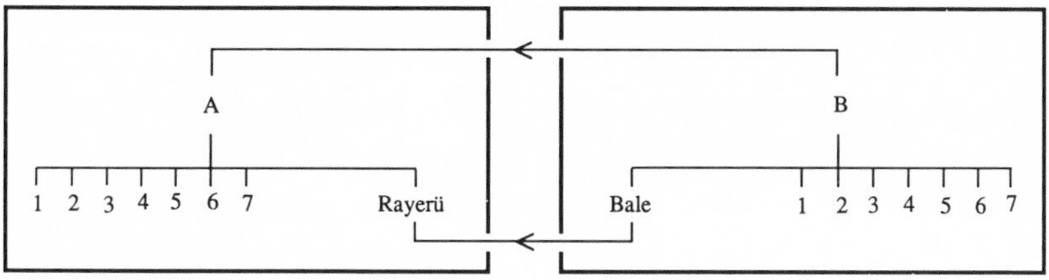

FIGURE 5. Kin ties in the Kelinji *Pāḍdana*.

A mother is supposed to look after the interests of her sons as well as her daughters. She is morally obligated toward her brother to marry her son to his daughter. And here there is only one of each. But a mother always does favor her daughter and a *podderü* cum (matrilineal) property group favors a daughter's children. The mother here stands for the perpetuity of the matrilineal property group at the expense of the *podderü* and its generational alliance: property versus kinship; matrilineality versus bilaterality; surface versus deep structure; *kavaru* versus *podderü*. She is a weak character, portrayed as sickly, offering excuses, sacrificing her son's interests. Rayerü, her son, not Bale's brothers, kills her.

The relationship that prevails is that between brothers-in-law. It is this relationship that symbolizes the *naṇṭer*, the unity of kin through alliance. It is the counterbalance to the *kuṭumba*. It ensures the generational promises of brother to sister.

Some final notes. Bale herself goes against the advice of her mother and her older brothers. Is this not wrong? No. She is innocent, completely trusting in the morality of the system. She goes with a pure heart. God will protect her. Interestingly, the god Narayana, despite the different name, appears to be that same god who controls the Siris in the Parnderü story and in the Siri myth (Claus 1975). It forces one to speculate whether there is not here a distinct religious system built around the *pāḍdanas* and their consistent kinship themes, replete with a pantheon, a morality to be enforced, and a ritual complex (the Siri cult) to activate and relate these dimensions.

Genres and Social Structure: Further Remarks

With these stories in mind, I want to return now to the problem of how the thematic content of genres is related to social structure and social ideology. The relationship is twofold: first, to the society at large, speaking to the ideological basis of a local Indian society, and second, to the performer and the performance context, correlating an appropriate time, place, and personnel (performer, audience) for the presentation of particular subject matter. There is nothing especially strange about the general relationship. We find analogous relationships in American popular culture, on television, say, where, taken collectively, the thematic content of a week's programming portrays many aspects of the ideological underpinnings of American society, while the particular time slots (daytime, nighttime, late-night, weekday, weekend, specials), each with distinctive thematic content and portrayed by stereotyped characters, are allocated for different audiences. In general principle, the folklore of India is not so very different.

What is different is the particular ideology and the specific breakdown of the proprieties that go into making up the different "time slots." There are, furthermore, no "actors" in the sense of the term in Western popular culture. Performers are "typecast" and are drawn from a familiar group of family, neighbors, and local "professionals." Mothers play "motherly roles," women play "women's roles," untouchables play "untouchable roles," and so on.

I do not want to appear to oversimplify the problems of genre definition and comparison by using the demystifying comparison to American television. One is still left with a great deal of ethnographic analysis and interpretation on both sides of the comparison. But we are in a situation where an analysis of American soap operas or *Star Trek* can provide insight into Indian folklore and vice versa. On the other hand, there are some genres on both sides that may lack their equivalents on the other. *Pāḍdanas* may be one of those genres. Let me try to identify the distinctive characteristics of the ballads' themes and link them to social ideology, on one hand, and the characteristics of the performance, on the other.

Internal: Themes

As I have already said, the dominant mood of the women's *pāḍdanas* is one of tragedy. More specifically, it is one of loss through the thoughtless, selfish action, or even the thoughtlessly spoken words, of one of the main characters. It is not simply a matter of the person's innate character. Tragedy is the result of a person's moral failings, weaknesses. It is that person's overemphasis of the self and the corresponding neglect of social obligations, usually involving neglecting to care for a female relative. The tragedy results in death, usually the death of a woman, and her death means the end of a descent line. The selfish person is often, but by no means exclusively, a man, and the victim of his rash, shortsighted, and selfish action is usually a woman who is in the social position to most benefit him in the long run. So, there is bitter irony along with the tragedy. But we can only understand the real source of the tragedy, the whole meaning of the piece, in relation to the larger web of social relations between groups. The group most frequently involved is that of a bilateral family, *maṇṭerü,* with its complementary halves: *podderü* (affines).

Often the death—and cessation of the family line—is caused by a family deity, Jumadi, whose role it is to protect the family and ensure its perpetuity. The deity is specifically linked to the manager of the matrilineal estate. Both the god and the man have the same sources of power and authority: the matrilineal estate, perpetuated in the line of female relatives. The deity's perpetual worship is simultaneously ensured by its protection of its worshippers. While the deity is often (not always, as we saw in Kelinji Bale) the instrument of tragedy, it does not act independently.[26] It carries out the will of the family, articulated by the family head. Both neglect of the family deity and selfishness (often equated in the *pāḍdana*s) bring ruin to and cessation of the family line.[27]

The stories we have looked at all involve two families linked as *podderü. Podderü,* although they have their independent concerns, are also entrusted with one another's perpetuity. It is a dual alliance system, familiar to anthropologists through the writings of Claude Lévi-Strauss, Louis Dumont, and Edmund Leach, in which the two partner groups form a unity greater than their parts. The morality of the *pāḍdana*s revolves around the morality of this alliance, not around that of the composite groups. And it is certainly not the morality of dyadic or even triadic relations between individual kin (Beck 1986, 1989). That may be (arguably) what folk tales are about, but the *pāḍdana*s consistently pit such individual motivations against their moral obligations to the larger group. More exactly, they demonstrate the principles of how that larger system works by showing the negative effects of individual deviance from them.

External

Content and Performers

Why is it a woman's genre? I have already pointed out that the disastrous and tragic consequences fall most heavily on women. This is not always the case, but it is so in the vast majority of *pāḍdanas*. Women, I would argue, are more dependent on the moral integrity of the system, less able to take independent action in the world at large. They are associated with the home, the family, while men have a life outside of it, albeit that their life outside the family is heavily determined by the status of the family. Women are not merely associated with the home (Ramanujan's *akam*) but are utterly dependent on the morality which they would hope governs the behavior of its individual members. They sing these songs to remind one another of the importance of family morality. It is they who suffer the consequences of its failure. And if the evil characters of the *pāḍdanas* are sometimes themselves women, they are always punished and it is a critical reminder that their own wrong actions, not just those of others, can result in disastrous consequences for their person. The women of the *pāḍdanas* are not all passive.

Women, more so than men, live their lives between two houses: their natal home and their husband's home. They are governed by the rules and regulations and the individual characteristics of the two houses. They serve as a link between the two houses. They have two stages to their lives. They have two statuses, two social structures within which they must live. This, of course, is true of other regions of India and many other cultures in the world. Indeed, these features serve to link the *pāḍdanas* with many other performance genres around India and the world in which women express, interpret, and share their double lives with one another. But what distinguishes the Tulu *pāḍdana,* within India at least, is the strength of the bond women, and even more so their children, maintain with their natal homes. This link is usually expressed through the relationship between a brother and a sister, *tagé* (older brother) and *tangaḍi* (younger sister). A woman relies heavily on this bond. The whole of the system of *āḷiya santāna* (matrilineal inheritance) can be implied by its mere reference. A woman trusts this bond, and the future of their family line, too, is entrusted in it. In each of the three *pāḍdanas* we have looked at, the heroine's fate, and that of her children, lay in the particular nature of her relationship with her brother. The tragedy is that one cannot always rely on this one bond, and that so very much—for both sides, and all together—hangs in its balance.

Types of Performers

As I noted earlier, the *pāḍdanas* are essentially a performance tradition, with the performance context defining the selection of particular pieces and their form of presentation (i.e., genre), and a broad distinction can be made between the contexts in which women sing and those in which men sing. While the field songs are a woman's subgenre, men sing *pāḍdanas* in the context of public rituals called *bhūta kōlas*.[28] More specifically, only men of certain castes sing *pāḍdanas*: the Pambadas, Paravas, and Nalkes, all castes of low standing, specialists in village-level ritual performances. In other words, to contrast correctly the social dimensions of the two subgenres, we must say that the field songs are known by a nonspecialist social category—women—while the ritual songs are sung by a social class of ritual specialists. One could go even further in distinguishing sub-subgenres, saying that the specific ritual song traditions are specific to certain castes, since: (1) each of these three castes specializes in the *kōla* traditions of certain deities and localities, and (2) even when there is an overlap (e.g., in the *kōla* of Maisandaya), the different castes perform it differently and sing very different *pāḍdanas* during the performance.[29] Thus one can collect *pāḍdana* repertoires for each of these subgenres and note similarities of many sorts within a given subgenre. In a few instances, one could collect a given story from all of the different subgenres and note the many sorts of differences between them (Claus 1988, 1989). This latter task is hampered by the fact that relatively few stories are sung by all groups.[30]

One of the major areas of interaction between the different *pāḍdana* traditions occurs via the women of the castes of ritual specialists, particularly the Paravas. As women, they sing in the fields with other women. As wives, mothers, and sisters whose menfolk perform the rituals, they are sometimes asked to sing the *pāḍdanas* during ritual performances. When this is the case, it has been my experience that they simply sing a (usually) shortened version of the field song; in other words, they sing as women, not as ritual specialists. It is here that the two traditions are partially linked.[31] But the degree to which women participate in these public rituals varies between these three castes of performers, and even from family to family within the castes. We are here in the realm of particularistic variation of individual family traditions, the competence of individual performers and the exigencies of particular performance events.[32]

Context and Performers

Why do women sing *pāḍdanas* in the fields? The setting is not, literally, "domestic," and, according to Ramanujan's categorization of genres into *akam* and *puṟam,* it would not appear to be a place where we would expect to find such a quintessentially women's genre.[33] Nevertheless, I think Ramanujan's distinctions do apply. In the Tuluva world view, fields, cattle sheds, women, and children are all thought of as being in the center of the home.[34] Theirs is not a physical, geographic conceptualization of the home, but a thematic one.[35] All of these items (cattle, paddy, women, and so forth) are at the generative, reproductive center of the family's existence. These are the entities that are most vulnerable and in need of male protection. The conceptual boundary, where male heroism arises, surrounds and protects this center. Furthermore, women do the majority of the agricultural tasks (transplanting, harvesting, threshing), especially those associated with the paddy plant itself. Men's work is associated with the physical field. Strictly speaking, women's *pāḍdana*s are not so much *field* songs as they are *paddy* songs, or, even more specifically, "seedling transplanting songs," *nēji naḍina pāḍdana,* a phrase by which they are often identified in Tulu. Women, rice, and family are linked in everyday life as much as in the allegorical world view. This linkage affects the genre system, too, even more deeply.

Why during transplanting?[36] Here, again, we must deal with subtle subgenre distinctions. There are two steps in the transplanting operation—pulling up the seedlings from their seed beds and replanting them in the growing field—and the songs sung in each operation are often regarded as different subgenres of *pāḍdana:* songs sung during the uprooting are distinguished as *sandi,* while those sung during replanting are *kabita*. In some parts of Tulunad this distinction is not made, and they are all called *pāḍdana*. But where the distinction is made, the songs I have translated above are categorized as *sandi.*[37] I have not collected many *kabita* (the distinction is not made in the area where I have done most of my collecting, and songs from the *kabita* repertoire are not frequently sung) or worked with them extensively.[38] Rhythms and melodies of the *kabita* are different from those of the *pāḍdana*s, and many women have told me that the reason they sing the different songs during the different operations is because the rhythm of the work is different and corresponds to the rhythm of the two kinds of songs.[39] Most of the *kabita* are much shorter than *sandi,* and, unlike *sandi,* each line sung by the lead singer is not repeated by the other women in the work team. Instead, a constant chorus is repeated at the end of each line. In one of the most popular *kabita,* the chorus is:

"Oh *work,* Oh *work,* Oh *work,* *work,* *work*"
O bēle, O bēle, O bēle, bēle, bēlā

The themes, too, of the *kabita* are quite different from the themes of the *sandi*. The *kabita* are regarded as being auspicious, while the *sandi* are regarded as "dangerous." The pulling up, the uprooting, is associated with the transplanting of a woman from her natal home to the home of her husband. The women are reminded of the delicate nature of the relations between *podderü,* the potentially disastrous events which could happen to them situated in the relationship between their two homes. The replanting and the *kabita* are associated with the husband's home: "work, work, work." But it is also associated with regeneration of their own matrilineal line and with fertility. The genre distinction, where it is made, is based on a metaphoric analogy between the two activities of transplanting and the two social structures in which a woman lives.

After writing the above, I was in a position to do some additional field work and encountered a woman, Ramu Muggerti of Katil, who was particularly informative about the analogy between the women and crops around which this subgenre distinction revolves. Before I quote her, I should mention that she (and her neighbors) do not use the term *sandi* in contrast to *kabita,* but instead, the word *pāḍdana* itself. *Sandi,* she says, are what men sing during the *bhūta kōla*s. I believe most women in that region follow this usage in ordinary speech, making distinctions in the term *pāḍdana* in different hierarchical contexts.

> The ancients made these customs. When transplanting [i.e., putting the seedlings into the growing field] the seedlings for the *anelü* crop [the monsoon crop, first of three crops] you mustn't sing *pāḍdana*s. You should sing *kabita*s and *ō bēle* songs [she implicitly makes a further sub-subgenre distinction between these two]. The *suggi* [the second crop, after the monsoons] is difficult. You shouldn't sing *kabita*s, only *pāḍdana*s. Look. The *anelü* [crop] is a whore. *Suggi* is a bride. It is a *satya* [true, pure] crop, help it! *Kolake* [the third crop] is a mother [*pedmēdi,* a woman who has recently given birth]. For that you can sing anything, *pāḍdana*s and *kabita*s.

This still does not explain why one sings *pāḍdana* (*sandi*) while uprooting the seedlings and *kabita* while returning them to the ground of the growing fields. The distinction is there during the *anelü* crop, but she (and others) explain this in terms of attitudes: during the planting they feel playful and they sing for fun. *Kabita*s are light, sometimes slightly obscene songs, sometimes complaining of women's work. Some (e.g., one called "The chasing [bull's] horn") ends with playful splashing, chasing, running, and falling in the soupy, muddy fields. But why there should be this consonance of planting and playfulness and sexuality will have to wait for another essay. I have now had the opportunity to collect a number of *kabita* and their associated play and see that this is a larger topic than can be covered in this chapter on *pāḍdanas* and their tragedies.

CONTEXT AND STYLE

Why are such themes expressed in a story which "must be sung"? The answer to this question—one which Ramanujan's distinction between *akam* and *puṟam* genres might not predict—is that these are clearly ritual texts: women's ritual texts. The stories are not to be just spoken in ordinary language.

The women's activity in the fields is not a purely secular activity. It is bounded by a number of ritual prohibitions (a woman may not enter the field during her menstrual period, for example) and has, as I have mentioned above, a number of ritual associations with fertility and regeneration. It is a place where a sacred power upon which humans rely for their continual sustenance is both strongly felt and very important. It is, like themselves, a female power.

And equally important, the contents of the texts are clearly concerned with morality and religion. They contain references to important deities associated with important religious cults. In many respects, the women's texts constitute a more elaborate source of exegesis for this religious complex than do the texts of the professional male bards. I do not think it is wise to view this situation as constituting two separate religions or even two separate cults. Their versions of these texts deal primarily with the family side of the religious and moral complex which, in other contexts, extends to the level of village affairs and the relationship between landlord and tenant (Claus 1979b). It is at that point that the men take over, with their texts and rituals. Women's rituals and men's rituals, women's texts and men's texts, men and women, family and society, are all linked. The *akam* and *puṟam* distinction still obtains, but their parallel ritual contexts and textual genres are complementary and even sometimes overlapping parts of a single whole. This is why, perhaps, it is often so difficult to perceive the subtle and often unlabeled genre and subgenre distinctions: they are thoroughly context-dependent.

Appendix

The following is a transcription of the opening stanzas of the Paramale Ballal *pāḍdana* summarized in prose form in the text. It was sung by two women, Payyu (the lead singer) and Kargi Mundaldaklu of Anjar village,

Udupi Taluk. Each stanza consists of two equal-length couplets, or four lines. In a couplet, the four-beat lines are grammatically marked, being generally a complete phrase or sentence. The second line generally consists of a formulaic repetition of the name of the speaker or actor or action. Musically, the *pāḍdanas* are quite simple, consisting of generally two or three tones (low, middle, and high). The couplets in a stanza are distinguished melodically, with the first ending on a higher tone than the second. The syllables italicized in the first stanza are those that are stressed throughout the piece. The last portion of each stanza, in boldface, is sung in unison, (*woipuni,* "pulling, plucking"), a distinguishing characteristic of *pāḍdanas*.

Payyu

1

*den*nana *den*nani*yéé, bal*lale
*par*amala *bal*lale*daa*.
*den*nana *den*nana*yaa*, *bal*lala
*par*amala *bal*lalo***yaa.***

denana denaanayéé ballaale
paramala ballalüyaa.
denana denanayaa ballaalü
paramala ballalüyaa.

As is true with most poetry, close literal translation of these lines and retention of their beauty are impossibly contradictory goals. Furthermore, like most oral narrative poetry, each stanza is filled with functional and formulaic verse. The first stanza, for example, is functional—it establishes the metric form and melody, using the meaningless sound, "dennana." It is found only in *pāḍdanas* and is thus the genre's performance marker. The first stanza also introduces the name of the main character, Paramale Ballal.

2

(y)eeridé manigaduu, leederü
paramala ballaledaa.
ekkaḍe pokkaḍeyaa, maaniga
jewula maaningad**aa.**

(y)eeriya maanigayéé
jewula maanigayaa.
ekkaḍe pokkaḍeyaa, maaniiga
jewula **maanigadaa.**

The first half of the second stanza can be roughly translated as "'Hey, Maniga,' called Paramale Ballal." The third line, consisting of the two words *ekkaḍe* ("a little while ago," but also a rare term for a solitary form of the mancala game by this name) and *pokkaḍe* ("for no good reason, simply") are strong in rhyme, but together have no currency in ordinary Tulu usage. Combined, they give the sense of whiling away time in idle pursuit, or, "Shall we play a little, Maniga?"

3

onji aaṭa gobbugayaa, maaniga
jewula maanigadaa
ekkade pokkaḍeyaa, maaniga
jewula maaniga**daa**

onji aaṭa gobbugadéé, maaniiga
jewula maaniganaa
ekkadé pokkaḍédéé, maaniiga
jewula maanigadaa

4

marata maneṭüyéé, ballale
pongara kaayiṭüyéé
enk aanda barpujiyéé, ballale
enk aanda teripuji**yéé**

marata maneṭüyéé, ballaale
enk aanda barandüyéé
pongara koṭṭeḍüyéé, ballale
enk aanda teri**pujiyéé**

The third stanza begins with the sentence, "Let's play a game, Maniga, Jewu Maniga." But we have to wait to the fourth stanza, Maniga's response—I don't know [how to play] with a wooden board, with *pongāra* seed pieces. I don't know [how]"—to be sure the game is *cenne,* played ordinarily on a wooden board with two rows of cupped depressions ("pits"), in which the small red seeds of the *pongāra* tree (a species of tamarind) are moved around. The game of *cenne* figures symbolically in several different ways in a number of *pāḍdanas* (Claus 1986). Thus the Tulu villager already has some idea of what is to follow.

We learn a lot about the relationship of the Ballal and Maniga from the reference to *cenne* in sentences of the fourth and fifth stanzas. In the fifth stanza, Maniga compares the Ballal's (her husband's) ordinary set with the expensive one at her uncle's house (her natal home).

5

yennala buuḍuuduyéé, ballale
    bangāra maṇegenaa
bangarina maṇegenaa, ballale
    bollina parelüy**éé**

yennala buuḍuuduyéé, ballaale
    bangārina maṇegenaa
bollina parelüyéé, ballaale
    paramala **ballaledaa**

In my house, Ballal,
    is a golden board.
Golden board,
    pieces of silver.

And so it goes. The story is built up in little pieces, consisting mostly of highly attenuated, but marvelously efficient, phrases and sentences in the confines of a tightly consistent poetic and melodic form.

Notes

1. Within both men's and women's subgenres there are additional levels of distinction (sub-subgenres). See Claus (1989) for a discussion of the versions of a single story sung in five different contexts.

2. There are several regional styles of singing *pāḍdana*s. Often they are sung by only two or three women out of a team of workers, with the others merely listening. A subgenre of *pāḍdana*s, called *kabita*s (discussed later in this chapter) is always sung with a large chorus.

3. In a sense, all of the occasions when *pāḍdana*s are sung are defined as rituals, with the possible exception of people singing for their own pleasure or comfort in their home. The field is a ritual area and the tasks of pulling up the young seedlings from their seed beds and planting them in the growing field are both ritual occasions. I shall discuss this later.

4. For each of the *pāḍdana*s I have a number of versions sung by different women of different castes. Two of them (Paramala Ballal and Parndédi) are known to be sung in some places during rituals (the *kōla*s of Jumadi performed by Paravas).

For the sake of clarity in the recording, I collected songs from women singing in pairs, not in the context of transplanting. The location was usually their own homes, during the day and during the months from January through June, when agricultural work is at a lull. Although this is not a traditional context, the women rarely felt uncomfortable with the situation and readily understood its advantages. In their minds, this was not merely an acceptable alternative, but in most ways one that was preferable to the normal context.

In my mind, the unconventional setting affects the performance in only two significant ways:

(1) In the recording context the songs tend to be longer and more complete in some respects. In the field, singing is frequently discontinued if there is objection by the team of women. Nonsingers may begin carrying on disruptive conversations. Sometimes there are objections to singing particular songs. Sometimes the women get bored with their singing. Sometimes there is objection to the way a lead singer is singing (e.g., if she leaves out an important detail or her version is seen as being unacceptably deviant). Sometimes only part of a song is known, but the women enjoy singing only the portion they know.

(2) In the field there is greater conformity between the lead verse and its repetition by the team of singers. In the recording context, with only two women singing, each singing in her turn alone, there are frequent discrepancies between their verses. Most of these discrepancies are "allo-semantic" and insignificant. The women themselves are not aware of them. When they are in the field and singing in a group, such individual discrepancies cannot be noticed. Only in the case of two women who sang many songs for me could I detect discrepancies that approached the character of a dialogue, with the second singer clarifying, interpreting, correcting, elaborating, or otherwise intentionally altering the lead singer's verse. There were a number of occasions when the women discussed the details that differed between the version they had just sung and other versions they knew.

5. In addition to the more theoretical papers discussed below, see also the research described in Beck (1982); Blackburn (1981, 1989), and Narayana Rao (1986).

6. Furthermore, most writers have felt frustrated in addressing these topics by the English words (and their associations) we must use to identify Indian genres: the genre systems of India simply do not break down in the same way they do in the West.

7. See also her earlier version of this paper in *Indian Folklore II,* entitled "Frames, Tale Types and Motifs: The Discovery of Indian Oicotypes" (1987).

8. Beck acknowledges Lévi-Strauss's work on the nuclear family as the source of her inspiration for the scheme (Beck 1986:77).

9. When *pāḍdanas*—as versions or references to the same ones sung by women in the fields—are performed by men in a public ritual context, they more clearly fall within the *puram* category. However, as I will discuss at more length at the end of the chapter, women, too, sometimes sing *pāḍdanas* at public ceremonies. But even when women sing among themselves in the fields, the language of their songs is very different from a narrative telling of the story (see Claus 1986c).

10. This brief account of Tuluva kinship applies only to the matrilineal castes. The majority of the rural non-Brahman castes are matrilineal, including the dominant Bant (Tulu: Okkelekulu) and the numerically preponderant Billava (Biruverü) castes. For a more complete discussion of Tulu matrilineal kinship, see my (1978b).

11. There is no change in the way any of the kin terms are used if and when the cross-cousins marry, other than that a man then refers to his spouse as "wife" (*boḍēdi*), rather than "cross-cousin" (*maitidi*): terms for the spouse's relatives remain the same. When one does *not* marry a cross-cousin, terms for the spouse's relatives become those used for the relatives of a cross-cousin. This kinship terminology system (called Dravidian kinship terminology in the anthropological literature) is thus distinctive in that it seems to imply cross-cousin marriage. One's "in-laws" are "cross" relatives, one's "cross" relatives are one's "in-laws."

12. Their father is *not* a member of their *kavaru* and his concerns in seeking a marriage partner for his children do not necessarily involve an interest in preserving their ritual status. In the search for a bridegroom, a woman's brother and maternal uncle play a more critical role than does her father.

13. In the *pāḍdanas*, Ballal is usually a surname of Jain overlords. The caste, called *māsādika jain*, "ordinary Jain," is matrilineal. Today, families of the Bant caste (matrilineal) also often have this name. In common usage it can refer to any family of the wealthy landlord class.

14. This is quite admissible, since this is the way a woman would describe the story of a *pāḍdana*. In the appendix to this chapter, I provide a transcription of one stanza of one of the many versions I collected between 1986 and 1989. For a complete description of the musical and poetic characteristics of different regional variants of this *pāḍdana* see my paper (in Kannada), "*Paramale Ballalavarana Paddananu*," forthcoming.

15. There is a version published in Kannada (Someshwar 1962). See also Claus (1986c).

16. It also has an unusually simple melody and meter.

17. See Claus (1987 and forthcoming) for a report on women's interpretations of this *pāḍdana*.

18. There are additional questions that arise from the full *pāḍdana:* Why does Maniga hold such animosity toward her family's *podderü*, her father's kin? Is there a story of how her mother was mistreated by the Bangera women? Or by the women in her father's family? Is there a story of how she died? Had her husband's family kept her jewelry, which rightfully belonged to Maniga?

If there is more to this story, I suspect it would be regarded as a separate, but linked, *pāḍdana*. This *pāḍdana*, as it stands, has the "feel" of a complete one.

19. There would have been no problem if Bikrama had married Maniga to his own son. This would have constituted a permissible patrilateral cross-cousin marriage, but then the alliance between Malla and Paddelü would not have continued on the basis of kin ties. And it is possible that Maniga would have rejected this marriage, too, unless the fortunes of Bikrama's children had prospered as a result of his own marriage. In any case, Bikrama and his son would then have had to provide Maniga with a bride-price of jewelry and sari and a palanquin, if they had the ability to do this. The fact of the story is, however, that he did not provide these things (or rather, he did so too late).

20. The version presented was collected from Kargi Mundaldi of Anjar village, near Hiriyadka, in 1975. S. A. Krishnaiah collected Kargi's version again in 1986 and found it to be very similar to the earlier one.

21. There is a version that begins with the same line (*mitt- onji Mallar- guttu, tirt- onji Mallar- guttu . . .*) and involves characters named Parndérü and Karnaga which has been published and translated into Kannada by K. Vadiraj Bhatt (1974: 156–61), in brief story form, under the title "Jumadi." Dr. Heidrun Brückner has collected four additional versions from two Pambada men, a Pambada woman, and a Parava woman (personal communication, 1987). All of these are of the short, Karnaga type.

22. A *guttu* is a Bant manor house.

23. To quote my earlier article, "Internal feuds often become bitter, and op-

posing factions (each headed by a woman) frequently resort to psychological warfare and avail themselves of the considerable arsenal of magical weapons dispensed for a fee by local sorcerers and bhuta priests. . . . A great many of the difficult cases of unwanted possession brought to the Siri cult are the result of a woman's secretly polluting the food of her sister's daughter, or influencing her sister's descendants through sorcery" (1986b : 282–283).

24. See also Claus 1979b and 1986b for other *pāḍdana* characters who emphasize their self-interest: "Competition and overstatement of the individual, the jealousy and animosity it is apt to engender, are all contrary to family prosperity" (1986b : 284).

25. The family deity is the instrument of the head of the family, just as the village deity is the instrument of the village headman (see Claus 1979b).

26. This is yet one more piece of evidence for the argument that I made some time ago (Claus 1973) that this class of deities and their activities, in Tulunad, at least, cannot be properly characterized independently of the social structure. By themselves, they cannot be equated with evil, or with devils; they are not merely lowly; they are not capricious; and they are not especially well understood in relationship to a hierarchy of gods. Their "dual character," as agents of affliction and cure, of protection and punishment, can only be understood in relationship to the social structure and the social action of their worshippers. I have discussed various dimensions of the interpretation of their character, as seen through their deeds, in other papers as well: Claus 1979a and 1979b.

27. Interestingly, the corporal punishment Kelinji metes out to his mother and sisters similarly ends his family line. However, it is clear he acts morally in doing this. The interpretation is apparently that he felt that such a degenerate line had no right to be continued.

28. For a description and discussion of the different public ritual contexts see Claus (1989).

29. A discussion of the differences in content and style of the various men's and women's *pāḍdanas* is far too large a subject for this chapter. A discussion of the differences I refer to may be found in Claus, 1989. There I describe the differences found within a single *pāḍdana*. In that case, the stories are relatively similar, although it is questionable still whether some of the versions can be regarded as versions of the same story, even though the Tuluvas so regard it. In other cases, there are so many differences it is hard to see the connection at all. Heidrun Brückner is currently working on a large collection of songs Pambadas sing in their *kōla* and *nēma* traditions; further characterization of the relationship between the two major genres of *pāḍdanas* will have to wait for the publication of her results.

30. The Parnderü *pāḍdana* is sung by different groups, but a comparative study has not yet been done.

31. Two other linkages must be mentioned: although the men of the performing castes sing a particular *pāḍdana* quite differently from the "same" (i.e., the same title) *pāḍdana* in the women's tradition, they often know the women's *pāḍdana* as spoken narrative in prose form, which they can provide as exegesis for otherwise arcane mention of proper names in their versions of the *pāḍdana*. This was first demonstrated to Heidrun Brückner and me by a Pambada informant whom Brückner interviewed while I happened to be present.

Secondly, women attend the public ritual performances, where they constitute at least half the audience. While the men of the performing caste, possessed, sing and dance the *pāḍdana* hero's character, there is nothing to prevent them from interpreting these actions from the perspective of their *pāḍdana*'s characterization of the story. Indeed, many times I have had women associate events in the story with actions in the ritual performance, and it has been one of my major resources for the interpretation of these rituals.

32. The exception is the women of the Parava caste, who regularly sing the *pāḍdana* during the ritual performance. Unfortunately, my experience with Parava women's *pāḍdanas* is rather limited, as is my familiarity with the Parava *kōla* performance tradition. However, what material I have suggests that the Parava women may have played an important historical role in disseminating and perpetuating the *pāḍdana* tradition.

33. The setting for the men's *pāḍdanas* is usually "public" and frequently includes the ritual setting itself. It frequently centers on male characters and focuses the narration on the activities of these men (for examples, see Burnell 1894–98).

34. See Claus 1979b.

35. In a sense, however, there is physical reality to this conceptualization since in Tulunad houses are not located in centralized, nucleated villages, but are dispersed among the fields, each in the center of their lands.

36. No songs are sung during harvest time, and I think it is safe to say that this silence is meaningful.

37. Although some literary scholars (e.g., Rai 1985) trace the word *sandi* to the Sanskrit *sandhi,* meaning "chapter of a long epic narrative," I believe it is derived from a Dravidian root, *cel-* (DED 2286), with the Tulu cognates *sanduni* ("to pass as time," "pass from this world"), *sandāvuni* ("to pay," as in paying a debt, fulfilling a promise), *sandāya* ("delivering over"), and *salaguni* ("to nourish," "shelter," "succor, take care of"). I have, in fact, noted that the word is pronounced *sanday* in some regions. If this derivation can be substantiated, there are clearly subtle and ramified connections between the kinship realm (the relations between *podderü,* a term that is itself derived from a word connoting an exchange that engenders "joining, partnership") and the paddy fields; the obligatory marriage exchanges between kin groups and the activity of transplanting and the moral obligations to care for and nourish something which one holds temporarily in trust for another.

38. See Rai 1985: 235–272.

39. This is a rather superficial distinction and does not reflect the abilities of the older and wiser women to analyze the difference in content as well.

References

Beck, Brenda E. F.

1982 *The Three Twins: The Telling of a South Indian Folk Epic.* Bloomington: Indiana University Press.

1986 Social Dyads in Indian Folktales. In *Another Harmony: New Essays on the Folklore of India,* Stuart H. Blackburn and A. K. Ramanujan, eds., pp. 76–102. Berkeley: University of California Press.

1987 Frames, Tale Types and Motifs: The Discovery of Indian Oicotypes.

In *Indian Folklore II,* Peter J. Claus, J. Handoo, and D. P. Pattanayak, eds., pp. 1–51. Mysore: Central Institute of Indian Languages Press.

1989 Core Triangles in the Folk Epics of India. In *Oral Epics in India,* Stuart H. Blackburn, Peter J. Claus, Joyce B. Flueckiger, and Susan S. Wadley, eds., pp. 155–175. Berkeley: University of California Press.

Bhatt, K. Vadiraj

1974 *Pāḍḍanagalu* (in Kannada). Kinnigoli (S.K.): Yugapurusha Prakatanalaya.

Blackburn, Stuart H.

1981 Oral Performance: Narrative and Ritual in a Tamil Tradition. *Journal of American Folklore* 94:207–227.

1989 Patterns of Development for Indian Oral Epics. In *Oral Epics in India,* Stuart H. Blackburn, Peter J. Claus, Joyce B. Flueckiger, and Susan S. Wadley, eds., pp. 15–32. Berkeley: University of California Press.

Blackburn, Stuart H., Peter J. Claus, Joyce B. Flueckiger, and Susan S. Wadley, eds.

1989 *Oral Epics in India.* Berkeley: University of California Press.

Brückner, Heidrun

1987 Personal communication.

Burnell, A. C.

1894–98 The Devil Worship of the Tuluvas. *Indian Antiquary* 23, seq.

Claus, Peter J.

1973 Possession, Protection and Punishment as Attributes of the Deities in a South Indian Pantheon. *Man in India* 53:231–242.

1975 The Siri Myth and Ritual: A Mass Possession Ritual of South India. *Ethnology* 14:47–58.

1978a Oral Traditions, Royal Cults and Material for the Reconsideration of the Caste System in South India. *Journal of Indian Folkloristics* 1, 1:1–39.

1978b Terminological Aspects of Tulu Kinship: Kin Terms, Kin Sets and Kin Groups of the Matrilineal Castes. In *American Studies in the Anthropology of India.* Sylvia Vatuk, ed. Delhi: Manohar.

1978c Heroes and Heroines in the Conceptual Framework of Tulu Culture. *Journal of Indian Folkloristics* 1 (2):28–42.

1979a Spirit Possession and Mediumship from the Perspective of Tulu Oral Traditions. *Culture, Medicine and Psychiatry* 3:29–52.

1979b Mayndala: A Myth and Possession Cult of Tulunad. *Asian Folklore Studies* 38, 2:94–129.

1985 The New Folklore: Review and Comment. In *Studies in South India,* Pauline Kolenda and Robert Frykenberg, eds., pp. 195–216. Madras: New Era Publications.

1986a Playing *Cenne:* The Meanings of a Folk Game. In *Another Harmony: New Essays on the Folklore of India,* Stuart H. Blackburn and A. K. Ramanujan, eds., pp. 265–293. Berkeley: University of California Press.

1986b A Story of a *Pāḍḍana:* Comparison of a Ballad Sung and Spoken as Conversational Narrative. Paper presented at the panel, "Speech, Text and Performance: Discourse in South and Southeast Asia," Conference on South Asia, Madison, Wis. (November).

1987 Tulu Pāḍdanagaḷu: Jijnyase. In *Mangala Thimaru* (in Kannada), Erya Laxminarayana Alva, ed., pp. 62–65. Mangalore: Siddhartha Mudranaalya.

1988 *Future Research in Tulu Culture.* Academy Silver Jubilee Lecture 4. Manipal (India): Academy of General Education, Manipal.

1989 "Behind the Text: Performance and Ideology in a Tulu Oral Tradition. In *Oral Epics in India,* Stuart H. Blackburn, Peter J. Claus, Joyce B. Flueckiger, and Susan S. Wadley, eds., pp. 55–74. Berkeley: University of California Press.

Forthcoming "*Paramale Ballalavarana Pāḍdananu*" *Janapada Gangotri* (in Kannada).

Claus, Peter J., J. Handoo, and D. P. Pattanayak, eds.

1987 *Indian Folklore II.* Mysore: Central Institute of Indian Languages Press.

Narayana Rao, Velcheru

1986 Epics and Ideologies: Six Telugu Folk Epics. In *Another Harmony: New Essays on the Folklore of India,* Stuart Blackburn and A. K. Ramanujan, eds., pp. 131–164. Berkeley: University of California Press.

Rai, Viveka

1985 *Tulu Janapada Sāhitya.* Bangalore: Kannada Sahitya Parishath.

Ramanujan, A. K.

1986 Two Realms of Kannada Folklore. In *Another Harmony: New Essays on the Folklore of India,* Stuart H. Blackburn and A. K. Ramanujan, eds., pp. 41–75. Berkeley: University of California Press.

Someshwar, Amrit

1962 *Pāḍdanagalu.*

Part II

Genres: Identification and Identity

Joyce Burkhalter Flueckiger

6. Genre and Community in the Folklore System of Chhattisgarh

> When I said we sing songs at our weddings, I didn't mean that *we* sang them; I meant Oriya women.
>
> —Oriya Kolta-caste woman, age 40

> In our Chhattisgarh, we dance the *suā nāc,* celebrate *gaurā,* and our girls plant *bhojalī* [seedlings] and sing songs to the goddess.
>
> —Chhattisgarhi village headman, age 45

Modern Chhattisgarh is a region of eastern Madhya Pradesh, bordering Orissa, comprised of five districts (or six, if Bastar is included). The region consists of a large, rice-growing plain, watered by the Mahanadi River and its tributaries, and the surrounding hill regions. Historically, the geographic barrier of hills has helped to isolate Chhattisgarh from surrounding regions and is a contributing factor in the development of Chhattisgarh as a politically and historically defined region. The Chhattisgarhi dialect of eastern Hindi also contributes to a sense of linguistic region. The word *Chhattisgarh* literally means "thirty-six forts," and, although they are not all historically documented, folk histories are able to name all thirty-six. Chhattisgarh as a "land of thirty-six forts" continues to be an important indigenous characterization of the region.

But more important to the perception of Chhattisgarh as a region than geographic, historical, or linguistic factors are cultural attributes considered by the regional population to be unique to Chhattisgarh. These include dress, jewelry, social institutions such as ritualized friendships, local festivals, and both verbal and nonverbal folklore traditions. A major factor contributing to this Chhattisgarhi cultural ethos is the high percentage of its tribal (*ādivāsī*) population (15.6 percent in Raipur District in the 1961 census), which in the Chhattisgarhi plain has generally acquired caste attributes and has been integrated into the local caste hierarchy. However, the *ādivāsī* castes have retained many of their own folklore traditions. Both *ādivāsī* and non-*ādivāsī* inhabitants of Chhattisgarh identify these traditions, more than any others, as being uniquely Chhattisgarhi, whether or not they directly participate in them.

When I first arrived in the Chhattisgarh region of central India to begin folklore fieldwork in 1980, I frequently asked villagers for a general repertoire of songs they sang, festivals they celebrated, or stories they told. A core repertoire of genres gradually emerged from the varied responses. Further, this repertoire was repeatedly identified—to me, as an outsider—with the Chhattisgarh region itself through phrases such as, "in our Chhattisgarh," "here in Chhattisgarh," "we Chhattisgarhi people," "these are our Chhattisgarhi customs." A strong identification was made between particular folklore genres and the region. Through oral commentary and metafolklore, it became evident that this general identification between genre and community was one of the primary indigenous organizing features of the system of Chhattisgarhi folklore. In this essay, I use this indigenous organization as a basis from which to explore a variety of ways in which Chhattisgarh folklore genres interact as a system; the categories of that system; and how these may be shifting with the impact of increased literacy and the spread of modern communication technology.

Folklore Genres as a System

Over the last two decades, scholarly interest in the interaction of folklore texts and contexts has given emphasis to performance and social contexts of particular genres and texts, but less attention has been drawn to the larger folklore systems of which they are a part—to the other genres within the system that contribute to their contextual arena. There have, of course, been notable exceptions: Roger Abrahams's early essay "The Complex Relations of Simple Forms" (1969) drew attention to folklore as a system and the relationship between genres; Dan Ben-Amos contributed an important essay emphasizing the differences between analytic and ethnic genres and their respective interaction within a system (1976). Richard Bauman has been interested in intertextuality on several levels, both in the relationships among several narrative genres in Texas (1986) and in genres as they are imbedded within other genres in the tradition of the Icelandic legends of *Kraftaskald* (1988). He points to scientific taxonomies, with their mutually exclusive categories, as exerting strong influence upon folklore categorization, which has resulted in an emphasis on genre autonomy (1988). Gary Gossen has taken on perhaps the broadest study of a folklore system within a specific culture, that of the Chamula Indians in Mexico (1974). He elicited an indigenous taxonomy of folklore genres and searched for an organizing feature of that taxonomy, which he found to be principles of time and space. He then used this primary feature as a basis from which to analyze several specific genres.

Within South Asian folklore scholarship, Susan Wadley has surveyed the folklore genres of a single village community in north India and suggested that the terminology for these genres tends to correlate with some aspect of their performance context (1975); however, the survey article did not expand further upon the indigenous system of organization. In her more recent work on the north Indian oral epic tradition of Ḍholā-Mārū (this volume; 1989), she has studied intertextuality by identifying numerous song genres incorporated for performative and thematic reasons into Ḍholā epic performance. A. K. Ramanujan (1986) has found that the south Indian categories of *akam* and *puṟam* (domestic and public) are useful organizing principles for Kannada folklore, although the terms themselves are from the Tamil classical tradition and are not known by most folk performers and their audiences.

The fact that inhabitants of Chhattisgarh often placed their various folklore genres within the larger category and repertoire of "Chhattisgarhi folklore" suggested to me a fieldwork and analytic methodology that would attempt to place representative genres within a system, rather than to analyze a single verbal genre as an autonomous artistic form. There are numerous ways in which genres work together in systems (formally, thematically, and contextually), but I wanted to begin to uncover indigenous perceptions of the system, its categories, and underlying principles. What did members of the folklore community talk about when they mentioned certain genres? What did they consider important about their folklore? How did they relate different genres to each other?

Indigenous Associations Between Genre and Community

The basic concept of folklore genres identifying social groups or expressing their identity is not unique to this chapter or to the Chhattisgarh folklore region (see, for example, Dundes 1983; Claus 1989; Badone 1987). However, what is unique is the concept looking at the relationship between genre and community as an indigenous organizing principle of a particular folklore system. Chhattisgarhi performers and audiences were more articulate about this relationship, about performance contexts and what might be called the "exteriors" of their verbal folklore traditions, than they were about their "interior" formal and thematic features, although the latter contribute to the constellation of features identifying and distinguishing any given genre. A pattern of terminology, organization (or categorization), and commentary about publicly performed genres gradually emerged in my conversations with Chhattisgarhi villagers and townspeople.[1] First, as Wadley found in northern India, the names of many publicly performed genres are based upon some aspect of their performance context, such as the festival in which they are traditionally performed, the term for the performer, or the major instrument used in performance. For example, songs sung during the *gaurā* festival are called *gaurā gīt* ("songs of *gaurā*") and narrative songs sung to the accompaniment of a large bamboo flute are called *bā̃s gīt* ("songs of the bamboo flute"). If the name of the genre does not itself reflect the performance context, much of the commentary about such a genre will.

Second, Chhattisgarhi folklore genres are perceived as belonging to specific social groups within the larger folklore region. This principle of categorization is verbalized repeatedly in metafolklore and indigenous oral commentary. The following are typical statements made by informants in discussions about particular genres:

> This is a Chhattisgarhi story, our story.
>
> We don't sing that, but *ādivāsī* [tribal] castes do.
>
> We know what *homo* is, but only unmarried girls sing it.
>
> We don't want to dance the *suā nāc* in town anymore; we'll dance only in our own Gond neighborhood.
>
> You'll have to come to our village for the *ḍālkhāī* festival if you want to hear those songs; other villages don't celebrate it anymore.

Members of Chhattisgarhi folklore communities make few broad categorizations or associations between individual genres, but when they do, it is most often on the basis of this kind of social organization. The Chhattisgarhi and Hindi words for song (*gīt*) and even story (*kathā* or *kahānī*) are attached to the names of several genres, but their usage is fluid, and strict boundaries between these formal categories are not maintained. Nor are genres called *gīt* necessarily associated with each other. A verbal dueling game (*khel*) and a festival-song genre (*gīt*) both performed by unmarried girls will be more frequently associated with each other than will be song (*gīt*) genres performed by these girls and those of male performers or married women. The regional epic Candaini is performed in both a *gīt* style and a *nācā* (or dance-drama) style. Both, however, are simply called "Candainī," unless the speaker wants to differentiate a particular performance. Candainī *nācā* is rarely associated with other *nācā*s, and *nācā* troupes who perform Candainī rarely perform other *nācā*s.[2] Further, Candainī *gīt* would rarely, if ever, be classified with the *gīt* sung by unmarried girls in their formation of ritual friendships. Thus, formal categories such as "song," "dance," or "narrative" do not seem to be as meaningful to the indigenous folklore community as are the social categories to which various genres belong.

Analytic Levels of Community

Beginning with the indigenous conception of an association between genre and community, I have identified three analytic levels of folklore communities in Chhattisgarh. The first level, which I have called the *folklore group,* is the level most frequently associated with a specific genre in conversations with inhabitants of the Chhattisgarh region. This is the group of people that participates in the genre directly, through performance—they are the singers, players, or dancers, and, for some nonprofessional genres, also the audience. The folklore group may be identified by more than one social variable—such as caste, age, gender, and marital status. Membership in some groups, those dependent on caste and gender, is relatively stable, while membership dependent on marital status or age is shifting.[3] The stability of some folklore groups may be even more fleeting—such as the folklore group (often composed of residents from several villages) created through the performance of a professional performer for the duration of a single night's performance. These performers, like the *kathānī kuhā* storyteller of eastern Chhattisgarh or the Oriya *bāhak,* singer/dancer who performs on the western border of the region, have the power to manipulate an audience into a cohesive body, which afterward dissipates again into diverse groups based on gender, caste, and village.

While folklore groups are often identified through indigenous oral commentary and metafolklore, such commentary does not always reveal "nontraditional" or newly emerging performance settings and participants; close ethnographic observation is necessary to identify all folklore groups associated with a specific genre. Local commentary may consistently identify a particular genre with unmarried girls, for example, but, in actuality, men and married women may also be singing the same genre in nontraditional contexts (see the discussion of *ḍālkhāī* that follows).

The second level of community identified by genre is the *folklore community*. For analytic purposes, identification of this community is perhaps the most interesting of the three, although this level is rarely verbally distinguished from that of "region" by members of the community itself. I have adapted the term and its definition from Dell Hymes's "speech community" (1974:51). The folklore community is one that shares both the knowledge of a particular folklore repertoire and the rules by which members of the community communicate through those genres. All members of a given folklore community will know and agree upon who is traditionally permitted to perform particular genres and under what circumstances. I include the word "traditionally" here, because with the spread of mass-media communication and modern literacy, some of these rules are changing and their regulation is not always clear.

A third level of community identified by folklore genres is that of the *folklore region*, the largest social and geographic grouping and, as mentioned above, one that is self-consciously expressed by inhabitants of Chhattisgarh. The folklore region is characterized by a shared repertoire of performance genres, but not necessarily by identical rules of usage for those genres. A single region may be composed of numerous folklore communities, whose repertoire of genres is similar but whose usage of those genres may differ. In many ways, a folklore region is "imagined" in the same way that, according to Benedict Anderson (1983), the nation is an "imagined community," because the members of the community "will never know most of their fellow-members, meet them, or even hear of them, yet in the minds of each lives the image of their communion" (1983:15).

As mentioned earlier, a common regional repertoire of Chhattisgarh itself was not difficult to determine, as many of its genres are believed to be of tribal (particularly Gond) origin. Pan-Indian traditions, such as Ramlila performances of the *Rāmāyaṇa* epic or *bhajan* devotional songs, were rarely, if ever, mentioned as part of this repertoire. Although members of the folklore region have a sense of a bounded region, determining its actual borders is difficult. One can conceptualize, however, what I call "isogenres" (equivalent to the isogloss of linguistics) for each genre of the regional repertoire, which show the geographic spread of its performance. The repeated overlap of such isogenres begins to build up the rough outlines of the folklore region (see the map in Figure 1).

The process of delineating a folklore region is particularly interesting in the border areas between two regions, where some of the isogenres of each region overlap. Working in these areas helps to identify what it is that gives definition to particular social groups or regions (Barth 1969). I did much of my fieldwork on the border between what I have called the Chhattisgarh and Western Orissa folklore regions, on the political border between the modern provinces of Orissa and Madhya Pradesh. A new, smaller cultural area, called Phuljhar, is defined by the overlap between the two folklore regions. Residents in this area say that Phuljhar is that area in which both Chhattisgarhi and Oriya, and a mixture of the two called Lariya, are spoken—and, I would add, in which both Chhattisgarhi and Oriya folklore genres are performed.

While performers and audience members of various folklore communities in Chhattisgarh have a strong sense of the folklore region, they rarely differentiate between "region" and "community" as I have defined them. They assume that the folklore repertoire of their local community is spread

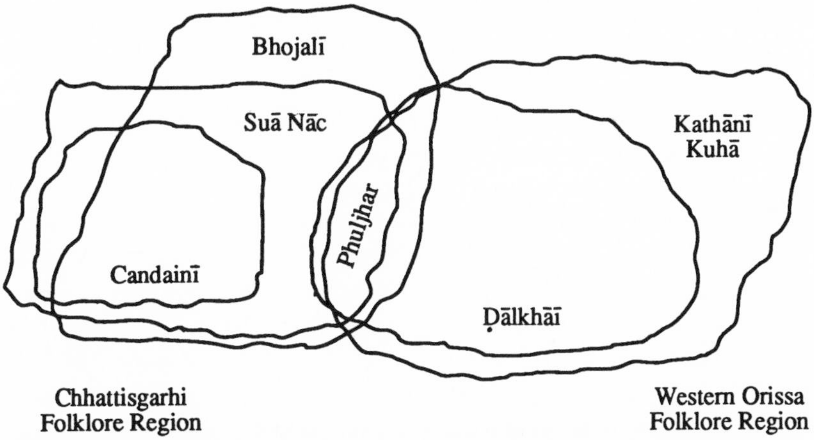

FIGURE 1. Isogenres indicating the Chhattisgarhi and Western Orissa folklore regions.

throughout the region and that its genres are regulated by similar rules of usage. Performers and audience members alike were usually surprised and sometimes disbelieving when I reported to them the degree of variation in rules of usage between various folklore communities I had visited in the course of my fieldwork.[4] The extent of variation between Chhattisgarhi folklore communities became apparent to me only because I lived in and traveled between villages and towns in both the border area of Phuljhar and the central plains around the city of Raipur.

An example of this variation can be found in the female festival and song tradition called *bhojalī*. The song tradition is identified as a single genre by its festival context as well as by repeated formal and thematic features. However, the tradition is performed primarily by married women in the central plains of Chhattisgarh, and only by unmarried girls in the hill areas of Phuljhar, only eighty-five miles away. In the plains area, *bhojalī* is identified as a goddess festival, associated with other goddess festivals in which possession of the participants by the goddess is a central feature; the festival songs revolve around the goddess and her worship. Ritual friendships, also called *bhojalī* may be formed at the end of the festival through the exchange of the immersed wheat seedlings, but this is optional. In the Phuljhar communities, within which only unmarried girls sing the *bhojalī gīt* and participate in the festival, ritual friendships are central to the festival and participation is limited to those who are going to form such friendships with each other. The two friends plant their seedlings together in one basket, and their growth is associated with the strength and life of the friendship. The seedlings are still worshipped as the goddess, but this is secondary to the formation of the friendship, as is confirmed by the absence of goddess possession. In this area, *bhojalī* is associated with other traditions belonging to unmarried girls, such as verbal dueling and other games, rather than with other goddess festivals, and the songs reflect the unique interests of this young, female folklore group.

Levels of Inclusivity in Folklore Communities

While there is often a single folklore group with which a genre is most frequently identified, there is rarely an exclusive one-to-one correspondence between a genre and a specific community. The nature and inclusivity of the community with which a particular genre is identified are dependent upon the identities of the speaker and listener and the wider context in which the statement is being made.

Early in my first year of fieldwork in Chhattisgarh, I was told by an upper-caste Oriya woman, "Of course, we sing songs at our [*hamar*] weddings." When I was invited to the wedding of her niece several months later, I took the six-hour bus trip back to her village in Phuljhar, attended the wedding, and waited to record wedding songs. After at least twelve hours of wedding rituals and celebrations, still not a single song had been sung, and I reminded my friend about her statement that they sing songs at their weddings. She laughed and said, "When I said we sing songs at our weddings, I didn't mean that *we* sang them; I meant Oriya women." Speaking to someone from outside of the folklore region, she was first identifying with the Oriya women of her community in general, which she typified by the traditions of *ādivāsī*-caste women (including their wedding songs), rather than by those of her own Kolta caste. This initially frustrating fieldwork experience revealed to me several dimensions of how genres help to identify, delineate, and give identity to communities at various levels.

Anthony Cohen (1982) has identified a similar variation of inclusivity in place-related identity in British rural communities as "ascending and descending 'levels.'"[5] In the Chhattisgarhi dialect, "we" or "our" can refer to communities of region, village, caste, age, or gender, and can be singular or plural; the word's inclusivity varies according to the context of the statement in which it occurs. The longer I lived in Chhattisgarh and the more familiar I became with the folklore system and its genres, the more specific informants became in identifying genres with smaller communities—the inclusivity of the communities they spoke about generally became more limited.

Male informants tend to associate themselves with more genres in which they do not directly participate as performers than do women. In general discussions, they often associate such genres with the wider communities of which they are a part, such as village or region, rather than with the more limited folklore group of performers only. Men often told me that "we sing the *suā nāc*," a genre performed exclusively by women. The "we" was used to refer to a broad community based upon decisive factors other than the gender of the performers. Women rarely identify themselves in this inclusive sense with male genres, and they spoke "on behalf of" the Chhattisgarh region less frequently than did their male relatives. This phenomenon may be partially attributed to the fact that women have less physical mobility than men, and thus they identify with more limited communities. It may also be due, in part, to the lower position that women occupy in the social hierarchy; those higher in the hierarchy (in caste, age, as well as gender hierarchies) more easily coopt the traditions of those below them in such discussions than vice versa.

Roger Abrahams has suggested that the manner in which folklore genres divide larger communities into smaller groups can indicate significant social categories within the larger community; the social and aesthetic organizations often reinforce each other (1969 [1976]: 194). This is exemplified in the Chhattisgarhi *bhojalī* and *javārā* goddess festivals and their associated verbal traditions, as they are performed in the plains of Chhattisgarh (see Figure 2). In both festivals, wheat or barley seedlings are planted, allowed to grow for ten days, and worshipped as the goddess; the presence of the goddess is affirmed through her possession of her devotees. The primary difference between the two festivals is that women sing the songs associated with the worship of the goddess in *bhojalī* and men sing *javārā* songs. This is the basis of the first distinction of groups indicated by both traditions and suggests a primary social division in the folklore community based upon gender. Gender distinction is characteristic of the Chhattisgarhi regional folklore system as a whole—while audiences may be mixed, there are no traditions (at least in the Hindu community) in which men and women perform together. In genres such as the dance-drama (*nācā*), female parts are played by males in female dress.

Next, a caste distinction among both *javārā* and *bhojalī* participants is indicated, although it is less accentuated in the male *javārā* tradition than in the female *bhojalī* tradition. Among female performers of *bhojalī*, there are no high- or even middle-caste women; they say they are afraid of becoming possessed by the goddess if they participate in the festival at any level, even simply as observers. Whether or not possession is present, there are few female traditions in Chhattisgarh in which women of different caste levels perform together. In the *javārā* tradition, men of all caste levels may participate in some way, as audience, singers, and/or devotees of the goddess. Caste distinction, as it is observed through the organization of the folklore system is typically less pronounced among men than women; they also perform together in other folklore genres, such as the *nācā* dance-dramas and *bhajan* (devotional) singing groups.

The social groups identified by the *bhojalī-javārā* traditions further suggest that the marital status of a male is not as significant as that of a female. Males are rarely segregated by their marital status for participation in most genres; widowers are not excluded from participation and unmarried boys have few unique public-performance genres: they generally participate with the married men in such performances. The female *bhojalī*

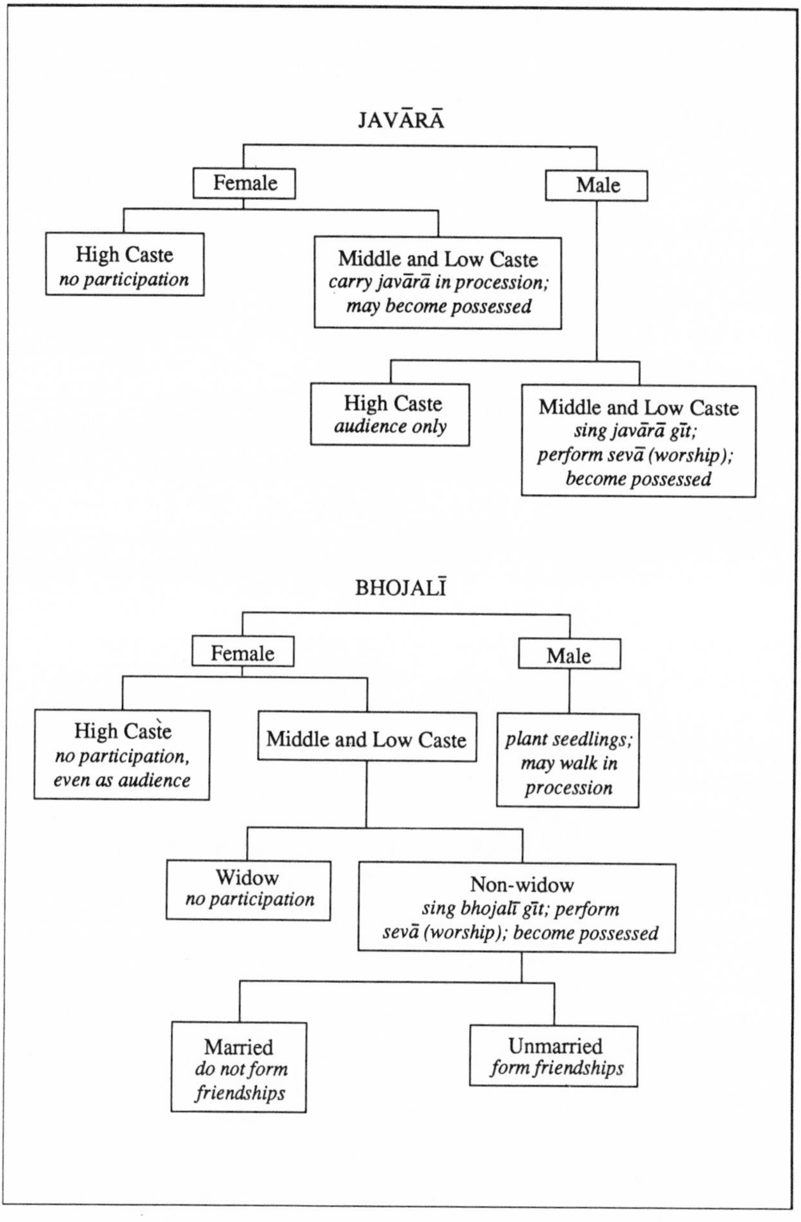

FIGURE 2. Social divisions indicated by the *javārā* and *bhojalī* festival traditions.

tradition, on the other hand, differentiates between categories of widow and non-widow as well as married and unmarried. In the Phuljhar area bordering Orissa, the unmarried category is given even more prominence in the *bhojalī* tradition; *only* unmarried girls sing the *bhojalī* songs. The fact that, in this part of Chhattisgarh, there are several publicly performed genres exclusively for unmarried girls (not true of the central plains area) suggests that this social category is given more recognition in Phuljhar, and possibly the rest of the western Orissa folklore region, than it is in the plains of Chhattisgarh.

Shifting Boundaries of Genre and Community

Increasing literacy, the spread and popularity of mass-media communication, and changing social institutions are affecting traditional associations between many folklore genres and their communities. Songs that used to be sung and heard primarily by women may now be heard blasting loudly over All India Radio's folklore programming, in village tea stalls, or at bus-stand ticket counters. In many villages, professional dance-drama troupes and storytellers are having to compete with what are called "video halls" (any kind of structure to which admittance is charged to view a Hindi film shown with a video machine, usually with two to three showings a day). One result of an increasing literacy rate has been the development of a perception of what it means to "act literate," action which sometimes precludes participation in certain performances and festivals. A school education has also resulted in a decreased interest in certain performance genres and a reemergence or realignment of other genres.

The Oriya festival tradition of *ḍālkhāī*, celebrated in the Chhattisgarh border area of Phuljhar, is one such tradition in transition. It is a festival of reversal traditionally associated with unmarried *ādivāsī* girls, often called a "*holī* for unmarried girls."[6] The girls spend the day singing and dancing outside of their village, during which time they may accost any passersby, mostly men, by surrounding them and trying to extort money from them. Today, the festival's most frequently mentioned characteristic is the songs the girls sing, called "*burā gīt*" (bad songs). Most of the songs are sexually suggestive, often centering on the Radha-Krishna theme (although in actuality they seem to an observer outside of the folklore system to be no more suggestive than several other traditions sung by this same folklore group).

Recently, the celebration of the festival has been discontinued in the Phuljhar area except for in one village.[7] This demise has occurred primarily at the instigation of the village male leaders, who feel that "our educated girls shouldn't be singing these kinds of songs." Many of the would-be participants are not themselves literate, but the village leaders are, and they have taken it upon themselves to insure that the girls of their villages "act literate." Thus increasing literacy seems to have had an indirect detrimental effect for the *festival* setting for the songs. However, the *ḍālkhāī* song tradition is alive and well outside of the festival setting, and as the performance context has shifted, so too has the identity of the community with which the genre is associated. Men and women of all castes and ages have begun singing *ḍālkhāī gīt*. The only explicit performance restriction is that they be sung outside the village, usually between groups of friends of the same or opposite sex as they are walking between their village and a destination such as the local bazaar or working in the fields (not in front of the foreign female fieldworker's tape recorder).

Sitting in a village courtyard, I once asked the women whom I was visiting if they could sing some *ḍālkhāī gīt* for me, since it was difficult to record them as they are sung outside the village or in the festival context in the one village in which it is still performed. Several women began singing short segments of *ḍālkhāī gīt* when a female member of the village headman's house came across the street to tell them that they should not be singing these songs in the village. After that, one of the women went into her house and brought out a small pamphlet of printed *ḍālkhāī gīt* and told me that these would be better for my purposes, since they were already written out. She tried to sing from the pamphlet, but had difficulty fitting the words into the *ḍālkhāī* tune she knew.

It may be that *ḍālkhāī gīt* gained their reputation for vulgarity, as "*burā gīt,*" when the identity of their folklore group changed, when they began to be sung outside the bounds of the festival, no longer restricted by ritual space and time, or by gender, caste, and age group. In any case, the genre is now identified more frequently with the Phuljhar folklore community of eastern Chhattisgarh, rather than with the folklore group of unmarried Oriya girls. It is called a "Phuljhar song," or an "Oriya song," more often than it is a "*holī* song for unmarried girls."

A second example of shifting boundaries and identification of social groups with a particular folklore genre is that of the *suā nāc*. *Suā nāc* literally means "parrot dance," and is a harvest dance and song tradition. The tradition has undergone numerous changes in performance context during the years in which I have done fieldwork in Chhattisgarh, beginning in 1980, and is an example of the ascending and descending levels of identification with a single genre. Traditionally, *ādivāsī* women dance around an image of a parrot in the courtyards of rural landowners; the eldest female householder gives donations of grain to the dancers in exchange for the latter's auspicious blessings to the household. As more and more *ādivāsī*-caste members moved into urban areas to work as daily laborers, *suā* dancers also began to dance in front of shops, and the shopkeepers gave them cash donations. At some level, as dancers/singers, as patrons, or as village-wide/urban-neighborhood audiences, the *suā nāc* has involved most segments of Chhattisgarhi society. As a public performance genre, the tradition serves to establish a communicative channel between high-caste patrons and lower-caste, *ādivāsī* dancers, between whom there is not generally such communication, particularly folklore communication. Because of the many levels of involvement in the tradition, as well as its wide geographic spread throughout the region, the *suā nāc* is an important genre in helping to define the Chhattisgarh folklore region.

The *suā nāc* is often identified by male informants with the region first, as "Chhattisgarhi," and only later as a female or *ādivāsī* tradition. Upper-caste women, on the other hand, most often identified it as an "*ādivāsī*" dance. Meanwhile, *ādivāsī* women were even more specific as to the nature of the social group to which the dance belonged—according to the age of the participants, their village or neighborhood, or the nature of their vow to the goddess the previous year for whose fulfillment the *suā nāc* is raising money. As a public dance tradition, the emphasis of the *suā nāc* is on the visual images of the tradition—the parrot, the grain, the dance—which reinforce a public image of women as fertile, auspicious, and life-giving, rather than on the verbal messages.

The song tradition of the *suā nāc* is also sung outside of the dance, however, by a wider group of low-caste women than is permitted to participate in the public dance. They sing these songs to other women of their own social, economic, and caste group, between whom a communicative channel is already present. In this context, the focus shifts to the verbal message of the text, which often differs significantly from the auspicious iconographic one of the dance; it gives voice to the private suffering to which a woman is born.

Increased literacy, changing social conditions, and mass-media technology (particularly radio) have all made an impact on the genre of *suā nāc* and on the communities with which it is identified. The few girls from *ādivāsī* castes who are "high-school pass" do not feel it is appropriate to dance in public the way the *suā nāc* troupes do. Further, because there was not a traditional economic relationship between dancers and shopkeepers in the urban areas, many other women, particularly the older ones, no longer want to dance in that context. I was told by several Gond women in the town of Dhamtari that "People think we'll dance, but why should we?" Neither they or the younger girls, however, have given up the songs and dance in their own neighborhoods.

One purpose of the *suā nāc* is for the dancers to raise money for the Gond *gaurā* festival, celebrating the wedding of Śiva and Pārvatī. (The same Chhattisgarhi word, *jhūpnā,* is used for both the dance movement of the *suā nāc* and that induced in festival participants by goddess possession.) In one Gond urban neighborhood, the women decided not to dance the *suā nāc* in town, but they did dance in an innovative setting around the *gaurā* festival images of Śiva and Pārvatī, before they were to be taken to be immersed in the town tank. The men of this neighborhood watched the women dance the *suā nāc* at the *gaurā* festival and a few even joined in singing some of the verses, a participation which the women did not appreciate. These days, such *ādivāsī*-caste women most often talk about the *suā nāc* as a Gond female tradition, rather than as a Chhattisgarhi one.

Because of its popularity throughout Chhattisgarh and the various levels of identification with the *suā nāc,* it is one of the genres frequently performed and recorded for the folklore programming of Akashvani (All India Radio). When I first moved to the town of Dhamtari and asked the Gond women who lived across the road from me when they began to sing and dance the *suā nāc* in the fall, several men listening to our conversation told me that I should turn on my radio on Wednesday afternoons; they suggested that is where I would hear the best singing, and I could just tape it directly from there. So, while live performances, particularly in the urban areas, may be becoming more private or limited, recorded, broadcast performances are available to all, regardless of caste or gender. The community associated with the genre is at the same time becoming more exclusive and more inclusive.

Pervasiveness of the radio in both urban and rural settings in Chhattisgarh, as well as the growing influence of modern cinema (in movie theaters as well as video halls) has affected another popular performance genre as well—that of Candainī, the regional oral epic of Chhattisgarh. I typify it as a "regional epic" because it is most frequently identified, by male and female members of the folklore community, with the folklore region of

Chhattisgarh, rather than with a single caste or age group; they often call the epic "our story" or a "Chhattisgarhi story." This broad level of identification with the epic may be relatively recent. The hero and heroine are from the local cowherding Rāūt caste, and the epic itself seems to have originated within this caste. It is now performed, however, by several other castes, including the Satnāmīs, a sect whose members converted from the untouchable Chamār leatherworking caste in the 1800s. It is difficult to determine the ways in which the epic story line and characters have changed since the Satnāmīs have become the primary performers of the epic, since we have few texts available to us from earlier Rāūt performances. Verrier Elwin recorded and translated parts of the epic more than forty years ago (1946), several episodes of which I heard performed in 1980; the contents of the episodes were strikingly similar. But several Rāūt audience members at one Satnamī performance told me that only Satnami singers give the major Chamar character as much voice in the epic as was given in the performance we were attending.

The performance style of Candainī has changed markedly as its performance community has grown and shifted. Professional and semiprofessional traditional Rāūt singers used to sing the epic with the support of a second human voice, but without instrumental accompaniment; such singers are now difficult to locate. When the Satnāmīs began to sing Candainī *gīt* (song) professionally and nonprofessionally, they added instrumental accompaniment—minimally, a tabla and harmonium—retaining the style of interactive singing with a companion.

Most recently, Candainī has begun to be performed in the *nācā* style. According to Rāūt and Satnāmī *nācā* performers, this dance/drama performance style developed approximately twenty years ago and is heavily influenced by the song and dance of modern Hindi cinema. The actors are in costume, and they speak in dialogue, sing, and dance. Musicians sit on the sidelines, accompanying the actors' songs or intermittently providing sung narration in the *gīt* style. *Nācā* audiences are unrestricted by age, caste, or sex and are drawn from entire villages or urban neighborhoods. The inclusivity of the audience contributes to the sense that Candainī is a regional epic. The *nācā* has become the performance style of choice in Chhattisgarh, almost exclusively for public, professional performances, as well as that most frequently broadcast over the radio. With a move toward broader, multicaste, urban and rural audiences, the language of performance (as well as musical style) has shifted from local variants of Chhattisgarhi toward a more standardized Chhattisgarhi approximating Hindi.

Conclusion

While the relationship between genre and community is a strong indigenous organizing principle of the Chhattisgarhi folklore system, the relationship has not been a static one, as evidenced in the *suā nāc*, *ḍālkhāī*, and Candainī traditions discussed above. Boundaries between communities and genres continue to shift and adapt with the introduction of new contextual features, such as a growing literacy rate, burgeoning communicative and mass-media technology, and changing economic and social relationships between patrons, performers, and audiences. A wider exposure to pan-Indian and regional traditions outside of Chhattisgarh has resulted in an increased identification of specific genres with the folklore region rather than with smaller folklore groups within the region. At the same time, traditions such as the *suā nāc* are being claimed by the folklore region, however, on another level, the folklore groups associated with them are becoming more self-restricted. The Gond women dancing the *suā nāc* in urban neighborhoods are aware at some level that the genre gives identity to their community and reflects and gives voice to their interests as women. As traditional settings for the dance are eroding in the towns and cities, they have discovered innovative contexts in which to maintain the tradition in order also to maintain their community.

The awareness of the power of genres to identify and maintain community is found on numerous levels throughout Chhattisgarh. In a discussion with a rather young village headman (age forty-five), who had come to his position through the recent acquisition of land rather than through heredity, he talked specifically about the role he thought folklore could play in establishing a sense of village identity and in improving village morale. He told me that he had introduced the *gaurā* festival to his village only seven to eight years earlier. Many of the daughters-in-law marrying into his village come from villages in which *gaurā* is a vibrant tradition, but for some reason it had not been celebrated in this village. So, the headman asked the women if they would be willing to introduce *gaurā* to their village of marriage. He thought this festival specifically would increase village cohesion because of the numerous folklore groups it could involve and the large public procession to the village tank which ends the festival. After several years of *gaurā* celebration in the village, the headman was satisfied with the results it had brought and was thinking of other new villagewide traditions which he could sponsor and "cause to be introduced" to the village.

Modern education and an effort by Chhattisgarhi literati to place Chhattisgarhi folklore within the broader schema of pan-Indian folklore have introduced another categorizing principle to the Chhattisgarhi folklore system, alongside that of genre and community. This is one based on formal distinctions, and its categories are *gīt, kahānī/kathā,* and *nāṭak/nācā* (song, story, and drama). All India Radio's folklore programming also relies on these distinctions. Although the terms *gīt* and *kahānī* are currently used by members of Chhattisgarh's folklore communities, they are not distinguishing categories of genres. It remains to be seen whether or not this system of formal genres will be adapted more fully, alongside of or replacing that of genre and community, by Chhattisgarhi performers and audiences in their oral commentary and metafolklore.

Recognizing indigenous genres and categories, their stability and flexibility, a scholar from outside a particular folklore system can begin to explore the interior of folklore texts in ways that are consistent with indigenous perceptions and understandings. In the folklore region of Chhattisgarh, one indigenous organizing feature of the folklore system is the identification of genres with communities. It is possible, however, that some of the changes restructuring these traditional associations may begin to affect the ways in which members of the folklore communities and the folklore region of Chhattisgarh perceive and structure their folklore system; and this restructuring may well affect the meanings of various Chhattisgarhi folklore traditions for those who perform them.

Notes

1. In my study of Chhattisgarhi folklore, I have worked primarily with publicly performed genres (these are also the genres that folklore community members tend to talk about most), rather than what I call "private genres," such as jokes, proverbs, and certain styles of folklore performance.

2. This phenomenon is not necessarily typical of epic traditions throughout India. Karine Schomer (personal communication, 1982) reports that singers of the Ālhā epic in north India do not consider the dramatic (*nauṭankī*) versions of the epic story to be "Alha"; although the Alha story is borrowed, the performance is still *nauṭankī*.

3. Dundes finds that many studies of identity and ethnicity fail to distinguish between such permanent and temporary identities (1983).

4. Fredrik Barth (1969) finds that this lack of awareness of cultural variation between similar communities is typical of most ethnic groups, including the Pathans with whom he worked.

5. Ellen Badone (1987) has applied Cohen's concept of ascending and descending levels to her data on geographic social groupings in Brittany. She argues

that "identity needs to be conceptualized in terms of a series of nested local, regional and national levels" (1987:186).

6. *Holī* is a festival of reversal celebrated in the spring by the larger Hindu community. The festival marks the end of the old year and the beginning of a new one. There is a general mood of license and reversals on that day, a relaxation of cultural norms, which is illustrated most vividly by the custom of "playing *holī*," spraying colored water at each other. Traditional hierarchical standards are broken: women may spray men, low-caste persons spray members of higher castes, and children may spray adults.

7. This village now takes a certain pride in its identity as the last village in the area in which the festival is still celebrated. It remains to be seen, however, how long a sufficient number of participants for the festival can be recruited, since the girls themselves are now aware that elsewhere "proper" girls are no longer participating. The number of participants has dwindled considerably over the last few years.

References

Abrahams, Roger

1969 Complex Relation of Simple Forms. *Genre* 2/2 (June):104–128. Reprinted in *Folklore Genres,* Dan Ben-Amos, ed., pp. 193–214. Austin: University of Texas Press, 1976.

Anderson, Benedict

1983 *Imagined Communities: Reflections on the Origin and Spread of Nationalism.* London: Verso.

Badone, Ellen

1987 Ethnicity, Folklore, and Local Identity in Rural Brittany. *Journal of American Folklore* 100:161–190.

Barth, Fredrik, ed.

1969 Introduction. *Ethnic Groups and Boundaries: The Social Organization of Culture Difference,* pp. 9–38. Boston: Little, Brown & Co.

Bauman, Richard

1971 Differential Identity and the Social Base of Folklore. *Journal of American Folklore* 85:31–41.

1977 *Verbal Art as Performance.* Rowley, Mass.: Newbury House.

1986 *Story, Performance, and Event: Contextual Studies of Oral Narrative.* Cambridge: Cambridge University Press.

1988 Contextualization, Tradition, and the Dialogue of Genres: Icelandic Legends of *Kraftaskald.* Lecture given at the University of Wisconsin, Madison.

Ben-Amos, Dan

1976 Analytic Categories and Ethnic Genres. In *Folklore Genres,* Dan Ben-Amos, ed., pp. 215–242. Austin: University of Texas Press.

Claus, Peter J.

1989 Behind the Text: Performance and Ideology in a Tulu Oral Tradition. In *Oral Epics in India,* Stuart H. Blackburn, Peter J. Claus, Joyce B.

Flueckiger, and Susan S. Wadley, eds., pp. 55–74. Berkeley: University of California Press.

Cohen, Anthony P.
1982 Belonging: The Experience of Culture. In *Belonging, Identity and Social Organization in British Rural Cultures,* Anthony P. Cohen, ed. pp. 1–18. Manchester: Manchester University Press.

Dundes, Alan
1983 Defining Identity through Folklore. In *Identity: Personal and Sociocultural,* Anita Jacobson-Widding, ed., pp. 235–240. Uppsala: Acta Universitatis Upsaliensis.

Elwin, Verrier
1946 *Folk Songs of Chhattisgarh.* Madras: Oxford University Press.

Flueckiger, Joyce Burkhalter
1987 Land of Wealth, Land of Famine: The *Suā Nāc* (Parrot Dance) of Central India. *Journal of American Folklore* 100:39–57.
1988 "He Should Have Worn a *Sari*:" A "Failed" Performance of a Central Indian Oral Epic. *The Drama Review* 116:159–69.
1989 Caste and Regional Variants of an Epic Tradition: The Lorik-Canda Epic. In *Oral Epics in India,* Stuart H. Blackburn, Peter J. Claus, Joyce B. Flueckiger, and Susan S. Wadley, eds., pp. 33–54. Berkeley: University of California Press.

Gossen, Gary
1974 *Chamulas in the World of the Sun.* Cambridge, Mass.: Harvard University Press.

Hymes, Dell
1974 Toward Ethnographies of Communication. In *Foundations in Sociolinguistics,* Dell Hymes, ed., pp. 3–86. Philadelphia: University of Pennsylvania Press.

Ramanujan, A. K.
1986 Two Realms of Kannada Folklore. In *Another Harmony: New Essays on the Folklore of India,* Stuart H. Blackburn and A. K. Ramanujan, eds., pp. 41–75. Berkeley: University of California Press.

Wadley, Susan
1975 Folk Literature in Karimpur. *Journal of South Asian Literature* 11:7–17.
1989 Choosing a Path: Performance Strategies in a North Indian Epic *Ḍholā.* In *Oral Epics in India,* Stuart Blackburn, Peter J. Claus, Joyce Flueckiger, and Susan S. Wadley, eds., pp. 75–101. Berkeley: University of California Press.

Susan S. Wadley

7. Why Does Ram Swarup Sing? Song and Speech in the North Indian Epic Ḍholā

This chapter arises out of a question that has been puzzling me for several years. The north Indian epic Ḍholā performed for me by a well-known artist, Ram Swarup, while said to be sung, is in fact filled with prose. Much of it is sung, but much of it is also narrated in prose. The puzzle is: Why the shifts? What is the value to singing? And what is the value to prose narrative?

In an earlier work (Wadley, 1989), I have demonstrated how music, as intertwined with speech (song or prose) structures the epic. Scenes, and episodes within scenes, are demarcated by verbal strategies that involve the use or nonuse of music—melody, instruments, and voice timbre. Clearly this musical structuring is one aspect of the shifting from prose to song. But the puzzle remained. Why shift to prose? Or better yet, why sing?

Ram Swarup gave part of the answer one day when I asked him how the epic should be properly performed. He is most vehement in his criticism of singers who cannot tell the story. He claims that beginning singers learn the various songs and then think that they can sing Ḍholā. But, he says, "From where will they get the story?" The metaphor that he used in describing proper singing is that of a road—you must choose the right road to get to the end of the journey. He expanded this basic metaphor by stressing that the sequencing is critical: you must not move from town A to C to B. Another time he commented, "Some singers are like this—they first reach Aligarh, then come back to Delhi, and again go back to Aligarh. They don't know where to sing each part of the story." Moreover, he adds, "It is impossible for someone to reach Delhi directly and not go through the middle towns." Hence the story must be told clearly and in proper order. It is not merely a collection of songs. Prose narrative obviously has something to do with this telling, although other Indian epics, such as Ālhā (Schomer, 1989), do tell their stories with few prose sections.

The hint here is that prose language is better, or at least better for giving some kinds of messages. The answer to my puzzle, then, must lie in the different kinds of speech acts that prose narration and song represent.

Ḍholā is performed in western Uttar Pradesh as a series of songs and chants tied together by a narrative thread. The region where this version is sung appears to encompass the districts south of Delhi, as far west as Agra and Bharatpur in Rajasthan and as far east as Fategarh and Bidaun. Agra and Mainpuri Districts mark its southern borders. In this region, Ḍholā is a named genre comparable to other song genres, connoting both a melody and a topic. The melody is also called *ḍholā* and the topic is any of the episodes of the larger epic. I am defining this regional version based on similarity in both story and performance style. Other regional variants of the Ḍholā tradition differ in both story and performance.

This variant is framed by an invocation to the gods and cannot begin without the singer's seeking the blessings of the goddess. But unlike some other Indian oral epics that are clearly mythological and tied to ritual (e.g., Gūgā, Pābūjī, Devanārayaṇ, Kanyaka), Ḍholā is performed primarily for the human audience, not the divine one. This difference in audience is critical because it allows the performer more freedom to innovate. He is not bound to a fixed text, as in Pābūjī, nor is there an audience of gods watching for errors in performance.

Ḍholā is a public performance genre (Blackburn and Ramanujan 1986) and is sung for entertainment. It is performed at district fairs, festivals, weddings, and other events demanding celebration and entertainment. It takes place on verandas, in rest houses, or in tents. The performers are all men, usually of middle castes, although I know of Untouchable and Muslim performers. The audiences are mostly men, with wealthy landowners as patrons. Ḍholā can be sung solo, with a partner, or with a troupe as a dance drama or folk opera. As a solo performance, it requires musical accompaniment, usually a *cikāṛā* (bowed two-string instrument), *ḍholak* (two-headed drum), and *cimṭā* (metal tongs). Often the solo singer plays the *cikāṛā*. When performed by a troupe, a harmonium replaces the *cikāṛā* and additional instruments may be added.

The epic is performed in episodes, never as a whole, with each night's performance usually being one episode. One famous singer from Mainpuri District said that there were 52 parts (*laṛāī*) to Ḍholā, but could name only 20.[1] If a long night is desired, two episodes are linked together. Each episode is further divided into parts containing several scenes. Scenes are marked performatively by heightened musical tension near the conclusion and by the singer then taking a short break.

This regional variant is a three-generational epic, primarily the story of Raja Nal, the son of King Pratham of Navargarh and his wife Manjha. Born in a forest, with the gods and goddesses in attendance, Raja Nal has a number of grand adventures. He has successive marriages, to Motini (the daughter of a demon) and Damiyanti (potential wife of Indra, tying Ḍholā to the *Mahābhārata*). Raja Nal fights one war with Phul Singh Panjabi and another with the King of Bengal. He eventually has a son Ḍholā, for whom the epic is named.

The history of this variant is obscure. But it is believed to be linked to the poems known as *Ḍholā-mārū,* written by medieval Jain poets. These poems tell of the marriage, separation, and ultimate reunion of Ḍholā, son of Raja Nal of Navargarh, and Maru, daughter of the Raja of Pingal/Pugal. This version appears in both English- and Hindi-language comic books and on the stage in urban centers such as Delhi and Jaipur.

Another variant, found in Punjab, modern Rajasthan, and Chhattisgarh, tells of the separation and reunion of Ḍholā and Maru, and contains introductory material about Raja Nal. Some versions use parts of the Nal-Damiyanti story derived from the *Mahābhārata* as background to the births of Ḍholā and Maru. The history of the association of Nal-Ḍholā and Nal-Damiyanti remains clouded, but some speculation is possible. Kusalalabh, a Jain poet who authored a version of *Ḍholā-mārū* in the sixteenth century in Rajasthan, notes in his prologue that Ḍholā's father's name is Nal and alludes to the Nal-Damiyanti story from the *Mahābhārata* (Williams 1976 : 68). Temple also remarks on this coincidence in *Legends of the Punjab* (1963). Further, in modern Rajasthan, *Ḍholā-mārū* and *Nal-Damiyanti* both form parts of the repertoires of folk opera troupes (*khyāl*). At some point, the apparent chance similarity in names became firmer. This is not surprising, for as Temple himself aptly stated in 1885: "The tendency of bards is to make their stories run in cycles. They love to connect all their heroes in some way or other" (1963 : ix). In western Uttar Pradesh, this chance similarity was expanded even further and the three-generational epic of Raja Pratham, his son Raja Nal, and his grandson Ḍholā developed. This variant exists primarily in the oral traditions of the area, although some locally printed versions do exist, including several titled *Nal*

Purāṇa, indicating that the western Uttar Pradesh variant is in fact much more the story of Nal than of Ḍhola. Recently, tape cassettes of Ḍholā have also been produced in Mainpuri District.

This discussion is based on the solo song performances of Ram Swarup in Mainpuri District, Uttar Pradesh. Ram Swarup left home in his early teens to learn Ḍholā and sang with various gurus for seven years, switching gurus as he found yet other styles being sung elsewhere. He took part in Ḍholā competitions in the 1950s and 1960s, attending some famous ones in Agra and Aligarh Districts. For about ten years, he headed a troupe of performers and set up his tent at district fairs, weddings, and other celebrations. He traveled as far as Delhi and Kanpur to perform. Finally, the demands of his family and land led him back to his village, where he works today as a farmer but sings Ḍholā frequently during the marriage season and travels throughout the district.

Ram Swarup usually performs at night on the veranda of his sponsor's house. Light is provided by a bulb hot-wired to a lamp pole or by kerosene lanterns. He is joined by Rajju, a tailor by caste, who plays the *ḍholak,* and Tilan, a Brahman by caste, who plays the *cimṭā.* Ram Swarup himself plays a *cikāṛā* as he sings.

I have transcribed here a portion of one episode of Ram Swarup's performance of "Motini's Wedding," one of the named chapters of Ḍholā. I have attempted to transcribe a performance score. All verse sections are sung or chanted; prose sections approximate ordinary speech. Each of the segments was later identified by the singer, and these identifications of prose type, chant, or song are indicated in the margin: *vārtā,* prose explanation; *dohā,* chanted couplet; *ḍholā,* sung in dominant *ḍholā* melody; *ḍholā dhār,* a stream of *ḍholā; ḍholā kā dohā,* a couplet song to the *ḍholā* melody.

In addition to designating the verbal aspects of this performance, I have indicated musical accompaniment, which plays a crucial role in structuring this performance. The *cikāṛā* is denoted in this score by a "(" for accent and "()" when accompanying a complete line, either sung or spoken, and by "n" when played as a solo interlude between lines of the text. The number (n) indicates the approximate number of beats, usually four, eight, or sixteen, of the musical interlude. The *ḍholak* (drum) is designated by a "*" for accents. When drumming accompanies sung or spoken lines, it is included in the "()" that marks the *cikāṛā,* for example, "(*)." The *cimṭā* is shown by "#" for accents and, like the drum, in "()" when used throughout a line with the *cikāṛā* for example, "(#)." Instrumental line accompaniments are indicated at the beginning of a line; accents are included between the lines of a text where they were played. Thus all three instruments together accompanying a line are denoted as "(*#)" before the text is given. An interlude marked "(8*#)" indicates an 8-beat line played on the *cikāṛā* with *ḍholak* and *cimṭā* accompaniment.

The episode from which excerpts are given begins when Raj Nal, the hero, goes to seek the sixteenth shell (*got*) used in a gambling game. His foster grandfather has been jailed for not bringing the full complement of sixteen shells to Raja Pratham who is actually Nal's true father. The sixteenth shell is with Motini, daughter of a demon, who will become Nal's first wife. The episode concludes with Nal's opening the hidden gate of the fort of the demon, where he will later meet and marry Motini.

1. *dohā* Sitting there was Behmata
Appearing to be 100 years old,
There at the ocean shore,
He found the old woman. (*#)

2. *vārtā* When he met Behmata, she was twisting the ropes of marriage [*juri*][2] and tossing them into the ocean. Some cross, some sink in the middle, some sink near the far shore, some sink immediately. *#

(4*#)

3. *dohā* When he saw the condition of the mother,
Raja Nal asked,
Oh mother, listen to me,
Oh what do you need? (*#)

4. *vārtā* He said to the old woman,

5. *ḍholā* Oh my mother, was there a quarrel between mother-in-law and daughter-in-law or brother?
(*#)

(8*#)

(*#) Oh my mother, was there a quarrel between mother-in-law and daughter-in-law?

(*#) Oh has your old man beaten you?
(*#) Oh why are you wasting your whole life sitting here by the ocean?

(6*#)

6. *vārtā* (*#) What does Behmata say?

(8*#)

7. *ḍholā* (*#) Oh son, there is neither fight between mother-in-law and daughter-in-law,
(*#) Nor has my husband beaten me.

(8*#)

(*#) Oh Karta[3] has sent me out of the country,
(*#) Oh son, I am making *juri* on the ocean shore,
(*#) Oh calf, I am giving the *juri*.

(8*#)

(*#) Oh son, some for the whole life, some for one half.
(*#) After twisting and twisting, I toss in the ocean.
(*#) My son, the old woman is speaking these words while working,
(*#) Sitting here, I am making the *juri*, my son.

(4*#)

8. *vārtā* (*#) Nal said, "What is *juri*?"
(*#) She said, "Son, for whom I twist *juri*, only he gets married, and for whom I do not make *juri*, he can put on any disguise, he can put on white powder, but there is no chance. [LAUGHTER]

(8*#)

9. *ḍholā* (*#) Now Nal said to the old lady,
(*#) Put a *juri* for me in the ocean,

(*#) Put a *juri* for me in the ocean,
(*#) In this way, mother, make a marriage for me.

(8*#)

10. *vārtā* (*#) So what does Behmata say?

(2*#)

11. *ḍholā kā dohā*
(*#) Oh my son, in which village do you live?
(*#) Who is your father, who is your mother?

12. *vārtā* (*#) What does Raja Nal say?

13. *ḍholā* (*#) Oh mother, my village is Dakshinpur
(*#) My name is Raja Nal.
(*#) I belong to the trader [*banyā*] caste.
(*#) In my house salt, pepper, and coriander are sold.

(8*#)

14. *vārtā* (*#) Then the old woman said, "Son, I don't have marriages for traders."

[LAUGHTER]

(8*#)

15. *ḍholā* (*#) And Nal became like a flame of fire,
(*#) If you will not make a *juri* for me, Mother,
(*#) I shall sever your head from your body,
(*#) Old woman, I shall leave you without life here at the ocean edge
(*#) Oh I shall force you to make my marriage.

16. *vārtā* He said, "You cannot save yourself without doing my marriage."

OH BROTHER YOU ARE SAYING SUCH WILD THINGS!

"Yes, you cannot be saved." OH SON
So the old woman said, "Oh my son, you are not a trader."
He said, "Mother, I am really telling you the truth. [LAUGHTER] Lakshmi Seth is my mother's father, Gopichand and Manekchand are both my (UNCLE) uncles. They are waiting in their anchored ship. I am truly a trader. There are hundreds of shops in my house."*

17. *dohā* Now Nal does not obey her.*
Oh he said to the old woman,
"Oh my mother,
Immediately do my marriage in the ocean." OH

(Raja Nal then convinces Behmata to make a *juri* for him, learns of his marriage to Motini, and is transported by Behmata on a magical raft to Motini's father's castle, which has no visible entrance.)

22. *vārtā* Then Nal saw neither gate, Behmata, nor the raft. He said, "Now I am in trouble. Now there is no way to escape. Tell me, if the demon comes, then the field will be clean [he will kill me] and my marriage will surely not occur." This is the situation.

23. *dohā* Nal's body begins to shake,
Oh in the fort of the demon,
Nal remembered his past life. (*#)

24. *vārtā* So what does Raja Nal do?(

25. *ḍholā* Oh he remembers all about Durga, (*#)

(8*#)

(*#) "Bhagvati, I am appealing to you,
(*#) You cut the cord in my mother's stomach,
(*#) You fed me the milk of the lioness."

(12*#)

(*#) Oh Nal shouted to the Protector of the Poor,
(*#) And Durga woke from her slumber,

(8*#)

And she called her langur,
(*#) Brought the lion from Kajriban,
(*#) Saddled the lion with green cloth,

(8*#)

(*#) And put a green cap on the langur,
(*#) The mother herself wore green bangles.

(8*#)

26. *vārtā* (*#) What is Durga doing?

(2*#)

27. *ḍholā* (*#) Bhagavati came to Danigarh.
(*#) She found Raja Nal standing there.

(4*#)

(*#) And she took Nal in her lap,
(*#) "Why are you sobbing, my beloved son?
(*#) "Oh tell me son, what is troubling your heart?"

28. *vārtā* (*#) What does Raja Nal say?

(4*(#)

29. *ḍholā* (*#) "Oh in distress comes misfortune, in adversity comes calamity.
(*#) "In distress, the bullocks don't lend a shoulder.

(8*#)

(*#) "In distress comes misfortune, in adversity comes calamity.
(*#) "In distress, the bullocks don't lend a shoulder.
(*#) "Then brothers and relatives don't speak to you,
(*#) "And descendants turn their backs."

(8*#)

30. *vārtā* (*#) What does Behmata say?

31. *ḍholā dhār*

(*#) When destruction comes to man,
(*#) "First, lightning falls on the brain,
(*#) "One's own mother is like a lion,
(*#) "And father seems like Yamraj.

(8*#)

(*#) "When destruction comes to man,
(*#) "First, lightning falls on the brain.
(*#) "One's own mother is like a lion,
(*#) "And father seems like Yamraj.

(8*#)

(*#) "Instantly the wind changes direction,
(*#) "Instantly the leaves fall from the tree.
(*#) "Sometimes there is yolk in the egg,
(*#) "Sometimes the birds fly from it."

(8*#)

(*#) "Sometimes the boat moves on a cart,
(*#) "Sometimes the boat goes across,
(*#) "Sometimes the boat moves on a cart."[5]

(Durga helps Nal to find the entrance to the palace. He enters and eventually marries Motini, who has the missing shell.)

Ḍholā performances are structured by the interaction of song and prose. Each scene or introduction of a new theme or character is marked by a chanted couplet, a *dohā* (see section 1). These couplets, whether occurring in the midst of a section of song or in a section of prose or at a transition point between song and prose (see sections 3 and 23), are never accompanied by instruments, though there is a melodic line. In a lengthy performance where the story is ultimately important, these scenic markers play a major role in focusing the attention of the audience on critical events.

Prose sections (*vārtā*) provide the "story line" of the epic; they allow narrative development and explanation. *Ḍholā* here marks the main song style used in this epic. *Ḍholā* is accompanied by the three instruments, becoming more rapidly paced as the singer shifts from individual verses (see sections 5, 7) to a long series of connected verses (section 31). This structuring is certainly part of the answer to my question, for it provides the framework for the epic performance. Yet it is only part of the answer.

Contrast for a minute the components of this epic: there is everyday prose—not formalized and not constrained by vocabulary, intonation, or rhythm. Ram Swarup's prose style is informal and everyday: it is in that sense conversational, as indeed his characters often converse with each other in long prose sections. These explanatory prose sections are, I think, very nonformalized. Ram Swarup explicitly called them "explanation" (*samjhānā*). In contrast are the chanted *dohā* couplets, defined by metrical patterns, choice of intonation, and rhythm of delivery. These chanted sections are highly formalized or "frozen" or certainly more frozen—and more formal—than is prose conversation.

My search for insight led me to the literature on ritual language, and through it to speech act theory. Ḍholā is not a ritual, yet the questions being asked of ritual language are most appropriate for seeking clues as to Ram Swarup's use of song and prose. The song portions of Ḍholā are largely formulaic and fixed, as is much ritual language.

Recent work by Bloch (1974), as expanded by Schieffelin (1985) and Brenneis (1987), develops an argument for the nontextual meaning of performed texts. Bloch argues that ritual language (and here I include song language, for it, like some formalized ritual language, is often "fixed" as a text) has lost its "propositional force" (following Austin) because its texts are predictable and redundant. One aspect of his argument is that ritual language, where choice is denied the speaker once an item is chosen—the

Lord's Prayer *must* be recited with each word correctly placed—has lost its propositional force, where propositional force is defined as "the ability of language to corner reality by adapting communication to past perception and connecting this with future perception" (Bloch 1974:67). A second aspect of meaning, however, is illocutionary force or performative force (see Austin 1962), the ability "not to report facts but to influence people." Bloch argues that speech that is highly formalized, such as some songs or prayers, communicates without (or with minimal) explanation. Yet these texts are still compelling through their "illocutionary" force. Ritual language is effective not because it conveys information or comments on a state of affairs or allows discussion of a point, but because it situates actors vis-à-vis other actors in a given context.

A comparable theory is that of Wheelock (1980, 1982), who proposes, following Searle, two kinds of speech acts: informing speech (a speaker conveys information to a hearer) and situating speech (speakers create situations by their utterances). For example, the narrative prose sections of epic are more "informing speech," while the song sections are more "situating speech," especially when we consider the tune as well as text. Ram Swarup's use of narrative tells the story, while his use of song creates a mood, through melody, rhythm, and text. The insights of these two authors crosscut one another and help us understand the role of prose and song in epic performance.

There is, however, a fundamental difference between Bloch and Wheelock. Bloch focuses on speech that is formal or fixed. Further, he is concerned with the political implications of this formality, with political oration with which the listener cannot argue. As he puts it, the fundamental question is "why would it be that traditional authority and religion tend to use a type of communication which excludes explanation and hides this exclusion?" (Bloch 1974:67) and hence also negates argument. Moreover, his claim that formal language has performance force and nonformal language has propositional force is in error. The guide on a Japanese bus tour speaks a formal language whose prime purpose is explanatory or propositional.

Nevertheless, Bloch makes an important point that is confirmed by the epic portion presented here. As language becomes more formal or fixed, the verbal interactions between speaker and hearer diminish. As we have seen, in the narrative sections of Ḍholā, the audience becomes part of the epic performance. But in the song portions, they are listeners. Likewise, woe unto those who interrupt the Japanese tour guide! Still, the audience continues to participate in the event during song portions, responding to the mood of the Ḍholā singer. Small donations to the singer occur only during songs. And the audience provides other nonverbal cues to the singer during this portion of the epic.

Wheelock's argument is not based on formal versus nonformal language, but rather on the intention of the speaker. As he says, "one must make a broad distinction between all those speech acts whose fundamental intention is the communication of *information* between a speaker and hearer, and those speech acts whose intention is to create and allow the participation in a known and repeatable *situation*" (1982 : 59). By not basing his definition on the formal characteristics of the speech event, he allows for the tour guide to give information in a fixed speech.

If we merge these two models, creating an axis of nonformal to formal language and another of informing to situating speech, we can begin to understand epic performance. (See Figure 1.)

First, there is everyday prose—not formalized and not constrained by vocabulary, intonation, or rhythm. These explanatory prose sections are, I think, very nonformalized and also provide the main story line. And there are chanted *dohā* couplets, defined by metrical patterns, choice of intona-

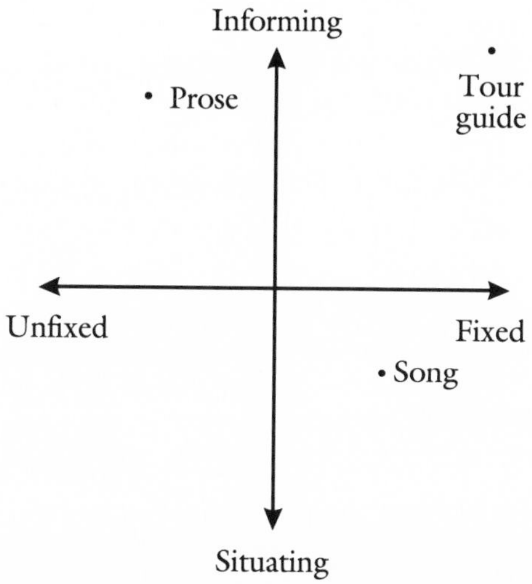

FIGURE 1.

tion, and rhythm of delivery. These chanted sections are highly formalized. Yet they are also informing speech. The fact that the *dohā* message is often repeated in prose, however, suggests that the main message of the *dohā* is to notify of change, possibly making it situating speech, rather than to clarify information. Hence *dohā* chants situate not through words, but through texture and tune. Meanwhile, their informing function is repeated. In the example above, this process occurs when Nal first speaks to Behmata in *dohā,* then in *vārtā.*

The songs of Ḍholā are also like ritual song—there is a denial, once a song is chosen, of choice of intonation and rhythm. Moreover, song is even more remote from normal speech than is chant. Song does allow creativity, as in song contests such as those once held for Ḍholā, or by putting more or less "expression" into song. Nevertheless, "the propositional force of all song is less than that of spoken words in an ordinary context" (Bloch 1974 : 70). Bloch further points out that many songs "predict the linguistic journey that the singer undertakes" (1974 : 70) and that to engage in a song requires one moment of will—once you take part, your route is chosen and fixed. Moreover, some songs allow no argument or reasoning.[4] So a second part of the answer to my question lies in the difference between speech acts that are informing and situating. In Ḍholā, prose is more informing and song is more situating.

But we still do not have a complete answer to the question, Why sing? To further answer it, we need to look more closely at song, as both a linguistic or semantic event and as a musical event.

Let us begin with music. First, we must recognize that our analyses of Indian folklore are overwhelmingly textual, yet much folklore is musical and all Indian epic is musical.

Song texts, following the argument given above, are primarily situating. Music is also situating.

> Music in any community is basically non-discursive; it does not predicate or make arguments. While music may be seen as communicating very significant messages, the ways in which meaningful work is accomplished are quite different from those involved in language-based notions of reference and usually depend heavily on the music's formal characteristics. (Brenneis 1987 : 238)

The meaning of a folksong performance cannot be understood by merely examining text, although the norm in studying South Asian folk traditions has been to consider only the text—and then not as literature, but as a cultural statement, ignoring the fact that the cultural statement embodies tune, linguistic structure, and performance.

The north Indian folksong genres with which I am familiar almost always have distinctive textural[6] and melodic patterns. Hence the choice of a particular melody may be the choice of a song genre. Grierson wrote in 1886, "In the country districts I have never heard of a new tune being invented. There seems to be a certain stock of melodies ready made, to which the words of every new song must be fitted" (1886:209). Song genres are melody-specific.[7] Moreover, the melody often has a textual pattern defined by rhyme and linguistic meter. And in addition to being melody-specific, many north Indian folksong genres are textural-specific: a specific linguistic structure is associated with a given genre. Finally, many song genres are sung by specified individuals only in certain cultural contexts, such as the marriage or birth songs of women or the Ālhā or *barāhmāsī* of men. Thus the choice of a song genre dictates, in addition to a specific text or content, (1) melody and rhythmic patterns, (2) a known textual pattern, and (3) a given theme and its associated connotations derived from its normal context. The result is a compact symbol form, a song genre. This multidimensional symbol situates audience and performer through text as meaning, conveying information. It also situates audience and performer through melody, rhythm, and linguistic structure, using nondiscursive elements of performance generally.

Let us look more closely at the musical message in Ḍholā. One aspect of Ḍholā not illustrated in the earlier example is the switching of song genres. Let us look at another portion of the epic.

In this episode, Raja Pratham has been reunited with his wife, Queen Manjha, after an absence of 12 years. Because Manjha has been gone for 12 years, Raja Pratham refuses to allow her in the palace until she bathes in the Ganges. Motini and Nal are very worried about this venture, as there have been bad omens about the trip. Manjha calls a maid and sends her to Nal to explain that she will be departing soon. This section begins when the maid reaches Nal's palace.

vārtā The the maid told him the story: she said to come quickly.

chhāp Sher Singh, resident of this village, gave one rupee.

ālhā And [he] rose immediately from his room.
Think of a lion, moving in the forest,

As he went his boots thumped loudly,
And his shield clanked on his shoulder.

vārtā What did he see?

ḍholā Oh, Nal glanced ahead:
A widow carrying an empty pot.

vārtā Nal thought, "Oh my mother has called, and these unlucky omens make me very fearful."

ḍholā How can one remain in peace when traveling on a road?
A crow cawing in a dry tree,
A crane alone, the pair separated,
Or a twitching on the left side of the body,
A deer alone, a pair of jackals,
Or meeting a shepherd riding on a buffalo.[8]

vārtā What did Raja Nal say?

chetvāni When destruction comes to man,
First lightning falls on the brain,
One's own mother is like a lion,
And father seems like Yamraj,
When destruction comes to man,
First lightning falls on the brain,
One's own mother is as ferocious as a lion,
And father seems like Yamraj,

Instantly the wind changes direction,
Instantly the leaves fall from the tree,
Sometimes there is yolk in the egg,
Sometimes birds fly from it.

nihalde Oh he went, then Raja Nal came in the palace.
The woolen wrap was spread, he sat on a stool.
The women speak to Raja Nal,
Then Motini notices her husband,
And she embraces Raja Nal.

In this short section, six different song/speech styles are identified by the singer: *vārtā,* speech or explanation, *chhāp,* the acknowledgment of a patron; *ālhā,* the warlike genre associated with the epic Ālhā; Ḍholā; *chetvāni,* a warning; and *nihalde,* a style named after a romantic epic of Rajasthan. The *chetvāni* used here is marked in linguistic texture and rhythm and stands in clear contrast to the surrounding verses.

Based on local song genres, each of these song styles is a symbol that can convey a particular mood to the audience. The audience knows *ālhā* by tune and rhythm and associates *ālhā* with matters heroic and military. The epic singer uses *ālhā* as a musical symbol to remind his audience of the heroic king marching off to war. Here Nal is not going to war, but the singer is able to convey by more than words alone the heroic nature of Nal as he goes to meet his mother. Likewise, the mood shifts suddenly as Nal is brought into the women's court where a genre, *nihalde,* based on a romantic epic sung in nearby Rajasthan, is used to seat Nal and for the greeting by his wife. What should be clear by now is that we are talking here of information conveyed not merely by texts but also by texture and tune. This leads us away from the textually based analysis of most Western writers.

Thus in Indian epic singing, the moods and characters of events and personae are conveyed by changing voices and situations through shifts in song genres. The shifting of genres is a critical component in developing the characters of the epic personae in any given epic performance. With no costumes or props, character can and must be conveyed orally. Most important, this character development is made not merely by words but also through the conscious choice of symbolically charged melodies, textures, and rhythms borrowed from the regional pool of genres.

A task for a later paper will be to examine more closely the song genres associated with particular character types or the moods of characters on specific occasions. Let me give two quick examples of what I expect to find.

Raja Nal, the epic hero, is usually portrayed as kingly warrior. As in the example above, he is often described with melodies taken from *ālhā.* Yet in one episode, where he is reluctant to fight a battle, his action is conveyed with *mālhār,* a women's genre of longing and pensiveness. The same words, sung in an entirely different melody, would have very different implications for Nal's character.

On a different note, Nal has two wives, Motini and Damiyanti. Motini, the daughter of a demon (or in some versions, a Brahman's daughter raised by a demon), is herself warlike and aggressive. She takes an active role in Nal's adventures and often gets him out of trouble. His second wife, Damiyanti, is much more passive; she follows Nal into exile and generally does his bidding. What would be revealing is the extent to which these two different characters' patterns are conveyed musically, as well as through our more commonly recognized "texts." My hypothesis is that there will be a significant difference in the song genre used to describe them and the genre used when they speak. By paying close attention to the song genres used, we can gain greater insight into epic character.

When a Ḍholā singer chooses to switch a song genre, he is making a major symbolic statement through music, not through words. The same basic text is conveyed as the singer adapts his words to his new melody, while the major symbolic message is conveyed in music. A text-only analysis would mask these crucial messages.

What does this tell us about singing epics, and Ḍholā in particular? Many oral epics in South Asia contain both song and prose elements, with greater and lesser degrees of fixity and choice. Ram Swarup says that he uses *vārtā,* prose, as explanation. At the same time he also makes the choice to open the epic up to argument. The interplay between singer and audience in prose sections reinforces this opening up. Here meaning depends upon rational discourse, on cornering a bit of reality.

Chanted and sung sections, on the other hand, derive their meaning from their performative and situating forces. Here other messages are being communicated. The concern is not to allow rational thought, but rather to create a mood, paint a word and musical picture, mark a change. Many nonverbal messages are being communicated to aid in creating meaning through illocutionary force—messages via intonation, melody, and drum patterns, all culturally understood and decoded (in part, at least) by the audience. The types of meaning may differ as we move across the continuum from everyday prose to formalized song, but the weight of meaning may in fact be heightened with the addition of nonverbal cues. Recognizing the nondiscursive elements of song as being part of the situating event is critical to understanding why Ram Swarup sings.[9]

Yet this analysis still ignores a final part of the puzzle. We must return to another facet of song as linguistic text, for song is also poetic. Poetic language and prose function differently. As Jakobson and Halle noted, "For poetry, metaphor, and prose, metonymy is the line of least resistance and, consequently, the study of poetic tropes is directed chiefly toward metaphor (1956 : 82). In *Fundamentals of Language* (1956), they defined two poles or axes of language: a paradigmatic axis based on selection and a syntagmatic axis based on combination. The first of these axes defines the creation of metaphor through similarity; the second defines the creation of metonymy by contiguity. Hence poetic language is largely metaphoric while prose is largely metonymic. As Lévi-Strauss might have put it, prose is concerned with syntagmatic chains and poetry with paradigmatic associations.

The epic with which we are concerned is both prose and poetry, both metonymic and metaphoric, or syntagmatic and paradigmatic. The structure of the song demands paradigmatic forms: the *dohā* couplets are formed of two lines, each made up of two parts. Consider the parallelism in the first *dohā*.

1. *dohā* Sitting there was Behmata
Appearing to be 100 years old,
There at the ocean shore,
He found the old woman.(*#)

In the first *ḍholā* song segment, we immediately have a fundamental reality of Indian family life stated, again in a parallel construction:

(*#) Oh my mother, was there a quarrel between mother-in-law and daughter-in-law?
(*#) Oh has your old man beaten you?

These parallel, paradigmatic constructions, what Jakobson called metaphoric language, are the building blocks of much of this epic. While many of the song segments contain information, and in fact carry the narrative thread of the story itself, they continually do so using a language built on parallelisms and stark contrasts. Consider the section from *ḍholā dhār:*

(*#) "One's own mother is like a lion,
(*#) "And father seems like Yamraj.

(*#) "Instantly the wind changes direction,
(*#) "Instantly the leaves fall from the tree
(*#) "Sometimes there is yolk in the egg,
(*#) "Sometimes the birds fly from it."

Here the juxtaposition of mother as Durga, father as the god of death, of the erratic weather and the birds leaving their eggs, conveys the true destruction of humans. In the second segment, the listing of inauspicious signs, again in the parallel language of poetry, has a similar effect.

> A crow cawing in a dry tree,
> A crane alone, the pair separated,
> Or a twitching on the left side of the body,
> A deer alone, a pair of jackals,
> Or meeting a shepherd riding on a buffalo.

The parallel constructions, the paradigmatic language, of poetry facilitate these kinds of messages. They are essentially metaphoric. Most other Indian epics are more heavily weighted toward song and hence metaphoric constructions. So why is epic metaphoric?

First, metaphor is a process of turning "from one domain to another" in order to accomplish "a creative transcendence" (Fernandez 1974). Metaphors bridge gaps. Normal language (prose) requires moving along gradients, not crossing from one category to another (Beck 1978). Ogden and Richards speak of metaphors, saying that they "provide . . . new, sudden and striking collocations of references for the sake of the compound effects of contrast, conflict, harmony . . . or [are] used more simply to modify and adjust emotional tone" (1960 : 240). But metaphors are more than just new bridges: some are basic to cultural understandings. They exemplify themes of a general nature. A metaphor is a "vehicle which orients actors towards the distinctive, intelligible and orderly views of experience which their culture provides" (Rosaldo and Atkinson 1975 : 44). When used in traditional cultural statements, metaphors isolate principles of order, emotional orientations, and cultural themes. While each metaphor is arbitrary, as a whole they signify and reflect an underlying system of meanings that reaffirms and constitutes that cultural system.

So I return to epic. Why does Ram Swarup sing? Epics, whether primarily associated with ritual, and hence fixed or frozen, or whether performed for entertainment, with a correspondingly looser structure, present fundamental orientations to the South Asian world. They are constructed largely in paradigmatic cum metaphoric language, while at the same time they are situating speech events. Through musical poetry, they are making fundamental statements about their world. Epics have a unique relationship with the community in which they are performed: they are "our story," and stand apart from other songs and stories because of community identification with them. As presentations of regularized world views, oral epics make a statement that other folk genres cannot. Hence epics are sung: through the non-discursive statements of music and with paradigmatic metaphoric constructions, they are not making arguments, but are stating fundamental realities.

So Ram Swarup sings for several reasons. He sings because music is a key structuring element of this epic. He also sings because sung speech is more situating than is prose and states truths with greater validity than does prose, being less arguable. He further sings because the nonspeech aspects of song, melody, and rhythm are key cultural symbols that add to the nondiscursive meaning of epic. Finally, he sings because the paradigmatic language of poetry allows for the stating of fundamental realities in a starker, clearer way than does prose, allowing for the building up of meaning through contrast and metaphoric constructions.

Let me conclude by turning my question around: Why then does Ram Swarup use prose? The answer lies in his concern for telling the story. The metaphoric language of poetry and song is not conducive to storytelling. Ḍholā is an epic performed for entertainment, not ritual. Hence the story is important. It has a dual role, and thus prose and poetry are both necessary. While Ḍholā does relate fundamental cultural categories, it also is an entertaining story.

Notes

1. The idea of 52 parts probably derives from the epic Ālhā, also sung in this region. Ālhā does have 52 parts.

2. *Juri* is literally the "pair" of a marriage, but here it is used as two ropes which the goddess twists together to float on the ocean.

3. Karta is the god who causes what was done to be written; that is, he writes one's fate and Behmata sees that it is carried out.

4. Obviously in extraordinary circumstances, you can argue with ritual speech: if not, our rituals would have been fixed aeons ago.

5. This translation originally appears in Wadley 1989: 82–90, and is reprinted by permission of University of California Press.

6. I am using textural here in the sense Dundes (1982) uses the term to imply the linguistic structure of an item of folklore, or song. Texture is thus distinguished from text by being concerned with linguistic structure rather than content.

7. Scott Marcus (forthcoming) uses this term.

8. These are all omens of impending disaster.

9. Wheelock talks of gesture, the use of props, etc. in his discussion of ritual language.

References

Austin, J. L.
1962 *How To Do Things With Words*. Oxford: Clarendon Press.

Beck, Brenda E. F.
1978 The Metaphor as a Mediator Between Semantic and Analogic Modes of Thought. *Current Anthropology* 19:83–97.

Blackburn, Stuart H., Peter J. Claus, Joyce B. Flueckiger, and Susan S. Wadley, eds.
1989 *Oral Epics in India*. Berkeley: University of California Press.

Blackburn, Stuart, and A. K. Ramanujan
1986 Introduction. In *Another Harmony: New Essays on the Folklore of India*, Stuart H. Blackburn and A. K. Ramanujan, eds., pp. 1–40 Berkeley: University of California Press.

Bloch, Maurice
1974 Symbols, Song, Dance and Features of Articulation: Is Religion an Extreme Form of Traditional Authority? *European Journal of Sociology* 15:55–81.

Brenneis, Don
1987 Performing Passions: Aesthetics and Politics in an Occasionally Egalitarian Community. *American Ethnologist* 14:236–50.

Dundes, Alan
1980 *Interpreting Folklore*. Bloomington: Indiana University Press.

Fernandez, J. W.
1974 The Mission of Metaphor in Expressive Culture. *Current Anthropology* 16:652–54.

Fox, James J.
1988 Introduction. In *To Speak in Pairs*, James J. Fox, ed., pp. 1–28. Cambridge: Cambridge University Press.

Grierson, George A.
1886 Some Bhojpuri Folk-Songs. *Journal of the Royal Asiatic Society* 18: 207–67.

Jakobson, Roman and Morris Halle, eds.
1956 *Fundamentals of Language*. The Hague: Mouton.

Lévi-Strauss, Claude
1966 *The Savage Mind*. Chicago: University of Chicago Press.

Marcus, Scott
Forthcoming The Rise of a Folk Music Genre: Biraha. In *Culture and Power in Banaras: Community, Performance, and Environment*, Sandria B. Freitag, ed. Berkeley: University of California Press.

Ogden, C. K., and I. A. Richards
1960 *The Meaning of Meaning: A Study of the Influence of Language upon Thought and the Science of Symbolism*. London: Routledge and Kegan Paul.

Rosaldo, Michelle, and J. M. Atkinson
1975 Man the Hunter and Woman: Metaphors for the Sexes in Ilongot Magical Spells. In *The Interpretation of Symbolism*, Roy Willis, ed. New York: Halstead Press.

Schieffelin, Edward L.
1985 Performance and the Cultural Construction of Reality. *American Ethnologist* 12:707–724.

Schomer, Karine
1989 Paradigms for the Kali Yuga: The Heroes of Alha and Their Fate. In *Oral Epics in India,* Stuart H. Blackburn, Peter J. Claus, Joyce B. Flueckiger, and Susan S. Wadley, eds. Berkeley: University of California Press.

Temple, Richard C.
1963 *The Legends of Punjab.* Vol. 2. Patiala: Department of Languages (Reprint).

Vaudeville, Charlotte
1962 *Les Duhā de Ḍholā Mārū.* Pondicherry: Publications de l'Institut Français d'Indologie, no. 21.

Wadley, Susan S.
1983 Dhola: A North Indian Folk Genre. *Asian Folklore Studies* 42:3–26.
1986 "And Raja Nal Said": Voices in an Indian Epic. Unpublished MS read at the 15th Annual Conference on South Asia, Madison, Wisconsin.
1988 Singing for the Audience: Aesthetic Demands and the Creation of Oral Epics. *Resound* 7:1–5.
1989 Choosing a Path: Performance Strategies in the North Indian Epic Dhola. In *Oral Epics in India,* Stuart Blackburn, Peter J. Claus, Joyce B. Flueckiger, and Susan S. Wadley, eds. Berkeley: University of California Press.

Wheelock, Wade T.
1980 A Taxonomy of the Mantras of the New- and Full-Moon Sacrifice. *History of Religions* 19:349–69.
1982 The Problem of Ritual Language: From Information to Situation. *Journal of the American Academy of Religion* 50:49–71.

Williams, Richard
1976 Ḍholā-mārū rā Duhā and the Rise of Hindi Literary Tradition. Ph.D. dissertation, University of Chicago.

Margaret Trawick

8. Wandering Lost: A Landless Laborer's Sense of Place and Self

This chapter addresses, in a small and local way, two rather large and abstract issues: one, the relation between art and life, and two, the relation between people and place. As regards art and life, no argument will be made, but an approach will be taken in which it will be assumed from the outset that an artistic performance is not an object that can be grasped in isolation from the life of the performer. Rather, the artistic act is continuous with the actor's ordinary life; it is a rendition into greater meaning of this life, and is as much dependent on it as a rosebush is dependent on its rose. A related assumption is that every human being is in some way an artist, a being driven, like the rosebush, to produce some rose, something of surprising beauty (the surprise is an important element here), even under the most adverse conditions. From this assumption, or belief, there arises an ethical injunction, which is that when we look at another human being, especially a human being in circumstances of poverty and abjection, we must force ourselves not to define that human being as equal to her material circumstances, or even as fully conditioned by them. We must recognize that person to be, like ourselves, not just a survivor (or subsister), but a creator, someone for whom creation may be even more important than survival.

As regards people and place, a more specific assertion will be made in this paper: namely, that for some communities (I would not say for all), a place is strictly identical to the people who occupy it. For such communities, place *is* people. On the face of it, this is probably not a very astonishing assertion. But as a fact among the Tamil Paraiyars who are the subjects of this paper, it has a number of rather interesting ramifications, some of which will be explored below.

The person whose life and work will be discussed in this paper is Cevi, a young agricultural laborer of the Paraiyar *jāti* living in the village of

Vattipaddi, near the larger village of Lingavadi, about twenty miles north of the city of Madurai in Tamil Nadu, south India. I must admit at the outset that I never got to know Cevi as a person, face-to-face, very well. She was one of over a hundred individuals around Lingavadi who, in 1984, for a project I was working on, were asked to speak about events in their lives that had been important to them, making special reference to personal relations and to feelings. The people who spoke for us were tape-recorded (they all knew about recording devices, as loudspeakers and cinema songs are omnipresent in Tamil Nadu), and knew that their recorded messages would be taken back to America (those among them who were literate and read the papers were familiar with the idea of America and were often critical of it) by a "white woman" (roughly identified with foreign wealth, Western movies, and British colonists), to be published in some form there. About half of the interview-cum-recording sessions were conducted by me. The remaining interviews were conducted by Kuppucami, a twenty-year-old college-educated Paraiyar man who lived in Lingavadi. All the people that Kuppucami interviewed (with the exception of two Muslim men) were Paraiyars of his own community. Cevi was one of these. Thus as Cevi talks for the tape-recorder, though we are her distant interlocutors, her immediate interlocutor is someone relatively close to her, and her speech is fluent and more natural when it would be if she had been trying to talk directly to me. I have gained this free-flowing text, as well as a kind of objectivity toward it (having met Cevi only once, and not having involved my life with hers, I have no strong feelings about her, as I do have about many of my other informants) at the cost of the deeper comprehension one acquires through personal engagement with and commitment to people. I offer no other excuses or justifications for the limited nature of the material I present here, except to say that I find this material too rich and informative in itself to be discarded just because some other information that would further enrich our understanding of it is lacking.

The tape-recorded texts that Cevi has given us are two. The first is a remarkable hymn to a goddess of the Melur Kuravar community, named Singamma.[1] When Kuppucami learned that I was interested in songs, he went to Cevi and asked her to record a song of her choice for me, because she has a reputation in her village for being a good, strong singer. After I heard the song, I asked Kuppucami to go back and have Cevi narrate her life story for us, which he did. This life story comprises the second text considered here.

Cevi's performance of this hymn is interesting not only for its beauty and its rich detail but also for the light it sheds on the unique and complex relationship that has developed between the Paraiyar community, to which Cevi belongs, and the Kuravar community, which the goddess Singamma represents. Both Paraiyars and Kuravars belong to the group of castes called untouchable (*tīṇḍā*) in Tamil. "Poisonous" might be a more apt translation of the term *tīṇḍā,* which comes from the verb *tīṇḍu,* meaning not only "defile by touch" but also "envenom, as a snake, by biting." People of Cevi's village use the term in both senses. Paraiyars are considered untouchable, defiling, or poisonous because their traditional occupation is to handle and process human and animal wastes and corpses, a set of tasks that the members of Cevi's community still perform conscientiously and sometimes competitively among themselves, like the funeral Brahmans in Benares (Parry 1982). Paraiyars are defiling also because they eat beef, though they revere living cattle, attributing protective spiritual powers to them and in general treating them more kindly as animals than do many members of higher castes. Most Paraiyars nowadays, like Cevi, earn their living as agricultural laborers, and are rooted by kin and property ties to particular locations. By training and in values they are farmers. What they know best is how to work the soil. Land they hold dear, the more so in that most of them are landless.

Paraiyars are not the lowest caste, however. As Moffatt (1979) has shown, Tamil untouchables consist of many groups which are not all equally ranked, but which form among themselves a caste hierarchy mirroring the caste hierarchy of the encompassing community.[2] Untouchables have their own "Brahmans," the elite among the outcaste, as it were. There is also at least one group of people whom the "mainstream" untouchables regard as untouchable to themselves. This last group, untouchable even to the untouchables, is the Kuravar community, the lowest caste of all.[3]

The term *kuṟavar* ("hill-dweller," "hunter") is a polite name for people known in some areas as *kuruvikkāraṅka.* The latter name derives from the word for small fowl (*kuruvi*), which Kuravar men hunt. Kuravars are elsewhere known as *narikkuṟavaṅka* ("jackal-hunters"), because they are said to hunt and eat jackals, scavenging wild animals that are more despised even than dogs in Tamil Nadu. Kuravars are known besides for keeping pigs, whose meat is avoided by many people of other castes because pigs feed conspicuously and abundantly on human excrement. In particular, however, Kuravars are famous for hunting and eating crows. In modern times, Kuravars may still be seen wandering with their rifles through fields and wastelands, with crows their principal quarry. While members of middle castes are not ashamed to hunt and eat wild fowl such as doves, only Kuravars will eat crows, for crows are, above all others, the birds of death. Crows, like some other birds, eat carrion. In ancient times, human corpses used to be offered by Tamil Jains to crows, and crows are still treated as the embodiment of dead ancestors and given offerings of rice on the festival day of *pōṅkal,* which marks the end of winter, the season of the crow, and the return of the life-giving sun. Paraiyars are despised by other castes for eating the meat of cattle, the purest, most life-giving of animals, whose destruction, therefore, is the gravest of sins. But as eaters of crows, Kuravars eat the eaters of death.

Eaters of wandering animals, Kuravars are themselves wanderers. While most Paraiyars are landless, hence impoverished and symbolically disembodied, Kuravars are even more conspicuously without a place. They have no fixed homes, no mud huts, but only rag-tents and a territory through which they roam, a territory which in no sense belongs to them. Their regular haunts are train stations, bus stops, markets, and festivals—crossroads of every kind. There they sell trinkets and are reputed also to survive by petty thievery and prostitution. The notion that Kuravar women sell their bodies together with their trinkets is helped along by their different style of dress—they wear a kind of skirt and blouse instead of the supposedly modest and respectable sari. The term *ciṅki* in Tamil means both Kuravar woman and whore. (The name Singamma, or *ciṅkammā,* according to the system of transcription used here, would be synonymous in Tamil with "Kuravar woman." Kuravars are said to hail from far-off north India, where "singh," meaning "lion," is a common surname. In Tamil also, *ciṅkam* means "lion.") In Tamil cities, Kuravar women are highly visible as they move through their daily rounds of urban food-gathering, picking through garbage bins and gathering rice off the polluted *eccil-ilai,* the "spittle leaves," thrown away by others after meals and feasts. To scavenge, to eat remainders, and to be themselves cast to the margins, left to drift with no permanent home—this is the *dharma* of Kuravars.

The Paraiyars who spoke to me on this topic seemed to have a somewhat ambivalent view of the people below them, the Kuravars. On the one hand, some Paraiyars seemed to romanticize the Kuravars, seemingly admiring their evident freedom, resourcefulness, and creativity, and occasionally singing for me, with evident enjoyment, rather raunchy songs which they said they had heard from Kuravars. On the other hand, they avoided contact with Kuravars, despised them for their dirtiness, and sang songs mocking them for lawlessness and brother-sister incest.

However, Cevi's rendition of the hymn to Singamma, the Kuravar goddess, does not fit this pattern. It is not sung in fun, but is straight and serious, and Cevi pours her heart into it, singing beautifully and with a high degree of control, yet almost weeping as she sings. Her rendition of the Singamma song, in fact, has several salient properties in common with Tamil "crying songs" (*ayiṟa pāḍḍu*) or laments. Each line is marked by a rapid rise to a peak in pitch, followed by a gradual descent to the original pitch level. Each line ends in the cry "*ammā*" ("mother"), with the final syllable "*mā*" drawn out into a descending glissando wail. Each line is sung in a single breath, reeling the breath out to its end, so that a deep and audible inhalation occurs at the completion of the line. Finally, the topic of this song, like the topic of all Paraiyar laments, is not just death, but the injustice of this particular death, with many comments as well upon the injustices suffered by low-caste women in life. The Singamma song differs from Paraiyar laments, however, in that its protagonist is able to come back from death and right the wrongs done to her. As Cevi performs it, the Singamma story, like many other Indian tales of apotheosis, moves through tragedy to triumph, and ends with a beautiful powerful woman, renouncing dependency, rising from defilement, death, and corrosion, and standing at last as a goddess, defiantly alone.

One question that may be asked of the moving performance Cevi offers us is: Why does she do it? Why does she choose the goddess of this most despised people to sing to, and why does she sing this particular song for us? As an untouchable singing to and about a being untouchable even to herself, is she perhaps saying something about the state of untouchability, about the state of being classified together with poison and corpses? Is she perhaps trying to move beyond the pecking-order mentality of caste, to create a more enlightened response to her own abjection? Out of the stench of pollution, to produce something not conditioned by that stench?

In another publication (Trawick 1990a), I have attempted to address these questions directly. Here I will not focus so much on the matter of untouchability, but will consider instead a closely related issue, the matter of homelessness in India. Homelessness and untouchability are related issues in India, not only because many people of Untouchable castes are without real homes but also because both homelessness and untouchability are states of bodily rejection. To be without a home in India is to be without people who will take you in, to be without people who will let you live with them. In a way, it is the farthest extreme of untouchability. It is no accident that the most untouchable people in south India, the Kuravars, are also the people most without a home.

I would like to present the full text of Cevi's performance here, since it is such a remarkable song, but space does not permit. Instead, therefore, I will give a summary of the story. This will be followed by a longer summary of Cevi's own life story as she narrated it to Kuppucami. Finally, a point-by-point comparison of Cevi's life story and the story of Singamma will be undertaken, and a few conclusions will be drawn.[4] A summary of the Singamma story as performed by a Kuravar priest in Melur is provided in the appendix. Readers may find it illuminating to compare the Kuravar version of the Singamma story with Cevi's version.

The Story of Singamma

The story of Singamma, as recounted in Cevi's song, is stark and elliptical. As it opens, we learn that Singamma is kept confined in the house by her brothers' wives. But one day, as she sees the women coming, she "puts on different clothes" and slips off to the market to sell trinkets. Her brothers weep when they come home and find her missing. They go to the market, where Singamma is playing cymbals (*ciṅki pōḍḍu*), selling songs for coins at the dried fish store (fish is a common symbol for female genitals in Tamil; fish spread out to dry evokes an image of women's legs spread out). One brother, "the lame older brother" (*nōṇḍi aṇṇan*), meets her there but does not recognize her, and again weeps when he returns home and cannot find her. Singamma, still in town at dusk, goes to a wedding feast, gathers up the leftover rice from discarded leaves there, and brings it back home in jars. For punishment, her brothers send her to a house in the forest and make her stay there, "grinding and pounding with a mortar." All four brothers go into the house, pull the doors shut and lock them, and the mortar stone pounds. Then Singamma says to them, or they say to her (it is unclear who the speaker is): "The sun has set on our good caste; we are excluded from caste" (*jātilēyum taḷḷuvaḍi*).

The lame older brother's wedding day arrives. Singamma is to cook and serve at the wedding feast, but the pots of rice and milk won't boil for her—the sun will not allow it. (The Tamil festival of the sun, celebrated around winter solstice time, is marked by the boiling of a rice-milk dish called *pōṅkal*. If the pot boils over, it means that the sun will bless the family with abundance in the coming year. If the pot fails to boil over, it is an evil sign.)

Singamma is again locked in the house, "weeping in her heart." But at dusk she declares, "If my honor [*patti*] is destroyed, let the doors of the house stay shut, but if my honor is undestroyed, let them open." The doors open, and Singamma flees. Her brothers come home and ask where Singamma is, and their wives say, "A husband has married her and taken her away." The brothers then dig holes in the floor inside the house. The holes are to be Singamma's grave.

Singamma is now with her mother. She lies down to sleep with her head on her mother's lap. Her mother tells her that because she is excluded from the caste and pots will not boil for her, her brothers are going to kill her. As she lies with her head in her mother's lap, she takes a louse comb in her hand and assumes the form of louse eggs. While she is in this form, her brothers pound rice for her mouth (rice is put in the mouth of corpses before burial) and drop chicken and crow meat in the holes in which she is to be entombed. The lame older brother weeps yet again, and then Singamma is killed and dismembered (*kulaicukum*). Only the heart of the mother (*attā*) is not made happy by this act, says the song.

Singamma is interred in the holes dug for her, and from them a poisonous red oleander (*cevvarali*) springs up. The lame older brother comes to the places where the oleander has grown. A poisonous earthworm (*pūnākam*) emerges from the oleander and tells the brother to build a palace there for Singamma. They crumble the house and build a foundation on that site; when they do so, an oleander bud blossoms for Singamma. Then the elder brother touches (*tīṇḍu*) the earthworm, which, in return, tells him a story. It says it once lived in the house. It says that Singamma's brother's wives saw it and told Singamma to catch it and take it away; both it and Singamma left the house, "weeping and sobbing." The earthworm concludes its story by saying, "Even if you build palaces, you may not stay. Only the lame older brother may stay."

All the brothers and their wives then come to that place to burn lime for mortar. As soon as they have burned and moistened the lime, buildings grow up in that spot. A woman comes to live there, and when she does so, the building in which she lives "leans over with its foundation." Singamma then appears to the woman. The woman asks her where she comes from. Singamma replies, "I came from within the house itself." Then, as the song goes, Singamma, having emerged from within the house, "rising up high, speaking with unsheathed energy, wearing pearls," addresses her lame older brother, telling him, "You are the one who killed me, who saw my sin, who undid me. That which entered the house truly was. Tell me to rise up outside. Now I will stand up straight and show you." She leaves the house, she goes outside, they raise her up. And the final stanza of the song says, "As soon as they raised you up, Singamma, your building, too, stood up tall."

Cevi's Story

Cevi's life history narrative is unusual in that she speaks mainly of other people and says very little about herself. In fact, she does not even appear as a minor character in the series of loosely connected events she recounts until near the end of the interview, when Kuppucami asks her about her own wedding and her subsequent married life, and even here she does not appear as an actor or speaker in the narrative, but only as someone to whom or for whom things are done or not done. The major part of the narrative has to do with the injustices suffered by Cevi's older sister.

Kuppucami begins by asking Cevi how many brothers and sisters she has. Cevi says there are six, then mentions that one older brother is dead, murdered:

> C: Of the six people, an older brother, one older brother died. When he was lying down, they wrongfully and mistakenly grabbed him and beat him and killed him.
> K: They beat him and killed him?
> C: Yes. Older brother.
> K: In what town did they beat him and kill him?
> C: In this town itself, appa [*uḷḷūrccilē tānppā*]. They beat him and killed him. They beat him and killed him. Older brother.

Cevi says no more about this event, but goes on to mention other siblings and to describe an event that happened to her parents when she was a child. I will quote her at some length here so that the reader can get a sense of her narrative style:

1. They beat him and killed him. They beat him and killed
2. him. Older brother. One older brother was married in
3. Lingavadi. He is alive in the house. An older

sister, the place where my mother was born, in East Valaccappaddi, in Valaccappaddi, in the place where she was born, to the younger brother who was born with her they gave older sister in marriage. Father, in that place, older brother, mother, to go, to come, keeping, father was thinking very much of mother [*ammāvē rōmpa karutuṇḍuḍḍāṟu*], he was not thinking [*karutāmē iruntirukkiṟāṟu*]. Then, mother, while he was spreading a chicken to split it, father split his hand. One of father's hands got split. Then, because of that, mother said she would not live [with him]. When she said she would not live [with him], we had lots of wealth and conveniences, father, even so, they took father to Melur, they took him to Madurai hospital, [the people of his] brothers' house itself [*paṅkāḷi vīḍu*], [the people of] father's younger brother's house [*cittappā vīḍu*], [the people of] father's older brother's house [*periyappā vīḍu*], and they had him admitted [*cēttuppiḍḍāka*]. When they admitted him like that, mother went, and she did not see him, she did not keep him. When he was just like that, then two of the younger brothers born with mother, both of them went, the coming, the going, they went and saw and came, then they said to father, "Til your hand is well, send the girl to me," so they said, and father listened. He listened and said, "Your younger sister says she won't live with me." "If the younger sister born with me says she won't live with you, how in the world do we make her live for you?" So saying, the two uncles born with mother, they said that and came back to Madurai. After they said that and came, [my father said,] "Go, I want to go see my wife, you go tell her to come." So saying, father waited. Then mother, from there, from Madurai, the one born with mother, the one who bore mother, the grandfather, and the father, both of them father and daughter, came to Madurai to see father. Father had broken his hand, no? They came to see that. As soon as mother went and saw, mother was very troubled.

43. "From now on I will not live with you at all," she
44. said to father right there. After they said that,
45. they left the hospital and took him outside and came,
46. they came, it is said. [The people of] father's
47. brothers' house [*paṅkāḷi vīḍu*], they brought him,
48. leaving all his belongings right there, they brought
49. father, they brought him to Kallantiri and they left
50. him there, it is said. Taking him to Kallantiri
51. [hospital], leaving him there to be, "You stay here,"
52. so saying, taking him to Kallantiri and leaving him
53. there, they came here. After they came here, "These
54. belongings, somehow we, keeping it for him, we . . .
55. even his wife says she won't live with him, [and] he,
56. from now on, somehow this hand is at fault [? *inta*
57. *kaiyi cōrammāyiruccu*]." So saying, "He will not keep
58. his life. He will die. He will die. For this child,
59. this girl child we must give away in marriage, no?
60. There in Valaccappaddi they will come to friendship
61. [*toyappukku vantiruvāṅka*]." So saying, "We will
62. have it all written into our name." So saying these
63. people of father's brothers' house, no?, found a way
64. for them to write it [i.e., sign over the father's
65. wealth to themselves]. As soon as they found a way to
66. write over father's belongings and wealth, then
67. what did they do?, quickly, they took father from
68. there in a car to the Madurai police station. Having
69. taken him there, father's handwriting [? *kai rēkai*],
70. they had it written that this man had no claim
71. [*pāttivam* < *pāttiyam*] to this wealth. Who? The
72. people who are there now, those people. As soon as it
73. was written and given to them, they put it in his
74. hand. Then father had lost his belongings, no? And
75. it is like that still; he has no claim. Afterwards,
76. we, we were four or five children. Then little
77. children, how are they going to work and earn money
78. and eat? So saying, there has to be a way to survive,
79. no? Father, working, working with his good hand, must
80. raise the children, bringing along his wife and also
81. bringing along his four children, so it happened.

82. Letting the children fly, mother left. Thinking just,
83. "We must not stay with him, he is going to take the
84. children and raise them," mother left. Afterwards,
85. thinking, "Having left the children, what are we going
86. to do? I must come back," she returned. Having come,
87. when she asked what happened to the woods and fields,
88. they wrote that there is not a thing left. Having so
89. written, "There is just a little bit, in an old field
90. there is just a little space," said [the people of]
91. father's brother's house, "Only what is in that, you
92. may take only from that mango grove, you may not take
93. from the other mango grove," they said it to mother
94. and father. "Then if you harvest it, only one bag of
95. paddy will come," they said. "If you plant cotton,
96. ten or twenty rupees of cotton will come. That is all
97. that will come." Keeping that, raising the children,
98. father and mother were living. While they were like
99. that, they performed a wedding for my older brother in
100. Lingavadi. Then, between Lingavadi and our people
101. there was a quarrel from past time, between father's
102. house and two people. Then three months after the
103. wedding, older brother went blind. . . .

The story told here may be paraphrased briefly. The narrator's father, while cutting a chicken, accidentally splits his own hand. When this occurs, his wife, the narrator's mother, fearing that the father has been so handicapped that he will be unable to work any more, deserts him and the children. The father's brothers take him to the hospital, where his wife's brothers also come to visit him. He asks them to bring his wife to him, but they say they cannot convince her to come if her will is against it. The wife's father then brings the wife to the hospital to see her husband. When she sees him, she repeats her decision that she will not live with him. Afterward, the father's brothers move him to another hospital, where they abandon him (when a poor person in India is hospitalized, relatives have to bring him food or else he will simply die there). Deciding that with his wounded hand he will not be able to work and support himself and will die, the father's brothers make plans for the future. One of the things they think of is that they will soon have to marry off his oldest daughter and this will take money. They consider that a marriage alliance with the people of Valaccappaddi will be advantageous. With these future plans in mind, before the father has even died, his brothers seek to legally appropriate his property. They do this by taking him to the police station and having him sign away all his possessions to them. The father recovers, however, and manages for a while to support his children by working with his good hand. The mother returns to live with them, and the father's brothers give him permission to cultivate a small portion of his former property and so support his family. The brothers do not give back to him the property they forced him to sign over to them in anticipation of his death. Though later in the narrative we learn that Cevi's father did not survive long, but died before she came of age and married, Cevi says, "Still he has no claim" to his former property. The dead father's having no claim means that his children have no claim to his land and must live at the mercy of the father's brothers.

If we look at the narrative style of this portion of Cevi's story, we find a number of textural patterns, patterns that recur again and again throughout the narrative, and that, I will try to show later, link up with the Singamma story in interesting ways.

First I should note that Cevi's speech style is liltingly musical. Like most Tamil villagers, she speaks very rapidly; every two or three seconds her voice rises to a high pitch, or drops to a sentence-final low, and she pauses, evoking an "mm" from her yes-sayer, Kuppucami. About half of her sentences repeat in participial form the predicate of the previous sentence, so that the end of the last sentence becomes the beginning of the next. This, combined with the falling and rising intonation, creates a rocking effect, which seems almost to lull Kuppucami to sleep. Occasional tag-questions wake him again, forcing him to respond. Important phrases are bracketed in pauses, murmured in low whispers, or conversely spat out in tense staccato syllables, reinforced by intonational parallelisms and much internal rhyme.

But when deprived of its music and put down on paper, Cevi's narrative (like many oral narratives) becomes choppy and hard to follow. Grammatically, it is fragmented and chaotic, or so it would be judged by Tamil pundits. Syntactic and lexical organizing and clarifying devices, present in written Tamil, are largely absent here. There is quite a bit of repetition, of stopping and starting over again, of self-correction, which comes out in the form of saying one thing and then immediately afterward saying something else parallel but contradictory to it (e.g., lines 10–11, 18–22, 37–40). There is also in Cevi's speech a kind of topic forefronting, in which the narrator says the name of a person somewhat in advance of when she actually starts talking about that person, sometimes several sentences in advance, so that the name seems for a while to be dangling there, unconnected to anything until the narrator picks up the thread to which the name belongs (e.g., lines 7–9, 11–14, 16–17). Often, several topics are forefronted simultaneously, that is, a series of key words is listed, before they are joined together into a sentence, as though the speaker were audibly laying the pieces of her thought before her before uniting them in a single construction. Different people and different voices become commingled. The boundary between quoted speech and Cevi's own voice is often unclear. The speech and action of several people is sometimes treated as though it were the speech and action of one person (e.g., lines 25–34).

Many of these features of Cevi's narrative can easily be attributed to the fact that Cevi is not a literate person. Her talk is not in any way modeled upon writing. What she says is heavily dependent for its meaning on many features of sound and context that do not come through in the transcribed text. Although an objective anthropologist would not evaluate Cevi's personality negatively for her way of speaking, in the Tamil world it is nonetheless true that Cevi's "poor" way of talking is inseparable from her moral and social status: she is "low" and her life is "bad." For the speaker, too, what she says must be part of what she is.[5]

The action of the story told by Cevi is dominated by coming and going, bringing and sending, keeping and leaving; the verbs "come" and "go" appear as fillers in many places (e.g., lines 8, 26). This incessant coming and going is one indication of what seems to be a strong preoccupation with place and placelessness in Cevi's narrative. People are always moving or being moved around; the moving is always a matter of what people are in what places; and the questions of who belongs where, what place belongs to whom, and who belongs with whom, are constantly being examined and reexamined.

The close identification of people with place is expressed in several distinct ways. First, Cevi has a habit of saying, "so-and-so's house" when she really means "the people of so-and-so's house." So, for instance, in this section of her narrative, she mentions *periyappā vīḍu* (father's older brother's house), *cittappā vīḍu* (father's younger brother's house), *pankāḷi vīdu* (brother's house), when in all these cases she is actually referring to the people having rights to a particular piece of property and not to a physical house at all.

Second, when a marriage is mentioned, the common way that Cevi refers to it is to say that so-and-so was married in such-and-such a place, as in lines 3–7, "An older sister, the place where my mother was born, in East Valaccappaddi, in the place where she was born, to the younger brother who was born with her they gave older sister in marriage." Or again, in lines 99–102, she says that her brother was married "in Lingavadi" and then, "between Lingavadi and our people there was a quarrel from past time, between father's house and two people."

Third, from time to time in the narrative, certain people are referred to as being "in the house." For instance, in lines 2–3, "One older brother was married in Lingavadi. He is alive in the house." Elsewhere, the convalescing father is said to be "in the house." Similarly, later in the narrative, an aged parent, a boy who has finished the tenth standard and is waiting for work, a girl who has come of age and is waiting to be married, all are said to be "in the house." But none of these people is actually confined to the house. The boy who has finished tenth standard travels around quite a lot, and the girl, the mother, the brother, and the father all go out to work every day. Considering all these cases, one surmises that to be "in the house" means to be okay, to be taken care of by others.

Given this identification of place with people, we now may begin to understand why, at the beginning of the interview, Kuppucami, upon learning that Cevi's older brother was beaten and killed by someone, does not ask what to us would be the obvious question, "Who did it?" but instead asks, "Where was it done?" It seems that, for people of Cevi's community, to ask "Where?" *is* to ask "Who?"

A certain characteristic of the world in which Cevi lives recurs six or seven times in the story she tells, and gives us a hint, or a partial answer to the question as to why people and place are so closely identified by Cevi and those around her. This real-world fact is the frequent co-occurrence of bodily destruction (illness or injury), fragmentation of the kindred group, uprooting or expulsion of someone from their home, and loss or fragmentation of property, especially land. Violence of kinsman against kinsman almost always has some or all of these consequences, and in Cevi's narrative, such violence is commonplace. Indeed, all of the events that Cevi describes in her narrative are composed of some combination of these four different kinds of breakage (body, kin group, land, land-body connection). It is no wonder then that her speech seems also to be, on one level, broken.[6]

After describing how her father lost his land to his brothers, Cevi tells of the following events.

An older brother becomes ill and is taken to the hospital. For the hospital expenses, money is needed. Cevi's father and her first older brother are unable to earn enough, so they sell, to the father's older brothers, the final tiny patch of land that has been left them, for one hundred rupees.

> You know those who are there today? [The people of] father's brother's house [*paṅkāḷi vīḍu*]. They wrote it over to them [*eṛutikkuḍuttiḍḍāka*]. As soon as they wrote it away, then between them and us there was no kinship [*urimai*]. Belongings, affection [*cōttu pattu*], in none of that was there any kinship. It had all gone.

The bond of affection and belonging between brothers is carried in the land and lost when the land is lost.

In the next and longest episode, Cevi's older sister comes of age and is married into Lingavadi.

> They brought her well, majestically, with all the proper rituals. But sister's husband kept her in a very countrified way [*rōmpa nāḍōdiṇḍu vaccukkoṅko*]. Then, when they are very countrified, from day to day it will be just like this. Once a month they will beat her, keep her, and being like this watch over her in violence. And when they were watching her like this, sister became three months' pregnant. And when he became angry, in purple violence beating her [*ūtāṅkōlaile aḍiccu*], breaking her skull, making the blood flow, he told her to go and sent her away. Sister, throbbing and burning, did not go to Komanampaddi [her parents' home], but came here to Vattipaddi [where Cevi herself subsequently married].

In Vattipaddi, the sister stays with the family of a medical practitioner named Pampaiyan. "Pampaiyan's house are very much kin to us, no?" (*pampaiyan vīḍu namaḷukku rōmpa urimaiyānavakuḷḷō*). But the husband comes there, beats her again and tells her she must not stay in Vattipaddi, but must go to Komanampaddi and he "puts her on the road."

At this point in the story, Cevi exclaims in outrage to her young male kinsman Kuppucami: "To beat her when she was three months pregnant—see the madness of it, boy!" (*pittunatē pārappā!*).

The sister goes go Komanampaddi, where she finds that her brother's wife has just died. She stays there for the funeral. She continues to stay there, thinking her husband will come and fetch her, but he never comes.

Her child, a son, is born. Her husband takes another wife and lives with this other wife. Then one day he gets into a fight with his second wife's family, "a hitting and grabbing fight. In the place where he married, [the people of] the house of that younger wife cut my sister's husband, they cut him on the hand, and sent him off with his blood." On his way out of town, bleeding, he passes through Komanampaddi, where his first wife is living.

> Then all the people gathered there said, "Oh no, how sad, your husband is cut and is going along bleeding." So they spoke. Then between sister and her husband the friendship [*toyappu*] had ceased. To clash is not friendship, is it? Then, in that place he married us, our husband, our child has been born, whenever it may be, we will join with that husband. We have written that between us as husband and wife there are no claims [*pāttivam illai*]. We have written that our kinship [*urimai*] is to the child. Tomorrow, if good or bad comes to the child, our husband must come, he can only come. However our husband is, older and younger brothers, opposing them all, I must go and see my husband in the stronghold of Madurai [*marutak-kōḍḍai-yile*]. So saying, older sister, bewildered and weary, taking a hundred rupees in her hand, started out, to see who? To see her husband.

The sister finds her husband in a bed (*poḍḍiyile*) in the Madurai hospital. When the two see each other, they both weep. Daily she visits him there, bringing him food and money and protecting his life. The son, now ten years of age, comes too, affectionately calling, "Father, father." Then the husband vows that he no longer wants the other wife. "You alone are my wife," he says.

> When he spoke, a woman's heart, in that place it causes it to be truly affected [*anta iḍattile pātikka tānē ceyyutu*]. Aha, our husband has come this distance, has spoken this far, for ten years our life has been ruined, but having been this way, from now on every day we will be together with our husband. In that place will be true kinship [*anta iḍattile urimai tānē irukkum*]. So spoke the heart of a woman, and older sister's thoughts were of kinship [*urimaiyā nenacciruccu*].

But when the husband is healed and returns back home, he changes his mind, and sends his first wife, Cevi's sister, away, telling her to leave him and the second wife alone. Still, while she lives with her parents in Komanampaddi, she continues to visit her husband in Lingavadi, borrowing hundreds of rupees and spending it on him. "In kinship [*urimaiyāvē*] she spent it."

Then one night the son also runs away from his mother: "Feeling kinship with the father [*appā mēlē urimai paḍḍu*], the son went off to Lingavadi." There he stays with his father's sister, who keeps him, "in great kinship." When the mother comes searching for him, her husband and his family send her away, saying, "What kinship is there between you and him? You go back and stay in your own house."

But Cevi's sister stays the night at her husband's house, and in the morning gets up, washes his clothes and his body, and ponders upon how she has spent so much on her husband to no avail, thus angering her natal family, "the people who are there," with her stubborn wifeliness. She thinks about how it is wrong (*urimai illai*) for her son to heed the father who deserted him, rather than the mother who cared for him for ten years.

There follows a kind of tug-of-war concerning where she is to live. Her husband's sister tells her to stay. Her husband's brother tells her to go. Finally she tells herself, "You must not go there. We must not come. We must not think of him as our husband." But she cannot maintain that frame of mind for long. She decides to have an ear-piercing ceremony for her son, now twelve, and says to herself, "I will come and go and ask my husband." But when she arrives at Lingavadi, her husband's kin tell her that he has left, and they ask her to stay. She answers angrily, "You say, 'Stay, stay,' on the morning my husband has gone."

"So saying, sister's mind was troubled," Cevi narrates. Then the husband's family tell her,

> "If you come and have the ear-piercing ceremony here, all the people of the jati who would come and give you things, they will take all those things they have come to give you and will keep them, they will not give them to you. In a former time, they would lovingly accept you. At this time, not desiring acceptance, you depart and go and stay. Wherever you are in your house, have the ear-piercing ceremony there." So saying, they sent her off.

The sister has the ear-piercing ceremony performed for her son in her own home. At that time, a relative convinces her that the boy should be sent to Bombay, to learn masonry work.

> Then sister signed him up [*eṛuti poḍḍu vaccu*] for that masonry work. This one boy, our life, he must make it a good life—so saying, she sent him to study there. Here, he did not know how to read, so what did she do, she sent him to Bombay. . . .
>
> "He may work for a mason's wages," they said, and, "We must send him to Bombay," they said, and "We will ask him," they said, and they wrote a letter on the very morning of that ceremony, and they took sister's son. Now sister is alone, and does some kind of work, just enough to eat, and for her part she sits in the house, while that boy is in Bombay.
>
> K: Does he send any of his wages to her?
>
> C: He has not sent any yet.
>
> K: How long has it been since he left?
>
> C: Now since he left—that ceremony was done, no? Three months have passed since that boy left, three months. Since he went, he has sent five or six letters, saying, "Mother, I am alive, I am holding on, I am in good shape, you stay there, mother. Don't you worry." In the letter he just sent, he told her to come. "Mother, you must come quickly," the boy wrote in his letter.

In the remainder of Cevi's narrative, at Kuppucami's urging, she tells something about her own married life. She explains how the people of her father's younger brother's house took on the job of arranging and paying for her marriage.

> The four people who were living there said, "For this girl, I am [responsible]. If any 'mistake' comes to this girl [i.e., if she is found to have any flaw], it is our responsibility." So the people of our father's younger brother's house spoke.

Cevi complains that when her father's brothers married her, they promised her a field and a garden, a set of cattle and a well, but after twelve years none of these things has been given her. "So far, they have not given anything, saying 'This ten cents is just for this girl.'" Cevi and her husband have a minute patch of land by the roadside (3/4 *kuṛi* = 108 square feet) and they also plant some things on the borders (*vārattile*) between other people's fields. Yet Cevi and her family have gotten along adequately. Her three oldest sons are in school. In the interview, she stresses the importance of education above all things in making a better life for her children.

When Cevi married, she and her husband were sent to live in a Muslim house (*rāvutta vīḍu*)—apparently a house that had been owned and abandoned by a Muslim family and then taken over by Cevi's father's brothers. At the end of the interview, Kuppucami asks Cevi if she has a family god (*kula tēvam*). Cevi answers with two names: Cinkampudukari, Cevukapperuman. Kuppucami asks if this deity has been any help to her. Cevi answers,

> The help he has given us is that we, husband and wife, have kept in good order. We have worked hard for our meals. Now for two years' time, for two years, that deity, we, in a polluted person's house [*oru tuṣḍakkāravuka vīḍḍule*], a Muslim house [*oru rāvutta vīḍu*], in the house of people of no particular caste [*entaccātikkāravuka vīḍḍulaiyum*], without making an error of hot or cold water, in a good way, our arms and legs must be well.
>
> Cevapperuman, you alone are our help. You alone must give health to our arms and legs. So saying, we pray only to that god. Now for these two years . . . since this small little boy [her youngest son] was born, well, a little well off, without debt or falsehood, we have been able somehow to eat. . . .
>
> Somehow, a bowl and a pot, what is needed for a house to survive—what way to buy them? For that, before, our husband worked very hard. Only if he labored very hard, only if he took up a shovel. . . . We were without rice. There was no rice. Now for two years, since this little brother was born, since then, because he took on the burden of going north and south a little bit, somehow a little cash has come into our hands. We are a little well off. We are able to eat a little to cool our hunger.
>
> K: Has the god helped you in any other way?
>
> C: He has not helped in any other way.

Let us return now, after this long interlude, to a consideration of the other text Cevi has given us in conjunction with this one, her hymn to the goddess Singamma. At the beginning of this chapter, I suggested that an artistic performance might be understood as a rendition into greater meaning of the performer's experienced life. One takes the substance of one's own life, whatever that substance may be, and one tries to make something better, truer, and more beautiful out of it—something, at least, that makes more sense, something more worth keeping, as memory, as part of self. Here we may consider Cevi's two texts, the one representing her life's raw material, the other representing the more perfect thing she would make out of this material, as illustrating this process of rendition-into-meaning of life, the artistic transformation of experience into knowledge.

Before considering the continuities between the two texts, we might note their differences: (1) The narrative is very fast and rather chaotic; many words and many events are packed into Cevi's hour-long talk. The song, by contrast, is slow, measured, and structured. (2) The narrative relates one episode of suffering and injustice after another. There is a tiny glimmer of optimism at the end. The song also tells of suffering and injustice, but at the end, justice triumphs. (3) In the narrative all the events, including the sufferings and injustices, are commonplace, even boring—Kuppucami yawns and loses the thread of Cevi's story from time to time. But the events in the song are gripping, extreme, bizarre, supernatural, astonishing. One might find them confusing, but one could hardly find them boring. Kuppucami is excited and proud to bring me this song. (4) Cevi's narrative style is low-key. She is not a dramatic storyteller. But she is a dramatic, powerful singer. In short, the song is in many ways better than the narrative. It is a more desirable gift-object.

Some of the more obvious similarities between the two texts may also be noted, before we consider the subtler, as it were subliminal, links between them. First, the key figure in both song and narrative is a battered woman; and second, this woman is not the singer/narrator herself, but someone worse off than the singer, with whom she evidently sympathizes. Third, in both texts, an evil collectivity of brothers, more or less undistinguished from one another as individuals, plays a prominent role. Fourth, both texts dwell upon the linked themes of bodily destruction, fragmentation of the kin group, and loss of place. In both, the central events entail violence of kin against kin, uprooting and confused wandering from one location to another. A fifth similarity is that in both texts there is a strong sense of moral outrage. People are not behaving toward each other as they should, and the pain of innocents results from this immorality.

The song, then, manifests the same basic preoccupations as are apparent in the narrative, but in more extreme form and with sharper resolution. For instance, in the narrative, the heroine is merely beaten; in the song she is killed and dismembered. In the narrative, the integrity of the heroine's womanhood is violated by her husband's beating her during her pregnancy. In the song the violation is stronger—she is raped by her brothers. In the narrative, the heroine into whose consciousness the narrator enters is only slightly removed from the narrator—she is her sister. In the song the heroine, with whose feelings the singer's feelings merge, is of a whole different caste, as well as of a different time and place from the singer—the embrace is wider, the message of solidarity among women stronger. One transformation that occurs, then, between life and song, is a clarification and strengthening of the meaning of certain kinds of relations and certain kinds of events.

Now we may begin to reconsider the identity of place and people and the close link between caste exclusion, or untouchability, and homelessness, or landlessness, that this identification of place with people implies.

We have already seen how important and complex the notion of "house" (*vīḍu*) is in Cevi's narrative. *Vīḍu* means not only an actual physical structure, but also a group of people related by kin ties to each other and to certain property. When a person moves from *vīḍu* to *vīḍu,* she not only changes location, she also changes the people with whom she lives, and her right to live in a certain place is determined by the nature of the ties she has with the people who already occupy that place and own it.

Closely related to the concept of *vīḍu* is the concept of *urimai,* a term that also appears frequently in Cevi's narrative. I have translated *urimai* as "kinship," but as Cevi uses the term it seems to mean something other than just a genealogical link between persons. *Urimai* exists in degrees that are not entirely determined by genealogical closeness or distance. One may behave in a fashion characterized by more or less *urimai,* at one's will. *Urimai* between uterine brothers may be broken completely, as may *urimai* between parent and child. All this we learn from Cevi's narrative. If *urimai* has a core meaning for Cevi, it would seem to be the feeling of rightness of people living together in the same place, taking care of each other materially, and sharing the same property. In a given context, the moral, or the affective, or the physical component of *urimai* may be stressed. They are all bound together.

A sense of wholeness is suggested by both *vīḍu* and *urimai*. But in Cevi's narrative, she dwells upon these two terms just because in her life the wholeness they offer is lacking. For Cevi and her people, no home is reliably home, no kin can be counted upon to recognize kinship forever.

There is a certain kind of person, writes Julia Kristeva, who "instead of sounding himself as to his 'being' . . . does so concerning his place: 'Where am I?' instead of 'Who am I?'" (1982: 8). Such a person is precisely one who has never been fully accepted or adequately identified by the normative social code, the order embodied in words, whatever that order may be. Kristeva refers to such a person as "the abject" or the "deject," one who is cast down and out. In Mary Douglas's (1969) terms, the abject is the polluted one, the one dwelling on the margins outside of wholeness and order, outside of the categories language creates. Thus, Kristeva argues, the abject challenges meaning: "It lies outside, beyond the set, and does not seem to agree to the rules of the game. And yet, from its place of banishment, the abject does not cease challenging its master. Without a sign, it beseeches a discharge, a convulsion, a crying out" (1982:2).

Kristeva argues that the abject lives in a twilight world—in terms of language, never perfectly coded; in terms of place, never perfectly grounded. Indeed, though he defines himself in terms of the ground on which he stands, this ground beneath him is not steady. It is broken into many parts, it trembles and it shifts, and it forces the one who lives on it always to keep on moving, always to keep on trying to build something solid, every day starting again. "For the space that engrosses the deject, the excluded, is never *one,* nor *homogeneous,* nor *totalizable,* but essentially divisible, foldable, catastrophic. A deviser of territories, languages, works, the deject never stops demarcating his universe whose fluid confines . . . constantly question his solidity and compel him to start afresh. A tireless builder, the deject is in short a stray" (1982:8).

Even if by accident, how well these words describe Cevi's world! And just as, for Cevi, the place of belonging constantly and treacherously shifts, so do the people of belonging, for people and place are one.

In the hymn to Singamma, a number of interwoven themes express this identity of place, body, and kin, or rather, the broken place, the broken body, and the broken kin group, that are the daily experience of the landless untouchable woman who sings the hymn. These themes also, in their various ways, bespeak the instability of the bond that holds the untouchable woman to each of these shattered entities. Here I will give names to the themes, and then discuss each of them in turn. They are: (1) anomalies of inclusion and exclusion, spatial and social; (2) fragmentation of body, place, and kin group; (3) partial attachment to places (wandering) and partial identification of persons (commingling of voices); (4) the power of death and remainders.

Anomalies of Inclusion and Exclusion

In the hymn to Singamma, as in Cevi's life-history narrative, there occur a number of problems and anomalies having to do with confinement in or exclusion from houses. Cevi introduces her performance of the hymn by stating that Singamma is "a child of the house of Kuravars" (*oru kuṟava vīḍḍuppillai*)—rather an ironic way of describing her, since real-life Kuravars have no physical houses. A second strange reference to houses consists in Singamma's being interred in the floor of one (in flagrant violation of Tamil convention, but perhaps echoing some more ancient custom?). There she is told to "stay and be happy" (in somewhat the same way as Cevi's sister is told to stay alone in a house where she does not want to be). A third strange episode involving houses consists in the erection of one upon the remains of another. (This also is a violation of Tamil building code, about which more will be said presently.)

Images of confinement and exclusion, wandering and bondage, are similarly interwoven. The song begins with Singamma being confined within a house and fleeing from it. The place where she stays after she flees is excluded, discarded ground—"the rocky wasteland of Melur" (*mēlur kallāṅkuttu, kallāṅkuttu poḍḍal*) it is called. On this rocky wasteland there occurs a wedding (the act of inclusion par excellence), where Singamma finds and gathers rice that has been discarded (excluded, remaindered). She is punished by being locked *in* a house that is *outside* the village—"yonder, in the forest," says the song. Finally, she demands that a house be built for her alone, and then she demands to be taken outside of it, so that she may stand up straight. Her brothers are ordered to build this house, and then they are told, "Even if you build palaces, you may not stay."

Even on the level of grammatical categories, states of exclusion and inclusion are repeatedly stressed, and then overturned, in this song. The key example of this scrambling of categories of inclusion and exclusion appears in the section describing the reason for the caste-exclusion of Kuravars. At the beginning of this section, the song tells how Singamma is punished by her brothers for leaving the house and going to the market. They lock her in the house alone in the forest:

> Leaving you within the house, Singamma
> All four doors they closed and locked and came, Singamma.
> All four men went inside the house, Singamma.
> And as they went inside the house, Singamma,
> the mortar stone pounds, doesn't it, Singamma.
> And as the mortar stone pounds, Singamma,
> all four doors they pulled shut and locked, Singamma.

This passage, though indirect, strongly implies gang-rape of Singamma by her four brothers. The image of incestuous multiple rape is linked to ambiguities concerning who is in what house with whom: have the brothers locked Singamma in the house and left her alone there, or have they locked themselves in the house with her?

The questions of incest and caste explusion, like the question of who is in what house, are, of course, themselves questions of inclusion versus exclusion. The dilemma that is suggested here is simple: to stay within the caste (as well as to abide by the rules of the caste system as a whole) we must marry within our group. But if we marry too closely within our group—that is, if we stress inclusion too heavily—we will be radically *excluded:* either we will be driven from our caste, or our caste will be driven from among the body of castes. The song proceeds:

> To them, to all four of them, Singamma,
> Singamma could give an answer, Singamma,
> On our [excl.] good *jāti,* Singamma,
> the sun has fallen and gone, Singamma, we [exclusive]
> From the *tāli* . . . from the *jāti* are excluded, Singamma.

In this passage, it is notable that the first-person plural forms, "*our* good *jāti*" and "*we* are excluded" are both grammatically exclusive rather than inclusive. In Tamil, the exclusive "we" (*nāṅkaḷ*), does not include the listener. But here, if the sister is addressing her brothers regarding "our" good caste, it would only make sense for her to use the inclusive form. If she is talking about her own exclusion from the caste, she should use the singular, not the plural form: "I am excluded," not "We are excluded." Whoever is speaking, though the *topic* of the passage is *exclusion,* the pronoun "we" should be *inclusive.*

Cevi's slip, saying *tāli* when she means *jāti* (and so correcting herself) is also telling. The *tāli* is the marriage necklace that a husband ties around his wife's neck on their wedding day. It is a powerful symbol for Tamils of the bound and confined state of married womanhood. The term *jāti* means caste. By accidentally substituting one word for the other, Cevi indicates how closely associated are the notions of confinement within marriage and confinement within caste. It is also interesting that she uses the locative here, saying "we are excluded *in* the *tāli* . . . *in* the *jāti*" (*tālilēyum* . . . *jātilēyum taḷḷuvaḍi*), when it would have made more sense to say "*out of* the *tāli*" (*tālileruntu*). Here it seems that the in-group/out-group ambiguity is striking at the heart of grammar.

Fragmentation of Body, Place, and Kin Group

One would be hard-pressed to find the life story of a deity in India that was not rife with all sorts of rule-breaking. Still, it is not unreasonable to think that people whose lives are especially damaged by adherence to the rules of Indian society might be especially inclined to break those rules in fantasy (so, as I have argued elsewhere [Trawick 1986], the most oppressed in India might very well be in some ways the most creative). I have tried to show here how broken into pieces is the world of Cevi's everyday life. Perhaps this is another reason why the song she sings is characterized by various kinds of normally whole things being broken into pieces.

I will only mention briefly at this point the various overt violations of Tamil social convention that take place in the story of Singamma: how she breaks out of the house against the will of her brothers, how she "wears different clothes"; how she sells herself in the market; how she gathers up polluted rice to take back home; how her sisters-in-law lie about where she has gone and drive her out of her natal home by ordering her to catch a poisonous worm; how her brothers rape, murder, and dismember her; how they bury her in the floor of the house; how they build one house upon the remains of another. I will only mention in passing also that the notion of code-violation is itself a difficult one in a society where there are, from the beginning, multiple codes. (The appropriation and legitimation of a multiplicity of codes-for-conduct and their subsumption into a hierarchical order can thus be seen as a very crafty defensive maneuver on the part of the code-makers.)

Just as, in this song, there is on the grammatical level a scrambling of the categories of exclusion and inclusion, reflecting perhaps a preoccupation with problems of belonging versus not belonging, so there is also a scrambling of the categories of singular and plural, perhaps reflecting a related preoccupation with problems of wholeness versus brokenness. Thus, many of the things that in the ordinary Tamil world are decreed to be singular come up plural in this song. For instance, when Cevi sings, "On our good caste the sun has fallen and gone" (*poṛutu viṛuntu pōyiḍḍāka*), the verb is given a plural personal marker. But even if the sun is personified, it should be singular, like any other deity. In Tamil, deities are invariably *avan* ("he," familiar, sg.) or *avaḷ* ("she," familiar, sg.). Consider the distant, all-encompassing unity that the fiery eye of the sun represents. Consider, in Tamil as in English, its powerful masculinity. In the song of Singamma, it is by the sun's authority that she is outcast(e), and again, that rice pots will not boil for her. By calling the sun plural, could Cevi be quietly shattering this authority?

But Singamma's own unity is also broken in the same way. Shortly before her death, she takes a louse comb in her hands and takes the form of louse eggs (plural). Lice, of course, with the eggs they lay, are small, inconsequential, and undesirable creatures that one seeks to exclude from one's hair. The instrument of their exclusion is the louse comb, which Singamma takes in her hand. Lice, besides being annoying, are also defiling, because they drink blood. High-caste people will not admit to having lice. So it is appropriate, if apparently bizarre, that the goddess of the Kuravars—the most defiled, excluded, and inconsequential of castes—should choose as her animal form louse eggs.

The fragmentation of Singamma's living self into louse eggs is followed by the fragmentation of her dead body and its burial, not in one hole but several. Both the louse eggs and the holes are specified as plural in the song.

Another plural presence in the song is the set of Singamma's brothers. Needless to say, it is not unusual or illegal for a woman to have several brothers. But the rape of Singamma by her several brothers contrasts sharply with the normal and, for Tamils morally most legitimate, sexual arrangement, marriage of one woman to one man (*oru āṇ, oru peṇ*—an oft-cited formula). And of course the one man should not be the woman's brother.

The plurality of the several brothers as against the one sister is further highlighted and made strange by Cevi's habit throughout the song of changing the number of brothers that Singamma has. The first stanza of the song begins, "There were five brothers, Singamma." In the 4th stanza, we learn that the five brothers have five wives. In the 5th stanza, it is down to four wives. In the 10th stanza there are five brothers again, in the 13th stanza only four. In the 49th stanza, the number of brothers becomes seven, in the 69th stanza, six. In the 85th stanza, there are again seven brothers, and they have four wives. All these changes in numbers go completely unexplained. It is as though the singer must defy even the pattern of expectations that she herself has set up. Or else it is (more likely) as though precision as regards numbers, adherence to the notion of fixed boundaries between entities, is not especially important.

Two other pluralities stand out in the song. When the brothers mix lime for Singamma's palace, not one building, but buildings (plural) grow up on that spot. And finally, when Singamma emerges, glorious and triumphant, from the buildings that have been built for her, she speaks out, and the song says, not "She spoke the truth," but "She spoke *truths*" (*uṇmaikaḷai colliḍuccu*), plural.

Partial Attachment to Places and Partial Connection with People

I have tried to show that, in Cevi's life-history narrative, the sense of belonging to a certain place and the sense of belonging to a certain people are one, so that place and people are in many contexts spoken of interchangeably. I have also tried to show that in Cevi's world, attachments to places and people are tenuous, so that wandering lost, coming and going continuously with no clear sense of where or with whom one is really supposed to be, seem to be the main activities that people engage in.

The text of Cevi's narrative manifests one other related property, and this is a near total merger in many places of Cevi's voice and consciousness with the voice and consciousness of her beleaguered older sister. It is a common characteristic of much informal Tamil narrative, as well as of many Tamil songs, that the distinction between reported speech and the speech of the narrator or singer is often very hazy. There tends to be no cue until the end of the reported speech that it is in fact not the narrator but someone else talking. This is a property of Cevi's narrative overall. But the older sister is treated in a different way from the other characters in Cevi's story, in that Cevi seems often to be inside this sister's mind. She does not report what the sister *said* in particular situations, but what the sister *thought,* very much as though she were describing her own thoughts. One imagines that Cevi must have had many conversations with this sister, given her advice, shelter, and so forth, but as far as the narrative is concerned, Cevi does not represent herself as a distinct character from the sister at all. There is no "I said" and "she said." There is only "she thought." This perfect unification of the voices and consciousnesses of the two women reminds me of the unification of the voices and consciousnesses of the *talaivi* and *tōṛi* (heroine and heroine's close friend or foster sister) in early Tamil poetry, where the *tōṛi* sometimes speaks the thoughts of the *talaivi* as though they were her own.

In other words, just as the characters in Cevi's narrative are not firmly grounded in one place, so Cevi the narrator is not firmly grounded in one voice, but dwells sometimes as much in her sister's mind as in her own.

The wanderings of the older sister, and the frequent entry of her thoughts into the mind of the narrator Cevi, find expression in the hymn to Singamma in a sharp and powerful way. Let us say that Cevi's feelings for Singamma are much the same as her feelings for her sister. Perhaps in some way to Cevi, Singamma is her sister, and both the goddess and the sister are also in some way herself. The wanderings of the sister in the narrative are echoed in the song in the wanderings of the goddess. As the sister wanders, her social identity and her attachments to others also shift. So, in the hymn to Singamma, just as Singamma the person physically wanders about, we find the *name* of Singamma wandering, its grammatical place shifting, its identification with various voices constantly changing.

The name "Singamma" is the refrain of this song. It is cried out repeatedly at the end of every line, regardless of the content of what is being said, as in, "They looked inside the house, Singamma, / and they cried with tears, 'Younger sister is missing,' Singamma." Thus the name Singamma plays the role that some chains of nonsense syllables play in other songs, grammatically superfluous, a filler between stanzas, which gives the performer time to think about what she is going to say next.

But "Singamma" is also a term of address in the song. Thus, near the beginning of it Cevi sings, "I am going to tell the story of your birth, Singamma, I am going to tell the story of your growth, Singamma."

Singamma is first outside the story in the sense of being a refrain, just a word tacked on at the end to keep time. Then she is outside the story in a different way: she is the person to whom the story is told. She is its audience. But she is also *inside* the story as its heroine, so as the story goes on, Cevi sings, Singamma you did this, Singamma you did that—"You put on different clothes, Singamma. . . . You went to the market to sell beads, Singamma," and so forth.

And finally, the name Singamma becomes even more deeply embedded in the story when in some stanzas it appears as ambiguously incorporated into the speech of one of the characters of the story, as when the brothers send Singamma into exile:

"Where have you been?" they ask you, Singamma.
They stand there asking, don't they, Singamma.
"In the forest, *ammā,* Singamma,
See that house, go there and stay, *ammā,* Singamma.
You will be pounding with the mortar, Singamma."

In some stanzas, Singamma speaks to herself, and then she seems to be saying her own name, divided from herself and reflecting upon herself:

Six o'clock has come, Singamma, Singamma.
If my honor is destroyed, Singamma, I, too
Must stay inside the house, Singamma, I am
A woman of perfect honor, Singamma, these
Four doors must open up, Singamma, Singamma.

Here, the words "I, too" (*nānum*) suggest that some "I" is identifying with some other "I," perhaps that the singer is telling Singamma, "I, too, Singamma (like you), am a woman of perfect honor." But the implied identification between singer and addressee remains always partial and ambiguous.

A similar partial and ambiguous identification is set up between Singamma and her mother:

In the lap of the mother who bore Singamma,
Being laid to sleep, Singamma, Singamma
Sleep won't come at all, mother, Singamma, Singamma
Must tell the order to the mother, Singamma.
The mother says, Singamma, Singamma,
Excluded from our caste, mother, Singamma,
The rice pot will not boil, mother, Singamma
Your brothers are going to kill you, Singamma, Singamma

In Tamil, *ammā* means "mother," but it can also be used as a term of address for any female human being. It would not be strange for a brother to call his sister *ammā* or for a mother to call her daughter *ammā*. So Singamma is addressed by her brothers and by her mother in the lines above as *ammā Singammā*, but the same *ammā Singammā* is echoed when Singamma speaks to her own mother (saying to her, "Sleep won't come at all, mother, Singamma") as though she is calling her mother by her own name.

Near the end of the song, Singamma addresses her elder brother and accuses him, saying,

> You are the one who killed me, Singamma
> The one who saw my sin, Singamma Singamma
> The one who undid me, Singamma . . .

And here again, it is as though she is calling one of her kinsmen by her own name.

There are also stanzas in which the name Singamma becomes split into two or three forms; one form a free-floating refrain, one form a term of address loosely bound to the content of the narrative, and one form an integral part of the narrative, tightly bound into the particular context and syntax of that stanza. For instance,

> To them, to all four of them, Singamma,
> Singamma could give an answer, couldn't she, Singamma?

> And in Singamma's grave, Singamma,
> And in Singamma's grave, Singamma, for you,
> A red oleander blossomed, didn't it, Singamma?

In this way the song expresses, more clearly than any analysis could, the fragmentation of the heroine, her lack of any one firm and unambiguous personal identity, her sometimes inside/sometimes outside status, her search for a place to be.

The Power of Death and Remainders

Kuravars and Paraiyars are said to be polluted and dangerous because they deal with remainders: corpses, feces, leftover food, skins, shells, seeds. Remainders/reminders. Reminders of what? Of the nonwholeness, the incompleteness of existence. No matter how much you try to sweep up, there is always some bit of dirt in a corner somewhere. Nothing can ever be perfect. Nothing is ever totally finished, past, and forgotten. Reminders/remainders. "Backward castes," still carrying habits that others have left behind, are themselves reminders living in leftover time, and, pushed to the edge of the village, they are themselves remainders living in leftover space.

If things were perfect and without remainders, though, things would never change; there would be no growth, no life. Indians know this very well. "Upon remainder the name and form are founded, upon remainder the world is founded. . . . Being and non-being, both are in the remainder, death, vigor." So speaks a certain Sanskrit remainder.[7]

In modern Tamil there is a whole body of folklore concerning the power and the importance of remainders, of leaving things imperfect. The image of a god should not be made perfect or terrible chaos will result. A house should not be perfectly finished, a brick should be left out. A transaction should not be perfectly finished, a rupee extra should be given. Something more should be left to the future, something should be left as seed.

Just as in the building of material works of art, so in the building of verbal works, the remainder is important in Tamil. One stylistic device which frequently occurs in all varieties of verbal art, and which Cevi employs very heavily in the hymn to Singamma, is enjambment. Enjambment appears when a metric line (or musical phrase, or set of words uttered in a breath) does not correspond with a grammatical sentence or phrase, so that the first word of a new sentence appears at the end of a metric line, and the sentence is completed on the next line. What results is a kind of verbal "remaindering." In the hymn to Singamma, the word that is most frequently so remaindered is *nī*, "you," so that many lines end, *cinkammā nī* "Singamma, you." What is predicated of "Singamma, you" is left to the next line. Meanwhile this "you," like the goddess herself, hangs in limbo.[8]

A related device, which might be called "predicate-chaining" is also very common both in Tamil spoken prose (including Cevi's autobiography) and in Tamil oral poetry (including the hymn to Singamma). Here the speaker or singer picks up the last part of the previous stanza or sentence or paragraph, and begins the new stanza or sentence with that same phrase. For instance:

> The wives of your five brothers, Singamma,
> Kept you inside the house, Singamma . . .
> And while you were kept inside the house, Singamma,
> The four women came, Singamma . . .
> And when the four women came, Singamma,
> You put on different clothes, Singamma . . .

Putting on different clothes, Singamma,
[you went] to sell beads and needles, Singamma . . .

In Tamil predicate-chaining, what is picked up to begin a new sentence is generally a participial phrase. If it was a finite verb phrase in the preceding stanza, it is converted to a participial phrase in the new one. These participles are themselves inherently dangling forms. Unlike finite verbs, they need something more to complete them. Their frequent use as a poetic device in both song and conversation bespeaks, like enjambment, a detotalizing vision of the world, a stress on the incomplete, the ongoing.

Cevi's hymn to Singamma stresses the theme of death and remainders very strongly. The entire song, indeed—though Cevi *says,* "I am going to tell the story of your birth, of your growth, Singamma"—is really devoted to the story of Singamma's death.[9]

The story of Singamma is one of a great many Indian tales about women who become goddesses by dying. In this song, however, the identification of the goddess with death, especially its physical aspects, seems more prominent than usual. For example, at several points in the song, Singamma's activity is associated with the loss of light, the setting of the sun, or the failure of the sun to exert its power. In other ways, also, it is suggested that Singamma's power is the power of death. The plant that grows from her grave, for instance, the red oleander (*nerium odorum carnea*), is a deathly poisonous plant. To consume even a tiny amount of it can be lethal. Finally, Singamma is identified with the earthworm (*pūnākam*) that emerges from the plant growing from her grave. This consumer and transformer of death's remains becomes, in the song, Singamma's only spokesperson.

The other direct references to remainders in the hymn to Singamma have already been spoken of: the leftover rice Singamma gathers, and the new house for Singamma built over the remains of the old. A new house must never be built over the remains of an old house, Tamil villagers say firmly, because there might be the bones of some dead animal there. Here the bones of Singamma herself are buried, and the place where her ending, her grave, was dug becomes the place where they dig her beginning.

Crumbling the hut, Singamma, for you
A foundation they dig, Singamma, Singamma,
And as they dig a foundation, Singamma, for you,
A bud comes and blossoms, mother, Singamma.

I will end this still-incomplete essay by comparing the denouement of the Singamma story with the end of Cevi's own life story, in which she tells how she and her husband have been forced to live in a Muslim house, a "polluted house," a "house of people of no caste"; and yet in this house, with the marginal land they cultivate near it, they have found some peace and some hope. It is as though, by placing their faith in remainders, they may perhaps see something new and good rise from the wreckage of their lives.

What are these remainders in which they place such faith? One is tradition: the family god, the set of values, the knowledge, the songs of their own past. Another is writing (what some people now call our human spoor, our calling card, the dried ink on the page): this quasi-magical thing which, as Cevi shows us, has exerted a terrible destructive power in the life of her family, is that which she now seeks, through the education of her sons and through the present inscription of her thoughts and words, to turn to her own advantage.[10] The third, finally, is Singamma herself, this goddess of cast-out people, whom Cevi has chosen to praise rather than to despise. Rather like her most famous compatriot, who became great of heart the day he realized he was not above blacks but was black himself, Cevi, I think, becomes great when she sings this song, recognizing her kinship with others poor even beyond her own poverty, filthy even beyond her own filth. Performing this difficult act, she makes something beautiful out of her terrible life, and so we should look up to her, and learn from her.

Appendix: Another Version of the Singamma Story

The shrine to Singamma sits outside the "mill-gate" of the Cooperative Milling Society, about two miles northeast of Melur. I am grateful to J. Bernard Bate for finding Vellacami, the Kallar exorcist (*kōḍāṅki*) working at this shrine, and recording Vellacami's rendition of the Singamma song for me. Though Vellacami is not himself a Kuravar, he is the one ritual specialist in regular contact with the spirit of Singamma, and his version of the Singamma story is regarded as authoritative by the people of Melur. Prior to his assumption of the role of Singamma-exorcist around ten years ago, people say, there was no ritual specialist for Singamma. The shrine also is new. Singamma herself is said to have died just thirty years ago.

In a subsequent publication I will discuss Vellacami and his work further, and will also discuss Kuravar interpretations of the Singamma story. Here I will sketch Vellacami's rendition of the song so as to give readers a sense both of the source of the Singamma story and of the distinctiveness of Cevi's performance of it. Vellacami's song, while telling essentially the "same" story as Cevi's song, differs from it in a number of remarkable ways.

In Vellacami's song, Singamma, an unmarried girl, comes with her family—both parents, her brothers, and her brothers' wives—on foot from the north to Madurai to see the Cittirai festival there. The hamlets and roads near Melur over which the family travels are named. The family camps out at last in a dark, thorny, flowery wasteland. The particular kinds of thorny shrubs (*iṇḍu, kaḍucānam, kārai*) that grow there are named, and their names are repeated again at the end of the song, as though to identify the location precisely. The place is called Thief-Stab Hill (*kaḷḷaṅkuttu mēḍu*) (cf. Cevi's mention of a "rocky wasteland hill," *kallāṅkuttu mēḍu*). In the morning, Singamma and her brothers' wives go to the Melur market to sell trinkets. There the brothers' wives deceitfully abandon Singamma, who is forced to return at dusk alone to the camp. The owner of a dried fish store sees Singamma begging alms, is struck by her beauty, and follows her, plotting to rape her. He is joined on the way by a headman of the goatherd caste. Together they lure Singamma into a lonely place, telling her that a wedding feast is going on and that all her caste-mates are gathered there, being fed. Singamma goes where they tell her, finds the place deserted, and weeps. The goatherd and dried fish merchant comfort the weeping Singamma and gain her trust by feeding her a feast of rice, vegetables, and dried fish stew. She eats, gathers up the remainders, and continues on her way. The two villains follow her a ways further, then overtake her, grab her hand, drag her into an empty goat stall, lock all the doors, and rape her, as she struggles, kicking, howling, and weeping. (Cf. Cevi's versions in which the girl's own brothers lock her up in a hut in an isolated place and rape her.)

In the morning, Singamma's brothers hear of what has happened to their sister and go to find her. As they arrive, Singamma's two rapists emerge from the goat stall, followed by Singamma herself, who curses the rapists and their families to be friendless "with no one to feed them a meal for seven generations." Seeing that Singamma is wearing new clothing and has brought with her good food, as well as a new grinding stone (which she has gotten from the market), the brothers suspect that Singamma has exchanged her sexual services for these gifts. A woman who has stayed the night away from home, they say, will ruin the caste. Singamma returns to the camp, combs her hair and adorns herself, and lays her tired head down on her mother's lap. The mother sings her a sweet lullaby, and Singamma falls asleep. Then, at midnight, as she lies sleeping in her mother's lap, the brothers split Singamma's head open with an axe. Hurriedly, they bury her body in the floor of the hut, hide the evidence of the burial, and flee before dawn with their families.

A few years later, the daughter of the villainous goatherd, just married, becomes possessed by the ghost of Singamma. The girl dances for days, singing incomprehensibly. The words of her song are the cries of a Kuravar girl, selling her wares in the marketplace. She chants the names of the small birds her people catch, and sings of a sparrow caught and trapped, a sparrow alighting within a virgin, a virgin caught and trapped like a sparrow. Thus she provides subtle clues as to the possessing ghost's identity and history. But still the surrounding crowd is mystified, and the elders keep asking, "Who are you?"

A spirit medium (*kōḍāṅki*) is summoned. With his help, the ghost of Singamma makes her identity known to the villagers who, impressed by the beauty of her dance and fearful of her power, initiate a fine festival for her, celebrating her "like a god." She tells the crowd that she wishes to return to Thief-Stab Hill, the site of her old home, her death, and her burial. And so she goes there. The thorny wasteland on which she is buried is razed, and a government spinning mill is built on the site. The spinning mill becomes Singamma's temple, and she reigns there, satisfied. Vellacami at the end of the song asks her to bless all those who sing of her and rejoice, all those who hear, and all those who read her story.

When I first heard Vellacami's rendition of the Singamma story, I was struck by its complete plausibility. All the events described in this song could (from my point of view) very easily have happened just as Vellacami describes them. The story makes perfect, logical sense, even though it is tragic and unjust. Cevi's rendition of the story, by contrast, contains many inexplicable episodes.

Stylistically, the two versions of the song are also quite different. Cevi's song is addressed to Singamma and much of the story as she sings it is told in the second person, while Vellacami keeps Singamma in the third person until the very end of his performance, when he addresses her, asking her blessing. Cevi repeats Singamma's name several times at the end of almost every line of her song, while Vellacami uses Singamma's name infrequently, and only referentially. Vellacami further distances himself from the story of Singamma by frequently using the reportative particle

-*ām* (usually glossed in English as "it is said" or "they say"), thus disclaiming responsibility for the factuality of the events he describes. The devices Cevi uses repeatedly in her performance to such powerful poetic effect—enjambment and pluralization—are completely absent from Vellacami's song. Vellacami accompanies himself on a drum as he sings. A steady, slowly accelerating drumbeat builds suspense up to the climactic rape and murder scenes. In the possession scene, the drumbeat suddenly becomes elaborate, fluid, and rapid as the Kuravar's marketplace chants are repeated.

Vellacami's main "job" as the *kōḍāṇki* of the Singamma shrine is to allow her spirit to possess him and speak through him on appropriate occasions. Thus, during his performance of the Singamma song, he assumes her voice during the possession scene, and only then. This scene is sharply divided from the rest of the performance by a radical change in drumming style and by a change from a proselike, sung narrative (the lines have no particular meter or length) to a highly rhythmic chant composed of a mixture of meaningful and semantically opaque syllables.

* * *

Research for this chapter was carried out under a Humanities Fellowship from the Rockefeller Foundation. Time to write it was provided by the School of American Research in Santa Fe, New Mexico. I wish to thank Lila Abu-Lughod, Arjun Appadurai, Frank Korom, David Ludden, Catherine Lutz, McKim Marriott, Margaret Mills, and Rajam Ramamurthy for their helpful comments on earlier versions of this chapter.

Notes

1. A note on genre. People in Tamil Nadu commonly sing songs addressed to gods. There are probably thousands of these. Their performance is not necessarily limited to a particular "ritual context," although the songs are most likely to be performed on the occasion of festivals to the gods in question. I have often heard young people singing songs to particular gods not so much because they were devotees of those gods as because they liked the songs. A god may even increase in popularity because of the release of some particularly attractive song addressed to him. (I am thinking here of the cinema song "Ayyappan.") I have not done any kind of extensive study of contemporary Tamil songs addressed to gods, and if such a study has been done by someone else, I am unaware of it. The "god-songs" (*tēvappāḍḍu, kaḍavuḷ pāḍḍu*) with which I am familiar generally stress the god's positive, auspicious attributes. Like the Singamma song, many of them seem pervaded with longing.

2. There is an unresolved debate concerning the degree to which south In-

dian people of untouchable castes accept the principle of caste hierarchy. Berreman (1971), Mencher (1974), and Gough (1973) argue that untouchables subscribe to an essentially egalitarian ideology. Moffatt (1979) argues that untouchables do not question the *principle* of social hierarchy; what they do sometimes question is their own place within the existing order. In my own work (Trawick 1986, 1988) I have tried to show that the verbal art of Tamil untouchables does covertly challenge some of the principles of caste hierarchy. A theme running through very many of their songs is the injustice of their fate. It is not implied that exclusion from the good things of life is all right for others but not for them. It is implied that the act of exclusion on the basis of pollution is itself an absolute wrong.

Nevertheless, it would be false to deny that untouchables believe in the reality of ritual pollution. And the fact that they have "their own untouchables" irrefutably bespeaks their acceptance, at least in some contexts and for some purposes, of "the system." I think the simple truth is that they are not firmly on one side or the other. They accept or deny hierarchy according to the situation they find themselves in. Many of the songs of Untouchables show strong *ambivalence* both toward their own status as persons in the community and toward the social order itself, which has afflicted them with that status.

3. Kuravars are found throughout south India and Sri Lanka. There are many named subdivisions of them. Kuravars from the Madurai area state that *Narikkuṟavaṅka* (jackal-hunters), *Kuruvikkāraṅka* (small-fowl-people), and "Kurava jati" (hunter caste) are all legitimate names for themselves. Because Cevi in the introduction to her performance refers to Singamma as "a child from the house of Kuravars," I have chosen to follow her lead in this chapter and to refer to the nomadic scavengers in Tamil Nadu as Kuravars. The situation is complicated by the fact that there exists in southern Tamil Nadu another low caste called Kuravars who are not nomadic and who are entirely distinct from the nomadic Kuravars discussed in this paper. The content of Cevi's song clearly shows that the Kuravars she refers to are not the settled laborers but the nomadic scavengers more commonly called Narikkuravars.

According to the report of the Kallars who maintain the Singamma shrine in Melur, most of those who become possessed by the spirit of Singamma are young women of the Paraiyar community, like Cevi herself. When they become possessed they dress in Narikkuravar clothes, chant in the Narikkuravar tongue, and demand Narikkuravar food (such as jackal-meat) as an offering.

The people of Melur, the exorcist Vellaccami, and the Narikkuravars who pass through Melur on their rounds all differ in their opinions concerning the precise community of nomads from which Singamma arose, and who the historic Singamma was is a matter that may never be determined. In any case, the cult of Singamma is not under the control of any of the nomadic scavengers, who know about this cult but are remarkably uninterested in it. Rather, the Singamma cult seems to be built upon the *image* of nomadic scavengers that people of other castes, especially Paraiyars, have developed. Cf. Moffatt (1979) and McGilvray (1983) on the relationship between Kuravars and Paraiyars in Tamil and Sri Lankan society.

4. My comparison of Cevi's life story and the life story of the goddess in whom she is interested is not without reason or precedent. Many observers have noted that in South Asia the personalities and life histories of deities and their worshippers tend to be intimately intertwined (Claus 1975; Kakar 1981; McDaniel 1989; Nuckolls 1987; Obeyesekere 1981; Roy 1972; Trawick 1980, 1982, 1990a, b, forthcoming). In Tamil Nadu it is common for individuals to consciously identify with and emulate particular deities, even when they don't formally worship those deities. Female identity in particular is tied up with the personalities of deities.

5. Literature describing relations between speech style and speaker personality (either as expressed by the speaker, or as interpreted by listeners) is massive (for example, Bakhtin 1984; Friedrich 1979a; Goffman 1981; Tannen 1984) although, of course, it would be a mistake to attempt to establish simple one-to-one linkages between particular stylistic features and particular personality "traits." Stylistic indices of a speaker's self-*image* are evident even on a commonsense level, and have been of interest especially to feminist sociolinguists in recent years. In the United States and elsewhere, females as well as members of other subordinate groups are often punished beginning in childhood for demonstrating high degrees of verbal proficiency. (In the United States, for instance, articulate and verbally powerful females are castigated and stimatized as chatterboxes, back-talkers, and nags.) Consequently they learn to keep their mouths shut. Females in American schools, though they are consistently better performers than males in written tests of verbal ability, learn not to exercise this ability in face-to-face encounters, but rather to remain mute, to be "dumb." Silence and *in*articulateness (in the presence of male peers, parents, teachers, et cetera) become their hallmarks. When they do speak, their speech is broken: that is, hesitant, audible only with difficulty, childlike, heavily qualified, and easily controverted and interrupted. The speaker must *assume* that she will not have her listener's attention for very long, therefore she learns to keep her messages not only "soft" but also simple and short. She then becomes defined as incapable of producing a sustained and coherent monologue, and it is concluded that the reason for her verbal incoherence is her inability to maintain an orderly train of thought (cf. Michaels and Cazden 1986). Because her communications necessarily are in pieces, she is viewed as scatterbrained. Disarticulation finally becomes a symptom of femaleness, as well as an expression of it. Women are flawed, therefore their speech must also be flawed, otherwise they are not true women (Lakoff 1975).

In the United States, moreover, since females are regarded as more emotional than males, females often "intentionally" adopt what could aptly be called broken speech (creaky voice, sobbing laughter, hesitancy and unevenness of breath, falsetto syllables, frequent self-interruption and self-correction, departure from established grammatical conventions and habitual speech patterns) to signal that they are overwhelmed by emotion, hence "out of control," hence both feminine and sincere. The incorporation of such "weeping features" into speech or song is a powerful and direct way of portraying feelings of grief, personal loss, and incompletion; indeed this set of features, together with the affective associations just named, may constitute a kind of sociolinguistic universal (Urban 1989).

In villages of Tamil Nadu, speech style is an important index both of gender and of caste status. Untouchables risk severe punishment if they adopt the habits, including speech habits, of higher castes. Criticism and complaint, if expressed at all, must be expressed by them in roundabout ways and with extreme circumspection. *Centamiṛ,* "high" or literate Tamil, is the language of privilege, of purity and of truth. Only the literate (viz., high-caste males, with few exceptions until very recently) are afforded the opportunities to master and wield it. *Koccai tamiṛ,* "low" or street Tamil, is thought to be crude, offensive, and incapable of expressing "high thoughts." This is the language attributed to low-caste people. Even certain high-caste women who live with literate, scholarly men and know by heart thousands of lines of "high Tamil" poetry (which they teach their children), may in ordinary conversation disclaim any knowledge of "beautiful words" and deliberately choose to speak "low" or "vulgar" Tamil as a way of challenging men's right to dictate the way women should speak (Trawick 1990b). Like American blacks, low-status Tamils escape becoming linguistic cripples because most of their verbal interactions are with each other, rather than with executors of the rules of the dominant culture. In their own world, they develop high proficiency at verbal art, encouraging, critiquing, and applauding each other's efforts from childhood on (cf. Heath 1983). And, for reasons that are partly aesthetic and partly political, they elaborate among themselves an esoteric language that remains partly or wholly opaque to "outsiders" (cf. Labov 1972; Kochman 1981).

Cevi, like others of her status, is certainly a victim of what McDermott (1985) calls "systematic inarticulacy." She is defined by people in authority over her as inarticulate, and she is forced by them to be this way, at least in her direct communications with them. And yet, I try to argue here, her very mistakes are eloquent.

6. "Partial isomorphisms," or similarities, between formal properties of a given discourse and properties of the topic of that discourse, are a common feature of poetic speech (Jakobson 1960; Friedrich 1979b), and indeed of casual conversation in general. Tannen (1984) has cogently argued that such iconicity—which runs the range from onomatopoeisis to complex parallelisms between syntax and history, verbal morphology and physical anatomy—may even be a necessary tool in the establishment of coherence in discourse. My suggestion that there may be an iconic relation between Cevi's grammatically fragmented speech style and the brokenness of the life she describes should therefore not raise any eyebrows. Of course, the discovery of poetic iconicity is always "after the fact," and the creation of such iconicity is in most cases not the result of conscious design. Therefore, it is generally futile to try to prove that a speaker intended a particular figure of speech to function as such.

7. This remainder, a leftover piece of lore from a time long past, is the Atharva Veda. It is cited by Kristeva (1982:76) in her argument suggesting that Indian consciousness defines the self in terms of place, and that such a self lives in a world of incomplete separations, of remainders (while a self defined in terms of *language* lives in a world of discrete categories and absolute divisions). In a subsequent publication, I hope to discuss Kristeva's argument more extensively.

8. Stylistic devices such as enjambment are inherently polysemous, just as words are. They can and do mean many things. Often in poetry and song, such

devices are used because of their ambiguity, because the artist desires to say more than one thing, to say contradictory things, to exercise his or her skill in the dream-like act of condensing several messages into a single image, or simply to avoid committing herself to, and reaping the punishment for, a particular statement which she nonetheless wishes to communicate. It is well documented that people in oppressed positions often express their opinions and desires indirectly and ambiguously (spirit possession is the classic example).

Given a text such as Cevi's, it would therefore be foolish to attempt to demonstrate beyond doubt that for some particular form some particular meaning is intended. Doubtless for any such text more than one meaning is intended by the artist, and others still may be read into it by the audience and developed further when members of the audience perform the text before others. In such a situation, the best one can do is seek to establish the plausibility of a particular interpretation by answering questions such as: Is this a meaning that a person such as the artist might want to convey? Is the form of the message consistent with the meaning we are attributing to it? Is the meaning we are attributing to this message congruent with other meanings that have been conveyed by the speaker herself in other messages, or by other speakers in similar situations? Is the meaning we are attributing to this message congruent with the apparent overall meaning(s) of the text at hand? In other words, does it fit? Does it make sense? Or not?

The subject of Cevi's song is a nomadic woman who is murdered and becomes a disembodied, wandering spirit. When Cevi uses enjambment in her song, she puts the name of this spirit at the end of the line, drawing out the final syllable and taking a deep breath before beginning the next line. The listener is made to wait, to find out what happens next to the subject, Singamma. I interpret Cevi's use of enjambment in this song as essentially iconic: the partial and temporary disconnectedness of the name mirrors the partial and temporary disconnectedness of the person to whom the name belongs. A simple, but powerful, poetic figure—the hanging voice as a sign of the homeless soul. Elsewhere, of course, similar devices might be used in different ways to different effects.

9. Cf. Blackburn (1988) on the emotional depth of death stories in Tamil. Blackburn argues that in the performance tradition he studied, Tamil people are inclined to identify and sympathize especially strongly with story heroes and heroines who die tragic deaths, and are likely to become possessed by the spirits of the protagonists when death stories are told; whereas stories of auspicious events evoke less powerful feelings.

10. Cf. Derrida (1974) on scription as spoor. Writing, Kristeva tells us, is a spatialization of thought. It takes us back to the world before language made thought immaterial and abstract. Writing is cathartic. It gives a place to our fears.

References

Bakhtin, Mikhail

1984 *Problems of Dostoevsky's Poetics*. Edited and translated by Caryl Emerson. Minneapolis: University of Minnesota Press.

Berreman, Gerald
1971 The Brahmanical View of Caste. *Contributions to Indian Sociology,* n.s. 5:16–23.
Blackburn, Stuart H.
1988 *Singing of Birth and Death: Texts in Performance.* Philadelphia: University of Pennsylvania Press.
Claus, Peter J.
1975 The Siri Myth and Ritual. *Ethnology* 14:47–58.
Derrida, Jacques
1974 *Of Grammatology.* Translated by Gayatri Spivak. Baltimore: Johns Hopkins University Press.
Douglas, Mary
1969 *Purity and Danger.* London: Routledge and Kegan Paul.
Friedrich, Paul
1979a Speech as a Personality Symbol: The Case of Achilles. In *Language, Context and the Imagination,* pp. 402–440. Stanford, Calif.: Stanford University Press.
1979b Poetic Language and the Imagination: A Reformulation of the Sapir Hypothesis. In *Language, Context and the Imagination,* pp. 441–512. Stanford, Calif.: Stanford University Press.
1989 Language, Ideology, and Political Economy. *American Anthropologist* 91: 295–312.
Goffman, Erving
1981 The Lecture. In *Forms of Talk,* pp. 160–196. Philadelphia: University of Pennsylvania Press.
Gough, Kathleen
1973 Harijans in Thanjavur. In *Imperialism and Revolution in South Asia,* K. Gough and H. P. Sharma, eds. New York: Monthly Review Press.
Heath, Shirley Brice
1983 *Ways with Words: Language, Life and Work in Communities and Classrooms.* Cambridge: Cambridge University Press.
Jakobson, Roman
1960 Closing Statement: Linguistics and Poetics. In *Style in Language,* Thomas Sebeok, ed., pp. 350–377. Cambridge, Mass.: MIT Press.
Kakar, Sudhir
1981 *The Inner World: A Psychoanalytic Study of Childhood and Society in India.* Delhi: Oxford University Press.
Kochman, Thomas
1981 *Black and White Styles in Conflict.* Chicago: University of Chicago Press.
Kristeva, Julia
1982 *Powers of Horror: An Essay on Abjection.* Translated by Leon Roudiez. New York: Columbia University Press.
Labov, William
1972 *Language in the Inner City.* Philadelphia: University of Pennsylvania Press.

Lakoff, Robin
1975 *Language and Woman's Place*. New York: Harper and Row.
McDaniel, June
1989 *The Madness of the Saints: Ecstatic Religion in Bengal*. Chicago: University of Chicago Press.
McDermott, Ray
1985 Lecture delivered to N.E.H. Summer Institute on Humanistic Approaches to the Study of Linguistics. Georgetown University, Washington, D.C.
McGilvray, Dennis
1983 Paraiyar Drummers of Sri Lanka: Consensus and Constraint in an Untouchable Caste. *American Ethnologist* 10 : 97–115.
Mencher, Joan
1974 The Caste System Upside Down, or the Not-So-Mysterious East. *Current Anthropology* 15 : 469–493.
Michaels, Sarah, and Courtney Cazden
1986 Teacher-Child Collaboration as Oral Preparation for Literacy. In *Acquisition of Literacy: Ethnographic Perspectives*. Norwood, N.J.: Ablex.
Moffatt, Michael
1979 *An Untouchable Community in South India: Structure and Consensus*. Princeton, N.J.: Princeton University Press.
Nuckolls, Charles
1987 Culture and Causal Thinking: Prediction and Diagnosis in Jalari Culture. Ph.D. dissertation, University of Chicago.
Obeyesekere, Gananath
1981 *Medusa's Hair*. Chicago: University of Chicago Press.
Parry, Jonathan
1982 Sacrificial Death and the Necrophagous Ascetic. In *Death and the Regeneration of Life*, Maurice Bloch and Jonathan Parry, eds., pp. 74–118. Cambridge: Cambridge University Press.
Roy, Manusha
1972 *Bengali Women*. Chicago: University of Chicago Press.
Tannen, Deborah
1984 *Conversational Style: Analyzing Talk Among Friends*. Norwood, N.J.: Ablex.
Trawick Egnor, Margaret
1980 On the Meaning of Sakti to Women in Tamil Nadu. In *The Powers of Tamil Women*, Susan S. Wadley, ed., pp. 1–34. Maxwell Center, South Asia Series. Syracuse: Syracuse University Press.
1982 The Changed Mother, or What the Smallpox Goddess Did When There Was No More Smallpox. *Contributions to Asian Studies* 18 : 24–45.
1986 Internal Iconicity in Paraiyar Crying Songs. In *Another Harmony: New Essays on the Folklore of India*, Stuart H. Blackburn and A. K. Ramanujan, eds., pp. 294–344. Berkeley: University of California Press.
1988 Spirits and Voices in Tamil Songs. *American Ethnologist* 15 : 193–215.

1990a Untouchability and the Fear of Death in a Tamil Song. In *Emotion and Discourse in Anthropology,* Catherine Lutz and Lila Abu-Lughod, eds. pp. 186–206. Cambridge: Cambridge University Press.

1990b *Notes on Love in a Tamil Family.* Los Angeles: University of California Press.

forthcoming Do Not Go Gentle: A Tamil Woman Sings About Her Death.

Urban, Greg

1988 Ritual Wailing in Amerindian Brazil. *American Anthropologist* 90: 385–400.

Carol Salomon

9. The Cosmogonic Riddles of Lalan Fakir

No folk poet has made a greater contribution to modern Bengali literature than Lalan Shah (Lālan Śāh), better known as Lalan Fakir. Lalan lived in the nineteenth century in the village of Seuriya (alternately spelled Cheuriya) in what is now Kushtia District, Bangladesh. He was a member of the Baul *sampradāy* (tradition), which is noted for its mystic folk songs generally termed *bāul gān* (Baul songs) in West Bengal, but in Bangladesh also named *bhāb gān* (songs for reflection). While there are numerous outstanding Baul poets, Lalan is considered to be the best of them all. Within the Baul *sampradāy* he holds a unique position. He is regarded as the *ādiguru* (first guru) of the Baul sect, the Lalan Shahi *sampradāy*. Twice a year, on the first day of Kārtik (October–November), his death anniversary, and on the full moon night of Phālgun (February–March), his devotees gather at the site of his *ākhṛā* (ashram) to sing his songs.

Lalan's songs have inspired many poets and authors of Bengal, most notably Rabindranath Tagore, whose thought and poetry were significantly influenced by Lalan. Tagore was one of the earliest collectors of Lalan's songs. He had in his private collection two notebooks in which an unknown scribe had recorded a total of 298 songs composed by Lalan.[1] Tagore is also credited with bringing the songs of Lalan to the attention of educated Bengalis; until he published twenty songs in the literary journal *Prabāsī* (vol. 15, *Āśvin, Agrahāyan, Pauṣ,* and *Māgh,* 1322 B.S., 1915–16 [*bāṃlā san* "Bengali Era"]), Lalan was little known outside village Bengal.[2] To this day, the songs of Lalan continue to be an inspiration to Bengali authors.

But while Lalan's songs are valued for their literary quality, their symbolic meaning is usually not comprehended by the uninitiated. This seems to be as much due to the audience's inclination to deny or close its eyes to the tantric sexual rites of the Bauls as to the ambiguity of the songs and the secrecy of the rituals. As Charles Capwell points out (1986 : 11–12 and chapter 2), Bengali society at large has an ambivalent attitude toward the Bauls. On the one hand, the songs of the Bauls and the humanistic beliefs they express draw the admiration of Bengalis, but on the other hand they find the more esoteric practices of the Bauls objectionable.

From Lalan's time to the present, his songs have been sung and admired all over West Bengal and Bangladesh. But in the last twenty-five years his popularity in Bangladesh has risen to new heights and he has attained the stature of a cultural hero. His remarkable talents as a poet first began to receive widespread recognition among Muslim Bengalis when, in the process of shaping a regional identity, they turned to their folk culture. In fact, the prevailing attitude of Muslim Bengali society toward Baul songs in general and Lalan's songs in particular, and toward the fakirs who sing them, can serve as a barometer of where it stands at any given time on the question of regional versus Islamic identity.[3]

During the late nineteenth century and first half of the twentieth, the reform movements set out to strip Bengali Islam of its local characteristics.[4] The Bauls, or *neṛār* fakirs, as they were also termed (see "The Baul *Sampradāy,*" below), were one of the main groups of fakirs denounced by the reformists for their heterodoxy. The mere fact that the Bauls are a musical tradition would have been sufficient cause for the reformists, who believed that music is forbidden by Islam, to oppose the Bauls. Their syncretic beliefs and sexual practices, of which the reformists had become aware, made the Bauls all the more vulnerable.[5]

They were denounced in *fatwa*s (legal decisions) for corrupting Bengali Islam with Hindu beliefs and practices. "Baul Dhvaṅsa Phatoyā" (Bengali for Arabic *fatwa;* Decision for the Destruction of the Bauls), written by Maulana Reyajuddin Ahmad in 1332 B.S. [1926] and revised and enlarged the following year, singles Lalan out as "the number one foe, a spy for the Arya Samāj [a Hindu revivalist organization], and a deceiver of six to seven million Muslims" (the Baul population as estimated by Ahmad, quoted in Caudhurī 1974a : 78).[6] The Bauls suffered physical attacks as well as verbal abuse. In 1947 Maulana Aphsaruddin Ahmed (1887–1959) disrupted the festival at Lalan's *ākhṛā,* then held on the full-moon night in the month of Caitra (March–April), and cut off the topknots of the Bauls who attended. Bauls did not congregate in large numbers again for a festival at the *ākhṛā* or in the surrounding area as long as Maulana Aphsaruddin was alive (Caudhurī 1974a : 39–40 and 1974b : 122). During the reformist period, public performance of the songs of Lalan and other Bauls became rare in East Bengal (Mansur Uddin 1978 : 24).

Soon after the formation of Pakistan, the Pakistani government's attempt to subvert the culture of its eastern half in the name of Islam, particularly its brutal suppression of the Language Movement (*bhāṣār āndolan:* the agitation to make Bengali an official language of Pakistan along with Urdu) in February 1952, brought about an abrupt change in the way Muslim Bengalis perceived their own cultural heritage. In their search for an identity rooted in the soil of Bengal, rather than based on Islam as practiced in Arabia, Muslim Bengalis exalted literary figures, whether Hindu or Muslim, who expressed nonsectarian humanistic beliefs. Foremost among them were Tagore, Nazrul Islam, and Lalan, who came to epitomize the Bauls, already symbols of Bengali folk culture.

The most telling indication of Lalan's rise in status in the period between the Language Movement and the emergence of Bangladesh is the new esteem accorded to the site of Lalan's *ākhṛā,* which had been the scene of reformist persecution of the Bauls. In 1962–63 a mausoleum was built over Lalan's grave and the Lalan Lok Sāhitya Kendra, or Lalan Folk Literature Center (the name was later changed to the Lalan Academy), was established beside it as an institute for the study of folk literature. The institute includes an open-air stage, used until recently for the biannual Lalan festival which once again drew a large number of Lalan Shahi fakirs.

To the reformists, Lalan was a Hindu masquerading as a Muslim. As Lalan grew in stature, however, some scholars went to the opposite extreme and began to claim him for Islam. Newly discovered legends published by these scholars ascribe to Lalan a Muslim birth, contradicting earlier biographical accounts according to which Lalan's parents were Hindus (see "Lalan in Legend and History," below) and creating a controversy that has polarized Bengali scholarship on Lalan from the 1960s until the present. Even Lalan's title Shāh (Persian for "king") is an Islamization of Sā̃i (< Sanskrit *swāmī* "lord"), which is the form of the name that occurs in the songs recorded in Tagore's notebooks. Lalan's songs, too, have undergone Islamization. In the edition *Lālan Śāh o Lālan Gītikā,* edited by Muhammad Abu Talib, Arabic and Persian words used in Bengali are spelled to reflect Arabic and Persian, rather than Bengali, pronunciation. Moreover, in at least one case, an interpolation intended to prove that Lalan was a Muslim has been introduced into the text of a song. (See the interpolation *khātnār jāt,* "circumcised caste" in vol. 2, no. 293.)[7] There can be no doubt that the desire to legitimize Lalan by turning him into a respectable Sufi, complete with his own shrine, was a motivating factor behind the construction of Lalan's mausoleum.

In independent Bangladesh, Lalan's popularity has continued to increase. A Lalan *pariṣad,* an organization that sponsors performances of Lalan's songs and also publishes the journal *Lālan Pariṣad Patrikā,* has been established in Dhaka, with branches in Jhinaidah, Rajshahi, Jessore, Khulna, and Chittagong. Lalan is the only folk poet whose songs are taught at the Silpa Kala Academy (Academy of Fine Arts) in Dhaka, and they are taught there not by an academically trained instructor, but by Khoda Baks Bisvas, a Lalan Shahi fakir from Kushtia.[8] Lalan's songs are frequently heard on radio and television. Professional singers (such as Farida Parveen) who are not themselves fakirs specialize in singing them much in the manner of singers specializing in Nazrul *gīti* or Rabindra *saṅgīt.* While most of the scholarship still focuses on the controversy over Lalan's birth, in the 1970s Bengali Muslim scholars, building on work done by Upendranath Bhattacarya, for the first time studied the esoteric aspect of the Lalan tradition.[9]

Yet as more emphasis is being placed on a pan-Islamic identity, ambivalent attitudes toward the tradition have once again intensified. When I first visited Seuriya in 1981, the Lalan festival in the month of Phālgun was a three-day event with the official program held on the stage of the Lalan Academy near the area where the fakirs were staying, whereas on my second visit in 1986, I found the festival had been curtailed to one night due to the withdrawal of government funding; the official program had been moved to a field some distance from the academy; and only a few fakirs had been selected to participate in it, the other fakirs had remained at the Academy, where they sang informally as they also had done on my previous visit. The new setting and altered program, I was told by one scholar, were intended to give the festival an air of respectability and make a favorable impression on government officials who are put off by ganja-smoking fakirs. In the process of nationalizing Lalan's songs and making him over to fit the image of a folk hero acceptable to the mainstream of Muslim Bengali society, it seems Lalan is not only being disassociated from his esoteric beliefs, but also from the very fakirs who carry on his tradition.

In what follows, I will first give an overview of Baul religion, placing special emphasis on Baul *sādhanā* (method of realization). Next, I will give a biographical account of Lalan. Finally, after a general introduction to his songs, I will treat in some detail a few songs Lalan composed in the form of cosmogonic riddles. Since the study of Lalan's songs and of his cosmogonic ideas is largely an unexplored field, what I will be presenting is only preliminary and will undoubtedly need to be revised in the future.

The Baul *Sampradāy*

The Baul *sampradāy* is a syncretistic tradition which draws from Tantric Buddhism (Sahajiya), Tantric Hinduism (both Vaishnava Sahajiya and Shaiva-Shakta), Gauriya Vaishnavism, and Islam. There are both Hindu Bauls, who are usually Vaishnavas, and Muslim Bauls, who are Sufis and are generally termed fakirs or *neṛār* fakirs rather than Bauls.

Neṛār fakir literally means "fakir with a shaven head." The term *nāṛā* or *neṛā* (fem., *neṛī*) originally referred to Buddhist *bhikṣus* and *bhikṣuṇīs* (monks and nuns; literally, male and female beggars), who shaved their heads and are believed to have followed the Sahajiya path of worship.[10] Some subsequently converted to Islam, while others became Vaishnavas.[11] After changing their religious affiliations, many *neṛās* eventually gave up the practice of shaving their heads, but continued to practice Sahajiya sexual rituals. It is clear from the use of the term *neṛār* fakir to refer to Muslim Bauls that some of the Buddhist *neṛās* became Bauls. It can be surmised that the *neṛās* had a strong influence on the development of the Baul *sampradāy,* particularly in respect to *sādhanā.*[12]

The Bauls, like other South Asian mystic traditions, reject caste, revere the guru or murshid as a representative of the Supreme on earth, and believe that the body is a microcosm of the universe—a belief they call *dehatattva* (the doctrine of the body). It is in their sexual rituals, however, that they break with many South Asian mystic traditions and most closely resemble the Tantric Buddhists, from whom they are descended, and the Vaishnava Sahajiyas, who share with the Bauls a common background in Buddhist Tantrism.[13]

Baul *Sādhanā*

Although Bauls all over Bengal practice basically the same *sādhanā,* the details of the rituals vary according to region and guru. The following overview of Baul sexual *sādhanā* during the three or three and a half days a woman is said to menstruate is based on the practices of the Lalan Shahi fakirs of Bangladesh. Only the most salient features of the rites are given.

According to Baul doctrine, the Supreme is present in the body in semen and menstrual blood. The Supreme in semen, on the one hand, is the *puruṣ,* the male principle, and on the other hand is the *īśvar,* who is both male and female. (Baul poets do not draw clear distinctions in their songs between these two aspects of the Supreme, so that it is frequently difficult to determine which one of them is being referred to.) The Bauls believe that the female as well as the male has semen.[14] The Supreme in semen resides in the *sahasrārcakra* at the top of the head,[15] also termed the *lā mokām* (Ar., *maqām*), or between the eyes in the two-petaled lotus, or *ājñācakra,*[16] but travels around the body, making one complete trip every month. Thus on each day of the lunar month, semen is found in a different part of the body. (Note that one of the names of the Supreme and one of the words for semen is *cā̃d* or *candra,* "moon.")[17] Whereas in a man's body the Supreme in semen remains passive, steady (*aṭal*), invisible (*nirūp*) and cannot be experienced, in a woman's body it is active, has the nature of bliss, and takes manifest form (*prakāśyarūp*) during menstruation.

Menstrual blood, which is believed to be the female procreative fluid and to contain the female principle, the *śakti* or *prakṛti,* is said by some to also come from the head.[18] Its appearance in the woman's *mūlādhār cakra,* at the base of the spinal column between the anus and the genital organs, is conceived of in the form of a blossoming flower. Bauls also refer to the *śakti* in terms of the *kuṇḍalinī,* envisioned as a coiled snake in the *mūlādhār* of each person.[19]

The goal of Baul *sādhanā* is to unite the dual polar principles of the Supreme and to reintegrate them into the Supreme in order to regain the original state of cosmic unity. The ritual to effect this reintegration, which reverses the process that leads to death and rebirth, consists of sexual intercourse involving seminal retention during a woman's menstrual period. (Since the Bauls believe that longevity is dependent upon the preservation of semen, the *sādhak* (male practitioner) attempts to prevent ejaculation also when a woman is not menstruating.) The *sādhak* draws a drop of menstrual blood into his penis by a process the Bauls refer to as *śoṣaṇ bān* (suction arrow) and yogic texts call *vajroli mudrā,* thus uniting semen and blood within his own body. Then, using yogic techniques of breath control, he takes his semen along with the drop of menstrual blood back to the *ājñācakra* or *sahasrār* via the middle of the three *nāṛīs* (channels), the *suṣumnā.*

Lalan Shahi fakirs believe that the Supreme becomes manifest in menstrual blood and can be "caught" at the start of the third day of menstruation. This is in contrast to some other Baul sects, which hold that the time for catching the Supreme is late on the third or early on the fourth day.[20] According to Baul belief, on this day the active form of the Supreme in female semen, frequently termed the *sahaj mānuṣ* (Natural Man) or the *adhar mānuṣ* (Uncatchable Man), desiring to unite with the *śakti* in menstrual blood, appears in the egg sac (*ḍimbakoṣ*) in the woman's *mūlādhār*, which is situated at the *triveṇī*, the junction of the three *nāṛīs: iṛā, piṅgalā,* and *suṣumnā*. The *sādhak* is able to tell when the Supreme is present by the sweet smell and taste of the blood. Whereas semen represents *prem* (love) and is referred to as *kṣīr* (cream), menstrual blood represents *kām* (lust) and is termed *nīr* (water). Just as the mythological swan separates milk from water, so the *sādhak*, through sexual intercourse, is said to separate *kṣīr* from *nīr, prem* from *kām*. The substance of the *adhar mānuṣ* is gradually thickened, producing an essence likened to butter (*nanī*). Once this is accomplished, the *sādhak* attracts it into his penis (see Das and Mahapatra 1958: no. 130, verse 2) and together with his semen, brings it up to his head, where the *adhar mānuṣ* is reunited with the *aṭal īśvar* (Bhattacarya 1971: 373). The resulting feeling of bliss that the *sādhak* experiences is what the Bauls call variously "catching the Uncatchable," "catching the thief," or "being dead while alive."[21]

As is apparent from the above description, Baul *sādhanā*, like tantric *sādhanā* in general, is described entirely from the male's point of view.[22] Thus Baul songs do not address the question of what a woman experiences during *sādhanā*. In fact, although there are female Baul singers and gurus,[23] there are few if any Baul songs by female composers. According to Riziya Khatun, the wife of Karim Shah, a Lalan Shahi fakir from Jessore, the ritual is performed primarily for the *sādhak*'s sake. He has to "catch" the Supreme already possessed by the woman. By transferring her power to him, the woman rejuvenates (*bā̃ciye rākhe*) the *sādhak*.[24] Although there is no parallel notion that the woman must obtain the Supreme from the man, she too is said to experience the blissful nature of the Supreme. For *sādhanā* to be successful, both *sādhak* and *sādhikā* must "die a single death"; together they must become "dead while alive."

Another ritual that the Bauls practice during menses is the ingestion of the four moons (*cāri candra*), or the four cups (*cār piyālā* [Pers. *piyāla*]), which are feces, semen, menstrual blood, and urine, and are identified with the four elements earth, air, fire, and water, the materials out of which man was created.[25] The *sādhak* takes the menstrual blood orally, puts a small amount either in a *mālui* (Skt. *mallaka,* a small, round coconut-shell vessel) or a *kisti* (Pers. *kashtī,* "boat," a larger, boat-shaped vessel) and then places half of the remainder in the *sādhikā*'s mouth. (Lalan Shahi fakirs believe the first drops of menstrual blood contain the most *śakti*.) The *sādhikā* takes his semen in the same way and shares it with him, also reserving some in the vessel.[26] Subsequently, a drink is prepared in the *kisti* of the four substances and sometimes a fifth substance, the fluid obtained from the woman following intercourse (*śṛṅgār ras*) is added. Before drinking the mixture, the *sādhak* and *sādhikā* (female practitioner) recite a *sodhan mantra* (mantra for purification), and after drinking it they smear it on their bodies. These substances are also taken either together or separately when the woman is not menstruating. *Strī bīrya*, the white female sexual fluid, then substitutes for menstrual blood.

The ritual drinking of the four bodily excretions is explained by the Bauls as a means to renew the body. Man depends on the elements for his very existence. Thus the excretion of the four substances homologous with the elements drains the body of its vital strength, while their ingestion reinvigorates it (Bhattacarya 1971: 424). Since the elements emanated from the Supreme, the consumption of the *cāri candra* or *cār piyālā* also effects reintegration into the Supreme. (Note in this connection that the *cār piyālā* are associated with the states of gradual absorption in God. See below, "The Riddle of the Flame.")

Lalan in Legend and History

Although many legends are told about Lalan, few details can be accepted as historical, particularly as regards the period of his life before he settled in Seuriya. There are basically two different stories of his origins. According to one, he was born a Hindu and according to the other, a Muslim.

The Hindu Legend

The earliest biographical sources unanimously state that Lalan was born in a Hindu Kayastha family, and most mention his connection with Cāpṛā, or the adjacent village Bhā̃ṛarā in Kushtia District; some say it was his place of birth, while others only say it was where members of his caste lived.[27] According to these sources, Lalan contracted smallpox while on a pilgrimage and was left for dead by his companions or by his parents. He was saved by a Muslim, some sources say by his guru Siraj Sai, and as a result became a fakir.

The legend ascribing to Lalan a Hindu birth cannot as a whole be taken as historical fact. The first two biographical accounts known to appear in print—an obituary article entitled "Mahātmā Lālan Phakir" by an anonymous author, published in the journal *Hitakarī* on October 31, 1890, just two weeks after Lalan's death,[28] and a biographical sketch by the historian Aksay Kumar Maitreya quoted in Tagore's niece Sarala Devi's article, "Lālan Phakir O Gagan," published in 1302 B.S. (1896)—state that there is no reliable source for Lalan's life and that all the information the authors were able to gather is based on hearsay; Lalan did not talk about his life, and neither did his disciples.

The Muslim Legend

In 1366 B.S. (1960), Shah Latiph Aphi Anhu reported the discovery of a manuscript dated 1303 B.S. (1897), purportedly written by Lalan's disciple Duddu Shah and containing an entirely different account of Lalan's life.[29] The text of this manuscript was first published in 1374 B.S. (1967) by Lutphar Rahman. The story of Lalan's life as related in this account is as follows: Lalan was born in a Muslim family in the village of Harishpur, Jessore District, on the first of Kārtik, 1179 B.S. (1772). His father, Daribullah Deoyan, and his mother, Amina Khatun, died when he was a young child. He was raised by Siraj Sai, a palanquin-bearer who also lived in Harishpur and who eventually became his guru. At the age of twenty-five, after the death of Siraj Sai, Lalan went to live in Navadvip in the home of a Hindu woman. One day, he attended a gathering of pandits, but as he was a Muslim he was not allowed to eat with them. Deeply offended, Lalan created the illusion that he was sitting next to each one of the pandits. Sometime after this incident, while traveling by boat from Kheturi (the birthplace of the famous sixteenth-century Bengali Vaishnava poet and theologian Narottam, and the site of a large *melā* [fair] established by him, which is held to this day and is attended by many Bauls), he was stricken by smallpox and thrown overboard. Instead of drowning, he floated to Seuriya, where he was saved by a man named Malam. Malam became Lalan's disciple and built an *ākhṛā* for him near his house.

The account of Lalan's Muslim origins is obviously apocryphal. The manuscript was discovered at just about the time when Lalan's songs were becoming a source of national pride for Muslim Bengalis and is clearly an attempt to claim him for Islam. The incident of Lalan's miraculous reduplication can, of course, be dismissed as impossible.

Lalan in History

While the circumstances of Lalan's early years will probably remain shrouded in mystery, there can be no doubt concerning the following widely known details of his adulthood: Lalan belonged to the Muslim Baul tradition, his guru was Siraj Sai, a fact Lalan himself reveals in the *bhaṇitās* (signature lines) of his songs, and he died in Seuriya on October 17, 1890,[30] at an advanced age.[31] Some further biographical information found in the *Hitakarī* obituary is less well known. (This account is the most reliable source for Lalan's life; it is the earliest, and it was written by someone who had met Lalan.) According to the obituary, Lalan had disciples—more than ten thousand, by common report—in almost every part of Bengal and lived in his *ākhṛā* in Seuriya with his wife and fifteen or sixteen disciples. In accordance with Baul doctrine, he had no children of his own. Contrary to the stereotypical view of the Bauls as homeless wandering minstrels, Lalan had a middle-class standard of living. He owned land and had almost 2000 *ṭākā* in cash when he died. He was buried on the site of his *ākhṛā* without religious ceremony.

An Introduction to Lalan's Songs

The Corpus

At least seven hundred different songs with Lalan's *bhaṇitā* have been published. Of these, 462 songs in the collection *Lālan-gītikā* (henceforth, LG), edited by Matilal Das and Piyuskanti Mahapatra (1958), can be identified with reasonable certainty as authentic and thus be considered the core of the Lalan corpus. This collection is based on the songs in Tagore's notebooks and on transcriptions of songs from a notebook which was found by Das in Lalan's *ākhṛā* in the early part of the twentieth century and which has since been lost. Although the songs are poorly edited, most scholars attest to their authenticity.[32] Moreover, they form a regular part of the repertoire of the Lalan Shahi fakirs. I have found from fieldwork in both West Bengal and Bangladesh that, unlike Bauls of other *sampradāys*, the Lalan Shahi fakirs have a distinct awareness as to which Lalan songs are genuine and which are not, and do not arbitrarily use Lalan's *bhaṇitā* in songs composed by other poets, as Bauls in West Bengal often do.[33] Whereas the Bauls of West Bengal have no specific training in Lalan's songs and usually know only a small number of them, the Lalan Shahi fakirs may spend as many as twenty years in apprenticeship to a guru, primarily, although by no means exclusively, learning the songs of Lalan.

Method of Composition

The weight of evidence indicates that Lalan was illiterate and that he composed his songs orally. Sometime after their composition, the songs are believed to have been written down by his disciples in notebooks (Bhattacarya 1971: 540). It is also thought that Lalan set his songs to his own tunes; however, it is not possible to determine whether the tunes sung today by the fakirs in Jessore and Kushtia, the center of the *sampradāy*, are the original ones. The tunes in this region are standardized, and there is a sense among the fakirs that they are traditional. In contrast, in other areas of Bengal, the songs are not sung to any fixed tunes; rather, a song can be put to any tune the singer chooses.

Not all scholars, however, agree that Lalan was illiterate. The breadth of his knowledge of Hindu (especially Vaishnava) and Islamic traditions and his poetic genius has led some scholars to argue that he knew how to read and write.[34] But this reasoning seems to stem from the stereotypical view of oral poetry as artless and lacking in complexity, and from the tendency to idealize cultural heroes. Upendranath Bhattacarya, author of *Bāṅglār Bāul O Bāul Gān* (The Bauls of Bengal and Baul Songs), the most comprehensive study of the Bauls to date, was the first to cast doubts on Lalan's illiteracy. He concedes (1971: 540) that it is possible Lalan composed orally, but rejects as unbelievable statements made by fakirs and previous biographers that Lalan was unable to read and write.[35] Yet the author of Lalan's obituary reported firsthand that Lalan was in fact illiterate, although his songs gave the impression that he was a great pandit (Caudhuri 1974b: 8).

Several scholars mention property deeds bearing Lalan's signature, but, to my knowledge, no photocopies of these documents have been published. The photocopies of two property deeds Muhammad Ābu Tālib provides in "Lālan-cariter Upādān Tathya o Satya" (1976: 18 and 22) are modern handwritten copies of the original documents, so their authenticity is unverifiable. Another property deed, however, published in *Lālan Smārak Grantha* (Caudhuri 1974b: opposite p. 1), bears the name Śrī Lālan Sā̃i at the top, underneath which is written: "*kalom* [pen] Śrī Śītal Śāhā." This seems to indicate that Śītal Śāhā (or Shah, a surname common among Muslim Bauls), who was one of Lalan's main disciples, signed the deed for Lalan. If so, this would be conclusive proof of Lalan's illiteracy.

Transmission

The songs of Lalan are orally transmitted from guru to disciple, or from one Baul singer to another. Bauls who are literate may record songs in notebooks, but they are not usually recopied to become part of a manuscript tradition. In Kushtia and in the neighboring district of Jessore, the songs have been handed down generally with only minor variation. The versions sung today are very close to those recorded in the Tagore notebooks. The songs have been transmitted with little change among Lalan Shahi fakirs in the main districts of the *sampradāy* because the tradition is a fairly recent one; many Lalan Shahi fakirs trace their spiritual line of descent (*silsila* or *guruparamparā*) directly back to Lalan in only two to five generations. Moreover, the fakirs place importance on memorizing the songs and reproducing them in performance as closely as possible to the texts taught by the guru.

Description of the Songs

Lalan's songs are short compositions consisting of a refrain and three or four rhymed verses ending in a *bhaṇitā*. His style is simple, colloquial, thought-provoking and full of vigor. The songs use a wide range of vocabulary, including Sanskrit and Sanskrit-derived words, Persian and Arabic words, even entire Arabic phrases from the Qur'an, and words from Kushtia dialect.

Lalan's songs are full of wry, often self-mocking humor. In typical Baul fashion, Lalan addresses his mind, calling himself "coward" or "fool" (*bheṛe*) or "king of bastards" (*bejātir rājā*). In many songs, the *bhaṇitā* serves as a punchline, giving an unexpected or funny twist to the songs: "Some will say Lalan the fool speaks nothing but gibberish" (LG no. 280); "Lalan says, What's a guru to you anyway, on a full stomach?" (LG no. 56); "Lalan asks, Does a fruit taste sweet if it's kicked until it's ripe?" (LG no. 447); "Lalan says, Why worry? Does Fate ever make revisions?" (LG no. 418). Sometimes the *bhaṇitā* is put in the mouth of his guru, Siraj Sai, who berates Lalan for his failure to see the truth: "Siraj Sai says, Lalan, you were only eager to fill your fat belly" (LG no. 398); "Lalan, you're walking in circles. You haven't a clue what to do" (LG no. 116); "Foolish Lalan even tries to swindle sadhus" (LG no. 444).

Imagery drawn from the activities of everyday life, such as fishing, farming, sailing, and litigation, are used as metaphors for Baul sexual *sādhanā*. To express esoteric beliefs and practices, Lalan often juxtaposes unusual words, painting surreal pictures. For example: "the trap in the house of the wind" (LG no. 49) signifies the yogic practice of breath control to catch the Supreme; "the city of mirrors" (LG no. 18) represents the place at the top of the head where the Absolute resides; and the boat loaded with the Ganges that sails on dry land (LG no. 184) symbolizes a woman's body when she is menstruating.

Lalan's songs treat a variety of subjects related to Baul religion. They revile caste, sectarian religion, and external rituals such as *pūjā, namāz* (Bengali *nāmāj*), and pilgrimage. They reject the authority of Hindu scriptures and the Qur'an; to Lalan, all scriptures are merely books written by men. They praise the guru or murshid and describe the Supreme in man, whom Lalan calls by such names as Man of the Heart (*maner mānuṣ*), Golden Man (*sonar mānuṣ*), Uncatchable Moon (*adhar cā̃d*), Unknown Bird (*acin pākhi*), Allah, Krishna, and Lord (*sā̃i*), as well as *sahaj mānuṣ* and *adhar mānuṣ,* mentioned above. The songs hint at the sexual *sādhanā* of the Bauls. And, finally, some of them concern the mystery of creation as the key to understanding the true nature of the Creator. It is these songs that are the subject of the discussion which follows.

Lalan's songs show the influence of both Bengali Islam and Vaishnavism. In those songs which draw from the Islamic tradition, Lalan sings of the creation of the world from divine light (*nūr*), of Fatima as the *śakti* of Allah, of the two doctrines the Prophet taught, one exoteric (*jāhir;* Ar. *ẓāhir*), found in books (*saphinā;* Ar. *safīna,* "boat"; in Pers. also, "a boat-shaped codex," and hence a general term for "book"), and the other esoteric (*bātin;* Ar. *bāṭin*), contained in man's heart or breast (*sinā;* Pers. *sīna*). He also sings about the superiority of *mārphat* (Ar. *maʿrifat;* mystical knowledge) to *śariat* (Ar. *sharīʾat;* Islamic law), and about the oneness of Allah, Muhammad, and man. He describes the murshid as the *barjakh* (Ar. *barzakh*), intercessor between man and God, and says that sainthood (*bilāyet;* Ar. *wilāyat*) is preferable to prophethood (*nabuyat;* Ar. *nubuwwat*), for sainthood concerns the secret doctrines of *mārphat,* while prophethood concerns the dictates of *śariat.* In songs on Vaishnava themes, Lalan tells of Krishna's boyhood pranks, such as his butter thief escapade, and of the loves of Radha, Krishna, and the gopis. He also sings of Caitanya as the dual incarnation of Radha and Krishna. Sometimes, the two traditions come together in the same song, as in this example:

Learn about *nāmāj* before you do it.
Keep your eyes on the human Mecca.
Fulfill man's desires

here and now, through man.
Handsome Kala plays in the world
of the human body.
(LG no. 294)

Here Lalan says that Kala (Krishna) is in the Mecca of the human body. By "*nāmāj*" he does not mean the external ritual of *namāz* practiced five times a day facing Mecca, but an internalized *namāz* performed all the time (*dāyemi;* Pers. *dā'imī;* Ar. *dā'im*). For Lalan, *namāz* is constant meditation on the guru or on one's beloved (see LG nos. 214 and 265).

Regardless of whether the songs use Vaishnava or Islamic terminology, whether the Supreme is referred to as Allah or Krishna and his *śakti* as Fatima or Radha, the underlying system the songs refer to is the same. In most cases, they cannot be fully understood apart from the tantric beliefs and practices of the Bauls.

The Cosmogonic Riddles

In the final section of this chapter, I will discuss at length four of the songs Lalan composed on the subject of cosmogony. Cosmogonic speculation is an important theme in the songs of Lalan because it provides the rationale for Baul *sādhanā.* According to Baul belief, ontogeny recapitulates cosmogony: the conditions that were present when the universe was created are recreated every month in a woman's body when she menstruates. Just as the Supreme became manifest on the cosmic waters to create the universe, so the Supreme becomes manifest in menstrual blood. By understanding the mystery of human birth, it is possible to understand the mystery of the creation of the universe and to attain the Supreme. Lalan sings:

Search for the root
to the vine
of your own birth.
Lalan says,
There you'll meet the Lord.
(LG no. 160)

The cosmogonic songs I will discuss are in *dhā̃dhā* or *hẽyāli* form. Both these terms are translated as "riddle," but they are used in a somewhat broader sense than the English word, to include paradox, enigma, and catechetical questions. Lalan's cosmogonic riddles often ask a series of questions on the mystery of creation. Sometimes they challenge the listener to solve a puzzle based on clues contained in the song. While Lalan did not compose songs that answer his riddles directly, as Bauls occasionally do, once in a while, possible solutions are found hidden in another song.

That the purpose of the riddles is didactic and that at least some part of their message is meant for those in the general audience who are willing to hear it became clear to me at two performances I attended in Bangladesh in 1986: one in the town of Jhinaidah, sponsored by the local branch of the Lalan Pariṣad, and the other in the village. Gopinathpur, near the town of Magura, sponsored by a local Hindu doctor on the occasion of his *hālkhātā* (a festival held on the opening of a new account book at the start of the year; by contributing what they could to the performance, patients who owed the doctor fees from the preceding year were forgiven their debts). Both performances were held in the form of competitions, between two Bauls or groups of Bauls, termed *pāllā gān* "song competition." The first party sang a riddle song which the second party attempted to answer with spoken commentary, quotes from other songs, humorous anecdotes (intended more to hold the audience's attention than to shed any light on the topic), and another riddle song on a related theme for the first party to respond to. Songs of other Baul poets, as well as those of Lalan, were sung. Although much of the commentary was in the enigmatic style of the Bauls, fairly explicit clues to the inner meaning of the songs were occasionally given.

Lalan's Cosmogonic Ideas

Before analyzing the riddles, I will present a survey of Lalan's cosmogonic ideas. In attempting to set forth his theory of creation, I encountered the following difficulties: First, Lalan does not give the myths in any detail. Rather, he merely alludes to them in cryptic riddle form. Second, the Bauls draw their cosmogonic ideas from many different traditions, which they reinterpret in terms of their ritual practices. Therefore, it is not always possible to trace the source of a myth given only as a riddle in the songs. Third, there is considerable variation in the cosmogony as related by different Baul poets. In the following discussion, I have tried to reconstruct the myths as far as possible from hints in Lalan's songs, but have used the songs of other Baul poets when they seemed consistent with Lalan's view of creation. I have also relied on explanations given to me by Khoda Baks and Karim Shah.

Lalan did not compose any songs describing the beginning of creation, but other Baul poets and Lalan Shahi fakirs mention a primal substance (*bastu*), often conceived of as a formless personal deity. This substance was made up of two elements, light (*nūr;* a symbolic word for semen) and water (*nīr,* a symbolic word for menstrual blood). The light pervaded the water, the poet Phulbas says, "as butter does milk" (personal collection).[36] Subsequently, Phulbas says, the "pearl-like" light was churned out of the water.

The story is reminiscent of the churning of the milk ocean for *soma,* which, in Vedic texts, is also equated with semen.[37] In fact, Lalan uses the image of churning the milk ocean in a song referring to sexual *sādhanā.* Just as light was separated from water in primeval times by churning, so in the ritual, through coitus, female semen has to be separated from menstrual blood to produce a concentrated form of the *adhar mānuṣ.* Lalan sings:

In the current of the churned milk ocean
nab that lover.
Keep your eyes on the liquid [*ras*]
where he can be caught.
(LG no. 42)

And in another song Lalan sings:

Milk and butter
are always mixed together.
Separate them with a churning stick.
(LG no. 64)

The word for light is Arabic *nūr.* The identity of *nūr* with semen can be traced back to early Muslim sources, which represent the luminous bodily substance of Muhammad as sperm.[38] This bodily substance, transmitted to Muhammad from his ancestors, is often depicted as a cosmic pearl possessing creative powers (Rubin 1975:97). According to Najm Daya Razi's (d. 1256) account of cosmogony, the prophets were created from pearly drops of sweat that emerged from Muhammad's light (Schimmel 1985:127). In the Indian tradition, as Mircea Eliade notes (1976:95), the equation of light with seed goes as far back as the Vedas. But it is probably the Buddhist tantric conception of *bodhicitta* (thought of enlightenment) as semen, and *prabhāsvara* (Clear Light), that most influenced the Baul equation of the Supreme with light and semen, given the fact that the roots of the Baul tradition are in Buddhist tantrism.

I might mention here that in the songs of Lalan and other Muslim Bauls, light does not always signify the Supreme in semen, either in its male aspect or its combined aspect. It also can refer to the *śakti* in menstrual blood and is sometimes termed *nūr jaharā* or *johurā* (Ar. *zahrā*, "luminous"; *al-zahrā* is the surname of Muhammad's daughter, Fatima).[39] Lalan sings:

> Two formless lights
> always float on the water;
> . . . .
> one is a man, the other, a woman.
> (LG no. 119)

In the Hindu tantric tradition, too, the *śakti* is a luminous principle (Goudriaan and Gupta 1981: 167–68).

The use of *nūr* to refer to the different aspects of the Supreme creates an intentional ambiguity that is typical of the symbolism of Baul songs. The purpose of this ambiguity is not just to conceal the true meaning of the song, but also to express the essential unity of the symbols.[40] Because one term can have more than one sense, in some cases it is possible to interpret a verse or a song in several different ways, all of which may be equally valid, as in this example:

> From light
> the whole world was created.[41]
> But they also speak of water.
> Can light be a watery substance?
> Lalan thinks so.[42]
> (LG no. 239)

By equating "light" with a "watery substance," Lalan may mean that light is the Supreme in semen, that it is the *śakti* in menstrual blood, and also that light (the male form of the Supreme) is identical to water (the female aspect of the Supreme); the two are in reality the same substance.

In several songs, Lalan refers to the birth of the Creator Niranjan from an egg floating on the cosmic waters. When he emerges, he is accompanied by the Pākpañjātan (Pers. *pākpanjtan*) "Five Holy People," the preexistent forms of Muhammad, Ali, Fatima, Hasan, and Husain, who are described as the ornaments on a star (*setārā;* Pers. *sitāra*). These songs hint at the principal role that Fatima, whom Lalan regards as the *śakti,* played in creation.

In *dehatattva* terms, Niranjan floating in an egg on the cosmic waters is the *adhar mānuṣ,* the active form of the Supreme, who appears in the egg sac in menstrual blood. Panja Shah sings: "The game of the egg is played in man" (Raphiuddīn 1968: part 2, no. 7). Lalan also sings:

> Find out about the light
> that surrounds Niranjan.
> Worship the light
> and you'll catch him.
> (LG no. 226)

The "light" here signifies menstrual blood. Ali, Fatima, Hasan, and Husain represent the four elements earth, air, fire, and water, and Muhammad is Divine Light. These five substances are conceived of as the five constituents of the body (M. E. Hak 1975 : 389).[43] According to Panja Shah, the Pākpañjātan surround the Absolute's seat in the *lā mokām* (Bhattacarya 1971: no. 309).

The story of Niranjan's birth from the cosmic egg is the myth of the *Hiraṇyagarbha* told in the *Ṛg Veda* (10.121), *Śvetāśvatara Upaniṣad* (3.4, c and 4.12, c), *Chāndogya Upaniṣad* (3.19), *Śatapatha Brāhmaṇa* (11.1.6, 1–2), and *Brahmāṇḍa Purāṇa* (1.3), among other Sanskrit texts.[44] According to the *Manusmṛti* (1.7–9), the Absolute deposited his seed on the primeval waters. The seed became a golden egg and from it Brahma, the Creator-god, grandfather of the whole world, was born. References to the myth are found in both Bengali Hindu and Muslim cosmogonic accounts. For example, the eighteenth-century Muslim poet Ali Raja says in his work *Jñān Sāgar* (Ocean of Knowledge): "One Lord Niranjan. One egg throughout the three worlds. One body in the world" (Śarīph 1969 : 416).

It is likely that both Islamic and Tantric Buddhist traditions played a part in the development of the Baul concept of the Pākpañjātan. The Shī'ī tradition recognizes the luminous preexistence of the five members of the Holy Family (including the first three imams Ali, Hasan, and Husain) and of the other nine imams (Ayoub 1978 : 29 and 54–57). Tantric Buddhism has a similar notion of five luminous Tathāgatas. They are described as having emanated from Ādi Buddha (First Buddha), are homologized with the five elements, and represent the divine in creation (Tucci 1937 : 347–50). (On the parallel notion of the four lights, see below, "The Riddle of the Flower.")

In the final stage of creation, the Creator, Allah, produces Nur Muhammad in anthropomorphic form from oozing drops of his light, and then, in the same way, Nur Muhammad creates the world. Lalan differentiates between the two forms of Muhammad termed *ḥaqīqa muḥammadiyya* or *nūr muḥammadī* by Sufi theologians; and the historical Muhammad considered the full manifestation of *nūr muḥammadī*.[45] In the body, Muhammad's light is identified with the *adhar mānuṣ* (see "The Riddle of the Flower.").

There is some difference of opinion among scholars as to how much, if at all, the indigenous Bengali tradition influenced the view of creation from drops of a liquid substance oozing from Nur Muhammad. Asim Roy (1983 : 129) notes the similarity of this myth with the *Śūṇya Purāṇ*'s account of the creation of Ādyā Śakti from the sweat of Niranjan's body and posits a synthesis of the Sufi concept of *nūr muḥammadī* with the popular notion of creation from perspiration. Annemarie Schimmel (1985 : 292–92, n. 20), however, points out that similar myths were recorded by Islamic theologians from at least the eleventh century on. (One such myth has been cited above.)

Thus far, the myth of creation from liquid light appears to be consistent with Islamic cosmogonic ideas. But there is a problem from the tantric point of view: the Supreme can only create in contact with the *śakti*. The Baul fakirs believe that Allah did not act alone to create Muhammad. The song by Phulbas previously quoted expresses this belief openly and in explicit sexual terms:

> The head of the *āliph* split
> and a drop of light fell.
> Mother in the form of Eve caught it.
> The Lord, our protector, was born
> in the form of *mim*.

The *āliph* (Ar. *alif*) represents Allah and is conceived of in the form of a *liṅga*. The *śakti* here is named Eve, whom the Bauls consider a form of Fatima. And the *mim* (Ar. *mīm*) signifies Muhammad. (How the Bauls view Muhammad's role in creation will be discussed below.[46])

The Cosmogonic Riddles

Of the four cosmogonic riddles included in this section, the first and second concern the *Hiraṇyagarbha* stage of creation, the third, a strange flower, and the fourth, the Prophet.

1. The Riddle of the *Hiraṇyagarbha* (a)

Whom can I ask this mystery?
Who will tell me?
No one I ask will say.
How can I found out?

On the day the bodiless Lord
floated in an egg on the water,
what form did he have?
In what form should we imagine him?
When the shining star appeared
the Five Holy People were its ornaments.[47]
Did that Merciful One have form then,
or was he formless?

Why did the Father of the World—
glory be to him—
call Barakat "mother"?
Wasn't he her husband?
Lalan keeps wondering.
(LG no. 223)

In many of his riddles, Lalan asks about the form of the formless Lord. It is an apparent paradox, Lalan says, that God is formless, and yet his creation has form:

It amazes me to see the Lord's play.
He gave form to creation,
but has he a form of his own?
Our Protector created man in his own image.
But if he has no form,
how was man created out of nothing?
(LG no. 281)

He resolves the contradiction by postulating three stages in the manifestation of the Absolute: *nīrākār,* "formless"; *sākār,* "with subtle form"; and *ākār,* "form."[48] Lalan sings:

> You were a light without form.
> Then you incarnated in the egg.
> In a subtle form, you created the world.
> Formed, you showed amazing love.
> (LG no. 202)

We are now ready to answer the questions in the second and third verses of riddle 1. We can say that when "the bodiless Lord floated in the egg on the water," he was formless (*nirākār*) light, but once he emerged to the company of the *pākpañjātan,* the preexistent forms of Muhammad, Ali, Fatima, Hasan, and Husain, he was *sākār,* "with subtle form."

Lalan does not describe the ornaments (i.e., the *pākpañjātan*) of the star (*setārā*). Other poets are more explicit; however, they differ widely in their descriptions of the ornaments and in their identification of them with the Five Holy People.[49] Although not directly related to the task of answering the questions asked in the song, I would like to quote one colorful description as an example of mythological embellishment in Baul doctrine. In Panja Shah's account of cosmogony, instead of a star, the Five Holy People ornament a luminous peacock. Panja Shah sings:

> In the peacock's nose was a nosepin.
> It's known as Hazrat Ali.
> Hasan and Husain
> are known as the two arm ornaments.
> The Prophet Muhammad was on the head.
> Mother Fatima was inside.
> (Shah 1890: 49)

According to a song attributed variously to Lalan (Talib 1968: vol. 1, no. 32) and Hatem (K. R. Hak 1985: no. 77), the star and peacock were different forms of the Prophet at different stages of creation.[50]

> First, the Prophet was Allah's light,
> second, a flower of the Tuba tree,[51]

third, the necklace of a myna bird,
fourth, a star and fifth, a peacock.

Barakat (blessings; auspiciousness) is an epithet of Fatima. She is the primal mother (*ādi mātā*), cause of creation. Lalan sings:

Prakṛti! Prakṛti created the world
and everyone in it.
Who can recognize that mother
without knowing the secret—
the mother to whom our Lord entrusted
religion and the world?
(LG no. 115)

The answer to the last question in riddle 1 is that Barakat is both the mother and the wife of the Lord. She is his mother because she gave birth to him. She was the water on which the cosmic egg was floating, the womb for God's seed. As a song attributed to Lalan explains:

When that jewel of a seed appeared,
mother took hold of it.
I heard he broke out of the egg
in the form of Brahma.
(Talib 1968: vol. 1, no. 264)

And she is his wife because creation proceeded from their union.[52]

2. The Riddle of the *Hiraṇyagarbha* (b)

On the day the Lord floated
in an egg on the water,
who was his companion?
Whom can I ask?

When he took a [subtle] form[53]
and emerged floating on the waves,
what was his name?[54]
The scriptures only drop hints;
they don't say.

Before he created the world,
who was there?
This story sounds impossible;
Two came from the creative power of one.

I can't know this power.
How do I catch the Uncatchable?
Lalan says, That light
is greater than the Prophet,
but not as great as Khoda,
some people say.
(LG no. 102)

I asked several fakirs the answer to the first question in riddle 2. They all replied that Fatima was the Lord's companion; she was the support for the cosmic egg. Phulbas provides a possible answer to the next question. According to him, the name of the Lord when he "emerged floating on the waves" was Ahad (Ar. *aḥad*, "the One"). In another verse of the song quoted above he sings:

Mother Johura in the form of Eve
was the receptacle for the uncatchable Lord.
He took a body in the shape of an *āliph,*
keeping his *mīm* form hidden
and became known as Ahad.

The significance of the name is that it differs from Ahamad (a name of Muhammad) only by the letter *mīm,* which itself often symbolizes the Prophet. Sufi poets all over the world are fond of this play on words.[55] As Edward Dimock (1987:378) explains: "*Mīm* is the principle of incarnation, and the relationship it states is that God is within man, āḥad within āḥamad. God is both formed and formless." But whereas most Sufis say that God and Ahamad are separated only by the letter *mīm,* the Bauls say that Ahamad is the manifest form of Ahad. In actuality they are one and the same.

The answer to the question, "Before he created the world, who was there?" turns on an understanding of the enigmatic statement: "Two came from the creative power [*kudrat;* Ar. *qudrat*] of one." The key to the enigma is found in another song by Lalan. He says: "Blood and semen—

they are the two. They were created from that flower" (LG no. 100). The flower represents the *śakti,* Fatima. She is "the creative power" of the "one" Allah, and from her came two—"semen and blood," that is all created beings, male and female. Thus it is Fatima who existed "before he created the world."

Lalan asks, "How do I catch the Uncatchable" without knowing "this power?" The question is unanswerable, for only through the *śakti* can the uncatchable Lord be caught. The *śakti* refers to both women in general, who are considered incarnations of the *śakti,* and also to the *śakti* in menstrual blood to whom the *adhar mānuṣ* is attracted. As Lalan puts it in another song: "Worship mother and you'll learn father's address" (LG no. 115).

The "light" that is "greater than the Prophet, but not as great as Khoda" probably also refers to Fatima, since her light, *nūr jaharā,* was created before the Prophet's light from the light of Allah. Elsewhere Lalan sings:

> There is a light
> that's the best of lights.
> Those who are clever know it.
> From the light of that light
> came Johura's light.
> (LG no. 226)

Thus Fatima, the *śakti,* occupies an intermediate position between Allah, the *aṭal īśvar,* and Muhammad, whose light, as we shall see, is equated with the *adhar* or *sahaj mānuṣ*.[56]

3. THE RIDDLE OF THE FLOWER

> Four colors in a single flower—
> How strangely beautiful
> that flower makes the city of love!
>
> The flower has a stem, but no roots;
> it has leaves, but no branches.
> This story is true,
> but who can I tell it to?
> Who would believe me?

The flower floats
from bank to bank
in the waters of creation.
A white bee hankers after its honey.

O mind, dive
into the Ocean of the Heart.
It is no ordinary flower
from which the Prophet was born.
Lalan says, Its roots are not in the ground.
(LG no. 96)

Riddle 3 differs from the others in that it describes the microcosm rather than the macrocosm. Much of the riddle has already been explained. The "four colors" of the flower in the "waters of creation" (the *śakti* in menstrual blood) are black or green, white, red, and yellow, colors associated with the blood of each of the days of menstruation (Bhattacarya 1971: 1055). These colors are also connected with four lights that are said to surround the Absolute in his place in the *lā mokām* and to be experienced by the adept during sexual *sādhanā*, when he brings his semen up to the two-petaled lotus (*ājñācakra*) (Bhattacarya 1971:475).[57] In addition, the four colors are identified with the *cāri candra* or *cār piyālā*, which represent the four excretions of the body on the microcosmic level and the four elements on the macrocosmic level. The *cār piyālā*, termed *jahari* (Ar. *jawharī* [?] "relating to essence"), *jabbari* (Ar. *jabbārī* [?] "relating to might"), *nuri* (Ar. *nūri*, "relating to light") and *chattari* (Ar. *sattārī* [?] "relating to protection"), are described as cups of light (*nūrer piyālā*) that were given to Muhammad by God (LG no. 270), presumably to use in creating the world. They are in turn associated with the three states of *fanā* (annihilation)[58] and the state of *baqā billāh* (subsistence in God, LG no. 227; see also the version in Tālib 1968: vol. 1, no. 76); with the angels Mikā'īl, Azrā'īl, Isrāfīl, and Jibrā'īl; with the four Sufi orders Chishtī, Suhrawardī, Qādirī, and Naqshbandī; and with four drinks, milk, honey, water, and light (Tālib 1968: vol. 2, no. 359).[59] It is not always clear how these various details correspond. Table 1 includes only what can be correlated with some certainty and is primarily based on the song in Tālib's collection just cited.[60]

The "white bee" hankering after the flower's honey signifies the *adhar mānuṣ* in female semen, which is attracted to the *śakti* in menstrual blood.

Table 1. The Four Colors and Their Associations

Color	*Element*	*Bodily excretion*	*Angel*	*Liquid*	*Sufi order*
white	air	semen	Jibrā'īl	milk	Chishtī
black/green	earth	feces	Isrāfīl	honey	Suhrawardī
yellow	water	urine	Mikā'īl	water	Qādirī
red	fire	menstrual blood	Azrā'īl	light	Naqshbandī

In a song by Panja Shah, it is expressly identified with Muhammad's light. Panja Shah sings:

The Prophet's light
shines in man.
Search your body
and you can find it.
Black, white, red, and yellow colors
surround the light's seat.
. . . .

The light has no hands, no feet,
no nose, no ears—nothing.
Bodiless, self-propelled,
it rushes to the *triveṇī*.
At that quay it becomes a bee
and drinks the lotus honey

You have to worship
that bee with great care.
I'm at a loss how to do it.
Poor Panja says, Only Fatima knows
how to care for the light.
(Bhattacarya 1971: no. 303)

4. The Riddle of the Prophet
My Prophet is the pilot
to the other shore.

You worship in vain
if you don't recognize him.
He is first and last,
concealed and clear.
The Prophet can take any form
anytime, anywhere.

From the Prophet's light
came sky and earth
water and wind.
Tell me what kind of seat
did he sit on?
Was he male or female then?

Allah and the Prophet
are two avatars—
like seed to tree.
I think that's the analogy.
Now use your good sense to deduce:
Is the tree greater or the fruit?
Find out!

He who has mastered
the truth of the self
can know about his secret affairs.
Our Lord appeared
in the Prophet's form,
through the grace of Darvesh Siraj Sai,
says poor Lalan.
(LG no. 269)

In riddle 4, Lalan refers to the Prophet as "first" (*āul;* Ar. *awwal*) because Nur Muhammad, the preexistent essence of Muhammad is God's first creation, and as "last" (*ākhir*) because the historical Muhammad is the "Seal of the Prophets." The light of Muhammad manifested itself in all the Prophets until it reached its full manifestation in the last Prophet, Muhammad. As Lalan puts it elsewhere, Muhammad is *hāyātul mursālin* (Ar. *ḥayāt al-mursalīn*), "the life of the Prophets" (Tālib 1968: vol. 1, no. 37; also LG no. 206, but the text is garbled). Lalan says he is "hidden" (*bātin*), since Nur Muhammad can only be known to those who possess secret knowledge. And he says he is "clear" (*jāhir;* literally, "manifest") for he lived in Mecca and Medina.

Whether Muhammad was "male or female," *puruṣ* or *prakṛti,* at the time of creation is an often repeated question in Lalan's songs. Lalan asks a similar question also in connection with the *mi'rāj,* Muhammad's heavenly journey (see LG no. 244). In Baul songs, the Prophet is an androgynous figure. Sometimes, as we have seen, he is equated with the *adhar mānuṣ,* which itself has both male and female characteristics; it is possessed only by the woman, is contained in the female equivalent of the male sexual fluid, and unites with the *śakti* in menstrual blood. And sometimes, as Lalan implies here, he is identified with the *prakṛti* or the *śakti.*[61]

Medieval Muslim poets, too, compared the love of Allah and Muhammad to that of *puruṣ* and *prakṛti* or *bhāvak* (male lover) and *bhāvinī* (female beloved). As Roy (1983 : 145), quoting from Ali Raja's *Jñān Sāgar* explains: "Love is never realized 'without a couple.' God created the world 'in duality.' He was 'alone in the beginning' and made his 'dual incarnation in Muhammad with love.' Together they were 'like *bhāvak* and *bhāvinī*' the dual representations of the creative truth in yogico-tantrism."

In Bengali Sufism the concept of the *nabī,* "prophet," was identified with the Hindu notion of *avatār,* "incarnation." Thus it is not unusual for Bengali Sufis to describe Muhammad as an incarnation of Allah. But Lalan says that "Allah and the Prophet are two *avatārs.*" The reason Lalan also calls Allah an *avatār* is probably that at the beginning of time he existed only in a potential state as the unqualified Supreme. Only when he emerged from the egg did he become the Creator. As previously indicated ("The Riddle of the Hiraṇyagarbha (a)"), Lalan says: "You were a light without form, / Then you incarnated in the egg" (LG no. 202). And Panja Shah explains (1890 : 36) that Allah and Muhammad were created from the same light: "The very light Allah came from, brother, the Prophet came from."

Lalan asks, "Is the tree greater or the fruit?" The metaphor of the seed, tree, and fruit appears in a number of Lalan's songs (e.g., LG nos. 269, 270, 272, and 278). It is a common image in Muslim Bengali literature to express the interconnection of God, the Prophet, and man. Roy (1983 : 158), commenting on the use of the image in *Nūr Jamāl* by the sixteenth-century Bengali poet Haji Muhammad, says: "He mentioned the cyclic process of creation as exemplified in the seed giving birth to the tree and the tree to the fruit and seeds again. This underlined that 'the one is three and the three is one.' The one is not 'affected' by the other, and the 'death of the fruit is not the end of the tree.'" But whereas Haji Muhammad rejects "a total identity of the creator and creatures," Lalan believes that

God, the Prophet, and man are one and the same. He sings: "The Prophet, man, the self or Khodā [Pers. *khudā*, "God"]—these three are never different" (LG no. 284). In other words, Lalan is asking: Which comes first, the chicken or the egg? The question has no answer. It is this identity of "the creator and creatures" that Lalan calls the "truth [or doctrine] of the self" (*ātmatattva*).[62]

At one of the riddle contests I attended in 1986, I observed the following incident. The program commenced in the usual fashion with speeches about Lalan by local dignitaries and scholars. When the performance was about to begin, Kaṇai Shah, a fakir in his eighties, suddenly stood up and burst out: "Everyone talks about Lalan and literature. You've heard these songs your whole life long. But I am Lalan. You are Lalan. We were all born in the same place he was. We've come to the very same place. But no one knows about his practices." He then began to recite a song describing the tantric *cakras*. The audience became furious, and he was forced to sit down. Kanai Shah reminded me of the Ancient Mariner: he had a strange story to tell, but no one wanted to hear it.

* * *

Research for this study was made possible in part by a grant from the Division of Research Programs of the National Endowment for the Humanities, which allowed me to prepare an edition and translation of Lalan's songs. This study would not have been possible without the insights into Baul songs and religion gained from discussions with many Lalan Shahi fakirs and Bangladeshi scholars on my field trips to Bangladesh in 1981 and 1985–86. I wish to express special thanks to the fakirs Khoda Baks Bisvas and Abdul Karim Shah, who gave generously of their time and knowledge. I would also like to thank my husband, Richard Salomon, as well as William Hanaway, Richard Eaton, David Shulman, Sarah Stroumsa, U. Rubin, Frank Korom, and David Cashin for their helpful comments. Of course, any errors in the presentation of the material and in the analysis of the songs are my sole responsibility.

Notes

Notes on transliteration. Persian (Pers.) and Arabic (Ar.) terms referring to religious concepts are transliterated according to Bengali orthography when a Bengali text is quoted or referred to; the standard Persian or Arabic form is generally given in parentheses only the first time a word appears. Islamic technical terms used in general discussion, however, are given in their standard forms. Except in a few cases, proper names in the text have been anglicized or given without diacritics. In the bibliography, however, authors' names appear with diacritics. Bengali *phakir* (Ar. *faqīr*) is transliterated *fakir*, according to common practice.

1. Visvabhararati University, Rabindra Sadan, nos. 138A, 1 and 2. According to a legend recorded by Upendranath Bhattacarya (1971 : 533; also noted in Capwell 1986 : 25) and still told today by Lalan Shahi fakirs, Rabindranath took Lalan's original notebooks from Lalan's *ākhṛā* in Seuriya when he was overseeing his family estate in Shilaidah, located a short distance from Seuriya. It was due to these notebooks, the Bauls say, that Tagore was able to become such a great poet.

2. See Capwell (1986, chapter 2) for a fascinating study of Rabindranath's role in fashioning the Bauls into "emblems of Bengali culture."

3. For a good overview on the subject of Bengali Muslim identity, see R. Ahmed 1983 : i–x.

4. As Rafiuddin Ahmed explains (1981 : 184): "The emphasis on an ethnic identity based on Islam induced, not quite logically, a contemptuous rejection of everything associated with the un-islamic land of Bengal—its language, culture, even personal and family names peculiar to Bengalis—in the belief that these were tainted by association with idolatrous Hinduism."

5. See the quote from Maulana Reyajuddin Ahmad's "Baul Dhvaṅsa Phatoyā" in Talib 1968: vol. 1, 63, note 1 (k).

6. *pahelā nambarer duśman, hindu āryasamājīder guptacar, ṣāṭ sattar lakṣa musalmānke bibhrāntakārī.*

7. The stanza containing the interpolation translates as follows:

A Muslim woman isn't circumcised.
A woman's a Brahman,
though she wears no sacred thread.
Enlightened brothers, you understand.
Lalan's a member of the circumcised caste.

Not only does *khātnār jāt* not make sense in the context of this song, but it is inconsistent with Lalan's teaching in general. (Cf. other songs by him on caste; for example, Talib 1968: vol. 1, no. 292.) Moreover, it makes the line hypermetric. According to the version of the song sung by the Baul Abdul Karim Shah, which I recorded on tape in 1981, the last line translates: "Lalan is a member of that very caste" (*lālan temni jātir ekjan*). That is to say, like a woman, Lalan is unmarked for caste.

8. After writing this paper, I learned that Khoda Baks has retired from the academy. I do not know if he has been replaced by another fakir.

9. See S. M. Lutfar Rahmān (1977) and Anwarul Karim (1980, based on his dissertation for Dhaka University completed in 1977).

10. Bhaṭṭacārya 1971 : 51 and D. C. Sen 1917 : 163–165. See also Capwell 1986 : 14–15.

11. On the conversion of the *neṛāneṛīs* to Vaishnavism, see D. C. Sen, loc. cit.

12. The word *nāṛā* occurs in at least three of Lalan's songs (Dāś and Mahāpātra 1958: nos. 14, 134, and 396). In nos. 14 and 396 Lalan says that the *nāṛās* are

the group one should join to escape from the cycle of birth and death for they are followers of the *ulṭa dāṛā* (opposite way, a reference to Sahajiya *sādhanā* involving the "return of semen" [see below, "The Baul Sampradāy"]) and travel on the path of Caitanya, the sixteenth-century Vaishnava reformer. And in no. 396 Lalan refers to the Supreme as *nāṛā ṭhākur,* "the Shaveling Lord."

13. On the Old Bengali Buddhist tantric songs, the *Caryagītis* or *Caryapads* (ca. tenth to twelfth centuries), as the precursors of Baul songs, see Capwell 1986: 33 and 83–84.

14. On female semen, see O'Flaherty 1980: 18, 21, and 33–40.

15. On the cranial location of semen, see O'Flaherty 1980: 45–46.

16. Muslim Bauls describe the body both in terms of the Hindu tantric *cakras* or centers (*mūlādhār, svādhiṣṭhān, maṇipūr, anāhata, biśuddhā, ājñā, sahasrār*) and Sufi *mokāms* (Ar. *maqām*) or stations (*nāsut* [Ar. *nāsūt*], *mālkut* [Ar. *malakūt*], *jabrut* [Ar. *jabarūt*], *lāhut* [Ar. *lāhūt*], and *lā mokām*). Although the standard number of *cakras* is six (*ṣaṭ cakra*) and *mokāms* four (*cāri mokām*), there are actually a total of seven *cakras* and five *mokāms*; the *sahasrār* and the *lā mokām* (literally, "no place") represent transcendent space and so are not counted. For the correspondences between *mokāms* and *cakras*, see Roy 1983: 175–77.

The *cakras*, which are conceived of as lotuses of varying numbers of petals, are often referred to in Baul songs by the number of petals rather than by name. In several songs (e.g., LG nos. 6, 134, and 232) Lalan mentions a hundred-petaled lotus not included in the standard tantric enumerations of the seven *cakras*, whose location I have not been able to determine. In almost all of these songs, the hundred-petaled lotus is mentioned together with the thousand-petaled one (*sahasrār*). The hundred-petaled lotus seems to have been adopted from the Sahajiya Vaishnava theory of the lotuses. Although its exact location varies according to the text, Sahajiya Vaishnava authors often place it in the heart, where the *anāhata cakra* (twelve-petaled lotus) is located in the standard tantric view (Bose 1930: 129). This location is corroborated by Bengali literary texts, which use this lotus as a metaphor for the heart. (See, for example, Tagore's novel *Cokher Bāli* [Calcutta: Biśvabhāratī Granthabibhāg, 1969], 239.) It is also possible, as suggested by Bhaṭṭacārya (1971: 365), that the hundred-petaled lotus is located below the navel. (See also Bose 1930: 126.)

17. The Vaishnava Sahajiya author Svarup Damodar Gosvami (n.d.: 115) describes the location of the "moon" on each day of the month.

18. The Vaishnava Sahajiya text *Bṛhat Nigam,* by Locan Das, contains the following lines (quoted in Bhaṭṭacārya 1971: 384): "Menstrual blood is in the *sahasrār* at the top of a young woman's head [flowing] in a hundred streams. The 'Man' (*mānuṣ*) moves around in her body. He worships sexual union and exists in the form of semen." The Baul poet Panja Shah (Bhaṭṭacārya 1971: no. 275), however, says that menstrual blood comes from the earth (*jamin,* a technical term for the *mūlādhār cakra*).

19. In Gosai Madhab Das's song (personal collection), "*Tumi age prabeś karo padmaban*" (First enter the lotus grove), a whole grove of flowers is surrounded by the *kuṇḍalinī,* described as the snake of illusion (*kāl nāginī*): "The lotus has eight petals. There are eight clusters (*mañjarī*). The snake of illusion surrounds [the grove] on all sides."

20. See Bhaṭṭacārya's discussion in 1971:415. In one song (LG no. 73) Lalan says: "The new moon day [*amābasyā*], the first [*pratipad*], the start of the second [*dvitiyār prathame*]—that's the time. Darvesh Lalan asks, Who comes at that juncture?" Since Bauls count the first day of menstruation as the new moon day, the technical term for the third day is "the second." In another song Lalan says, "Why do you die wielding the plow on the new moon day and on the first?" Here the "plow" signifies the penis and "to die" means to ejaculate. The first two days of menstruation are considered days of lust, when it is difficult for the *sādhak* to control his semen. See also LG no. 26.

21. Since each person is a microcosom of the universe, it is theoretically possible for the *sādhak* to unite male and female principles without engaging in sex, and some Bauls do speak about reaching a stage where they no longer need a female partner (see Capwell 1986:49). But this is unusual and there is no evidence in Baul songs for *sādhanā* without a woman.

22. Goudriaan remarks (Gupta, Hoens, and Goudriaan 1979:34), "Indeed, Tantrism seems to be inspired by a genuine awe for the female as the seat of reproduction, the source of all life. But it would again be wide of the mark to state that it acted as a liberating force which aimed at the improvement of the social status of women. . . . The sādhaka is the bee, woman the flower which is left behind when the nectar of siddhi has been gathered [Bose, *Sahajiya Cult,* pp. 76f., referring to the Bengali text Premavilāsa]."

23. The Baul poet Madan Fakir had a female guru named Anandamohini. He mentions her in the *bhaṇitā* (signature line) of his song (Bhattacarya 1971, no. 445), *Yathā garal tathāy sudhā* (Where there's poison, there's also nectar).

24. Describing tantric ritual, O'Flaherty remarks (1980:269), "Tantrism retains the ancient yogic concept of the man's need to retain his semen but adds to it the even more ancient concept of his rejuvenation through consuming the woman's seed." See also ibid., 270.

25. Capwell (1986:22) notes that this ritual is mentioned in the Buddhist *Hevajra Tantra,* which dates as far back as the end of the eighth century.

26. The eleventh-century Hindu treatise on Tantrism, *Tantrāloka,* by Abhinavagupta, refers to a ritual that bears a striking resemblance to this practice: The semen is "passed back and forth from the mouth of the woman to the mouth of the man, and finally poured into a concecrated vessel" (Eliade 1976:101, quoting J. L. Masson and M. V. Patwardhan, *Śāntarasa and Abhinavagupta's Philosophy of Aesthetics* [Poona: Bhandharkar Oriental Research Institute, 1969], p. 43).

27. Maulavi Abdul Wali, in "On Curious Tenets and Practices of a Certain Class of Faqirs in Bengal," published in 1900, is the only author to give this account who does not link Lalan in some way with these villages. In his opinion, Lalan's native village was Harishpur, in the district of Jessore, the home of many famous Bauls, including Lalan's disciple, Panja Shah. Harishpur is mentioned as Lalan's birthplace in accounts ascribing to Lalan Muslim origins.

28. Caudhuri (1974b:3–5) is of the opinion that the author of the obituary was the co-editor of *Hitakarī,* Raicaran Das.

29. "Bāul Kabi Duddu Shah," *Samakāl* (Caitra, 1366 B.S. [1960]), p. 603 (cited in Mitra 1980:97). A similar account is given by Panja Shah's son Khondakar Raphiuddin in the introduction to his collection of Baul songs, *Bhāb-saṅgīt* (1968).

He may not have been aware of the biography of Lalan attributed to Duddu Shah, as he makes no mention of it. In addition to these accounts, several other versions of the Muslim legend have been published. See, for example, Talib's biographical sketch of Lalan (1968, vol. 1, 1–44).

30. The *Hitakarī* obituary, which is the original source for Lalan's date of death, states that Lalan died on Friday, October 17, but does not give the year. Moreover, the copy of the obituary preserved in Lalan's *ākhṛā* that was examined by several scholars has no date of publication. (I do not know if this is the only extant copy, but it is the only one that has been mentioned.) Still, there can be no doubt concerning the year in which Lalan died, since 17 October was not a Friday in any other possible year. On the dating of the issue of the journal containing the obituary, see Bhattacarya 1971 : 538–39.

31. Most accounts of Lalan's life say that Lalan lived to be 116. Considering the absence of any knowledge about Lalan's origins and the propensity to exaggerate the longevity of sages, such a long life span must be regarded with suspicion.

32. Mitra (1980 : 266–267), however, believes that Tagore's notebooks contain the entire corpus.

33. This was first brought to my attention by Khoda Baks when he remarked that a song I had attributed to Lalan (*Cā̃der gāye cā̃d legeche* [Moon is stuck to moon]), in my address to the Seuriya Lalan festival held in March 1981, was not an authentic Lalan song, although Bauls in West Bengal consistently place his name in the *bhaṇitā*.

34. Lalan's speculation on the symbolic significance of Perso-Arabic letters may indicate that he was familiar with some of their shapes, but it is not sufficient evidence for postulating that he could read and write Persian or Arabic. Most, although not all, of the letter symbolism is conventional.

35. Since Bhattacarya published his account, many stories intended to prove that Lalan was literate have appeared in print, but all of them can be summarily dismissed as apocryphal. To cite two examples: Rahman quotes a story in his article, "Lālan Śāher Jīban Kathā" (1970 : 255) to the effect that Lalan, before his death, threw all his handwritten notebooks into the Kāligaṅgā River. And according to Talib, (1968: vol. 1, 36) not only could Lalan read and write Bengali, but he was also proficient in Arabic and Persian. He states (1968: vol. 1, 33) that Lalan opened a school at his *ākhṛā*, where he himself instructed students in the Qur'an.

36. The song opens with the line: *ei duniyāy elo nabī jagatke karte uddhār* (The Prophet came to this world to save it).

37. See O'Flaherty 1980 : 24–28 and Eliade 1976 : 105.

38. For example, Ibn Qutayba (d. 279) records the following verses attributed to the Prophet's uncle, al-'Abbās b. 'Abd al-Muṭṭalib (quoted in U. Rubin 1975 : 90):

> Then you descended to earth, not as a human being,
> Nor as a morsel of congealed blood—
> But as a drop of sperm [within Adam's loins].
>
> . . . .
>
> When you were born, the earth shone
> and the horizons beamed with your light.

For more details, see Rubin's article on Nūr Muhammad cited above. I am grateful to Hananya Goodman for bringing this article to my attention.

39. See the verse of LG no. 226 translated under "The Riddle of the Hiraṇyagarbha (b)".

40. On the many symbolic meanings of words in the *sandhābhāṣā* (intentional language) of the *Caryagītis,* see Eliade 1969 : 249–59 and Kvaerne 1977 : 37–60.

41. For LG *phul* read *kul.* Emendations to LG are based on the readings of the Tagore notebooks, on my discussions with Khoda Baks, on comparative evidence of other songs, and on consistency with Baul religion, philosophy, and symbolism.

42. *lālan bhābe tāi;* the line may also be translated: "Lalan wonders about it."

43. Islam only recognizes four elements, but the Baul concept of the *pākpañjātan* is probably a transformation of five-element symbolism.

44. See Das Gupta's remarks on "the conception of Nirañjana" as "a replica of Prajāpati Brahmā" (1969 : 326–28).

45. On *ḥaqīqa muḥammadiyya,* see Schimmel 1985 : 132–43.

46. Two of Lalan's songs allude to four states of creation. In one (LG no. 374), Lalan sings: "I heard, before the four states the Lord took refuge in love" (*rāg,* a symbolic word for menstrual blood). And in the other (LG no. 270), he sings: "Find out! Before the four states who was in the vessel of love?" These are either the first or last four of a total of eleven states termed *kār.* According to Khoda Baks they are: (1) *andhakār* (darkness); (2) *dhandhakār* (the term is obscure; it may be related to the word *dhundhukār* which appears in the chapter on cosmogony [*sṛṣṭipattan*] in the Medieval Bengali Buddhistic *Śūnya Purāṇ* and which Das Gupta [1969 : 311] translates as "darkness and haze"); (3) *kuyokār* (fog); (4) *nairākār* (formlessness); (5) *ākār* (form); (6) *sākār* (with subtle form; in Lalan's songs that refer to the three stages in the manifestation of the Supreme, *sākār* precedes *ākār;* see the discussion under "The Riddle of the Hiraṇyagarbha (a)"); (7) *dīptākār* (shining); (8) *hāhākār* (the sound *hā hā,* a cry of distress); (9) *huhukār* (the sound *hu hu,* according to Khoda Baks, made by the egg breaking); (10) *śūṇyakār* (emptiness); (11) *nīrākār* (water).

I have heard several Baul songs that mention the eleven states, although none describes them in any detail. Rupcad, in one verse of his song (personal collection), "O from what light was the Prophet's light created?" (*O re kon nure nur nabī paydā*), enumerates the first seven *kār*s and in the next verse says: "There were eleven states. If you know about them, tell me. What form did the Lord take in each state? Why did he keep four states secret?"

47. For LG *bāhan* read *gahanā,* and for *pāy* read *pāk.*

48. In both Islamic and Hindu tantric traditions, there are three stages in the manifestation of the Absolute. According to Sufi theologian Abdul Karim al-Jili's scheme of ontological evolution as set forth by R. A. Nicholson (1983 : 97), they are: Absolute Being or Pure Thought (*al-Dhat-al-Wujūd al-muṭlaq*), Abstract Oneness (*Aḥadiyya*), and Unity in Plurality (*Waḥidiyya*). In Hindu tantrism the stages are: supreme (*parā*), subtle (*sūkṣma*), and gross (*sthūla*) (Gupta et al. 1979 : 50).

49. See, for example, song no. 205 in Mansur Uddin (1984), attributed to

Lalan but probably not authentic, and *Tālināma bā Śāhdaulāpīnāmā*, by the eighteenth-century Sufi poet Sekh Cad (Śarīph 1969 : 55).

According to one Islamic tradition (Suyūṭī, *La' ālī* I, 395–96; Dhahabī, *Mizān*, II, 495–96; *Lisān al-Mizān*, III, 346; cited by Rubin 1975 : 99), the image (*ṣūra*) of Fatima is described as a body of light wearing a crown on its head representing Ali, and two earrings, symbolizing Hasan and Husain. Thus the association of the preexistent forms of the Pākpañjātan with ornaments is also found in Arabic sources.

50. The sixteenth-century poet Saiyad Sultān, in his materpiece, *Nabībaṃśa* (1978, vol. 2, 6), states that the Prophet took the form of a peacock at the order of God and sat on the heavenly tree meditating on Him. Khoda Baks, however, identifies the shining star and peacock with Fatima. His interpretation thus agrees with the Islamic tradition mentioned in note 49.

51. Name of a tree in paradise.

52. In the Buddhist tantric tradition, Prajñā is first the mother and then the wife of Buddha; and in the Śākta tradition, Ādi-Śakti is the mother and wife of Śiva (Das Gupta 1974 : 97, note 5). See the last verse of LG no. 153 for another riddle on the dual role of the *śakti*.

53. The meaning of the word *payār* in the Bengali text of the song is obscure. The word commonly means "a meter consisting of fourteen syllables to a line," which obviously does not fit the context. Rahman in his unpublished dissertation "Baul Sādhanā o Lālan Śāh" (1977 : 295), glosses the word with *sūkṣma*, "subtle," but provides no explanation. For lack of an alternative, I have tentatively accepted his definition. To my knowledge, this is the only occurrence of the word in Lalan's songs.

54. The referrent of the pronoun *se* (he or she) is not clear. It is also possible to translate the verse as referring to the "companion" rather than the Lord.

55. Lalan, too, composed several songs on the subject. See, for example, LG no. 280.

56. This interpretation of the song is not definite. It is possible to also interpret the "companion" and the "light" as referring to the *adhar mānuṣ*. I have discussed the problem at length in an unpublished paper, "The Enigma of the Ajān Mānuṣ (Unknown Man)," which I read at the seminar "Enigmatic Modes of Expression" held at Hebrew University in Jerusalem in 1988–89.

57. As in the light symbolism of the *pākpañjātan*, so in the ecstatic experience of colored lights, both Buddhist tantric and Islamic influences are likely. See Eliade 1976 : 98–100 and 114; Tucci 1935 : 348–50; and Corbin 1978.

58. *fanā fi' sh-shaykh* (annihilation in the spiritual guide), *fanā fi'r-rasūl* (annihilation in the Prophet), and *fanā fī Allah* (annihilation in Allah).

59. The song is by the Baul poet Duddu Shah. Talib incorrectly attributes it to Lalan.

This set of associations resembles the theory of the five Paṇḍits, or Priests, of the Dharma cult who are associated with five directions, five cups with five kinds of liquids, five colors, etc. It also resembles the theory of the five Tathāgatas or Dhyānī Buddhas, the source of the theory of the five Paṇḍits. See Das Gupta 1969 : 302–10.

60. The set of associations varies somewhat, depending on the source. See, for example, the table in M. E. Hak (1975 : 416) based on Bengali Sufi yogic texts.

61. Panja Shah clearly connects Muhammad with *prakṛti* in his instructional treatise *Chahi Iski Chādeki Gaohor* (The True Essence of Pure Love [1890 : 39]) when he remarks that the *yugal rūp* (joint form) of Allah and the Prophet are in the *lā mokām*. *Yugal rūp,* or *yugal mūrti,* is the image of lover and beloved, and in Vaishnavism of Radha and Krishna.

62. See Dimock's discussion (1987 : 378) of Vaishnava, tantric, and Sufi influences on this doctrine.

References

Ahmed, Rafiuddin

1981 *The Bengali Muslims, 1871–1906: A Quest for Identity.* Delhi, New York: Oxford University Press.

1983 (ed.) *Islam in Bangladesh: Society, Culture, and Politics.* Dhaka: Bangladesh Itihas Samiti.

Anonymous

1890 Mahātmā Lālan Phakir. *Hitakarī* (Oct. 31) 1 : 101. Reprinted in Caudhurī 1974b : 7–10 and Mitra 1980 : 67–71.

Ayoub, Mahmoud

1978 *Redemptive Suffering in Islam: A Study of the Devotional Aspects of Āshūrā in Twelver Shī'ism.* The Hague, Paris, and New York: Mouton.

Bhaṭṭācārya, Upendranāth

1971 [1968] (1378 [1371] B.S.) *Bāṅglār Bāul O Bāul Gān.* 2nd ed. Calcutta: Orient Book Company.

Bose, Mamindra Mohan

1930 *The Post-Caitanya Sahajiā Cult of Bengal.* Calcutta: University of Calcutta.

Capwell, Charles

1986 *The Music of the Bauls of Bengal.* Kent, Oh.: Kent State University Press.

Caudhurī, Ābul Āhsān

1974a *Kuṣṭiyār Bāul Sādhak.* Dhaka: Naoroj Kitābistān.

1974b (1380 B.S.) (ed.) *Lālan Smārak Grantha.* Dhaka: Jātiya Grantha Kendra.

Corbin, Henry

1978 *The Man of Light in Iranian Sufism.* Translated by Nancy Pearson. Boulder, Col. and London: Shambhala.

Dāś, Matilāl, and Pīyūṣkānti Mahāpātra, eds.

1958 *Lālan-gītikā.* Calcutta: Calcutta University.

Das Gupta, Shashi Bhusan

1969 [1946] *Obscure Religious Cults.* 3rd ed. Calcutta: Firma K.L. Mukhopadhyay.

1974 [1950] *An Introduction to Tantric Buddhism.* 3rd ed. Calcutta: University of Calcutta.

Devī, Saralā
1896 (1302 B.S.) Lālan Phakir O Gagan. *Bhāratī*. Bhādra: 275–281. Reprinted in Caudhurī 1974b: 27–35 and Mitra 1980: 73–81.
Dimock, Edward C., Jr.
1966 *The Place of the Hidden Moon: Erotic Mysticism in the Vaiṣṇava-sahajiyā Cult of Bengal*. Chicago and London: University of Chicago Press.
1987 The Bauls and the Islamic Tradition. In *The Sants: Studies in a Devotional Tradition of India*, Karine Schomer and W. H. McLeod, eds., pp. 375–388. Delhi: Motilal Banarsidass.
Eliade, Mircea
1969 [1958] *Yoga, Immortality, and Freedom*. Translated by Willard R. Trask. Bollington Series LVI, 2nd ed. First Princeton/Bollington paperback printing. Princeton, N.J.: Princeton University Press.
1976 *Occultism, Witchcraft, and Cultural Fashions*. Chicago and London: University of Chicago Press.
Goudriaan, Teun, and Sanjukta, Gupta
1981 *Hindu Tantric and Śākta Literature*. A History of Indian Literature, J. Gonda, ed., vol. 2, fasc. 2. Wiesbaden: Otto Harrassowitz.
Gupta, Sanjukta, Dirk Jan Hoens, and Teun Goudriaan
1979 *Hindu Tantrism*. Handbuch Der Orientalistik, J. Gonda, ed. 2 Abteilung: Indien, 4. Band, 2 Abschnitt. Leiden and Köln: E. J. Brill.
Hak, Khondkār Riyājul, ed.
1985 (1391 B.S.) *Bhāb Saṅgīt*. Lok Sāhitya Saṃkalan 40. Dhaka: Baṃlā Ekāḍemī.
Hak, Muhammad Enamul
1975 *A History of Sufism in Bengal*. Dhaka: Asiatic Society of Bangladesh.
Karim, Anwarul
1980 *The Bauls of Bangladesh*. Kushtia: Lalan Academy.
Kvaerne, Per
1977 *An Anthology of Buddhist Tantric Songs: A Study of the Caryagīti*. Oslo: Universitetsforlaget.
Mansur Uddīn, Muhammad
1984 [1961] (1368 B.S.) *Hārāmaṇi*. Vol. 5. Dhaka: Bāṃlā Ekāḍemī.
1978 [1965] (1384 B.S.) *Hārāmaṇi*. Vol. 7. Dhaka: Bāṃlā Ekāḍemī.
Mitra, Sanatkumār, ed.
1980 (1386 B.S.) *Lālan Phakir Kabi o Kābya*. Calcutta: Pustak Bipani.
Nicholson, Reynold Alleyne
1983 [1921] *Studies in Islamic Mysticism*. Lahore: Hijra International Publishers.
O'Flaherty, Wendy Doniger
1980 *Women, Androgynes, and Other Mythical Beasts*. Chicago and London: University of Chicago Press.
Rahmān, S. M. Lutfar
1967 (1374 B.S.) Lalan Sāher Jīban Kathā. *Sāhitya Patrikā*. Barṣa. Re-

printed in 1970 (1377 B.S.). *Pūrbapākistāner Prabandhasaṃgraha,* Maitreyī Devī, ed., pp. 215–293. Calcutta: Saṃskṛta Pustak Bhāṇḍār.
1977 Bāul Sādhanā O Lālan Śāh. Unpublished Ph.D. dissertation. Dhaka University.

Raphiuddīn, Khondkār, ed.
1968 (1374 B.S.) *Bhāb-saṅgīt.* 2nd ed. Dhaka: Khondkār Raphiuddin.

Roy, Asim
1983 *The Islamic Syncretistic Tradition in Bengal.* Princeton, N.J.: Princeton University Press.

Rubin, U.
1975 Pre-existence and Light: Aspects of the Concept of Nūr Muḥammad. *Israel Oriental Studies* 5:62–119.

Śāh (Shah), Khondakār Pāñja
1890 (1297 B.S.) *Chahi Iskichādeki Gaohor.* Harishpur: Pāñja Śāh.

Saiyad Sultān
1978 *Nabībaṃśa.* Ahmad Śariph, ed. *Saiyad Sultan Biracita Nabībaṃśa.* 2 vols. Dhaka: Bāṃlā Ekāḍemī.

Śarīph, Ahmad
1969 (1375 B.S.) *Bāṅglār Sūphī Sāhitya.* Dhaka: Baṃlā Ekāḍemī.

Schimmel, Annemarie
1975 *Mystical Dimensions of Islam.* Chapel Hill: University of North Carolina Press.
1985 *And Muhammad Is His Messenger.* Chapel Hill and London: University of North Carolina Press.

Sen, Dineschandra
1917 *The Vaisnava Literature of Medieval Bengal.* Calcutta: University of Calcutta.

Svarūp Dāmodar Gosvāmī
n.d. *Āśray Siddhānta Candroday bā Svarūp Dāmodar Gosvāmīr Kaṛcā* (9th ed.), Hārādhan Baiṣṇab Ṭhākur, ed. Malda: Manīndranāth Adhikarī.

Tālib, Muhammad Ābu
1976 Lālan-cariter Upādān: Tathya o Satya. In *Lālan Sāhitya o Darśan,* Khondakār Riyājul Hak, ed., pp. 1–61. Dhaka: Muktadhara.

Tālib, Muhammad Ābu, ed.
1968 (1375 B.S.) *Lālan Śāh o Lālan Gītikā.* 2 vols. Dhaka: Baṃla Ekāḍemī.

Tucci, Giuseppe
1935 Some Glosses upon the Guhyasamaja. *Mélanges chinois et bouddhiques* 3:339–353.

Wali, Maulavi Abdul
1900 On Curious Tenets and Practices of a Certain Class of Faqirs in Bengal. *Journal of the Anthropological Society of Bombay* 5/4:203–218.

Wilma L. Heston

10. Footpath Poets of Peshawar

The footpaths of Peshawar's Bazaar of the Storytellers provide a focal point for the transmission of verses by a group of poets considered within Pakistan to be folk poets. This chapter begins with the general background for this study and then continues with a description of the Peshawar area. The next section describes various modes of transmission of Pashto verse; the final section presents some views expressed by these poets about the knowledge they use in producing their poetry.

General Background

The composition of poetry is an old and honored tradition in South Asia. However, until the nineteenth century, only a small portion of this was available in written form. Each copy of a book had to be written individually; the preservation of manuscripts took time and money. Our knowledge of the literatures of South Asia has thus inevitably tended to be dominated by documents (and languages) associated with the ruling or religious establishments and with the comparatively wealthy individuals who could afford handwritten manuscripts. The result is that our knowledge of popular literatures of South Asian villagers and urban masses has had major gaps.

The lack of easily available documentation for pre-nineteenth-century popular literatures of South Asia provides an easily understandable reason for their neglect by Western scholars, particularly with the often formidable barriers of language. However, the introduction of inexpensive printing techniques in the nineteenth century and the introduction of cassette recording techniques in the mid-twentieth century have now provided not only new modes of transmission for these literatures but also an ample stock of new materials for the researcher. These materials have sometimes been utilized, but with a few exceptions,[1] attention has been given to the subject matter or to particular themes (for example, death or battle) and epics (for example, *Ālhā* or *Rāmāyaṇa*), rather than to the processes of creation and transmission (or, in economic terms, production and distribution) of this literature.

If our knowledge of popular literature, and poetry in particular, has been and still is limited, our knowledge of its poets is still more limited. Even for the classical poets of the past, biographical information in South Asia has tended to be minimal—passing references in court histories or in some other work of art or literature; the major source of information has been the works themselves. Coming into the modern period, the sources increase, but again the focus of attention is on poets of literary (and literate) circles. We thus have a gap in our knowledge of poetry for the non-elites but also a gap in our knowledge of its poets. In hopes of making a small contribution toward filling this gap, this chapter will discuss these Pashto poets and the processes of transmission of their work. The footpath (in American usage, the sidewalk) where the poets' products are sold is used as an identifying term for these poets; the content of poetry is treated in this paper only in terms of some general indication of subject matter; attention is instead focused on the form in which it is physically transmitted.

This chapter has developed as an extension of a book of translations of Pashto verse narratives, *The Bazaar of the Storytellers* (Heston and Nasir 1988).[2] Many of these poets are unschooled and some are illiterate, like those whose Pashto verses Darmesteter cited a century ago.[3] This was particularly interesting to me because my conventional middle-class American background has led me to associate the writing of poetry with advanced (i.e., at least college level) education, and to consider the promotion of poetry (including support of the poets) as one of the cultural contributions of the academic establishment and intellectual elite.[4] The same cultural bias makes me use the phrase "writing" poetry unthinkingly; in fact, neither a mechanical translation nor (for many of these poets) the mechanics of the process justifies the use of "writing" poetry; the remainder of this chapter will usually substitute "producing," "composing," or a similar verb.[5]

Peshawar and the Region

The city of Peshawar is the capital of Pakistan's Northwest Frontier Province (NWFP). Within Pakistan, English is the language of education at the university level and is the "international" language, paralleling the status of English in India. The national language is Urdu, a language not indigenous to Pakistan and used (in 1981) as a household language by only 7.6 percent of the country's households, mostly urban (24.4 percent); it was spoken by only 1.3 percent of rural households (Addleton 1986:70). The Urdu-speaking households have been predominantly immigrants (*muhājirs*) from India; inter-regional marriages and the influence of urban culture are now adding a younger generation of Pakistani-born Urdu speakers. Urdu not only acts as a lingua franca, but also dominates the Pakistani intellectual scene; the educated upper-class elites are to varying degrees literate (able to read and write) in Urdu and/or English, but are very often not literate in their household language.

The regional languages of Pakistan include both halves of the Indo-Iranian language family; Peshawar, located on the western side of the Indus, is in that half of Pakistan where Iranian languages predominate. The majority language of the NWFP, and the language with which this chapter is concerned, is Pashto, an eastern Iranian language spoken in northwestern Pakistan and in Afghanistan. It is a language which has been compared to an archeological museum (MacKenzie 1987:549) because it preserves a rich heritage of lexical information both from its own tradition and from the languages with which it has come in contact.

The city of Peshawar, like many cities of the subcontinent, has an Old City and a Cantonment; the latter was for British military and civil establishment in the days of the Raj and continues to be much more westernized than the Old City. The language of the Old City itself is not Pashto but Hindko, a language with a rich (and unstudied) oral literature which has been finding its way into print only in the last few decades. It is the language of the traders and craftsmen of the Old City, and the language to which many Pashto speakers shift after living for a generation or two in the Peshawar metropolitan area. This leads to the viewpoint of some Peshawaris that Pashto is itself essentially a village or folk language (regardless of the respect with which it may be treated by members of the Pashto Academy). This attitude is complemented by a feeling among some Pathans that the tribal man is the "real" Pathan. In this sense, the city of Peshawar can, at best, act as an intermediary for Pathan culture, but cannot itself (almost by definition) be a center for that culture. This linguistic situation with Peshawar and its surrounding districts thus contrasts with many major cities elsewhere in the subcontinent, where the city functions naturally as a promoter of the language and culture of its surrounding districts or province.

The Old City of Peshawar, like many other old cities of South Asia, has both traditional bazaars, such as a bird bazaar, a jewelry bazaar, and brass bazaar, and more modern additions, like Cinema Road, which supply inhabitants of both the city and the surrounding countryside with goods and services. The bazaar which particularly attracts both tourists and tribesmen, and which is a common means of approach to the other Old City bazaars, is Qissa Khwani Bazaar, the Bazaar of the Storytellers. Today, this bazaar does not appear to have much relationship to the product for which it was named; no storytellers stand on the footpaths or in the streets. However, the bazaar has been in the past, and still is, a center or hub for the transmission not only of Pashto stories in verse but also of other forms of poetry; it thus provides a geographical reference point for this chapter.

Transmission

Poetry can be transmitted by the poet himself or by an intermediary. Because I am particularly interested in the relationship of twentieth-century technology to traditional forms of literature, I have concentrated on poetry that is transmitted through intermediaries. Many of these intermediaries have clustered around Peshawar's Bazaar of the Storytellers during the past decade, forming a network convenient for themselves and for the Pashto poets from outlying areas, while continuing a tradition implied by that bazaar's name. The first two parts of the following section examine transmission of folk poetry by intermediaries through song and through print. The final part discusses some forms of transmission by the poet himself.

Two points should be noted here. First, although song and print are treated separately, there is continual interplay between the two forms. Singers may use printed forms as prompts, and verses that prove popular in sung form may then be put into print.[6] Second, just as poetry can be transmitted by the poet or an intermediary, so also can information about the poet's knowledge be derived from the poet or an intermediary. For some poets, this may indeed be the only source of information, and a few of these points are discussed below in the context of transmission through print.

Transmission Through Song

In Pashto, there is an extremely close tie between music and verse, with a one-to-one correspondence between (vocal) musical forms and poetic forms. This parallel in form would be equivalent in English to having a sonnet be a form of music, or a sonata be a form of verse; the parallel extends from the shortest Pashto verse form, an asymetric and anonymous couplet called a *ṭappa,* and continues through to the longest form, called variously a *badala, dāstān,* or *qiṣṣa.*[7] Similarly close ties between musical and poetic forms apparently have parallels elsewhere in South Asia, although published documentation of this is still difficult to find.[8]

Examples of some of these verse forms, such as the *rubāʿī, qaṣīda,* and *ghazal,* appear in volumes of classical Pashto poetry (such as that of Khushhal Khan Khatak), where they follow the classical Persian tradition with respect to rhyme scheme. Classical Pashto verses continue to be popular in sung form, and could be heard on TV-Pakistan in the fall of 1987.

In the footpath poetry discussed below, there are additional forms of poetry, such as *chārbaita, loba,* and *nīmakai,*[9] which are completely absent in classical *diwāns* (collections of verse by a single poet) and the names of which are not even glossed by nineteenth-century British dictionary compilers. Furthermore, in this footpath poetry, Persian verse terminology loses its original significance; a *rubāʿī,* for example, no longer need be a quatrain, but may be a poem of six or seven couplets.[10] There is thus a range of Pashto poetry which can be documented only by going outside the classical, textual tradition; music is one source for this documentation.

Transmission via a singer

Before the advent of modern recording technology, the transmission of poetry by a singer to a listener was direct (i.e., the singer and listener could see each other). Among the direct transmitters were the *qiṣṣa-khwāns*, usually translated as "storytellers," such as the blind Sayyid Nur, who by 1983 was a beggar in Peshawar's Old City, and his now-deceased brother, Sayyid Muhammad, who was once interviewed by Mumtaz Nasir of Lok Virsa.

The interview with Sayyid Muhammad (ISM) includes three stories which he was asked to "say" (the verb used is *wayəl,* the most commonly used verb meaning "to say") and which he then sang, getting increasingly hoarse as he reached the third story.[11] Two of these stories were religious verse narratives and the third was a romance, a verse narrative about Yusuf Khan and Sher Banu which was written about twenty years ago by Ali Haydar "Joshi," translated into French by Johnson (1982:97–120) and into English (Heston and Nasir 1988:70–87). Despite his being blind, this singer's rendition of this story was obviously taken from the printed text that has been available to literate and sighted readers; it included the poet's pen name (*takhalluṣ*). The source of the remaining two stories is not known, but the singer did not make any claims to having versified them himself; my impression is that these were parts of originally longer texts now mostly forgotten.

In the past, the Bazaar of the Storytellers (Story-singers?) was said to include not only these male street singers, but also female entertainers who lived in the upper stories of the buildings along Qissa Khwani and sang; singing thus transmitted poetry. The limited number of references to these singers, however, suggests that they were working within a light classical framework, rather than a folk tradition.[12]

In addition to singers who hope to find audiences on the street, there are and have been professional singers hired to sing for private gatherings, and especially for festive occasions such as weddings and circumcisions. A number of relatively successful singers keep "studios" in upstairs rooms (*bālā-khānas*) behind the Bazaar of the Storytellers (Pusht-Qissa Khwani).

Among these Pashto singers is Fazli Qayyum, who is regularly invited to the annual folk festival in Islamabad; his songs have also been recorded on commercial cassettes. Although Fazli can sing a variety of forms of Pashto music, he does not specialize in singing Pashto *g͟hazals*, thus differentiating him for several Pashto *g͟hazal* singers popular on television, whose singing style sounds (to me) heavily influenced by (or derived from) Urdu *g͟hazal* singing.

Fazli comes from the Mohmand Tribal Agency, and is without land to support his family; his main source of income is from singing. He is not from a family of musicians and has not had formal training, thus contrasting with the classical singers of the subcontinent.[13] He keeps a large stock of poetry in both printed and handwritten form, and is an active collector and transmitter of both old and new Pashto poetry; he also is a mine of information on the works and whereabouts of writers of popular Pashto verse. Without a telephone, but using the adjacent bazaar networks, he can give directions for finding a local poet quickly or can collect other musicians to accompany him or to comment on a researcher's questions.

The only other bazaar in Peshawar which (to my knowledge) acts as a center for Pashto poetry transmission in musical form is Dab-gari Bazaar. The musicians here are said to be instrumentalists or less successful singers. A number of Afghan refugees have had rooms in this area, including the currently very successful singer, Shah-wali, who still had his name on a building there in January 1988.

The most eye-catching items offered by this bazaar are quilts and mattresses. Many of the quilts are in bright colors with gold trim and seem gaudy to some Western eyes; an American anthropologist suggested to me that the purchases are made particularly for brides in the villages around Peshawar. The bazaar also offers less colorful quilts and mattresses on a rental basis for customers who have to provide hospitality for large numbers of people; the market as a whole thus provides an inflow of potential purchasers of musical entertainment (poetry transmission) for weddings and similar occasions.

Teahouses (*qahwa-khānas*) also provide a place for transmission of poetry in the bazaar itself. This was, for example, a place suggested to me by one member of the Pashto Academy for hiring a singer for a relatively inexpensive afternoon of poetry singing.[14]

Transmission through cassettes

A technological development of the past few decades which has provided Pashto music for the masses is the audiocassette; this has become a major medium for the transmission of Pashto poetry, offering remote villagers a chance to hear the most popular Peshawar singers and thus acting as an intermediary between themselves and the poet. These cassettes are sold in and around the Bazaar of the Storytellers, both on the footpaths and in the shops behind it, going on down to Cinema Road.[15] There are literally hundreds of cassettes available, usually sold by the name of the singer and the form of music. The two major forms of sung Pashto poetry in cassette form are verse narratives (*badalas*) and *ghazals*, but tapes of other forms can also be purchased. The verse narratives may themselves include non-narrative forms inserted at various points within the story.[16]

The sale of cassettes is not limited to Peshawar; shops selling tapes of Pashto music are scattered throughout the towns and villages of the NWFP, where they can sometimes be heard before they are seen. The cassette shops in a town are usually grouped together, and each shop plays one or more tapes full blast, leaving no doubt about the location of that bazaar. However, sometimes a shop sits in comparative isolation; one such shop in Barikot has over it a large sign in the shape of cassette complete with Sony brand name and the shop name as printed on a cassette label, providing a means of shop identification far beyond earshot.

Peshawar dominates the production of cassettes of Pashto poetry in musical form. The claim of being the first major producer of Pashto verse narratives (and the owner of a big shop in 1982) has been made for Sher Baz Khan by his younger brother (IBSBX); Sher Baz Khan is from Darra Adam Khel, a town better known to foreigners for its hand-manufactured guns. His tapes are usually preceded by, and interspersed with, advertisements for his shop. When other dealers copy his cassettes, they often tape their own advertisements at the beginning of a tape; however, at some later point, Sher Baz Khan's name can usually be heard, thus providing in the tape itself a history of the circulation of that tape.

Sher Baz Khan not only acts as a producer of music but also as a patron of poets; his name is sometimes included in a couplet within the narrative (see, for example, Heston and Nasir 1988 : 229, 262, in stories about Kamal Khan and Multan Khan, both Afridis), offering an obvious parallel to other forms of art where a patron is given explicit recognition within the work which he has financed. Conversations with poets likewise attest to their having been commissioned to versify the story of a particular local hero for cassette recordings by a music-store owner. The cassette producer thus has a role in both creating and transmitting poetry, and at the same time can perpetuate the fame of his favorite heroes.

One poet, Rafiq Jan, has produced cassette tapes of his own poetry, "hiring a singer to record his poems to the traditional musical accompaniment of harmonium, rebab, and tabla" (Edwards 1987a : 3); the distinction between poet and singer is thus maintained. This poet had himself been the owner of a shop dealing in cassette tapes, and would thus have already been familiar with the business of tape reproduction and distribution.[17]

Mixtures

The line between direct personal transmission by singers and impersonal transmission through cassettes is blurred. Cassette shops in 1986 were selling *maidānī* (lit. "field,") recordings. These tapes are made during a wedding or some other festive occasion and then copied and sold to a cassette dealer; remarks of the listeners and the firing of guns (usually festive) can be clearly heard in the background, thus differentiating them from what would be expected in a recording made for commercial purposes. The recording of commercial cassettes may, in its turn, be enjoyed as a private performance when a cassette shop dealer himself (IBSBX) turns the recording of a particular singer into a social occasion, inviting his friends and hoping for a more inspired performance by the singer. Although the more sophisticated equipment and professional staff used for a commercial recording can eliminate a considerable amount of background noise, some residual of performer-audience interaction (such as an appreciative *wah, wah* from a listener or the naming of a particular member of the audience by the singer) is often detectable to the buyer of the finished product.

A recent development in the cassette marketing can be seen in the boxes in which cassettes are enclosed. Five years ago, the tapes were generally copied and sold in what was probably the original box from the manufacturer (usually Sony, Maxell, or TDK); the name of the verse narrative would be written by hand with a black pen on the inside cover of the box. Printed labels were generally limited to the name and address of the shop on the cassette tape itself. Now, however, the cassettes are being sold with various kinds of covers, often with pictures that have little or no relation to the contents. For example, a cassette of the Sher Baz Khan Music Center (mentioned above), which now uses Cinema Road as its location, has pictures of seven different girls (including one in Western shirt and slacks) on a narrative cassette sung by Ahmad Gul about Kaka Sahib. A cassette from the International Cafe and Music Center has a girl in a tight, red Western-style short-sleeved blouse and a black hat trimmed with a red bow or flower for Wahid Gul's rendition of the very traditional story of Sayf-ul Muluk, a story usually associated with a lake of the same name located in northern Pakistan. Another cassette of the Sarhad Cassette House offers the same story by the same singer in a cassette box with a girl in Pathan dress, hand at one corner of her mouth in a flirtatious pose familiar from South Asian films. These three cassette covers all have their covers and labels written in Urdu (rather than Pashto) style script, again reflecting the multilingualism in the Peshawar area.

In contrast, a cassette from EMC (an acronym nowhere spelled out on the tape for a company said to be one of the largest cassette producers in the country) portrays the cassette singer, Wahid Gul, who was probably the most popular of the verse narrative singers in 1982 and 1983; he is shown with rings on his fingers and microphone in his hand. The inside of the cassette cover gives the name of the poet, Jamal (see below) along with the name not only of the singer, but also of the ṟebab player (*ṟebab nawāz*), Amir Hamza; the tabla player (*tabla nawāz*), Jamal; and the harmonium player, Azmat. Information about the poet and the recording artists, as given by EMC since 1986 or earlier (perhaps in an effort to offer the buyer something he would not get by copying someone else's tape) [18] will surely make studies of Pashto music and related poetry much easier in the future.

VCR

The transmission of sung poetry through video cassettes has already begun. The video cassettes are now being made informally from Pakistan-TV programs [19] or movies; they can also be purchased as a separately produced tape. So far, however, I have seen these cassettes sold only in shops, not on footpaths, so they are excluded from consideration here.

Transmission Through Print

Publication

Another mode of poetry transmission is in written form, an impersonal and (in and of itself) a non-oral form of transmission. The British introduction of new printing techniques in the nineteenth century resulted in a great increase in the supply of popular literature in the subcontinent. This included poetry and prose published in chapbooks in various languages. Pritchett (1985) has traced the publication of a number of stories (*qiṣṣa*s) in Hindi and Urdu back to the early nineteenth century. Some of the stories which she finds in Urdu are also found in Pashto verse form; at least one of these is translated from Urdu.[20]

Book publication in Pashto began at least as early as 1863 (Rafi 1975, no. 1180: a Bible published by Stephen Austin). The first two Pashto stories (*qiṣṣa*s) in verse (which I have so far found) were published in Delhi, one in about 1877 and another in 1881.[21] By the first decade of this century, when Lahore was the capitol of the area that now includes the NWFP, at least four publishers in Lahore had printed Pashto verse narratives.[22]

Pashto verse narratives were published in Peshawar as early as 1885;[23] that city dominates the Pashto chapbook market in Pakistan, with Quetta as a second important source of publication.[24] The Peshawar publishers, like the cassette dealers, are now clustered around the Bazaar of the Storytellers, as usually indicated on the cover and/or title page. The publishers of both narrative and shorter forms of verse tend to be the same; there are half a dozen who have been active in the past five years. These publishers publish not only different forms of verse, but also other genres of Pashto (prose, drama, children's stories, and so on); they also publish in other languages, including Persian.[25]

The absence of any date of publication in these chapbooks makes it difficult to judge the volume of chapbook poetry being transmitted through publishers at any given time. Several publishers list publications on the back of their chapbook covers; three of these (Rahman Gul, Islami Kutub Khana, and Nurani Kutub Khana) list more than forty titles.[26] Five publishers have published most of the chapbooks I have purchased within the past five years (the aforementioned three plus Qadimi Kutub Khana and Zeb Art Publishers).

The title page of the chapbooks usually includes a price, either printed or handwritten; the prices generally increase over time and as the number of pages increase.[27] I use an increase in the printed price of otherwise identical chapbooks as an indicator of a new edition. The inference to be drawn from a price (invariably higher) written in by hand over an earlier printed price is not so obvious without information on who did the writing.

For the publication of these chapbooks, the final manuscript of these chapbooks is written out by a calligrapher on "butter paper," which is much like a fine grade of American supermarket waxed paper. This may be financed and supervised by the poet or by the publisher, but after the calligraphy is finished and the verses have gone to the publisher, the poet is generally separated from his work.[28] This thus contrasts with, for example, Slater's folk poetry in Brazil, where "most poets are vendors or publishers" (Slater 1982 : 25).

The calligraphed "butter paper" is used in a photo-offset process; an interested passerby can easily get invited inside a shop to watch the flash go off. The makeshift tangles of electrical wiring look like something from a Rube Goldberg cartoon and the flash equipment would not look too modern for an early Charlie Chaplin movie. In nice weather, the plates may be taken out into the lanes, where men from the shop sit patiently touching them up. The drums of big printing machines, sometimes electrified and sometimes hand-turned, roll the finished pages onto tables which may extend outside the shop itself. Inside the shop, background noise from the banging of the trays of steel balls used to clean the plates (when not reused by one publisher or another) makes conversation virtually impossible. Small handpresses for block printing are also in use, usually operating with a team of two men, one laying down fresh sheets of paper and the other dropping the press and pulling out the printed copy, piling up pages almost as quickly as the electrically operated machines. These small presses produce, among other things, labels used on cassette tapes of sung poetry.

Place of sale

These chapbooks, like the cassettes, are also sold in and around the Bazaar of the Storytellers, where the transmission of this poetry takes place on the footpaths and in little shops. Some of these shops are maintained by the publishing houses; they sell not only their own chapbooks but also those of other publishers. Chapbooks from Peshawar can also be found for sale on the footpaths of smaller towns in the NWFP, along with an occasional chapbook printed locally; finding a chapbook not locally published on the footpaths of Peshawar is (in my experience) quite unusual.[29]

Of greatest relevance for this study is the fact that these chapbooks are *not* sold in major bookstores of the Old City such as the University Book

Agency, or in Cantonment stores such as the London Book Store; a request for them meets with a blank look of disbelief ("Why would you want those?") or a (polite but barely concealed) sneer of disdain and directions elsewhere.[30] The marketplace itself thus provides a sharp demarcation between this "footpath" poetry and "literary" poetry in Pashto.

The chapbook as product

An examination of the chapbooks themselves illustrates the diversity of footpath poetry in terms of poetic form and subject matter; the contents (implicitly and sometimes explicitly) suggest some of the sources (i.e., "knowledge") and the paths of transmission. The variety in chapbook covers is a quick (though not always reliable) indicator of content; the uniformity of size (usually about 4¾ by 7 inches or (less often but especially for longer volumes) about 5½ by 8½ inches) makes them easy to spot in the marketplace.

There are two basic categories of published poetry; narrative (a single story) and mixed (a collection of various verse forms). Neither of these is a tight category, however; a verse narrative will almost always be interspersed with shorter forms such as *rubā'īs* or *g͟hazals*. Similarly, a collection of poetry often includes one or more short narratives, usually labeled *qiṣṣas*. The one feature common to both kinds of chapbooks is that they begin with verses in praise of God and (usually) the Prophet (e.g., a *ḥamd* and a *na't*), a practice also found in other Islamic literatures.

The differences in content are reflected in the covers. Verse narratives more often have pictures on the covers, particularly if they have romantic subject matter, while collections of mixed verse tend to have nonpictorial designs; there are, however, numerous exceptions. The covers are not signed with the illustrator's name; stylistic affinities suggest that publishers employ the same artist for more than one cover.[31]

Both the author's and the publisher's names usually appear on the cover. When an author's name is omitted on both cover and title page, it can still be ascertained by looking within the verses for the author's name and/or pen name (*takhalluṣ*); these names are generally found (alone or in combination with the poet's village name) in both narrative and most shorter forms of Pashto verse.[32]

Narrative poetry. The verse narratives, whether in chapbook or cassette form, are concerned mainly with love or battle, or both; the story titles with two names (male and female) are usually romances and the titles with a single name are usually martial in nature. Chapbook covers, however, sometimes give only a hero's name; for example, a chapbook (CNM-šA) which has only Prince Aurang's name written on the cover, has a title page saying that it is a romance with the Fairy Tajbari.[33]

There are a wide range of *romances,* varying in sources from the traditional tales that have circulated for centuries in the Middle East to events which have taken place in Pakistan during the past few decades. Perhaps the single most popular story (in terms of number of versions in circulation at a given time) is Yusuf and Zulaikha, the same Joseph of the Book of Genesis, whose story is also retold in the Qur'an; at least four Pashto versions have been printed as chapbooks during the past five years.[34] Another popular romance is the story of Prince Bahram and Gul Andam; one edition (CF-BGa-1) by Fayyaz[35] was reissued in 1987 by the same publisher and with the same contents but with a different cover (CF-BGa-2). Like Joseph and Zulaikha and other stories, such as Laila and Majnun, Shirin and Farhad, Sayf-ul Muluk and Badiʾ-ul Jamal (variously *badī* or *badrī;* see, for example, Abbasi 1969 : 123 [*badrai*], Cejpek 1968 : 633 and Ghazanvi 1978 : 105 [*badī*]), this story (or references to it) can be found in the classical and folk literature in Persian and other languages of the Middle East (see, for example, Cejpek 1968 : 631–633). Some very traditional stories have cover illustrations that are modernized; for example, a recent edition (CN-LM-2) of the Middle Eastern classic, Laila and Majnun, as it was versified in Pashto at the turn of the century, has the hero in Western-style shirt and pants (or jeans) with beads around his neck.

The sources of some verse narratives can be found within the chapbook literature itself as, for example, when a character from one story takes on a title role in another story. For example, the story of Gul Andam (CF-BGa, above) includes an episode about Dev Turaban, who then has his own story written by another poet (CIš-DT); the latter story has been available in a chapbook with its cover picturing Dev Turaban carrying Gul Andam from a bed in the lower part of the cover and with a couplet describing the event also written on the cover. Chapbook inscriptions are not always so informative, however; the same chapbook cover mentions wondrous *rubāʾīs* (*ʾajība rubāʾ īyāt*) which are not to be found (in distinguishable form, at least) in the text itself. This chapbook also includes at the end a Birbal Nama in prose about the Emperor Akbar and Mulla Do-piyāza (see below), the latter being a stock folk figure around whom a number of humorous anecdotes in prose have accumulated.

Other romances, such as the story of Sher Alam and Memunai, sometimes called the Pashto *Otello,* are taken from the local culture. For these, the word "romance" is perhaps misleading because, in contrast to the romances of Iranian tradition, where (after numerous adventures and separations) the hero and heroine live happily ever after and may even produce offspring (see Hanaway 1974 : 5), the Pashto romances usually end with the hero and/or heroine dead. The stories might better be called tragedies, and the mortality count by a story's conclusion can bring to mind a Verdi opera, perhaps because both have plots based on conservative societies with strong honor codes.

Several versions of the Sher Alam and Memunai story have been in circulation in the last five years. One edition of the story of Sher Alam–Memunai, subtitled "A Tale of Stormy Grief" (*tufānīghham*), was written by Wali Muhammad (CWM-šA/M-1; translated in part by Heston and Nasir 1988 : 49–65) and was available in the bazaar in 1983; the publisher's name on the cover (Awami Kutub Khana) differs from that on the title page (Rahman Gul).[37] The cover illustration shows a mountain setting, with the slain heroine lying face down with head and arm resting on a large stone, red blood dripping on the bright green grass, and orange leaves in the immediate foreground; a scene with the murdered heroine is as integral to this story as a bedroom scene with the strangled Desdemona is to *Otello*. This same cover-page illustration with the dead heroine was also used with a change in the publisher's name to match the publisher's name on the title page. Another and somewhat different version of this romance was written by Jamal of Sangar (see below) and has been recorded in cassette form (translated by Johnson 1982 : 132–141).[38]

Although some covers depict incidents identified with a particular story, they may be used by another publisher for a quite different story. For example, a (N)urani Kutub Khana edition (CAAš-AX/DX-1) of Abu Ali Shah's late nineteenth-century versification of *Adam Khan and Dur Khanai,* sometimes called the Pashto *Romeo and Juliet,* has a cover showing a man, a woman, and a rebab (the musical instrument played by the story's hero); the same cover was also used by a Rahman Gul edition (CA-Da/Da-1) of the quite different story of Prince Heart-increasing (*dil-afzā*) and Princess Heart-dazzling (*dil-afrūza*). The latter story by Nurani Kutub Khana had a much different cover with the prince and princess in costumes, the faces and ornate surrounding borders vaguely reminiscent of a seventeenth- or eighteenth-century Persian manuscript painting; its contents had been recalligraphed (CA-Da/Da-2). The contents of the Pashto *Romeo and Juliet* (CAAš-AX/DX-1) are distinguished by the fact that page 13 is printed upside-down. Another publisher's edition of this story (CAAš-AX/DX-2) has a cover with no illustration, but page 13 is also upside-down; one set of text plates have obviously been either reused or rephotographed.

As befitting this classic of Pashto romances, these have not been the only two editions of *Adam Khan and Dur Khanai* available during the past five years; still another chapbook edition of this same romance (CAAš-AX/DX-3) has been published which includes five film songs at the end of the book, following the verse narrative. Unlike either the verse narratives or most other verse forms of this study, the film songs do not include the name of the poet/lyricist.[39] These chapbook versions are quite different from the seventeenth-century version published by the Pashto Academy, which has been available through the University Book Agency.

Stories transferred from South Asia's Hindu/Sanskritic tradition are notably absent; for example, the Fort William derived texts of *Simhasan battisi* (Thirty-two Throne [Tales]) or *Baital paccisi* (Baital's Twenty-five [Tales]) relating to the cycle of folktales about Raja Vikram, discussed by Pritchett (1985: 56–78), are not in evidence.

The sources for tales of battle (sometimes called *jańg-nāmas*) are generally more limited than the sources of romances; the subject matter is usually concerned either with the early days of Islam or with local events. The covers of these stories also show less variety than those of the romances; comparatively few of them are illustrated. One of the few illustrated covers for a local story shows a scene of a local fort with mountains in the background, much like what can actually be seen in the NWFP and what is described in the story (CMAA-BM: translated in Heston and Nasir 1988: 189–210). The chapbook includes a preface by the poet, Muhammad Ali "Arif," saying that he did "much research" (*ḍer taḥqīq*) for the story. He is apparently an ambitious writer; he includes a list of local heroes about whom he intends to write. These stories had not yet come into the marketplace (so far as I know) in 1987. Although this poet has not yet been interviewed, one might infer from his description of the villagers as being very simple, uneducated, and unskilled (*sāda bāda be ʾilma be hunara*) that he has had some formal education.

Mixed-verse forms: in general, the verses within chapbooks with various forms of poetry are not arranged in any formal order. An exception which might first be mentioned is a *diwān* by Ali Haydar "Joshi," whose narrative poetry was sung by the street singer mentioned above. This diwan (CAHJ-dj) is alphabetized according to the last letter of the last word of the couplet. It is thus a much more formal arrangement of poems than the usual chapbooks of non-narrative poetry. His chapbook, "Alien Grief" (CAHJ-pg), has the more usual variety of verse forms, such as *rubāʾīs*, a short story (*qiṣṣa* about Abu Talib), *chārbaitas*, *qitaʾ*s (fragments), *nīmakais*, *ghazal*s, and (more unusual) even some short prose selections, with no discernible organization as to either rhyme or form. Most of the poems are titled by form, but some indicate content: "Charbaita of My Youth," "Charbaita in a New Style," "Heaven and Hell" (*jinnat dozakh*), "Elegy" (*marsiya*), "Advice" (*naṣīḥat*) (CAHJ-gh: 18, 21, 24, 35, and 49). Curiously, there is no *ḥamd* or *na't* at the beginning, but there is a prose section concerning the Haj and some verses that give thanks to the Prophet.

Sometimes, a chapbook's title indicates a single narrative but it is in fact a mixture of various forms of verse. One example of this is a "story" (*qiṣṣa*) of *Three Girls* (Cšš-DJ), published by Zeb Art Press, a relatively new entrant into the Pashto chapbook publishing field. The poet, whose pen name is Shakir and who has not yet been interviewed, must be fairly versatile at versification, for he has also written at least one long verse narrative, the *Longing for the Red Doli* (Cšš-RD), which is a continuous narrative of about one hundred pages (about eight hundred couplets), mostly in rhyming couplets (*masnavī* form).[40] He has also written a story of Sher Dil the Dacoit (Cšš-DD), which is unusual in two respects. First, the author calls the hero a dacoit. Although it is true that the British have considered many heroes of the local verse narratives as bandits, dacoits, or savages and barbarians,[41] the Pashto poets do not generally use the term "dacoit" for the hero of either chapbooks or cassettes.[42] Second, this story of Sher Dil, which on the front cover and title page is called a *qiṣṣa*, is a drama in prose, one of the two examples which I have so far encountered of a footpath poet also writing plays.[43]

Some poets write chapbooks of religious verse; when the covers of these chapbooks are illustrated (usually with a mosque or Ka'ba in Mecca included), they tend to be an accurate indication of the nature of the contents. Among the authors of chapbooks with religious covers are the already mentioned Ali Haydar "Joshi" (CAHJ-din) and Abdul Wahab of Lohar Kili (CAWD-qt), who also wrote a narrative about Chamnay Khan (translated in Heston and Nasir 1988: 289–301). Other poets who write religious verse include Molawi Abdullah of Nowshera (CAN-pa) and Mulla Ahmad Jan (CAJ-qa); the latter has published a lengthy Pashto version of Amir Hamza (CAJ-AH).

One chapbook (CAWT-tt) by Abdul Wahid "Thekadar" ("Contractor") has a collection of various kinds of verses that can be sung.[44] It is appropriately named *Ṭang Ṭakor*, "music; sound; musical beat"; its simple two-color cover has musical instruments including a rebab, clay pot (*mangai*), and tambourine (*duff*).

The calligraphed forms of these printed texts of Pashto poetry (like those also in Persian and Urdu) either align couplets in a series with a straight margin on the left, or else group the two halves of a couplet either by indenting both halves or alternate couplets or by indenting the second hemistich of each couplet. In one chapbook (CAWT-SX), however, many of the poems are arranged with a series of indentations to form patterns on the page, often a zigzag like the letter *Z*, with an extra "zig" on the top. This chapbook's cover has a picture of a fairy, thus illustrating the book's title: *Sundar Khāperai,* "The Beautiful Fairy"; the combination of a Sanskritic and a Pashto word in the title would perhaps sound strange to an Afghan. The book's paper is rough and the illustrations are crude, but the page formats could certainly attract the attention of a footpath browser.

Sometimes the covers are pictorial representations of the titles of collections of mixed forms of verse. For example, a chapbook with the title *Camel-driver and Caravan* (CDXX-ck) shows a man leading a string of two camels; the second camel is being ridden by a woman with a green dress and red shawl. A chapbook with the title *Torn Collar* (CFGN-sg) has a man in a kurta and vest ripping open his shirt, exposing his chest. This chapbook includes several short stories (*qiṣṣa*s) in verse, such as a thirty-one-couplet story about Shirin and Farhad and a forty-three-couplet story about a gazelle and the Prophet Muhammad, as well as *loba*s, *rubā*ʾ*ī*s, *g͟hazal*s, and *chārbaita*s, all shorter forms of poetry.

A few chapbooks of mixed poetry which I have collected are the output of small presses rather than major chapbook publishers; these are mainly from printers outside Peshawar. For example, *Tears of the Pen* by a young poet, Zeb (CMZZ-qo), was printed in Nowshera, rather than Peshawar; it has a picture of the young author on its cover. Both it and another locally printed chapbook (CRXR-zt) give information not only about the size of the printing (1000 in both cases) and the price (printed on the reverse of the title page), but also about the date of publication in a fashion similar to that seen, for example, in Pashto Academy publications.

Direct Transmission

In addition to the preceding forms of transmission, where there are intermediaries such as a singer (in person or on tape) or a publisher, there have been, and still are, traditional forms of transmission directly between poet and audience.

One of these forms of transmission is the poetry contest, in which the poet of one village challenges the poet of another village. This is a custom distinct from *mushā*ʿ*ira*s;[46] it is well remembered in villages of the Charsadda, Nowshera, and Mardan area, but seems to have died out today.

Elderly poets describe how the contests took place with one poet "throwing" difficult lines to the other for him to complete with the same rhyme.[47] A winning poet was the pride of his village; he was backed by his khan, who would assure the poet of an appropriate revenue as he went to challenge, or stayed home to receive the challenge of, a poet from another village. Elderly poets can still recite with glee the verses of their successes half a century ago (IJT). The setting for this contest was the *hujra,* or male guest house, a distinctive feature of Pathan villages. The *hujra* is also the place in which poetry was (and is) transmitted in musical form.[48] The existence of poetry contests in Hindi-speaking areas of India, as mentioned by Susan Wadley in this volume, suggests that these contests may be a more general South Asian phenomenon which, to my knowledge, has not yet been documented.[49]

In addition to transmission by poets in the formal context of a contest (and, of course, in informal situations as well), there are also poets who sing their own verses. In general, the footpath poets thus far interviewed have not brought attention to their own singing skills (or lack thereof), perhaps because of social stigma attached to being a professional musician or the feeling that it is undignified for men of a mature age, such as most of the poets we interviewed. Occasional remarks dropped in conversation, however, indicate that the voices of several now elderly poets were enjoyed by their contemporaries in their youth.

There are also poets who can sometimes be seen singing their own verses on the footpaths of towns outside Peshawar. One such poet is Afsar Jan of Mardan, who improvises his verses as he goes along. His voice does not have the quality that will earn him any income from commercial cassette producers or from singing privately at a wedding or other festive occasion. His work is not available for transmission in printed form; once sung, his poetic improvisations disappear (unless a folklorist happens to be passing by). As a transmitter only of his own work, he contrasts with the *qiṣṣa-khwāns* and other professional singers who transmit the verses of a number of poets. He thus can be regarded as an extreme (or minimal) case of a transmitter, and the footpath is for him a place for direct transmission of his poetry, rather than transmission in printed or recorded form.

From his own standpoint, however, Afsar Jan is a poet, rather than a singer; he thus contrasts with the other poets discussed below only because he sings his verses in public in hopes of getting a little money and because he has not produced any poetry for indirect transmission.[50] For that reason, his views on poetic composition will be discussed below.

Knowledge

The remainder of this chapter will discuss the knowledge used for poetic composition, using materials from a sample of interviews with Pashto folk poets. Most of these poets had never been asked for any kind of interview before; many of the points raised by the interviewer were prompted by curiosity about one or more of the poets' verse narratives and related biographical data rather than by a systematic attempt to fill in a conceptual framework about what makes a poet. The poets themselves quoted extensively from their own verses but almost always from nonnarrative forms; it is hoped that a study of their recitations can at a later time be integrated with their published verses and additional interview material specifically concerning nonnarrative verse composition, a topic not fully explored in previous interviews.

Afsar Jan

The poet-singer Afsar Jan is a woodcutter by occupation; he was about 65 years old (according to his own estimate) at the time of the interview. He explains his poetry as having started from two sources. The first source was the cinema; he saw his first movie (an Indian movie, since this was before partition), when he was quite young, maybe sixteen years old. There were girls dancing openly, and he fell in love with the heroine; his heart was filled with feelings of love and separation, a classic theme of love poetry, films, and popular music in South Asia.[51] Therefore he started composing poetry with the help of the rhythms (? *sāz*) of the film songs (*filmī sandarī*). The second source of his poetry was love for the girl who would become (and who still was, at the interview) his wife. He had first met this girl at the ford (*gūdar*) of a stream, one of the few traditional meeting places of hero and heroine in Pashto narratives (see, for example, Heston and Nasir 1988 : 202). He talked to the girl and even held her hand, but she told him that this was not a good way to do things, so he asked his mother to arrange a marriage with her. This was done, but it was a long wait for the wedding because of the high bride price that was demanded. During this period of separation when he was thinking about this girl, his ideas developed and he began composing poetry about love and beauty. Thus, as he put it, "my teacher [*ustād*] was the girl and my love for her, and the movies were my education." In addition, Afsar Jan was obviously aware of the subject matter of traditional romances of South Asia, since he could sing his own version of, for example, Gul and Sanobar.

RAFIQ JAN

Rafiq, who uses Jan as his pen name, is from the Mohmand tribe, which inhabits both sides of the Pakistan-Afghanistan border; he was born in the village of Lalpura, near Jalalabad, in Afghanistan. His education was limited to learning to "read" the Qur'an, and it was through this that he learned the mechanics of writing, since the Pashto script is based on the Arabic script. In this he is fairly typical of a number of folk poets, for in the villages, especially in the tribal areas in Pakistan and in Afghanistan, classes given by the mullas have long been the only form of education available. Rafiq Jan began composing poetry at the age of twelve, but he did this secretly because his father was a very pious man.[52] His first poem was a *chārbaita,* a short form of poetry, and it was only later than he began producing verse narratives, which he refers to as *dāstāns*.

Rafiq Jan has used political events in Pakistan as poetic source material; one of his verse narratives (available only in cassette form) concerns a conflict with the British which took place in the Bazaar of the Storytellers on April 23, 1930,[53] continuing in a long tradition of poetry celebrating Pathan resistance to outside rule.[54]

When Rafiq Jan began producing narrative poetry about events in Pakistan that took place prior to his arrival there, his sources of information (knowledge) were old men (*spīn-gīray*s, lit., white-beards) in the community. His use of this information is clearly evident: almost half of one verse narrative is recounted as if in the words of an old man who witnessed the events (Heston and Nasir 1988 : 307–316).

Rafiq Jan came to Peshawar before the Russian invasion; he has friends and relatives on both sides of the Afghanistan-Pakistan border. He began producing a considerable amount of political poetry against the Marxist government in Afghanistan after the 1978 coup d'état. These poems, which were circulated in cassette form, "played an important role in providing a culturally-constituted ideology of resistance that helped lay the foundation for a national movement" (Edwards 1987a : 3) against the Russian-backed regime.

JAMAL OF SANGAR

Like Rafiq Jan, Jamal of Sangar is also a Mohmand; also like him, his education was religious: he learned to recite the Qur'an by following the text and learned about the Qur'an through a translation. Jamal knew from the first stage of his youth, from the age of about eight or ten, that he was going to be a poet. He thus contrasts with the woodcutter, Afsar Jan, who needed the motivating force of love to begin his poetic career. The materials used for his poetry in this period were from his own life experience: "We said what we saw." It is perhaps his highly developed sense of observation that has given his narrative poetry its "down-home" imagery with, for example, heads flying in battle like bits of cucumber or piling up on the ground like windfall fruit (Heston and Nasir 1988 : 155–160).[55]

Somewhat later, at an age between twenty and forty, he began producing narrative poetry. For information on the stories which are about Pathans, he went to the places where the events were supposed to have taken place. Thus, for the story of Momin Khan and Shirinai (CJS-MX/š: the story of "much grief" also contained in the cassette mentioned earlier), Jamal went to the village in Afghanistan where the events were supposed to have taken place; there he got the story from an old man who repeated what his father had told to him.

Similarly, for the story of Sher Alam and Memunai (the Pashto *Otello* discussed above), Jamal went to the village of Memunai and talked with Haji Muhammad Gulab, "whose house was just above that of Memunai."[56] This poet is thus doing the work of (what I might call) a folklorist; he draws, immediately at least, on oral, rather than written tradition. However, he would more likely view himself as an investigative reporter, because his underlying presumption, sometimes stated explicitly, is that these are true stories of actual events, rather than either an accumulation of myth and legend or the outcome of creative imagination. He is thus like other poets who, for example, insist that their poems don't have five grams of falsehood in them; or cite only a few names so "I won't write this story with mistakes of my own"; or even specify what is unknown: "Countless Englishmen were killed but history books say nothing about the casualty count" (Heston and Nasir 1988 : 215, 219, 240).

For Jamal's verse narrative about Mir Khatam (translated in Heston and Nasir 1988 : 154–161), in which the alleged events took place not in this region but in the Middle East of more than a millenium ago, the source of the story was a particular mulla (IJT), a religious personage who could be presumed to be the most knowledgeable source on such matters. Thus although the mulla may have relied on written sources, the poet himself used oral (not written) sources.[57]

At the time when this interview was made, Jamal was 65; he had stopped producing narrative poetry and had turned to religious poetry as a result of making the Haj in 1975. This poetry had not yet been published in 1988, although his secretary (or clerk: *munshī*) had a copy of it. This secretary writes down Jamal's poetry and then takes it to Peshawar for publication in chapbooks (which may in turn result in cassettes). A *munshī* (or, for other cases, a *kātib*) thus plays an important, though rarely acknowledged, role in transmission of poetry when a poet is not literate.

Ali Haydar "Joshi"

Perhaps the best known of these NWFP folk poets is Ali Haydar, whose pen name is "Joshi." He says he was born in 1916. He is one of the poets said to have had a pleasant singing voice when he was young.[58] He has long been a friend of Mumtaz Nasir at Lok Virsa, and (at least in part because of this), he has been written up several times in Urdu newspapers (for example, *Jang*). Joshi now lives in Takht-Bha'i, near Mardan, although the place name he uses in his poems is Ismaila (often "Smela" in local pronunciation), a village which he left because of a (typically Pathan) feud. He is a quite prolific poet; twenty-one titles are listed on the last page of his *diwān* (CAHJ-dj).

Joshi draws heavily on his own experiences and includes remarks about them even in his verse narratives. For example, in a story about Ramdad Khan (see Heston and Nasir 1988 : 165–187), a Pathan hero celebrated in other, shorter verse forms as well as in Joshi's narrative, Joshi compares his own life to that of Ramdad and compares women's conduct today with that of an earlier and more virtuous time (op cit.: 184). In his research for this narrative, he followed the already mentioned pattern of going to the villages where the story took place (e.g., Hari Chand and Koper) and talking to the people there about the events. This story brought Joshi considerable popularity and was made into a movie (available on videocassette in 1986) in which he played the role of the hero's father, thus acting out the events and feelings he had expressed in his poetry.

One of Joshi's most popular verse narratives is a "romance" about Yusuf Khan and Sher Banu (mentioned above in connection with the street singer); this story was also made into a movie, now available on videocassette. This story has some supernatural elements, including five holy men (*pīrs*) with special powers, who give the heroine the ability to cover a large distance in thirty steps, and some jinns who bring women and a bed to a mosque at night for the pleasure of a yogi (*jogī*). (The latter event evidently caused difficulty for the singer of a Lok Virsa recording; he emended yogi to student (*ṭālib*). Although these supernatural elements suggested (to me) a source outside the local culture, the narrative's social structure with the paternal male cousins as villains gives the story an appearance of being typically Pathan; it is certainly classified as "one of our stories" by many Pathans, both educated and uneducated, with whom I have talked.[59] Joshi, in his own account (IAHJ-1) of his source material, says that he first found this story when he got some medicine at a local fair (*melā*) where it had been wrapped in a sheet of manuscript. He then went back to the seller and got more of this manuscript, which was in Persian (*fārsī*), and it was from this that the story was written.

Having found that many of these footpath poets are in fact nonliterate, I wondered whether Joshi was perhaps an exception to the footpath poets and had received a classical education that included Persian. In an interview this past year (IAHJ-2), Joshi was asked specifically about his education. Like Jamal of Sanger and Rafiq Jan, he too had a religious education at the mosque (*jomāt*). On then being asked about how he could read this story in Persian, he said that he took it to a learned man who knew Persian and could explain it to him so that he could then render it in Pashto verse.[60] In this way, the research for the narrative was still oral, even though at an earlier level, the source of the story is (or was) in book form, thus illustrating a mechanism for transmission of knowledge both between book and oral traditions (as, for example, that diagrammed by Blackburn and Ramanujan [1986:5]) and between the literatures of two distinct languages.

Jamshed of Topi

Jamshed said he was "about fifty" in 1987 (though his birth certificate date would make him 55). He is one of the most educated of the folk poets whose narratives I have translated; he went to school through "matric." (that is, through tenth grade). More important than the number of years of schooling, however, is that "matric." implies a Western-style education (whatever the medium of instruction), rather than just the primarily religious education at a mosque or *madrasa*. His mother tongue (*mādarī zabān*) is not Pashto but Urdu, which is also the language in which he was educated; he is thus unschooled with respect to Pashto. He has written poetry in Urdu as well as in Pashto and has been invited to Urdu and Pashto *mushāʿiras* in Peshawar. Jamshed now prefers writing in Pashto because, he says, if he writes in Urdu, people won't understand it.

In regard to the technical side of poetry, Jamshed feels that there is not much meter (*wazn*) in Pashto, which makes composing Pashto poetry easy; he learned some of the rhyme forms while listening to the radio. Although he has Western schooling, he considers himself a folk poet, contrasting folk poets (*ʾawāmī shaʾirān*) with the literary poets (*adabī shaʾirān*) like Pareshan Khattak (then the president of Pakistan's Academy of Letters).

Although my concern with Jamshed was as a poet, he has also written several dramas; he is thus another of the rare examples (so far as I know) of a footpath poet who has written in a quite different genre. And although he considers himself a folk poet, he has received national recognition with financial rewards, such as Rs. 2000 from former president Ayub Khan for a book about the 1965 war between Pakistan and India.

Jamshed began writing poetry in about 1946 when he was "very young" (at about 14 years of age), and his family had returned from Bombay and Hushangabad. His first piece of poetry was a *chārbaita,* which he still can quote, for *chārbaitas* were very much the style (*riwāj*) then. He was active in the Muslim League and wrote poetry for it; he first attracted local attention at a political meeting when he was invited to recite poetry in front of Qayyum Khan.

Jamshed says that his poetry is improvised (*fiʾl-badīha*); he has written twelve books of it. His first book was *Dīn Dunyā* (*Religion and the World*), a book of counsel and advice of a religious nature, which was printed in Peshawar by an early publisher of folk verses. His second book, *da Haq Wīna,* was of a similar nature, and it was only for his third book that he wrote a historical narrative in verse. This was about Pir Baba (*Balkhī aw Qadrai*), a very famous local holy man, and was written at the request of Maulana Abdul Qadir, then director of the Pashto Academy, who gave Jamshed five hundred rupees "from his own pocket" for it. Among his other books is *Garden of Love* (*Gulzār-i ʿIshq*), which includes a variety of poetry, because "some people like one thing and some like another." In whatever he writes, he always includes three or four *rubāʿīs*.

In 1964, Jamshed published a verse narrative about Ajab Khan (translated in Heston and Nasir 1988 : 267–285) which tells of Ajab's 1923 kidnapping of a British officer's daughter in retaliation for the alleged British violation of Pathan women's purdah. Both U.S. and U.K. newspaper reports at the time presented the Pathan kidnapper as a savage barbarian, rather than as a heroic avenger of mistreated local women. Now, however, Ajab Khan has become a national hero in the struggle for independence; the story of the kidnapping has been made into movies, in Urdu and Panjabi (I am told) as well as in Pashto; the latter also is now available on videocassette.[61]

One point which might be mentioned about this story is the matter of the killer of the kidnapped girl's mother. Jamshed's version has the hero killing the mother, a deed certainly inconsistent with Pathan codes of conduct which abhor physical injury to women (except in retribution for dishonoring the family). Despite the fact that most printed accounts of 1923, as well as more recent retellings in Pakistani newspapers and magazines, usually say that the hero's brother, Shahzada, was the killer, Jamshed attributes it to Ajab Khan because, as he says, "that's what people think."[62] Oral tradition (or public opinion) thus takes precedence over most newspaper accounts.

Although Jamshed himself is educated, he has taken an interest in unlettered poets; among his projects was a collection of two hundred *chārbaitas* by unlettered poets for Maulana Abdul Qadir, thus offering another example of a way in which the folk poet himself acts as folklorist. In Jamshed's opinion, this traditional kind of poetry is in the process of dying out, since the young men writing poetry now are educated;[63] this again points to the perceived distinction between the poetry of literate and nonliterate poets.

Saifur Khan Saifur

Saifur Khan, who uses "Saifur" as a pen name, was interviewed on January 3, 1988, when he was "three or four years less than sixty" in age; he died the next day. He was then on a pension; he had been last employed as an antimalaria worker and "in service" for twenty-five years. Like Jamal of Sangar, he feels he was born a poet and his only teacher was God (ISXS); as a young man, he went into the woods (*zangal*), and had what must have been a mystical experience (complete with a voice calling him by name), which is reflected in his verses.

Saifur Khan was from a poor family which could not afford even schooling at a mosque for him. However, he did learn how to read and write from a little girl when he was young, through the process described by other unlettered poets (for example, by Iwaz Khan). The girl went through the letters of the alphabet, first explaining them individually, *alif, be, te,* and so on. Then she showed him how the letters are joined, *be* with *alif* is *bā, te* with *alif* is *tā,* and then *alif* plus *be* plus the vowel points to distinguish *ab,* from *ib,* and so on, in a process much like children's primers in Pashto (or college workbooks of introductory Urdu). After that, Saifur says, he went on to Arabic in the Qurʾan; he also claimed to understand Farsi. Later he learned English; he found the English alphabet very short of letters: it has only one *z* ("zed") while Pashto (like Persian or

Urdu) has four (*zāl, ze, zād,* and *zā*). Furthermore, English is short of *d*'s, because it does not have *dāl* and *ḍāl,* and it needs to use two (!) letters to make *kha* or *sha.*[64]

RAVAIL KHAN RAVAIL

Ravail Khan, who uses Ravail as a pen name, began writing when he was in the fourth standard. He is one of the few poets who claims to have had teachers (*ustāds*), whom he then names. His chapbook, *Heartbeat,* includes a number of *lobas*, a form of poetry not often seen in classical Pashto poetry. Perhaps most interesting of these is his *loba* (CRXR-zt: 20) of the Tangewal (the tonga man), in which he specifies the style (*tarz*) by using an Urdu couplet, thus providing an unquestionable example of how poetry of one language can influence another in an area of multilinguals.[65] Perhaps following the model of the teachers who helped him, he has been helpful in distributing a recent volume of poetry of Zeb, a young man who was introduced as one of the up-and-coming folk poets.

ABDUL WAHID THEKADAR

Abdul Wahid, the poet whose story of "The Beautiful Fairy," mentioned above, was in zigzag form, uses *ṭhekādār* ("Contractor") as a pen name; the name indicates one of his occupations. He produced his first poem, a *chārbaita,* at the age of ten or twelve. He didn't have to write it, but just opened his mouth and God made the words come out. Unlike most other poets, Thekadar did not need to have a *munshī* for his verses; instead, he had students who remembered his verses and wrote them down for him, thus playing their role in the transmission of his verses to the footpaths of Peshawar and from there into more general circulation.

Conclusion

These poets are a small sample of those whose work is available on the footpaths of Peshawar and other towns of the NWFP. Although their craft is traditional, the knowledge that they use for technique and content generally has not been transmitted linearly in a South Asian pattern of father to son or of teacher (*gurūs* or *ustāds*) to student. Instead, these unlettered poets appear randomly and spontaneously in villages of the NWFP where, despite a lack of education and, indeed, of much financial encouragement, each develops his own talents. Their acquired knowledge comes from their own experiences and from oral sources within their own culture. The development of nineteenth-century printing techniques and twentieth-century recording technology now offers tangible evidence of a continuing tradition of verse composition while providing village poets with new channels into the ever-increasing stream of poetry flowing from the footpaths of Peshawar.

* * *

I would like to express my thanks to Lok Virsa and its former director, Uxi Mufti, for making its research materials available to me. The chapbooks and tapes of Lok Virsa's library were my first encounter with the Pashto verse narratives; the interviews of poets (as field reports in Urdu translation) were the initial stimuli for a study of the poets themselves. My collections of material were funded by the American Institute of Pakistan Studies and the Smithsonian Institution's SFCP program, to whom I wish to express my thanks.

Notes

1. One notable exception is by Pritchett (1985), who examines popular printed Hindi/Urdu prose literature of the subcontinent in the nineteenth and twentieth centuries. The only study of South Asian literatures which I have seen that uses materials offered by cassette technology is Johnson (1982); like most studies using chapbook material, hers too focuses on content rather than on the phenomenon of this particular medium of transmission. In an anthropological context, Edwards (1987b: 5 and elsewhere) gives explicit recognition to the significance of the tape medium.

Outside South Asia, the study by Slater (1982) of Brazilian stories in verse (including a story traceable to a South Asian Jataka tale of King Shibi and the dove) explicitly relates marketing form to genre. Her work not only examines this genre, but also describes the poets and their views about their work; despite the distance and the considerable cultural difference between Brazil and Peshawar, the attitudes of the poets and the production and distribution of their work show a number of similarities.

2. Much of the material for this chapter was collected by my coauthor for *The Bazaar of the Storytellers*, Mumtaz Nasir Khan, of Lok Virsa's staff, to whom I am much indebted. The earliest interviews used as source material for this chapter were made by Mumtaz Nasir in conjunction with recordings of Pashto verse narratives; others were added when the decision was made to translate a group of these narratives into English (Heston and Nasir 1988). The poets who compose these narratives were found to produce other kinds of verse as well; there were also

many poets whose poetry was not included in the translations. The interview base was therefore expanded to include other poets whose work is available in a form transmittable through the marketplace. A considerable portion of these interviews is taken up by the poets' recitations of their own poetry; it was often with considerable difficulty that the flow of verse was stopped. It is hoped that the poetry and the comments of the poets can eventually be integrated into a single monograph.

3. Darmesteter 1888, section 139; however, he does not consider these poets as Afghans, but instead calls them "Indiens afghanisés," because "L'Afghan ne connaît que deux métiers: guerrier et agriculteur" (p. 140). This appears to follow from his equating of poets with the musician class/caste (*ḍoms*). The equating of these two groups is strongly at variance with my own experience, where none of the folk poets so far interviewed claim to be professional musicians, and they would probably dislike being considered as such.

4. This is a model which also seems more or less applicable to one group of poets within Pakistan's NWFP who are associated either with the University of Peshawar (including the Pashto Academy) or with various schools and colleges in smaller towns in the NWFP. They are now being written up in, for example, the *Frontier Post,* Peshawar's English-language newspaper, usually as poets of Swat, poets of Malakand, and so forth; their bio-data as given in the newspaper usually include mention of some college education and often the information that they are or have been teaching at a local school or college. The typical popular poet of Slater's Brazilian study likewise appears to come from a relatively educated class, where his "superior education and experience necessarily set him apart from the masses from which he originally came" (Slater 1982 : 177); an illiterate poet is noted as such (ibid., 250). (To be set against this, however, is the belief that "the poet learns his craft from no one; he learns everything alone" [ibid., 165].)

5. I am much indebted to Margaret Mills for pointing out in an earlier draft the incongruity of saying that illiterate poets write narrative verses. In fact, the Pashto verb most often used in these contexts was some form of "to say" (*wayəl*). Unfortunately, it is somewhat difficult to gauge the extent to which this is the effect of the interviewer's questions on the respondent's answers. For example, Jamshed of Topi, the most schooled of the poets discussed in this study, did use the verb "write" (*likəl*) in connection with a now deceased poet, Aman Gujerati, who wrote a widely circulated version of Gul and Sanobar. However, when Jamshed was asked what poetry he himself first began making (*sha'r . . . shurū' kawəl*), the interviewer's question and the respondent's answer both used the verb "say" (IJT). Beyond this, there is the lexical problem that (if available dictionary citations and my own impressions are to be trusted) verbs meaning "to say" (*wayəl*) or "to do, make" (*kawəl*) rather than "to write" (*likəl*) are standardly used with nouns such as *sha'r,* "poetry" or *nazm,* "verse" even if the poet uses a pen in the process. This paper's use of "composing" or "producing" is thus only a makeshift solution to alert the reader to a point which will need further research for clarification.

6. See the story introductions and endnotes in Heston and Nasir (1988) for some of these relationships in narrative verse. It is my impression that narrative cassette stories are greater in number than narrative chapbook stories, undoubtedly reflecting the greater relative costs of printing, (especially since the performance necessary for producing a cassette can also be enjoyed as a consumption item).

However, I have worked mostly with longer narratives (e.g., one or more cassettes in length), and have systematically investigated neither shorter performances (private or commercial) of these narratives nor commercial cassettes of non-narrative forms. I would guess that much of the shorter forms of chapbook poetry is never recorded commercially.

7. The terminology regarding narrative forms is rather loose. For example, Lal Jan (ILJ) first says that *dāstān, qiṣṣa,* and *badala,* are just dialect variations between Mohmands, Yusufzais and Afghans, respectively; he later qualifies that, saying that *dāstān*'s are short—10–15 minutes—and *badala*s and *qiṣṣa*s go on for an hour.

8. Cf. Wadley, this volume.

9. Bukhari and Hamdani (1966) include definitions and examples of these with (Urdu) translations. Their example (ibid., 27–28) of a *chārbaita* rhyme scheme is *aa bbb aa ccc aa . . . fff aa,* differing from that of, for example, Darmesteter (1888 : 141); the latter thinks the *miṣra* (often called a *ṭappa* in Pakistan) is the most original of Afghan forms and comments on its similarities to the Multani *ḍoṛhā*. Another view of the *chārbaita* is that it "is made up of at least sixteen lines, and the upper limit is infinity. . . . Sometimes all the verses rhyme together . . . sometimes only the first and the last, and so on" (Anon. 1962 : 19), a statement which seems well suited to the chapbooks I have collected.

10. Joshi, for example, has *rubāʾī*s of 4, 5, 6, 7, and more couplets (CAHJ-pg: 33, 32, 13, 43, 15–16); the *rubāʾī*s of the young poet, Zeb, alternate between 6 (CMZZ-qo: 22, 24, 32, 33, 35) and 7 couplets (CMZZ-qo: 15, 17, 19, 26, 28, 33, 36), and a *g͟hazal* may have a repeated refrain (CFGN-sg: 34–35).

11. It thus seems that the translation of *qiṣṣa-khwān* should include "story-singer" as well as "storyteller" (thus paralleling the reciting/singing translations possible, for example, in the phrase *naʾt-khwān*). This is perhaps partly because Pashto does not have a common simple verb equivalent to *gānā* of Hindi/Urdu and instead uses a construction of noun plus inflected verb; it is in any case one more example of the problems of crosscultural translation.

12. Thus IAX, where a singer refuses to entertain a rich khan because he was uneducated and wanted to hear a *rāg* inappropriate for that time of day.

13. This is not to imply that all "folk" singers are untrained; Fazli Rabi, for example, mentions a teacher (*ustād*) with whom he has studied (IFR).

14. Male dancers (*lakhtays*) whose favors are for sale can also be seen in the upstairs rooms of these teahouses, thus offering another example of the alleged link between prostitution and music (and thus poetry) in the South Asian subcontinent. This is not intended to imply that all teahouses offer this specialized form of entertainment. There are many teahouses where music can be heard only from a cassette or radio. I have not yet been able to find in Peshawar any tea- or coffeehouses offering poetry recitations on a regular basis, as has been found in Iran.

15. In 1982 and 1983, I was unable to find Pashto verse narratives in the Cantonment cassette shops, which seemed then to be selling mainly Urdu songs.

16. For example, see (in translation) Heston and Nasir 1988: 155–158, where the unnumbered couplets are called *miṣra*s in a parallel chapbook.

17. Rafiq Jan's occupational record goes from day laborer and sometime smuggler of tea and petty merchandise to tea-shop owner to owner of a cassette

shop selling "mostly bootlegged scores from Indian and Pakistani films" (Edwards, 1987a: 1).

18. Also included is the name of the verse narrative, both the *badala, Momin Khan and Shirinai,* and the story (*kahānī*), *Ḍer Gham,* "Much Grief." The use of these two terms, *kahānī* (a Hindi/Urdu word) and *badala* (a Pashto word) is curious. In a parallel chapbook, both the names of the characters (Momin Khan and Shirinai) and the phrase, *ḍer gham,* "much sorrow" appear on the cover (CJS-MX/š); the cassette producer has taken the phrase as a title for the story.

In 1986 I purchased another EMC tape of *Yusuf Khan-Sher Banu,* sung by Sayyid Mohammad, which also had both a picture of the singer and the information regarding the poet and accompanists. The cover had "Azim Khan Production—Karachi, original sound track recording" (in Urdu script). The tape itself had a "Qandahar Music Center, Kabari Bazaar, Peshawar" sticker on it. In a conversation with Brian Silver (2 April 1988), he said that the head of this company complained of the difficulty of making money on cassettes when the standard practice is to make copies of tapes rather than to buy new ones.

Still another picture of Wahid Gul appeared on a cassette from Khan Music Center (Karachi) which was purchased in Barikot in 1985, but not the name of the *badala.* In Kohat, the Bokhari Music Center (Main Bazaar, Kohat) had a tape of *Ajab Khan* with a girl dancing on the cover, but no mention of the poet's name; in the film version of *Ajab Khan,* there are several female characters, but there are none in the verse version by Jamshed of Topi.

19. As Pakistan-TV expands its programs, it makes a deliberate effort to take local culture into account (making for a potentially interesting study of multilingualism and the media in a developing nation). The Pashto *g͟hazal*s sung on television are often "classical" in style, undoubtedly reflecting the more educated tastes of the program managers; the poets who appear on the programs can be considered members of the literary establishment. Curiously, some Pakistanis have told me that the best videocassettes of Pashto music are now coming from Afghanistan.

20. Urdu stories that are also found in Pashto verse include, for example, *Bahram Gor* published in 1845 (?), *Four Dervishes* in 1801 (a Fort Williams publication), *Gul and Sanobar* (with a French translation from Urdu published in 1876) and *Laila and Majnun* in 1846 (Pritchett 1985: 194, 21, 197, 199). These Urdu stories themselves have Persian origins, and it is difficult to know definitively whether any particular Pashto poet is using a Persian or an Urdu version as his immediate source. When a source is specified, it is most often Persian, a "higher" culture language relative not only to Pashto but also to Urdu. However, the combination of three factors: (a) that a Persian source is *not* specified, (b) that there was a very large output of these certain stories as chapbooks in Urdu, and (c) that various words and phrases are calqued on or borrowed from Urdu in the Pashto versions, suggests to me that Urdu has played an important role in the transmission of some Pashto versions of these widely known tales. Furthermore, there are some cases in which an Urdu version is specified as a source, as with a turn-of-the-century version of *Gul and Sanobar* (see CAG-G/S, first couplet, page 3).

21. Rafi 1975: no. 1169 in 1295 HQ (a story of Mansur Hilaj in *maṣnavī* form) and no. 1168, respectively.

22. Rafi (no. 1128, p. 680) includes another story of Niʾmatullah (*Akhtar Numir Afghani*) published in Lahore in 1912/1331. The publisher, Mandir Singh, is the same publisher who printed no. 1132, also in 1912. Other Lahore publishers include Haji Abdul Khaliq (no. 1137), Sundar Singh (no. 1138), Mirza Mohammad Sadiq (no. 1140). Printing was also done in Lahore for other NWFP publishers; thus Mulla Saidan Shah of Mardan has a *qiṣṣa* printed in Lahore in A.H. 1317 (c. A.D. 1898) (Rafi 1975: 1143). This is perhaps the same Saidan Shah referred to by Abu Ali Shah in the preamble to his *Adam Khan-Dur Khanai* (e.g., CAAš-AX/DX-2). Could the publisher, Ghulam Mursalin (Rafi no. 1146, 1226, 1228), be the Ghulam al-Mursalin mentioned by Niʾmatullah (Heston and Nasir 1988: 93)?

23. Darmesteter (1888–90: 141, fn. 3), for example, mentions Niʾmatullah's version of *Nimbulla and Dimbulla* (translated in Heston and Nasir 1988: 92–113). One (presumably more recent) copy of this is held by Lok Virsa's library, but I was not able to find any version in the chapbook markets between 1982 and 1987.

24. Thus in a bibliography of folk literature in all the regional languages of Pakistan published by Lok Virsa (Jatoi 1980), only 3 of over 52 citations of Pashto folk literature in the "Folk Tales" category were not published in Peshawar. These remaining three were published in Swat (Niʾmatullah's version of *Laila and Majnun*), in Quetta (a collection) and in Darra Adam Khel (*Dre Nangiyālay*) (ibid., 31, 42, 27). For "Folk Songs," there is a somewhat larger cluster of Pashto publications in Quetta (e.g., ibid., 55, 57, and 58), but Peshawar publishers still dominate his listings.

25. A mixed prose and verse *qiṣṣa* in Persian about Najma Shirazi (144 pages long), which I purchased in 1986, was published by Nurani Kutub Khana. Commenting on this paper, Margaret Mills told me that this was the most commonly performed romance in Herat in the early 1970s; she has one version from Tehran and one from Peshawar. It is her impression that, as a producer of Persian chapbooks available in Afghanistan, Peshawar far exceeded Kabul, and was second only to Tehran.

26. Over the period from 1982 to 1987, a large number of these publications continued to be listed, but other titles were added or dropped. I suspect that these lists are not reliable indicators of what is actually available in the market at a given point. I have found several books that have gone out of print in the last five years. One of these was the story of Naik Akhtar (CNM-NA), a romance probably of Persian origin set in the time of Sultan Mahmud of Ghazna (r. 999–1010), a historical figure and patron of literature about whom stories have accumulated and who plays a role in this story. It was in print in 1983, but out of print in late 1987. This chapbook's cover is particularly interesting in that it shows a woman (presumably the heroine, who is supposed to be very pious) alone reading a book held in the kind of stand usually used for the Qurʾan with a mosque and the Kaʾba are reflected in a mirror in the background.

27. A 286-page edition of a story about Amir Hamza (CAJ-AH), purchased in 1986, had a price of Rs. 12 stamped on the cover; a 64-page copy of a Pashto romance (CWM-šA/M-2) with a smaller and more common page size purchased in the same year had Rs. 2.50 printed on the title page. Most of the printed chapbooks I purchased during 1986 and 1987 were Rs. 3 or 4. Thus Rs. 3, for example, for a 96-

page romance [CJS-MX/š] and 64 pages of religious poetry [CAWD-dqm] and Rs. 4 for 64 pages of more religious poetry by the same poet [CAWD-qt]), when the exchange rate was about 16–18 Rs./U.S. dollar.

28. There are a few exceptions where poets have themselves financed the publication by a small printing shop; the exceptions thus far noted have been for printing jobs done outside Peshawar city.

29. I did find a Swat edition of *Laila and Majnun* in Peshawar (CN-LM-1).

30. This is an asymmetric relationship, since books (usually secondhand) from the University Book Agency are sold on the footpaths or in the small shops of Qissa Khwani. This situation may be changing; in early 1990, the University Book Agency did have for sale a small selection of chapbooks.

31. Thus CAJ-AH, Cšš-šDD, Cšš-DJ, and CDXX-ck are all published by Zeb Art Press; all four also have the same printer's name (A. Z. Tabassum) printed on their covers. Those covers are stylistically closely related to (and perhaps by the illustrator of) three covers (CN-LM-2, CIš-DT, and CF-BGa-2) published by Rahman Gul, which do not have a printer's name on them. These latter three stories themselves are traditional, and at least one (CF-BGa-2) is a reprint, with a change of cover from another quite different (presumably earlier) style (CF-BGa-1).

32. The major exception in this folk poetry is the *ṭappa,* or *miṣras*; thus the Pashto *rubāʾīs* of folk poets (e.g., AWD-az: 27) have one more point of contrast with the Persian *rubāʾī,* where a *takhalluṣ* is not included and attribution can be a real problem. *Lobas* (e.g., AWD-az: 13–14) and *chārbaitas* (e.g., AWD-az: 23) can also include a *takhalluṣ.*

33. The story includes a fight with a demon (*dew*) from Jandol, today a part of the NWFP. The inclusion of a flight to Majandaran (surely Mazanderan) raises the possibility that this is a story of Persian origin which at some point was transferred through a Hindustani dialect that substitutes for *z.*

34. These four are CMB-YZ, CšRA-YZ, CAJH-YZ, and CGšN-YZ; the first of these is the only chapbook I have collected that is printed in Kohat.

35. See Bukhari and Hamdani 1966:202–205 for biographical information.

36. Anecdotes about Mulla Do-piyāza are also printed separately. One edition (C-MDp) has a cover with a king, presumably the Emperor Akbar, in the background; the stories usually include Akbar and/or his vizier, Birbal, as characters. The deeds of Mulla Do-piyāza (none so far found entirely in verse) perhaps deserve some independent study; Pashto versions have been published as far away as Delhi and as early as 1896 (A.H. 1313) in a combination of prose and verse (Rafi 1975: no. 1129). Their appearance in various chapbook editions illustrates one more way in which folk material combines and recombines for the enjoyment of successive generations.

37. The publisher listed on the cover of CWM-šA/M-1 is Awami Kutub Khana, but the publisher on the title page is Rahman Gul, who in 1987 was using the same picture, but with the blue title and couplet at the top replaced by a title in black and white and with the red section, which has the publisher's name at the bottom, replaced by his own in black and white (CWM-šA/M-2). This type of phenomenon creates some special problems for bibliographies of chapbooks.

38. Johnson's version is probably the same as "Shair Alam Mamonei," by

"Jamal Shair of Ghandaw," listed by Jatoi (1980: 60), who also lists a "Amir Ghulam Sadiq" version of "Memone-e-Shir Alam," about which I have no further information.

39. This seems likewise to be true of the chapbook film lyrics. These chapbooks sometimes feature a particular singer, for example, "The Nightingale of the Frontier, Mah-jabin Qizalbash" (purchased in Peshawar, 1987), who is pictured in plump pulchritude on the cover; others are more general, listing both the name of the film and the name of a (probably playback) singer. The film song chapbook covers show some similarity to the recent cassette covers.

40. The cover of this chapbook shows a girl (presumably a bride) dressed in red and crouched in a blue-curtained, green-topped *dolī* (litter) that is suspended from a single long pole and carried by two barefooted men wearing red turbans and yellow kurtas with rolled up pants, a more realistic cover than is generally seen in romances. The carrying of the bride from her parental house to the groom's house (and sometimes also circling once or more through the village) is a traditional feature of village Pathan weddings. Red is the color associated with marriage clothes (as white has been in the United States); the longing for a red *dolī* thus implies a desire to be married. *Dolī*s have also been used for nonceremonial occasions, providing a form of enclosed transport for women in purdah; I have heard stories about events when the women in families of khans living in Peshawar two generations ago were carried from one house to another by this means. I have also heard that NWFP *dolī*s differ from those of other parts of South Asia, but I have not been able to document the variations (e.g., the number of poles [one or two] and the position of poles [above, below or in the middle of the enclosure]) of this rapidly disappearing form of transport.

41. Some (usually Westernized) Pathans would agree, as, for example, in the case of Chamnay Khan (see Heston and Nasir 1988: 289–301).

42. For example, in a list of over fifty *badala* cassettes compiled in 1983, Fazli Qayyum has one named simply *Dako*; another story called *Yusuf Mafrur* (*Joseph the Fugitive*) may also fall into this category. The nonurban nature of Pashto folk poetry probably also precludes narratives about the Peshawar *badmāsh*es, who played a role in a 1987 TV drama. They appear to share certain characteristics of the Persian *lūtī*. The lack of popularity of dacoits in Pashto contrasts with, for example, the bandit/outlaw folk heroes studied by Kathryn Hansen (1983).

43. I do not know anything about theater tradition in Pershawar or whether this particular play was ever performed. In conversation on April 2, 1988, Kathryn Hansen said that Sher Dil the Dacoit is also the hero of an Indian film; this may be purely a coincidence of names. There is also a recent Urdu film, *The Dacoit's Daughter* (*Daku Kī Larki* [sic]), wherein the dacoit is named Sher Dil (reviewed in *The Pakistan Times Overseas Weekly*, May 8, 1988: 10); unless it is assumed that the latter begins with a second marriage of Sher Dil, it is not related to the Pashto version. However, the role of the moneylender as villain in the Urdu versions probably parallels the role of a *ṣeth* in the Pashto version.

44. The edition listed in the folk song section of Lok Virsa's bibliography (Jatoi 1980: 69) gives a price of Rs 2, whereas my edition has Rs 4.50 printed on the inside cover and therefore is (I assume) a later edition.

45. Over 90 percent of the Hindu-Urdu *qiṣṣa* publications listed by Pritchett (1985:181–190) are in printings of 1000 or a multiple thereof, suggesting that this is a standard unit of print.

46. For example, Jamshed of Topi, who has himself been invited to participate in mushairas (*mushāʿira*), says that these contests are not the same as a mushaira (IJT).

47. The term used is *shand* (IJT), which might be translated as "sterile" or "barren" lines; I have not seen this word used elsewhere and it may be a purely local usage.

48. Lindholm (1982:22–24) discusses the *betək* (sic) as a replacement for the *hujra*. However, I was taken to both an old and a new *hujra* (still under construction) of Abdullah Khan of Village Hajizai, near Shabqadar. It should perhaps be noted that the new *hujra* was adjacent to the compound where the khan's wives and children were living, thus fitting a description of Lindholm's description of *betək,* although the term used was *hujra*. Lindholm includes a cassette deck as a prestigious item in a *betək,* thus providing another example of how new settings continue to offer ways for transmitting traditional poetry.

49. Additional comparative material may be available from Brazil: see Slater (1982:9, inc. fn. 19), who also notes that the tradition of verbal dueling goes back to the Greeks and Romans. It is not clear from Slater's remarks whether the "spirited exchanges in verse" are for the purpose of testing the technical skills of the poets or for more general purposes, such as disparagement of the character or ancestry of the poet.

50. Although this study has focused on poets whose work has reached the marketplace, there are certainly many other respected local poets whose work is not found in published chapbooks or commercial cassettes. In April, 1986, for example, Fazli Qayyum helped Mumtaz Nasir in locating Qalandar Baba of Bada Bher (a village near Peshawar) and bringing him to Green's Hotel in Peshawar for an interview. Qalandar Baba's entrance into the hotel created great excitement; he obviously was known and respected by the Pashto-speaking staff. He was invited by the manager to stay for lunch, and by the time he came downstairs to the lobby, a small crowd of perhaps a dozen local businessmen and members of the hotel staff were waiting respectfully to escort him into the dining room.

51. This is not intended to imply that verses concerned with expressions of love and separation are limited to South Asia; it is well attested in genres as diverse as American popular songs and Zulu women's songs (for the latter, see Joseph, 1987). However, my general impression of Pashto, Urdu, and Persian love poetry and Urdu films and film songs suggests a commonality of imagery and modes of expression which contrasts with, for example, American popular song lyrics.

52. Edwards (1987a:1) says that Rafiq Jan's father was a mulla and that as a boy, "he began imitating his father who wrote verse in praise of the Prophet Mohammad." The apparent contradiction regarding writing of verse is perhaps related to the dichotomy in attitudes toward religious and secular verse.

53. The episode is now commemorated by a small monument on the footpath in Qissa Khwani Bazaar. This "massacre," when the "brutality of the Raj . . . cut down hundreds of people" (*The Frontier Post,* April 24, 1987) and "women

and children were mercilessly killed" (*The Frontier Post,* Jan. 21, 1988), receives attention in local newspapers both on the anniversary of this event and at other times of year.

54. Verses of the seventeenth-century classical Pashto poet, Khushhal Khan Khattak, celebrated resistance to Moghul rule. Somewhat later, Darmesteter (1888) included examples of folk poetry about battles against the British in Afghanistan as late as 1880 (so dated on p. CCXIII). Edwards (1987a:2) mentions another narrative by Rafiq Jan concerning an incident in 1935, when the Mohmands attacked a British road building crew on the Nahakki Pass. Rafiq Jan is only one of many poets writing in this tradition; six other stories from cassettes which extol in verse the deeds of Pakistani folk heroes in their struggle for independence from the British are translated by Heston and Nasir (1988).

55. However, Edwards (1987a:16) cites an example by Rafiq Jan, wherein cucumbers are mentioned in a similar martial context ("The skull of an enemy is like a cucumber to them"), raising the possibility that some of these images have wider usage than has yet been documented.

56. The pronunciation of the heroine's name has a long *ā* as the second vowel in Jamal's version; this variant is here ignored for purposes of exposition.

57. It is not stated when this "Landi" mulla's information came from an oral source, from another Pashto version, or from a source in some other language. Hamdani (1981:74) gives the text of an Ahmad Jan version of the Amir/Mir Hatim story which he says comes from an Urdu source; I have not yet been able to locate any Urdu versions. Jamal mentions that Mir Khatam is one of Amir Hamza's men; there is a Pashto version of Amir Hamza by Mulla Ahmad Jan (CAJ-AH); perhaps this is the textual source from which Jamal is working.

58. According to Benedicte Grima Johnson, Joshi continues to sing informally; she has made some tape recordings of his singing. It would be interesting to know how often he sings with, for example, men of his own age group.

59. Similarly, also in surveys of Pashto literature, e.g., Abbasi, 123.

60. This raises the question of how many poets who cite books (e.g., Heston and Nasir 1988:223) can be assumed to have actually read them.

61. The movie version gives Ajab Khan a fiancée. This is perhaps not simply a means of adding romance for a "better" movie; Abbasi (1969:123) lists "Ajab Khan and Nazo" as a popular local story.

62. *The Herald* (April 1983:73) includes an account by Mollie Ellis which says that her mother was killed by Shahzada, Ajab Khan's brother; Shoaib Sultan's article in *The Frontier Post* (Nov. 13, 1987:3) also attributes Mrs. Ellis's death to Shahzada. However, an article by Niloufer Khan in *The Muslim Magazine* (July 22, 1983:4) does attribute Mrs. Ellis's death to Ajab Khan (as a result of the movie's influence?).

63. Although the question of whether new young men are waiting in the wings is open to question, the older practitioners are certainly dying off. From Jamshed, we learned that Aman Gujerati, a poet who wrote a well-known Pashto version of *Gul and Sanobar* (translated from a commercial cassette by Johnson [1982:121–130]) had died only a year or two ago, in Takht Bha'i, the town of Ali Haydar Joshi, when he was one hundred seven or eight years of age.

64. The perceptive Saifur does not, however, get perfect marks in phonetics; he equates the English phoneme represented by *th* with the aspirated *t* of Urdu.

65. This *loba* uses the refrain "I am a Tangawal," reminiscent of the "I am a Truck Driver" Pashto cassette circulating in Peshawar during 1986.

References

'Abbasi, Shah Muhammad Madani

1969 *Pashto zaban aur adab ki tarikh* (in Urdu). Lahore: Central Urdu Board.

Addleton, Jonathan S.

1986 The Importance of Regional Languages in Pakistan. *Al-Mushir* 28, 2 (Summer).

Anonymous

1962 Pathan Folk Songs. *Pakistan Quarterly* 10, 4 : 17 : 23.

Blackburn, Stuart H., and Ramanujan, A. K.

1986 *Another Harmony: New Essays in the Folklore of India*. Berkeley: University of California Press.

Bukhari, Farigh, and Raza Hamdani, compilers

1966 *Pushto Sha'iri*, vol. 1 (in Urdu). Karachi: Anjuman-i Taraqqi-i Urdu.

Cejpek, Jirí

1968 Iranian Folk-literature. In *History of Iranian Literature*, J. Rypka, ed., pp. 607–648. Dordrecht: Reidel.

Darmesteter, James

1888–90 *Chants populaires des Afghans*. Paris: Imprimérie nationale.

Edwards, David B.

1987a Words in the Balance: Honor and Sacrifice in the Poetry of the Afghan Jihad. Paper presented at the American Anthropological Association Annual Meeting, Chicago.

1987b The World Turned Upside Down: Poetics of Order in the Afghan Resistance. Paper presented at the American Ethnological Society Annual Meeting, St. Louis (Spring).

Ghazanvi, Khatir

1978 [*Sarhaddī Romānī Kahaniyā̃* (in Urdu; English title page: Romantic Tales from Frontier [sic]).] Islamabad: National Institute of Folk and Traditional Heritage.

Hamdani, Raza

1981 *Razmiya Dāstānē* (in Pashto and Urdu; English title page: *Razmia Dastanain (Epics)*. Islamabad: National Institute of Folk and Traditional Heritage (Lok Virsa).

Hanaway, William L., Jr., trans. and ed.

1974 *Love and War: Adventures from the Firuz Shah Nama of Sheikh Bighami*. Delmar, N.Y.: Scholar's Facsimiles Reprints.

Hansen, Kathryn.

1983 [*Sultana the Dacoit* and *Harishchandra:* Two Popular Dramas of the Nauṭanki Tradition of North India.] *Modern Asian Studies* 17 : 313–352.

Heston, Wilma L., and Mumtaz Nasir
1988 *The Bazaar of the Storytellers*. Islamabad: Lok Virsa.
Jatoi, Iqbal Ali
1980 *Bibliography of Folk Literature*. Islamabad: National Institute of Folk Heritage (Lok Virsa).
Johnson, Benedicte Grima
1982 Les Contes legendaires pashtun: Analyse et traduction de cassettes commercialisées. Mémoire presenté pour une maîtrise d'études iraniennes. University of Paris.
Joseph, Rosemary M. R.
1987 Zulu women's bow songs: ruminations on love." *BSOAS* 50, 1 : 90–119.
Lindholm, Charles
1982 *Generosity and Jealousy: The Swat Pukhtun of Northern Pakistan*. New York: Columbia University Press.
MacKenzie, D. N.
1987 Pashto. In *The World's Major Languages*. Bernard Comrie, ed., pp. 547–565. London: Oxford University Press.
Pritchett, Francis
1985 *Marvelous Encounters: Folk Romance in Urdu and Hindi*. New Delhi: Manohar.
Rafi, Habibullah
1975 *Pashto Biblography* (sic: English title on cover:). Kabul: Pashtu Academy. Vol. I: 1975; vol. II: 1977.
Slater, Candace
1982 *Stories on a String*. Berkeley: University of California Press.

Interviews

The following interviews were used for this chapter but are cited only in cases where the source of a particular statement might not otherwise be obvious.

IAA: Aurangzeb "Aurang" (poet)
IAHJ-1: Ali Haydar "Joshi" (poet)
IAHJ-2: Ali Haydar "Joshi" "
IAJ: Afsar Jan (poet/singer)
IAWT: Abdul Wahab "Thekadar" (poet)
IAX: Abdul Khaliq (publisher)
IBSBX: Younger brother of Sher Baz Khan (cassette dealer)
IDAXA: Dil Aram Khan "Arif" (poet)
IFR: Fazli Rabi (singer)
IJS: Jamal of Sangar (poet)
IJT: Jamshed of Topi (poet)
ILJ: Lal Jan (Radio Pakistan)
IQB: Qalandar Baba (poet)
IRJ: Rafiq Jan (poet)

IRXR: Ravail Khan "Ravail" (poet)
ISMX: Sayyid Mohammad Khan (poet)
ISXS: Saifur Khan "Saifur" (poet)

Chapbooks

Peshawar (QX) = Qissa Khwani Bazaar, Peshawar

CA-Da/Da-1 *Dil-afza Shahzada aw Dil-afruza Shahzadagai,* by Amanat. Peshawar (QX): Rahman Gul Publishers. (Oversize)

CA-Da/Da-2 *Dil-afza Shahzada aw Dil-afruza Shahzadagai,* by Amanat. Pehsawar (QX): Qadimi Kutub Khana. (Oversize)

CAAš-AX/DX-1 *Adam Khan—Dur Khanai,* by Abu Ali Shah. Peshawar (QX): (N)urani Kutub Khana.

CAAš-AX/DX-2 *Adam Khan—Dur Khanai,* by Abu Ali Shah. Peshawar (QX): Nurani Kutub Khana.

CAAš-AX/DX-3 *Adam Khan—Dur Khanai aur film sandare.* Peshawar (QX): Rahman Gul Publishers.

CAG-G/S *Qissa da Gul aw Sanobar bi-zabani afghani,* by Aman Gujerati. Peshawar (QX): Rahman Gul Publishers.

CAHJ-din *Da Iman Nakha,* by Ali Haydar "Joshi." Peshawar (QX): Islami Kutub Khana.

CAHJ-dj *Diwan-i Joshi,* by Ali Haydar "Joshi." Peshawar (Mahalla Jangi): Zeb Art Publishers.

CAHJ-pg *Parde Gham,* by Ali Haydar "Joshi." Peshawar (QX): Islami Kutub Khana.

CAHJ-YZ *Hikayat La-Jawab,* by Ali Haydar "Joshi." Peshawar: Islami Kutub Khana.

CAJ-qa *Qisas al-anbiya,* by Mulla Ahmad Jan. Peshawar (QX): Nurani Kutub Khana.

CAJ-AH *Dastan-i Amir Hamza,* by Mulla Ahmad Jan. Peshawar (QX): Qadimi Kutub Khana.

CAN-pa *Parwaz-i Aql,* by Molavi Abdullah of Nowshera Kalan. Peshawar (QX): Islami Kutub Khana.

CAWD-az *Akhira zamana,* by Abdul Wahab "Dasti." Peshawar (QX): Nurani Kutub Khana.

CAWD-dqm *Da qadrat tamasha,* by Abdul Wahab "Dasti." Peshawar (QX): Haji Fazli Ahad Industries.

CAWD-qt *Da gabr manzil,* by Abdul Wahab "Dasti." Peshawar (QX): Nurani Kutub Khana.

CAWT-tt *Tang Takor,* by Abdul Wahid "Thekadar." Peshawar (QX): Haji Fazli Ahad Industries-Tajran Kutub.

CAWT-SX *Sundar Khaperai,* by Abdul Wahid "Thekadar." Peshawar: New Eagle Star Printing Press.

CDXX-ck *Carawan aw Karawan,* by Diyar Khan Khamosh. Peshawar: Zeb Art Press.

CF-BGa-1 *Bahram Gul-andam* (on cover), by Fayyaz. Peshawar (QX): Rahman Gul. (10/83)

CF-BGa-2 *Qissa da Shahzada aw Gul-andama,* by Fayyaz. Peshawar (QX): Rahman Gul. (Purchased 2/86, with different cover but same contents as CF-BGa-1)

CFGN-sg *Sire garewan,* by Fazli Ghani Mujahid. Peshawar (QX): Qadimi Kutub Khana.

CGšN-YZ *Dastan-i Shirin o Tarikhi Yusuf o Zulaikha,* by Gulab Shair Nishta of Charsada. Peshawar (QX): Rahman Gul Publishers.

CJS-MX/š *Der Gham: Qissa da Momin Khan-Shirinai,* by Jamal of Sangar. Peshawar (QX): Rahman Gul Publishers.

CJT-AX *Ajab Khan Afriday: Nar Pakhtun,* by Jamshed of Topi. Peshawar: Islami Kutub Khana. (Purchased 1982).

CIš-DT *Qissa da Dey Turaban,* by Ibrahim Shah. Rahman Gul: Peshawar (QX).

CMAA-BM *Qissa da Bakht Munir,* by Muhammad Ali "Arif." Rahman Gul: Peshawar.

CMB-YZ *Qissa da Hazrat Yusuf al-Ma'ruf Bibi Zulaikha 'Ashq,* by Malal Baba of Kohat. Kohat: Kitab Gohar.

CMš-MDp *Mulla Do-piyaza aw Birbal,* by Sayyad Mastan Shah. Peshawar: Zeb Art Publishers. (Prose)

CMZZ-qo *da Qalam Okhke,* by Muhammad Zeb "Zeb." Nowshera.

CN-LM-1 *Qissa Laila Majnun,* by Ni'matullah (as *takhullus* on pp. 2 and 54 but not on title page or cover). Mingora (Swat): Islam Beg Store.

CN-LM-2 *Qissa Laila Majnun,* by Ni'matullah. Peshawar (QX): Rahman Gul Publishers.

CNM-šA *Qissa (da) Shahzada Aurang aw Khaperai Tajbari,* by Nur Muhammad of Nowshera. Peshawar: Islami Kutub Khana. (Purchased 2/86; 11/87)

CNM-NA *Naik Akhtar aw Bibi Husn Banu,* by Nur Muhammad Ustad of Noshera. Peshawar: Islami Kutub Khana.

CRXR-zt *Da zra takor,* by Rawail Khan "Rawail." Peshawar: Shahin Bargi Press.

CšRA-YZ *Khakle qissa da Yusuf,* by Sayyid Shah Rasul 'Abidy. Peshawar: Zeb Art Publishers.

Cšš-šDD *Qissa da Sher Dil Dako,* by Shakir-ullah Shakir. Peshawar (Mahalla Jangi): Zeb Art Publishers.

Cšš-DJ *Qissa da Dreyo Jinako,* by Shakir-ullah Shakir. Peshawar (Mahalla Jangi): Zeb Art Publishers.

Cšš-RD *Nawe qissa da sare dolai arman,* by Shakir-ullah Shakir. Peshawar (Mahalla Jangi): Zeb Art Publishers.

CWM-šA/M-1 *Sher Alam and Memunai: Tufani Gham,* by Wali Muhammad. Cover: Awami Kutub Khana; Title page: Rahman Gul Publishers, Peshawar.

CWM-šA/M-2 *Sher Alam and Memunai: Tufani Gham,* by Wali Muhammad. Cover and title page: Rahman Gul Publishers, Peshawar.

Part III

Tradition: Persistence and Divergence

Peter Manuel

11. The Popularization and Transformation of the Light-Classical Urdu *Ghazal*-Song

One may speak, in the most general sense, of two major sociohistorical developments which have influenced the course of Indian urban music over the last 150 years. The first of these is the decline of Indian feudal society and the subsequent emergence of modern, capitalist socioeconomic classes. The second is the advent of industrial technology and, in particular, the mass media. These developments have had prodigious and diverse effects upon urban musics, influencing the nature of patronage, dissemination, audiences, musical meaning, and style. Some musical genres have fared poorly in the transition period; *dhrūpad,* the favored classical genre of the Mughal aristocracy, has become an archaic and peripheral curiosity on the musical scene, while many folk genres—including the practice of beggars singing Urdu couplets—have virtually disappeared. In their place have emerged new hybrid musics, most notably, of course, the commercial popular musics associated with the mass media. These musics may be regarded as archetypically syncretic in their combination of Indian, Western, rural, urban, traditional, and modern features—characteristics that reflect in their own way the emergence of modern Indian urban social classes.

In evaluating the cultural ramifications of these two sociohistorical trends, the fate of the Urdu *ghazal*-song over the last century is of particular interest, for it is one of the very few musical genres which not only enjoyed wide popularity in the nineteenth century, but also has earned genuine mass appeal in the present. A study of the *ghazal*'s successful transition from court to cassette, and from courtesan salon to concert hall, serves to illustrate the protean versatility of the *ghazal* itself, and the commercial assets and aesthetic costs of such adaptability; on a broader level, the development of the modern commercial *ghazal*-song embodies and reflects the interlocking dialectics—tradition versus modernity, elite versus mass, Hindu versus Muslim, nationalism versus internationalism, and corporate manipulation versus grass-roots spontaneity—whose negotiation and interaction animate modern Indian culture as a whole.

The Traditional Urdu *Ghazal*-Song

Properly speaking, the term *ghazal* denotes a literary genre, although it is common parlance to speak of it as a musical idiom as well. The *ghazal* as a poetic form originated in Arabic literature, but was carried to far greater heights in Persian poetry, especially in the work of Sa'di (d. 1292) and Hāfez (d. 1390). *Ghazal* subsequently became an important literary genre in several other Middle Eastern and Central Asian languages. While the Persian *ghazal* enjoyed a long and distinguished career in India, by the eighteenth century it had given way to the Urdu *ghazal*. The latter, while developing a distinctive character obliquely reflecting its own sociohistorical circumstances, tended nevertheless to adhere to the form, imagery, and even traditional content of its ancestor. The Urdu *ghazal* continues to enjoy prodigious popularity in north India and Pakistan—a popularity, indeed, incomparably greater than that of any poetic form in the West.

Formally, the *ghazal* consists of a series of rhymed couplets in the scheme *aa ba ca da* and so on; the "a" lines contain a double end-rhyme, which poses special challenges for the author. The verses are set to strict poetic meters based on Arabic prosody (whose rules are observed faithfully even by illiterate poets). The couplets are unified only by meter and rhyme rather than by content; thus, each couplet is intended to constitute a discrete entity—like a pearl in a necklace, to use the familiar metaphor.

In practice, the fragmentary nature of the *ghazal* is mitigated by the use of stock themes and imagery, which facilitates the epigrammatic condensation so essential to the form. Most couplets tend to deal with unrequited love, as perceived or imagined by the male persona. Frequent use is made of traditional symbolic imagery, in which, for example, the lover is likened to a moth that circles and eventually immolates itself in the candle, which itself represents the beloved.

> Now only betrayal remains, and the memory of fidelity,
> Where there was once a candle, now lies only the dust of the moth.[1]

Other common themes (which often conflate with that of unrequited love) include mystical longing, contempt of Islamic orthodoxy, celebration of madness and inebriation, and philosophical speculation.

Who in the desert will see springtime?
For whom does the flower in the jungle bloom?[2]

In modern times, traditional symbology has also been used to convey sociopolitical themes, most notably by the late Faiz Ahmad Faiz.

<u>*Gh*</u>*azal*s are ideally intended not to be silently read, but to be declaimed—archetypically at a poetry reading (*mushā*ʿ*ira*). Indeed, the <u>*gh*</u>*azal,* with its extended end-rhymes, incessant meter, romantic imagery, and flowery Persianized diction, lends itself naturally to musical rendering, and appears to have existed as a musical genre well before its introduction to South Asia. In India, <u>*gh*</u>*azal* has long been the basis of several musical styles, most notably *tarannum* (a semimelodic chanting style used in *mushā*ʿ*ira*s), *qawwālī* (Muslim devotional song), and the more genteel semiclassical style of rendering.

In the light-classical style, a solo vocalist sings the text, accompanied by melodic instruments (generally, harmonium and/or *sāraṅgī*) and the tabla drum pair. The melodic structure generally conforms to an *asthāi-antara* pattern, in which the "a" lines are sung to a precomposed tune (the *asthāi* or *sthāi*), while the nonrhyming first lines of couplets are sung to a florid, more melismatic melody (the *antara*), which may be loosely improvised. During the *antara* the artist may endeavor to interpret the text through extended and varied melodic elaboration, in the process building up a degree of suspense in anticipation of the end-rhyme and completion of the couplet. Each couplet (*she*ʾ*r*) is generally followed by a *laggī* section in which the tabla player improvises. The form may be schematized as shown in the table.

	Text	*Rhyme*	*Melody*
1st couplet	1st line	a	*asthāi*
	2nd line	a	*asthāi*
(*laggī*)			
2nd couplet	1st line	b	*antara*
	2nd line	a	*asthāi*
(*laggī*)			
3rd couplet	1st line	c	*antara*
	2nd line	a	*asthāi*
(*laggī*)			

<u>*Gh*</u>*azal*s may be set to classical *rāg*s (modes), or to melodies that do not correspond to any *rāg*. Simple *tāl*s (meters) are generally used, espe-

cially *kaherva* (eight beats) and *dādrā* (six beats). While one cannot speak of any explicit written or oral theory of *ghazal*-singing, purists and aficionados do articulate high aesthetic standards relating to such matters as proper enunciation and phrasing, expressive interpretation, and judicious use of word-painting; hence they are quick to criticize such faults as distortion of the text through rhapsodic but incorrect phrasing, and, even worse, mispronunciation of Urdu phonemes (some of which do not exist in Hindi or other Indian languages). Since *ghazal* is not a classical music genre, however, this unwritten aesthetic is far from standardized, and opinions differ as to what sorts of indulgences constitute prevarications from good taste.

Because *ghazal,* as a Muslim-oriented light-classical genre, lay outside the tradition of Sanskritic-based music theory, there are very few references to *ghazal*-singing prior to the nineteenth century. Evidence suggests that it was a popular aristocratic genre from well before the Mughal period (see, e.g., Umr 1975 : 374), but it is not until the emergence of Lucknow as a cultural center in the late 1700s that *ghazal* appears to have burst into lavish court and elite patronage and, at the same time, into historical daylight. *Ghazal* played an important part in the flowering of Indo-Muslim culture based in nineteenth-century Lucknow, which had replaced war-ravaged Delhi as the center of fine arts patronage in North India.

The efflorescence of Lucknow society can be seen as a transitional phase in the emergence of modern North Indian culture. From one perspective, it resembles the vibrant and colorful sunset of Indian feudal culture, animated by the sybaritic *nawāb*s (especially Wajid Ali Shah) who immersed themselves in music and dance, and by the declining *zamīndār* (hereditary landlord) aristocracy which, although unable to adapt to the capitalist land-tenure systems introduced by the British, attempted to perpetuate their role as patrons of fine arts. From another angle, the period foreshadows the present in the emergence of a new, protocapitalist class of commercial speculators and absentee landlords (*tāluqdār*s), who, while relatively ignorant of the finer aspects of Mughal culture, gradually came to assume the support of the fine arts. Given the *nouveau arrivée* nature of this class, it is not surprising that its constituents tended to patronize lighter, more accessible genres like *ghazal* and *ṭhumrī,* rather than the austere *dhrūpad,* and that Urdu poetry itself became markedly more shallow, sentimental, and sensuous in this period.[3] As before, *ghazal* continued to be performed primarily by courtesans, who were recognized and celebrated to an unprecedented degree as custodians of the fine arts.

Contemporary chronicles attest to the extraordinary popularity of *ghazal* in Lucknow during this period, and especially during the decades preceding the Mutiny of 1856–58.[4] While the *tāluqdār, zamīndār,* and court aristocracies were clearly the most enthusiastic patrons of the art, descriptions by Abdul Halim Sharar (1975 : 33, 174) and others seem to suggest that *ghazal* was also widely enjoyed by members of the urban lower classes. Theodor Adorno has written nostalgically of the late 1700s in Europe as perhaps the last period when a work of art, such as Mozart's light opera *The Magic Flute,* could appeal to both elite and lower classes, in an era before the vulgarities of the popular music industry, the defensive esotericism of serious composers, and the reification of all works of art under advanced capitalism (Adorno 1976 : 22). One has the impression—whether accurately or not—that the nineteenth-century *ghazal*-song enjoyed a similar status in contemporary North Indian urban culture on the eve of the modern era.

The recording industry got off to a remarkably early start in India, for by 1902 the Gramophone Company of London had already produced over five hundred discs of various types of music (Gronow 1981 : 251). *Ghazal*s sung by prominent courtesans appear to have figured prominently in these and subsequent releases, especially since the genre, with its accessible style and use of Urdu (rather than a regional language), was already popular throughout urban North India.

The early *ghazal* recordings of singers like Gauhar Jan and Janki Bai document the turn-of-the-century style, which may well have resembled that of the Lucknow era. These *ghazal*s are remarkably classicized in their use of a wide variety of *rāg*s and in the emphasis on virtuosity in the form of breathtaking, fast melodic runs (*tān*s). Less apparent in recordings, although described by informants, was the use, in performance, of histrionic stylized gestures, facial expressions, and declamation techniques (e.g., alternating whispering, singing loudly, and imitating sobbing). Such mannerisms, referred to as *nakhra* (lit., "blandishments, coquetries"), were trademarks of the courtesan style, which was, after all, designed to entice men on a very mundane level aside from its aesthetic appeal.

Courtesan culture, however, was doomed to gradual extinction, as a casualty of the transition to bourgeois patronage. The new Victorian-influenced middle class that was emerging throughout urban India regarded the red-light districts—including the courtesans and their music—with embarrassment. And as the nationalistic bourgeoisie eventually turned to patronize the fine arts, the public concert hall replaced the courtesan salon as the home of music and dance. The most talented courtesans were able to effect this transition, performing *ghazal, ṭhumrī,* and *kathak* dance for their new patrons, or finding employment in film, theater, or folk drama troupes like those of *nauṭankī;* most of the remainder were obliged to rely on prostitution, which in turn became for the first time the primary business of the red-light districts.

The *Ghazal*-Song in Mid-Century

The *ghazal*-song itself did not decline with the courtesan world; rather, its inherent versatility enabled it to adapt to changing patronage and modes of dissemination. By 1950 the genre comprised a continuum of styles oriented, to a large extent, toward discrete audiences.

The light-classical *ghazal* continued to be a vital and popular style, although it differed substantially from its turn-of-the-century parent. The seductive *nakhra* was disappearing, inappropriate as it is to the concert stage; perhaps for related reasons, the practice of performing seated mimetic gestures (*abhināya*) was also largely abandoned as an archaicism too redolent of the brothels. As microphone amplification came into vogue, singers began to emphasize subtle vocal nuances rather than volume and strength. Moreover, the use of difficult *rāg*s and virtuoso *tān* techniques declined; the new *ghazal*-song instead resembled modern *ṭhumrī* in stressing emotive text interpretation (*bol banāo*) in a leisurely tempo. Begum Akhtar (d. 1974) was the most influential figure in this trend. It could be said that with her limited vocal technique she would have been unable to duplicate the virtuoso pyrotechnics of a Gauhar Jan even if she had wanted to; but the pervasiveness of her own *ṭhumrī*-oriented style reflected a broader trend in audience aesthetics (Ranade 1974). At worst, the new style lent itself to sentimentality; talented singers, however, found it a vehicle for a greater range and depth of emotional expression than appears to have been possible in the old courtesan style.

A somewhat different approach to the light-classical *ghazal*-song was developed by Barkat Ali Khan (1910–63) and, to a lesser extent, his elder brother Bade Ghulam Ali Khan, representing the Patiala *gharānā* (hereditary musical lineage). Like Begum Akhtar, Barkat Ali stressed emotive elaboration of text rather than displays of virtuoso technique. His style differed, however, in its profusion of intricate, difficult zigzag melismas and ornaments more reminiscent of *ṭappa* than *ṭhumrī.*

While Begum Akhtar continues to serve as a model for many singers, Barkat Ali's style seems to have perished with him, largely, no doubt, because modern light singers lack the formidable vocal technique and improvisatory fluidity required to do it justice.

The semi-classical *ghazal* of this period, although widely disseminated on records, should not be thought of as a popular music per se, if by "popular music" we mean a genre whose stylistic evolution has been inextricably linked to the mass media and to the mass production of recordings for sale on a commodity basis. By mid-century, however, a commercial counterpart to the light-classical *ghazal* had emerged, disseminated to some extent on records, but, more commonly, in the context of Indian film.

Within a few decades of the advent of the sound film in India in 1931, the Indian film industry has mushroomed into one of the world's largest. Almost all commercial films have been musicals, generally interspersing song and dance sequences with romance and melodrama. Despite occasional light social commentary, the films tend to avoid any portrayal of poverty, basing much of their appeal on lavish sets, extravagant effects, and synthetic Western-style luxury. As such they serve as escapist fantasies, in many respects promoting the consumerist and bourgeois values of the corporate Bombay upper class that produces them, rather than those of their diverse and largely lower-middle-class audience; in this regard, it has become commonplace among some Indian intellectual circles to regard the effects of the films as profoundly alienating.[5]

Film songs, like the movies themselves, have been generally produced by relatively small coteries of artists working in the studios of Bombay and Madras. In accordance with the pattern of monopoly capitalism, the film music industry has sought to appeal to and create a relatively homogenous mass audience, rather than attempt to represent and respond to the traditional aesthetic tastes of the many dozens of diverse linguistic and ethnic groups in India. Hence, film songs have tended to follow certain formulaic patterns, such as: use of simple, singable tunes; combinations of Western and Indian instruments; predominantly modal melodies, with occasional harmonies added in the ensemble backing; *kaherva* and *dādrā* meters; sentimental solo vocal style; simple diatonic modes rather than difficult classical *rāg*s with augmented intervals and oblique passages; absence of improvisation; elaborate ensemble arrangements, juxtaposing sectional passages in contrasting orchestral timbres, and often combining indigenous instruments not normally played together (e.g., *shahnāi* and sitar); and the use of varied ensemble interludes and other techniques which often lend the music a progressive, goal-oriented, sectional format rather than a simple strophic structure, in accordance with bourgeois aesthetics.[6]

Finally, for several decades, the vast majority of all North Indian film songs (including film *ghazals*) were sung only by four or five vocalists. Lata Mangeshkar and her sister Asha Bhosle dominated the repertoire. Among male vocalists, Kishore Kumar, Mohammad Rafi, and especially Talat Mehmood sang the majority of film *ghazals*. In the two decades before his death in 1987, Kishore Kumar featured in roughly sixty percent of film songs recorded in Bombay (Rahman 1987 : 81–82). The hegemony of these few singers and the three or four leading music directors may be contrasted with the extraordinary diversity of vocal styles in regional Indian folk musics, and well illustrates the manner in which a corporate music industry may tend to superimpose a common-denominator, mass-produced product on its audience, effectively creating and manipulating taste rather than responding to it. Thus, while Adorno may have overstated his argument that formulaic homogeneity is an unavoidable concomitant of popular music in capitalist societies, such would seem to be the case, to a large extent, with Indian film music.

Ghazals had long constituted one of the largest categories of Indian film songs since the inception of the genre.[7] Thus the film *ghazal* emerged as an important genre, on the whole conforming to the stylistic parameters mentioned in the preceding paragraph. Not surprisingly, it has been held in contempt by many singers and aficionados of classical and semiclassical music, who deplore its crass sentimentality, the absence of improvisation and *bol banāo,* the frequently maudlin texts, and the mangling of Urdu phonemes by Hindu singers.[8] These purists, of course, have been sorely outnumbered by the film *ghazal*'s new audience, which indeed could now be counted in the hundreds of millions. The *ghazal* had thus successfully negotiated the transition from court and courtesan salon to mass dissemination, becoming in the process an archetypical example of a reified, commodified music, a catchy, tuneful *song* rather than an elaborative process. In its melodic and textual simplicity, its sentimental and manneristic vocal style, and its heavy reliance on formulae in order to achieve commercial success, the film *ghazal* would seem to constitute an extreme example of what Adorno would consider "pre-masticated" music, whose digestion requires little discernment or effort on the part of the listener.

Ghazal in the 1970s and 1980s

Since the early 1980s, the urban music scene, and with it the *ghazal,* underwent a limited but significant reorientation. The primary catalyst was the vogue of cassettes, which have come to surpass both records and radio as a medium of music dissemination, and which now rival even the cinema in this regard. Cassettes and players are cheaper, more durable, and more portable than records and record players; more important, mass production of cassettes costs enormously less than that of records and, of course, movies, and thus the cassette boom has for the first time enabled diverse ethnic and lower-middle-class groups to have direct access to production and dissemination of music via the mass media.

The results of this development have been numerous. Throughout the country, small-scale cottage cassette companies have arisen, many of which produce stylized versions of regional and often lower-class folk musics, constituting new and diverse regional popular musics. These backyard cassette industries are able to respond to local tastes in a manner that the monopolistic film studios have been unable or unwilling to do. The new cassette-based pop musics have thus undermined the hegemony previously enjoyed by the cinema in the world of popular music; at present, for example, film music comprises less than half of cassette sales. *Ghazal* has played an essential role in the boom of cassette-based musics;[9] indeed, the two trends have gone hand-in-hand, for the cassette boom has also contributed to the unprecedented vogue of *ghazal* in the last two decades.

In general, film music is spoken of as being in a state of decline, both in terms of quality and quantity of output. Competition from television and video, coupled, in some states, with high entertainment taxes, has bankrupted hundreds of movie halls. Most of the superstar vocalists mentioned above are either retiring or deceased. Modern films in general, with their emphasis on *masālā*—"spice," that is, violence and action—lend themselves less well to sentimental and melodious musical scores than did their melodramatic predecessors. Most important, however, is the challenge to film music posed by the cassette vogue. In recent years, film music directors have employed, to an unprecedented degree, singers who have already established their reputations outside the cinema world, and especially in the field of cassette-based *ghazal* (Rahman 1987: 81–82).

As in previous decades, one may speak of a continuum of *ghazal* styles. On one end lies the film-style *ghazal*, which may be said to resemble that of preceding decades, occasional usage of synthesizers and other modern instrumentation notwithstanding. Many of these songs exhibit elaborate complexity and sophistication in parameters of orchestration and arrangement; but in terms of vocal melodies, the modern film *ghazals* are, if anything, even simpler in style than their predecessors, with at least one leading film music director (Kalyanji, of Kalyanji-Anandji) stating that "every song should be as simple as a nursery-rhyme" (in Marre and Charlton 1985:142).

The film *ghazal*s have been overshadowed, however, to some extent, by the emergence of a handful of *ghazal* "superstar" singers who have based their appeal largely on cassette dissemination. In the seventies the dominant figures were two Pakistanis, Mehdi Hasan and Ghulam Ali, who promoted a new style of singing which, whether termed pop or light-classical, came to replace the older style associated with Begum Akhtar and her imitators. Ghulam Ali and Mehdi Hasan both have some training in art music, and in concerts and live recordings they often improvise extensively. In semi-classical tradition, they generally prefer simple harmonium and tabla accompaniment. Both have smooth, supple, and "sweet" voices; microphone-bred as they are, they tend to croon softly rather than to declaim at full volume as their predecessors did.

In the music of Ghulam Ali and Mehdi Hasan, the distinctions between pop and light-classical become ambiguous. Some of their renditions of *ghazal*s are complex and challenging, and are clearly aimed at connoisseurs; Ghulam Ali's most popular *ghazal*, "Chupke chupke," with its complex melody and its use of the seven-beat *rūpak* (or *mughai*) *tāl*, may be taken as a case in point. Yet both these singers also record in film-oriented styles, eschewing improvisation, being backed by large ensembles, and in many cases, employing simple songlike settings (see, e.g., Mehdi Hasan's "Bāt karnī mujhe").

In the 1980s, the pop-classical distinction became even more blurred with the rise of a new generation of singers who, while employing the basic style of Mehdi Hasan and Ghulam Ali, are either unwilling or, more likely, unable to execute the fluid and often complex improvisations of the latter vocalists. Although vocalists frequently employ chordal accompaniment, their melodic settings of *ghazal*s are often simpler, reflecting a new synthesis of the light-classical tradition with the "nursery-rhyme" aesthetic. Foremost in this group of vocalists are Anup Jalota, Pankaj Udhas, and the duo Jagjit and Chitra Singh. In the hands of these singers, the *ghazal* has achieved a vastly broader popular base than before, whether in spite or because of the fact that many of their recordings and performances eschew features associated with the previously dominant film style (e.g., heavy orchestration). This new brand of singers has taken the soothing character of Mehdi Hasan's singing to a new extreme. In their soft vocal timbre, bland diatonic melodies, slow tempi, and leisurely, relaxed style, they convey a mellow, placid urbanity that is quite uncharacteristic of the traditional courtesan style. At the same time, the unhurried ease of the presentation style, coupled with the very use of Urdu poetry (however simplified), continues to suggest an aristocratic ambience and ethos.[10]

It seems clear that the audience—both intended and actual—of the new crossover *ghazal* is the burgeoning Indian middle class. In particular, the crossover *ghazal* appears to be aimed at the casual bourgeois music-lover who lacks deep understanding of art music, of the traditional *ghazal*, and, in many cases, of any Urdu diction beyond the most elementary level; at the same time, the crossover *ghazal* listener prefers melody to the current disco-oriented film music, and is aware that his social class has inherited from its feudal predecessors the role of fine arts patron. Expatriate professionals constitute a significant portion of this audience, as is illustrated by the singers' frequent foreign tours, with ticket prices occasionally reaching as high as $100. In its eclectic style, the crossover *ghazal* can thus be seen as a response to the growth of the new Indian middle class, and can be contrasted in that sense with the older film *ghazals* of Talat Mehmood—evidently aimed at a lower-middle-class, musically unpretentious audience—and the semiclassical *ghazal*, with its connoisseur patrons.

The Indian bourgeoisie is predominantly Hindu; in recent decades, Sikhs have also come to constitute a significant part of the north Indian business class. It is significant that very few of the current *ghazal* stars are Muslim, although *ghazal* has traditionally been a Muslim specialty (since most Hindustani musicians have been Muslim, and Urdu is the language of north Indian Muslims). The success of Jagjit Singh—perhaps the most gifted singer-composer of the new *ghazal* style—marks the entry of Sikh musicians into national renown. The prominence of non-Muslim singers in the realm of *ghazal* can be seen as a contemporary example of the Hindu-Muslim cultural syncretism that has characterized much of Hindustani musical history, even if it is perhaps better regarded as a "Hinduization" of the *ghazal* rather than an Islamicization of Hindu listeners.

This Hinduization is most clearly evident in the dramatically simplified Urdu used in modern *ghazal*-songs. In accordance with the decline of Urdu in India as a whole, most contemporary singers and their poets tend to avoid any but the most familiar Urdu words in order to be understood by their Hindi-speaking listeners. Urdu's decline, far from being an inevitable result of Partition, has been actively promoted by the federal and state governments' defunding of Urdu education and the systematic purging of Urdu words, however commonplace, from Hindi radio and television broadcasts. The Urdu words (along with English loan words) are generally replaced with obscure Sanskrit-derived terms, many of which are unintelligible even to educated Hindi-speakers. Quratallain Hyder writes:

> This deterioration of the ghazal reflects the rapid socio-economic changes which are taking place in our multi-lingual society. Urdu has, by and large, taken a back seat. Politically, it has become a thorny problem and it has only reemerged as a kind of entertainment industry. . . . The ghazals have come back as essentially Urdu exotica. The erotic pop variety is as hollow and crass as the video-cassette culture of the new rich in which it is flourishing.[11]

Indeed, it is paradoxical that the *ghazal,* in however Hindified a form, should achieve such unprecedented popularity at a time when the Urdu language is all but dying in India. Meanwhile, the traditional *ghazal*'s stylized poignancy and metaphorically antinomian praise of intoxication have given way to sentimental clichés and sybaritic celebration of drinking for its own sake. What remains in the modern *ghazal*-song are verses that sound like Urdu, phrases that sound like improvisation, and mannerisms that sound like emotive expression; the result, from the viewpoint of many purists and connoisseurs, is music that is tuneful, soothing, competent, slick, and, in general, kitsch.

In its aristocratic ethos, the crossover *ghazal* may be contrasted with another category of popular music that, together with *ghazal,* has usurped the hegemony of mass-produced film music. I am referring here to the vast panoply of stylized folk musics which have emerged in different forms throughout the country. On one level, these can be seen as products of the cassette boom, which has extended mass media technology to all but the most indigent and isolated classes and ethnic groups. On another level, the new syncretic pop-folk fusions are responses to the continued migration of country people to the cities, where they enjoy even greater access to the mass media and develop new social identities and correspondingly new aesthetic needs. Hence, for example, the appearance, in Gujarat, of such hybrids as "disco *garba*" (*garba* being a widely popular folk song and dance). The flowering of stylized versions of Punjabi folk musics—especially pop *bhāngra*—is particularly remarkable and vital. These musics have no elitist pretensions, nor are they aimed at a *nouveau arrivé* bourgeoisie; rather, their appeal seems to be based on regional identity and the inherent, often rustic, buoyancy of the music. The emergence of such regional fusions of folk and popular musics illustrate the extent to which Indian popular music, despite the previous hegemony of the mainstream Hindi film style, may be growing increasingly more diverse and democratic as regional and lower-middle-class groups gain control over the means of musical production. Such heterogeneity allows the "crossover" *ghazal* of Pankaj Udhas and others to flourish as a distinct popular music genre, largely independent of the former hegemony of the film-style *ghazal*. It has also led to the emergence of pop *ghazals* sung in Punjabi, Gujerati, Marathi, and other languages.

Conclusions

The changes in Indian musical life in the last century have been as dramatic as the broader social, economic, and technological transformations during the same period. The advent of new classes—especially, the modern urban middle class—has engendered new musical styles; the spread of the mass media has spawned an entirely new category of music, based on mass dissemination and sale as a commodity. These and other changes have redefined the nature of the dialectic interaction of city and village, tradition and modernity, aristocracy and lower class, and commerce and creativity.

The *ghazal*-song has succeeded remarkably well in adapting to these changes while retaining its traditional formal structure and poetic content. At the same time, given the fundamental sociohistorical developments to which it has had to respond, it is not surprising that its style has changed beyond recognition. Needless to say, the new *ghazal* styles—indeed, like all music and art—must be understood as inextricably related to their historical contexts rather than as being autonomous art forms evolving along purely abstract lines. Similarly, they should be seen as active agents in the formation of new social identities rather than as passive superstructural reflections of socioeconomic developments.

In sophistication and complexity of improvisation—the prime criterion by which the light-classical *ghazal* was traditionally judged—the *ghazal* has naturally suffered in the process of being adopted by a social class untutored in Indo-Muslim high culture. In many respects, the changes undergone in the emergence of a popular music are irreversible, related as they are to the formation of modern technology and social classes. Other aspects of the process—such as corporate hegemony of the music industry, and the role of music in reinforcing dominant class ideology—should never be taken for granted, and it is in the objective questioning of such phenomena that the evolution of musical forms ceases to be of purely academic interest.

Notes

1. "Ab jafā hai na wafā yād-e-wafā bāqī hai / thī jahāṅ sham'a wahāṅ khāk hai parvāne kī" (Fani Badayuni).

2. "Kauṅ vīrāne meṅ dekhegā bahār / phūl jangal meṅ khile kin ke liye" (Simab Akarabadi).

3. Further discussion of these phenomena in relation to *ṭhumrī* can be found in Manuel 1983, 1986. For a more favorable interpretation of Lucknow poetry, see Petievich 1986.

4. See, e.g., Ruswa 1961, and Vidyarthi 1959.

5. See, e.g., Krishen 1981.

6. See Manuel 1985 for further discussion of this phenomenon.

7. The majority of Indian film songs do not adhere to any particular identifiable or traditional formal structure, although most tend to use some variant of *asthāi-antara* form, as does the *ghazal*-song itself.

8. See, e.g., Durry 1972:23.

9. See, e.g., Dubashi 1986:112.

10. Unlike *qawwālī*, the "crossover" *ghazal*, with its relaxed, urbane, complacent, and now thoroughly bourgeois ethos, would be a highly unlikely vehicle for the rendering of any kind of political or socially critical verse.

11. "A Tradition Betrayed," *Times of India*, May 19, 1989. Similarly, music critic Subhash Jha writes, "The ghazal has been so bastardized in the '80s that its filmy versions sound more unfeigned than the non-film exertions, with their fake feelings and canned 'wah-wah's [bravos] ("They're ghazals—believe it or not," *Times of India*, Sept. 13, 1989).

References

Adorno, Theodor
1976 *Introduction to the Sociology of Music* (reprint). New York: Seabury.

Dubashi, Jagannath
1986 Cassette Piracy: High Stakes. *India Today*, March 31, 1986, p. 112.

Durry, Kaokab
1972 Ghazal: The Dying Swan. *Lipika* (February): 21–24.

Gronow, Pekka
1981 Record Industry Comes to the Orient. *Ethnomusicology* 25,2:251–284.

Hydar, Quratallain
1989 A Tradition Betrayed. *Times of India*, May 19, 1989.

Krishen, Pradip
1981 Introduction. *India International Centre: Quarterly* (March): 3–9.

Manuel, Peter
1983 Thumri in Historical and Stylistic Perspective. Ph.D. dissertation, University of California, Los Angeles.

1985 Formal Structure in Popular Music as Reflection of Socio-Economic Change. *International Review of the Aesthetics and Sociology of Music* 16(2):163–180.

1986 The Evolution of Modern Thumri. *Ethnomusicology* 30,3:470–490.

Marre, Jeremy, and Hannah Charlton

1985 *Beats of the Heart: Popular Musics of the World.* New York: Pantheon.

Petievich, Carla

1986 The Two-School Theory of Urdu Literature. Ph.D. dissertation, University of British Columbia.

Rahman, M.

1987 Filling the Void. *India Today,* Nov. 30, 1987, pp. 81–82.

Ranade, Ashok

1974 The Musical Evolution of the Gazal. *National Centre for the Performing Arts: Quarterly Journal* 3,1.

Ruswa, Mirza

1961 *Umrāo Jān Adā.* Karachi: Urdu Academy.

Sharar, Abdul Halim

1975 *Lucknow: The Last Phase of an Oriental Culture.* Translated by E. S. Harcourt and Fakhir Hussein. Boulder, Col.: Westview Press.

Umr, Mohammad

1975 *Hindustānī tahzīb kā musalmānoṅ par aṡar.* New Delhi: Publications Division.

Vidyarthi, Govind, trans.

1959 Melody Through the Centuries (a chapter of Mohammad Karam Imam's early nineteenth-century treatise, *Ma'danul Musīqī*). *Sangeet Natak* 11–12:13–26, 33.

Donald Brenneis

12. Aesthetics, Performance, and the Enactment of Tradition in a Fiji Indian Community

Introduction

In an essay on his childhood in Trinidad, the late Shiva Naipaul wrote:

> It is in [an] elementary sense that I assert my own lack of a culture, the unnerving perception of having been disinherited a long time ago, of having been cut off without a penny and cast adrift. I was not trained to anything; I was heir to no coherent and clearly identifiable body of tastes, prejudices, loyalties and behavior. The "culture" that would have provided me such a training did not exist. It was already disintegrated—reduced, at best, to a nostalgic ruin—by the time I was born . . . I was a waif, inhabiting a makeshift world in which all the landmarks had been effaced. (1985 : 24)

Subramani, a young, urban Fiji Indian poet and essayist, has a similar perspective:

> The Indo-Fijians have been in Fiji for a hundred years. The younger generations do not have any of the Indian languages except a little Hindi. Although a literature in Hindi exists, so far no writer of any distinction has emerged. Hinduism no longer governs the life of Indo-Fijians. Their religious zeal manifests itself only when threatened by other religions as happens invariably during political elections. . . . The arts and crafts brought by the indentured Indians have either vanished altogether or exist in a transmuted form. Contact with India is still maintained mainly through Bombay movies, visiting cultural troupes and occasional package tours to the holy places. (1979 : xi)

Although Naipaul and Subramani are writing of their own particular experiences, they articulate a view of overseas Indian communities echoed, albeit far less eloquently, by many folklorists and social scientists. The model of immigration is a model of loss. Both writers have objectified culture, treating it as "a bounded entity made up of bounded constituent parts" (Handler and Linnekin 1984 : 287). For Naipaul and Subramani the constituent elements of "Indian" culture—arts, language, religion, loyalties—have vanished; without a coherent body of such constituent parts, culture itself is lost. Many anthropologists working in overseas Indian societies have been preoccupied with one institution—caste—as definitive of Indian society and, therefore, with its loss or retention as the key for understanding how "Indian" an overseas community remains (cf., Schwartz 1967; Mayer 1973; Jayawardena 1971). For many folklorists the "things" of which culture or tradition is made are texts. Pandit Usarbudh Arya's work in Surinam, for example, is basically an inventory of genres and song texts, a checklist for what has fallen away and what has been retained (1968). The resilience of a tradition is measured by how well it keeps the past intact. From this perspective, "culture," unfortunately, is always easier to lose than to regain. Deracination is inevitable, with the missing elements to be replaced by class consciousness or by an increasing absorption into dominant culture. In the case of Fiji and other overseas Indian communities, the image is one of a shattered continuity.

On the other hand, in contemporary Fiji there is a counterposed discourse of primordial, inevitable loyalties and identities. In the period between the two 1987 coups, an emblematic incident occurred outside the national Legislative Council building. "About a dozen Taukei [Fijian nationalist] men, in traditional warpaint and armed with spears and war clubs, were chanting war songs and performing war dances around a *lovo* [earth oven] they had constructed in ancient times, the *lovo* pit was where Fijian cannibals cooked human flesh, usually [sic] prisoners of tribal wars, and performed tribal rituals" (*Overseas Fiji Times* 1987a : 1). When a Fiji Indian politician from the ousted coalition government passed by, these men chased him into a tourist hotel, where they beat him with their war clubs. Their spokesman claimed, "We just want to show . . . that this *lovo* is going to be the ultimate end. This is not a threat to anyone. All we are trying to say is that if all else fails, this is going to be the end" (*Overseas Fiji Times* 1987a : 1).

Fiau Tabakacoro, a historian and member of the Great Council of (Fijian) Chiefs, recently said of Fiji Indians that "This is not their country . . . they still speak Hindi. They still eat curry. They are not Christians. . . . How do you compete with a race that has thousands of years of what we call civilization. . . . When the first Indians arrived in Fiji in 1879, my great-grandfathers were just about 10 years from eating each other" (Kristof 1987:6). Finally, the Welsh wife of Ratu Meli Vesikula, the minister for Fijian affairs under the new government, stated in an interview that "Your race gives you leanings and feelings—that's something over which no laws have control" (*Overseas Fiji Times* 1987b:7).

The Fiji Indian dilemma is to be caught between, on the one hand, an image of cultural loss, of the disappearance of those "things" which make them truly Indian, and, on the other, an inescapable racial identity. They are trapped by other people's theories, and by the discourses those people use to shape reality. Are Fiji Indians really people without culture but with an inescapable identity?

My intention is to propose an alternative approach to questions of Fiji Indian tradition, one guided not by a concern for measuring the loss of cultural content but by an interest in understanding the discourse—the ways of talking and conceptualizing—within which Fiji Indian residents of one small rural community interpret, shape, and evaluate their experiences. I am not claiming that we as folklorists should not be concerned with questions of the historical continuity of texts, but rather that an apparently straightforward "before and after" comparison is likely to be misleading for several reasons. First, the notion of a bounded, internally integrated but sharply delineated single tradition from which those texts taken as definitive can be lost is, in the case of Fiji, highly inappropriate. As John Kelly has pointed out, "Fiji Indians have—from the beginning of indenture—found in the *plurality* [my emphasis] of systems the paths and practices that make sense to them" (1988:40). There is no single antecedent culture.

Second, a primary focus on textual continuity can easily obscure the active role which contemporary Fiji Indians play in defining their own culture, whether through the creation of new texts or the reinterpretation of old ones. If, as Handler and Linnekin (1984:287) argue, tradition is a "process of interpretation, attributing meaning in the present through making reference to the past," it is unlikely that people abandon such complex interpretive work on leaving the homeland. Indeed, one would expect an even stronger concern for locating present experience in terms of the past. I am primarily concerned here to avoid the kind of analysis which can lead us to the neglect or misconstrual of the ideology and practice of Fiji Indians themselves.

In looking at the ways in which Fiji Indian culture represents a transformation of traditions in new circumstances, I want to focus on those notions through which local people themselves evaluate the effectiveness of performances, rather than rely upon the more customary criteria of textual provenance and pedigree. What rings true to them? How is their experience of such events defined and interpreted? In what sorts of local theories is it rooted? Particularly, in turning to those practices we might identify as "folklore," how might performance bring Fiji Indian identity to life?

One of my concerns in this chapter is to provide a more adequate representation of Fiji Indian culture in its own terms. Here I am motivated by a sense that the Fiji Indian story is at a potentially tragic impasse, and that more needs to be told of it. I am also concerned with several broader theoretical issues in folklore, ones having to do with the relationships among text, context, and meaning. The critical junctures for examining such questions are those events in which texts come to life through performance.

With the rise of the performance model in folkloristics (see, for example, Bauman 1977; Hymes 1975) has come a shift in focus from text to performer. Roger Abrahams's (1968) rhetorical theory, for example, brought such questions as performers' intentions and the creative strategies they developed for meeting those goals to the center of folkloristic discourse. His research focused primarily on the compelling but variable logics associated with different genres; subsequent rhetorical studies have considered a wide range of textual and stylistic devices and the ways in which they shape particular texts.

In order to provide the most comprehensive account of performance possible, however, we must also consider the other side of the event, that is, the audience. A focus on performers, their rhetorical intentions, and the communicative devices through which they deploy various idioms to pursue their goals must be complemented by attention to their audiences and to those local theories and understandings that inform their responses. If performers' rhetoric works, how does this happen? Audiences are not solely targets for logical traps; they are, rather, active interpreters, critics, and respondents.

In a recent article (Brenneis 1987) I have suggested the notion of "social aesthetics," a cluster of community theories fusing intellectual sense-making activity with local aesthetic criteria for coherence and beauty and with ethnopsychological notions of personhood, emotion, expression, and experience. These concerns must, to draw on Herzfeld's discussion of a similar notion, "correspond intelligibly with local social theory, with indigenous ideas about meaning, and with criteria of style, relevance and importance" (1985 : xv). Such a social aesthetics may be helpful as a notion for interpreting the role of performance—and for approaching the questions of authenticity mentioned above—in a range of societies. It also can provide a tool for understanding the roles of the audience and the expectations and values that members hold. The notion further brings together folkloristic questions with the social and cultural practices with which they are inherently entangled.

Ater a brief introduction to Bhatgoan, a rural Fiji Indian village, I will characterize several aspects of a Fiji Indian social aesthetic. I then turn to the more detailed discussion of two genres of song performance in the community, looking at their transformation in the Fiji context.

Bhatgaon: A Fiji Indian Community

Bhatgaon is a rural village of 671 Hindi-speaking Fiji Indians located on the northern side of Vanua Levu, the second largest island in the Dominion of Fiji. The villagers are the descendents of north Indians who came to Fiji between 1879 and 1919 as indentured plantation workers. Bhatgaon was established in the early 1900s and now includes ninety households.[1] There has been little migration to or from the village for the past twenty years. Most families lease rice land from the government of Fiji, and, although they may work as seasonal cane cutters or in other outside jobs, most men consider themselves rice farmers. Leaseholds are generally small, and rice farming does not afford Bhatgoan villagers the same opportunities for wealth available in sugarcane raising areas. All villagers speak the local dialect of Hindi and also command to varying degrees a more formal Hindi, called "sweet" or "radio" Hindi; some speak English or Fijian as well.

Social life in Fiji is quite different from that of the north Indian communities from which villagers' ancestors came. In Bhatgaon, hierarchical caste organization has been replaced by a loose system of egalitarian but ambiguous and flexible relationships. The overdetermined social system in India has been replaced at the local level by relationships in many ways underdetermined (for a more detailed discussion, see Brenneis 1979). Notions of a somewhat delicate relative equality inform quotidian relations within the face-to-face community, but the local community is embedded in a larger stratified society. Motivated by frequently opposed local and broader interests, villagers must attend to both vertical and horizontal relations.

In this chapter, I focus on the local community, a context within which egalitarian ideology and practice are expected to obtain. While for some villagers no relations of superior and subordinate are present, such equivalence rarely extends through the entire community. Women and younger males are often excluded. Beyond this, such egalitarianism often implies a certain social sensitivity. One is concerned to maintain one's standing as an "equal," and perceived affronts by others pose serious threats. There is, in addition, a heightened emphasis on one's own political autonomy and that of others, whether as target or as something to protect.

The most important organizations in the village are religious societies. Three sects are represented in the village: Sunni Muslims, orthodox Hindus or *sanātanīs*, and reform Hindus or *ārya samājīs*. Orthodox Hindu practice centers on the worship of Rām, Sītā, Hanumān, and other figures from the *Rāmāyaṇa;* worship services are led by professional priests or *paṇḍits* who claim Brahman ancestry. Aside from the belief that *paṇḍits* should be Brahman, little emphasis is placed upon caste identity. The reform Hindu group, the *ārya samāj,* is monotheistic and iconoclastic. It was founded in northwestern India in the late nineteenth century by Swami Dayanend Saraswati. *Samājī* teachings were introduced to Bhatgaon in 1933 by a village youth who heard a missionary singing *samājī* songs at a religious fair; he became interested in the sect. In its early years in Fiji, the *ārya samāj* organization actively proselytized and used various channels, including religious singing, for this missionary activity. The term *maṇḍalī* denotes both the local associations of the two Hindu sects as well as the weekly prayer and fellowship meetings these groups hold.

As long as no problems are posed for the broader society, there is rarely much external interest in maintaining order in Bhatgaon, nor are many political or administrative resources available to its residents. In the absence of institutionalized offices within the community, social and political relations are constantly being negotiated and tested. Individuals are unlikely to intervene in the conflicts of others; there are few if any third parties to whom one may turn. One problematic aspect of social life in Bhatgaon is the achievement of any decision-making or dispute management at levels above that of the coresident family. Negotiation between contending parties is very unlikely to succeed, as a direct discussion of disputed issues usually leads to injured feelings and even stronger hostility. On the other hand, obtrusive attempts by third parties to assert authority or intervene in the disputes of others may well be seen as socially presumptuous and lead to conflict between them and the original disputants. This recurrent impasse in the maintenance of social order mirrors a broader conundrum in Bhatgaon society: how can one at the same time be publicly recognized as effective and accomplished—whether in political, religious or other activities—while not offending others? A second problematic issue, that of sociability, is in some ways the inverse of the leadership problem discussed above: given the kinds of limits posed by egalitarian sensitivities in Bhatgaon, how can and do villagers have a good time *together*?

Social life in Bhatgaon has a generally amorphous and negotiable quality. Aesthetically marked activity in such a community is often strikingly concerned with the constitution of contexts within which interaction can occur. Public performance—verbal, musical, ritual—is an achievement, often allowing times of negotiated social order and sociability in an otherwise very flexible world.

A Fiji Indian Social Aesthetics

The system of social aesthetics in Bhatgaon has a number of distinctive elements. First, it underlies verbal and musical performances alike. I was directly guided to this understanding by villagers, in whose discussions it became increasingly clear that, for them, a common aesthetics encompasses both verbal and musical performance. This underlying system focuses primarily on the organization of performance as social practice. As social practice, performance almost inevitably involves more than one actor; one can rarely conduct aesthetically marked discourse by oneself. A second distinctive element of their social aesthetics is that it makes an explicit link between theories of performance and the language of emotion and experience. It is indeed very difficult to separate ethnopsychological from aesthetic notions; in articulating the bases of their enjoyment or appreciation of particular events, villagers also articulate their sense of self and experience.

Third, aesthetic theory in Bhatgaon is internally quite complex and multivalent. While the means through which different experiences are effected are taken to be relatively invariant, the characteristics of those contrasting experiences differ in systematic ways and are, further, all included within the same broader discourse. Fourth, Fiji Indian rural society is dramatically different from that of north India; it poses new problematic questions requiring new solutions, ones often phrased in a classical Hindu idiom but with still emergent implications.

In Bhatgaon villagers' discussions of emotions and aesthetic experience, two features are salient. First, the word in local Hindi for emotion (*bhāv*) is the same as that for gesture or display. Bhatgaon social aesthetics explicitly links feeling and display. Second, none of these "feelings" seem to be individually experienced ones, at least as people spoke of them. *Bhāv*—"feelings"—are not viewed as internal states. Rather, moods seem to be located in events themselves.

Bhāv is most frequently used in compound constructions in religious discourse, as in *prembhāv,* which carries the multidimensional meaning of (1) a situation of interpersonal amity, (2) the display of the mutually respectful and amiable demeanor that embodies this amity, and (3) the experience of that state. *Prembhāv* is definitively associated with the weekly meetings of religious groups and through those events with such performance genres as *parbacan* (religious speeches) and *bhajan kavvālī* (*kavvālī*-style hymns).

Moral didacticism—the willingness to teach and be taught—is a critical component of *prembhāv*. Clearly defined solo turns, a focus on moral and spiritual improvement—on the message—and the willingness of others to attend to what any individual is saying or singing are among the features encoding *prembhāv* and enabling its experience. It is critical to note that they are features which cannot be enacted by an individual alone; the discourse of amity is necessarily interactional.

This Bhatgaon aesthetics and the system of ethnopsychological theories intertwined with it are social theories in two senses. First, they are shared understandings, the emerging product of ongoing social learning, negotiation, and modification. Second, they include necessarily interactive behavior for their enactment and experience. Important aesthetic experiences in Bhatgaon are located in events themselves, and especially in the constellations of persons and performance styles conventionally associated with their different varieties.

The term *bhāv* is related etymologically to the dramaturgic and psychological notion of *bhāva* in Sanskrit poetic theory. In part this reflects historic factors. There is a much more direct link between Indian village culture in Fiji and literate north Indian Hindu traditions that there might be for most mainland rural Indian communities. Hindu missionaries, both orthodox and reform, have been very active in Fiji, drawing upon and using a wide variety of textual materials, which have been subsequently adopted by villagers. The *ārya samāj* missionaries, particularly, took classical Hindu notions such as *bhāva* as rhetorical foci in their proselytizing literature. In this adaptation the implications of the term have been transformed; *bhāv* has been relocated from the individual to the realm of *rasa*.

The performances associated with one *bhāv* or another are rationalized, explained, and understood in relation to *printed* sources—hymnals, tracts, books of religious exempla, usually published in India. For a variety of reasons, village epistemology has privileged the written or printed over the orally transmitted. This is a change from many Indian traditions in which knowledge is allocated in terms of who one is, as in a putatively unbroken line of Brahmans (see, for example, Staal 1961).[2] In Fiji, there is open access to knowledge and an obligation to share it; *śikcā*—giving instruction—is critical. The warrant for such present practice is thought to lie in a distant past, one which the printed word can illumine despite the discontinuities and distortions in orally transmitted materials.

Devotion and Abuse

In this section I want to consider two genres of song relatively popular in Bhatgaon. Both have north Indian antecedents, but, I will argue, they have been dramatically transformed in terms of performance style and its implications. In this section I will be drawing my comparative examples primarily from the work of Edward O. Henry, an ethnomusicologist who has conducted research in Indrapur, a pseudonymous village near Varanasi (1973, 1976a, b).

The first genre is called *harīkīrtan* in Indrapur and *bhajan* in Fiji. Both terms mean "devotional songs." This is a male genre. In both Indrapur and Bhatgaon, the song texts are drawn from familiar sources, especially the *Rāmāyaṇa* of Tulsidas. In both communities, men sing from hymnals published in Agra, Varanasi, Delhi, or elsewhere. The texts are often in praise of a specific deity or narrate a specific incident from the epic. In Bhatgaon, another range of texts is found among *samājīs*; these are hymns, published in India, some praising the founder and early heroes of the sect, others expounding on particular religious doctrines.

The texts are similar if not identical between India and Fiji. As is often the case, the vernacular publishing industry is so widespread that the sorting out of "traditional" and "published" texts is quite difficult; something analogous to a broadside publication tradition clearly flourishes in India. Does textual similarity, however, equal continuity of tradition? Where are the differences, if any?

They lie in the style of performance and in the implications attributed to those styles by local communities. In India, *harīkīrtan* singing is choral and antiphonal. Extended strophic forms dominate; the internal structural units are rhymed couplets. Steady rhythm is maintained throughout, with cadential duplet over triplet patterns. Considerable repetition is evident, with lines being sung back and forth between the two choruses. This is not to say that such antiphonal choral singing is the only variety of village hymn singing, but it is the most common in Indrapur.

In Fiji, *bhajan* are sung in what is called the *kavvālī* style; they are solo throughout. The texts are broken into shorter verses and characterized by much less repetition. The singer accompanies himself on the harmonium, others back him on various percussion instruments. In contrast to the invariant tempo of the North Indian group, *harīkīrtan, kavvālī*-style pieces alternate between slow and fast sections. Except for this characteristic alternation, the Fiji Indian style is not the same *qawwālī* as that Muslim devotional genre with which Indianists, Indians, and Pakistanis are familiar.

In both India and Fiji, such hymns are sung in group gatherings, usually in the evenings. In India they are often sung on religious holidays; in Fiji they usually are part of weekly *maṇḍalī* services. When people are asked why they sing these devotional pieces, the differences between Indian and Fijian performances become even more marked. In India the stated goal is *mastī* or "intoxication," the direct, individual experience of relationship with the divine, unmediated by ritual status, that is, caste (cf. Henry 1973 : 150–160). Beyond this, those singing together are often from a wide range of castes. In singing they have a common relationship with the deity and thus an asocial relationship with each other for the moment, one without hierarchy—of situated equality. The social semiotic here is not one of inversion but of the temporary collapse of hierarchy, of social distance disappearing in the face of proximity to the divine. In aesthetic or evaluatory terms, the fact of fullhearted participation is considered more important than its quality.

In Fiji, on the other hand, the goal of *bhajan*-singing is *śikcā*, "instruction." Clarity, not intoxication, is central. The quality of performance is central; bad singers are not asked to perform. One sings, further, to a human rather than divine audience. The Fiji Indian value on teaching and the highly stylized marking of the performance genre make relationships of teacher and taught, leader and led, momentarily axiomatic, taken for granted in a usually highly flexible and amorphous social world. Beyond this, from the audience's point of view, the performance leads to the experience of *prembhāv*, of amity, in terms of local aesthetic discourse.

Bhajan kavvālī and the experience of *prembhāv*, of which it is an essential constituent element, work not through the blurring of social differences, as does hymn singing in India, but through the temporary creation of a clearcut social order, the position of the singer as teacher validated by the importance of his message, as is the role of the audience as student. Singers' virtuosity is prized. They can excel without occasioning the resentment and revenge of others because their messages are valuable for all involved and because the medium through which messages are carried is stylistically so highly marked and demanding.

It is critical to point out that this kind of song reflects a Fiji-born performance style combined with an unequivocally Indian text. These are highly valued performances, part of an elaborated realm of discourse about central religious practices and experience, lodged within the framework of *bhāv* theory. I want to turn now to a second type of song, one not highly valued in Fiji.

Invective Songs

In this section I will deal with invective songs, a variety of song text referred to in north India as *gālī* ("slanders") and in Fiji referred to as "challenge songs." The texts themselves are remarkably similar in the two countries. They are generally considered obscene, accusatory, and very humorous because of their shocking nature. Many of the same kinds of behavior are considered worthy of insult—familial irresponsibility and incest (especially improper relations with one's sister), miserliness, sodomy. Let me give several examples, first from Indrapur:

> Brother, Patna is a pleasant city; brother, Patna is a pleasant city.
> Corrupted in childhood, Henari Ram and Ram Sagar Mishra are
>   the sons of whores.
> Their sister was corrupted by Ram Chandra.
> They eat from their sister's earnings; tears come into their eyes.
> Henari and Ram Sagar eat from the earnings of their sisters;
> they submit themselves to sodomy.
> Brothers, Patna is a pleasant city.
>
> (Henry 1976a: 8)

And from Bhatgaon:

> "You're going to beat me up? You and who else?
> Who will dare to boast in front of me?

We will beat you and break off your head;
streams of blood will flow. Who will come to your aid?
Your mothers and sisters will mourn after your death;
your wife will become a widow, and who will care for her?
Your sister has become a whore, and she roams from village to
village.
She's become a whore, and who will pay her price?"

(Brenneis and Padarath 1975:288)

Both these songs are locally and spontaneously composed, but they draw on the same insult tradition. A textualist might point to this similarity as evidence that Fiji Indians are maintaining tradition, even if not a very savory aspect of it. And, indeed, the transmission here is clearly not through printed texts.

When one considers performance, however, the picture is quite different. In India *gālī* is a performance genre usually limited to weddings. Such songs are sung by the female relatives of the bride (*ghartiya*) to male relatives of the groom (*baratiya*) as they arrive at the bride's parents' house for the wedding; they may also be sung by the groom's female kin to affinal men (Henry 1976a:10). Such singers are all lower in status than their immediate addressees and audience.

When women sing these remarkably abusive songs, the only response which the *baratiya* can—and indeed must—make is to give money to the singers. Money is traded for insult. The reason given for such performances is that they are *maṅgala,* "auspicious." The social semiotic of *gālī* singing at weddings hinges on the skewed nature of the social relationships of those involved and on the situated overturning of everyday hierarchical relations. Wedding *gālī* represent a Turnerian antistructure (Turner 1969) analogous to Holi and other north Indian festivals of inversion in which the orderly world is reversed and in which those on top must, for the moment, listen in silence.

The other reported event in which *gālī* figure in north India is reminiscent of ancient Greek practices known as *aischrologia,* the "hurling of abuse" at gods during seasonal festivals.[3] Freeman (1977) has provided a detailed account of such abuse in the Bhubaneshwar Lingaraj festival in Orissa. Again, the publicly acknowledged motive for the practice is its auspiciousness. The songs are sung by the charioteer, abusing the god, local officials, priests, and the ordinary citizen, as in this example directed at policemen controlling the crowd:

> The cows went to the cattle pen;
> the police inspector gentleman gave the order
> to count the tits of those two sisters-in-law.
> (Freeman 1977: 884)

This is a singularly mild example of such texts.

In Fiji, the primary context for such performances is the competitive, invitational song challenges with two teams from two different religious groups. The performers are teams of social equals. Both sides sing, in turn, but, with few exceptions, no one wins or loses. Song challenges end when both sides are chastised by outside audience members for their bad behavior. Such songs may also be used in competitions between coreligionists from different villages who gather at wedding parties. Here, again, abusive songs are traded, but both sides are ultimately chastised for their raucous goings-on. No one wins. What is critical to both contexts is that it is an exchange, not a one-way hurling of abuse. Men who should be equals exchange insults before an audience, which in this case serves a third-party role. Frequently, such challenges occur when tensions between groups are high. The reason given is *manoranjan* ("entertainment"). Such events represent not antistructure but moments of structure—of socially tolerated and guided, if not positively valued, competition of equals. Further, they are ritually established moments of equivalence, orderly points of departure for future relations.

It is critical to note that the reason given for abusive singing is entertainment, not auspiciousness. But it is not a practice of which people are particularly proud. In contrast to the good work which *bhajan* do, invective is considered *fakūtiya,* "worthless." It is, further, outside the valorized tradition of social emotions or *bhāv*. The transmission is by word of mouth, not through print. Favorite compositions might be recorded in private notebooks, but they are definitely not published.

So, in the case of *bhajan kavvālī,* no direct Indian antecedent is available, at least in terms of the combination of text, performance style, and generic label. They represent a Fiji Indian piecing together of elements from disparate sources, including Muslim religious songs and film music. Direct continuity is not part of the picture. But *bhajan kavvālī* represent a powerfully legitimated form, one deriving its authority from several sources:

(a) The Indian provenance of the texts and the fact that they are usually printed; their print-mediated transmission gives them legitimacy.

(b) The local social aesthetic, giving value to particular kinds of performance and shaping audiences' experience of them. This is linked to *ārya samāj* ideology, itself a late nineteenth-century transformation of an imagined Vedic past.

Gālī are clearly directly descended from antecedent traditions in a more direct manner. The texts are very similar and are traditionally transmitted, at least in terms of their general content. The performances are radically different, however. They are closer to an orthodox notion of "folklore," but, while enjoyed, they are devalued as less legitimate than the Fiji-born styles.

Conclusion

The Fiji Indian case raises some more general issues related to the themes central to this volume. Questions of knowledge and transmission are critical. The central role of printed texts in the largely literate community of Bhatgaon allows relatively open access to publicly prized varieties of knowledge. With study and guidance one can master religious doctrine; concomitant with such mastery is the requirement that one share it through public teaching. Sacred knowledge, a monopoly in many South Asian communities, has been radically democratized in Fiji.

Performance becomes the critical nexus of text, performer, and audience. Attending to the text alone can lead analysts into trouble, and a consideration of performers' intentions and strategies is not enough by itself. Audience understandings must also be considered in order to explain the effectiveness and implications of particular events. Investigating such a social aesthetic can help illumine the ways in which local people conceptualize, discuss, and evaluate their own experiences.

The system of social aesthetics in Bhatgaon provides a clear case of "tradition" in the sense that Handler and Linnekin propose, a process of "attributing meaning to the present through making reference to the past" (1984 : 287). The past in question is a temporally distant Hindu India, one far different from that from which villagers' elders emigrated. Recreating that more immediate past is irrelevant; that model of loss does not obtain. Fiji Indians are, rather, engaged in the emergent and ongoing symbolic construction of a new culture at the same time contemporary and traditional. They draw upon a range of sources and practices: direct oral transmission, the reworking and reinterpretation of published texts (themselves reinterpretations), and purely local creations.

The traditions of Bhatgaon are clearly invented ones. In contrast to the invented traditions considered by Hobsbawm (1983a, 1983b) among others, those found in Bhatgaon are neither engendered by dominant political groups nor manufactured from whole cloth. Instead, they draw in complex ways on past resources and present concerns. To gain understanding of this ongoing process, it is vital that one pay attention to what the inventors themselves have to say about the process, particularly in contrast to the models through which others define and regard them.

Notes

1. The "ethnographic present" for this article is 1972.

2. That Fiji Indians are not alone in privileging written texts is evident from Appadurai's study of the constructed past(s) of a South Indian temple, in which "*textual evidence* [emphasis in original] for the authority of any charter is superior to any other kind" (1981 : 204). Such textual primacy may in part reflect the considerable history of conflict and formal litigation concerning that temple.

3. Several participants in the South Asia Seminar discussion of this chapter have pointed out the long if dishonorable tradition of aischrological practice in Hindu, Buddhist, and Jain texts; it is clear that such abusive performances were often considered supernaturally effective and, at times, highly auspicious.

References

Abrahams, Roger D.

1968 Introductory Remarks to a Rhetorical Theory of Folklore. *Journal of American Folklore* 81 : 143–158.

Appadurai, Arjun

1981 The Past as a Scarce Resource. *Man,* n.s. 16 : 201–219.

Arya, Usarbudh

1968 *Ritual Songs and Folksongs of the Hindus of Surinam.* Leiden: E. J. Brill.

Bauman, Richard

1977 Verbal Art as Performance. In *Verbal Art as Performance,* R. Bauman, ed., pp. 3–58. Prospect Heights, Ill.: Waveland Press.

Brenneis, Donald

1979 Conflict in Bhatgaon: The Search for a Third Party. In *The Indo-Fijian Experience,* Subramani, ed., pp. 57–64. St. Lucia: University of Queensland Press.

1987 Performing Passions: Aesthetics and Politics in an Occasionally Egalitarian Community. *American Ethnologist* 14 : 236–250.

Brenneis, Donald, and Ram Padarath

1975 "About those Scoundrels I'll Let Everyone Know": Challenge Singing in a Fiji Indian Community. *Journal of American Folklore* 88 : 283–291.

Freeman, James M.

1977 Rites of Obscenity: Chariot Songs of Eastern India. *Journal of Popular Culture* 10 : 881–896.

Handler, Richard, and Jocelyn Linnekin
1984 Tradition, Genuine or Spurious. *Journal of American Folklore* 97: 273–290.

Henry, Edward O.
1973 The Meanings of Music in a North Indian Village. Ph.D. dissertation, Department of Anthropology, Michigan State University, East Lansing.
1976a Vindicating *Gali* Songs: Insult Songs Which Promote Social Cohesion. *Journal of Social Research* (India) 19:1–13.
1976b The Variety of Music in a North Indian Village: Reassessing Cantometrics. *Ethnomusicology* 20:49–66.

Herzfeld, Michael
1985 *The Poetics of Manhood: Contest and Identity in a Cretan Mountain Village*. Princeton, N.J.: Princeton University Press.

Hobsbawm, Eric
1983a Introduction: Inventing Traditions. In *The Invention of Tradition,* Eric Hobsbawm and T. Ranger, eds., pp. 1–14. Cambridge: Cambridge University Press.
1983b Mass-Producing Traditions: Europe, 1870–1914. In *The Invention of Tradition,* E. Hobsbawm and T. Ranger, eds., pp. 263–307. Cambridge: Cambridge University Press.

Hymes, Dell
1975 Breakthrough into Performance. In *Folklore: Performance and Communication,* D. Ben-Amos and K. Goldstein, eds., pp. 11–74. The Hague: Mouton.

Jayawardena, Chandra
1971 The Disintegration of Caste in Rural Fiji Indian Society. In *Anthropology in Oceania,* L. R. Hiatt and C. Jayawardena, eds., pp. 89–119. Sydney: Angus and Robertson.

Kelly, John D.
1988 From Holi to Diwali in Fiji: An Essay on Ritual and History. *Man,* n.s. 23:40–55.

Kristof, Nicholas D.
1987 In a South Seas Eden, a First Taste of Race Strife. *New York Times,* May 1:6.

Mayer, Adrian C.
1973 *Peasants in the Pacific: A Study of Fiji Indian Rural Society*. Berkeley: University of California Press.

Naipaul, Shiva
1985 Beyond the Dragon's Mouth. In *Beyond the Dragon's Mouth,* Shiva Naipaul, ed., pp. 3–43. New York: Viking Penguin.

Overseas Fiji Times
1987a Taukei Gang Bashes Richard Naidu. Sept. 18:1.
1987b Ratu Meli Who? Oct. 16:7.

Schwartz, Barton M.
1967 *Caste in Overseas Indian Communities*. San Francisco: Chandler Publishing.

Staal, F.
1961 *Nambudiri Vedic Recitation*. The Hague: Mouton.
Subramani
1979 Introduction. In *The Indo-Fijian Experience,* Subramani, ed., pp. ix–xii. St. Lucia: University of Queensland Press.
Turner, Victor W.
1969 *The Ritual Process: Structure and Anti-Structure*. Chicago: Aldine.

Stuart H. Blackburn

13. Hanging in the Balance: Rāma in the Shadow Puppet Theater of Kerala

Folklore within a great civilization is bound to present anomalies; one of these in India is that folk variants of its most popular folktale have been rarely collected and studied. Scholars have long acknowledged that the Sanskrit variants of the Rāma story developed from and are transmitted by oral traditions, but (until recently) precious little research has ventured beyond that assertion.[1] Change has come over the past three decades, dating roughly from Bulcke's 1962 study, in a series of full-length analyses and translations of folk and popular variants of the Rāma story.[2] This new research has done more than simply demonstrate the importance of folk Rāmāyaṇas; it has presented us with yet another example of the complicated texture of Indian culture. The Rāmāyaṇa tradition, we now see more clearly than before, is a crisscrossing of Sanskrit texts, *bhakti* transformations, folk inversions, theatrical amplifications, oral epic sequels, and heterodox revisions—not to mention women's folk songs, political slogans, and proverbs.

This apparently impenetrable textual tangle may provide a new perspective on an old issue: the elusive relation between the different layers of Indian culture. How do the various streams of this civilization, from the Vedic to the video, cohere in a whole?[3] In approaching this question, the *bhakti* Rāmāyaṇas offer particular promise because they are themselves comminglings of tradition, an interweave of theology and local religion.[4] For instance, the *bhakti* concept of the avatar has been understood as an historical linchpin between Brahmanical worship and folk cults. Moreover, when the *bhakti* Rāmāyaṇas are orally performed in a folk setting (as they often are), we are presented with a rich cross section of part of the Indian cultural design.

The analysis that follows examines the Kampaṉ Rāmāyaṇa as performed in the shadow-puppet tradition of Kerala.[5] In discussing this *bhakti* text in folk performance, we will consider how local culture receives the theology of *bhakti,* especially how the avatar fits with the local world view. As will be shown, when Rāma truly descends and appears as a leather puppet on a white cloth screen in rural Kerala, the theology of perfection gives way to the principle of balance.

Kampan Text and Folk Performance

Even the title of Kampaṉ's epic poem (A.D. 12th c. ?) *Irāmāvatāram* (Rāma-avatār) is unambiguous: Rāma is a god, an avatar sent to rid the world of *rākṣasas*.[6] Widely considered one of the finest literary works in Tamil, the poem has achieved a unique cultural status as *the* Tamil Rāmāyaṇa. Its approximately 40,000 lines have become a vehicle for philosophical discourse, for meditation, and (if one is lucky enough to be a *rākṣasa* hurling himself against Rāma's arrows) for liberation. How and when the text came to be performed as a shadow puppet play in Kerala is unknown, although a date after A.D. 1500 seems likely.[7]

In any case, the Kampaṉ text is sung today in more than one hundred goddess temples in central Kerala. The puppeteers actually sing only about 1,200 of Kampaṉ's more than 10,000 verses; they also sing other verses (roughly 10 percent of the total performance) that have no identifiable textual source and were probably composed and transmitted through the oral tradition of the puppeteers. The Kampaṉ verses are carefully memorized and recited with near word-for-word fidelity to their printed versions.[8] Each verse is followed by an oral commentary that first glosses the meaning and then launches into whatever topic the individual puppeteer chooses.

Essentially, however, the shadow puppet performances of Kampaṉ are verbal ritual. The recitation of the verses is an indispensable ceremony in the annual festival at the Bhagavati (Kālī, or sometimes Kaṇṇaki) temples in villages and towns in central Kerala. The performances are, in fact, an extended *pūjā,* a ritual shower of words that continues without interruption (even for a moment) from late night to early morning for eight nights, or twenty-one nights, or, on occasion, for sixty consecutive nights. The performances are also directly linked to the Bhagavati temple by a small procession led by the priest (*vellicapād*), who carries a white cloth that becomes the puppeteers' screen and the lighted lamp that creates the shadows on the screen. On some occasions, Bhagavati's sword is also presented to the troupe leader, who lights a small fire on its blade and then touches the tip to the head of the other puppeteers as they stretch in full *namaskāram* at his feet.

Other rituals could be cited, but these should demonstrate that Kampaṉ's *Rāmāyaṇa* has become firmly embedded in local folk Hinduism. The avatar, it would appear, has landed upright; this, however, is not the case. The curious truth is that Rāma *bhakti* (in the sense of personal, emotional experience or intimate relation with a god) is conspicuously absent. The performance is a *pūjā* to the goddess, and most expressions of *bhakti* during the singing are to Śiva.[9] The puppeteers do recite verses (from their own tradition and not from Kampaṉ) that praise Rāma's powers and stress the necessity of direct experience, but these are outnumbered by verses praising Śiva by more than five to one. Furthermore, there are very few Rāma temples in the area where the puppeteers perform, and these few are generally not patronized by the villagers who sponsor the puppet shows.

Instead of fusing classical with folk elements in the Kerala shadow puppet tradition, the avatar highlights their differences. A clear example of these differences lies in the opening images in Kampaṉ and in shadow puppet play texts. Kampaṉ begins with a long paean to the Sarayu River, and then describes the perfection of Ayodhyā, and its king, Dasaratha. Here, in David Shulman's term, is an icon of virtue:

> The king of that splendid city
> was king of kings,
> Over all the seven worlds,
> alone,
> he wielded his straight staff—
>
> (Shulman 1985: 47–48)

The shadow puppet text opens up quite differently. Bhumi Devi, Mother Earth, is overburdened with the weight of the *rākṣasas*' evil; the weight must be shifted and equilibrium regained. Bhumi Devi goes first to Indra to ask his help, but the king of the gods confesses that he is helpless against a Rāvaṇa who once conquered him; Bhumi Devi then journeys to Brahmā, who explains that he also cannot fight Rāvaṇa because the demon-king is actually his lineal descendant; Śiva too begs off, claiming that Rāvaṇa and his clan are his devotees. It is thus left to Viṣṇu to defeat the demons and restore the status quo on earth. The Rāma avatar in the shadow puppet play, then, performs a balancing act, shifting the weight of the *rākṣasas*' evil.

It is important to note, however, that the avatar itself is unbalanced; Viṣṇu is fit for the theological mission precisely because he has no relation to the demons. In Kampaṉ's *bhakti* epic, the Rāma avatar derives its power from isolation, but when the text is performed on the Kerala puppet stages, all this changes. To examine this movement from isolation and perfection to relation and balance, let us look closely at one section of the puppet performance—its opening scenes.

Although the puppeteers' texts begin with the Bhumi Devi story just mentioned, the performance selects another, much later scene with which to open the narrative. The first night in the string of performances is devoted to special ceremonies followed by a long, detailed summary of the story, from the Bhumi Devi episode through Rāma's birth, marriage, and exile until he, Lakṣmaṇa and Sītā have come to Pañcavatī. It is only on the second night that the narrative proper begins. The puppeteers' first two verses describe the beauty of the Godāvarī River; the first, one of Kampaṉ's finest, is an extended metaphor:

"Look, brother, here is the Godāvarī
    lying as a necklace on the earth
    nourishing this rich soil
    rushing over waterfalls
    flowing through Pañcavatī
    in clear, cool streams—
Like a fine poet's verse."[10]

The puppeteers' commentary (abridged) follows:

> Just look, Lakṣmaṇa, we've traveled a long time, taking Sītā through these dangerous dark forests, and finally here is this beautiful river. From what the poets have said, it must be the Godāvarī. Of all the rivers in Bhārata, including the holy Gaṅgā, they say it is the most beautiful. In this verse, you see, the word *puvi* means *bhumi:* Bhumi, goddess of earth, wears the river like an ornament. But the river is more than a sparkling jewel. It is like a person whose two hands cradle the land, supporting the pious Brahmins who recite the *Rāmāyaṇa,* the *Bhāgavata Purāṇa* and the other sacred books that tell us when to marry, how to live the four stages of life, when and where to travel, how to perform *dharma* and sacrifices with mantras and oblations.

And the Godāvarī feeds this special spot of five landscapes, which is called "Five-Lands" [*pañca-vatī*].[11]

I said that the verse compares the river to a necklace, but realize also that the river flows, it moves, like a poem. The word "verse" (*kavi*) in these lines means poetry, especially Vālmikī's epic (*kāviyam*), which is packed with meanings. For instance, you need one commentary (*pata urai*) to give you the literal meaning and another (*visēṣa urai*) to tell you the hidden meanings. The Godāvarī, you see, is like that. It has the same sound, beauty and movement.

The puppet performance, like Kampaṉ's text, opens with a river as a symbol of perfection; but here the image is doubled because the avatar, too, is present. The perfection of Pañcavatī, an earthly reflection of Rāma's piety and righteousness, is heightened also by the fearsome danger at its edge. In the third verse (from Kampaṉ), Rāma speaks to Lakṣmaṇa:

"Sandalwood, eagle-wood, champuka, snake-jewel,
  Asoka, silk-cotton, and pepper trees—
Rising up
  high above us on the banks,
Those forests
  are full of *rākṣasas*;
But we, too,
  will perform *tapas* here."

The commentary (abridged) follows:

You see, Lakṣmaṇa, there are five kinds of trees here, just like the five types of land; and that's why it's called Pañcavatī. We heard that many demons live here and commit the five heinous crimes of lying, stealing, drinking, killing, and abusing one's guru. But don't worry, brother. That's the very reason that we must perform austerities on earth, isn't it? To root out evil and protect the good. The demons have attacked *dharma* since the beginnings of time, especially here in Pañcavatī. So we must stay and destroy them.

At the very outset, in these initial three verses, the folk performance plunges headlong into the central conflict of the epic: divine perfection threatened by evil. This much the folk tradition has received from the *bhakti* text; it does not (and cannot) reject the avatar. It does, however, realign the ethical positions of Rāma and *rākṣasas*.

The moral scales tilt abruptly when the story of Śūrpaṇakhā's son, Sambukumāraṉ, is inserted into the performance. This episode is not found in either Vālmikī or Kampaṉ, but it is widespread in both folk and literary texts of the Rāma story in India and Southeast Asia.[12] The episode fits smoothly into the epic: before Rāma, Lakṣmaṇa and Sītā arrive at the banks of the Godāvarī, Sambukumāraṉ has already begun a long, arduous *tapas* to Śiva by hanging upside down in a tree. When Lakṣmaṇa enters the forest to chop wood with which to build a hut, the stage is set for the first encounter between the forces of virtue and evil.

At this point, the first cracks appear in the smooth surface of the avatar-mission. Once Lakṣmaṇa is on his own, the brave warrior hears strange noises:

> "Bears and tigers everywhere!
>   now a lion's rushing me!
> Better run for cover and shoot;
>   but, look, that's no lion—
> Only cuckoos and doves chattering away."

Lakṣmaṇa's next mistake is not so humorous; when he hacks away at a tree, he kills Sambukumāraṉ and sets in motion the chain of events that lead to Sītā's capture and near death. This is the same Lakṣmaṇa who later proudly announces that "I will protect the south [side of the hut] and keep Sītā from harm."

Rāma's earlier declaration of his dharmic mission (see commentary above) now sounds hollow, too. The avatar has come to "root out evil and protect the good," but his own brother has murdered an innocent *rākṣasa* (proving farsighted Sītā's fears that this would occur). Yet, in Kampaṉ the imagery of perfection continues:

> Like the great Vedas
>   which drive out confusion,
> Like the pure milk ocean
>   surrounding Vaikunta itself,
> My brother has built a hut
>   as wonderful as the Gaṅgā![13]

But the viewer knows that the sword used to build the hut is stained. Lakṣmaṇa's act may have been inadvertent, but its presence in this variant of the Rāma story cannot be accidental, for it constitutes an ironic inversion of the very purpose of the avatar: the evil in the forest is afoot—let loose by those sent to remove it.

Into this ominous scene steps Śūrpaṇakhā. Looking for her son, who has gone to do *tapas* in the forest, she is startled by his bloody body:

"Is cruel death your reward
  for long *tapas* to the gods?
Wearing fresh flowers you came
  and you wear them now,
Riding to Śiva's heaven
  in death's golden bier;
I've lost you forever,
  my son, Sambukumāraṉ."

It can't be true . . . are you really dead? You came here to win liberation and got death. Is this everyone's fate who worships Śiva? Or your special fate? Where are you now? Somewhere on the journey to heaven . . . who knows?

"Covered with turmeric and ash,
  I prayed at Śiva's feet for a son;
Now your golden body
  lies in little pieces;
Who did this, Sambukumāraṉ?
  Who makes me collapses in grief?"

I chanted and meditated on Śiva's name for months, and finally you were born. But now . . . is this Śiva's boon? Did my *tapas* win your death?

"Your killers have gone,
  but not escaped;
It might be the Great God,
  or the Flower-God
  or the husband
  of the red-lotus goddess;

No matter who it is,
I'll follow his trail,
Find him
and drag him to Laṅkā."

Hah, let them try to escape! They can jump off this earth, and I'll follow. Revenge will be mine, no matter who it is. He might be the strong Indra, who once imprisoned the gods and has performed so many sacrifices and victory marches. Or it might be Brahmā, the flower-god, who creates birds, animals, humans, and the other 80,000 lakh creatures in our world. Even if Nārāyaṇa, consort of Lakṣmī, did this evil deed, he will not escape. Killer of my son, whoever you are! I will find and imprison you in Laṅkā, and no one ever escapes from the hands of my brother, Rāvaṇa.

These three verses are the centerpiece of the Sambukumāraṉ episode. Sung in a pained voice that slowly draws out the words and compresses emotions to pinpoints, they resemble the traditional Tamil dirge (*oppāri*). As in many of those songs, Śūrpaṇakhā here cries out against a breakdown in religious logic: piety is rewarded with death. The angry, mocking tone of her appeal for justice from an uncaring god is one of the few expressions of *bhakti* in the puppet play; but it is addressed to Śiva, not Viṣṇu or Rāma.

Śūrpaṇakhā's initial appearance in Kampaṉ is very different. She is presented in two verses (not used by the puppeteers) as lethal danger: "a congenital disease about to strike its victim."[14] Then follows her infatuation with Rāma. On the white cloth screen, however, the demoness first appears as a victim, not a cause, of evil. When the puppet play scene ends, Śūrpaṇakhā wanders off into the forest as a mother grieving for the death of her only son. Rāma and Lakṣmaṇa never learn the identity of the *rākṣasa* they killed, but the viewers already have, and with this knowledge they watch the remainder of the epic story unfold. They cannot, however, view it as Kampaṉ presents it because the moral positions of Rama and the *rākṣasas*, so clear-cut in the Godāvarī verses that open the performance, have now shifted forever.

In this way, the Sambukumāraṉ episode provides the background to the fateful meeting between Śūrpaṇakhā and Rāma in the next scene. The effect of this episode is thus due as much to its placement in the narrative as to its contents; altering a narrative by inserting prior events is an Indian storytelling device not lost on the puppet play tradition.[15] Positioned immediately before Rāma encounters the *rākṣasas*, the Sambukumāraṉ episode recasts their relationship; because the avatar has lost its isolation and perfection, some greater balance between good and evil is possible.

When Śūrpaṇakhā and Rāma do meet, the puppet play returns to the Kampaṉ text, which it follows for the remaining twenty-five verses and three hours of performance on this second night. Nevertheless, by altering several verses, even only slightly, and by appending their commentary, the puppeteers continue to narrow the ethical distance between avatar and *rākṣasa*. As we shall see, Rāma is more than a little interested in Śūrpaṇakhā, and she defends herself by explaining that *kāma* is not only not evil but necessary to the proper working of the world.

The angry Śūrpaṇakhā is suddenly transformed when she spies Rāma on the riverbank. But first she must change her outer form to match this new emotion. Her oversized arms and squat legs, missile-like breasts and bumpy nose clearly will not do; she chants Lakṣmī's mantra and her demon puppet is replaced by a beautiful (human) puppet. All this is found in Kampaṉ also, but the puppeteers add something else: Śūrpaṇakhā is a devotee of Lakṣmī and did *tapas* to her in order to receive this special boon that changes her into a lovely woman. Like Sambukumāraṉ, she is a demon-devotee and no simple embodiment of lust.

Rama's reaction to Śūrpaṇakhā suggests that he is less than an incarnation of divine purity. Whereas Kampaṉ's verses (although comparing Śūrpaṇakhā to Lakṣmī in one of the many cases of mistaken but perceptive identifications in this scene), are restrained, the puppet play rings with Rāma's excitement (in commentary):

> Well, well . . . who is this lovely lady? Nowhere in these worlds of innumerable creatures have I seen any woman so incredibly beautiful! I must meet her personally. [Rama puppet moves toward Śūrpaṇakhā] . . . What have I done to deserve this [meeting with you]? Certainly my acts of *dharma* and piety could not bring this much fortune. There's so much I want to ask you. . . . Oh, soft, lovely peacock, tell me your name.

Even more revealing is the puppeteers' rewording of the verse in which Rāma first speaks to Śūrpaṇakhā. Kampaṉ's verse turns on a juxtaposition in the last line, which (according to the editor of the Kampaṉ text) underlines the incompatibility between Rāma (*vēta mutal* = source of the Vedas) and Śūrpaṇakhā (*pētai* = young/ignorant girl). What makes Śūrpaṇakhā *pētai* (the editor tells us) is her ignorance of Rāma as a god. The folk verse simply eliminates this juxtaposition altogether by dropping *vēta mutal* and making *pētai* an endearment by adding "peacock" ("lovely peacock [*pētai mayilē*]").

The separation between all-knowing god and deluded demon that recurs in Kampaṉ is undermined again by an alteration of a single letter in a later verse. When Rāma explains that humans cannot marry *rākṣasas*, he is forced to suppress a laugh (*nakai*) at Śūrpaṇakhā's stupidity (again, her *pētai*) because, as the editor points out, "loud laughter would not be appropriate to his excellence [*mēṉmai*]." In the folk verse, however, Kampaṉ's *nakai* becomes *vakai* and the sense of the entire verse changes. Rāma does not laugh at Śūrpaṇakhā; instead her beauty [*vakai*] pulls at his heart. The puppeteers also explain that the "dark rain-cloud edged in white," which in Kampaṉ describes Rāma's body, now describes Śūrpaṇakhā's hair. In Kampaṉ the silly (again *pētai*) demoness deserves secret mockery, but for the puppeteers Rāma is far too infatuated to laugh. Rāma does reject the offer of marriage, but there is no mockery in his words. He suppresses his desire, not his contempt for Śūrpaṇakhā.[16]

Śūrpaṇakhā herself is not unaware of Rāma's attraction to her. After she explains her family background and Rāma asks why, if her family is so distinguished, she walks alone in a wild place, she says (in commentary), "Frankly, since you are probably a god, you ought to know the answer to that. No, I think you ask just to hear an answer from me." After accusing Rāma of "chatting her up," however, she does offer an explanation of her behavior: *kāma*.

Śūrpaṇakhā's defense of *kāma* in Kampaṉ is confined to one (very moving) verse: "It may not be proper for women of high rank to speak when *kāma* afflicts them, / but what I feel is killing me. / I have no one; / please protect me from this work of Kāma deva."[17] Her defense, in effect, is a confession that only enables Rāma to see through her disguise and denounce her as "base" (*noyyal*) and "shameless" (*nāṇ ilaḷ*).[18] Otherwise, Śūrpaṇakhā's defense is deceit, an unsuccessful attempt to convince Rāma that she has renounced evil (*tī*) and has embraced the way of *dharma*. In one verse, she plays the silly [*pētai*] lover who imagines that Rāma's momentary silence indicates his desire for her.[19] Kampaṉ's Śūrpaṇakhā, in short, is a fool, whose words and actions reveal what they are intended to conceal.

In the puppet play, as already noted, Śūrpaṇakhā knows that Rāma is attracted to her. She does not resort to wheedling deceit or pretence of virtue. She declares her *kāma* in the Kampaṉ verse given above, but also explains it (in commentary):

> There's no right or wrong in this . . . it's the work of that Maṉmataṉ [Kāma deva]. You see, he holds five arrows and each has a different quality, causing different effects in whomever it hits. The worst is the red-lotus arrow; when that pierces your heart, it intensifies the *kāma* already present in you. If you have a little desire, it grows and grows until you can bear it no longer. I'm sure that Kāma has hit me with that red-lotus arrow. Please help me, make love to me, marry me, and release me from this pain!

Then, in the next verse, after Rāma condemns her as "base" and "shameless," Śūrpaṇakhā rises to her own defense:

> What you say, sir, may be true. But remember that I have not come of my own free-will. Kāma's arrows have driven me here. Understand that this lust is not mine; it's part of nature and can be relieved. You must know that saying about *kāma:* 'Kāma is the source of the whole world; it's impartial.' You see, *kāma* is everywhere, in every one of us, in every kind of being. If a man desires a woman and wants to marry her, that's *kāma;* it's a neutral force. Like the proverb says: 'Love [*kāma*] is blind.'[20] But it takes intelligence and strength to know how to act on *kāma,* and when. If it is not satisfied somehow, it brings great pain, even death. Even though the *sastras* say that we must avoid this disease of *kāma,* it's not that simple. Our bodies are a balance [*cāmaṇam*] of the three *guṇas*: *sattva, rajas, tamas*. If you eliminate *rajas* in order to avoid *kāma,* you lose the other twelve emotions that come with *rajas*. Get rid of *kāma* and there's no balance. Of course, no one wants *kāma* just to keep balanced, and *kāma* needn't be this strong. It's swirling around in me in hot gusts of air.

The topic of *kāma* takes us back to the beginning of our discussion, to the evil in the forest surrounding the perfection of Pañcavatī. Śūrpaṇakhā's love for Rāma is also mirrored by Rāvaṇa's love for Sītā, and both are clear manifestations of the demonic force that Rāma must defeat. Through Śūrpaṇakhā, the Kerala folk tradition, however, takes a different view of *kāma:* it is morally neutral and not unique to *rākṣasas*; it is natural and necessary, and should not, and probably cannot, be eliminated. *Kāma,* the puppeteers say, should be moderated but not altogether denied. Indeed, as we have noted, Rāma is himself not entirely free of *kāma;* and, in some folk traditions, even Sītā harbors desire for her ten-headed captor.[21]

In this defense of *kāma,* the puppet play expresses a Hindu world view that predates the Upanishadic and later *bhakti* attitudes toward evil. It is a world view based on the concept of balance, especially between the "strands" (*guṇas*) that form the person and material world, as found in the Upanishads.[22] But this search for harmony is also very old in Tamil culture, where it is the basis of the siddha medical system and, as Val Daniel has shown recently, continues to guide lives in contemporary Tamil Nadu.[23] This deeply rooted sense of balance is challenged by the ideological thrust of the avatar, and the shadow puppet play reacts by seeking equilibrium in the realigned relation between Rāma and Śūrpaṇakhā. If, as Bob Goldman (1984 : 52–59) has argued, the *rākṣasas* represent the dark forces "exiled" from Rāma, then the folk tradition only seeks to restore an original unity.

Finally, this shift accompanying the transposition of Kampaṉ's epic into the puppet theater of rural Kerala is visually clear in the positionings of the characters on the white cloth screen. The long (40 to 50 foot) screen is divided into two sides from the very first moment of performance, when the Brahman puppets are placed in its center. During the actual narration, each puppet enters and remains on only one side of the divide. Rāvaṇa, the *rākṣasas*, the unreformed monkeys, and Laṅkā stand on the puppeteers' left; Rāma and his associates, the gods, the rehabilitated monkeys, and Ayodhyā are on their right. For most of the more than one hundred hours of performance, the puppets stand in a static tableau, facing the figures on the opposite side of the screen. A character who does cross over (e.g., Sītā, Hanumaṉ, Angada, Vibhīṣaṇa) signals a dangerous shift, an imbalance. Indeed, on the final night, when Rāvaṇa is defeated and removed from the left side of the screen, the dramatic tension is deflated (although Vibhīṣaṇa is quickly crowned to restore the balance). This final triumph is dictated by Kampaṉ's text, but the folk performance cares little for the defeat of one side by the other and thrives instead on the relations, and half-hidden intimacies, that connect them.

Performing Kampaṉ's text as a shadow puppet play does not create the integration of classical and folk cultures that we might expect, for the theology of the avatar violates the basic principles of the local world view. In the opening scene of Bhumi Devi, in the killing of Sambukumāraṉ, in the intimations of Rāma's interest in Śūrpaṇakhā, in the justification of *kāma,* and in the tableau of characters, the moral isolate is brought into relation with the rest of the world. In the hands of the puppeteers, the Rāma story becomes not the conquest of evil by good, but the complication of a theology of perfection by a principle of balance. When the avatar truly descends and appears on the white cloth screen in Kerala, Rāma hangs in the balance—a symbol of the creative tension between the *bhakti* and folk streams of Indian culture.

Notes

An earlier version of this paper is published in Thiel-Horstmann (1990).

1. For bibliographies of Rāmāyaṇa studies, see Gore (1943); Smith (n.d.). One of the earliest full-length studies of folk variants of the Rāma story is Sen (1920).

2. Important recent work includes Hein (1972); Sweeney (1972); Sarma (1973); Ramaswami (1978); GoldbergBelle (1984); Lutgendorf (1985); Raghavan (1975, 1980); Iyengar (1983); Thiel-Horstmann (1990).

3. Vedas and videos, as the editors reminded me, derive from the same root ("to know") and are perhaps more compatible than we might fear.

4. On *bhakti* Rāmāyaṇas, see Brockington 1985; Bulcke 1962; Hart and Heifetz 1988; Hein 1972; Naidu 1971; Schechner and Hess 1977; Whaling 1983.

5. Seltmann 1986, the only full-length study on the Kerala folk tradition, focuses primarily on the theatrical elements: puppets, iconography, and so forth. See also Venu (1981); Blackburn (1987).

6. See Shulman 1979 for a clear exposition of Rāma as avatar in Kampaṉ.

7. For a discussion of the relevant historical data, see Blackburn 1987.

8. My source for the Kampaṉ text is the edition by Vai. Mu. Kōpālakiruṣṇamācāriyar 1926–39.

9. The considerable influence of Saivism on Kampaṉ is widely acknowledged, but goddess cults also appear to be important links between the bhakti epics and folk tradition: Kampaṉ's own son is named "Ampikāpati"; and, in the popular story of Mayili (Mahi), Rāvaṇa, Rāma and Lakṣmaṇa are delivered in a sealed box to the temple of Bhadrakālī.

10. The Kampaṉ verse is *puviyiṉukku.* Its double meaning (*cilēṭai*) is that all the qualities attributed to the river are equally attributable to poetry.

11. This is an interesting folk etymology, utilizing the "five-landscape" (*aintiṇai*) concept from classical Tamil poetics to explain Pañcavatī.

12. Variants of the Sambukumāraṉ episode are found in the shadow puppet traditions in Andhra Pradesh and Karnataka, the Sanskrit *Ananda Rāmāyaṇa,* the Jain *Paumacariyam,* the Telugu *Raṅganātha Rāmāyaṇa,* the Kannada *Torave Rāmāyaṇa,* to name only major texts.

13. In Kampaṉ, this verse (*mayam nīṅki*) occurs not in the Śūrpaṇakhā episode, but in the much earlier episode of building a hut at Chitrakuta.

14. The Kampaṉ verse is *nīlam mā.*

15. The avatar concept itself is an example of this backward-building tech-

nique of Indian narratives; the insertion of a prior divine birth radically alters a story by shifting the hero to a new theological status.

16. The Kampaṉ verse (*aruttiyal*) reads:

> When the *rākṣasa* spoke,
>   Rāma, that white-edged rain cloud,
> Laughed inside and mocked her:
>   "Lady, it is not proper
>   for a human to marry
>   within the easy demon clan,
> So wise poets have said."

The folk verse reads:

> "Oh, *rākṣasa* lady,
>   your beautiful hair shining
>   like a rain cloud edged in white
>   pulls at my heart!
> But you are an easy *rākṣasa* woman,
>   and I am a human—
> We can never marry,
>   so the wise poets say."

17. The Kampaṉ verse is *tām oṟu*.

18. See Kampaṉ's verse *cēn uṟa*.

19. The Kampaṉ verse is *pēcalaṉ*.

20. The standard form of this proverb is "love [*kātal*] is blind." Replacing *kātal* with *kāma* (with its intimations of passion and lust) makes Śūrpaṇakhā's point.

21. In variants of the Rāma story, Kaikeyī or her servants tease Sītā (when she returns with Rāma from Laṅkā) about her relations with Rāvaṇa; eventually, they force her to draw Rāvaṇa's picture, on her toe or on palm-leaf, which then comes to life in her bedroom.

22. For a description of the *guṇa*-theory in Sāṁkhyā, see Larson 1979.

23. The siddha medical system seeks to maintain a balance between air, water, and fire, sometimes expressed as a humoral balance between bile (*pittam*), phlegm (*kapam*), and wind (*vāyu*). See Daniel (1984), Egnor (1978), Zvelebil (1973).

References

Blackburn, Stuart H.

1987 Epic Transmission and Adaptation: A Folk Rāmāyaṇa in South India. In *The Heroic Process: Form, Function, and Fantasy in Folk Epic,* Bo Almqvist et al., eds., pp. 569–590. Dublin: Glendale Press.

Brockington, John
1985 *Righteous Rāma: The Evolution of an Epic*. New Delhi: Oxford University Press.
Bulcke, Kamil
1962 *Rāma Kathā: Utpati aur Vikās*. Allahabad: Prayag.
Daniel, Valentine
1984 *Fluid Signs: Being a Person the Tamil Way*. Berkeley: University of California Press.
Egnor, Margaret Trawick
1978 The Sacred Spell and Other Conceptions of Life in Tamil Culture. Ph.D. dissertation, University of Chicago.
GoldbergBelle, Jonathan
1984 The Performance Poetics of Tōlubommalāṭa: A South Indian Shadow Puppet Tradition. Ph.D. dissertation, University of Wisconsin, Madison.
Goldman, Robert, ed.
1984 *The Rāmāyaṇa of Vālmikī*. Princeton, N.J.: Princeton University Press.
Gore, A. N.
1943 *Bibliography of the Ramayana*. Poona: n.p.
Hart, George L., and Hank Heifetz, trans.
1988 *The Forest Book of Kampaṉ's* Rāmāyaṇa. Berkeley: University of California Press.
Hein, Norvin
1972 *The Miracle Plays of Mathura*. New Haven, Conn.: Yale University Press.
Iyengar, K. R. Srinivasa, ed.
1983 *Asian Variations in Rāmāyaṇa*. New Delhi: Sahitya Akademi.
Kōpālakiruṣṇamācāriyar, Vai. Mu., ed.
1926–39 *Kamparāmāṇayam*. Madras: The Editor.
Larson, Gerald James
1979 *Classical Sāṁkhyā: An Interpretation of its History and Meaning*. 2nd ed. New Delhi: Motilal Banarsidass.
Lutgendorf, Philip
1985 The Life of a Text: Tulasīdāsa's *Rāmacaritamānasa* in Performance. Ph.D. dissertation, University of Chicago.
Naidu, S. Shankar Raju
1971 *A Comparative Study of Kampa Rāmāyaṇam and Tulasi Rāmāyaṇ*. Madras: Madras University.
Raghavan, V.
1975 *The Rāmāyaṇa in Greater India*. Surat: South Gujarat University.
1980 (ed.) *The Rāmāyaṇa Tradition in Asia*. New Delhi: Sahitya Akademi.
Ramanujan, A. K.
1981 *Hymns for the Drowning: Poems for Viṣṇu by Nammāḻvār*. Princeton, N.J.: Princeton University Press.

Ramaswami, S.
1978 Tamiḻaka Tōlpāvaniḻal Kūttu. Ph.D. dissertation, Madurai-Kamaraj University.
Sarma, C. R.
1973 *The Rāmāyana in Telugu and Tamil: A Comparative Study*. Madras: Lakshminarayana Granthamala.
Schechner, Richard, and Linda Hess
1977 The Ramlila of Ramnagar. *Drama Review* 21,3 : 51–82.
Seltmann, Friedrich
1986 *Schattenspiel in Kerala*. Stuttgart: Steiner.
Sen, D. C.
1920 *The Bengali Rāmāyaṇas*. Calcutta: Calcutta University.
Shulman, David
1979 Divine Order and Divine Evil in the Tamil Tale of Rama. *Journal of Asian Studies* 38 : 651–669.
1985 *The King and Clown in South Indian Myth and Poetry*. Princeton, N.J.: Princeton University Press.
1986 Battle as Metaphor in Tamil Folk and Classical Traditions. In *Another Harmony: New Essays on the Folklore of India*, Stuart Blackburn and A. K. Ramanujan, eds., pp. 105–130. Berkeley: University of California Press.
Smith, Daniel H.
n.d. Reading the Ramayana: A Bibliographical Guide to Indian Variants on the Rama-theme in English Translations. Typescript.
Sweeney, Amin
1972 *The Rāmāyaṇa and the Malay Shadow-Play*. Kuala Lumpur: National University of Malaysia Press.
Thiel-Horstmann, Monika, ed.
1990 *Contemporary Rāmāyaṇa Traditions*. Wiesbaden: Otto Harrassowitz.
Venu, G.
1981 Tolpava Koothu. *Journal of the National Center for Performing Arts* 10 : 25–36.
Whaling, Frank
1983 *The Rise of the Religious Significance of Rāma*. New Delhi: Motilal Banarsidass.
Zvelebil, Kamil
1973 *The Poets of the Powers*. London: Rider.

Alf Hiltebeitel

The Folklore of Draupadī: Saris and Hair

In the immediate sequel to the famous dice match episode of the *Mahābhārata* in which the heroine Draupadī is the last stake wagered and lost by her Pāṇḍava husbands, her Kaurava captors first drag her by the hair and then order her disrobing. This double theme involving Draupadī's hair and saris has preoccupied me for some time. My initial concern was to explore its rich cosmological and theological implications in classical sources.[1] In this chapter I would like to address some folkloric material bearing on the same twin subjects that has come to my attention over the last six years, and discuss it toward some additional ends, taking up the wider issue of pan-Indian *Mahābhārata* folklores, and raising the question of the relation between the distinctly Tamil folklore about Draupadī that is found in her cult and wider pan-Indian themes. Are Tamil and other south Indian *Mahābhārata* folklores (some of which are almost certainly older than the Draupadī cult) a source of diffusion for similar themes found elsewhere in India? Or does the classical epic just suggest common folk responses? Is there a sort of "underground" *Mahābhārata,* one that is perhaps even reflected in the Sanskrit epic itself but also different from it in certain basic accentuations concerning the goddess? What are some of the features that distinguish *Mahābhārata* folklores from other Indian folklores? And how are folkloric themes concerning the *Mahābhārata* related to distinctive modes of transmission and performance? How and why is the *Mahābhārata* linked with certain regional folk epic traditions and not with others? And in such regional folk epic traditions where there is a connection, how do we understand their portrayals of virgin heroines at the center of conflicts over land? Draupadī's saris and hair provide a fitting entrée into the problematics of such questions.

That the Sanskrit *Mahābhārata* is itself a repository of folklore has not, of course, gone unnoticed. But little consistency has emerged from the appreciation of this fact. Walter Ruben (1944), for instance, used a comparative method to try to explain away all the episodes involving Krishna as folkloric intrusions. N. B. Patil (1983) claimed the status of folk motif for virtually any narrative element in the epic that caught his eye. And Georges Dumézil tried to distinguish mythic, epic, and what can be called folkloric levels in certain episodes: for instance, at Draupadī's *svayaṃvara,* the "myths" that explain her polyandry by the intercessions of Śiva in her former lives; the main "epic"-"heroic" narrative itself; and the "romanesque" fatality of Kuntī's mistaking Draupadī for alms, and telling the Pāṇḍavas, her sons, to "share it all equally" (1974 : 109–10). Though I once looked at these matters much as Dumézil did (Hiltebeitel 1976 : 27–33) and would not dispute that there may be some value in retaining such "levels" as heuristic devices, I am now sensitive to their being rather arbitrary in general. Moreover, in the specific case of the *Mahābhārata,* they become means to deceive ourselves into missing the work's integrity.[2]

In this vein, much has been gained recently by A. K. Ramanujan's placement of epic at the *puṟam* end of the folklore spectrum that runs from *akam,* the "interior" of heart and home, to the *puṟam* exterior of the public arena. As Ramanujan shows, at this *puṟam* pole, epic has affinities with drama, and introduces tragic modes that are not found in *akam* genres (1986 : 41–51, 71–72). All of this is very suggestive for interpreting *Mahābhārata* folklores and their modes of transmission and performance. Even the Sanskrit *Mahābhārata* itself is proverbially not to be read in the home, as it arouses family conflict; whereas the *Rāmāyaṇa,* by way of contrast, should be read in the home because it portrays ideal family conditions.[3] And beyond the Sanskrit *Mahābhārata,* one finds further suggestive ways in which *Mahābhārata* folklore has distinctive features in relation to drama, and to other "mythic" and "epic" folklores. According to Gustav Oppert (1893 : 97–98), whereas the *Rāmāyaṇa* is favored above all by Brahmans, the *Mahābhārata* is adopted by Śūdras.

The ways in which different folk dramas are patronized in India suggests such a pattern. Best known are the Rās Līlās of north India, which are about Kṛṣṇa's youth among the cowherds (Hein 1972; Hawley 1981), and the Rām Līlās, also from the north, performed in connection with the fall festival of Dasarā (Schechner and Hess 1977; Schechner 1983 : 238–293). *Mahābhārata* drama cycles are less common and less well known. The Rās and Rām Līlās seem to be largely the expressions of high caste traditions of Brahmans and kings and of pan-regional values.[4] *Mahābhārata* dramas are sometimes sponsored at these levels, as for instance with the Kathakaḷi and Kūṭiyāṭṭam (Zarilli 1984). But they are sometimes also found with deeper roots in more regionally intensive, cult-specific forms, tied in with the values of lower castes, and in particular the dominant landed castes that sponsor most of the festivals in which the plays are performed. Most similar to the mix of drama, recitation, and ritual found in the Draupadī cult are the so-called Pāṇḍav Līlās celebrated in the mountains of sub-Himalayan Garhwal. From the recent fieldwork of William S. Sax, we know that the Pāṇḍav Līlās, or Pāṇḍava Plays, involve ritual dramas sponsored by dominant caste Rājputs or Kṣatriyas (warriors), who claim descent from the Pāṇḍavas and regard their region as one in which certain epic events—the Pāṇḍavas' births, their Himalayan ascent to heaven—took place. The Pāṇḍavas are regarded as "personal deities" (*iṣṭadevatās*). The *līlās* are ways of worshipping Kālī, for Draupadī is regarded as Kālī's *avatāra*. They enact epic scenes, include a mix of bardic recitation and dance-drama performance, induce possession by both actors and audience, and evoke animal sacrifices through portrayals of death scenes (Sax 1986; 1987).

Such features are all paralleled in the south Indian Draupadī cult. Draupadī festivals are sponsored mainly by Vaṉṉiyars, a regionally dominant landed caste in the South Arcot District of Tamilnadu where the cult is centered. Vaṉṉiyars who are connected with the Draupadī cult claim to have originally been Kṣatriyas and, like the Pāṇḍavas, to have Draupadī as their *kuladevatā*, or "family deity." Draupadī cult martial traditions are in fact linked up with the royal fort and regional mythology of Gingee, the medieval Nāyak kingdom or "viceroyalty" under the Vijayanagar "empire." For instance, Gingee is often regarded as the site where Draupadī took a second birth to help one of Gingee's ancient kings, a close descendant of the Pāṇḍavas, to overcome the demon of the Gingee Forest. Though Draupadī is an incarnation of Śrī, the goddess of prosperity, as she is in the classical epic, she takes on the "form of Kālī" (*Kālīrūpa*) as well as traits of Durgā in gaining revenge for her violation by the Kauravas. Her festivals combine local ritual, recitation of the *Mahābhārata* in Tamil, and night-long plays. At the largest festivals, there may be over sixty days of off and on ritual, fifty afternoons of recitation, and eighteen nights of dramas. Shorter festivals combine these elements in smaller but similar proportions, also frequently emphasizing the number eighteen in some fashion (for instance, eighteen days of recitation, or ten days' recitation plus eight of dramas), since the festival commemorates the epic's eighteen-day war.

The ways that the *Mahābhārata* roots itself at these social and regional levels need to be considered in connection with the way certain folk epics in other parts of India link themselves with the *Mahābhārata,* and involve similar mixes of drama, bardic recitation, and "hero cult" ritual. I will return to this problem, or set of problems, in closing.

Draupadī's Hair and Saris in Her Tamil Cult

In the Draupadī cult, images of Draupadī's hair and saris cannot be dissociated from the primary natural elements of earth, water, and fire.[5] In what follows, one must keep in mind the cult's ritual cycle, with its sequence of ceremonies that involve earth trampling, fire trampling (*tīmiti*) the crossing of a ditch of water called the "milk pit" (*pāl kuḻi*), and in which women who cross the coals often wear brilliant yellow (*mañcaḷ*) saris and loosened hair. The mythology of the Draupadī cult firewalk bears out the relevance of these images, for among the accounts of how Draupadī protects her devotees as they cross the coals, one hears sometimes that she does so by throwing the end of her sari over them, and sometimes that she does the same with her unseen flowing hair (Hiltebeitel 1988 : 437).

The twin themes of hair and saris had already coalesced into a resonant symbolic unit in Bhaṭṭa Nārāyaṇa's Sanskrit drama *Veṇīsaṃhāra,* "The Binding-Up of the Braid," probably from the early eighth century. For with Bhaṭṭa, two things happen that recur in the Draupadī cult but are not found in the Sanskrit epic. First, Duryodhana replaces Karṇa in ordering the disrobing, so that he becomes responsible for commanding the violations of both the sari and the hair. And second, Bhaṭṭa initiates the device of alluding to the two violations together, recalling them jointly and repeatedly, at least once in every act, as the *keśāmbarākarṣaṇa,* "the pulling of the hair and the garments" (Hiltebeitel 1981 : 183 and n. 12).

This double accentuation recurs in the Tamil *Mahābhārata* of Villiputtūr Āḻvār, a text composed around 1400 within the area of the Draupadī cult heartland, at the very point where Draupadī makes her celebrated vow:

> He who brought me without fearing into the court of kings, touching my saree, touching my hair [*tukil tīṇṭi aḷakam tīṇṭi*] which was made fragrant, its garland surrounded by swarms of bees, kings—not until the victory drums roll on the battlefield, having cut off [their] crowned heads, smelling of raw meat, the hot blood falling, will I take up and bind my dishevelled hair. (*Villipāratam* 2.2.255)

As Richard Frasca (1984 : 145), David Shulman (1985 : 14) and I (1988 : 198) have all sensed, the *Villipāratam* is quite possibly responsive to early developments of the Draupadī cult itself. It is in any case most definitely responsive—like the largely lost ninth-century *Makāpāratam* of Peruntēvaṉār—to prior south Indian *Mahābhārata* folklores (Hiltebeitel 1988 : 15 and *passim;* Venkatesa Acharya 1981 : 307–31). More to the present point, it is the text that is usually used for recitation and exposition of the epic by the *pāratiyārs* or *pārata piracankis*, the professional itinerant "bards" who sing from and expound upon this *Mahābhārata* at Draupadī festivals. And it is further the version of the *Mahābhārata* that stands most directly behind the *Terukkūttu* dramas that are performed at Draupadī festivals. I will not attempt here to illustrate the many and often contrasting ways in which both the *pāratiyārs* and the dramatists introduce "folk" themes that go beyond Villi's classical text (itself enriched by folk traditions, as just noted). Suffice it to say that just as each *pāratiyār* makes his own folk-classical weave (with variations sometimes stimulated by the particular requirements of local festivals), so does each drama vary in the same way, with some far closer to Villi than others, but here again differing from troupe to troupe, performance to performance, and also from printed to handwritten to oral-performed variants. The drama that deals most centrally with Draupadī's saris and hair, "Dice Match and Disrobing," has a printed chapbook version by a poet named Irāmaccantira Kavirāyar (1977), who lived sometime in the early nineteenth century and seems to have played a major role in launching the transformation of this folk drama tradition into a chapbook folk literature (Hiltebeitel 1988 : 157–67). I cannot go here into the variance from such chapbook texts that is found in performance; although it is considerable, performed versions do seem to retain basic elements of the structure of the chapbook versions as well as many songs and proverbial images.[6] Irāmaccantira Kavirāyar stays closer to the *Villipāratam* in "Dice Match and Disrobing" than he does in certain other dramas performed at Draupadī festivals that he also authored. And in general, he stays closer to Villi than other authors within the same genre. With these points in mind, let us observe some of the ways that he situates this "classical" theme in his folk theatre composition. Taking things in order, we will look first at the hair pulling, then at the sari pulling, and finally at the vow. Throughout this discussion, one must keep in mind not only Irāmaccantira Kavirāyar's text, but details and variations of performers. The quite skeletal text tells us virtually nothing about staging and "props," matters that are clearly decisive for our subjects.

According to Irāmaccantira Kavirāyar's text,[7] Duḥśāsana seizes Draupadī by the hair. Actually, in performance he swings her by a stick or a length of wound cloth that each holds at opposite ends, Draupadī holding the end of her hair to her end of the stick or cloth to indicate that it is her hair's extension. The Duḥśāsana actor will often pause at this point to make a gesture of worship (prayer, devotional salute, sometimes even lamp-waving or *dīpārādhanā*) toward Draupadī's image (brought on a *tēr* or "chariot" to watch the play) to beg the goddess's forgiveness for this violation that he performs only out of professional duty (Hiltebeitel 1988 : 234). Once Duḥśāsana has thrown her around the stage and to the ground, Draupadī sings a deep and defiant lament (*pulampal*), one that Irāmaccantira Kavirāyar indicates is precisely the "lament of Draupadī when Duḥśāsana touches Draupadī's hair" (*tuṟcātaṉaṉ turōpataiyai mayirai toṭṭapōtu turōpatai pulampal;* 1977 : 67; henceforth referred to as CTU).

> Alas, [I am] a sinner, O god
> Can this injustice be, O god?
> My *kūntal* [hair knot] that has been decorated and stroked [or loosened; *kōti*] by my lords [my husbands/kings; *maṉṉavar*], can this fool touch it, O god?
> My *kūntal* that is praised and touched by my war heroes, can a low person [*pulaiyaṉ*] touch it, O god?
> My *kūntal* that is touched and unfolded by my husbands [loved ones; *kaṇṇālar*], can a base person [*kaṭalyaṉ*] touch it, O god?
> That *kūntal* that is arranged and stroked [*kōti*] by my battle heroes, can a fool touch it, O god?
> My *kūntal* that good pure heroes adorn with flowers, can an evil person touch it, O god?
> The *kūntal* that smells sweetly from being adorned with fresh jasmine, alas, it rolls in the dirt [*maṇ*], O god.
> The *kūntal* to which I applied *campaṅki* oil, alas, it rolls on the earth [*tarai*], O god.
> My *kūntal* that shines after running through it with a comb, alas, it rolls on the street [*teru*], O god. (CTU 67)

The *kūntal* (colloquial *koṇṭai*) is a powerful symbol and is a resonant term, as we shall see, throughout Draupadī cult folklore. The opening four lines attribute the touching, arranging, loosening, adornment, and praising of Draupadī's *kūntal* alternately to the Pāṇḍavas and to battle heroes. And the fifth and sixth lines bring in flowers, indicating that it is specifically pure heroes who adorn it with jasmine. Obviously, the Pāṇḍavas are war heroes and pure, but the alternation suggests a ritual nuance as well. The touching, arranging, loosening, adornment, and praising of Draupadī's *kūntal* are also done by Draupadī's worshippers: by the actors who act out her dramas, and by the *pūcāris* and other temple officiants who handle and adorn her icons. Indeed, we shall soon discuss a myth that is precisely about a *pūcāri*'s handling of Draupadī's hair. There is further an erotic-yet-defiling ambience to the symbol. Draupadī describes the loosening of her *kūntal* in terms of a love and affection between her and her husbands that is violated by Duḥśāsana's defiling—indeed, outcaste-like—touch. But the defilement works both ways, as the stick or cloth would seem to symbolize, for Draupadī is menstruating. Moreover, as Duḥśāsana is quick to point out in reply, the erotic connotation of Draupadī's marital status—her polyandry—invites its own defiling interpretation. Says Duḥśāsana: "As soon as five men's hands fall on you, you wicked cheat, does your body emit fragrance? Will it grow [*vaḷarntupōmō*]? As soon as the hands of those five who keep you fall on you, having become proud, if you experience my hand, will all the shining diminish? With five [already], let it become six. What is that! Get up and come!" (CTU 68). Also interesting in the lament is its conclusion: first the transition from the fragrance of jasmines to the rolling of Draupadī's hair in the dirt, on the earth, and finally in the street. The connection between fragrance and the earth already typifies Draupadī in the Sanskrit epic from the moment of her birth (*Mahābhārata* 1 : 155.43), and recalls the association between smell and the earth that is found in classical Indian philosophical systems (Biardeau 1971–72 : 41). The culminating line brings all this down literally to the "street" (or *teru*) level—and smells—of the *terukkūttu*.

As to the disrobing scene, we must again look beyond Irāmaccantira Kavirāyar's text to what is done in performance. In all cases, performance of the disrobing scene is regarded as highly inauspicious, and is sometimes omitted from a festival on this account. Draupadī stands on the musicians' bench behind the stage screen (held by two members of the troupe), and behind Draupadī is Kṛṣṇa, either in back of her on the platform itself, or above (sometimes flute in hand) on the greenroom roof. He holds the end of a yellow or even gold sari, *mañcaḷ* in Tamil, that passes from his hands over Draupadī's shoulder. Simultaneously, another *mañcaḷ* cloth—

symbolically identical with the sari that passes from Kṛṣṇa to Draupadī—may be placed in front of the processional icon of Draupadī that would normally "watch" the drama from her "chariot" at the back of the audience. The Draupadī actor folds "her" hands in the devotional salute and repeatedly cries out "Kōvintā! Kōvintā!" (the Tamil vocative for Govinda, a name of Kṛṣṇa). The *mañcaḷ* sari is said to represent her chastity (*kaṟpu*) as well as the source of all the other saris that proceed from Kṛṣṇa's graceful response to her prayers for his protection. The actual disrobing is done in either of two ways. Usually, Duḥśāsana reaches under the screen and grabs hold of what he takes to be the bottom of her sari. But he is foiled by what turns out to be a long chain of saris tied end to end, and eventually linked to form a revolving circle.[8] The more he pulls, the more the circle goes round and round, resulting in his bafflement and exhaustion. Alternately, in a scene repeated several times, one or more additional saris may be placed loosely around Draupadī, and while Duḥśāsana pulls violently as she prays, the Draupadī actor twirls as the saris come off—always leaving, of course, the one sari underneath to confront Duḥśāsana with the impossiblity of this task.[9] I will return to the circle of saris tied end to end, for it is a fitting metaphor for much that goes on in the *terukkūttu* handling of Draupadī cult folklore. In either case, however, it is of interest that Duḥśāsana charges repeatedly that Draupadī frustrates him by some magic craft or use of mantras (CTU 82–84; Hiltebeitel 1988 : 271–272). The scene has both theological subtlety and high dramatic intensity, often involving possession. But the audience also registers that either device is an obvious sleight of hand, one which Duḥśāsana is being portrayed as too arrogant, violent, and ignorant to see through. The contrast between what is obvious and what is subtle, or intangible, is fittingly portrayed by this perhaps universal symbol of veiling, illusion, and fabrication (Eliade 1963 : 180–82; Neumann 1963 : 226–234, 250, 284).

The disrobing scene also provides Irāmaccantira Kavirāyar an opportunity to rework into local idioms some of the cosmological themes concerning the *pralaya* ("dissolution" of the universe) that figure in classical versions (see note 1). Once again, the disrobing portends the disruption of the ordered relation between the elements. When the miracle of the disrobing ends and Draupadī stands vindicated, the Kuru elders rise and speak these "softened words":

To the five she is the goddess [or wife; *tēvi*], to others, she is the mother.

She is the goddess Earth [*pūmitēvi*], she is Fire's self-manifestation [*akkiṉicorūpi*]

She is the goddess of this lineage [*kulatteyvam*]. Is there any other like her?

(CTU 86; Hiltebeitel 1988 : 264)

In contrast, after the hair-pulling and just before the disrobing begins, Draupadī asks Dhṛtarāṣṭra:

O king of the Kuru dynasty who sees the greatness of the *kula,*
Do you allow this cruelty in your *kula,* O father-in-law?
If you permit these faults in the presence of the elders, my father-in-law,
Will the rain fall? Will the world survive [*maḻai peyummō vaiyakam uyyumō*]?

(CTU 73; Hiltebeitel 1988 : 265)

There are repeated references to the fires that will erupt in the form of Draupadī's vengeful anger (CTU 68, 85; Hiltebeitel 1988 : 271, 274). Duḥśāsana compares the impossibility of disrobing her to the use of a well-sweep (*eṟṟam*) to drain the seven seas (CTU 86). But most interesting, once again, are two contrasting evocations of Draupadī's relation to the earth. First Duḥśāsana tells her that by stripping her he will reduce her to "an open ground," a "desert" (*veṭṭaveḷi;* CTU 83; Hiltebeitel 1988 : 272). But when he finds he cannot do this, he complains: "Millions and billions, beautiful and variegated, [crores of sun-bright saris of many kinds, emerging variously (?)], as the winged white ants [*īcal*] come out of an anthill [*puṟṟu*] in a great exodus [*perum pōkku*], how many crores of saris must I remove?" (CTU 85).[10] Not to be reduced to a barren ground or desert, Draupadī is the earth in its most resourceful and inexhaustible aspect, and in a form, moreover, that connects her with other rural and village goddesses whose cult centers on the plenitudinous mysteries of the anthill, or, more correctly, the termite mound (Irwin 1982; Meyer 1986 : 29–30, 58–59, 65, 121–122, and s.v. "termite hill" in index).

Finally, let us see how Irāmaccantira Kavirāyar handles the vow Draupadī makes to bring about her rebraiding. Having seen Duryodhana expose his thigh to her and having responded in dialogue to his various taunts, telling him, among other things, that "vultures will peck at your thigh so that it will become a filthy place producing wriggling worms,"

Draupadī's closing statement is as follows (first in meter and closing in prose):

> Having been made to stand in the royal presence, having touched my *kūntal* and sari [*kūntaluṅtukiluntīṇṭi*],
> the one who did this, growing weak in the future together with his kin [*vēr:* that is, "roots"] on the battlefield,
> [until] your head [is] severed without beating the unequaled war drum of victory,
> I will not, taking it, braid my shiningly spread out *kūntal*.
>
> Listen, you kings in the *sabhā!* If in the future, on the battlefield, I do not tie up my hair [*mayirai*] standing on the chest of the man who has done this disgrace of touching my hair and saris [*kūntalai-yum tukilun tīṇṭi*], having made me stand in the royal *sabhā,* then I am not Draupadī. (CTU 88; Hiltebeitel 1988 : 30, 236–37)

Irāmaccantira Kavirāyar in effect doubles the compound illusion to the hair and saris that is found in, and no doubt drawn from, Villi. Be it noted, however, that neither Villi nor Irāmaccantira Kavirāyar gives us a fully operative festival version of Draupadī's vow. In fact, the passage leaves it rather vague whether she is referring to Duḥśāsana or Duryodhana. For a fuller and clearer expression of her own vow, we may turn to another chap-book drama called *Turōpatai Kuṟavañci,* one that is far less classically based and therefore probably freer to bring out the cult-related themes. Disguised as a gypsy fortune teller, Draupadī tells Duryodhana's wife and mother of the fate that awaits him and him alone.

> She [Draupadī] went to dwell in the forest, saying, "On the battlefield [*paṭukaḷam*] I will put up my *kūntal*, which was spread out in the great *sabhā.*"
> She went to dwell in the forest, saying, "In the war I will put up my *kūntal,* which was spread in the great *sabhā,* O mother."
> She went, saying, "I, one woman, spread my hair and stood; as a result everyone in the country had to keep their hair spread."
> When the battle takes away the army on the eighteenth day, standing on the king of the earth, the Ammaṉ will tie up her *kūntal*.

Seizing the lord, *aiyō,* the king who rules the country, standing on your husband, the Ammaṉ will tie up her *kūntal.*
Taking up a handful of blood, combing her hair, separating his ribs for a comb,
the chaste woman [*pattiṉiyāḷ*], taking up the fourteen intestines on both sides, gathering up her hair on the battlefield [*paṭukaḷam*], the Ammaṉ will tie up her *kūntal.*
After the differences have vanished, Pāñcāli will come, she said, after crushing the decorated crowns of the hundred and one [the Kauravas plus Jayadratha, their brother-in-law].
Having seized and cut off all the heads of her relatives [*paṅkāḷis*], the chaste woman, having put up her hair, will come to rule the earth [*pattiṉiyā talaimuṭittu pār āḷa varuvāḷ*].
(Taṉikācala Mutaliyār 1979: 44; Hiltebeitel 1988: 306–7)

It is in the final scene of the drama *Patiṉeṭṭām Pōr,* or "Eighteenth Day War," the play that closes the cycle of festival dramas, that the hair-tying, *kūntal muṭittal,* at last comes to pass in the fashion thus anticipated. I note only that in my experience it is invariably Kṛṣṇa who ties the red or orange flowers into Draupadī's hair. The scene is then replicated later in the same morning with the anointing of Draupadī's processional icon atop Duryodhana's effigy on the ritual battlefield called the *paṭukaḷam,* in this case with her hair tied by the hands of local villagers, or by the *pāratiyār.* And often the rebraiding of the icon on the effigy is complemented and doubled by a reappearance of members of the troupe, who this time not only repeat Draupadī's rebraiding but show the dishevelment of the now widowed Peruntiruvaḷ, wife of Duryodhana, lamenting and carrying a winnow.

In fact, one could trace the double theme of hair and saris through the drama cycle, and indeed the cult, as a whole. The drama cycles often begin with the play *Kaṇṇaṉ Jalakkirīṭai,* "Kṛṣṇa's Water Sports," which culminates in Kṛṣṇa's stealing of the saris of the Gopīs (who, before bathing, loosen their *kūntal*s; Hiltebeitel 1988: 186–90). The Kṛṣṇa who steals the saris of the Gopīs replaces the saris of Draupadī. Or alternately, a festival drama cycle may begin with the play *Turōṇāccāri Yākacālai,* "Droṇa's Sacrificial Hall," which tells about the births of Aśvatthāman and Draupadī, and introduces the folk theme that Aśvatthāman is born from a horse that is fed with a plate of rice that Śiva has ejaculated into after seeing Droṇa's wife Kṛpī appear before him naked and with her hair down as well (idem., 190–195). The disguise themes are enriched, with Bhīma and Arjuna in transvestite roles, wearing saris (idem., 296–298, 336–343). Indeed, again in terms of the theme of illusion and fabrication, it is not insignificant that all parts are played by male actors. At some level it must register on viewers that if Draupadī (or the Gopīs, or Kṛpī) were actually stripped on stage it would be quite out of character. In both the dramas and the *Villipāratam* there is the prophecy by Sahadeva that the only way to avoid war would be to bind Kṛṣṇa and shave off Draupadī's hair (idem., 313). Villi also introduces the notion that Karṇa has an instantly combustible sari that he uses to test whether women who claim to be his mother are telling the truth: only Kuntī can wear it unharmed (idem., 314–16). Throughout the battle scenes, rolled-up cloths, and sometimes saris, are used for heads. And when Duryodhaṇa is disemboweled, his guts can be represented by another *mañcaḷ* sari (idem., 421). Then there are some scenes involving the end-pieces of saris which I will turn to shortly.

Beyond the *Villipāratam* and the dramas, one finds these themes further articulated in popular cult myths. One sometimes hears that from the beginning of Draupadī's forest exile to the end of the war, the period that she wears her hair disheveled, she takes on the "form of Kālī" (*kālirūpam*), her Viśvarūpam or "Universal Form." While her husbands sleep, she roams about the forests from midnight to 3:00 A.M., devouring whatever comes her way (wild animals, domesticated animals, even humans). And during the war she goes out at the same time to consume the bodies of the dead. There are several stories that spin off these themes that I will not go into here (idem., 289–295). Suffice it to say that they are linked with the disheveled Kālī through their evocations of the forest, the battlefield, and the crematorium.

As we begin to address the issue of *Mahābhārata* folklores outside the Draupadī cult, one more myth is instructive. It is a story known in the immediate Gingee area, and apparently rarely if at all known outside it. It supplies a sort of oral *sthala purāṇa* of Draupadī's "original temple" (*āti kōvil, āti pīṭam*) just north of the Gingee Fort in the village of Mēlaccēri. This village, also known as *paḻaiya ceñci,* or Old Gingee, marks the site where Draupadī is said to have taken second birth to come to the aid of a certain king Cunītaṉ, a descendant of the Pāṇḍavas, to rescue him and his Gingee kingdom from the Gingee or Mēlaccēri Forest Demon (the forest is just west of the Mēlaccēri Draupadī temple). Different versions of this story give the king different names, but I cite here the most complete and informed version I found, that of the Mēlaccēri temple's *pūcāri,* in which the king is the same Cunītaṉ, presumably later in life.

When Cunītaṉ was ruling Old Gingee, there were ten acres of land near the temple for a flower garden to supply the *pūcāri* with flowers for the temple *pūjās*. It was the custom that each day, after the flowers were placed on the Ammaṉ, that the *pūcāri* would bring them before the king, as *prasādam*. One day, without the *pūcāri* knowing it, his concubine, seeing the beautiful flowers on the icon, took them off and placed them in her *kūntal,* just to enjoy them. After some time, she removed them and put them back on the Ammaṉ. Unaware what she had done, the *pūcāri* then came and removed the flowers from the Ammaṉ and sent them with various other *pūjā* articles to the king's palace.

When they reached the palace, there was one hair lying in the flowers. The queen noticed it and asked the king: "How can there be a hair in the flowers? It is a stone icon [*kal-cilai*]. Does a *cāi* [a god(dess] have a *kūntal?*" The king immediately called back the *pūcāri* and demanded an answer. The *pūcāri* had never seen the hair, and knew nothing of how it got there. He was blinking, and could not answer. In rising anger, the king said: "I will give you a week. If you can answer my question in one week, well and good. Otherwise you will be punished with death."

When the *pūcāri* returned to the temple, he unburdened his troubles to the Ammaṉ. He wept, he prayed, he did daily and nightly observances at the temple, never returning home, always imploring her: "Somehow you must show your hair to the king." At last the Ammaṉ appeared in his dream, and said: "On Friday let the king and queen come before my image. If you do the regular *apicēkas* and *pūjās* on that day, and place a white screen [*veṇtirai*] before me, then I will show my *kūntal*.

The next Friday the *pūcāri* did a *pūjā* in the presence of the king and queen. Only he could see the icon, as the screen was in front of it. Again the king asked: "Can a stone icon have a *kūntal?*" As soon as the raja stepped forward to peer over the screen, the Ammaṉ flashed the dishevelled hair of her *kūntal* out over the screen and into his eye. Yet at this point only the *pūcāri* could see the Ammaṉ's real form. The king still had a doubt: the *pūcāri* could have pulled a trick. "It may be hair, but is it the Ammaṉ's? He is going to lose his life, so he has resorted to some trick." Thinking that it was artificial, the king touched the Amman̲'s hair and pulled one piece of it. When he did this, he heard the sound made when a hair is pulled. The root of the hair came over the screen and into his hand, and he saw that it was tipped with blood. Immediately he became blind.

At once the king fell at the *pūcāri*'s feet, asking his forgiveness for causing him so many hardships and doubting him, praising his devotion as firmer than his own, and imploring him to "Pray on my behalf to Amman̲ to restore my eyesight." The *pūcāri* prayed, and at last one night the Amman̲ appeared in his dream and said the king would get back only three-fourths of his vision, not all of it, as he had tested her. The next day, after the *pūjā*, the three-fourths of his vision returned. In gratitude, the king then ordered the construction of various additions to the temple.

The blind king is a symbol that has in fact one of its most powerful expressions in the *Mahābhārata* itself, in the person of Dhṛtarāṣṭra. Indeed, from a certain angle, it is Dhṛtarāṣṭra's blindness that allows the dice match, and the hair-pulling and disrobing that result from it. The pulling of just one hair is sufficient here to evoke the dire consequences of the epic precedent. The hair tipped with blood recalls the connection between Draupadī's menstruation and the hair-pulling in the *sabhā*. The blinded Cunītan̲ is in this regard no less a descendant of the Kauravas than the Pāṇḍavas. Just as it is the vow Draupadī makes concerning her hair that leads to the punishment of the kings who violate her in the *Mahābhārata*, so it is again with her hair that she punishes the king of Gingee for doubting her miraculous power and violating the sanctity of her icon.

Aside from its evocations of the *Mahābhārata*, this myth is of interest for its variations on certain South Indian mythic themes, and more specifically as a variant of two myths that tell essentially the same story: one from Puri in Orissa that has been set forth by Frédérique Marglin (1985: 92–93), and one from Śrīkākulam in Kṛṣṇa District, Andhra, that was kindly summarized for me by David Shulman.[11] What is most striking is that the Draupadī cult myth is the only one where the icon in question is that of a goddess. In the two others, the priest's concubine takes the flowers from an icon of Viṣṇu, which (or who) must eventually grow hair in a corresponding fashion to exonerate the priest from the charges of his royal patrons. It would seem that in this case we have an essentially royal myth that probably circulated during the Nāyak period outside the Draupadī cult, and was adapted to the latter only in a very local tradition. Yet how much more powerful an image it is in the goddess's case!

Loose Ends and Closing Circles

In the rest of this chapter, let us begin to explore some of the ways that the Draupadī cult is not on the receiving end, but part of—and in some cases perhaps even the source of—wider networks of folk *Mahābhārata* transmission. I return to the circle of saris linked up end to end. We have seen how this image of grace and illusion works in the text and performance of "Dice Match and Disrobing." One must appreciate, however, that the end piece of the sari (in Tamil, *muntāṉai,* colloquial *muntāṇi*) is itself a powerfully operative symbol of Draupadī cult dramas and folklore. We have seen that Draupadī drapes the end piece over the coals to protect her fire-walking worshippers. In the performance of "Dice Match and Disrobing," Duḥśāsana begins his attempted disrobing by grabbing hold of what he thinks is the end of Draupadī's sari (and in cases where the Draupadī actor twirls, Duḥśāsana actually does hold her *muntāṉai,* though not her "real" one). And at the other end of this endless circle, it is Kṛṣṇa, holding one end of the special *mañcaḷ* sari, who provides Draupadī with its other end as the piece to place over her shoulder, again covering the Draupadī actor's real sari, but as if it were truly her own. Margaret Trawick Egnor enriches our appreciation of this moment, commenting on the use of the term "a young girl's garment" for the shoulder-piece in the crying songs of the Paṟaiyar women: "'A young girls's garment' [*cittāṭai* is the top piece draped over the shoulder, worn by girls come of age but not married. The same garment is tied on the statues of female deities, because a deity is always young and always a virgin" (1986 : 307). Draupadī, whose virginity in her cult will be discussed further, is thus in an iconic pose, with the loose piece of *mañcaḷ* sari over her shoulder being the only one untied in the whole dramatic scene, and the one that accounts symbolically for the linking of all the others. As with the hair, here too we have a symbol of binding and loosing, knotting and unraveling. Indeed, one senses that the hair and the saris are again complementary, for it is while the hair is unraveled that the saris are linked. Each binding and unraveling further points to the collaboration of Kṛṣṇa and Draupadī, Viṣṇu and the goddess: for just as Kṛṣṇa provides the *mañcaḷ* sari at the disrobing, so he resets the blood-symbolizing flowers into Draupadī's hair when he reties her *kūntal*.

I know of three instances in Draupadī cult folklore where the *muntāṉai* is used as a symbol, and in each case, I would argue, the single unbound end pieces in these episodes evoke the linked *muntāṉai*s of "Dice Match and Disrobing." In one instance, Arjuna disguises himself as a woman (really a multiform of Durgā, called Vijayāmpāḷ, "Mother Victory") to seduce Pōrmaṉṉaṉ (Draupadī's temple guardian and servant-to-be) into giving up his *pūjā* implements so that they can serve Draupadī as the weapons by which she will be able to win the eighteen-day war and retie her hair. In one variant of this story that I have not found in any of its dramatic renditions, Pōrmaṉṉaṉ accompanies Arjuna-Vijayāmpaḷ who says "she" has to urinate. Pōrmaṉṉaṉ insists on holding the end of "her" sari, so as to be sure "she" does not disappear. Arjuna then "disrobes" behind a bush, ties the other end to the bush, and makes off with the *pūjā* items.[12] In this comic inversion, Arjuna, not only a multiform of Durgā but a stand-in for Draupadī, disrobes himself and leaves Pōrmaṉṉaṉ, standing there with the end of a sari, as demonic and dumbfounded as Duḥśāsana (they are made up identically in the dramas and often played by the same actors). A second use of the *muntāṉai* is made in the dramas. At the end of the Pāṇḍavas' year spent incognito in Virāṭa's kingdom, Virāṭa interrupts his dicing with the disguised Yudhiṣṭhira to protest the latter's seeming belittlement of Virāṭa's son. He throws the gambling pieces at Yudhiṣṭhira and wounds his forehead. Draupadī then steps forth and stanches the bleeding with the end of her sari. As it stands, the use of the sari here can be traced to the *Villipāratam,* for in the Sanskrit epic Draupadī uses a golden bowl. The important thing in all cases is that she keeps the blood from touching the ground, for as Yudhiṣṭhira soon explains, had it done so, it would have destroyed Virāṭa's kingdom. This alone is a sufficient evocation of the war to come (Hiltebeitel 1988: 300–301). With the *muntāṉai* replacing the golden bowl, however, we have also an evocation of the link between saris and blood at the disrobing. And as our third piece of *muntāṉai* folklore will make clear, it also "ties in" with the miracle of the saris as well.

The play that precedes "Dice Match and Disrobing" in Draupadī's festival cycles is the play *Irājacūya Yākam,* "Rājasūya Sacrifice." In fidelity to the structure of the *Mahābhārata,* it portrays the great sacrifice of royal consecration that entitles Yudhiṣṭhira to paramountcy over the other kings, and spurs the embittered Duryodhana to initiate the dice match. At the Rājasūya, a pivotal episode involves the vilification of Kṛṣṇa by Śiśupāla that results in Kṛṣṇa's beheading of this incarnate demon with his discus in the very midst of the *sabhā*. Draupadī cult folklore has made this scene the prelude to Kṛṣṇa's rescue of Draupadī at the disrobing. In the drama, when Kṛṣṇa throws his *cakra* he cuts his finger. Out comes Draupadī. Holding the *muntāṉai* of her sari, she offers it to Kṛṣṇa to stanch his blood. Delighted with her show of compassion, he promises that should she ever need help, he will find a way to return her favor in kind. The drama cycle once again reminds us that what will link the ends of the saris together at "Dice Match and Disrobing" will be the ominous theme of blood. Indeed, let us recall King Cunītaṉ and the blood-tipped piece of Draupadī's hair.

There is also a popular and less ominous variant of this story that is known outside the drama cycle.

> Once while the Pāṇḍavas and Kṛṣṇa were swimming in a tank, wearing only their loincloths, Kṛṣṇa lost his in the water. When everyone finished bathing, he remained there, hesitating and feeling shame. No one understood why he wouldn't come out. Meanwhile at a neighboring tank, Draupadī and her maids were also bathing. She observed the scene, understood, tore of a piece of her *muntāṉai,* and threw it to Kṛṣṇa, from one pond to the other. Kṛṣṇa caught it and used it as his loincloth. Then he came out of the water and told Draupadī: "In my life, I won't forget this kind of help. Out of gratitude, I will repay it in kind when the occasion comes." (Hiltebeitel 1988 : 227)

Here it is not the somber theme of end pieces tipped in blood that links Kṛṣṇa and Draupadī but the more amusing byplay on sexual modesty (*veṭkam*) Krishna will make his loincloth from the portion of the sari that covers Draupadī's breasts. For the tiny piece of cloth that Draupadī throws to him, she will get in return the inexhaustible flood of saris. Indeed, one is reminded further of Kṛṣṇa's theft of the saris of the bathing Gopīs, from the play that often starts the drama cycles. How appropriate it is that Draupadī should be promised unending saris for rescuing Kṛṣṇa from the same impasse in which he had left the Gopīs (Hiltebeitel 1988 : 226–227, little modified).

I have gone to such length in trying to show the interconnectedness of this folklore within the Draupadī cult not only because that is the best way to appreciate it, but because it provides us with a slender entrée into the problematics of transmission, by which from here on I mean diffusion.[13] The variant of Kṛṣṇa's promise that is found in the heart of the drama cycle is known in a north Indian variant. Susan Wadley has found the northern variant told in connection with the ceremony of sisters' tying the protective string called *rākhī* around their brothers' wrists: "One time Bhagavan Krishna's hand was cut and bleeding. When Dropadi saw this she immediately tied a piece of cloth from her dhoti [sic] on her brother's hand. Because of this tying, Shri Krishna saved Dropadi's honor at the time of Dusharsan's taking her sari" (Wadley 1976 : 158). The folk epic setting is not stipulated, but one sign suggests that this northern variant has a southern source. It draws upon the apparently southern theme, richly underscored in the Draupadī cult, of Draupadī being Kṛṣṇa's *taṅkai*, his younger sister (Hiltebeitel 1988 : 226–227). Since this concatenation of themes is so richly interwoven in the Draupadī cult, it seems that the best argument one could make here is that this fragment of North Indian *Mahābhārata* folklore has traveled not only up from the south, but from the Draupadī cult itself.

There are no doubt other cases where *Mahābhārata* folklores from diverse parts of India could be traced with similar probability to Draupadī cult sources. At present, however, I know of no other instances where this is likely outside of the south (that is, in fact, outside Tamilnadu and Andhra Pradesh). Karthigesu Sivathamby argues that the various south Indian and Tamil Sri Lankan drama forms that draw on the *Mahābhārata* (he includes *terukkūttu*) "indicate a common prototype" that itself results from a fusion of epic material with local legends (1981 : 360). I doubt, however, that there is a coherent folk epic prototype outside the Sanskrit epics themselves. Even the theme that recurs most prominently in the south Indian vernacular retellings and folk dramatizations of the epic—Draupadī's vow to rebraid her hair with blood—is told very differently from region to region: sometimes it is Duryodhana's blood, sometimes Duḥśāsana's and sometimes the mingling of both (Hiltebeitel 1981 : 180, n. 3; 1988 : 409, n. 19). The prominent differences in the ways that the *Mahābhārata* is treated in vernacular retellings and regional drama forms suggest that it is not so much a common folk prototype that shapes them as the different regional mythologies (Hiltebeitel 1988 : 148). Yet south Indian folk variants of the *Mahābhārata* would seem to have a relatively strong interconnectedness that lessens as one moves to the north. The themes I have highlighted in this chapter do not seem to have the same prominence in the Pāṇḍav

Līlās of Garhwal. Similarly, the tantric accentuations of Draupadī's connections with hair and blood in Nepalese *Mahābhārata* folklore are certainly different from what one finds in the south: in a Nepalese account, when Duḥśāsana is decapitated two spouts of blood shoot from the wound, one for Bhīma to fulfill his vow to drink Duḥśāsana's blood, and the other for Draupadī to fulfill her vow to wash her hair in it (Anderson 1971 : 235; Hiltebeitel 1988 : 409). There is, however, need for further research and information to clarify these relative consistencies.[14]

In one respect, though, we are now, I think, at a point where we can begin to say something more significant on the relationships between regional folk *Mahābhārata* traditions throughout much of India, including north and south. Here, however, it is not a matter of vernacular and regional reworkings of the epic itself such as one finds in the Tamil and Garhwali "*Mahābhārata* cults," but of the ways in which the *Mahābhārata* impacts upon distinctive regional folk epics. As numerous scholars have noted, a number of regional Indian folk epics are linked with the *Mahābhārata*. Such linkages would seem to be more widespread than with the *Rāmāyaṇa*, although the latter are not unknown, as John D. Smith has shown in his discussions of the Pābūjī epic from Rajasthan (1986, 1989, and forthingcoming [a]).[15] Where it is a question of regional folk epics linked with the *Mahābhārata*—such as the Tamil *Elder Brothers Story*, the Telugu *Epic of Palnāḍu*, and the *Ālhā* of the Hindi-speaking heartland of north India—the epics seem to be connected with regionally dominant landed caste traditions, although this is far clearer in the two southern examples, where regionally dominant castes are prominent in sponsoring the hero cult festivals that celebrate these folk epics, than it is for the *Ālhā*, which is without such festivals and without any single caste or caste cluster that predominates among its reciters or listeners (Schomer 1984). In any case, the *Ālhā* evokes a past and lost age of regional Kṣatriya dominance. Let us note that what I am suggesting here about the social and landed background of regional folk epics linked with the *Mahābhārata* is what we find also in such *Mahābhārata* cults as the Draupadī cult and the *Pāṇḍav Līlās*. Folk epics linked primarily with pastoralist castes, such as the *Kāṭamarāju Kathā* discussed by Velcheru Narayana Rao and the above-mentioned *Pābūjī* epic, by contrast, do not seem to be connected with the *Mahābhārata*.[16] Upon reflection, however, if further research bears out these patterns, it should not be surprising. The *Mahābhārata* is precisely the classical epic that concerns the issue of Kṣatriyas and the land. It is thus quite logical that regional folklores about dominant landed castes, those castes that translate Kṣatriya values into local and regional terms, should link themselves with it.

So far, however, though linkages between regional folk epics and the *Mahābhārata* have been noticed, they have not been adequately interpreted. All too often one hears it implied that they are meaningless afterthoughts, tagged on to what is allegedly genuine about the regional folk epics, whether it be their true "historical" cores or their regional counterculture ideology (Roghair 1982: 92–93, 136–137; cf. Hiltebeitel 1984). Or the connections made by the folk epics themselves are seen as a kind of superficial register of deeper connections: motifs that recur in the Indo-European heroic life cycle, and are virtually universal (Beck 1982: 122–123, 126–28, 132). To be sure, the connections which the folk epics make with the *Mahābhārata* may look superficial and rather arbitrary. There is no obvious consistency from one regional folk epic to another in the ways they link up with the *Mahābhārata*. *The Epic of Palnāḍu*, for example, occurs at the juncture between the Dvāpara and Kali *yuga*s, thus replacing the *Mahābhārata* war in that interval and relegating it back to a time within the Dvāpara *yuga* (Roghair 1982: 97, 108, 154, 165, 320). The great battle of the *Ālhā*, on the other hand, comes to an end when the Kali *yuga* is one-fourth over (Waterfield and Grierson 1923: 273). Certain *Mahābhārata* themes and episodes—dice matches, disguises, various types of births, marriages, and deaths—recur in the regional folk epics, but with no repeated pattern. And certain heroes and heroines of these regional folk epics are said to be incarnations of *Mahābhārata* heroes and heroines, but each folk epic seems to make its choices of who gets incarnated from the *Mahābhārata*'s vast cast of characters quite differently.

Yet scholars cannot afford to treat such correlations as superficial or random, any more than the "catalogues of divine incarnations" in the *Mahābhārata*. The correlations are consistently different, but they are consistently there, and we must find the right questions to ask of them. To my mind, it is the failure to formulate one pair of questions that is at the center of this current malaise. Those questions are as follows: What is the role of the goddess in the *Mahābhārata* in relation to Draupadī? And what is the role of the goddess in the regional folk epics in relation to the heroines who are linked with Draupadī? Others have appreciated the centrality of the goddess in relation to the heroines of the regional folk epics (Beck 1982: 49–52, 122, 128–136; Roghair 1982: 91–92, 121–123; Smith, forthcoming, but without appreciating that this centrality involves a reinterpretation of what are essentially *bhakti* images of the heroine-as-goddess in the classical epics. The problem is most acute in John D. Smith's case, when he observes that "goddesses are relatively unimportant in the *Mahābhārata* and the *Rāmāyaṇa,* but they play a major rôle in many vernacular epics," often bringing about "a war of destruction that will annihilate the heroes" (Smith, forthcoming). What about Draupadī? Or even Sītā? In suggesting that these are the right questions, I am, of course, aware that I am generating them in part from what I have found in the Tamil Draupadī cult, which in effect stands midway between the classical *Mahābhārata* and such regional folk epic traditions. I am further suggesting that amid the various and seemingly arbitrary clusters of incarnations in the different folk epic traditions, there is one central consistency. That is a heroine who represents the goddess through an imagery that clarifies itself, at least in some small but significant part, in relation to the imagery of Draupadī: not the Draupadī of the classical epic, however, so much as the Draupadī of the Draupadī cult.

In the folk *Mahābhārata* of the Draupadī cult, Draupadī is a virgin, a *kaṉṉi:* she has no sexual relations with her five husbands, who are not the fathers of her five children (Hiltebeitel 1988:293–295). In fact, Tanaka (1987:409, n. 2) reports from a Draupadī festival in Tamil Sri Lanka that Draupadī is said to wear a yellow sari because it "is the colour of a virgin." She also has what I call low-status ritual service companions or guardians—one of them the above-mentioned Pōrmaṉṉaṉ and the other a Muslim—who ostensibly help her Kṣatriya husbands win the *Mahābhārata* war, but also serve the purpose, as guardians of the virgin goddess, of handling the impurities of bloodshed required by the *Mahābhārata*'s sacrifice of battle. These minimal features recur in the three regional folk epics just mentioned that link up with the *Mahābhārata.* There are the low-status ritual service companions (Cāmpukā in the *Elder Brothers Story;* Kannama and others in the *Epic of Panāḍu;* the four Banāphars and the one Muslim Mīrā Tālhan, the reincarnation of Bhīma, in the *Ālhā*) who serve not only the dominant caste heroes who represent the Kṣatriya ideal, but the heroine from that real or purported Kṣatriya caste who represents the virgin goddess. In each case this virgin heroine is the pivotal female figure in bringing about the climactic episodes of the respective great battles. And in each case, it is the nonconsummation of her marriage that stands as one of the primary fatalities that shapes the deaths of the major heroes: the real or purported Kṣatriyas no less than the low-status service companions. Finally, each of these "Kṣatriya" virgin heroines is linked directly with Draupadī. Taṅkāḷ in the *Elder Brothers Story* and Bēlā in the *Ālhā* are reincarnations of Draupadī.[17] And Māncāla in the *Epic of Palnāḍu* has a pet parrot named Draupadī, the parrot itself being one of Draupadī's iconographic emblems and a metonym for her forest wildness in the Tamil Draupadī cult (Hiltebeitel 1988: 263–264).

The consistencies in the ways these three regional folk epics tie such *Mahābhārata*-related themes together are, of course, enlightening for their contrasts with the *Mahābhārata*. It makes a large difference whether Draupadī is a sexually active wife who incarnates the goddess primarily in the form of the fickle and favor-bestowing Śrī, or a virgin who incarnates the goddess primarily in the destructive capacities of Durgā (with shades as well of Kālī). In the first case, she is an image of the "prosperity" of the sacrifice that will always accrue ultimately to the rightful kings, who happen to be her husbands. In the latter, though, she is an image of the goddess of victory to whom warrior heroes willingly and chastely dedicate—that is, sacrifice—their lives in battle. Bēlā in the *Ālhā* and Māncāla in a variant of the *Epic of Palnāḍu* (Chandra Sekhar 1961: 184) actually disguise themselves as warriors to avenge the deaths of their husbands: the husbands who leave them virgins.[18] In all this, the regional folk epics introduce a tragic modality that is absent in the *Mahābhārata*. In the classical epic, the Pāṇḍavas, wedded to Śrī, are victorious. But in the regional folk epics, there is a turning of the tables. In two of them, the *Ālhā* and the *Elder Brothers Story,* it is the reincarnated Pāṇḍavas—still the central heroes—who must taste defeat. And in the *Epic of Palnāḍu,* in which it is not the Pāṇḍavas who are reincarnated but their son Abhimanyu, as the eldest of a set of seven youthful brothers, death in battle comes to one and all. In the regional folk epics, the links between the virgin goddess and the land require the regional heroes to authenticate the sacrifice of battle in these different, but still victorious, terms; ultimately, that is, through their own pure self-offerings to the territorial goddess.[19]

Beyond the links mentioned already (reincarnations, Māncāla's parrot), these three regional folk epics vary in the extent to which they go further in linking their virgin heroines with Draupadī. In each case, however, there is at least one moment where we are reminded of the hair and the saris. Māncāla's case, again the least conspicuous and most uncertain, concerns the sari. At the crucial point where Bāluḍu, her husband, is finally alone with her, she must allay his advances and prevent her disrobing to guarantee that he will die as the "bridegroom of battle." This she accomplishes by breaking her pearl necklace (which was given her by Brahma Nāyuḍu, Viṣṇu incarnate: the figure who corresponds to Kṛṣṇa then setting Bāluḍu to the task of finding the strewn pearls, and hiding "the chief pearl in the folds of her garment."[20] In Taṅkāḷ's case, once her twin brothers (incarnations of Arjuna or Yudhiṣṭhira and Bhīma) have died, she burns alive their widows (with whom the chaste brothers had never slept), and then "tying her sari tightly, and letting loose the thousand strands of hair," she sets out to find—and momentarily revive—the brothers (Beck 1975:284). Earlier in this folk epic, Taṅkāḷ's and the twins' mother, Tāmarai, whose penance is compared with that of Arjuna, had twice been dragged by the hair: once by her clansmen, once by their "black watchman" (idem., 90–92, 152–153). In these cases it is rather clear that the *Mahābhārata,* and probably the Draupadī cult itself, are being evoked, but in fragmented ways.[21]

But the richest evocations of Draupadī are those involving Bēlā in the *Ālhā,* and it is worth summarizing the pertinent portions of that epic to show how this is the case, and to suggest something of the deep (and not superficial) level at which the *Mahābhārata* imbricates such regional folk epics.[22] Bēlā is the reincarnation of Draupadī. Her brother Tāhar is the reincarnation of Karṇa. And their father is Prithīrāj Cauhān, king of Delhi, who draws the kings of Mahōbā and Kanauj into the pyrrhic war that, even though he wins it, leaves the Rajputs decimated and North India open to the Muslim takeover at the beginning of the thirteenth century.

When Bēlā reaches age twelve, her father sends Tāhar out with the customary challenge-invitation to all the *rājā*s to come seek her hand by fighting. But Prithīrāj instructs Tāhar not to go to Mahōbā lest the "low"-caste Banāphars seek the bride. The Banāphars are in some accounts reputed to have Ahīr, or cowherd, mothers; primary among them are Ālhā, reincarnation of Yudhiṣṭhira, and Ūdan, who seems in certain respects to recall Kṛṣṇa but is not identified as any hero's reincarnation.[23] The conditions are too severe for any of the *rājā*s to seek the bride. Finally, the Banāphars learn of the situation and force Tāhar to accept the betrothal of his sister to the prince of Mahōbā, whom the Banāphars serve and treat in many ways as a brother, the Chandēl Rājput prince Brahmā, son of the Mahōbā king Parmāl. Brahmā is the reincarnation of Arjuna. It is the Banāphars who meet all the challenges that secure his wedding, upstaging all the Rājputs in Prithīrāj's entourage as well as Parmāl.

When it comes to the offering of presents to the bride, "Bēlā sees the pearls sent her by Parmāl and throws them away, crying that they are poor ornaments of modern times. She must have the jewels of the Dwāpara Yuga (or the age when she existed as Draupadī)" (Waterfield and Grierson

1923 : 198). Ālhā secures these, showing his willingness to offer his head to Śāradā Devī, the patron goddess of Mahōbā, and then learning where Draupadī's treasure has been buried. Note here again the link between the goddess, the heroine, and the land which yields the treasure. Draupadī's treasure seems to include only jewels, and no saris. But we have seen in the case of Māncāla how jewels and saris are linked as symbols of the heroine-goddess's apparel (see Hiltebeitel 1980–81, 1985 : 41–48).

The Banāphars then accompany Brahmā to the wedding ceremony and protect him through the seven circuits around the wedding post as Prithīrāj's allies try to kill him. Finally, Brahmā is invited into the women's apartments to eat the wedding breakfast, and "Ūdan insists on accompanying him as 'best man.'" When they are seated, Chauṇṛā, Prithīraj's Brahman minister and an incarnation of Droṇa, who has dressed himself as a woman, stabs Ūdan in the side. Bēlā then comes, "cuts her little finger, puts her blood into the wound, and it heals at once" (Waterfield and Grierson 1923 : 199). One is struck by the similarities between this incident and Draupadī's stanching of Kṛṣṇa's blood in the folk reworkings of the Rājasūya. That episode too hinges on Kṛṣṇa's status as the "best man": he throws his discus at Śiśupāla, and as a result cuts his finger, because Śiśupāla had challenged Bhīṣma's assessment that Kṛṣṇa was the best man among all present. Yet what is striking here is the seeming inversion. Draupadī does not take the tip of her sari to stanch the cut in Kṛṣṇa's finger. She cuts the tip of her own finger to heal the cut of Ūdan. Considering that she never has sexual relations with Brahmā, and thus never joins blood with him in that metaphoric sense, this mixing of blood with Ūdan must have some special significance. In any case, even after all these trials the Mahōbā party does not get to take the girl home, for Prithīrāj reveals at the last moment that "it is the custom of his house never to send the bride to her husband's home immediately after the wedding, but that he will let her go in a year" (idem., 196–199).

This promise Prithīrāj has no intention of keeping, and it is its breach that leads to final war. He conspires with Tāhar and Chauṇṛā to deceive Brahmā by again dressing Chauṇṛā as a woman, this time to look as if he is Bēlā. When Brahmā rides forth from Mahōbā to receive his bride, the disguised Chauṇṛā and Tāhar mortally wound him and return to Delhi. Here, the interests of Bēlā and the Banāphars finally converge: the Banāphars seek to avenge the dying Brahmā by bringing Bēlā to him; and Bēlā writes to Ūdan to bring her "home" to Mahōbā so that she can be with her dying husband. Ūdan disguises the Mahōbā and Kanauj forces and gets Prithīrāj to hire them to guard Bēlā, since they are great warriors and he fears Ūdan's attack. Ūdan plays dice with Lākhan, the prince of Kanauj and incarnation of Nakula. As he throws, Lākhan says, "If Bēlā is true I win" (idem., 262). Bēlā overhears and sends a servant girl to find out who is taking her name in vain. In effect, her chastity, like Draupadī's, has become the decisive stake of a dice match. When she finds it is Ūdan, she curses him for allowing Brahmā's fall, and he tells her what he had done to try to avoid it. She then tells him of her seven births, from the first, when she and Brahmā were fish,[24] to her sixth as "Draupadī, the wife of Arjuna, but called the wife of five husbands," and this one, the seventh, as Bēlā, "imprisoned by her father, who has killed her husband." In all seven, she says, "she has had the same fate, never to be really united with her beloved" (idem.).

It is not clear whether this recurrent separation reflects the situation in the classical *Mahābhārata*, where Draupadī's polyandry might be said to prevent her from being "really" united with Arjuna, or the situation in a folk epic perception of Draupadī like that in the Draupadī cult, where Draupadī is a virgin. Whatever the case, Bēlā then prods Ūdan and his men to bear her away to Brahmā, revealing that two of them—Lākhan and the Muslim Mīrā Tālhan—were previously her husbands Nakula and Bhīma. These two then conduct her litter out of Delhi. She pauses to collect her jewelry, worship the goddess, and prophesy that in three months and seventeen days Delhi will be sacked and every woman there become a widow. After various skirmishes, she is brought before Brahmā (262–263).

Arriving, she tends to him and "utters a great cry of 'Awake, awake, my beloved,' and he returns to consciousness" (265). He calls her a traitor's daughter and orders her dismissal, but she convinces him that she shares his cause. He replies that "if anyone will bring him the head of Tāhar he will live again" (idem.). Bēlā then promises to kill her own brother: Karṇa reincarnate, a fitting echo of the undying hostility and incompatibility of Karṇa and Draupadī.[25] Disguised as Brahmā, whom she presents as having recovered from his wounds, Bēlā demands the remaining half of her own dowry and challenges Tāhar to bring it lest she burn down the city of Delhi. While she fights her brother her sleeve is torn, revealing her woman's bangles. Chauṇṛā warns Tāhar, but too late, and she decapitates Tāhar and brings this head to Brahmā. Brahmā challenges her to become a satī and then dies, thankful to her for having shown him his enemy's head. Bēlā then calls for Ūdan to help her perform satī by obtaining wood for her funeral pyre from her father's grove of sandalwood. The Mahōbā and Kanauj forces cut down the sandal and bring it to Mahōbā after routing the Delhi army, but Bēlā says it is damp, and that she now needs the dry sandalwood from the twelve pillars in her father's audience-chamber. Ūdan is reluctant: it will mean certain death for all. But she threatens curses and insists the time for satī is short. And so the great war is joined. After several battles, the sandal pillars are brought to Mahōbā. Bēlā instructs Ūdan to build the pyre. "She puts on all her ornaments, dresses herself in her bridal array, and ascends" to join the corpse of her husband (271).

Hearing of her intention, Prithīrāj and his forces now arrive to protest that only a Rājput of the Mahōbā Chandēl family of Parmāl and Brahmā can light the pyre, not any of the low-caste Banāphars. But Bēlā has commanded Ūdan to light it, and so he intends to do. Grave fighting then erupts again, with many dying, including Mīrā Tālhan. And in the midst of all the fighting, while her pyre remains unlit, "as no one had been able to set the fire alight, Bēlā lets her hair hang loose. A flame issues from it, and the pyre at once bursts into a blaze, so that with the corpse she is consumed" (271). The battle continues while the pyre burns, and after nearly all the great heroes beside Ālhā and Prithīrāj have died, all the other widows consume themselves in it (273).

What is striking is that the Draupadī who is incarnated in Bēlā is more like the Draupadī of Draupadī cult folk traditions than she is like the Draupadī of the classical *Mahābhārata*. Not only are there the themes already noted: her virginity, her low status and Muslim guardians, her healing of Ūdan. The closing episode of creating the purifying satī pyre for all the heroes' widows also has a close counterpart in Draupadī cult mythology, where the corresponding myth explains Draupadī's postwar firewalk. And there satī is the analogous scene, already noted, in which Taṅkāḷ brings about the satī of her sisters-in-law in the *Elder Brothers Story* (Hiltebeitel 1988:440–42). Let us just note that unlike Bēlā, Draupadī and Taṅkāḷ do not die in the fires they set. Neither of them, however, sets the fire with her hair, although, as noted earlier, Draupadī may protect her firewalking devotees' crossing of the fire with her invisible spread of hair. In terms of violent and destructive power, the only comparable scene involving Draupadī's hair is that of her Mēlaccēri temple icon. And here there is a curious correspondence, for one of the names I have found for the Gingee king who gets the hair of the icon flashed in his eyes is Pirutivīrāja, quite plausibly a Tamil equivalent for the name Prithīrāj (idem., 99–100). Is it possible that this name retains a memory of Rājput folklore? It is not only the Telugu Nayaks who held sway in Gingee. So also, for a brief period, did the Rājput line of the ballad hero Rāja Desing, from Bundelkhand, the region of Mahōbā. It is admittedly a long shot, but the hair of the icon that blinds king Cunītaṉ-Pirutivīrāja could in some minds have been linked with the hair that lit the fire in defiance of King Prithīrāj of Delhi.

In short, and in closing, there may well be an underground folk *Mahābhārata*. But it cannot be monolithic. It has no prototype outside the Sanskrit text (which can never be assumed to have fallen out of the "folk epic" frame of reference). If such a folk *Mahābhārata* exists, however, it would seem to be centered on images of the goddess and the control of the land. Its lines of transmission and adaptation are too vast to ever trace fully. But those lines that do emerge suggest the crossing of many geographical and linguistic boundaries, and symbols and motifs that recur in a wide spectrum of "reflexive" and interpenetrating genres: from *Mahābhārata* vernaculars to folk dramas, from folk dramas to ritual idioms, from ritual idioms to temple tales, from temple tales to sisters' tales, from sisters' tales to regional folk epics, from regional folk epics to *Mahābhārata* vernacularizations.

Notes

1. In 1979 I wrote an article (Hiltebeitel 1979) in which I tried to bring into one focus a discussion of Draupadī's saris and hair, themes that were treated separately in Hiltebeitel 1980 and 1981. Some of the cosmological and theological formulations worked out in those papers remain significant for the present discussion. I argued that the epic Draupadī is already an image of the goddess in her totality: not only as Śrī-Lakṣmī, whom she explicitly incarnates, but as Bhūdevī (the goddess Earth), Kālarātri (the "Night of Time"), Mūla-Prakṛti (primal matter), and with intimations of Durgā and Kālī; in her relations to Viṣṇu-Kṛṣṇa and to figures linked with Śiva; in her role with respect to the turn of the *yuga*s and the relieving of the Earth's burden; in relation to the Earth's potential dessication (it is the solar Karṇa who orders Draupadī stripped) and resubmergence at the "occasional" *pralaya*, the *pralaya* at the end of a *kalpa* that burns and dissolves the Earth as the nucleus of the triple world through the agencies of fire, wind, and water; and in connection with symbols that portray the further potential for the unmixing and unleashing of all the elements—earth, water, fire, air, and ether—that is prelude to the final dissolution or *prākṛta pralaya* with its "unbraiding" of the "strands" or *guṇas* of matter (see especially 1981: 210–211). I will argue here that Draupadī's saris and hair retain such theological and cosmological resonances in Draupadī's cult folklore, especially in connection with the elements earth, fire, and fluids (a triad of elements that also finds vivid staging in the Peter Brook "Mahābhārata").

2. Dumézil treats these three levels hierarchically and, in effect, chronologically, with myth the most privileged and formative, epic its "transposition," and the "romanesque" as afterthought, introduced to tie the other two together. There

is no reason to accept either the chronological or the hierarchical implications of such formulations in the supposed formation of the text. As concerns *Mahābhārata* folklore, the categories themselves would seem to collapse, or at least be continually permeable.

3. This is a well-known maxim, but I can cite it only from oral traditions such as the mention of it by Robert P. Goldman and A. K. Ramanujan at different conferences.

4. The chief boy actors in the Rām Līlā at Ramnagar (Varanasi) "must be brahmans, well-behaved, with 'good looks'" (Schechner 1983:265); indeed, the Maharaja himself is a Brahman (266).

5. Let me insist again on the continuity between classical and folk perceptions of the *Mahābhārata;* cf. note 1.

6. Frasca 1984:1–400, translates a performed version of the first part of this play. I discuss the relation between this performed version and the corresponding portion of Irāmaccantira Kavirāyar's text in Hiltebeitel 1988:228. n. 7; 230–231.

7. I thank Pon Kothandaraman of the Department of Tamil Literature, University of Madras, for his help with my reading of these passages. Responsibility for all errors is, of course, my own.

8. Richard Frasca indicates (personal communication) that in performances of this play by troupes in North Arcot the chain of saris was not linked up to form a circle. As I have seen it performed at Tindivanam (1981) and Mēlaccēri (1986), the first saris are pulled out straight, linked end to end, without forming a circle. Then, when Duḥśāsana tries again, the circle is formed.

9. Both versions can be seen in my video film, "Lady of Gingee: South Indian Draupadī Festivals, Part I" (available through University of Wisconsin, South Asia Films). See also Hiltebeitel 1988:236 and n. 22.

10. The bracketed addition is found in a different edition of Irāmaccantira Kavirāyar's play (1968:80). The Tamil of the addition reads: "*koṭi cūriyap pirakācamāṇa cēlaikaḷ, vitavita vācamakōcaramāy.*" The question mark raises my uncertainty about the closing part.

11. For summaries of the three versions, further discussion, and different considerations, see Hiltebeitel 1988:93–97.

12. My thanks again to Madeleine Biardeau for supplying me with this amusing variant; see Hiltebeitel 1988:344 and n. 15.

13. With regard to the classical discussion of folklore diffusion by Kaarle Krohn, the following reservations may be noted as bearing on distinctive features of Indian *Mahābhārata*-related regional folklores: (1) The statement that the "most nationalistic creation of a people, its heroic poetry, seldom spreads across linguistic boundaries" (1971:146), would be inadequate to describe the Indian situation, and may likewise be inadequate to describe the Indo-European situation (see Hiltebeitel 1976:57–59). (2) The use of terms like "hallucinatory forms," "fantasy," and "superstition: (Krohn 1971:59, 138, 168–169, 170–171) are inadequate to account for the fluidities within what Krohn calls the "basic form" of this folklore; the distinctive features of this "basic form" are the presupposition of a "classical" *Mahābhārata* and the armatures of ritual. (3) The emphasis on "mechanical laws of thought and imagination in the rich variation of oral tradition" over and against "creative pro-

duction" (97–98) seems to push what are otherwise good insights to an unnecessary "superorganic" extreme; cf. Dundes 1965:219–220.

14. More work needs to be done to see whether a similar interconnectedness can be found in the north relative to the south. So far, from what is known of folk *Mahābhārata* traditions in Garhwal, the Kurukṣetra area, Nepal, and through the *Ālhā* (see below), there is nothing to suggest a comparable contiguity.

15. I thank John D. Smith for letting me see this latter work in advance of publication.

16. The *Kāṭamarāju Kathā* is associated with Golla herders (Narayana Rao 1986:141, 144), the *Pābūjī* story is patronized primarily by the Rebārī caste of shepherds and camel herders (Smith 1986:53).

17. Beck 1982:182, indicates that Taṅkāḷ is considered an incarnation of Draupadī only in written versions of the *Elder Brothers Story*. The fact that this relation is not found in the bardic version she recorded does not, however, guarantee that it is not found in oral variants at all.

18. Each goes to battle in her husband's guise, riding his horse.

19. I would like to thank Arjun Appadurai for his editorial reflections on the anthropological implications of the argument here, suggesting that "the underlying structure which accounts for the hook-up of Draupadī as a goddess to the problem of landed dominance, has to do with the link of purity, power, and status," and more particularly that the "purity of women is crucial to land-holding groups" as an index of such groups' control of, and rivalries over, the power and fertility of the soil (personal communication). For background, see Yalman 1963; Tambiah 1973:92–110; Hart 1973, Rajam 1986. See also Narayana Rao 1986:143 and, for some supportive data and thoughts of my own, Hiltebeitel 1988:8–9, 32–39, 74–75, 101–2, 222–23, 293–94, 397–98. The folk epics of Telugu trader castes also accentuate the role of virgin heroines, but in significant contrast with the emphases in the Telugu "martial epics" of landed castes; see Narayana Rao 1986:134–49, most notably the "central theme" contrast between "protection of caste integrity" in the trader caste epics with the "control of territory" in the "martial epics" (140) and the corresponding heightening of "control of women" by men in the martial epics (146). Cf. the virginization of Kaṇṇaki in folk variants of the "non-martial" *Cilappatikāram* (Beck 1972).

20. Roghair 1982:324 and 326. The former has "his garment," the latter "her garment." I assume the latter is correct.

21. Tāmarai's *tapas* pillar is much like the *tapas* tree that Arjuna climbs in Draupadī cult rituals; see Beck 1975:129–38.

22. On *Ālhā* variants, see Grierson 1985a and 1985b; on the less "mythological" (if not necessarily more historical) versions in the *Pṛthvirājā Rāso* and the *Paramāla Rāso,* see Dikshit 1977:141–54; Tod 1972:1, 489:96. What follows relies primarily on the so-called Elliot *Ālhā,* partly translated, with the rest summarized in Waterfield and Grierson (1923); on the collecting of the text itself see idem., 10–13. A more extensive discussion of the *Ālhā* is in preparation for my third volume of *The Cult of Draupadī.*

23. On the Ahīr mothers, see Waterfield and Grierson 1923:15, 59–60, 182. Along with those remarked upon below, Ūdan holds the following reminders of

Kṛṣṇa: he is dark (99, 204, 207); he is the youngest of the Banāphars; offered kingship, he refuses it to remain Brahmā's guardian (241); he uproots a post he is tied to (213); he plays the flute (75, 88, 97); he dances like a peacock (84); his future bride compares him with Kṛṣṇa and says their bed would be like Viṣṇu's heaven (92); and Mahōbā "was empty, as a garden without a bird, a court without a sovereign, a night without the moon, a lake without a lotus, a tree without its leaves, or a wife without her husband" (253). This is the language of *viraha*.

24. The implication that not only Bēlā and Brahmā but Draupadī and Arjuna were in their "primal" incarnation two chaste fish cannot help but remind one of the rich Draupadī cult fish symbolism connecting Draupadī and Arjuna, most notably the requirement at Draupadī's *svayaṃvara* (marriage choice) that Arjuna must win her by shooting his arrow through an elevated fish (see Hiltebeitel 1988: 21, 196–211). Like the folklore of Draupadī's saris and hair, the fish-target theme can be traced through other regional folk epic traditions linked with the *Mahābhārata;* see Roghair 1982: 148, 152 for the *Epic of Palnāḍu,* and Grierson 1885b: 258 for a variant of the *Ālhā.*

25. Note that their brother-sister relation can be taken as another strategy to preclude their marriage; on Draupadī and Karṇa's incompatibility in the *Mahābhārata,* see Hiltebeitel 1980: 103; 1988: 315–316.

References

Anderson, Mary

1971 *The Festivals of Nepal.* London: Allen and Unwin.

Beck, Brenda E. F.

1972 The Study of a Tamil Epic: Several Versions of *Silappadikaram* compared. *Journal of Tamil Studies* 1: 24–38.

1975 *The Story of the Brothers. An Oral Epic from the Coimbatore District of Tamilnadu.* Translated and privately circulated by the author.

1982 *The Three Twins: The Telling of a South Indian Folk Epic.* Bloomington: Indiana University Press.

Biardeau, Madeleine

1971–72 Brāhmaṇes et potiers. Article liminaire. *Annuaire de l'École Pratique des Hautes Études* 89: 31–55.

Chandra Sekhar A.

1961 Fairs and Festivals: 6. Guntur District. Part 7B of *Census of India 1961,* vol. 2: Andhra Pradesh, Delhi: Manager of Publications.

Dikshit, R. K.

1977 *The Candellas of Jejākabhukti.* Delhi: Abhinav Publishers.

Dumézil, Georges

[1968] 1974 *Mythe et épopée, vol. 1: L'Idéologie des trois fonctions dans les épopées des peuples indo-européens.* Paris: Gallimard.

Dundes, Alan

1965 *The Study of Folklore.* Englewood Cliffs, N.J.: Prentice-Hall.

Egnor, Margaret Trawick

1986 Internal Iconicity in Paṟaiyar 'Crying Songs.' In *Another Harmony:*

New Essays on the Folklore of India, Stuart H. Blackburn and A. K. Ramanujan, eds., pp. 294–344. Berkeley: University of California Press.

Eliade, Mircea

1963 *Patterns in Comparative Religion.* Translated by Rosemary Sheed. Cleveland and New York: Meridian.

Frasca, Richard

1984 The Terukkūttu: Ritual Theatre of Tamilnadu. Ph.D. dissertation, University of California, Berkeley.

Grierson, G. A.

1885a The Song of Alha's Marriage: A Bhojpuri Epic. *Indian Antiquary* 14:209–227.

1885b A Summary of The Alha Khand. *Indian Antiquary* 14:255–60.

Hart, George L., III

1973 Woman and the Sacred in Ancient Tamilnad. *Journal of Asian Studies* 32:233–250.

Hawley, John Stratton

1981 *At Play with Krishna: Pilgrimage Dramas from Brindavan.* Princeton, N.J.: Princeton University Press.

Hein, Norvin

1972 *The Miracle Plays of Mathurā.* New Haven, Conn.: Yale University Press.

Hiltebeitel, Alf

1976 *The Ritual of Battle: Krishna in the Mahābhārata.* Ithaca, N.Y.: Cornell University Press.

1979 Draupadī's Garments, Draupadī's Hair: Two Intangibles of the Goddess. Paper delivered at Association of Asian Studies Regional Meeting, George Washington University, Washington, D.C.

1980 Draupadī's Garments. *Indo-Iranian Journal* 22:97–112.

1980–81 Sītā *vibhūṣitā:* The Jewels for Her Journey. In Ludwik Sternbach Commemoration Volume, *Indologica Taurinensia* 8–9:193–200.

1981 Draupadī's Hair. In *Autour de la déesse hindoue,* Madeleine Biardeau, ed., pp. 179–214. *Puruṣārtha* 5.

1984 Two South Indian Oral Epics. *History of Religions* 24:164–173.

1985 Purity and Auspiciousness in the Sanskrit Epics. In *Essays on Purity and Auspiciousness,* Frédérique Apffel Marglin and John Carman, eds., pp. 41–54. *Journal of Developing Societies* 1.

1988 *The Cult of Draupadī, 1. Mythologies: From Gingee to Kurukṣetra.* Chicago: University of Chicago Press.

Irāmaccantira Kavirāyar

1968 *Śrī Makāpārata Vilācam allatu Cūtu-Tukilurital.* Madras: Ar. Ji. Pati Company.

1977 *Śrī Makāpārata Vilācam allatu Cūtu-Tukilurital.* Madras: Irattiṉa Nāyakar and Sons.

Irwin, John

19xx The Sacred Anthill and the Cult of the Primordial Mound. *History of Religions* 21:339–60.

Krohn, Kaarle
1971 [1926] *Folklore Methodology*. Translated by Roger L. Welsch. Austin and London: University of Texas Press.
Marglin, Frédérique
1985 *Wives of the God-King. The Rituals of the Devadasis of Puri*. Delhi: Oxford University Press.
Meyer, Eveline
1986 *Aṅkāḷaparamēcuvari: A Goddess of Tamilnadu, Her Myths and Cult*. Wiesbaden: Franz Steiner Verlag.
Narayana Rao, Velcheru
1986 Epics and Ideologies: Six Telugu Folk Epics. In *Another Harmony: New Essays on the Folklore of India*, Stuart Blackburn and A. K. Ramanujan, eds., pp. 131–66. Berkeley: University of California Press.
Neumann, Erich
1963 *The Great Mother: An Analysis of the Archetype*. Translated by Ralph Mannheim. Princeton, N.J.: Bollingen Series.
Oppert, Gustav
1893 *The Original Inhabitants of Bharatavarṣa or India*. Westminster: Archibald Constable & Co.; Leipzig: Otto Harassowitz.
Patil, N. B.
1983 *The Folklore in the Mahabharata*. Delhi: Ajanta Publications.
Rajam, V. S.
1986 *Aṇaṅku:* A Notion Semantically Reduced to Signify Female Sacred Power. *Journal of the American Oriental Society* 106:257–272.
Ramanujan, A. K.
1986 Two Realms of Kannada Folklore. In *Another Harmony: New Essays on the Folklore of India*, Stuart H. Blackburn and A. K. Ramanujan, eds., pp. 41–76. Berkeley: University of California Press.
Roghair, Gene H.
1982 *The Epic of Palnāḍu: A Study and Translation of Palnāṭi Vīrula Kathā*. Oxford: Clarendon Press.
Ruben, Walter
1944 Krishna. Konkordanz und Kommentar der Motive seines Heldenlebens. *Istanbuler Schrifter,* No. 17. Istanbul.
Sax, William S.
1986 The Pāṇḍav-Līlā: Self Representation in a Central Himalayan Folk Drama. Paper presented to the Graduate Seminar on South Asia, University of Chicago.
1987 Ritual and Performance in the Pandavlila. Paper presented at the American Academy of Religion Annual Meeting, Boston.
Schechner, Richard
1983 *Performative Circumstances from the Avant Garde to Ramlila*. Calcutta: Seagull Books.
Schechner, Richard, and Linda Hess
1977 The Ramlila of Ramnagar. *The Drama Review* 21, 3:51–82.
Schomer, Karine

1984 Cycle and Episode in a North Indian Oral Epic. Paper presented at the Association of Asian Studies Annual Meeting, Washington, D.C.

Shulman, David Dean

1985 *The King and the Clown in South Indian Myth and Poetry.* Princeton, N.J.: Princeton University Press.

Sivathamby, Kartigesu

1981 *Drama in Ancient Tamil Society.* Madras: New Century Book House.

Smith, John D.

1986 Where the Plot Thickens: Epic Moments in Pābūjī. *South Asian Studies* 2:53–64.

1989 Scapegoats of the Gods: The Ideology of the Indian Epics. In *Oral Epics in India,* Stuart H. Blackburn, Peter J. Claus, Joyce B. Flueckiger, and Susan S. Wadley, eds. Berkeley: University of California Press.

Forthcoming Pābūjī the God. Chapter 5 of the author's forthcoming book on the Pābūjī epic.

Tambiah, S. J.

1973 Dowry and Bridewealth, and the Property Rights of Women in South Asia. In *Bridewealth and Dowry,* Jack Goody and S. J. Tambiah, eds., pp. 59–169. Cambridge: Cambridge University Press.

Tanaka, Masakazu

1987 *Sacrifice for Power: Hindu Temple Rituals and Village Festivals in a Fishing Village, Sri Lanka.* Senri: National Museum of Ethnology.

Taṉikācala Mutaliyār, Tiṇṭivaṉam

1979 *Turōpatai Kuṟavañci Nāṭakam.* Madras: Irattiṉa Nāyakar and Sons.

Tod, James

1972 [1829] *Annals and Antiquities of Rajasthan or the Central and Western Rajpoot States of India.* London: Routledge and Kegan Paul.

Venkatesa Acharya, Kumbaluru

1981 *Mahabharata and Variations: Perundevanar and Pampa (A Comparative Study).* Kurnool: Vyasaraja Publications.

Wadley, Susan

1976 Brother, Husbands, and Sometimes Sons: Kinsmen in North Indian Ritual. *Eastern Anthropologist* 29:149–70.

Waterfield, William, trans. (partial), and George Grierson, ed.

1923 *The Lay of Alha. A Saga of Rajput Chivalry as Sung by Minstrels of Northern India.* London: Oxford University Press.

Yalman, Nur

1963 On the Purity of Women in the Castes of Ceylon and Malabar. *Journal of the Royal Anthropological Institute of Great Britain and Ireland* 93:25–58.

Zarilli, Philip

1984 *The Kathakali Complex; Actor, Performance, Structure.* New Delhi: Abhinav Publications.

Velcheru Narayana Rao and David Shulman

15. The Powers of Parody in Nāyaka-Period Tanjavur

We may begin with a folktale, recorded at the turn of the century, but presenting itself as belonging to a period much like that which will occupy us below—seventeenth-century Tanjavur, before the final collapse of the Vijayanagara superstate:[1]

> In the town of Tanjavur there lived a poor but clever Brahmin priest named Keśava Bahaṭṭa. He earned about two pennies [*paṇam*] a day, one of which he would spend on his household expenses; with the other penny he would hold court each night on a cot hidden in the back room of a vast, seven-storied mansion owned by the rich merchant, Navakoṭi Nārāyaṇa Ceṭṭi. The mansion opened on to West High Street in Tanjavur, but each night Keśava Bhaṭṭa would crawl into the back room from a door in East High Street, where he would be served, as he sat on his cot, by a carpenter, a cobbler, an oil-vendor, and a maker of turbans—each of whom received a quarter of a penny for their service. The carpenter would bring the cot, the oilman would keep two torches burning, the cobbler would bring a pair of costly shoes, and the tier of turbans would adorn the Brahmin's head with a regal turban. In addition, four peons were engaged, for ten gold coins a month, to wait upon the Brahmim, who insisted that he be called the "Subahdar of the Cot." At the tenth hour of the night, the lights would be extinguished, the shoes and turban would be removed, the carpenter would carry away the cot, and Keśava Bhaṭṭa would dismiss his servants and return home. The merchant, Navakoṭi Nārāyaṇa Ceṭṭi, had no knowledge of these nocturnal events in the back of his palace.
>
> After one month, the Subahadar of the Cot had a problem: he paid the four artisans every night, but how was he to pay the four

peons their golden coins? Seeing no way out, he decided to die by hanging himself from a tree in the garden of his house. As he placed the rope around his neck, a voice rang out: "Dig at the root of this tree, and you will find seven pots of gold, each with a lakh of gold coins."

The Subahdar came down from the tree, dug up the pots full of gold, and hid them without informing his wife. He paid the four peons their salary, gave them an additional five gold coins as a present, and then sent two of them on a mission to the capital city of Vijayanagara; there they were to deliver the seven pots of gold (except for a hundred coins from each pot, which the Subahdar kept in reserve for himself) to Indumukhi, the favorite courtesan of the emperor, with a letter which read: "Having heard of your unparalleled beauty, and without wishing to rival the Emperor, your lord, we are sending you this small gift, to cover one day's expenses for your ladyship; please favor us by accepting it. (Signed), the Subahdar of the Cot."

When Indumukhi received the gold and read the letter, she was amazed: what great lord could send such an enormous sum as payment for one day's expenses? She was unable to form a clear impression of the Subahdar from the peons who had brought his gift. But, believing him to be the wealthiest man in the whole world, she sent back with these peons a costly throne inlaid with diamonds and other precious stones, with a letter thanking the Subahdar for his gift and declaring herself to be his humble maidservant. After twenty-one days' journey, the peons arrived back in Tanjavur.

There they were amply rewarded by the happy Subahdar. But what was he to do with the precious gift? Having heard of a still more beautiful courtesan called Nurzana, concubine to the Emperor at Delhi, he decided to send the throne to her with a note similar to the previous one. So the peons set off for the three-months' journey to Delhi, where Nurzana, in her turn, was astonished to receive, as a "small gift" from the Subahdar of the Cot, a throne such as even the Emperor of India had never owned. And she wrote back to the Subahdar, thanking him and expressing the hope that someday, perhaps within a year or two, she would be able to visit him in person. Since this visit was still an indefinite wish, and no counter-gift had come back to Tanjavur, the Subahdar put the matter out of his mind and enjoyed his subahdari for an entire year.

But his peons, who had become rich from his presents, became the talk of the town, and soon everyone knew of the Subahdar of the Cot and his nightly council in the Ceṭṭi's house. Finally, even Navakoṭi Nārāyaṇa himself heard of the matter and paid a sudden visit, one night, to the back quarters of his palace. Furious, he had his servants seize the Subahdar, whose peons and other servants fled for their lives. Keśava Bhaṭṭa explained to the merchant how he had come to play at being a subahdar, but he said nothing about the treasures and correspondence with Indumukhi and Nurzana; Navakoṭi Nārāyaṇa Ceṭṭi laughed at the tale, took pity on the poor Brahmin and his pretense, and, as punishment for his pride, took him into his service as his head cook.

Késava Bhaṭṭa served the merchant faithfully and well, and soon became, in addition to being cook, his adviser on various affairs; he also managed to bring his former peons into the Ceṭṭi's service. After one month, Nārāyaṇa Ceṭṭi, acting on the Brahmin's advice, set off with a large entourage on a pilgrimage to Benares, in the hope of being granted a child by the god. On the way he visited various other sacred shrines and rivers, including the Tuṅgabhadrā, in the vicinity of Vijayanagara city. He stayed for several days in the city, where, one night, he caught a glimpse of a woman of unearthly beauty in the top story of a fine palace. Nārāyaṇa Ceṭṭi fell madly in love. But the woman was none other than the courtesan Indumukhi, jealously guarded by the emperor from contact with any other man. After three days, the merchant, sleepless and haggard from hopeless desire, confided in his cook, Késava Bhaṭṭa: "I would," he said, "give all my wealth for a single moment with that lady." Said the Brahmin: "I can arrange it for you—and it is enough if you give me but half of your vast riches and restore me to my Subahdari in the back of your palace." The incredulous Nārāyaṇa Ceṭṭi agreed.

At the Brahmin's insistence, the merchant clothed Keśava Bhaṭṭa in his own fine garments and jewels, and retired himself, in the guise of a humble servant, to an inner chamber. The Subahdar's former peons were also royally attired, and the two of them who had formerly gone on the mission to Indumukhi were sent to her again with a letter summoning her to the Subahdar's presence. In a moment, she stood before him and shyly and humbly offered to serve him as his slave. The Subahdar, however, did not even glance in her direction. "You surely understand," he said, "that we are far above your humble company; but if you are true to your promise, and as a sign of your faithfulness, I order you to go at once to the next room and offer your service to one of our attendants, who is waiting there." Like a slave at the master's command, Indumukhi at once entered the inner chamber, where she spent the night with Navakoṭi Nārāyaṇa Ceṭṭi.

By morning, she was back in her palace, and Keśava Bhaṭṭa had resumed his place in the kitchen. At his urging, the pilgrimage proceeded as planned, while he continued to act as the merchant's servant—although Nārāyaṇa Ceṭṭi now treated his cook with new and signal respect. He questioned him many times as to the secret of his power over Indumukhi, but to no avail; and he never ceased to marvel at the fact that all his wealth had been quite useless, and that only the word of his Brahmin cook had brought the woman to his bed. Upon their return from Benares to Tanjavur, Navakoṭi Nārāyaṇa Ceṭṭi kept his word and gave half his riches to the Brahmin; his great palace was also divided, so that the Subahdar of the Cot could now hold court, openly and lavishly, in the eastern half, where he had once kept his nocturnal councils. Thus a few months went by.

One day a letter arrived by messenger addressed to the Subahdar of the Cot. In it was a message from Nurzana, the Delhi Emperor's concubine, announcing that she would be arriving the day after tomorrow in Tanjavur and would come to pay her respects to the Subahdar in person. This news threw the Subahdar into consternation: he was now, it is true, a wealthy man in his own right, but surely not nearly as wealthy as Nurzana must imagine from his former gift. How could he receive her without disabusing her of her illusion? Unable to resolve this dilemma, he decided to kill himself and went back to his garden to hang himself on the tree. Once again, as he was arranging the rope, a voice from heaven spoke to him and asked him what he wanted. "I wish to keep Nurzana away from Tanjavur," said the Brahmin, "and I cannot do so without help from the gods." "What is it you need?" asked the voice. Said the Brahmin: "I must borrow the services of Rambhā, Urvaśī, Tilottamā, and the other *apsaras*es for two hours in the morning, the day after tomorrow. They are to collect cow dung on Trichy Road, on the outskirts of Tanjavur; if questioned by Nurzana, they must state that they are the sweepers in the house of the Subahdar of the Cot. After the two hours, they can return to heaven." The god agreed to this request.

When the morning came, slightly before sunrise, a hundred divine women took up their posts on Trichy Road, at the entrance to

> Tanjavur, where they began collecting cow-dung in baskets made of gold. Soon the retinue of Nurzana appeared, with the courtesan herself in a fine palankeen carried behind. Seeing the amazing apparition on the road, the entire company came to a halt. Nurzana opened the curtain to see why they had stopped. Struck by the great beauty of the women before her, she asked them who they were. "My lady, we are the sweepers of the Subahdar of the Cot," they replied; "each morning we collect cow-dung to smear upon the walls of our lord's house." And they went on with their work without waiting for Nurzana to reply.
>
> The courtesan from Delhi was overcome with fear and wonder. For some moments she gazed at the women as she thought to herself: if these women, who are as beautiful as the very *apsaras*es of heaven, are merely the sweepers in the Subahdar's service, how great must be the beauty of the ladies in his palace! And, unwilling to put this observation to the test, she ordered her palankeen to be turned away from Tanjavur. (Natesa Sastri 1908 : 506–521)

This powerful tale is a story about power, about what constitutes and enhances and preserves power—that is, money, honor, display, and the various modes in which they come into play. Or, focusing on the central issue of the story from a different vantage point, we might say that this is a story about the compelling and creative power of illusion in the service of politics and status. Like so many folktales, this one is seriously engaged in articulating a particular vision of reality—one which is endowed with attributes of autonomy and cultural expressivity and also, we believe, with systemic features. We have before us the rudiments of a folk countersystem, with its own semantics and values, yet profoundly linked to what we shall refer to here, for the time being, as the courtly system of Nāyaka literature.

The poor Brahman, Keśava Bhaṭṭa, becomes, in effect, a king (note the symbolic interweaving of the two normally separated roles).[2] He does so with only very partial premeditation—his whole career actually begins with a private fantasy, which he insists on enacting even though he lacks the means to sustain it. At the end of the first month of his "subahdari," which is almost his last, he reaches the point of suicide because of this very disability. And this same point is later reached again, when he is actually at the height of his success, but again threatened with the ultimate disaster, a puncturing of the regal illusion from an outside source. Something here is, apparently, basic: "kingship" begins, we might hypothesize, as a kind of uncertain gamble, and can always revert to being no more than that. The king is a dice-player, as we well know from other Indian tales. But it is just here, in the élan with which he plays his game, that his power is forged. On the one hand, this power derives from the outrageous manipulation of illusion, a creative pretense lived out to the limit in circumstances that make its survival seem, at best, precarious. On the other hand, the very extremism in evidence here—playing the game, and investing in it, to an ultimate degree—seems to carry within it a certain coercive potential: this is what we see on the two occasions, at the beginning and at the end of the story, when Keśava Bhaṭṭa reaches the point of attempting suicide to avoid abandoning the illusion. In both cases, this ultimate threat, an all-or-nothing cast of the dice, produces the necessary result.

But there are other, more tangible aspects to the logic of this game. If kingship is a brazen gamble, the nurturing (in others) of an illusion heightened, we might almost say existentially, to the point of absurdity, then the economic basis of this traffic in pretense seems to lie in forms of asymmetrical exchange. The aspiring ruler has to give—in fact, he must give all, or nearly all, he has—and the resulting imbalance is the medium of his self-assertion and the precipitating cause of others' recognition of this claim. Service and other obligations flow necessarily out of the initial gift. But the game is one of one-upmanship, and the counter-gift inevitably follows, and inevitably produces a counter-counter-gift, elevated to a wider or still higher sphere (thus the movement in our story is from Tanjavur to Vijayanagara to Delhi to, at the end, the heaven of the gods). Each new round in the cycle raises the ante—this is not a system of orderly, reciprocal mutuality, or of redistribution rooted in reciprocity, but of symbolic interdependence in a competitive mode which constantly enlarges the sphere of interaction and pushes the major actors into new, more elaborate, and more risky exchanges. These are carried out in two disparate coinages, so to speak—one wholly material, and the other moral. Service can generate dependency, or the need to fulfill an obligation, no less than a gift of gold. It is this duality that the poor Brahman subahdar/cook/servant uses to capture his Ceṭṭi patron's "real" fortune.

Both coinages are, however, consistently inflated, as everyone knows—especially the folktale-teller, outside the story, and the Brahman hero within it. This is important: in a way, the entire tale is predicated on this awareness. The question is not, essentially, how real the illusion is—that is more a question for the royal court—but how effectively it can be used.

We see this most clearly at precisely the point where "reality" has seemingly destroyed the illusion forever—when the "subahdar" has had to confess his counterfeiting and has reverted to the status of servant, cook, and (Brahmanical) *mantrin* to the Ceṭṭi lord. If it were only a question of distinguishing true from false, the story should have ended here. Instead, "illusion" penetrates it in the alluring form of Indumukhi and, in the hands of the Brahman purveyor of illusion, will be externalized in concrete, and highly lucrative, form. A similar magical manipulation will take place at the conclusion of the story, with equally successful results (though not without another resort to the coercive suicide motif). In any case, the courtly investment in projected power displays is here turned on its head. The illusion of power turns out to be more real than nakedly visible power or accumulated wealth. Note, too, that in our tale there is no question of a zero-sum game, with an inevitable loser. The mode is rather that of having one's cake and eating it—perhaps, indeed, a dominant attitude in the south Indian folktale.[3]

And the lessons of the tale, for our purposes in approaching the court literature of this period? We note the existence of a countervision of power informed by a curious ambivalence. Power, we learn, is precariously balanced in falsehood—the tale itself consistently and deliberately punctures regal pretense as illusion. Note that major episodes of the story turn upon a kind of a fortiori argument: if the subahdar calls this a humble gift, what is the real measure of his wealth? Or, explicitly, at the conclusion: if these divine women are his sweepers, how beautiful must the ladies of his harem be? The hidden tenor of this logic might perhaps be formulated as follows: if such is the truth of kingship for Keśava Bhaṭṭa, how much more must this be the case for the Nāyaka king (or the local zamindar!). But—this is the other side the coin—the story also shows us how regal counterfeit comes true. Exposing the hollowness of the display does not preclude our successfully imitating it. In fact, the mimetic aspect of the story is at least as salient as its satirical, debunking quality. And, indeed, this is what we might expect—because the countersystem presented to us by the south Indian folktale is, not only in this case, much more extensive and complex than the analogous Bakhtinian ideal of an earthy, corporeal "grounding" in relation to the high culture's high-flown ideals (though these elements, as we shall see, do also exist in the context of seventeenth-century Tanjavur). The folktale is, precisely, a parody of, not a foil to, high-caste, Sanskritic models, a parody which is in some sense mortgaged to its object, which it only partly assimilates to its own radical, folk perspective. Indeed, mimesis infuses parody with its most penetrating power.

To pursue this a step further: parody, as the theorists of comedy have usually recognized, pivots on a hinge that swings in two directions—both toward, and away from, the parodied subject (which the parody partially constructs). By its very nature, it is simultaneously mimetic and subversive. Its mode is ambivalence, never simple, overt hostility. As Margaret Rose remarks in a recent study of literary parody, "Unlike satire . . . parody includes the 'victim' or object of its attack within its own structure" (Rose 1979 : 50). We will find this distinction useful as we turn to the literature of the Nāyaka court. Clearly, questions of illusion, identity claims, and self-awareness will remain highly relevant to our analysis. We can also hazard the hypothesis, on the basis of our story, that parody both embodies, and may reflectively illuminate and define, a more flexible ontology than is normally present in satire, which depends strongly on the perceived "reality" of its object; the complex parodic universe, even as it undermines the taken-for-grantedness of one reality, is perfectly capable of creatively investing in another, no less tenuous but possibly more compelling construction (think of Quixote). We can observe this process at work in several of the Nāyaka sources. For now, let us restate the analytical premise that has emerged from the above discussion, and which will guide us in what follows, in more abstract and formal terms: satire operates, in effect, with a single dominant code and in the context of clearly articulated boundaries of identity, reality, and ethical judgement; parody deliberately mingles domains and superimposes or interweaves contrasting visions, including competing notions of the real, while always allowing for the presence of at least two operative codes (cf. Duisit 1978). Keśava Bhaṭṭa's kingship is rooted in illusion, an illusion that is systematically exposed by the tale as part of its basic "programme"; the other essential thrust of the story is to establish this illusory kingship as entirely real.

Nāyaka Court Drama: The *Yakṣagāna* Corpus

We turn now to the literature of the Nāyaka courts of the late sixteenth and seventeenth centuries in Tamilnadu—a period when this area was ruled by three imported Telugu warrior dynasties established in the political centers of Senji in the north, Tanjavur in the Kaveri Delta, and Madurai in the south. In particular, our interest will focus on the Tanjavur court and on one of the major genres to emerge there—the so-called *yakṣagāna* dance dramas in Telugu. Unlike the *yakṣagāna* folk dramas still current in Karnataka (see Ashton and Christie 1977), the Telugu works of this class are cast in a resolutely classical mould—couched, for the most part, in "high" literary Telugu, each play with its clear attribution of authorship and a fixed text (although we should remember that these texts, as we have them in the surviving manuscripts, are really only scripts for performance). These plays, a large and fairly coherent corpus, constitute one of the major contributions of the southern poets to Telugu literature; we would also be justified in seeing them as perhaps the outstanding expression of the Nāyaka court's own image of itself, an image projected internally, to an audience of courtiers, poets, and the extended royal family, in a manner somewhat analogous to that of the Elizabethan court masques.

One of the most salient features of the genre is its incorporation of satirical, parodic, burlesque, or farcical elements, often in most unexpected ways and at critical points of the drama. Unexpected—because the *yakṣagānas,* certainly those of the common and heavily conventionalized romantic variety, seem intent above all upon constructing a familiar pattern of lyrical illusion centered on the figure of the king, patron of the drama and primary spectator at its performance. A synthetic version of this romantic type would go something like this: the king, duly eulogized in the opening verses as a paragon of virtue and of physical form, leaves his palace for his daily ritual procession (*ulā*), which takes him through the courtesans' quarter of Tanjavur; there, the women who see him from behind their latticed windows enter frenzied and hysterical states, sensuously and exhaustively described; one of these women exceeds the rest in the intensity of her love and somehow manages to assert a claim on the parading hero, perhaps by catching his eye, in any case arousing him to a reciprocal fury of desire. This mutual passion must now follow its inexorable course: each of the lovers suffers, alone, the torments of separation (*viraha*); the king may try to forget his sorrow by a hunting expedition, or by holding to his usual routine in the court, but these bring only temporary relief; sleepless, hallucinating, burned by the usually cooling rays of the moon, the woman reproaches Manmatha, god of desire, for having inflicted such misery on her; perhaps a *kuṟatti* or *kuṟavañci* tribal woman will come to tell her fortune, to comfort her with a prophecy of eventual union with her beloved; eventually, always through the intercession of a messenger or messengers (*dūti,* Tam. *tūtu*), this happy prophecy is fulfilled, and the courtesan joins the king's harem (as one among hundreds of other women—this is, we recall, a daily ritual). Note that the *yakṣagāna* always ends happily, with *sambhoga,* after what is in effect a rather moderate delay in gratification (unlike the pattern of the classical Sanskrit *nāṭaka,* for example). The king, whose infinite desirability is clearly one of the central themes of these plays, enacts the role of the delicate, not to say effete, *dhīralalita* hero of the Sanskrit *alaṅkāra* tradition, which is now brought down to earth, made accessible and visible to the eyes and ears of everyone at court.[4]

This is the essential pattern of the *Vijayarāghavakalyāṇamu* by the Brahman poet Kōnēṭi Dīkṣitulu, perhaps the most rounded and complete of all the Telugu *yakṣagānas,* from the end of our period. It is a fascinating play, precisely because of this all-embracing quality, which offers us a glimpse into the full-fledged self-vision, or, perhaps, self-serving illusion, of the Tanjavur court. It is thus important for us to observe the following scene at court, where the lovelorn king, Vijayarāghava, has convened his Brahman pandits for the usual displays of erudition and literary skill.

The poets and pandits arrive together, pushing and shoving one another on their way into the court, shouting in Tamil and Telugu:

—Hey, take it easy!
—Ayyā Ayaṅgār, why are you poking me?
—Where's your dhoti, Appan Ayaṅgār?
—Mādhava Śāstri, don't fall all over me!
—Gōpāla Bhaṭlu, what's happened to your turban?
—Wake up, Peddi Bhaṭlu!
—Koṇḍu Bhaṭlu, what's wrong with your earrings?

Seated at last, after prostrating before the king, they begin their program with a verse by Ciṭṭābaḷa Sōmayājulu:

Mannārudāsabhūpāla mahanīyaguṇāmbudhe
acañcalābhaktir astu bhavān gopālapādayoḥ

O King Mannārudása [Vijayarāghava], ocean of superb qualities,
may you have steadfast devotion to the feet of Gopāla.

Gōvinda Bhaṭlu has an objection: By Pāṇini 6.3.34[5] the crucial compound should read *acañcalabhakti,* not *acañcalābhakti;* if the poet is capable, let him answer this point. Sōmayājulu answers sarcastically: "Oh, you've got the *sūtra* quite correctly. Doesn't it say that before *priya* etc. the use of a masculine ending is prohibited? I've won this argument." Here the *madhyastha*-arbitrator has to intervene (he is still fixated on the use of the word *striyāḥ,* literally "women [gen.]", in the *sūtra*): "Stop this, look how many leaps you've taken! Are you saying that your wife is like a man [*puṃvad*] or not?"

This literalistic objection degenerates into further coarse remarks, which Sōmayājulu puts an end to by reminding his opponent that he is in the presence of the king; and, anyway, it is poetry (*kavitva*) that is the primary discipline (*pradhānavidya*). Time, then, for *samasyāpūraṇa,* the improvising of verses around a single line given by the opponent. Sōmayājulu offers the line: *vidyānidhir vijayarāghavasarvabhaumaḥ* Gōvinda Bhaṭlu easily completes the first three lines of the verse:

sadyo dadhāti sukaviprakarepsitārthān
hṛdyānavadyatarapadyaraseṣv abhijñaḥ
pradyotanapratimabāhumahābhirāmo—
vidyānidhir vijayarāghavasārvabhaumaḥ

He grasps at once the meanings intended by good poets;
he is familiar with the flavors of delightful verses;
he is gloriously handsome, his arms radiant as the sun—
is that treasure-house of wisdom, Vijayarāghava, King of the World!

But this modest display is, of course, only the beginning; another poet comes to the fore, one Sakalavidyāsārvabhaumuḍu, "King of all Sciences," who is able to improvise not only in Sanskrit but also in Prakrit, Śaurasenī, Māgadhī, Paiśācī-Cūḷikā, Apabhraṃśa, and Bhāṇḍīra (mixed). Another poet, Madhurakavi, translates these laudatory verses on the king into a Sanskrit *chāyā.*

Tiring of poetic contests, the pandits turn to logic (*tarka*). As our two original antagonists, Sōmayājulu and Gōvinda Bhaṭlu, are haggling over issues of causality, Sōmayājulu cites the case of a donkey who, arriving by chance (*daivād āgata*), stumbles over a pot; what is the cause (*kāraṇa*) of this donkey? The hackneyed example infuriates his opponent:

Gōvinda Bhaṭlu: "Why bring a donkey as an example?
Sōmayājulu: Because you, with your vain boasting, are a donkey.
Gōvinda Bhaṭlu: And you, by your boasting, are a dog.
Sōmayājulu: You're a hog.
Gōvinda Bhaṭlu [to the arbitrator]: Did you hear what he said?
Arbitrator: Isn't it bad enough that you heard it, do I have to hear it too?

Sōmayājulu: I'm expounding, and he keeps interrupting out of context. Are you really the son of a scholar?
Gōvinda Bhaṭlu: Yes, and until yesterday you were just a servant boy; now you've put on a turban and call yourself a scholar's son!
Sōmayājulu: And you were carrying kindling-wood for a choultry from some little lord's camp [*sāmantuni pāḷēnanuṇḍi*]. Now you're passing yourself off as a scholar who can dispute in court.
Gōvinda Bhaṭlu: What about you, until yesterday you were carrying out the choultry's garbage on your head—that's how you became bald and have to wear a hat. Why are you barking like a dog?
Sōmayājulu: You're braying like a donkey!
Gōvinda Bhaṭlu: I'll slap your cheeks.
Sōmayājulu: I'll knock out your teeth.
Arbitrator: What a fine discourse you're giving [*doḍḍa prasaṅgam cēsirōyi*]. You're both superb.
King [smiling]: They always dispute just like this. If you ask them to give a discourse, they grab one another's tufts and start kicking.
(Kōnēṭi Dīkṣitulu 1956 : 136–147)

Soon this edifying spectacle comes to an end, so that the king can return to the serious business of being miserably in love. The courtly satire speaks for itself: it is a kind of intellectual slapstick, realistic enough in its own way, which provides a certain relief from the neuraesthenic torments of the two lovers and from their conventional lyrical effusions. In general, this is a simple instance of well-targeted satire; but it is also worth noting, at least, that embedded within this satire, and thus perhaps contaminated by something of its spirit, are the series of improvised panegyric verses on Vijayarāghava, the drama's hero and king.

This is one type, the simplest to understand, of Nāyaka-period comedy at court. The next step involves weaving the comic antithesis far more intimately into the structure of the work, in true parodic fashion, so that it becomes a self-conscious commentary on the images and identities of the main protagonists. A good example is the *Hēmābjanāyikāsvayaṃvaramu* of Mannārudēva (Vijayarāghava's son), one of the most intriguing of the romantic *yakṣagānas*, which tells of the lovesickness and courtship of the god and his consort at Maṉṉārkuṭi, and of the Nāyaka king's necessary intervention to make their marriage possible; the play concludes with a ribald scene at the time of the wedding, in which the wives of the Brahman priests who have come to officiate exchange obscene comments on the realities of married life (see Narayana Rao and Shulman, forthcoming). The slow, lyrical progression from the lovers' first glimpse of one another to their final union here culminates in a moment of delightful comic deflation.

Tirukkuṟṟālakkuṟavañci

An interesting variation on this pattern of structural assimilation of the parodic, from a slightly later period, appears in the Tamil *kuṟavañci* plays. Although this genre has much older roots in Tamil literature,[6] and also exists in parallell expressions in the Tamil folk and folk-epic tradition,[7] its mature form as an integrated dance-drama complete with three major episodes seems to have emerged from the Tanjavur court: Pāpanāca Mutaliyār's *Kumpēcar kuṟavañci nāṭakam,* from the late seventeenth century (the reign of the Maratha king Ekoji, who is mentioned in the work) is the first full-fledged exemplar of the mature style, which has clearly assimilated the impact of the *kuṟavañci* episodes from the Telugu *yakṣagānas,* of Nāyaka times.[8] By far the most illustrious example of this type of work is Tirikūṭarācappakkavirāyar's *Tirukkuṟṟālakkuṟavañci,* which won the patronage of the Madurai Nāyaka ruler Muttuvijayaraṅgacokkanātha in the early eighteenth century. Let us look briefly at the composition of this uncannily moving poem.

Like so many of the *yakṣagānas*, this *kuṟavañci* begins with an *ulā*—the god's procession around the streets of Tirukkuṟṟālam. Here he is seen by the heroine of the play, Vacantavalli, who immediately falls into the usual state of utter incapacitation and lovesick stupor. The first third of the drama is given over to her lyrical laments, replete with the verbal plays and the standard tropes of the classical tradition:

Sleep?
Sleep doesn't come
any more.

Forget him?
The one who played this trick
on me?
I *can't* forget him.

You tell me that whoever is born a woman
should know no passion,
and I know it's true—

know, too,
that I am nothing, now
but passion
for that great lord. (43)

He saved three good demons from the Tripura fire,
but he won't put out the fire of desire
that is driving me mad.
He drew the mighty mountain to him
to make it his bow,
but he won't take my breasts, tall as mountains,
in his hands.

He drank poison and made it nectar,
a gift to the gods—
but he won't give me the joy
of draining poison
from my eyes, long as spears.

Everyone praises him,
the lord of Kuṟṟālam,
and he has compassion
for them all

and no compassion
at all
for me. (41)

Thus our heroine, in her sweet sorrow: but the real hero of the work, as we can see, is, of course, the god for whom she longs, thus exemplifying the yearnings of all his devotees. Like other Tamil *bhakti* poems of the medieval period,[9] the *kuṟavañci* mediates the god's presence—a presence usually enacted through an unsettling series of withdrawals and absences—by displacing our attention to another figure, who becomes central, expressive, and active in a way that the impassive deity cannot. The primary focus is thus on the inner emotional world of the worshiper (here, as so often, given a feminine persona and voice). In this sense, the mature *kuṟavañci* is perfectly in line with a central thrust of the medieval *bhakti* literary tradition (and, for that matter, with its analogues in the "secular" poetry of the royal courts).[10] But Tirikūṭarācappakkavirāyar also goes a step farther, a step which locates him at the end of the medieval period, in the Nāyaka tradition of reflexive and disjunctive parody incorporated into the texts of the parodied norm (as in the case of the courtly *yakṣagāna,*). For the *kuṟavañci* now unfolds into two further "acts." First, the Kuṟatti or Kuṟavañci fortuneteller, the gypsylike folk heroine familiar from folk-epic and local myth, arrives with her professional paraphernalia (her basket, her magic wand, *māttiraikkōl*) and her colorful costume; in a humorous scene that follows certain set patterns, she reads the heroine's palm, immediately determines the nature of her illness and the object of her love, and, in a delightful punning verse, assures her that the god will come to claim her as his lover. The heroine, though at first reluctant to concede that the Kuṟatti has made a correct diagnosis, loads her down with costly jewels and other presents. Then, in the concluding section of the play, we meet the Kuṟatti's husband, the exuberant bird-catcher Ciṅkaṉ—a Tamil Papageno—and his friend Nūvaṉ, as they set their traps for the birds on the Kuṟṟālam mountain. Ciṅkaṉ is looking for his wife—"Ciṅki," as he calls her—but first he has work to do; he sings, in a comic representation of Kuṟavar dialect, of the dignity of his profession:

> "Even the gods never looked down on bird-catching in the wild—didn't Rāma chase after a crow? Śiva wears the feather of a heron in his matted hair; Murukaṉ, with a child's mischief, took the peacock for himself; the god of this good town [= Śiva again] gave a goose to that Brahmin (Brahmā) to ride on; and the Thief [= Viṣṇu) has stolen an eagle as his mount!
>
> So come on, Kuḷuva—set the traps and catch those birds!" (95.4)

This, after the high-flown devotional rhetoric of Vacantavalli's love for the god of Kuṟṟālam, who is suddenly, marvelously reduced to the level of a Kuṟavaṉ hunter of birds! Ciṅkaṉ coarsely but delightfully unravels the whole fabric of delicately contrived emotion that the poet has woven for us in the earlier part of his work. We will not attempt to do justice to the rich blend of punning, earthy, idiomatic speech that Ciṅkaṉ displays; but we should note that his thoughts, throughout this section, keep reverting in the most explicit, frankly sensual manner to his absent wife. He sings freely and joyfully of the intimate details of their lovemaking, which he hopes to resume without delay. Meanwhile, the birds escape his traps; he decides he can stand it no more, sets off through the world in search of his lost Ciṅki:

she is black and beautiful, and, it turns out, something of a nymphomaniac, and also very fond of toddy; who knows what man might have caught her eye? She is always eager for love, could turn the head of Manmatha himself (120); she is as lovely as the long hair of the lord of Kuṟṟālam when he goes forth in procession (116; once again the hidden tenor of the poem reappears!) Ciṅkaṉ offers Nūvaṉ all his magic powders (for which the Kuṟavar are famous in Tamil folklore (if only he will find his wife for him. But, as it turns out, Nūvaṉ's services are unnecessary; Ciṅkaṉ is by now back in the streets of Kuṟṟālam, where suddenly he sees his beloved on her way back from Vacantavalli:

When they saw each other
there
in the land of Kuṟṟālam's lord
    who wears the cold, crescent moon,
the ocean of passion
reached high tide:

and like the shore that stands alone
against the ocean's flood,
only the city street
remained a barrier
between them. (122)

Their happy meeting is marked by yet another comic dialogue. Ciṅkaṉ cannot quite identify the various new ornaments his wife is wearing:

—Where did you go, without telling me? It's been so many days!
—I was telling a lady's fortune, at some length.
—When I look at you, it's strange—I'm a little bit afraid.
—No need to be afraid—just tell me what's the matter.
—What's that viper coiled around your foot?
—It's an anklet [*cilampu*] given me for telling fortunes in the Cēlam country.
—What about the dead frog on your other foot?
—That's a bell for my ankle, given by the women in the temple of the Kuṟṟālam god.
—And that slimy worm wound around your little toe?
—It's a toe-ring I got in Kandy, a long time ago.

—You have a bird's nest hanging in your hair!
—It is a clasp from the people of Kurukaiyūr (Āḻvārtirunakari).

And so on: Ciṅkaṉ slowly works his way up, from toe to tip (in the reverse direction, *nakhaśikhāparyantam,* from the courtly tradition of describing divine women, from the head down). We observe another characteristic exercise in ludicrous misperception. Soon Ciṅkaṉ is pleading for a kiss, even tries to disrobe his wife in the street, at midday, in full sight of everyone; she objects, perhaps a little halfheartedly, certainly in teasing tones, to this shameless behavior. They settle on retiring to a hidden spot where he has set his traps for the birds (126.15).

And the moral: "Stop circling the world from place to place, you poets—say the name Kuṟṟālam just once, and the god of the waterfall that never goes dry will keep us out of the mire of rebirth" (127).

What an end to what began with the traditional lugubrious rhythms of love-in-separation, south Indian *bhakti*-style! We must get used to these happy endings that Nāyaka-period poetry, in Tamil as well as Telugu, so unexpectedly supplies. And also, to the remarkable and sudden reversals of direction, to the opening up of the poetic work to comic, contrapuntal themes which may even, as in the present case, overwhelm it and reformulate its initial premises. The *Tirukkuṟṟālakkuṟavañci* is an outstanding example of this process; so brazen and dynamic is the comic finale to the work, and so successfully integrated into the whole, that, rather than parodying the supposedly "serious" love theme of the heroine and the god, it in effect turns the latter itself into a somewhat absurd, parodic imitation of the Kuṟavar's rude and sensual romance. As in the case of *A Midsummer Night's Dream,* the comic subplot comes not merely to illuminate but actually to dominate and to set standards for the entire play. The reversal could hardly be more complete, and it is consistent in other ways as well: note the Kuṟatti's autonomy, sophistication, and outspokenness, all of which give her the upper hand in relation to her rough-hewn husband, and which compare favorably with Vacantavalli's supine state. In any case, both instances of love achieve a successful conclusion (although Vacantavalli's remains in the form of a promise), and this happy tendency reaches out to include the relations of the devotees and their god, in rather striking contrast to the classical norms of frustration and unsatisfied desire. All in all, this subtle synthesis of conventional, high-strung lovers' longing, in the *bhakti* mode, and its gentle and overtly sensual parodic counterpart follows an optimistic logic of celebration—a logic that lacks the cutting edge of earlier courtly satire, but that incorporates the court poets' fascination with innovative and antithetical comic experimentation.[11]

There are other examples of this fascination in the Tamil literature of the seventeenth and early eighteenth centuries; one important pattern is the creation of textual doublets or "echo-texts," one of which parodies the conventionalized (usually romantic) sentiments of the other.[12] Another possibility is the complete internalization of the echo, as in the Sanskrit *Viśvaguṇādarśacampū,* a satirical portrait of seventeenth-century Tamil Nadu by Veṅkaṭādhvarin, who divides his work into two voices (belonging to two traveling *gandharvas*, flying over southern India)—one of them a positive, "optimistic" viewer who always seeks the good quality in any place or event, the other a sardonic pseudo-*nāstika,* who consistently undermines his comrade's delusion. The resulting bifurcated picture served as a model for a number of similar works, for example, Rāmacandramakhin's *Keralābharaṇa* on the whole of the south, but concluding happily in Kerala. Or the entire work may unfold through a disjointed double register by sustained play with paronomasia, as in the *śleṣa*-dominated dream-romance of Kaṭikai Muttuppulavar, *Camuttiravilācam.* These patterns, taken as a whole, reveal a consistent cultural trend toward internalized parodic commentary and cognitive disjunction, which we have already seen to be a dominant feature of the literature of the Nāyaka court. Let us return, now, to this court, to the most richly conceived and extravagantly executed of all surviving Naỹaka court comedies, the *Annadānamahānāṭakamu* of Puruṣottama Dīkṣituḍu, which must, we feel, be seen as the farcical and deliberately parodic counterpart of the romantic *yakṣagāna,* corpus as a whole. In what follows, we will attempt to give an overview of this unusual work by summarizing and translating selected passages; this synopsis will then allow us to highlight certain general features of Nāyaka court drama and to suggest tentative historical (cultural-historical) conclusions.

"Love in the Soup-Kitchen" (*Satramarulu nāṭakam*)[13]

The play opens with the usual *kaivāramu* praises for the king, Vijayarāghava, blessed with the grace of his family deity, Rājagopālasvāmi of Maṉṉārkuṭi, conquering hero who smashed the forces of the Pāṇḍya and Tuṇḍīra kingdoms (i.e., Madurai and Senji—a somewhat inappropriate epithet for this most unmilitary of Nāyaka kings). Vijayarāghava's former births are mentioned: Marutta in the Kṛtayuga, Nābhāga in the Tretā,

Yudhiṣṭhira in the Dvāpara; now he is King of Tanjavur, so beautiful in form that he drives courtesans to distraction (*vilāsinījanamōhanarūpadhēyuṇḍavai*), and so lavish in his generosity that he constantly feeds one hundred lakhs of Brahmans (*anavaratasatalakṣaviprābhīṣṭamṛṣṭānnapradātalu*). It is this unending feast (*tadīyārādhana*) of ghee, jaggery, *payasam,* cakes, curd, and rice that the poet, who names himself at the opening, has made into the drama called *Tañjāvūr'annadānamahānāṭakamu,* which, he tells us, has three main *rasas*—*śṛṅgāra, hāsya,* and *adbhuta*. Coming to this play from the other *yakṣagāna* dramas, we might not yet suspect that this introduction, with its gradiloquent title, its resort to the *rasa* terminology of the Sanskrit poetic tradition, even, perhaps, its depiction of the Nāyaka king in the audience, is couched in wryly ironic, tongue-in-cheek tones.

But we are soon disabused. We meet, at the outset, the royal official in charge of the Tanjavur *satram,* or choultry, Nellūri Ellamma Rāju, as he tries in vain to get his Tamil accountant (*kaṇakkapiḷḷe*) to render intelligible account of the choultry's finances. "You're just lying there scratching yourself as if you'd drunk buffalo milk—what's going on?" The accountant passes the buck: "Sir, if these Brahmans and the rest spend their time chatting up the dancing girls [*kūttaḍiyāḷ, koḍaṅgaṭṭiyaḷ*], to whom am I to render account?" He has been out on tour, in Tiruvālūr sīma; someone else has reported to the palace. How can he be held responsible? And so on—the dialogue, carried on in the colloquial Tamil of the seventeenth century as heard and recorded by native Telugu speakers, is meant to evoke not only the official apparatus charged with *annadāna,* the gift of rice, at Tanjavur, but also the vast quantities involved in this daily ritual of such central symbolic importance for the Nāyaka kings. "Our ruler," says the *satrādhikāri,* "will not tolerate any failings in feeding these lordly Brahmins, these Vaiṣṇava kings [*vīravaiṣṇavasārvabhaumulu*]. Even if they are only Brahmins by virtue of wearing the sacred thread, they must not go hungry in Tanjavur. Is everything ready—the banana leaves, the curries and rice, the salt, *dal,* condiments, *pāyasam,* pickles?" The cooks assure him that all is ready, and the Brahmans begin to arrive—from Maharastra, Bengal, Kashmir, the Pāṇḍya country, from Kāśī and Kurukṣetra, Kāmbhoja and Pāñcāla, famine-stricken Badari, Kedāra, Prabhāsa, the Naimiśa forest. Among them are the true heroes of this play, the Telugu Brahman Pappu Tippābhaṭlu[14] and his family (including his wife, Ellamma, and their sons Mañcigāḍu, Pedda Bhikṣālugāḍu and Pinnabhikṣālugāḍu).

They are hungry, can hardly wait for the choultry's doors to open. But Tippābhaṭlu wants to establish his Brahman credentials; he blesses the choultry official: *maṅgalāni bhavantu*. This is followed by a flood of Sanskrit gibberish (*hariḥ om. kośam dakṣiṇaḥ pakṣaḥ. kuppa uttaraḥ pakṣaḥ . . . gampam nimpayati*).[15]

Manager: Tippābhaṭlu, from what Veda is this?
Tippābhaṭlu: From the fifth Veda.
Manager: The fifth? I thought there were only four. What *aṣṭaka* is it from in this fifth Veda?
Tippābhaṭlu: The one after the eighth!
Manager: Excellent, Tippābhaṭlu. You're a fine Brahman. Can you cast horoscopes?

Of course he can, though he has trouble reading certain of the letters in his almanac. Eventually, after a brief scatological exchange, he draws a picture of the heavens: Udayam is in the east, Chatram is near the king, Bharaṇi is in the box, the Ram is in the goat herd, the Bull is in the cow herd, the Twins (Mithunam) are where men and women are copulating, the Crab is in its hole, the Lion is in the forest, Virgo is in her father's house, Libra is with the Seṭṭi merchant, Scorpio is in the cow dung, the Bow is with the archer, Makaram is in the ocean, the pot is at the potter's house, Pisces is in the pond, and everything is in place.

This learned discussion is interrupted by the arrival of the courtesans (*bhōgālavāru*) seeking gifts (*tyāgam*). They will provide the second major axis of the play (after the central topic of food and feeding). First, as they sing a love poem about Vijayarāghava, they must be introduced to the innocent Tippābhaṭlu:

Tippābhaṭlu: What's all this noise?
Manager: The courtesans have come here in the hope of receiving gifts.
Tippābhaṭlu: Are courtesans women? Are all of them women, or only part of them women?
Manager: O Tippābhaṭlu, what a great connoisseur [*rasikuḍu*] you are!
Tippābhaṭlu: You mean the dancers are the honorable and respected Lady Whores [*lañjammagāru*]?
Manager: How can you call them honorable and respected?
Tippābhaṭlu: Why not? Don't you know the mothers, Pōlakamma, Nūkalamma, Puṭṭalamma, Ekkalamma, and Lañjamma? [He is referring to Telugu *grāmadevatā*, village deities.] Anyway, what do these courtesans do?

Manager: They collect gold.
Tippābhaṭlu: Only gold, not silver?
Manager: They take gold for sleeping with you.
Tippābhaṭlu: If they take gold for sleeping, maybe they take silver for staying awake.

By now, the courtesans' interest is aroused; perhaps they can gain something from this learned Brahman (*agnihotracintāmaṇi, vedamūrti*). They sing a *pada* for him: "How can love ripen without intimacy?" He becomes curious:

Tippābhaṭlu: Mañcigāḍu, is that a big spoon she's holding in her hand?
Mañcigāḍu: It's a ladle.
Tippābhaṭlu: Isn't a ladle a spoon? Anyway, what's that noise coming from it?
Mañcigāḍu: Father, a cat is meowing inside it.
Veṅgasāni [a courtesan]: Sir, we can see you have fine taste in music. Now that you've shaken your head, it's time to shake your hand a little too.
Hāsyagāḍu [a clown, suddenly present in this group]: Lady, he'll die if he has to give money.

As the courtesans become more determined, and more provocative, Tippābhaṭlu begins to respond without quite understanding why:

Tippābhaṭlu: Something's coming up inside me.
Tallubhaṭlu [another Brahman]: Must be your stomach.
Hāsyagāḍu: Maybe it's that basket you're lifting.
Tippābhaṭlu: O, not that—it's a kind of feeling . . . Its still coming on, still coming. . . .
Tallubhaṭlu: If you're looking at that big stick in the hand of the whore, maybe you have to pee.
Tippābhaṭlu: Hold on!
Tallubhaṭlu: Hold? Why hold on—what are you giving me, a cow [*godāna*]?

Tippābhaṭlu now knows what he wants and sings a crude, unintentionally comic verse, ludicrously couched in the elevated, lyric *śārdūlavikrīḍita* meter: "The cuckoos are nesting, making much noise; Manmatha is shooting. You've seen my pain over and over—is that your *dharma*? I'm a Brahman, very pure. O Lañjamma, won't you make love to me?"

The courtesan, the hideous hag Veṅgasāni, is alarmed; things have gone too far: "Your wife is the one who should make love to you." Tippābhaṭlu wants to bow at her feet. She protests: "Tippābhaṭlu, you're a Brahman! If you bow at the feet of a whore, *she* gets the sin." The clown has his own suggestion: "Leave the whores alone. If you want to bow at someone's feet, try mine—it's less dangerous." Tippābhaṭlu is already chasing the courtesan around the stage, despite her panic-stricken cries: "Just looking at you makes me sick." Nothing can deter him any longer: "You are the god of my temple," he tells her; he will give her his sacred *darbha* grass, an ocher robe—after all, he is a Ṛgvedin, he assures her—he will break his sacred thread, offer her all the fruits of his worship of Garuḍa in Kāñcipuram (*kañcigaruḍaseva*—a Telugu expression denoting useless and never-ending service). Veṅgasāni is saved, temporarily, only by the arrival of a group of Tamil Brahmans, who develop their own comic dialogue with and about the courtesans.

The two groups, Telugu- and Tamil-speaking Brahmans, eye one another suspiciously. Our hero, Tippābhaṭlu, invites one of the Tamilians, Appam Vātyār, to sit down. The latter turns to one of his friends:

> Appam Vātyār: Tippābhaṭṭaṉ is inviting me to sit. Is this place pure enough?
> Nāñjin: Must be pure.
> Appam Vātyār: How do you know?
> Nāñjin: There's Mahājanamāṇikyattāḷ.
> Appam Vātyār: O, now my mind is at ease [*yinnekkonnō manaśuddhi yācci*].
> Ambirāya: What, Appam Vātyār, have you been drinking *nēpāḷam* herbs for constipation [*malaśuddhi yāgharudukku*]?
> Appam Vātyār: No, you idiot, I said *manaśuddhi,* not *malaśuddhi!* Don't you know what it says in the *Liṅgapurāṇam:*

veśyāyā darśanaṃ puṇyaṃ sparśanaṃ pāpanāśanam
śayane sarvatīrthāni suratam mokṣasādhanam/

> "Seeing a courtesan is auspicious; her touch destroys all evil.
> Her bed is the abode of all sacred sites; making love to her is the way to Release."

Soon it transpires that Appam Vātyār knows these ladies very well—or should, at least, know them:

> Appam Vātyār: Who is she?
> Mahājanamāṇikyattāḷ: Don't you recognize Pernāṭṭu Māṇikyattāḷ? After all you've been through together? After you deflowered her at the time of her consecration as a *devadāsī,* you hung around her for three whole years. Have you forgotten?
> Appam Vātyār: Oh, so this is Ternāṭṭu [sic] Māṇikyam. How are you, my dear?
> [She kicks him.]
> Appam Vātyār: O Ambirāya, I am blessed by the touch of Pernāṭṭu-māṇikyattāḷ's sacred foot.

Pursuing this logic, he will soon declare that if she bites him, his whole body will become pure. Meanwhile, the predictable competition develops between the Telugu and Tamil Brahmans over the courtesans' attentions. The Tamils try to convince Mahājanamāṇikyam that she belongs to them: "You used to dance in that *agrahāram;* didn't you enjoy that one-sixteenth of a share that Cevvappanāyaka gave our grandfather there? Now Pappu Tippābhaṭṭaṉ with his eighth of a share is dancing around here. But when the Ceṭṭi was making trouble for you last year, who bailed you out? *We* did!" This seems to convince the lady: "If you're so rich, why do I have to go hunting around elsewhere?" Now Appam Vātyār can take a moment to admire his catch:

> Appam Vātyār: Hey, Nāñjan—she's a little small up front, but her back and her breasts are really big [*munnedu cinnedu, muduvum mārum yallām akhaṇḍamay irukkurudu*].
> Hāsyagāḍu [interposing with a characteristic naive but suggestive remark]: Appam Vātyār, look at *my* back, just like a slab for pounding sandalwood. . . . Why are you staring at her breasts? Look at me!

But Mahājanamāṇikyam wants the Brahman's upper cloth as payment for her songs—the cloth given his grandfather, he tells us in another comic verse, by Kṛṣṇadevarāya himself! The Tamil Brahmans begin to extricate themselves from the situation, leaving the girl to "that Telugu," as they call him; anyway, they note, he's a heavyset man, and they don't want to tangle with him.

Tippābhaṭlu meanwhile offers *his* upper cloth (after his wife refuses to part with her sari); but when the courtesan, Veṅgasāni, takes it, he runs to the Manager to complain that she has stolen it. The Manager wearily promises to provide him with another.

At last, it is time for lunch; the erotic slapstick gives way before more pressing preoccupations. The manager calls the Brahmans to enter according to order (*krama*):

> Manager: Let the lame Brahman come in.
> Tippābhaṭlu: Listen, Mañcigāḍu, he's calling the lame Brahman first. How is he related to the Manager?
> Mañcigāḍu: He's the brother-in-law of the husband of the granddaughter of his maternal aunt.
> Tippābhaṭlu: If that's the case, we can go in just like that lame Brahman. [Leaning on a stick, chanting the Veda, he limps toward the choultry.]
> Manager: Hey, I called the lame Brahman, what are you doing here?
> Tippābhaṭlu: In this village, is anyone more lame than I?
> Manager: You're not lame; you're bluffing. Let the short Brahman come in!
> Tippābhaṭlu: Listen, Mañcigāḍu, he's calling the short Brahman. How is he related to the Manager?
> Mañcigāḍu: He's the elder brother of his paternal uncle.
> Tippābhaṭlu: Then we, too, can go in.

Again the Manager stops him; instead, he calls the tall Brahman. How is this one related to the Manager? Mañcigāḍu suggests: "He's his mother's husband." Another attempt to tiptoe past the door, this time while singing the praises of Vijayarāghava, hero of Tanjavur; and, when challenged by the Manager, Tippābhaṭlu proudly asserts, "I'm as tall as the *gopura* at the Mannāru shrine." Blocked again. This time the stammering Brahman is invited in, and Tippābhaṭlu joins the queue. A Brahman wife asks him whom she resembles, and he tells her she is just like the heavenly courtesan Rambhā; she reciprocates by comparing him to the god Nārāyaṇa himself.

Now the Brahman who has carried a *kāvaḍi* from Benares is invited in. What is his relationship to the Manager? Mañcigāḍu: "He's one of his fathers." This is Tippābhaṭlu's chance. He grabs Tallubhaṭlu's *kāvaḍi* and heads for the door. The Manager stops him: "Bathe and then come."

> Tippābhaṭlu: Mañcigāḍu! The Manager says we have to bathe. The river is too far away. We could try the moat, but it's full of crocodiles.

> Before you know it, we'll miss lunch. We can at least wet the end of our tufts of hair and re-tie them. Quick, pass a little urine.
> Mañcigāḍu: Father, I can't.
> Tippābhaṭlu [in desperation, to his wife]: Now, of all times, he can't pee!
> Yallama [Tippābhaṭlu's wife]: What can I do about it?
> Tippābhaṭlu: OK, Mañcigāḍu, take some water from Prōlubhaṭlu's pot for our tufts.
> Manager: You've already had your bath?
> Tippābhaṭlu: O yes, sir, we've bathed. Look at my wet tuft.
> Manager: Where did you bathe?
> Tippābhaṭlu: In the river.
> Manager: And just where is the river?
> Tippābhaṭlu: Um, over there, beyond the trees, to the south.
> Manager: Some Brahman you are. Nothing but lies. Wait, wait, come on. Our king respects all Brahmans, we mustn't put them to the test. No matter what you may be, we must offer you worship. Come and eat.

And Tippābhaṭlu joins the throng of pushing, scrambling Brahmans, each fighting for a place before one of the banana leaves.

We can look briefly at the final scene, which resumes the erotic encounter with the courtesans but also turns it in a new and somewhat surprising direction. Having feasted to his fill, and beyond it, Tippābhaṭlu invokes the blessings of the god, Rājagopālasvāmi, and then summons the Manager to his side.

> Tippābhaṭlu: We have eaten excellent food, by the mercy of our ruler. But we have one more request.
> Manager: How fortunate. Tell us what it is.
> Tippābhaṭlu: You tell him, Appam Vātyār.
> Appam Vātyār: I don't know Telugu; tell him yourself. You ate in the king's choultry; now tell him what is missing.
> Tippābhaṭlu: To tell you the truth, Manager, we're a little shy to say it.
> Manager: *You,* shy?! Just tell me.
> Tippābhaṭlu: Appam Vātyār, please!
> Appam Vātyār: Tippābhaṭṭa, do you think I know what you're hollering about in that outlandish Telugu?
> Tippābhaṭlu [reluctantly giving in]: In that case—it's the whore.

Appam Vātyār [in Tamil]: All he ever talks about is that whore; just tell him you want her for free.
Manager: What about the whore?
Tippābhaṭlu: Make her do it with me, for once. That is our humble request.
Manager [laughing]: Hey, Veṅgasāni, Jakkula Raṅgasāni, Sānimuddu, come here. Tippābhaṭlu and Appam Vātyār have come from a long ways away. They are very worthy people. They can't just sit around doing nothing. Please satisfy them.
Courtesans: It's Veṅgasāni that he's fallen in love with, why come to us?
Manager: Jakkula Raṅgasāni, Paṭakasānimuddu, is this how you please your customers? What difference does it make? Isn't it your business to fall in love, to make others fall in love, to be mad, to drive others mad, and to use your tricks to keep everything for yourselves?
Courtesans: Just as you say, sir.
Manager: Tippābhaṭlu, as long as you look like this, women will turn away from you in disgust. Use your great ascetic powers, take on a handsome form for making love, as the great sage Cyavana once did.
Tippābhaṭlu: Whatever you say.

As Tippābhaṭlu temporarily disappears from the stage to perform this metamorphosis, the courtesans beg the Manager to give them gifts (*bahumānam*) in his own right; he asks them to perform a song composed by the king, Vijayarāghava. They sing a punning Telugu love *padam* in the style current in Tanjavur:

He gave me a paltry five coins [*ayidu varālu*], and when I asked why,
he said slyly, "You're a very auspicious lady [*ayiduvarālavu*]—or so I thought!"

He's good with words, that Mannārudeva; how can I praise him?

I told him, "You're so good at loving, you have tied me with golden chains [*saripenalu*]; but he turned it back by saying, "Won't you embrace me just the same [*saripenal'iyyavāy*]?"

This is the teasing, playfully irate tone that always predominates in the *padam* poems—a poetry of love for the god or king as seen through the eyes of a jealous, repeatedly betrayed, still impassioned woman. Note that in this case the hero and lover is none other than the king himself, who is also said to have composed the verse (about himself! praising himself!) and who must also be assumed to be listening to it from his seat in the audience. The *padam* marks a moment of transition in this play, to a conclusion informed by a somewhat gentler, perhaps even poignant irony (as we find in the *padam* corpus generally). For this is the moment when Tippābhaṭlu reappears; and, miraculously, he is no longer the grotesque and ludicrous old Brahman lecher but, rather, now bears the alluring form of a new avatar of Manmatha, the god of love (*navyamadanāvatāruṇḍu*).

He, too, sings a *padam*, this time an erotic dialogue couched in a more appropriate idiom than that of his earlier attempt at poetry:

—Won't you let me trace a pattern with my fingernails on your breasts?
—No, you musn't touch me now.

—But I love you—please embrace me!
—You're my friend, why be so hasty?

—Won't you kiss me, play with me?
—No, I know what games you play!

—Take me, master me, let's make love!
—You're the god with eyes as arrows; don't I know your tricks [*nī māya vinnānu lēra*]?

The crudeness and obscenity of the Tippābhaṭlu we have grown to know and admire have been replaced by the coquetry and innocuous banter characteristic of the courtly *padam* tradition. Note that the *padam* incorporates a dialogue reflecting both parties to the love relationship, the urgent suitor and the coy, playfully elusive courtesan—certainly a change from Tippābhaṭlu's earlier stance of crudely single-minded pursuit of his own lust. We may mourn the transformation as a loss, but not even Tippābhaṭlu himself can deny its effectiveness; indeed, in the final dialogue of the play, we hear him giving voice to a strange and somewhat moving confusion about his identity

Tippābhaṭlu/Manmatha: [16] Uttarādi Veṅgasāni!
Veṅgasāni: What is it?

Manmatha: Jakkula Raṅgasāni!
Raṅgasāni: What is it?
Manmatha: Paṭaka Sānimuddu!
Muddu: What?
Manmatha: Where are we?
Muddu: We're in the temple.
Manmatha: Where is the temple?
Muddu: In the fort.
Manmatha: Where is the fort?
Muddu: In Tanjavur.
Manmatha: Oh yes, is that the Tanjavur where our king feeds a lakh of Brahmans?
Veṅgasāni: Hey you old Brahman, have you forgotten yesterday's feast, when you sat in the row with your wife and children and gorged yourself on lentils, *pāyasam,* pickles?
Manmatha: Veṅgasāni—who am I?
Veṅgasāni: You're the new Manmatha, aren't you?

But by this point, Tippābhaṭlu, or Manmatha, is beyond words; he mutters incoherently, as he loses consciousness; somehow he sings a final verse:

I can't bear to be away from you, even for a single second.
I am intoxicated beyond thought or measure—won't you kiss
    my lips?

And with this unthinkable intoxication, as the courtesans dance, the drama comes to an end.

The *Annadānamahānaṭakamu,* or *Satramarulu nāṭakam,* is surely one of the most remarkable literary creations of the Tanjavur Nāyaka court. It deserves a detailed study, which would, inter alia, classify the various types of comedy it presents and analyze the "calculus of comic permutations" embodied by its characters. In the present context, we will limit ourselves to a brief list of selected features, which relate either to the general problems of Nāyaka kingship and society or to the specific question of the role of the folk sources and folk themes in the literature of the Nāyaka court:

(1) Most obvious, perhaps, is the "Bakhtinian" side of this play—the obsession with food and sex (rather than love), the emphasis being, clearly, on the pursuit of oral appetites; or, more generally, with the body's assorted apertures. The action is grotesque rather than pornographic, and

never far from scatology; its verbal abandon, focusing on crudely physical images—the view from the bottom up, so to speak—stands in fine contrast to the usual high-caste Hindu fastidiousness about bodily orifices and excretions. As such, it clearly has an affinity with certain representative folk-literary types—one thinks, for example, of the obscene songs associated with the *bharaṇi* festivals to the goddess (a "carnivalesque" mode, to pursue the Bakhtinian analogy),[17] or, perhaps even closer in language and tone, with the comic introduction and interludes in the South Indian shadow-puppet theatre, which also plays with obscenity, scatological humor, homosexual innuendo (as with the Hāsyagāḍu), and incongruous sexual alliances (see GoldbergBell 1984; Shulman 1985:204–10). But there is an equally striking contrast with the rest of the romantic *yakṣagāna* corpus, as we have already indicated. We have no doubt that this contrast is intentional; indeed, the *Annadāna* is, in a sense, deliberately keyed to the dramas of courtly life and love in a way that allows it to serve as reflexive commentary upon them. It even follows the same structure that we find in the *abhyudaya-kāvyas* from Tanjavur,[18] which show us the king's daily routine (described as a kind of divine ritual), especially concentrating on the elaborate and highly conventionalized descriptions of his meals and his lovemaking (always with a courtesan). These are the two major subjects of our play as well. But where Raghunātha Nāyaka dines in state, with elegant abandon, served by an endless host of delicate women, our rough Brahman heroes attempt to elbow their way violently into the choultry, where they will gorge themselves in a Rabelaisian mode. And while Raghunātha performs the leisurely daily rituals of falling in love, pining for his beloved, excoriating Manmatha in measured, elevated verses, meeting the girl's messenger, arranging a rendezvous, and, at long last, as evening descends, slowly undergoing the tedious process of seduction and the inevitable lovers' quarrels and reconciliations that follow it, Tippābhaṭlu and Appam Vātyār pursue their prostitutes briskly, ludicrously, and wholly directly. They are prepared to delay their satisfaction only for one purpose—just long enough to eat. On the one hand, we have courtly manners, grace, a dignified and cultivated indirection; on the other, desire at its coarsest and most absurd. It is difficult to avoid the feeling that the farce aims at piercing the veil of sustained romantic, regal illusion, thereby revealing the raw reality of human drives that lies behind it.

(2) This disintegration of illusion goes still deeper. We must remember that this play was performed at court, with the king as spectator. As with other works of the *yakṣagāna* type, the *Annadāna* helps to articulate

a certain vision of kingship and identity. These plays show us the king and his court as they wished to project themselves publicly, to themselves and to others. In part, of course, the projection in evidence in our play is highly positive and flattering to the king, who is intent upon feeding Brahmans of any kind, and at any price. The ironies of farce are bracketed, as it were, by a wholly "serious" ideology which casts the king in the role of magnanimous patron and donor. On the other hand, Vijayarāghava is also present within the erotic fantasy-zone of the farce, as author and subject of one of the love poems (and thus as a potential target for ridicule, along with all the rest of the apparatus of love in its courtly guise). Once the disjunction of irony is allowed to open up—and the entire play is, after all, a vehicle for just such an opening—it is virtually impossible to limit its range. Our play, seen in the context of the *yakṣagāna* corpus as a whole, presents this disjunction as part and parcel of the court's self-awareness; as such, it casts the whole of the kingly role in a new, corrosive light. Probably more than earlier South Indian conceptualizations of royal identity, Nāyaka kingship, in its public aspects, seen from within, knows itself to be constructed at least in part around illusion.

(3) But it is an illusion that manages to realize itself: this play is not, or not only, an anti-Brahman satire (it was, we recall, composed by a Brahman) any more than it is an outright attack on the ideology of the court. Like the folktale with which we began, it is a parody, with both the parody's traditional double hinge and something of its playful ontological assertiveness. Comic debunking remains heavily mortgaged to its lampooned ideals. Look at the end of the drama—the actual transformation of our ignorant, lascivious, miserly, repulsive Brahman into a *real* incarnation of Kāma, the god of love. This is the point where illusion, knowing itself as such, recreates itself as real. We may be reminded of the triumphant conclusion achieved by the Subahdar of the Cot, whose royal pretense turns out to be more powerful than kingship itself. Here the Brahman's successful transition to a more attractive identity remains unexplained, the result not of any wisdom, or of a skill in manipulating illusion, but, apparently, of the sheer magic of desire. Such happy fantasies are, perhaps, no more improbable than the burlesque caricatures that fuel the play from the start. But the process as a whole is remarkably similar to what we have observed in the opening tale: the comic parody of illusion ultimately issues into another, still more compelling and motivating illusion, visibly and externally established and confirmed. Unlike the companion-examples of the Vidūṣaka in Sanskrit drama, or the tales of the south Indian court Jester,

Tenāli Rāma—both of whom offer a kind of consistent cognitive disillusion—the Nāyaka farce, like the tale of Keśava Bhaṭṭa, goes through the more complex and intriguing process of taking illusion apart and then putting it back together again.

(4) Finally, in addition to sharing in this way something of the countervision of the folktale, and, in particular, its characteristic parodic double code, the Nāyaka court drama recalls another semirealistic trait of folk literature—the extension of the social universe to include types and themes normally beyond the pale of "high" literary depiction.[19] We see the all-too-believable Brahman ignoramus, with his irritable wife and foolish sons; the cynical and ugly prostitutes; the lazy and inefficient accountants; the harassed Manager of the choultry, with his Brahman cooks. As Aristotle recognized, comedy tends, almost by default, toward a relative realism. If we look beyond the Telugu poetry of the court to other genres, in Tamil and Sanskrit, prevalent in this period, we can add to our list the Kuṟavar fortune-tellers and bird-catchers of the *kuṟavañci,* the Kaḷḷar horse thieves of the *Noṇṭināṭakam,* the peasant farmers of the *Paḷḷu,* the dancers, procurers, and prostitutes of the *Viṟali viṭu tūtu,* the sycophantic poets and conjurers, the astrologers and quack doctors, and the avaricious moneylenders of Nīlakaṇṭha Dīkṣita's *Kaliviḍambana* and a series of similar compositions, and other, similarly convincing types. All of this is newly integrated into the formal literature of the period. We should not look only to the folk traditions as potential sources for this new universe of character and theme; there are also important precedents from within the rich (though often neglected) tradition of Sanskrit comedy and farce, from Kṣemendra to the writers of medieval *bhāṇas* and *prahasanas* (Siegel 1987). In any case, whatever the sources from which the Nāyaka poets drew, we would be justified in regarding the integration they achieved—both of hitherto unknown or excluded types and themes and, above all, of the disjunctive, parodic counterpoint now radically internalized within the "high" tradition—as their most creative contribution to the reformulated culture of their time.

Can we, in conclusion, offer any explanation for this innovating form of integration that we have found at the Nāyaka courts?[20] No doubt there are factors in the domains of Nāyaka-period society and political economy, both of which reveal far-reaching transformations, which moulded the literary forms that we are studying here. The seventeenth century was a time of rapid social change in Tamil Nadu, of economic and demographic expansion, and of apparent fluidity and "experimentation," as Sanjay Subrahmanyam has suggested,[21] in the structuring of the political and symbolic realms; these forces are reflected in the expansion of the literary horizons and in far-reaching experiments such as we have seen in the courtly drama. There is a certain boldness in the incorporation of satire, or in its domestication as parody, which seems very much in keeping with the new spirit of the Nāyaka age (in contrast, for example, with the lyrical heyday of imperial literature at sixteenth-century Vijayanagara). But it is never very satisfying to invoke the intangible spirit of a period in lieu of explanation. So we would like to conclude with three analytical considerations, of a structural or dynamic nature, which may at least point us in the direction of a possible (though clearly partial) understanding of this development.

There is, first, a simple law of compensation at work. As mentioned earlier, Nāyaka courtly poetry presents us with the most striking hyperbolic inflation of royal claims and images ever witnessed, to this time, in south India. Unlike earlier Tamil or Telugu kings, the Nāyakas were not at all hesitant to proclaim themselves gods, or to identify their palace with the temple, or to display symbolically the actual superiority of their power over that of the very deities they worshipped. Indeed, it is this last feature that is truly significant: the mere rhetorical identification of ruler and deity counts less than the attempts to enact, in various symbolic media, ritualized processes that treat the king as god or that demonstrates the god's complete dependence upon him.[22] All of this exists at Tanjavur in the context of the extreme conflation and interpenetration of hitherto disparate symbolic spheres (Narayana Rao and Shulman, forthcoming). The process also entails a peculiar type of Sanskritization, which identifies the individual king with the aesthetic models of Sanskrit poetry and drama and thus visibly grounds these models in the physical reality of the court: the hero of courtly drama is no longer a figment of imagination or a paragon drawn from the mythic or legendary past—an Udayana or Duṣyanta—but is incarnate before his courtiers' eyes; indeed, they can observe him both on stage, within the drama, and as the chief spectator outside it, stolidly observing himself. This aesthetic modeling of the king begins, it seems, in Kākatīya-period Andhra,[23] and is probably a distinctive Telugu legacy to Nāyaka Tanjavur, which takes it to new lengths—and which also develops a characteristic response, by balancing the hyperbolic assertions with an internalized satire of them, indeed of all extravagant pretensions. These two vectors have an innate, logical connection.

Second, we can sense that we are dealing with a new and more complex construction of the self, including the social self. This is not only a cognitive or conceptual issue but actually informs virtually all cultural domains. For example, the art of this period is often criticized as "baroquely" overembellished and ornate; but we might do better to see it as inherently and necessarily elaborate, finished, and complex.[24] The entire South Indian cultural past, with its diverse institutional and ideological components, has, as it were, collapsed into the various expressive forms of this period, which have organized themselves by making a new, and generally rather comprehensive, selection; in the process, they have also reached out toward hitherto neglected elements and sources. Part of this process of seeing and projecting an image of the self seems to involve a new kind of "otherness," of alien perception, such as we might expect from the transplanting of a language and its classical literature to another setting. The Telugu courtly ethos, moving south, observes, is stimulated by, assimilates, and thus legitimates and extends conspicuous features of its new environment, including some never adopted by the political center before. This is a creative movement, not based on opposition—Telugu and Tamil, despite the surface frictions apparent in the *Annadānamahānāṭakamu,* develop a selective symbiosis which persists in the Tamil country for some three centuries—but it entails, at least for the Telugu poet, a more complex vision of his cultural identity. We can hear this in Tippābhaṭlu's concluding speech, with its convincingly articulated quandry: Where am I? Where is Tanjavur? "Veṅgasāni—who am I?" Nowhere is the complexity more in evidence than in the productive disjunction that the comedy activates and brings to the fore.

Finally, the resulting combination of inflated royal claims and their simultaneous undermining seems well suited to the structure of Nāyaka political reality. What we see in courtly farce and parody is the understandable attempt to have one's rhetorical cake and eat it: the double code of parody allows, more effectively than any other literary mechanism, the conditional assertion of a highly inflated imperial kingship in conditions that effectively preclude its realization. The Nāyaka has, it is true, a certain tenuous power, though much of it depends upon transparent illusion, as he knows all too well; he does transcend his titular overlord in the decaying Vijayanagara center, by now dependent on its erstwhile servants for support; this little, local king will make every effort to take this equation to its symbolic and rhetorical extreme. But even, or especially, in his own court, his claims to divinity ring true only to the extent that they are also shown to be hollow. It is not by chance that the parodic idiom adapted for this purpose is drawn in part from the preexisting, highly articulate and ambivalent vision of the south Indian folk tradition.

* * *

The authors wish to thank the National Endowment for the Humanities, which has supported the research presented here. We are also indebted to V. S. Rajam for the long hours she spent helping us decipher the colloquial Tamil portions, recorded in Telugu script, of the *Annadānamahānāṭakamu*.

Notes

1. Like most folktales, this one is undatable. It also conflates various historical periods (note the use of the Mughal administrative term *subahdar* and the role of Delhi in a text which depicts Tanjavur as part of the Vijayanagara state system). We feel that, given this latter orientation as well as the well-known conservative tendencies of the Tamil folktale, we can speak of a continuity in perception and self-understanding that reaches back toward Nāyaka Tanjavur.

2. There is also a pun implicit in the subahdar's title: *kaṭṭil ēṟa*, "to sit on the cot," is a Tamil idiom meaning also "to mount the throne" (Fabricius 1972, s.v.). The folktale literalizes the idiomatic metaphor, making the cot into a real throne.

3. Striking examples of this attitude can be seen in several of the tales collected and introduced by A. K. Ramanujan in a forthcoming volume.

4. This pattern goes back at least to the Kākatīya period, and to the model of the *Pratāparudrīya*, which makes Pratāparurdra the hero of the exemplary *udāharaṇa* verses. See discussion in the final section of this chapter, below.

5. "*striyāḥ puṃvad bhāṣitapuṃskād anūṅ samānādhikaraṇe striyām apūraṇīpriyādiṣu*": a feminine (adjective or noun) before another feminine in composition takes the corresponding masculine form when available, except in the case of feminine-ending *ū* or before ordinal numbers or the word *priya* and so forth, when they are in the same case relationship. (So: *darśanīyabhārya* but *kalyāṇīpriya*.)

6. The prehistory of the genre is discussed at length by Mu. Aruṇācalam in his introduction to the collection of four *Kuṟavañci* (1980 : 1–29); see also Muttuccaṇmukaṉ and Mirmalā Mokaṉ (1977). A precursor of the figure of the *kuṟatti* soothsayer, the *akavaṉmakaḷ*, appears already in Caṅkam poetry (e.g., *Kuṟuntokai* 23). The theme survives in the medieval genre known as *kuṟam* (e.g., *Mīṉāṭciyammai kuṟam*), in the single *kuṟam* verses that find a place in the *kalampakam* compositions, and in the purāṇic traditions of sites such as Tirupati (where Viṣṇu/Veṅkaṭeśvara himself becomes a *kuṟatti* to further his cause with his bride-to-be, Padmāvatī). We are preparing a detailed study of the genre in Telugu and Tamil.

7. Thus *Turōpatai kuṟam*, and so forth: see Hiltebeitel 1988 : 301–9.

8. E.g., *Vijayarāghavacandrikāvihāramu* of Kāmarusu Vēṅkaṭapatisōmayāji, in Gaṇṭi Jōgisōmayāji 1956 : 47–56.

9. E.g., in genres such as *kōvai* and *ulā;* on the former, see Cutler 1987.

10. Note that nondevotional *kuṟavañcis*, with the same format, also exist, e.g., *Carapēntirapūpālak Kuṟavañci*. We can also trace the evolution of the genre in this direction via earlier experiments, e.g., the anonymous *Tañcai Veḷḷaip Piḷḷaiyār Kuṟavañci* from the time of Vijayarāghava (one of the oldest available works in this genre: see the edition by Cokkaliṅkam [1965]). Here the heroine's love for the god is missing—she is, instead, a wife deserted by her husband because of barrenness; the *kuṟatti* promises her that, by the grace of Veḷḷaip Piḷḷaiyār, her husband will come back to her and she will bear children. Later *kuṟavañci* poets such as Pāpanāca Mutaliyār and Tirikūṭarācappakkavirāyar pursue the logic of love-in-separation to its usual limit by giving the god the role of absent or denying lover.

11. Not surprisingly, the revival of the *Tirukkuṟṟālakkuṟavañci* by Rukmini Devi in puritanical, mid-twentieth-century Madras entailed the bowdlerization of the text: the entire concluding episode of Ciṅkaṉ and Ciṅki—the high point and necessary denoument of the play, in our reading—was excised from the Kalākṣetra version.

12. Thus the *Kūḷappanāyakar kātal,* which we read together with the *Kūḷappanāyakar viṟali viṭu tūtu,* both by Cupratīpakkavirāyar: see Shulman, forthcoming.

13. This is the title given in the colophon to the work, in contrast to the far more pretentious (and probably ironic) title mentioned in the preface (*Annadānamahānāṭakamu*). As in other cases, the existence of two titles may well reflect the work's popularity.

14. The *iṇṭipēru* or ancestral (village) name Pappu may be meant as a pun on *pappu,* lentils or split pulse; the hero is thus "Lentils Tippābhaṭlu," just as later we will meet Appam Vātyār, "Pastry Vātyār."

15. The last phrase is an absurd Sanskritization of Telugu *gampa,* "basket," and the verb *nimpu,* "to fill"—thus, no doubt, "he fills my basket."

16. The stage directions simply call him Manmatha.

17. E.g., at Koṭuṅkōḷūr; and cf. the essay by Donald Brenneis in this volume.

18. E.g., the *Raghunāthanāyakābhyudayamu,* by Vijayarāghava Nāyaka, on his father, Raghunatha.

19. It is important to note that the farce is also linguistically realistic in a way that the high-flown romantic dramas are usually not: its characters speak in a comic imitation of Telugu Brahman or Tamil Brahman colloquial idiom. (Aside from the colloquial diction, Telugu Brahman pronunciation is also caricatured by the consistent substitution of *ṣ* for *ṭ*.)

20. For an intriguing parallel in eighteenth-century France, see Isherwood 1986.

21. Private communication, February 1988; and see Subrahmanyam 1987.

22. This is the criterion—the actual worship of the ruler in some form—that Kulke (1978 : 3) rightly establishes as necessary for any real divine kingship; we agree with his rejection, on this basis, of such kingship for Hindu India generally, but would wish to posit the Nāyakas as an innovating exception.

23. With the *Pratāparudrīya,* subsequently imitated in many works, including an *alaṅkāra* work from Tanjavur with Raghunātha as the subject of the exemplary

verses, Kṛṣnakavi's *Raghunāthabhūpālīya*. (We are preparing an edition of this text.)

24. Here we are inspired by Breckenridge's discussion of "scale" in relation to this period.

References

Tamil, Telugu, and Sanskrit Texts (by title)

Annadānamahānāṭakamu of Puruṣottama Dīkṣituḍu
1956 In *Yakṣagānamulu* (*Tañjāvūru*), vol. 2, Gaṇṭi Jōgisōmayāji, ed., pp. 191–234. Kākināḍa: Andhra University.

Camuttiravilācam of Kaṭikai Muttuppulavar
1956 Madras: South Indian Saivai Siddhanta Works Publishing Society.

Keralābharaṇa of Rāmacandramakhin
1985 E. R. Ramabai, ed. Madras: Elango.

Kuṟavañci (by various authors)
1980 Mu. Aruṇācalam and Irā. Iḷaṅkumaraṉ, eds. Madras: Government of Tamil Nadu.

Raghunāthanāyakābhyudayamu of Vijararāghava Nāyaka
1951 N. Venkataramanayya and M. Somasekhara Sarma, eds. Tanjavur: Sarasvati Mahal Library.

Tañcai Veḷḷaippiḷḷaiyār Kuṟavañci
1965 Vī. Cokkaliṅkam, ed. Tanjavur: Sarasvati Mahal Library.

Tirukkuṟṟālakkuṟavañci of Mēlakaram Tirikūṭarācappakkavirāyar
1980 Madras: South India Saiva Siddhanta Works Publishing Company.

Vijayarāghavacandrikāvihāramu of Kāmarusu Vēṅkaṭapatisōmayāji
1956 In *Yakṣagānamulu* (*Tañjāvūru*), vol. 2, Gaṇṭi Jōgisōmayāji, ed., pp. 3–66. Kākināḍa: Andhra University.

Vijayarāghavakalyāṇamu of Kōnēṭi Dīkṣitulu
1956 In *Yakṣagānamulu* (*Tañjāvūru*), vol. 2, Gaṇṭi Jōgisōmayāji, ed., pp. 69–188. Kākināḍa: Andhra University.

Viśvaguṇādarśacampū of Veṅkaṭādhavrin
1934 Madras: Vāviḷḷa Rāmasvāmiśāstrulu and Sons.

Other Works

Ashton, M., and B. Christie
1977 *Yakṣagāna, A Dance Drama of India*. New Delhi: Abhinava Publications.

Breckenridge, Carol Appadurai
1985 Scale and Social Formation in South India, 1350–1750. In *Studies on South India: An Anthology of Recent Scholarship and Research*. R. E.

Frykenberg and P. Kolenda, eds., pp. 51–66. Madras: New Era Publications.

Cutler, Norman

1987 *Songs of Experience: The Poetics of Tamil Devotion*. Bloomington: Indiana University Press.

Duisit, Lionel

1978 *Satire, parodie, calembour: esquisse d'une théorie des modes dévalués*. Stanford, Calif.: Stanford French and Italian Studies, Vol. XI, Anma Libri.

Fabricius, Johann Philip

1972 *Tamil and English Dictionary*. 4th ed. Tranquebar: Evangelical Lutheran Mission Publishing House.

GoldbergBelle, Jonathan Robert

1984 The Performance Poetics of Tōlubommalāṭa: A South Indian Shadow Puppet Tradition. Ph.D. dissertation, University of Wisconsin, Madison.

Hiltebeitel, Alf

1988 *The Cult of Draupadī, I. Mythologies: From Gingee to Kurukṣetra*. Chicago: University of Chicago Press.

Isherwood, Robert M.

1986 *Farce and Fantasy: Popular Entertainment in Eighteenth-Century Paris*. New York and Oxford: Oxford University Press.

Kulke, Hermann

1978 *The Devaraja Cult*. Ithaca, N.Y.: Cornell University, Department of Asian Studies.

Muttuccaṇmukam (Piḷḷai) and Nirmalā Mokaṉ

1977 *Kuṟavañci*. Maturai: Muttuppatippakam.

Narayana Rao, Velcheru, and David Shulman

1990 Marriage-Broker for a God: Vijayarāghava Nāyaka in the Tanjavur Yakṣagānas. In a volume edited by Hans Bakker. Groningen.

Natesa Sastri, S. M.

1908 *Folklore in Southern India*. Madras: Natesan.

Rose, Margaret A.

1979 *Parody/Meta-Fiction*. London: Croom Helm.

Shulman, David

1985 *The King and the Clown in South Indian Myth and Poetry*. Princeton, N.J.: Princeton University Press.

Forthcoming Poets and Patrons in Tamil Literature and Literary Legend. In a volume on patronage in India, Barbara S. Miller, ed.

Siegel, Lee

1987 *Laughing Matters: Comic Tradition in India*. Chicago: University of Chicago Press.

Subrahmanyam, Sanjay

1967 Trade and the Regional Economy of South India, ca. 1550 to 1650. Ph.D. dissertation, University of Delhi.

Afterword

Arjun Appadurai

Afterword

This volume is one of a series of recent publications which leaves little doubt that the study of folk expression and performance in South Asia has come of age (Beck 1982; Blackburn and Ramanujan 1986; Blackburn 1988). That is, in richness of method, complexity of data, and subtlety of interpretation, South Asian folkloric studies no longer occupy that strange semiperiphery between studies of folk phenomena in Europe and America on the one hand, and of native performances and practices in allegedly untouched small-scale societies on the other. India, in particular, has always held a certain fascination in the comparative study of Indo-European mythology and folklore. But it must now be seen as a place where problems of literacy (both in its broad cultural sense and its narrow, technical sense) and orality, textuality and history, genre and gender, have not only entered the mainstream of folkloric studies, but have begun to generate ideas and possibilities to which analysts of cultural forms working elsewhere in the world will need to attend. South Asia is thus no longer grist for a mill constructed elsewhere, but its voices (both indigenous and scholarly) can now play a central role in building folkloric discourse generally. But what are the special directions in which the present volume points us, both in regard to the folklore of South Asia and in regard to folklore generally? Below are discussions of three areas wherein the time may be right for the radical rethinking of folkloristic ideas, in light of the kinds of arguments that are represented in this volume.

The Lore of the Folk

Folklore is the term that needs to be problematized, since neither of its lexical components is any longer usable in a simple and straightforward way. This view, which I develop in this section, carries to a terminological level observations and auto-critiques that have been made by the best minds in folkloristics in the United States and have received fresh impetus within folklore studies recently (Bauman 1989; Kirshenblatt-Gimblett 1988). *Lore* is a problematic word, laden with earlier European conceptions about the knowledge and beliefs of others. Like the word *belief* (Kopytoff 1981), *lore* is a term that implies knowledge that is somehow more weak in its epistemological foundations, more evanescent in its relationship to social life, and more hazy in its grasp on history, than words like *knowledge, theory,* and *world view*. Each of these latter terms has its own problems, but they do not definitionally privilege the knowledge of the observer over the knowledge of those persons and traditions of which he or she speaks. *Lore* is a poor word to describe the very rich variety of texts and of practices, of strategies and of structures, of arguments and of counterarguments that are contained in this volume.

The same is true of the prime component of the term *folklore,* the word *folk*. Again, while anthropologists have spoken of primitives, savages, and exotics in other parts of the world (and have rightly been castigated for the implicit meanings of these terms), the term *folk* has, until recently, been reserved for our own historical predecessors in the Euro-American West (Handler 1988; Herzfeld 1982). The "folk," in *folklore* were typically regarded as existing in complex, preindustrial social formations, but were not seen as "natives," "primitives," or "savages." That is, as many folklorists have recognized in the last two decades, especially in the United States, the idea of the "folk" is not only a romantic idea, but also an intrinsically self-referential and essentialist idea, which did facilitate the kind of fantastic and horrifying spectacle of nationhood which the Nazis erected around the German term *volk*. Of course, in recent years, the majority of those who practice folklore do not operate with such assumptions, but the master term under which they operate, and the master narratives underlying this term, imply problems that are not yet wholly behind us, whatever our departmental and disciplinary affiliations. Anthropologists and folklorists will need to continue to reflect critically on their practices, in order to fully exorcise their romantic prehistory and their tendency to deny "coevality" (Fabian 1983) to the people they study (Appadurai 1988).

Both the "lore" we have gathered in this volume and the "folk" who produce and enjoy it, are far more complex realities than these terms have allowed us to imagine. What these essays show is that any artificial homogeneity implied by the term *folk* masks many social diversities: of class, of gender, of region, of skill, of taste, and of temperament. What is more, the idea of the "folk" in South Asia creates an illusion not just of synchronic homogeneity but also of historical and geographical fixity. The essays in this volume show that such fixity is not characteristic of the complex temporal dialogues and polylogues that performers, patrons, and audiences have been engaged in for centuries in South Asia. As to their "lore," it comprises many levels of knowledge and of understanding, of belief and of irony, of certainty and of doubt, of "common" sense (Geertz 1975) and of "uncommon" possibilities. Pleas for terminological rehabilitation, such as this one, are fraught with peril, especially when we are concerned with the discursive habits of "fields," "departments," and "disciplines" in the modern university. Disciplinary labels carry deep epistemic and political force, as do master terms such as *folk, native,* and *primitive,* which always threaten to drag anthropology and folklore back into aspects of their prehistories with which most contemporary practitioners are deeply uncomfortable. The material from South Asia, and the material in this volume more particularly, suggest that such reconstruction is urgent and now under way.

Performance, Textuality, and History

The essays collected here suggest that the time is now ripe for a full and direct encounter between the problematics of performance and textuality, on the one hand, and of social and cultural history, on the other. These materials, that is, drive our attention outward from the "text" toward contexts, occasions, and what we might call the variety of *regimes of reception* in South Asia, that is, those social and historical formations within which tales and texts, songs and poems, are produced; which they simultaneously represent and inflect; and in which the literacy of audiences and patrons, in different regions and periods, is constituted. The turn to "performance" in much recent folklore (Abrahams 1977; Bauman 1989; Limon and Young 1986) does, of course, imply a deep attention to context. But the prevailing sense of context tends to be relatively small-scale and confined to a variety of immediate and intricate micro-features of performance. This is not surprising, given the profound influence of the sociolinguistic models of the 1960s and 1970s on such work, as well as the related influence of ethnomethodology and conversation analysis, as represented by such theorists as Garfinkel, Goffman, and Sacks. What the South Asian material contained in this volume invites us to do is to move toward somewhat larger-scale ideas of context, in which broader ideological frameworks, historical currents, and social formations are brought into the conceptualization of context.

A few examples of the push outward from the texts: Alf Hiltebeitel's chapter drives us out of the folk Draupadī stories and performances into larger questions about kingship, gender, and territory in north and south India. The paper by Narayana Rao and Shulman makes us wonder why irony and satire become the central rhetorical devices of what we might call not just "theatre-states" (in the sense of Geertz 1980) but "mimic-states," states that are elaborate mimetic statements referring to earlier or imagined political orders. Ann Gold's chapter, based on Rajasthani materials, forces us to ponder the ambiguities of power, as it is shared between men and women in Rajasthan. Since the stories she recounts are told today, do they cast light on the complex cultural debates surrounding the *satī* death of Roop Kanwar in 1988? Gender and illusion were clearly present in this extraordinary event in recent history. There seems little doubt that this peculiar reenactment of martial Rajput ideals by men who are today truck drivers and grain traders, and Rajput women as wives, sisters, and mothers, must have involved a very complex form of "deep play" (Geertz 1973) in the mutual perceptions of the sexes in present-day Rajasthan. The debates over the sense in which Roop Kanwar was a moral agent in choosing her mode of death will surely profit, eventually, from understanding the role of narratives in empowering popular imagination and unleashing buried conceptions of gender and agency.

Likewise, Margaret Trawick's paper on an Untouchable Tamil woman singer forces us to reflect not only on the sociopoetics of reflexivity, but also on the multiple levels of "quotation" involved in the relationship of this woman to other Untouchables, and of untouchables as a class to their caste superiors. These songs, and others like them, take on the emotional force they do because they are *commentatorial* as well as *constitutional*. That is, they represent strategies of irony and satire from "below" and they are simultaneously constitutive of liveable identities in a situation of devalued roles for many individuals in South Asia.

Thus, in all such powerful events of singing and telling, we must recognize that social life is constantly being rethought, rephrased, repositioned from the point of view of the teller. The more positivistically inclined among us might well ask what this sort of repositioning means in terms of the objectively given realities of caste in South Asia. The answer must be provisional: such tellings are part of the habitus of caste and the history of the next few decades will show whether such tellings will ignite new narratives of class, of protest, and of social exit, or simply reinforce and replay older strategies of containment and upper-caste hegemony. In all these cases, and virtually every other chapter in this volume raises similar questions, the texts we read and their contexts, like translucent eyes, are instruments for seeing history and social life, while, through their subtexts and structures, they show us something of social life and history in the modes of the tellings themselves. There is also the meta-historicist puzzle raised by this method; were texts of this sort always a part of agency and history in the way that has been suggested? And did we miss this dimension in the past (and in regard to the past) because our methods were insufficiently sensitive? Or is such a mutually interrogative relationship between text and history a relatively recent fact about the South Asian expressive world, and our discovery of this relationship wholly a matter of methodological serendipity?

Perhaps most important, many of these essays (and the essay by Ramanujan is an excellent example), revolve around materials which show not cultural consensus but debate, on central matters of power, of status, of gender, of genre, and of reality itself. It would be easy enough to say that these materials show us a polyphonic situation, but it is important to note how often this polyphony expresses "essentially contestible" (Gallie 1964) ideas and "internal cultural debates" (Parkin 1978). We are reminded, once again, that the "folk" (themselves multiple) have many "lores."

Of course, this "opening out" from texts and tellings to social life and history writ large could not be accomplished without a great deal of attention to detail within these materials, and that is also what we learn from the care with which these essays have been written and argued. These texts may be translucent, but they are by no means transparent. To decide what they "mean" or "say" in regard to their larger contexts requires close attention to their "inner" dynamics: these may be dynamics of meter or prosody, tone or style, structure or ethos. Thus, to make these texts look *out*, one must first take a hard and close look *into* them. What is true of the texts that the authors have analyzed is equally true of many of these essays themselves, for these essays collectively suggest ways of linking "text" and "context" that are neither textually naive nor socially reductive.

The problem of how these texts and performances come to take on certain historical and social meanings brings to the fore a central problem for all enterprises such as this one. How are these texts received and understood by their audiences? Here it is clear that much work remains to be done, largely in regard to method. If, as most of the authors in this volume seem to agree, objective survey methods of the traditional social-science variety are not adequate to handle the subtleties of reception, what kind of theory of reader, listener, viewer do we need? This is a very large and looming problem in cultural studies generally today, and interpretive approaches to the problem of the audience are nowhere highly developed. But the essays in this volume point to the need for further work in this area, work that pays equal attention to the politics of texts and the textualities embedded in politics. Equally, these essays force us to reflect on the complexities of cultural literacy in a civilizational setting such as South Asia, where a multiplicity of media and modes confront each other, and where reading, seeing, and listening constitute an ever-shifting synesthetic balance for audiences, audiences whose own cultural literacy emerges in the trajectories of local society and history. Thus problems of genre, of cultural literacy, and of taste need to be conjoined in order to produce a genuinely powerful "reception" theory, which can accommodate both genre diversity and contextual variation and turn the issue of "cultural literacy" from a quantitative (Hirsch, Kett, and Trefil 1987) and canon-centered issue (Bloom 1987) to a processual and contextual issue. While no single volume can be expected to resolve a problem of this scope, the authors represented here certainly show that the prerequisite of a powerful theory of reception is a thorough understanding of the dynamics of intertextuality in a complex civilization. To explore these dynamics, these authors attend to how songs and texts are mutually referential, how silences are culturally formed, and how textual and existential strategies intermesh with each other, in a process that is ineluctably historical. This leads me to my final concern, the problem of folk modes of knowledge and transmission in what Walter Benjamin called "the age of mechanical reproduction" (Benjamin 1936).

Folk Knowledge and Electronic Media

It is a truism that once we have mechanical modes of reproduction in the arts, exemplified in records, films, cassettes, and books, the "folk" world of production, performance, and reception is somehow dramatically transformed. At least two essays in this volume (those by Heston and Manuel) deal explicitly with this shift, though several other contributors allude to this process in the last few decades. There are many problems to be considered here: problems of authenticity and survival; of reproduction and of media reach; of textual durability and thus of fixity. There are those who welcome the new, "mechanical" modes of reproduction in the folk arts, for they promise better archiving of folk materials; higher incentives for folk artists because of the commercial possibilities inherent in the new media; and the inherently wider availability of folk materials due to the portability and durability of these new "textual" envelopes. Others worry that these new envelopes contain the seeds of rot: of homogenization and of sterility; of commercial corruption and of the loss of the anonymous but individual voice of the traditional performer; of wide distribution at the cost of contextual authenticity and serendipity; and of the loss of control of the product by its producers.

This is, of course, another very large problem in contemporary cultural studies which affects debates over: museums and world fairs; national festivals and staged folk events; and electronic-media impact on existing linguistic, aesthetic, and social forms. This volume can hardly solve the many problems contained here, but certainly these essays suggest that electronic media do not enter a simple prior situation of clear-cut genres, anonymous "authors," and highly localized and time-bound audiences. For centuries in South Asia, texts and performance styles have circulated over large spaces; they have been edited and modified to suit local exigencies and tastes, and interacted in complex, intertextual ways. Thus, the complexities of mechanical reproduction do not impinge on a prior world of generic simplicity, audience fixity, and social confinement. So we must be careful not to assume that the new modes of reproduction are in every respect as new as they might first appear. More importantly, there is some reason to suspect that "authenticity" is a false issue that we have counterposed to the world of mechanical reproduction (Appadurai 1986; Spooner 1986, Handler 1986), an issue largely of our own making, growing out of certain special problems involving Western philosophy and aesthetics in the last few centuries.

There is a great deal of evidence to show that indigenous traditions have always been plastic and pluriform, that certain forms and texts were standardized over large spaces and long periods, and that individual "signatures" and prestige are not wholly a product of the new mechanical age. Indeed, if we take the case of music, the argument that a vibrant and diverse folk culture is giving way to a sterile and homogeneous "mass" culture may well be wrong. After all, the emergence of the *ghazal* as a *semiclassical* form available to a wider audience is not necessarily a sign either of sterility or of homogenization. That a popular contemporary vocalist like Anoop Jalota can today sing *ghazal*s at large concerts for the middle and lower-classes of cities, whereas the *ghazal* previously required and imposed more stringent criteria for literacy and appreciation, is not by itself the sign of any degeneracy, except from an unargued elitist perspective. Rather, as music, the novel, television, and tape cassettes begin to enter the fields of the epic, the folksong, and traditional performances generally, what is emerging is a whole new series of hybrid forms: disco-*garba,* semi-classical *ghazal,* cinematized epics, tape-recorded devotional hymns and songs, wedding videos, and a host of other hybrids.

These hybrids belong to an explosively growing middle-class culture and what has elsewhere been called its "public culture" (Appadurai and Breckenridge 1988). These newly emergent hybrid forms, and the middle-class, cosmopolitan cultural world to which they belong, do not necessarily constitute a degenerate and kitschy commercial world, to be sharply contrasted with a folk world we have forever lost. In fact, it may be the idea of a folk world in need of conservation that must be rejected, so that there can be a vigorous engagement with the hybrid forms of the world we live in now. If we embark on this task, our understanding of the textual and intertextual complexities of the past will stand us in good stead, and we are not likely to plunge into a premature requiem for the "lore" of the "folk." Rather, we can reinvigorate our commitment, as students of alternative ways of knowing, of narrating, and of remembering, to incorporate "mass" forms into our field of investigation. Such study is surely urgent, since the present turns into history ever faster, and the task of interpretation, as far as popular forms are concerned, applies as much to the historical present as to the past.

I shall conclude by returning to a topic alluded to in the introduction, the current controversy over *The Satanic Verses* by Salman Rushdie, a controversy that is not likely to have died out by the time this book is available in print. If there are any lessons that can be learned from this collection, they are: that the forms of "magic realism" are many; that the traditions in which they have been produced and enjoyed are multiple; and that it is not just a modern privilege to have blurred the lines between fantasy, history, and satire. Such modern and postmodern enterprises have many earlier prototypes and precedents, so that the sensibilities of those who have rioted and killed over the publication of this work may be products not solely of their manipulation by contemporary politicians and publicists. They may, in fact, constitute a new twist in an old politics of genre, which has been internationalized and inflamed by ideas of fiction and artistic freedom that are both recent and parochial (that is, confined to the Euro-American ecumene over the last three centuries). The claims of those who argue that these values have universal currency will have to be made (and judged) in a crowded, embattled, diverse, and transnational discursive space. The politics of folklore is now close to home.

* * *

I am grateful to Margaret Mills for helping me to discriminate between the walking habits of angels and of fools, and for helping to take the lead out of parts of my prose.

References

Abrahams, R. D.

1977 Towards an Enactment-Centered Theory of Folklore. In *Frontiers of Folklore,* William Bascom, ed., pp. 79–120. Boulder, Col.: Westview Press.

Appadurai, Arjun

1986 Commodities and the Politics of Value. In *The Social Life of Things: Commodities in Cultural Persepctive,* A. Appadurai, ed., pp. 3–63. New York: Cambridge University Press.

1988 Putting Hierarchy in Its Place. *Cultural Anthropology* 3/1 (February): 36–49.

Appadurai, Arjun, and C. Breckenridge

1988 Why Public Culture? *Public Culture* 1 (Fall): 5–11.

Bauman, Richard

1989 American Folklore Studies and Social Transformation: A Performance-Centered Perspective. *Text and Performance Quarterly* 9/3 (July): 1–10.

Beck, Brenda E. F.

1982 *The Three Twins: The Telling of a South Indian Folk Epic.* Bloomington: Indiana University Press.

Benjamin, W.

1969 [1936] The Work of Art in the Age of Mechanical Reproduction. In *Illuminations,* translated by Harry Zohn. New York: Schocken Books.

Blackburn, Stuart H.

1988 *Singing of Birth and Death: Texts in Performance.* Philadelphia: University of Pennsylvania Press.

Blackburn, Stuart H., and A. K. Ramanujan, eds.

1986 *Another Harmony: New Essays on the Folklore of India.* Berkeley: University of California Press.

Bloom, A. D.

1987 *The Closing of the American Mind.* New York: Simon and Schuster.

Fabian, J.

1983 *Time and the Other: How Anthropology Makes Its Object.* New York: Columbia University Press.

Gallie, W. B.

1964 *Philosophy and Historical Understanding.* New York: Schocken Books.

Geertz, Clifford

1973 Deep Play: Notes on the Balinese Cockfight. In *The Interpretation of Cultures,* pp. 412–53. New York: Basic Books.

1975 Commonsense as a Cultural System. *Antioch Review* 33:5–26.

1980 *Negara: The Theatre-State in Nineteenth Century Bali.* Princeton, N.J.: Princeton University Press.

Handler, R.

1986 Authenticity. *Anthropology Today* 2/1:2–4.

1988 *Nationalism and the Politics of Culture in Quebec.* Madison: University of Wisconsin Press.

Herzfeld, M.

1982 *Ours Once More: Folklore, Ideology and the Making of Modern Greece.* Austin: University of Texas Press.

Hirsch, E. D., J. Kett, and J. Trefil

1987 *Cultural Literacy: What Every American Needs to Know.* Boston: Houghton Mifflin.

Kirshenblatt-Gimblett, Barbara

1988 Mistaken Dichotomies. *Journal of American Folklore* 101/400 (April–June): 140–155.

Kopytoff, I.

1981 Knowledge and Belief in Suku Thought. *Africa* 51/3:709–723.

Limon, J., and M. Young

1986 Frontiers, Settlements, and Development in Folklore Studies, 1972–1985. *Annual Review of Anthropology* 15:437–460.

Parkin, D.

1978 *The Cultural Definition of Political Response.* London: Academic Press.

Spooner, B.

1986 Weavers and Dealers: The Authenticity of An Oriental Carpet. In *The Social Life of Things: Commodities in Cultural Perspective,* A. Appadurai, ed., pp. 195–235. New York: Cambridge University Press.

Contributors

Arjun Appadurai is professor of Anthropology at the University of Pennsylvania, where he is co-director of the Center for Transnational Cultural Studies and associate editor of *Public Culture*. He is the author of *Worship and Conflict Under Colonial Rule* (New York, 1981) and editor of *The Social Life of Things* (New York, 1986).

Stuart H. Blackburn is the author of *Singing of Birth and Death: Texts in Performance* (Philadelphia, 1988) and co-editor of *Another Harmony: New Essays on the Folklore of India* (Berkeley, 1986) and *Oral Epics in India* (Berkeley, 1989). He teaches at University High School in San Francisco, and is now finishing a book on the performance of the Rama story as shadow puppet play in Kerala.

Donald Brenneis is Professor of Anthropology at Pitzer College. He has conducted research in Fiji and southern Nepal. He is the author of numerous articles on sociolinguistics and folkloristics, co-editor of *Dangerous Words: Language and Politics in the Pacific* (New York, 1984) and *The Audience as Co-Author* (Amsterdam, 1986), as well as current editor of *American Ethnologist*.

Peter J. Claus is Professor of Anthropology at California State University, Hayward. He is the author of numerous articles concerning kinship, ethnomedicine, folklore, and folk religion in south India, and has co-edited *Indian Folklore I* (Mysore, 1981), *Indian Folklore II* (Mysore, 1987), *Folktales of India* (Chicago, 1987), and *Oral Epics in India* (Berkeley, 1989). He is currently completing a book with Frank J. Korom titled *Folkloristics and Indian Folklore*.

Joyce Burkhalter Flueckiger is an independent research scholar and editor in Madison, Wisconsin, where she received her doctorate in South Asian Language and Literature in 1984. She is co-editor of *Oral Epics in India* (Berkeley, 1989) and *Boundaries of the Text: Performing the Epics in South and Southeast Asia* (1990). She is also the author of several articles on genre, folklore systems, and performance in central India.

Ann Grodzins Gold is Visiting Assistant Professor of Anthropology at Colgate University and a Visiting Fellow in the South Asia Program at

Cornell University. She has done fieldwork on Hindu pilgrimage, women's songs and stories, and Nath oral epics in Rajasthan's Ajmer district. She has published several articles on spirit possession, shrines, and folklore, and her book *Fruitful Journeys: The Ways of Rajasthani Pilgrims* (Berkeley, 1988) received the Hans Rosenhaupt Memorial Book Award from the Woodrow Wilson Fellowship Foundation. She has recently completed an annotated translation and interpretive analysis of the Rajasthani tales of King Gopi Chand and King Bharthari, and three chapters for a co-authored manuscript on women's lore and lives in rural North India.

Benedicte Grima received her doctorate at the University of Pennsylvania in 1989. She is currently an independent researcher working with Afghan refugees in Pakistan. She is the author of several articles on Paxtun oral narrative, and founding co-editor of the *Middle East and South Asia Folklore Newsletter.* Her book, *"The Misfortunes Which Have Befallen Me": Paxtun Women's Life Stories* forthcoming (Austin).

Wilma L. Heston is an independent scholar and senior fellow in the Oriental Studies Department at the University of Pennsylvania. She is the author of two books: *Isfahan Is Half the World* (Princeton, 1983), a translation from Persian of Jamalzadeh's *Sar o Tah-e-Yak Karbas,* and *The Bazaar of the Storytellers* (Islamabad, 1988), a translation from Pashto of fourteen verse narratives. She is currently preparing a Pashto-English dictionary in collaboration with the Pashto Academy in Peshawar.

Alf Hiltebeitel is a professor in the Department of Religion at George Washington University. He is the author of *The Ritual of Battle: Krishna in the Mahabharata* (Ithaca, 1976, reprinted Albany, 1990) and *The Cult of Draupadī I: Mythologies from Gingee to Kuruksetra* (Chicago, 1988), as well as the editor of a collection of essays titled *Criminal Gods and Demon Devotees* (Albany, 1989).

Frank J. Korom is a Ph.D. candidate in the Department of Folklore and Folklife at the University of Pennsylvania. He is the author of *Pakistani Folk Culture: A Select Annotated Bibliography* (Islamabad, 1988) and a number of articles dealing with folkore and religion in South Asia. He is currently completing a book with Peter J. Claus titled *Folkloristics and Indian Folklore.*

Peter Manuel has researched and published extensively on musics in India, Cuba, and Spain. An accomplished sitarist, he is the author of *Popular Music in the Non-Western World: An Introductory Survey* (Oxford,

1988) and *Thumri in Historical and Stylistic Perspective* (Motibal Banarsidas), and several articles. He currently teaches ethnomusicology at Columbia University.

Margaret A. Mills is an associate professor in the Department of Folklore and Folklife at the University of Pennsylvania. She is the author of *Rhetorics and Politics in Afghan Traditional Storytelling* (Philadelphia, 1991), and of a number of articles on folktales in Afghanistan and on theoretical issues pertaining to the study of gender.

Velcheru Narayana Rao is Professor of South Asian Language and Literature at the University of Wisconsin, and a well-known literary critic and scholar of Telugu. He is the author of numerous articles on the folk and classical literature of India, and more specifically on the contemporary literature and culture of Andhra Pradesh. Along with Hank Heifetz, he has also co-translated a volume of Telugu poetry titled *For the Lord of the Animals: Poems from the Telugu* (Berkeley, 1987).

A. K. Ramanujan is William E. Colvin Professor in the Department of South Asian Languages and Civilizations, the Department of Linguistics, and the Committee on Social Thought at the University of Chicago. A poet, writer of fiction, translator, and scholar, he is a recent recipient of the MacArthur award. He is the author of many articles and books, including *The Interior Landscape* (Bloomington, 1967), *Speaking of Siva* (London, 1973), *Hymns for the Drowning* (Princeton, 1981), and *Poems of Love and War* (New York, 1985).

Carol Salomon is a research assistant professor in the Department of South Asian Languages and Literature at the University of Washington. She received her doctorate at the University of Pennsylvania in 1983. She has worked on medieval Bengali narrative poetry and conducted fieldwork in West Bengal and Bangladesh on Baul songs. She is currently completing an annotated translation of the songs of Lalan Fakir.

David Shulman is a MacArthur Fellow and Professor of Indian Studies and Comparative Religion at Hebrew University in Israel. He has published a variety of articles and books on south Indian religion and literature, as well as a volume of poetry in Hebrew. Among his best-known works are *Tamil Temple Myths: Sacrifice and Divine Marriage in the South Indian Tamil Tradition* (Princeton, 1960) and *The King and the Clown in South Indian Myth and Poetry* (Princeton, 1985).

Margaret Trawick is Assistant Professor of Anthropology at Hobart and William Smith Colleges. She is the author of *Notes on Love in a Tamil*

Family (Berkeley, 1990). Her other major publications include articles on Ayurveda, spirit possession, Tamil folklore and literature, and the poetics of resistance in modern south India. She is currently working on a book on the varieties of Indian feminism.

Susan S. Wadley is Professor and Chair of Anthropology at Syracuse University. She is the author of *Shakti: Power in the Conceptual Structure of Karimpur Religion* (Chicago, 1975) and co-editor of a number of books, the most recent being *Oral Epics in India* (Berkeley, 1989). She has written extensively on women, folklore, and religion in India.

Index

This book has been set in Linotron Galliard. Galliard was designed for Mergenthaler in 1978 by Matthew Carter. Galliard retains many of the features of a sixteenth century typeface cut by Robert Granjon but has some modifications which gives it a more contemporary look.

Printed on acid-free paper.